CHRISTIANITY IN A REVOLUTIONARY AGE

A History of Christianity
in the Nineteenth and Twentieth Centuries

VOLUME III

THE NINETEENTH CENTURY
OUTSIDE EUROPE:

The Americas, the Pacific, Asia, and Africa

CHRISTIANITY IN A REVOLUTIONARY AGE

A History of Christianity
in the Nineteenth and Twentieth Centuries

VOLUME III

THE NINETEENTH CENTURY OUTSIDE EUROPE

The Americas, the Pacific, Asia, and Africa

KENNETH SCOTT LATOURETTE

Sterling Professor of Missions and Oriental History, Emeritus,
and Associate Fellow of Berkeley College in Yale University

GREENWOOD PRESS, PUBLISHERS
WESTPORT, CONNECTICUT

The Library of Congress has catalogued this publication as follows:

Library of Congress Cataloging in Publication Data

Latourette, Kenneth Scott, 1884-1968.
    The nineteenth century outside Europe.

    (His Christianity in a revolutionary age, v. 3)
    Bibliography: p.
    1.   Church history--19th century.   I.   Title.
II.   Series.
BR475.L33 vol. 3 [BR477]   270.8s [270.8'1]   72-11978
ISBN 0-8371-5703-X

To all, both past and present,
who as his secretaries have aided the author,
these volumes are gratefully
and affectionately dedicated

Originally published in 1961
by Harper & Brothers, New York

Reprinted with the permission
of Harper & Row, Publishers, Inc.

First Greenwood Reprinting 1973

Library of Congress Catalogue Card Number 77-138141

ISBN 0-8371-5700-5 (Set)
ISBN 0-8371-5703-X (Vol. III)

Printed in the United States of America

CONTENTS

Chapter I

INTRODUCTION   I

Chapter II

THE UNITED STATES OF AMERICA: The Setting and the Distinctive Characteristics of the Christianity Which Emerged   4

Chapter III

THE UNITED STATES OF AMERICA: Countering De-Christianizing Trends and
Winning Peoples of Non-Christian Ancestry   16

Chapter IV

THE UNITED STATES OF AMERICA: The Development of Ecclesiastical Organization and Leadership   84

Chapter V

THE UNITED STATES OF AMERICA: Movements Emerging from Christianity   112

Chapter VI

THE UNITED STATES OF AMERICA: Christianity and Education   140

Chapter VII

THE UNITED STATES OF AMERICA: The Response of Christianity to Intellectual
Currents   152

Chapter VIII

THE EFFECT OF CHRISTIANITY ON THE UNITED STATES OF AMERICA   200

Chapter IX

THE CHRISTIANITY OF THE UNITED STATES OF AMERICA AND THE WORLD-WIDE
SPREAD OF THE FAITH   242

Chapter X

BRITISH NORTH AMERICA   247

Chapter XI

GREENLAND; THE BRITISH, DANISH, AND DUTCH WEST INDIES; THE BRITISH AND
DUTCH ENCLAVES ON THE MAINLAND OF SOUTH AND CENTRAL AMERICA   277

Chapter XII

LATIN AMERICA   284

Chapter XIII

AUSTRALIA   353

Chapter XIV

NEW ZEALAND   371

Chapter XV

INTRODUCTORY TO THE WORLD OUTSIDE "CHRISTENDOM"   378

Chapter XVI

WESTERN ASIA AND NORTH AFRICA   384

Chapter XVII

INDIA   400

Chapter XVIII

SOUTH-EAST ASIA AND THE FRINGING ISLANDS   416

Chapter XIX

CHINA   431

Chapter XX

KOREA   446

Chapter XXI

JAPAN   450

Contents vii

Chapter XXII

THE ISLANDS OF THE PACIFIC 458

Chapter XXIII

AFRICA SOUTH OF THE SAHARA: MADAGASCAR 463

Chapter XXIV

THE WORLD OUTSIDE "CHRISTENDOM": A Summary Retrospect 481

Chapter XXV

THE FORESHADOWING OF GLOBAL COÖPERATION AMONG PROTESTANTS 484

Chapter XXVI

RETROSPECT AND PROSPECT 491

BIBLIOGRAPHY 497

INDEX 515

AUTHOR'S ACKNOWLEDGEMENTS

IN CONNEXION with the present volume the author is deeply indebted to Dean Emeritus Luther A. Weigle and Professor Sydney E. Ahlstrom. Both read the chapters on the United States of America and made valuable suggestions. But for them the following pages would be guilty of more omissions and errors than they now contain.

CHRISTIANITY IN A REVOLUTIONARY AGE

*A History of Christianity
in the Nineteenth and Twentieth Centuries*

VOLUME III

THE NINETEENTH CENTURY OUTSIDE EUROPE:

The Americas, the Pacific, Asia, and Africa

CHAPTER I

Introduction

W E NOW pass to the portion of the world which lies outside Europe. It embraces the large majority of mankind and most of the land surface of the globe. It was profoundly affected by the revolution which had its origin and earliest developments in Western Christendom. In the nineteenth century it was beginning to feel the impact of that revolution, in extensive areas with sweeping results. The impact was intensified as the century hastened to its culminating catastrophe in World War I.

The world outside Europe was in two divisions, which for the most part were sharply defined. One was what might be called the larger Europe. It was made up of lands which at the outset of the nineteenth century were sparsely settled, whether by non-European or European peoples. It included the Americas, Australia, and New Zealand. Into its relatively vacant spaces Europeans poured, mostly from Western Christendom, and new nations either came into being or, already in existence, grew with breath-taking rapidity. Non-Europeans were found in it—American Indians, Australian aborigines, Maoris, Africans, and, in the Americas, Negroes whose ancestors had been imported as slaves, and a few from Asia. But they were minorities surrounded and dominated by mounting majorities of European birth or ancestry. The other division was one in which non-Europeans were in the overwhelming majority and Europeans were mostly merchants, government officials, plantation owners, or missionaries.

In that first division, the larger Europe, Christianity was the hereditary faith of most of the peoples of European descent, but it was not at all clear that it would be perpetuated in the new environment. Its responses to the revolutionary forces of the age varied from region to region and from country to country. In Canada the reaction differed from that in the United States and in both it was quite unlike that in Latin America. In Australia and New Zealand the record of Christianity was not exactly parallel to that in Canada—although all three were in the British Empire. Yet in all these areas those who bore the Christian name far outnumbered adherents of any other faith.

In the second division Christians, where they were found at all, were, with the exception of the Philippines and a few regions in Western Asia, minorities and usually very small minorities. In some regions Christianity did not arrive until the nineteenth century, and in a few it had no representatives even at the close of the century. Most of the small Christian groups were dominated by missionaries, for they were so young and so recently planted that little or no indigenous leadershsip had emerged. Yet nearly everywhere the Christian minorities were growing through fresh conversions, and by the beginning of the twentieth century indigenous leaders were beginning to appear, precursors of the many who in that century were indications that the faith was firmly planted.

It is to the regions and countries in the first division that most of the ensuing volume is to be directed. That is partly because in them the numbers of professed Christians and the churches were many times larger than in the second division. It is also because the question arose whether in the face of the revolutionary forces stemming from Western Christendom Christianity would accompany the migrants from Europe and would survive transplanting. Important, too, were the changes wrought in Christianity and effected by Christianity in its new environments. As the century progressed, this larger Europe loomed ever more prominently. Increasingly it moved away from its colonial status, not only politically but also culturally and economically. In varying degrees its Christians and its churches had a growing place in the world religious scene. Their share in the propagation of the faith among the peoples of the second division mounted until, after 1914, they provided the majority of the Protestant missionaries in those portions of the globe and contributed increasingly, although still not as much as Western Europe, to Roman Catholic missions. This meant that more and more the Christianity, and especially the Protestantism, in the lands embraced in the second division bore the impress of that of the larger Europe. In the adjustments in methods and the response in thought, worship, and organization to the revolutionary forces of the age the Christianity of the younger portions of the Occident became important for Christianity as a whole and had significant repercussions upon the Christianity of the older sector of the Occident.

Because of its dimensions, the vigour of its people, and its rapidly mounting population and wealth, by the end of the nineteenth century the United States of America was beginning to emerge as a major factor in the affairs of mankind. By the mid-twentieth century it shared with Russia the perilous distinction of being the leading power on the planet. While it did not become as nearly preponderant in the religious as in the economic and political spheres, the United States had more and more to be reckoned with in any comprehensive survey of Christianity. Especially was this the case in Protestantism. We must, therefore, devote a larger proportion of the current volume to the United States than to any other one country.

Emphasis on the newer portions of the Occident must not cause us to neglect that larger segment of mankind which lies outside the Occident. From its inception Christians have claimed that the Gospel is for all men. Great seers among them have dreamed of seeing all men made disciples, baptized, and taught to observe all that their Lord had clearly commanded the little group of his intimates.[1] They have affirmed that it is the purpose of God to unite all things in Christ, both in heaven and on earth,[2] that Christ is to reign until He has put all enemies under His feet,[3] and that God Who revealed Himself and acted through Christ is to reign forever and ever.[4] The brief century and a half covered by these volumes is quite too short a time to determine whether these dreams are to be realized. But it should enable us to gain some inkling as to whether that majority of the human race which lies outside the Occident is to give allegiance to the Christian faith. Upon that majority the revolutionary forces proceeding from Western Christendom impinged in these decades with startling effect. In great areas they shattered the inherited cultures and elsewhere modified them profoundly. To what extent and in what ways did Christianity enter into the incursions from the Occident, and what were the nature and strength of the Christian communities which arose? A detailed account has earlier been given by the author.[5] Here we can take the space only for a brief summary, centring upon the methods by which Christianity was planted, the nature and strength of the resulting communities, and the effects upon the peoples among which they were gathered.

[1] Matt. 28:19, 20.
[2] Eph. 1:10.
[3] I Cor. 15:25.
[4] Rev. 11:15.
[5] Latourette, *A History of the Expansion of Christianity*, Vols. IV–VII.

CHAPTER II

The United States of America: The Setting and the Distinctive Characteristics of the Christianity Which Emerged

WE HAVE already sketched the pre-nineteenth-century course of Christianity in the United States of America.[1] We have noted the place that Christianity had in the history of the Thirteen Colonies which became the United States. We have remarked that the Christianity was predominantly Protestant, but that on the eve of independence only a small minority of the population were members of churches, and this even after the Great Awakening which swept through the Colonies in the first half of the eighteenth century. We have called attention to the fact that the Puritan-Pietist-Evangelical strains were more prominent in the Protestantism of the new nation than in the Protestantism east of the Atlantic and that they were strengthened by the Great Awakening. We have seen that the movements which issued in the independence of the Thirteen Colonies were deeply indebted to those strains and that the ideals of the infant nation owed much to Puritanism. We have said something of the quarter-century from 1789 to 1815 during which the United States felt the repercussions of the contemporary revolutionary storm in Europe and was drawn into a late stage of the Napoleonic Wars. Deism and other sceptical currents irrupted. Yet Protestantism in the United States came to 1815 on a rising tide of awakenings and revivals of the Pietist-Evangelical kind. Some Protestant denominations achieved national organizations. New denominations arose. The Roman Catholic Church, although represented only by a small minority, was given the beginnings of a hierarchy. The ties between Church and state, already looser than in Europe, were further weakened: the tradition was being established of what in Europe was called "a free Church in a free state."

As we outlined the fashion in which, during the nineteenth century, the revolution in Western Christendom[2] mounted and proliferated we mentioned some of the influential intellectuals in the United States who departed from the

[1] Volume I, Chapters III, IV.
[2] Volume I, Chapter V.

historic Christian faith—Ralph Waldo Emerson, William Graham Sumner, John Dewey, and the militant sceptic Robert G. Ingersoll. To them should be added for the fore part of the century Thomas Paine (1737–1809), whose influence continued after 1815, and Thomas Cooper (1758–1839), scientist and friend and disciple of Joseph Priestley, who came to the United States with the latter in 1794 and who had a notable and stormy career as teacher, college president, pamphleteer, and controversialist.[3] The list might be greatly lengthened, especially for the latter part of the century.

THE CHALLENGE OF THE REVOLUTIONARY AGE

In a great variety of additional ways the United States was drawn into the mid-current of the revolutionary age. Here were a threat and a challenge to Christianity.

Some of the forces which swept the United States into full stream in the multiform revolution of the day and which posed serious problems for Christianity entered from Europe—the intellectual movements especially. The theories associated with the names of Darwin and Huxley had a wide circulation. Herbert Spencer, who applied them to social evolution, was read in university circles. The advances in the knowledge of geology in which Lyell had a leading part became known and set the stage for the Darwinian hypotheses. English poets, essayists, novelists, and playwrights who popularized the issues raised by the new discoveries and theories became household names and their books were found in the homes of thousands. Among them, on the positive side, were Tennyson and Browning. On the questioning side, departing, sometimes reluctantly, from the faith, were such authors as Thomas Carlyle, Leslie Stephen, Matthew Arnold, George Eliot, Thomas Hardy, and, puckishly, towards the latter part of the century, Bernard Shaw. Continental authors were read, usually but not always in translation. In some circles such names as Goethe and Ibsen were familiar. Books presenting the radical critical approach to the Bible and Jesus were circulated. Translations were published of Strauss's *Leben Jesu* and Renan's *Vie de Jésus*. The former especially appears to have been extensively read. In more restricted circles, largely those professionally interested, German and British critical studies of the Scriptures were known. American editions of translations of Nietzsche, Schopenhauer, and Feuerbach, in several instances more than one, evidence of their popularity, made familiar the thoroughgoing scepticism which they represented.

In several aspects of the revolution the United States shared with Western Europe as an originator and made distinctive contributions. In the ideals and structure of government and society it strongly reinforced the kind of democracy which was indebted to Anglo-Saxon Protestantism. Its example had wide

[3] *Dictionary of American Biography*, Vol. IV, pp. 414–416.

repercussions throughout the world, and especially in the Americas and Australasia. Although the Industrial Revolution did not begin in the United States, it made itself felt early in the nineteenth century, and before the outbreak of World War I brought the century to an end, that country had developed to an outstanding degree the processes and structures arising from the factory system. It added many inventions which were to affect profoundly the life of mankind —among them the cotton gin, interchangeable parts in the manufacture of arms and machinery, the electric telegraph, the telephone, the incandescent electric light bulb, and the airplane. In the United States railways had the largest mileage of any country, the petroleum industry had its earliest extensive development, and towards the end of the century automobiles began to appear.

With industrialization came other developments. Some were characteristic accompaniments regardless of the country where industrialization occurred. They included the growth of cities, of an urban proletariat, and of what was usually termed the middle class—although in the absence of a landed aristocracy inherited from feudalism this term was less applicable in the United States than in Europe. Other developments either were not found in Europe or existed in different forms. Among them were an enormous immigration from Europe, at first mainly to the north-eastern states, which provided unskilled labour for the industries and the construction of railways, and, in the fore part of the century, the burgeoning of the plantation system in the South, based upon Negro slave labour, by which the cotton was grown for the factories of Britain and the North.

Partially as an accompaniment and sequel of the Industrial Revolution came the growth of sectionalism. The South, rural and producing cotton through the labour of Negro slaves, became a highly self-conscious section in contrast with the North-east, which was being rapidly industrialized. Rivalry and strains ensued, culminating in the costly Civil War (1861–1865), the prostration of the South, and the abolition of slavery. After the war the South continued to have its distinct life and traditions.

A prominent feature of the history of the United States was geographic expansion. It was akin to the empire-building which was prominent in the experience of European nations. But in the United States empire-building differed significantly from that of Western European powers: for the most part it was movement into contiguous territory thinly occupied by non-white peoples. Only late in the century did it jump the oceans and include other cultural traditions —in Samoa, Puerto Rico, Hawaii, and the Philippines. Most of the expansion of Russia was also into contiguous land territories, but much of it annexed regions which were the historic homes of peoples of high and alien civilizations. In the United States, in contrast, the paucity of the indigenous non-white population made possible the early integration of the new territories in the form of states of equal legal status with the original thirteen. The Indians were not easily or quickly assimilated and constituted a continuing problem, but they were small minorities.

In the United States an accompaniment of the Industrial Revolution and territorial expansion was a prodigious growth of population, caused partly by a high birth rate and partly by the immigration which, attracted by the demand for unskilled labour in the mines, factories, and railway building and by the vacant lands in the West, poured into the country. The flood continued to mount until World War I. In 1800 the population of the country was 5,300,000. By 1830 it had risen to 13,000,000. In 1850 it was 23,000,000, in 1880, 50,000,000, and in 1910, 93,500,000. The last figure was more than two and a half times that of France and considerably more than that of Germany in the same year.

Cities grew by leaps and bounds. In 1799 only six had a population of more than 8,000. In every decade to 1920 the cities with a population of more than 8,000 doubled. In 1880, 28.6 per cent. of the population of the United States was urban—that is, in cities of more than 8,000. In 1910 45.8 per cent. of the population was urban, and in 1920, 51.4 per cent. of the population was in that category.[4]

Constant in the United States was the westward movement of population. Earlier this meant the advance of the frontier. By the end of the century the frontier had largely disappeared but the Western states continued to grow by migration from states to their east.

Because of the setting, in the United States the revolutionary age confronted Christianity with challenges both like and unlike the ones it faced in Europe.

The challenge was like that of Europe. Here, too, were the intellectual currents which for many undermined or weakened the Christian faith. Here were growing cities and industrial centres where the patterns of life made difficult or impossible the kind of parish organization for religious instruction, public worship, and the administration of the sacraments through which the churches had earlier ministered to their constituencies. Labourers in the factories and mines tended either to form no ties with the churches or to drift away from such as they had. The mounting complexity of life and the multiplication of competing activities and amusements made the churches and their services simply one of many interests—in contrast with the older Europe, where the parish church had had a central place in the life of the community. In all these aspects the challenge was fully as great as in Europe.

In at least one respect the challenge was not as acute as in Europe. The weakening of the tie between Church and state and the non-existence of an established religion—for the last traces of it which persisted in the original states were cancelled early in the century and it was non-existent in the newer states—

---

[4] *The Encyclopædia Britannica,* 14th ed., Vol. XXII, p. 735.

made for the absence of the anti-clericalism which was strong in a number of European countries.

Some challenges which did not exist in Europe seemed to render the prospect for Christianity more grim than in the older Christendom. At the outset of the nineteenth century the de-Christianization of the portions of the population which by ancestral ties belonged to the faith appeared to be far advanced and the westward movement of population was augmenting it. When the United States came into being only a small minority of the population were communicant members of churches and the large majority had not even been baptized. Most of the immigration in colonial days had stemmed from other than religious motives, and baptism and attendance at church services were much less a social convention than in the mother lands. The dwindling tie between Church and state and the disappearance of such establishments as remained further weakened whatever of conventional conformity to religious customs had survived. As the multitudes poured westward, their tendency was to drop such adherence to the churches as they may have had in the older states. Many who had been members of a church in the home from which they came did not reëstablish that tie in their new home. Sunday observance with attendance at church services was ignored, and the day was used for amusements, numbers of them crude and even contrary to Christian morality.[5]

A similar challenge was the immigration from Europe. Most of it came from countries where one or another of the churches was established and where baptism and often confirmation were universally observed social conventions. Now, in a land where these sacraments were lightly held, would the immigrant, whether Roman Catholic, Protestant, or Orthodox, observe them or would he drop all ties with his ancestral church? Jews were increasingly numerous and for the most part held to their hereditary faith—or at least, even when secularized, to some of its customs.

Negroes constituted a challenge without exact parallel in Europe. Here were several millions, until the 1860's mostly slaves, from completely non-Christian backgrounds. Could they be won to the Christian faith in a country where the de-Christianization of the white population was threatened?

The Indians, a much smaller but widely scattered minority, also non-Christian by heritage, were comparable to the pagans who confronted the Orthodox Church in large sections of the Russian Empire.

Distinctive Characteristics of Christianity in the United States

As it dealt with the challenges presented by the United States, Christianity in that country developed characteristics which made it distinctive. While being

---

[5] For a few of many examples, drawn from different sections and periods, see Richards, *Samuel J. Mills*, pp. 105 ff.; Stewart, *Sheldon Jackson*, pp. 112–114; Johnson, *The Frontier Camp Meeting*, pp. 9–16; Barclay, *Early American Methodism*, Vol. I, pp. 218, 219.

clearly in the historic stream of the faith, it became different from that in Europe and, indeed, from that in any other country. Much of the difference was the result, directly or indirectly, of the response to the challenges of the revolutionary age. Most of it was evidence of vitality within Christianity which enabled it to adjust itself to conditions in the United States.

A characteristic already mentioned was the separation of Church and state and the absence of an established church. The Congress of the national government was prohibited by the first amendment to the constitution from making any "law respecting an establishment of religion, or prohibiting the free exercise thereof." Even before this amendment, the constitution had expressly declared that "no religious test shall ever be required as a qualification to any office or public trust under the United States."[6] The motives and precedents which led to the incorporation of these provisions were of mixed origin. Some stemmed from John Locke and the Enlightenment. Others sprang from a feature of the life of the country which in time was to become even more pronounced: the multiplicity of denominations and the unwillingness to accord any one of them a favoured place. The example of several of the original states, notably Rhode Island and Pennsylvania, where religious liberty and the absence of an established church were already in effect, either fully or partially, was potent. Before the placing of these provisions in the constitution of the United States the struggle for religious liberty had been won in some of the states which had had an established church. In that achievement leaders of minority groups, especially the Presbyterians and the Baptists, had been prominent.[7] After the adoption of the national constitution such remnants of establishment as continued in the states were fairly early erased. The last to disappear was in Massachusetts in 1831–1833.[8]

In the separation of Church and state the United States was not unique. As we have seen, in the nineteenth century the trend in Europe was in that direction. We are to note that elsewhere in the Americas during that century it became general, although not universal. It also prevailed in Australia and New Zealand. In the twentieth century it continued to mount in Europe. The example of the United States reinforced the trend.

The separation of Church and state did not mean that either the national government or the state governments were anti-clerical or anti-Christian. The President took the oath of office on a Bible. The two houses of the Congress and the armed forces had chaplains. Some state constitutions declared belief in God a prerequisite to office or to serving on a jury. Several specifically acknowledged God and expressed gratitude to Him. A few made acceptance of the Old

---

[6] Article VI.
[7] Stokes, *Church and State in the United States*, Vol. I, Chaps. 4, 5, 7, 8; Pfeffer, *Church, State, and Freedom*, pp. 115 ff.
[8] Stokes, *op. cit.*, Vol. I, p. 426.

and New Testaments a condition of office holding.[9] An annual day of Thanksgiving was observed by several individual states and, in the later decades of the century, on a national scale and by presidential proclamation.[10] The century saw nine nationally proclaimed fast days. Legislation was passed to safeguard the observance of Sunday.[11]

Another distinctive characteristic of the Christianity of the United States was variety. In no other country were as many kinds of Christianity represented. Indeed, never in any one country had Christianity presented such a coat of many colours. Here was both a cause and an accompaniment of the separation of Church and state and religious liberty. The number of denominations represented, even in colonial days, presented an obstacle to preference to any one of them. The adoption of freedom of religion favoured the development of variety. Fully as important was immigration. The vast flood which swelled to more than a million a year on the eve of World War I attained larger dimensions than any other similar movement in history. Most of it was from Europe; some from the Middle East. It was therefore predominantly Christian in ancestry and in at least nominal allegiance. It brought with it adherents to every numerically major and practically all minor Christian confessions and denominations. As we have suggested, the immigrants did not necessarily hold to the faith of their fathers. But many did so. In consequence, by 1914 nearly every kind of Christianity found anywhere else in the world was present. Here was the Protestantism of Europe in its manifold manifestations. The Roman Catholic Church was strong. The several national Orthodox Churches were represented, although not all of them in organized form. Among the immigrants were members of most of the older churches of Asia.

Associated with the variety of Christianity in the United States was the weakness of the territorial parish as compared with its position in Europe. In most countries in Europe the vast majority of the population were members of a particular church: since the initial conversion of the land, for purposes of administration and the better care of souls, the area had been divided into parishes. Before independence, in such of the colonies as had an established church, a similar pattern prevailed, but seldom with the efficiency of that in the Old World. With the passing of establishment and the multiplication of denominations the parish as known in Europe was either non-existent or weak. Some churches, accustomed to the parish structure in Europe, attempted to reproduce it, but only infrequently were they able in what they called the parish to win or maintain the adherence of all within its borders. Smaller or larger number became members of other denominations or had no church connexion.

In the United States the confessions and denominations imported from

[9] *Ibid.*, pp. 620, 621.
[10] Pfeffer, *op. cit.*, p. 223.
[11] *Ibid.*, pp. 227 ff.

the Old World did not exactly reproduce either the relative strength or the complexion which was theirs in their original habitat. Roman Catholics, for instance, were in the minority; the Orthodox were even more a minority; Lutherans were not as prominent as on the continent of Europe; the Episcopalians, while important socially, constituted a much smaller proportion of the population than they did in England; Presbyterians were not as outstanding as in Scotland; and the Reformed did not loom as large as in the Netherlands and Switzerland. Methodists and Baptists, although minorities in England, the country of their origin, together totalled more than half of the Protestants and outnumbered the Roman Catholics. Each confession and denomination developed features which reflected the environment of the United States, but without severing its fellowship with its adherents in the rest of the world.

Particularly significant was the numerical strength of the Baptists and Methodists and such denominations of indigenous origin as the Disciples of Christ and the Christians. They appealed to the rank and file, especially of the older stock, were in the Puritan-Evangelical tradition akin to Pietism, and produced relatively few scholars and outstanding theologians.

To the bodies claiming the Christian name brought by the immigrants, others were added which were indigenous to the United States. We have mentioned[12] those born out of the awakenings which began shortly before 1815—the United Brethren in Christ, the Evangelical Association, the Cumberland Presbyterian Church, and the movements stemming from Barton W. Stone and Alexander Campbell which called themselves respectively Christians and Disciples of Christ and eventually largely coalesced. To them others were added in the nineteenth century. Outstanding were the Church of Jesus Christ of Latter Day Saints (the Mormons), the Church of Christ Scientist (the Christian Scientists), many pentecostal groups, diverse forms of adventism, and Jehovah's Witnesses. All were sprung from Protestantism, but together they constituted only a minority, although a substantial minority, of the Protestants of the country.

The Christianity of the United States, and especially Protestantism, gave birth to new movements or adopted and adapted movements which originated in Europe. Although they were not denominations they increased the variety presented by the faith. Among them were the Young People's Society of Christian Endeavour, begun in the United States, and the Young Men's Christian Association, the Young Women's Christian Association, and the Sunday School, which were born on the other side of the Atlantic, but which had their largest development in the United States. They were among the evidences of the abounding vitality of Christianity in the United States in rising to the challenge of the revolutionary age.

Another manifestation of the vitality and an outstanding characteristic of Christianity in the United States was the mounting proportion of the population

[12] Volume I, pp. 192–195.

who were won to membership in one or another of the churches. The percentage of the population holding membership in the churches is said to have risen from 6.9 in 1800 to 15.5 in 1850, 35.7 in 1900, and 43.5 in 1910.[13] Although these figures are in part conjectural, they seem to be sufficiently near the truth to indicate a substantial and fairly steady gain in meeting the threat to de-Christianization which was one of the challenges of the day. While church membership was not a guarantee of profound Christian conviction and for many might arise merely from conforming to a social convention, the fact that it was growing so pronouncedly was in contrast to the contemporaneous decline in church attendance in some European cities and to the active anti-clericalism in several Roman Catholic lands.

In general, the increase came about in three ways. One of these was the winning of the partially de-Christianized among the older American stock—descendants of those who had come to the country in colonial days. A rapidly growing number were from those who were non-Christian by ancestry—mainly Indians and Negroes. Much success was registered in holding to the churches the nineteenth-century immigration. The immigrants tended to gather into ethnic churches and in the first generation found in them convenient centres of association in which they could meet those of their own background and hear their native tongue. Yet adherence to a church was not automatic: initiative and religious conviction were essential on the part of at least the leadership. As the second and third generations appeared, of children born in the United States for whom English was the customary speech, a very large proportion held to the denominations of their fathers. However, as the twentieth century progressed, the ethnic lines were increasingly blurred and were less determinative in denominational affiliations.

The growth in church membership among the older American stock and the Negroes was mainly in Protestant bodies which had been represented before 1815. It took place in large degree through methods which had become familiar previous to that year and which were still another characteristic of the Christianity of the country. In them revivals akin to the Great Awakening, the Second Great Awakening, and the camp-meetings had a major part. The denominations which profited most were the Baptists, the Methodists, and the Christians and Disciples of Christ. Presbyterians, Congregationalists, and a few other bodies which had been firmly rooted in colonial days also gained, and to some degree through these means. Roman Catholics, scantily represented as they were in the Thirteen Colonies, made little headway among the older American stock and the Negroes. Their increase came almost entirely through nineteenth century immigration. Although the Lutherans had been more substantially rep

<hr>

[13] Dorchester, *Christianity in the United States*, p. 750; Weber, *1933 Yearbook of the American Churches*, p. 299.

resented before independence than the Roman Catholics, their growth in the nineteenth century was chiefly through immigration.

As a kind of corollary it followed, as another characteristic, that the Christianity of the United States was predominantly Protestant and that the tone of that Protestantism was largely determined by the Protesantism of the pre-nineteenth-century stock. Both Roman Catholics and Lutherans had an increasing role as their constituencies were augmented by immigration and as in the second and third generations the constituencies ceased to be foreign. Throughout most of the nineteenth century, however, the Roman Catholics especially were looked upon by the older stock as aliens.

Another characteristic of the Christianity of the United States was what may be called its activism. The people were engaged in occupying a vast area and in developing its resources. They were more interested in doing than in reflecting. The urgent tasks of building a new country were compelling. Absorbed in winning a partially de-Christianized population and the large non-Christian Indian and Negro elements, and in holding to the faith the immigrants of Christian background, the leadership and much of the rank and file of the churches were absorbed in expansion and organization. In addition, nineteenth-century Protestantism of Anglo-Saxon provenance was heir to the dream which had inspired many of the founding fathers, especially in New England and Pennsylvania, of building in the New World, remote from the evils of the Old World, a fully Christian society. The dream persisted and gave rise to extensive movements for moral and social reform—among them those directed against slavery and intemperance, and, in the latter part of the century, what was called the Social Gospel.[14]

Profound thought provoked by the challenges of the revolutionary age was not lacking. At the proper place we must call attention to it and attempt to summarize it. Some of it was radical and some conservative. However, more than in Europe the intellectual responses to the challenges were of the kind which appealed to the masses and tended to be superficial and to over-simplify the issues. One cause for the rather cursory dealing with the challenges was the activism which was prominent in the Christianity of the country. Another was the fashion in which the non-Christians and the partially or completely de-Christianized were won to church membership. Here was a kind of popular lay Christianity, predominantly Protestant.

The lay character of the Protestant Christianity of the United States was parcularly marked. Lay men and women were active in the churches and in many organizations related to the churches—among them the Sunday Schools, the Young Men's and Young Women's Christian Associations, and the Young People's Society of Christian Endeavour.

[14] See especially Niebuhr, *The Kingdom of God in America, passim.*

The movements towards unity among Christians and the differing attitude towards them were still another feature of the Christianity of the United States The picture was mixed. In no other country did coöperation among so many religious bodies have so extensive a development. More local and state council of churches were created than in all the rest of the world and the national Fed eral Council of the Churches of Christ in America which came into being late in the century was a pioneer in the diversity of the denominations associated with it. In the twentieth century such bodies continued to multiply. In addition on Protestant initiative ways were devised through which Protestants and Ro man Catholics worked together in particular enterprises and at times the col laboration embraced both Christians and Jews. Protestants of the United State had a mounting and at times an outstanding share in organizing coöperative enterprises on a world scale, notably the World's Student Christian Federation the World Missionary Conference which met in Edinburgh in 1910, and, after 1914, the International Missionary Council and the World Council of Churches In the twentieth century, with the growth of cities and especially of suburban districts and with the rapid shifts of population, denominational difference tended to fade and community churches arose: some either were only loosely affiliated with existing denominations or had no denominational tie and were purely local; others were federations of existing congregations of different de nominations; still others drew together in what was essentially a new denomi nation. Here and there, especially after 1914, were fusions on a national scale of ecclesiastical bodies closely related in doctrine and polity. In the Young Men's and Young Women's Christian Associations, originally begun by Protes tants of the Evangelical tradition and always under lay leadership, Protestant of many denominations, Roman Catholics, and at times Orthodox were drawn together as individuals in fellowship for specific purposes and some Jews were served. On the other hand, unions of churches on a national scale into fresh ecclesiastical bodies of denominations of differing traditions were not as inclu sive, even in the first half of the twentieth century, as in several other countries —Canada, Japan, China, the Philippines, Thailand, and India, for example. A larger proportion of Protestants remained aloof from coöperation than in Eu rope. Tensions also developed between those who held to traditional formula tions of the faith and those who sought adjustment to the new currents. They were both within and between denominations. They were no more acute than similar ones in other countries, but in the numbers involved they loomed larger than elsewhere.

In spite of tensions and the resistance of a number of denominations to coöp eration with other denominations, a common pattern tended to develop in the Protestantism of the United States. Increasingly all denominations tended to use the same methods and the same hymns. For years what were known as the

International Lessons were followed in Sunday Schools regardless of the denomination.

A kind of Christianity developed, notably among denominations which had been longest in the country, bearing the distinctive marks of the United States. The family likeness was most conspicuous in Protestantism. But features of it were detectable in the Roman Catholic Church.

One of the distinctive tokens of the Christianity and especially of the Protestantism of the United States was the fashion in which it conformed to the ethos of the country. It both helped to shape that ethos and was shaped by it. It tended to be domesticated in the small-town society and mentality which characterized the United States through much of its history, particularly before the growth of the large cities, and later to bear the marks of the suburban areas in which it flourished. It sought to transform some features of the nation's life. It also tended to fit into it in an almost hand and glove fashion. In its very variety it reflected and reinforced ethnic, class, and racial stratifications and attitudes.

A highly important characteristic of the Christianity of the United States, and particularly of the Protestantism of the country, was the mounting role played in the total Christian scene, to some degree because of the wealth and material strength of the country, especially after 1914, to some because of the vitality of the Christianity of its people. Increasingly, the Protestantism of the United States placed its stamp on the Christianity outside Europe and had repercussions in Europe.

In the succeeding chapters we will have occasion again and again to recur to these characteristics and to note their relation to the revolutionary age. Partly because of the unprecedented and unparalleled variety of the Christianity of the United States the record is extraordinarily complex—more so than in any other country. It will not be easy to compress it within the dimensions imposed on us by the necessities of our task, but we will attempt to outline what, from the standpoint of the revolution which marked the age, were the most significant features. This initial enumeration of the main characteristics of the Christianity which emerged may help in affording perspective amid the many facets and details.

CHAPTER III

The United States of America: Countering De-Christianizing Trends and Winning Peoples of Non-Christian Ancestry

THE growing proportion of church members in the population of the United States in the face of the challenges presented by the revolutionary age was one of the striking features of the record of Christianity after 1815. As we have suggested, the increase was estimated to have been more than six-fold in the eleven decades from 1800 to 1910. It was unequalled in the nineteenth century in any other country of predominantly Christian ancestry and was surpassed only in Africa south of the Sahara, India, Burma, Indo-China, the East Indies, the islands of the Pacific, China, Korea, and Japan, where at the outset of the century the number of Christians was very small and percentage-wise mounted rapidly in the course of the hundred years. In gross numbers the gains in the United States were greater than in any other country or region.

The striking numerical increase was realized partly through the winning of millions from the partially or completely de-Christianized descendants of those who had come to the Thirteen Colonies before separation from the British Empire. It was also realized partly through holding to the churches the nineteenth-century immigrants from Europe and their children. A substantial minority came from the Indians, the Negroes, and the few tens of thousands of non-Christians from East and South Asia. We can best describe what was achieved by summarizing successively the record in each of these groups.

GAINS FROM THE OLDER STOCK: GENERALIZATIONS

The gains from the older stock were primarily by Protestant denominations which were in the country before 1815. In 1815 only a very small minority of the population was Roman Catholic. So far as the others and their immediate forebears had ecclesiastical connexions, they were or had been with one or another of the Protestant denominations. In the nineteenth century the energies of the Roman Catholic Church were almost completely absorbed in providing for those of its children who poured into the country from Europe after 1815.

While the existing Protestant bodies made some attempts to win them and the immigrants of Protestant background, their chief energies were devoted to the un-churched of pre-Revolutionary ancestry. Roman Catholics put forth efforts to convert Protestants. However, before 1914 their numerical success was slight. Except through marriages across confessional lines, until after that year relatively little success was had by Protestants in drawing Roman Catholics into their fellowship or by Roman Catholics in bringing Protestants into their fold. The Protestant denominations of Anglo-Saxon origin, longer identified with the life of the country, had missions among the nineteenth-century immigrants of Protestant provenance, mainly Lutheran or from the union churches of Lutherans and Reformed, which attacted scores of thousands. But the large majority of the German and Scandinavian immigrants of Protestant background were gathered into Lutheran churches or the Evangelical Synod in which the Lutheran and Reformed heritage was combined. The chief successes of the Protestant bodies which had been part of the colonial scene were among those of colonial ancestry.

Protestant Gains from the Older Stock on the Westward-Moving Frontier

Major numerical gains of pre-nineteenth-century Protestant bodies were on the westward-moving frontier. The advancing frontier was a continuing factor in the life of the United States. It was part of that explosion of the population of Western European stock which was a striking feature of the revolutionary age. It had been present in colonial days and persisted throughout the nineteenth century. At the beginning of that century frontier conditions still existed in most of the original thirteen states. In several they continued for more than a generation and in some mountain districts they were found even in the twentieth century. However, the frontier of settlement quickly advanced into the Mississippi Valley and by mid-century had reached the Pacific Ocean. In the latter part of the century the intervening territory was occupied. In the twentieth century the westward migration of population swelled to even larger proportions, but in most places the pioneer stage had passed.

The spread of Christianity westward was by a variety of channels and agencies. Some groups brought a congregational organization from their original home. Here and there colonies were formed for a religious purpose. There was much lay initiative in conducting Sunday Schools or forming churches. Many clergymen went west and as individuals carried on their ministry. The camp-meeting was long a favoured means. Methodists with their system of supervised circuit riders and groups known as classes were important. Baptists, Disciples of Christ, Christians, and some other denominations in which the autonomous congregation was the unit and which made no exacting requirements for the education of their ministry appealed to frontiersmen. Christians in the older

part of the country brought into existence societies which supported missionaries, aided educational institutions, or sent literature to the frontier. Some of
the societies were denominational, others interdenominational, and still others
undenominational but supported by many different churches. We can obtain
something of an impression of what occurred if we take up these instruments
of the westward expansion one by one. For the most part they were operating
at the same time and each reinforced the others.

Here and there a party which moved westward together constituted themselves a church before they left their old home. Thus we hear of early Baptist
churches in Kentucky and Tennessee organized respectively in Virginia and
North Carolina before their members started across the mountains.[1] In 1795 a
Congregational church was solemnly inaugurated in Granville, Massachusetts,
composed of members who were to found Granville, Ohio.[2]

Colonies that sought to build communities which would fully exemplify
Christian principles established themselves on vacant lands on the frontier. Of
these the largest, of which we are to say more later, was the Church of Jesus
Christ of Latter Day Saints, the Mormons. Numbers of other and smaller groups
cherished a similar dream. Some were from the older states and some from
Europe. Thus Tallmadge, Ohio, begun by a Congregational clergyman from
Connecticut, was born of such a purpose.[3] More widely known was Oberlin, in
the same state, named for the Alsatian pastor but also founded by native Americans, which had as its aim the glorification of God, service to men, and assistance to the conversion of the world and the bringing in of the millennium.[4]

Individual laymen were active and at times preceded the clergy in commencing religious organizations. Thus the first Baptist church west of the Rocky
Mountains was organized in 1844 in Oregon in the home and at the instance
of a layman.[5] The Sunday school was a convenient instrument for lay activity.

Numbers of clergymen made their way to the frontier and, often supporting
themselves by farming or teaching school, preached on Sundays. Many of them
had slight formal education, spoke the language of their hearers, and had a
method of approach which appealed to a population among whom schools were
scanty. Typical of many was Joab Powell (1799–1873). Born of Quaker stock
in Tennessee, in his twenties he experienced conversion and a call to preach as
a Baptist minister. Like numbers of pioneers, he grew restless as the country
around him became better peopled, moved across the Mississippi to Missouri

---

[1] Benedict, *A General History of the Baptist Denomination in America and Other Parts of the
World*, pp. 799, 811.

[2] William T. Utter, *Granville, The Story of an Ohio Village* (Granville, Ohio, Granville Historical Society, 1956, pp. xii, 347), pp. 32–36.

[3] Bacon, *Leonard Bacon*, pp. 22–29.

[4] James H. Fairchild, *The Colony and the College, 1833–1883* (Oberlin, E. J. Goodrich, 1883
pp. 377), pp. 9 ff.

[5] C. H. Matton, *Baptist Annals of Oregon* (McMinnville, Ore., The Pacific Baptist Press, 2 vols
1906, 1913), Vol. I, pp. 1, 2, 39, 43.

then the western outpost of settlement, and was there for twenty years, farming and preaching. Again gripped by the lure of the frontier, in 1852 he made the six-months journey by wagon to Oregon and in that land, on the farthest edge of the United States, won local fame as an itinerant preacher of revivals. Stentorian of voice, a giant in frame, utterly fearless, with a lively sense of rough humour, and possessed by a deep convictiton of the necessity of conversion and holding that conversion should be followed by righteous living, he is said to have been the means of bringing over three thousand to a Christian commitment.[6] Hundreds of others, like Powell with little formal education, had a somewhat similar record in other parts of the country.

Camp-meetings were widely employed on the frontier. The beginnings dated from around the turn of the century and took place in Kentucky.[7] Precisely when and where the first camp-meeting was held is uncertain. Although 1800 is sometimes given as the date, gatherings akin to camp-meetings appeared in connexion with the awakenings in the closing decade of the eighteenth century and the opening decade of the nineteenth century.[8] In the frontier society, where most of the population lived on isolated farms under crude physical conditions, camp-meetings afforded a means of social intercourse. Families would come from the surrounding countryside and camp in a grove, sometimes for several days. In a number of the early camp-meetings the occasion was "sacramental," involving preaching and exhortation to self-examination and repentance in preparation for a communion service. The Presbyterian James McGready (c. 1758–1817)[9] had much to do with their inception. A preacher with a voice like that of a Boanerges and with great physical energy, he fearlessly denounced sin. He moved many, among them Barton W. Stone, a leader of revivals in Kentucky and one of the originators of the churches bearing the simple name of Christian.[10] The camp-meetings were often marked by extreme physical and highly emotional phenomena—weeping, falling to the ground, jerking, shouting, barking, leaping, and dancing. They were not unlike the accompaniments of similar movements in the Middle Ages and of the preaching of John Wesley, Jonathan Edwards, George Whitefield, and others in the Evangelical and Great Awakenings. The "physical exercises" were frowned upon by some preachers and encouraged by others.[11] In the early camp-meetings Presbyterians, Baptists, and Methodists worked side by side. They preached universal redemption, free and full salvation, justification by faith, regeneration by the Holy Spirit, and the joy of a living religion.[12] The hearers often came under deep conviction of sin and

[6] M. Leona Nichols, *Joab Powell: Homespun Missionary* (Portland, Ore., Metropolitan Press, 1935, pp. 116), *passim*.
[7] Volume I, pp. 191, 192.
[8] Johnson, *The Frontier Camp Meeting*, pp. 30–32.
[9] *Dictionary of American Biography*, Vol. XII, pp. 56, 57.
[10] Volume I, p. 193.
[11] Cross, *The Burned-over District*, pp. 8, 9.
[12] Johnson, *op. cit.*, p. 35.

then, sometimes after a prolonged period of despair, entered into the peace of forgiveness and acceptance by God. Here was another expression of the Pietist-Evangelical form of Protestantism which we have met again and again in the seventeenth, the eighteenth, and notably the nineteenth centuries. The Methodists and Baptists especially gained in numbers through the camp-meetings. In Indiana in the 1830's and 1840's the followers of Barton W. Stone made much of them.[13]

The Methodists seem to have employed the camp-meetings more systematically than any other denomination. None of their official bodies appear formally to have approved them, but Francis Asbury, the bishop who more than any other one man was responsible for the organization and early growth of Methodism in the United States, was quick to seize upon them as a means of reaching the frontier.[14] Partly through Methodist hands the camp-meetings were given orderly physical patterns. The favoured form of the camp was circular, with fringes of tents around a central place for the assembled congregation. Sites were acquired and equipment provided where camp-meetings could be held year after year. By 1838 the "Old North-west" was said to be dotted with such grounds.[15]

In connexion with the camp-meetings popular hymns were written and compilations of hymns were published and circulated. They became a kind of folk music, with short, simple lines and words and melodies that sang themselves into the hearts of the rank and file.[16]

The camp-meeting reached others than the pioneers of the older white stock. In the South Negroes also attended, sometimes segregated from the whites. Here and there Indians came and were deeply moved.[17]

As a region outgrew the frontier stage the camp-meeting tended to decline and to be succeeded by more staid forms of periodic assemblies and summer camps. However, when the frontier moved westward, especially into the "Old South-west," the camp-meeting followed it and was repeated where conditions resembled those once prevailing in the earlier-settled portions of the West.[18]

The Methodist message and methods were peculiarly fitted to the frontier and early rose to meet the challenge. The message of repentance and salvation was preached in terms and in language which appealed to those having little or no formal education. The assurance that, in contrast with the doctrine of election, it was possible for any and all to fulfil the conditions for acceptance by God attracted many. Since Whitefield and Wesley had early established the custom of preaching in the open air, Methodists had a tradition congenial to the kind

13 *Ibid.*, pp. 67, 73.
14 *Ibid.*, pp. 81–85.
15 *Ibid.*, pp. 112, 113.
16 *Ibid.*, pp. 192 ff.
17 *Ibid.*, pp. 114, 115, 119.
18 *Ibid.*, pp. 242 ff.

of society common on the frontier and took kindly to the camp-meeting.

The circuit rider was a natural outgrowth of the methods employed by Wesley. On the frontier with its thinly scattered population the circuit rider filled an important function. He travelled incessantly, usually on horseback but sometimes on foot, preaching wherever he could find a hearing—in log cabins, taverns, courthouses, schoolhouses, or outdoors. One circuit was 475 miles in length and four weeks were required to traverse it.[19] Another stretched to 500 miles, and much of it was without roads.[20] Most of the circuit riders used the colloquial speech and mixed informally with the groups they met. Fairly typical was the occasion when a circuit rider turned a dance in an inn into a prayer meeting and organized the converts into a Methodist class with the landlord as the leader.[21] Often the circuit rider was ready at repartee. Again and again he faced ridicule and violence and at times met them with a strong arm.[22] Normally the circuit rider was unmarried and subsisted on a very small salary. If and when he married he was assigned a residential post. Francis Asbury (1745–1816), the organizer of the Methodist Episcopal Church, never married. Worn out by his incessant travels, he died the year after 1815.[23] William McKendree (1757–1835), the first American-born bishop, also remained a celibate. A native of Virginia, he had been a presiding elder west of the Appalachians and in 1808 was elected to the episcopate. On Asbury's death, eight years later, he became senior bishop. His duties took him over much of the nation, but he spent his last days in Tennessee.[24]

The Methodist Church possessed other features which fitted it to meet the challenge of the frontier. It had lay as well as ordained preachers, a tradition established by Wesley in England. It organized small groups of believers into what were called classes, with lay class leaders, a provision also having its rise with Wesley and peculiarly adapted to the frontier with its scattered and sparse population which made difficult individual care by ordained pastors. Its system of districts with annual conferences and appointments by the bishop, soon with the advice of the presiding elders, furthered skilled supervision.

The Methodist Church, especially on the frontier, had much that was akin

[19] *Autobiography of James B. Finley*, pp. 193, 194.
[20] *Circuit Rider Days Along the Ohio. Being the Journals of the Ohio Conference from Its Organization in 1812 to 1826*, edited with introduction and notes by William Warren Sweet (New York, The Methodist Book Concern, 1923, pp. 299), p. 51.
[21] Johnson, *op. cit.*, pp. 144 ff.; *Autobiography of Peter Cartwright, the Backwoods Preacher*, edited by W. P. Strickland, pp. 207, 208; Posey, *The Development of Methodism in the Old Southwest*, pp. 35–47.
[22] Finley, *op. cit.*, p. 196; Cartwright, *op. cit.*, pp. 141, 188, 287 ff.
[23] Volume I, pp. 190–193.
[24] Robert Paine, *Life and Times of William McKendree, Bishop of the Methodist Episcopal Church* (Nashville, Publishing House of the Methodist Episcopal Church, South, 1922, pp. 549), *passim;* E. E. Hoss, *William McKendree, A Biographical Study* (Nashville, Publishing House of the M. E. Church, South, 1924, pp. 206), *passim.* On the difficulties of travel faced by McKendree in the West, and fairly typical of the frontier, see Barclay, *History of Methodist Missions*, Vol. I, pp. 216, 217.

to the early Franciscans—the dedicated poverty, the joyous preaching of salvation, an orderly structure marked by occasional dissensions and storms, and the third order of laity, who did not take the vows of the full members but who shared their faith and gave themselves to works of piety and benevolence.

Baptists, Christians, and Disciples of Christ also were singularly adapted to the frontier, although in some respects in ways which contrasted with those characteristic of the Methodists. Like the latter, their clergy were usually men of slight education who spoke the language of the common man. While, in contradiction of the Methodist Arminianism, many Baptists believed in predestination and election, not all did so. As time went on, in practice the majority of Baptists proclaimed that Christ's death was for all and urged all men to repent. The form of organization prevalent among Baptists, Christians, and Disciples, with its autonomy of the local congregation and the theoretically equal voice of every member in the decisions of the congregation, appealed to a frontier society which was extremely democratic and which held that each must prove his worth by his achievements. The democracy of the frontier of the United States had antecedents in the Puritan-Evangelical ethos, in itself a preparation for the message of salvation by faith and the appeal to the will of the individual to repent and accept the salvation freely offered by God.

Of the numerous societies which sprang up in the older parts of the country and which had as their objective or at least one of their chief objectives the spread of the Gospel and the nourishing of the Christians on the frontier, a few must serve as examples.

As the strongest denomination numerically and in geographic compactness at the beginning of the century, the Congregationalists were especially active in forming such societies. Missionaries early went from Connecticut, and in 1798 the Missionary Society of Connecticut was formed.[25] It sent representatives to Vermont, western New York, and the Western Reserve in Ohio, for here settlers from Connecticut were numerous. In 1814 the Massachusetts Missionary Society (organized in 1799) was supporting thirty preachers. The Hampshire Society, with its base in the portion of the Connecticut River Valley which lay in Massachusetts, had missionaries in the West.[26]

The Presbyterian General Assembly sent ministers to serve the settlers of Presbyterian ancestry, largely Scotch-Irish. In 1816 it created its Board of Home Missions in succession to an earlier standing committee which had home missions as its responsibility.[27]

In 1826 the American Home Missionary Society was organized. It was in-

[25] Edwin Pond Parker, *Historical Discourse in Commemoration of the One Hundredth Anniversary of the Missionary Society of Connecticut* (Hartford, The Case, Rockwood & Brainerd Co. 1898, pp. 40), *passim.*

[26] Cross, *op. cit.,* pp. 19–22.

[27] William Warren Sweet, *Religion on the American Frontier,* Vol. II, *The Presbyterians 1783-1840, a Collection of Source Materials* (New York, Harper & Brothers, 1936, pp. xi, 435), p. 32.

tended to be an agency for uniting the efforts of several denominations in a comprehensive plan for reaching the nation. At the outset and for some years Congregationalists, Presbyterians, the Reformed, and the Associate Reformed joined in it. Eventually, since the others withdrew to form their own agencies, its support came only from Congregationalists. In 1893, in recognition of the change, the name was altered to the Congregational Home Missionary Society.[28] Its activities were chiefly north of the Ohio River, in the regions between that Old North-west and the Rockies, and along the Pacific coast. Some of its agents went to particular areas as bands made up of those graduating in the same year from the Yale Divinity School or Andover Theological Seminary. Several took the initiative in founding colleges.[29]

One of the outstanding missionaries of the Presbyterian Board of Home Missions was Sheldon Jackson (1834–1909). A native of New York State, he served the Board in Minnesota and in the vast region of the Rocky Mountains, travelling by crude methods of transportation, preaching, organizing churches, sometimes helping to erect church buildings with his own hands, recruiting and assigning missionaries, and raising funds. He served not only the whites but also the Indians. When the Rocky Mountain states began to pass out of the pioneer stage, Jackson moved on to Alaska, recently purchased by the United States from Russia. He there gave himself primarily to the Eskimos, starting schools for them and importing domesticated reindeer from Siberia to augment their food supply. He lived to see the gold rush to the Klondike, with its influx of miners and the rough frontier society which it created.[30]

Largely at the instance of John Mason Peck (1789–1838), in 1832 the American Baptist Home Mission Society was organized and adopted all of North America as its field. From early in the 1800's Baptists had been sending missionaries to the West and had formed local and state societies for that purpose. Peck had already travelled widely in Illinois, Indiana, and Missouri, establishing Bible societies and Sunday Schools, editing a religious journal, and beginning a college. Under the society whose founding he stimulated, Baptists sought to develop a comprehensive programme for reaching the vast continent which they envisaged as its responsibility.[31]

The Methodists were not content with their system of circuit riders super-

[28] Goodykoontz, *Home Missions on the American Frontier*, pp. 173–179; Walker, *A History of the Congregational Churches in the United States*, pp. 328, 329; Clark, *Leavening the Nation*, pp. 59 ff.

[29] Clark, *op. cit.*, pp. 70–72, 109, 110, 134–136, 209–311; George F. Magoun, *Asa Turner. A Home Missionary Patriarch and His Times* (Boston, Congregational Sunday-School and Publishing Society, 1889, pp. 345), *passim;* Ephraim Adams, *The Iowa Band* (Boston, The Pilgrim Press, rev. ed., no date, pp. xx, 240), *passim;* Truman O. Douglass, *The Pilgrims of Iowa* (Boston, The Pilgrim Press, no date, pp. xiv, 422), *passim.*

[30] Stewart, *Sheldon Jackson, passim.*

[31] White, *A Century of Faith*, pp. 28–49; Rufus Babcock, *Memoir of John Mason Peck D.D. Edited from His Journals and Correspondence* (Philadelphia, American Baptist Publication Society, 1864, pp. 360), *passim;* Goodykoontz, *op. cit.*, pp. 202, 203.

vised by presiding elders, conferences, and bishops. They organized societies to inaugurate and assist missions both at home and abroad. When, in 1820, the General Conference organized the Missionary Society of the Methodist Episcopal Church, the primary concern was the United States, and especially assistance to the "itinerating system" and its extension in the rapidly increasing new settlements. Indian missions were one of the objects and foreign missions were envisioned as a possibility, but it was to the advancing frontier that the Society was intended to direct its major efforts.[32]

Partly to meet the challenge of the frontier, in 1820 the General Convention of the Protestant Episcopal Church organized what a year later was named the Domestic and Foreign Missionary Society of the Protestant Episcopal Church in the United States of America. In 1835 the base was so broadened that all members of the church were considered as members of the society. Moreover, in that year the General Convention adopted the policy of electing missionary bishops to serve in states and territories not organized as dioceses. The way was thus prepared for the nation-wide extension of the church and for planning on a national scale.[33] An effective agent of the new policy was found in Jackson Kemper (1789–1870). He had long been interested in the West and was appointed the first missionary bishop. His initial jurisdiction was Missouri and Indiana, but it was later broadened to include "the North-west." Over this vast area he travelled indefatigably. He sought to recruit clergy from the Eastern states, but they proved to be ill adapted to the frontier. To fill the gap he began Kemper College in Missouri, but it did not have a long life. He then founded Nashotah House in Wisconsin and, a high-churchman, established it in that tradition. As dioceses were carved out of the huge area for which he was responsible, he confined his efforts to Wisconsin.[34]

Zealous though the Congregational, Presbyterian, and Episcopal missionaries were, they did not succeed in attracting as large constituencies on the frontier as did Methodists, Baptists, Christians, and Disciples of Christ. They stressed an educated ministry, and men with that kind of preparation did not know how to appeal to the rank and file. Their congregations were gathered chiefly from the minority who had some formal education and a degree of culture.

Congregationalists and Presbyterians, the former especially, through the schools and colleges which they founded did much to raise the level of education in the West. Several of the representatives of the American Baptist Home Mission Society promoted education and inaugurated colleges. Without losing their touch with the common man, the Methodists too laid the foundations for

[32] Barclay, *op. cit.*, pp. 205–208.

[33] *Proceedings of the Board of Missions of the Protestant Episcopal Church in the United States of America at their forty-first annual meeting . . . October, 1876,* appendix, p. 3; Manross, *A History of the American Episcopal Church,* p. 257.

[34] *Dictionary of National Biography,* Vol. X, pp. 321, 322; Addison, *The Episcopal Church in the United States 1789–1931,* pp. 140–144.

colleges and universities which were to become prominent. But it was the Congregationalists and Presbyterians who led in education, in the kind of preparation which would be important as the West passed out of the pioneer stage and began to feel the full impact of the intellectual currents of the revolutionary age challenging Christianity.

A number of societies, some undenominational and others denominational, sought to meet specialized needs on the frontier, but most of them did not direct their efforts solely to that region. Thus in 1816 the American Bible Society was organized. The British and Foreign Bible Society, formed in 1804, had stimulated the creation of numbers of Bible societies in the Continent of Europe. In the United States its example proved contagious. Between 1809 and 1815 more than a hundred Bible societies, some local and some state-wide, came into being. To the state societies the British society gave financial assistance. Partly as a result of visits to the Mississippi Valley by Samuel J. Mills and his reports of the spiritual destitution on that vast frontier, the American Bible Society was born. It, too, was assisted by an initial grant from the British and Foreign Bible Society. Somewhat on the British pattern, numerous auxiliary societies sprang up. The American Bible Society did not confine its efforts to the frontier but planned on a nation-wide scale and early began to establish agencies in other lands.[35] In 1825 the American Tract Society was begun, with the Religious Tract Society having its seat in London and dating from 1799, as a prototype.[36] Not far from the same time, in 1824, in that early heyday of effort across denominational lines, the American Sunday School Union was constituted.[37] In 1828 it adopted the ambitious programme of bringing into being a Sunday School wherever a sufficient constituency could be found in the United States and its territories.[38] The Methodist Book Concern, established in 1789, in 1820 opened a branch office in Cincinnati.[39] The year 1824 saw the inauguration of the Baptist General Tract Society. In 1840 it became the American Baptist Publication Society.[40] Through its colporteurs it distributed literature and organized Sunday Schools on the frontier and later built chapel cars to utilize the railways to reach the new settlements. Several societies were organized to assist colleges in the West. The chief one was the predominantly Congregational and Presbyterian Society for Promoting Collegiate and Theological Education in the West.[41]

[35] Dwight, *The Centennial History of the American Bible Society*, Vol. I, pp. 8 ff.
[36] *First Annual Report of the American Tract Society Instituted at New York, 1825* (New York, 1826, pp. 48), *passim*.
[37] A. A. Brown, *A History of Religious Education in Recent Times*, pp. 18–24.
[38] J. O. Oliphant in *Church History*, Vol. VII, p. 133.
[39] Barclay, *op. cit.*, p. 218.
[40] Newman, *A History of the Baptist Churches in the United States*, pp. 426, 427.
[41] Tewksbury, *The Founding of American Colleges and Universities Before the Civil War*, pp. 7–12.

PROTESTANT GAINS FROM THE OLDER STOCK IN THE LONGER-SETTLED SECTIONS:
THE EVANGELISTS

By what methods did the Protestant bodies which had come down from colonial days seek to check the de-Christianization of the older American stock
in the longer-settled portions of the country? What were the results? The frontier moved westward or retreated into the valleys and uplands of the Appala-
chian Mountains. As vast areas passed out of the pioneer stage, roads improved,
towns and cities had a rapid growth, living standards became higher, and the
level of education and of culture was raised. The methods adapted to the frontier were quickly outmoded. The earlier type of camp-meeting dwindled and
was succeeded by less highly emotional assemblies and camp sites with more
physical comforts. A ministry with more formal education was required if
Christianity was to keep pace with the changing conditions. Yet sophistication
did not immediately come to the rank and file, even in the towns and cities.
The kind of approach adapted to the highly educated who were aware of the
subtleties of the intellectual challenge of the revolutionary age would not meet
the needs of the majority.

Out of the Protestantism represented in pre-nineteenth-century days came
men and methods adapted to the new conditions. Many of the men were pastors of local congregations. Others were professional itinerants—"evangelists."
In community after community they held "protracted meetings," daily for a
week or more, in which they presented the Gospel, sought to bring conviction
of sin, urged repentance, and pointed the way to assurance of salvation. They
continued the Pietist-Evangelical tradition and message. Better educated than
the average preacher of frontier days, they were near enough to the level of the
majority of their hearers to be on common ground with them and so to win a
response. Their number was legion and we can take the space to mention only
a few of the more outstanding.

In New England, where the level of education in the first part of the century
was as high as anywhere in the country, two men, Nathaniel William Taylor
(1786–1858) and Lyman Beecher (1775–1863), were outstanding.

Taylor, grandson of a distinguished Connecticut clergyman who was one of
the Old Lights who had not believed in the Great Awakening, and son of a
prosperous business man, while a student in Yale had come under the influence
of its president, Timothy Dwight (1752–1817).[42] Dwight, a grandson of Jonathan Edwards, was prominent as an able opponent of the Deism and scepticism
which, associated with the French Revolution, were popular among many students. Under Dwight revival after revival broke out in Yale. In that atmosphere
Taylor was converted after a period of deep depression, studied theology with
Dwight, and was his secretary. Like Dwight, and true to the inherited Augus-

[42] Volume I, pp. 190, 196.

tinianism and Calvinism, he believed that he could not be sure of his salvation but cherished a degree of hope which gave him joy. From 1812 to 1822 he was pastor of the First (Centre) Church of New Haven, one of the most important in the Congregationalism of the day. Handsome, eloquent, with a dignity which bordered on arrogance, he sought above all to convict men of sin and to lead them to Christ. Under his preaching revivals occurred in 1815, 1816, 1820, and 1821. In 1822 he became the first professor of theology in the newly organized Yale Divinity School. There he had a profound and wide influence on theological thought to which we must recur. His concern always was the conversion of sinners and their growth in the Christian life.[43]

Lyman Beecher, older than Taylor, like him a graduate of Yale where he was also under the influence of Dwight, was the son and grandson of blacksmiths and so from a very different social background. He formed a deep attachment to the younger man and the two became fast friends. Lyman Beecher sired a family of distinguished sons and daughters, but in his own right he was one of the outstanding clergymen of his day and leader in revivals. From 1810 to 1826 he was pastor of the Congregational Church in Litchfield, Connecticut, a village then marked for its intellectual life. He laboured for revivals, not only in his own parish but elsewhere, and with striking success. He wished them to be preached by clergymen who were settled in parishes rather than by itinerants without regular pastoral charges, and he helped promote a method in Connecticut by which the state was covered systematically by ministers who, each with his own parish, would devote part of their time to itinerant preaching. He worked for a continuous revival. In 1826 he was called to the pastorate of the Hanover Street Congregational Church in Boston to combat the Unitarianism which had that city as its main stronghold. His preaching led to notable revivals. He also attacked the Roman Catholicism which, through immigration, was increasing in that erstwhile Puritan capital. In 1832 he became the first president of Lane Theological Seminary in Cincinnati and pastor of the Second Presbyterian Church in that Ohio city. There he not only furthered revivals but also became the storm centre of a theological controversy in which he was brought before the Presbyterian General Assembly on the charge of heresy—an incident in the struggle over the issues posed by the revolutionary age which will later command our attention. He retired in 1850, in his mid-seventies, and spent most of his remaining years in Brooklyn with his famous minister son, Henry Ward Beecher.[44]

A friend of Lyman Beecher, but unlike him an itinerant evangelist, without a settled pastorate and unmarried, Asahel Nettleton (1783–1843), was noted in his day as a preacher of revivals which issued in conversions, usually without

[43] Mead, *Nathaniel William Taylor, passim.*
[44] Beecher, *Autobiography, Correspondence, etc., passim;* Mead, *op. cit.,* pp. 76–79; Edward F. Hayward, *Lyman Beecher* (Boston, The Pilgrim Press, 1904, pp. 114), *passim.*

the extreme emotional accompaniments and the censoriousness for the "unconverted" which sometimes marked similar movements. A farmer's son, he, too, was a native of Connecticut and a graduate of Yale under Dwight. Before he entered college he had had a profound religious experience marked by deep conviction of sin and despondency followed by a sense of inward peace. Yet, like Taylor and Dwight, he never expressed a high degree of confidence that he was a child of God and said, "the most that I have ventured to say respecting myself is, that I think it possible I may get to heaven." He wished to be a missionary in other lands and was a friend of Samuel J. Mills, who more than any other one man was responsible for the beginning of foreign missions from the United States. He was unable to fulfil that purpose and instead gave himself to the work of an evangelist, chiefly in Connecticut, Massachusetts, eastern New York, and also in Virginia and North Carolina. In doing so, he always sought to coöperate with pastors and not to criticize them. Some of his preaching was in communities without a pastor. In his later years he was on the faculty of the Theological Institute of Connecticut (later the Hartford Theological Seminary), which owed its origin to protests against the theology Taylor was teaching in Yale.[45]

Charles Grandison Finney (1792–1875) was even more prominent than Taylor, Beecher, and Nettleton and in influence was the outstanding American evangelist of the first half of the nineteenth century.[46] Born in Litchfield County, Connecticut, of old New England stock, as a young child Finney was taken by his parents to central New York, then on the frontier. There, in pioneer conditions, he came to maturity. Tall, handsome, full of energy, fond of outdoor sports, and with a strong musical bent, he had some formal education but decided not to go to college and through individual study and teaching school sought to obtain the equivalent of what he might have acquired at Yale. He became a lawyer, led the choir in the local Presbyterian church, but scoffed at the dogma which he heard from the pulpit and at the practices of professed Christians. When he was twenty-nine, after a profound religious crisis he was converted. He began immediately to testify to his new-found faith, a revival broke out, and his father and mother were converted. Although from objections to the doctrines taught there he refused to go to Princeton Theological Seminary, a presbytery ordained him. He first preached in frontier villages in northern New York. There his earnestness, his homely illustrations, his avoidance of the ordinary pulpit conventions, and his vivid portrayal and denunciation of sin brought conviction to hundreds, some of them previously noted for their

---

[45] Bennet Tyler, *Memoir of the Life and Character of Rev. Asahel Nettleton, D.D.* (Boston, Doctrinal Tract and Book Co., 1850, pp. 367), *passim; Remains of the Late Rev. Asahel Nettleton, D.D.,* compiled by Bennet Tyler (Hartford, Robins and Smith, 1845, pp. 408), *passim.*

[46] Of the large literature by and about Finney, see *Memoirs of Rev. Charles G. Finney, Written by Himself* (New York, A. S. Barnes, 1878, pp. xii, 477); and George Frederick Wright, *Charles Grandison Finney* (Boston, Houghton Mifflin Co., 1893, pp. vi, 329).

godlessness. He also proclaimed the wonders of God's grace. Revival after revival was stirred by his preaching, with physical and emotional accompaniments. He moved to more settled portions of central New York and similar scenes followed his preaching, with marked moral improvement in entire areas.

Criticism of Finney's methods developed. In it Beecher and Nettleton joined. A meeting of interested ministers from New England and New York in 1827 brought better understanding but not full agreement. Later, however, it was on Beecher's invitation that Finney held meetings in Boston.

In spite of criticism, Finney's influence spread. He preached in cities on or near the Eastern seaboard. For months he was in Philadelphia. For a year in 1830–1831 he was in New York City, and many leading lawyers and business men were among the converts. He made the acquaintance of Arthur and Lewis Tappan, wealthy philanthropists, and was given their full support. In Rochester, a growing city in upper New York, he introduced the practice of the "anxious seat," pews at the front of the room to which those who were ready to repent of their sins and to consecrate their whole hearts to God were invited to come for personal conversation and direction.

Although Finney held to what might be called New School Calvinism, the Old School Calvinists believed that he was acting against sound doctrine when he urged his hearers to repent on the assumption that they could if they would and become at once the inheritors of the divine promises of acceptance and salvation. The Old School Calvinists held that only the elect could be converted, that conversion was wrought directly on their hearts by God, and that the function of the preacher must be limited to recommending to his hearers the use of the means of grace and waiting on the Lord to transform their desires by His sovereign grace. Finney became increasingly dissatisfied with Presbyterian forms of procedure, his friends organized the Broadway Tabernacle in New York City as a Congregational church, and in 1836 at his request he was released by his presbytery and his name was erased from its roll.

In his later years Finney was a resident of Oberlin, Ohio. He went there in 1835 to take charge of the theological education which was being begun in that infant idealistic community. According to the original plan he was to spend half of each year there and half as pastor of the Broadway Tabernacle. However, the strain of the double duty became too great and in 1837 he resigned his New York post and made Oberlin his centre. From 1835 to 1872 he was pastor of the First Congregational Church in that village and from 1851 to 1866 was president of the college. He gave part of each year to evangelistic meetings elsewhere. In 1849–1850 and 1859–1860 he was in Great Britain and reinforced the Evangelical movement in that country. As we have seen, the inception of the Young Men's Christian Association in London was deeply indebted to him—although through his writings rather than through his spoken words.

Finney had high ideals for the Christian life and believed that it was possible to attain them. He stressed not only conversion but also sanctification. He held that many of the popular amusements were inconsistent with the Christian profession and were a hindrance to growth in Christian character. He taught total abstinence from the use of alcohol and tobacco and looked with disfavour upon tea and coffee. A Mason before his conversion, he later came out emphatically in opposition to that order.

Finney gave impetus to some of the movements for reform. Although he made conversion primary in his preaching, he was against Negro slavery. Some of the most active abolitionists were among his converts and friends. He endorsed the interracial policy of Oberlin and the coëducation of the sexes for which the institution stood.

That Finney had an outstanding role in reaching the partially de-Christianized of the older American stock was due partly to his native ability, even more to his profound conviction, and in no small degree to the fact that he was a child of his generation and could meet others of it on their own ground. Reared, as many of them had been, on the frontier, like them with the westward movement of the frontier he had acquired more education than would have been possible in frontier days. He spoke their language and appealed to beliefs which they might outwardly deny but which were part of their inheritance—in the Bible, in a life of misery or bliss beyond the grave, in sin, and in the necessity of conversion through faith in what God had done in Christ and commitment to Christ—in other words, the Pietist-Evangelical legacy. Most of his later evangelism was in the growing cities, to which thousands with his background were going. Although he worked out a theology, it was not particularly original. It grappled with the questions propounded by Calvinism to the methods of evangelism prevalent in the older Protestantism of the United States of his time rather than with those with which theology and Biblical scholarship were confronted in Europe by the revolutionary age.

Symptomatic of the growing concentration of life in the cities and of the increasing role of lay leadership was what was called the prayer-meeting revival of 1857–1858. It began in New York City in September, 1857, in a noon prayer meeting for business men. Prayer meetings multiplied at other hours of the day and in most of the larger cities and towns. Their emphasis was upon prayer rather than preaching. Significantly, they were interdenominational. Physical and nervous excitement were noticeably absent. Laymen were prominent in the leadership. Large accessions to the churches followed.[47] As we have seen, the movement spread across the Atlantic.

Dwight Lyman Moody (1837–1899) was the most prominent evangelist in the second half of the nineteenth century. By his rearing, experience, and per-

---

[47] Weigle, *American Idealism*, pp. 182, 183; Frank Grenville Beardsley, *A History of American Revivals* (New York, American Tract Society, 1904, pp. 352), pp. 213 ff.; Smith, *Revivalism and Social Reform*, pp. 63–79.

sonal characteristics, as well as by his deep and unquestioning faith, he appealed to many of the older American stock and to men of affairs from that stock who, like himself, were largely from humble rural backgrounds but through their own efforts had become successful in business in the burgeoning towns and cities. They tended to dismiss as irrelevant issues raised by the intellectual movements of the age, accepted the Scriptures as the inspired word of God, and were activists, impatient with theological debate. Even more than his predecessors, Moody concentrated his efforts on the cities, the nerve centres of the revolutionary age. Unlike the other evangelists whom we have mentioned, he was a layman and remained such to the end of his days. He had only a smattering of formal education, but by reason of his transparent sincerity, informality, and good sense he had a striking influence on university students and graduates. Moreover, when he was convinced of their Christian faith and character, he welcomed the coöperation of Biblical scholars such as George Adam Smith and of cultivated men such as Henry Drummond who were familiar with modern science and the issues raised by evolution.[48]

Moody was born in Northfield, a village on the Connecticut River, in northern Massachusetts. He was of old New England stock. His father, a brickmason, died when he was four years old and his mother reared him. A healthy, lively, wholesome, warm-hearted, quick-tempered lad, given to pranks, he left school at the age of thirteen to go to work on neighbouring farms. Like many other country boys of the day, at seventeen, restless and ambitious, he went to Boston to seek his fortune. There he was employed in a shoe store owned by his uncles. In Boston he became a member of the Young Men's Christian Association. There, too, through a Sunday School teacher, he had what he regarded as his conversion and joined a Congregational church. The only church in his native Northfield was Unitarian and he had been baptized in it, but so little had been his early religious instruction that the Boston church kept him waiting for a year to acquire more knowledge of Christian doctrine before it would admit him to full membership.

In 1856 Moody did as many another youth from the East was doing: he went west. In the young and growing city of Chicago he was soon on the way to success as a salesman of shoes. He gave an increasing amount of his time to religious work. He filled pews which he rented in a Congregational church with men from hotels, boarding houses, and the streets. He taught a Sunday School class of boys whom he gathered from the slums. In 1858 he organized a Sunday School around which he developed a programme of evangelism, prayer meetings, social recreation, and welfare work. Soon, after a sharp inward struggle, for he could have acquired a fortune in business, he decided to devote his time entirely to religious enterprises. In this he was aided by his wife, Emma C.

[48] A standard life, sympathetic, by a son, is William R. Moody, *D. L. Moody* (New York, The Macmillan Co., 1931, pp. 556).

Revell, a Baptist of English birth, who reinforced his purpose and helped him to acquire some of the social graces which were alien to his rearing. Believing that as a Christian worker he could not consistently enlist as a soldier in the Civil War, he gave himself unstintedly to those who did so and coöperated with the National Christian Commission. After the war he served as president of the Chicago Young Men's Christian Association. Out of his Sunday School came evangelistic meetings for the parents of the children. Although for a time he demurred, wishing the converts to join one of the neighbouring churches, a union or interdenominational church sprang up—after his death called the Moody Memorial Church. He held evangelistic meetings in Chicago and elsewhere.

Following preliminary visits in 1867 and 1870, from 1873 to 1875 Moody was in the British Isles. He took with him as a singer Ira D. Sankey (1840–1908).[49] Sankey, with a good untrained baritone voice, usually accompanying himself with a small reed organ, sang simply, with careful enunciation and much feeling and expression, and with a sense of the dramatic. Beginning without publicity and in the face of some criticism, the Moody and Sankey meetings mounted in attendance and were said to have stirred Britain more than any of that nature since Wesley and Whitefield. Moody and Sankey were again in the British Isles in 1881–1884, and once more their meetings were thronged. The year 1891 saw Moody for a fifth time in Britain, chiefly in Scotland.

The fame of the British meetings brought Moody many invitations in the United States. As a rule he required the coöperation of churches across denominational lines and efficient preliminary preparation, organization, and publicity. He did not criticize the clergy, wished those converted in his meetings to identify themselves with existing churches, and had no ambition to start a new denomination.

In his methods and message Moody both resembled and differed from his predecessors in seeking to bring the Gospel to the masses. Like the frontier preachers and Finney, he spoke the language of the people and reinforced his message by homely terms and vivid, pungent illustrations. Like them, he had a passion for conversions. Unlike most of them he discouraged emotional and physical manifestations and stopped them abruptly if they broke out in any of his meetings. After his first few years, in contrast with the others we have mentioned, although he denounced sin in scathing fashion he did not attempt to frighten his hearers with the prospect of certain judgement but emphasized the love of God. To him Christianity was the Gospel, "Good News," that "God so loved the world that He gave His only begotten Son, that whosoever believeth in Him should not perish but have everlasting life." Men such as Dwight and

[49] Ira David Sankey, *My Life and the Story of the Gospel Hymns and of Sacred Songs and Solos* (Philadelphia, P. W. Ziegler Co., 1907, pp. 410); *Dictionary of American Biography*, Vol. XVI, pp. 352, 353.

Taylor were never assured that they were among the elect. Moody, however, was joyously certain that by God's grace he had entered on eternal life. He encouraged others to the confidence that they could have the same experience. Also in contrast with some who went before him, he was not interested in the intricacies of dogma. With them, he accepted the Bible as God's Word and made much of its study, but in it he saw the beliefs held in common by those of the Pietist-Evangelical tradition and not the issues which had divided them.

Like other awakenings in the Pietist-Evangelical succession, the Moody revivals found expression in hymns. Moody and Sankey were responsible for *Sacred Songs and Solos* and *Gospel Hymns Numbers 1, 2, 3, 4, 5, 6*, of which millions of copies were sold. These collections reinforced the Evangelical pattern which was common in the older American stock.

Moody was intensely practical and insisted that conversion, if genuine, would issue in good works. He practised what he preached. The enormous profits from his hymnals and other books he devoted to causes which he favoured. Among them were the Northfield Schools—one for girls in Northfield and one for boys at Mt. Hermon a few miles away—for those who without them might have found it difficult or impossible to obtain an education. He organized a school in Chicago for training for religious work men and women who were unable financially to go to college or theological seminary. He also raised many thousands of dollars for objects in which he believed, among them buildings for Young Men's Christian Associations.

Although with only a common school education and quite aware of his lack of a university background, at the height of his career Moody gave much attention to undergraduates and greatly impressed many of them. In his years in Britain in the 1880's, for example, he held meetings in Cambridge and Oxford. At the outset in both universities faced with rowdyism, he won his way and many of his hearers were permanently changed. He spoke in many colleges and universities in the United States. He held summer conferences for students, first at Mt. Hermon in 1886 and later in Northfield. From the Mt. Hermon gathering came the Student Volunteer Movement for Foreign Missions, which in the course of succeeding years enlisted thousands of young men and women for service abroad. At his invitation J. E. K. Studd, later Sir Kynaston Studd and Lord Mayor of London, visited colleges and universities in the United States and Canada, telling of the awakenings in the British universities. Through Moody a great impetus was given to the Student Young Men's Christian Associations, then near their inception and for years the chief channels of voluntary student religious activities in American colleges and universities. In their student days men such as John R. Mott and Sherwood Eddy were profoundly stirred by him. Both were to be evangelists in many different parts of the world.[50]

[50] Shedd, *Two Centuries of Student Christian Movements*, pp. 229 ff.; Mathews, *John R. Mott,*

The later decades of the nineteenth century saw many other itinerant evangelists, but none of them with such widespread or profound influence as Finney and Moody. Rodney ("Gipsy") Smith (1860–1947), English born, a son of gipsies, converted when he was sixteen, did most of his preaching in Britain but made repeated visits to the United States, largely in connexion with Methodists.[51] Reuben Archer Torrey (1856–1928), much moved by Finney's writings and later by the example of George Müller, was pastor successively of several churches. There his ministry was marked by revivals. He was chosen by Moody to be the first superintendent of the Bible institute which the latter founded in Chicago and later added to the post the pastorate of the church which Moody had begun in that city. Together with a singer, Charles McCallon Alexander (1867–1920), he held evangelistic meetings not only in the United States but also in Australia and Great Britain.[52] John Wilbur Chapman (1859–1918), declared by Moody in 1895 to be "the greatest evangelist in the country," a Presbyterian minister who held pastorates before giving himself to itineracy, and at one time moderator of his church, like Torrey did not confine his efforts to the United States but engaged in evangelistic "campaigns" in Australia, Asia, and the British Isles. He developed what he called the "simultaneous evangelistic campaign," dividing into districts the cities where he held meetings, each with a preacher and song-leader, with Chapman himself speaking in a large centrally located hall.[53]

The most famous evangelist on the eve of 1914 was William Ashley Sunday (1862–1935), better known as Billy Sunday. Sunday's father was of fairly recent German immigrant parentage and his mother of the older American stock. His formal education was slight. He was in professional baseball, in 1886 was converted in the Pacific Garden Mission in Chicago, in 1888 married an active Presbyterian who became his lifelong able assistant, soon began to give full time in the Young Men's Christian Association in the Chicago slums, and in the 1890's became an assistant and close personal friend of Chapman. Eventually he was ordained as a Presbyterian minister.

When Chapman became a pastor in a Philadelphia church, Sunday continued itinerant evangelism. For several years he confined his efforts to towns and smaller cities in the Middle West, largely in his native Iowa. There he gradually developed the methods which attracted nation-wide attention. He held his meetings in great tents and then in wooden "tabernacles" erected especially for the purpose. He had a careful business organization and demanded the coöperation

World Citizen, pp. 33 ff.; Sherwood Eddy, *Eighty Adventurous Years. An Autobiography* (New York, Harper & Brothers, 1955, pp. 255), pp. 26, 27.

[51] *Gipsy Smith, His Life and Work, by Himself* (Chicago, Fleming H. Revell Co., 1902, pp. 330), *passim*.

[52] George T. B. Davis, *Torrey and Alexander. The Story of a World-wide Revival* (Chicago, Fleming H. Revell Co., 1905, pp. 257), *passim*.

[53] *Dictionary of American Biography*, Vol. IV, p. 19.

of the churches. He became increasingly informal on the platform, using ex-
pressive, colloquial language and antics suggesting vaudeville, shedding his coat
and vest as he warmed to his message. He encouraged applause in his audiences,
had large massed choirs to lead the singing, attacked saloons, liquor, gambling,
dancing, swearing, smutty stories, and card-playing, and encouraged those professing conversion to come down the aisles to the platform—"hitting the sawdust trail," it was called—and shake his hand. He sought to bring about civic
and community moral reform. He came out strongly for prohibition. His was
a cheerful, happy religion. He applied to his "revivals" the advertising, promo-
tional, and other organizing methods of the contemporary American business
world. Frank, honest, with a charm which won his way with large audiences
and with individuals, he never spared himself but exuded energy. His pulpit
acrobatics left him perspiring and exhausted. He had no scruples about accepting large "free will offerings" and, although he regularly gave a tenth to what
he deemed worthy causes, he did not, as had Moody, devote what eventually
was a large income to philanthropic enterprises.

Not far from 1911 Sunday began to move out of the towns and smaller cities
of the Middle West into other parts of the country and to larger cities. Among
other centres he held meetings in Philadelphia, Boston, Washington, and, as a
kind of climax, in New York City in 1917. He gradually built up a large staff
to assist in one form or another of his campaigns and for some years paid them
out of his own pocket. For twenty years his song-leader was Homer Alvin Rodeheaver, who had great skill in "warming up" the city audiences with preliminary "inspirational" song services. Rodeheaver emphasized the more cheerful
songs, such as "Brighten the corner where you are."

Like Moody, Sunday discouraged the kind of emotionalism which had characterized the camp-meetings and even the early meetings of Finney. His revivals
were orderly and respectable. He became a national figure and was a friend of
Theodore Roosevelt, William Jennings Bryan, and John D. Rockefeller, Jr. He
was not blind to the social evils of his day and not only stood for prohibition but
also excoriated child labour and the exploitation of the poor by the rich. Sunday
was not a profound theologian and, with Moody, he held that those who acknowledged Jesus Christ as their personal saviour could be assured that they
were children of God and now had eternal life.

Sunday's appeal was most effective among the middle income groups of the
older American stock and, in proportion to the population, more in towns and
small cities where that element constituted a larger percentage of the population
than in the great cities where the nineteenth-century immigration congregated.
Many who "hit the sawdust trail" were already members of Protestant churches
which served the descendants of the pre-nineteenth-century population. Gains

in church membership through his campaigns were substantial but were also mainly from that portion of the nation.[54]

We have devoted so much space to the Protestant efforts to counter the de-Christianization of the older American stock on the frontier and in the longer-settled portions of the country because of their importance in shaping the Protestantism of the country and in affecting its response to the revolutionary age. Through these efforts striking progress was made against the threatened de-Christianization. They greatly strengthened the Pietist-Evangelical strain of Protestantism. Before 1815 that strain was already relatively more prominent in the new nation than anywhere in Europe. By the methods employed to meet the challenge of de-Christianization it became predominant in the Protestantism of the United States, most markedly in the Protestant bodies which had been represented there before 1815. It was much less characteristic of the Protestant bodies arising out of the nineteenth-century immigration. When it appeared among them it was usually in forms quite different from the ones which came out of the awakenings and revivals that penetrated the pre-nineteenth-century stock. The awakenings and revivals were furthered by thousands of pastors and itinerant evangelists and became a normal feature of much of the older Protestantism of the country. The revivalism and its accompanying evangelism issued in the phenomenal growth of denominations which were either minorities or non-existent on the other side of the Atlantic—especially the Baptists, the Methodists, and the Disciples of Christ and the Christians. These denominational families in their several branches eventually enrolled the large majority of the Protestants and together were more numerous than the Roman Catholics and Orthodox, even after the vast immigration of the nineteenth century had flooded the country and especially the cities with the hereditary children of these churches. The revivalism gave wide currency to theological attitudes which both reflected the spirit of the nation and shaped it. It stressed the importance of the decision of the individual and thus was congenial to and reinforced the individualism and the kind of democracy already deeply indebted to the Puritan-Pietist tradition of colonial days. The trend which we have noted in evangelism to insist on the full ability of every man to accept the salvation offered through Christ became progressively more marked. In practice it was a repudiation of the Augustinian-Calvinistic doctrine of election. Even Finney, Chapman, and Sunday, ordained Presbyterian clergymen though they were and theoretically committed to the Westminster Confession, in their appeals to the unconverted ignored the belief in election so clearly set forth in that document. Methodism had always been Arminian, as had been important Baptist groups. Most of the

[54] William G. McLoughlin, Jr., *Billy Sunday Was His Real Name* (University of Chicago Press, 1955, pp. xxix, 325), *passim;* William T. Ellis, *"Billy" Sunday, The Man and His Message* (Philadelphia, The John C. Winston Co., 1917, pp. 450), *passim.*

Baptists who by their confessions of faith held to election, in their preaching ignored it. Disciples of Christ and Christians had never subscribed to it.[55] The assumption of the infallibility of the Scriptures and some other convictions which underlay revivalism ran counter to the intellectual currents of the revolutionary age. The conflict was to lead to vigorous debate and deep division in Protestant ranks.

COUNTERING DE-CHRISTIANIZING TRENDS; THE SUNDAY SCHOOL

The Sunday School, although of English origin, had its largest development in the United States. It was a major instrument in countering de-Christianization and, especially as a channel for reaching youth, made major contributions to increasing the membership of Protestant churches. It was a potent ally of revivalism, for those trained in it were prepared for the appeal of the evangelists. From the Sunday Schools, either their present or former pupils, came a large proportion of the converts of the revivals. During the nineteenth century the curriculum of the Sunday Schools was Bible centred and inculcated a familiarity with the text of the Bible and the Evangelical-Pietist interpretation of the Bible which prepared those who had attended them for the appeal of the evangelist. The Sunday Schools became almost universal among denominations which ministered primarily to the older American stock. Eventually they were adopted by many of the Protestant bodies whose constituencies were chiefly from the nineteenth-century immigration.

Some kinds of Sunday Schools for the religious instruction of children had existed in the colonies in the sixteenth and seventeenth centuries, but the movement begun by Raikes quickly achieved popularity.[56] Soon after 1815 unions for the promotion of Sunday Schools were begun in a number of cities—for example, in New York and Boston in 1816 and in Philadelphia in 1817. In 1824 the American Sunday School Union was organized. By 1830 some of the leading denominations had also inaugurated Sunday School unions.[57] The American Sunday School Union drew its membership from many denominations and within a few years hundreds of auxiliary unions were formed. The leadership was largely lay. Literature, including lesson materials, was produced. Missionaries were early employed to organize new Sunday Schools.[58] In 1830 the American Sunday School Union resolved to establish within two years "a Sunday School in every destitute place where it is practicable throughout the Valley of

---

[55] Smith, *Revivalism and Social Reform*, pp. 80–94.

[56] Ferguson, *Historic Chapters in Christian Education in America*, pp. 14–16; M. C. Brown, *Sunday-School Movements in America*, pp. 19–26; A. A. Brown, *A History of Religious Education in Modern Times*, pp. 48, 49; Rice, *The Sunday-School Movement and the American Sunday-School Union*, pp. 42–48.

[57] A. A. Brown, *op. cit.*, p. 50; Fergusson, *op. cit.*, pp. 20–22; Rice, *op. cit.*, pp. 49–79.

[58] Rice, *op. cit.*, pp. 90–100.

the Mississippi."[59] It thus was reinforcing other agencies, such as the American Bible Society, in seeking to win the de-Christianized on that vast frontier. National conventions were held, essentially for laymen. The training of teachers, also chiefly lay, was promoted. In it a young Methodist minister, John H. Vincent (1832–1920), was prominent.

In the Fifth National Sunday School Convention, held in Indianapolis in 1872, a plan for Uniform Sunday School Lessons was adopted and an International Sunday School Committee was appointed. Through the Uniform Sunday School Lessons teachers and students of all age groups were to study the same passage of the Bible at the same time. Canada was represented on the Committee and Great Britain had a corresponding committee. Therefore the lessons were in fact international. They were also interdenominational. The action of the Convention was largely due to a Chicago business man, a Baptist and a friend of Moody, Benjamin Franklin Jacobs (1834–1902), for forty-five years a Sunday School superintendent. His purpose was the achievement of a Protestant community religion rising above denominations and centred on a common study of the Bible. It was to be disseminated through Sunday School classes functioning through a system of township, county, state, provincial, and international conventions. The goal was a saved and united community. By the inclusion of Canadians as delegates, in 1875 the National Sunday School Convention became the International Sunday School Convention. Most of the denominations fell into line.[60] Jacobs was long the commanding figure. He sought to extend the programme to other nations. The International Sunday School Association was organized, with Jacobs as its leader. Through its growing staff, Sunday Schools using the Uniform Lessons proliferated. Enrolments vastly increased. By 1875 the Uniform Lessons were in use in nineteen nations, and by 1905, seventeen million pupils were said to be studying them.[61] Partly through Vincent and William Rainey Harper (1856–1906), the latter the first president of the University of Chicago, the training of teachers was improved.[62]

The vitality of the Sunday School movement was also seen in a number of efforts to improve the curriculum, whether through modifying the Uniform Lessons, introducing completely new ones, or constructing graded series designed to meet the needs of the several age groups. Some were by denominations. Partly under the influence of Harper, Erastus Blakeslee (1838–1908) worked out a series of graded lessons which were promoted by the Bible Study Union, an organization formed in 1891. The Sunday School Council of Evangelical Denominations for a time was a formidable rival of the International Sunday School Association. In 1914 the International Lesson Committee was

[59] A. A. Brown, *op. cit.*, p. 56.
[60] Weigle, *American Idealism*, p. 199; Fergusson, *op. cit.*, pp. 36–47.
[61] Benson, *A Popular History of Christian Education*, p. 210.
[62] Fergusson, *op. cit.*, pp. 49 ff.

reorganized to include representatives of these two bodies and of the denominations. International Graded Lessons were developed.[63] In 1903, largely at the instance of Harper, the Religious Education Association was initiated to make the Sunday School more effective by the adaptation of its materials and methods of instruction to the several stages of the moral, mental, and spiritual growth of the individual, and better to utilize the home, the day school, and all other agencies for the education of youth in religion and morals.[64] Some of the developments in Sunday School curricula late in the nineteenth century reflected efforts to take account of the application of nineteenth-century historical methods to the study of the Bible.

Henry Clay Trumbull (1830–1903) was prominent in the Sunday School movement and was outstanding in encouraging it in winning individuals to a commitment to the Christian faith. Of old New England ancestry, he was converted through the personal appeal of a friend, was profoundly influenced by Finney, early began a mission Sunday School, served as chaplain in the Civil War, and for many years was an agent of the American Sunday School Union. In 1875 he became editor of *The Sunday School Times.* Through its columns and other writings he made major contributions to the general movement both in the United States and in other lands. His deep concern for the conversion of those with whom he came in contact was illustrated by his widely read book, *Individual Work for Individuals: A Record of Personal Experiences and Convictions.*[65] In it he made clear his belief in the kind of conversion characteristic of the Evangelical tradition, with a quiet confidence that any one could give himself to Christ as his saviour and by so doing enter now into eternal life. His was the kind of faith which inspired the Sunday School movement at its inception and for many years thereafter and made it an instrument for countering the threat of de-Christianization.

THE NINETEENTH-CENTURY IMMIGRATION: ITS EXTENT, CHARACTER, AND CHALLENGE

The "new Americans" of the nineteenth-century immigration posed a complex problem. They were mostly from Europe. A few were liberals who came to escape political reaction. For a smaller number the motive was religious. For

---

[63] *Ibid.;* M. C. Brown, *op. cit.,* pp. 153 ff.; Benson, *op. cit.,* pp. 212 ff.; A. A. Brown, *op. cit.,* pp. 101 ff.; Frank Glenn Lankard, *A History of the American Sunday School Curriculum* (New York, Abingdon Press, 1927, pp. 360), pp. 272 ff.

[64] Henry Frederick Cope, *The Evolution of the Sunday School* (Boston, The Pilgrim Press, 1911, pp. vii, 240), pp. 201 ff.

[65] Published by the American Tract Society, New York, 1901, pp. x, 186. On Trumbull himself see Philip E. Howard, *The Life Story of Henry Clay Trumbull, Missionary, Army Chaplain, Editor, and Author* (Philadelphia, The Sunday School Times Co., 1905, pp. xv, 525), *passim.* On his comprehensive view of the Sunday School see H. Clay Trumbull, *Yale Lectures on the Sunday-School: The Sunday-School, Its Origin, Mission, Methods, and Auxiliaries* (Philadelphia, John D. Wattles, 1888, pp. xiii, 415).

the overwhelming majority the attraction was economic opportunity. Most of them were peasants, unskilled labourers who tended to congregate in the industrial, commercial, and mining centres in the North. Many, largely Germans and Scandinavians, hewed out farms on the westward-moving frontier. Only the minority were from Great Britain, akin to the majority of the older stock.[66]

From 1820 to 1865 England was said to be the source of 744,285; from Ireland, afflicted by famine due to the failure of the potato crop and by other ills, 1,880,943 are reported to have come; and Germany was the fatherland of 1,545,-508. In these years a few thousand came from Switzerland, the Netherlands, and France, but, in contrast with the latter part of the century, only 16,776 were from Russia, Italy, and Poland.[67] This meant that in the first half-century after 1815 those of Anglo-Saxon stock who by ancestry were Protestant and who were easily assimilated to the older stock and found themselves at home in its churches were less than a fifth of the new arrivals; that the Roman Catholics, heretofore a small minority, were largely augmented by the Irish and a substantial proportion of the Germans; and that to the Lutherans, a minority during the colonial period, were added some hundreds of thousands from Germany of Lutheran background or of the mixture of Lutheran and Reformed which was found in several of the German states.

The second half of the century witnessed a sharp shift in the sources of the immigration. In 1882, for example, 27.7 per cent. were from Great Britain and Ireland, 38.7 per cent. from Germany, and 16.3 per cent. from Denmark, Norway, and Sweden. In 1902, 7.4 per cent. were from the British Isles, 4.2 per cent. from Germany, 8.7 per cent. from Scandinavia, 28.6 per cent. from the Hapsburg realms, 28.6 per cent. from Italy, and 17.2 per cent. from Russia. Those from Russia were mainly Jews, but a substantial number were Poles.[68] Those from Austria-Hungary were largely Roman Catholic by heredity, and those from Italy and Poland were almost entirely so. Roman Catholics were also augmented by the immigration of French Canadians. In 1901 over 900,000 of that background were said to be in the United States, chiefly in New England.[69] Mexicans, at least ostensibly Roman Catholic, moved across the border into the South-west and in 1910 were said to total 221,915.[70] Legal restrictions on immigration from East Asia kept down the number of Chinese and Japanese. In 1910 the continental United States was said to have 71,531 of the former and 72,157 of the latter.[71]

[66] Handlin, *The Uprooted, passim.*

[67] John Spencer Bassett, *A Short History of the United States* (New York, The Macmillan Co., 1914, pp. xv, 885), p. 461.

[68] John R. Commons, *Races and Immigrants in America* (New York, The Macmillan Co., new ed., 1920, pp. xxix, 242), pp. 71, 87.

[69] Bracq, *The Evolution of French Canada*, p. 214.

[70] Manuel Gamio, *Mexican Immigration to the United States* (University of Chicago Press, 1930, pp. xviii, 262), p. 2.

[71] Eliot Grinnell Mears, *Resident Orientals on the American Pacific Coast. Their Legal and Economic Status* (New York, Institute of Pacific Relations, 1927, pp. xvi, 526), p. 412.

Protestant Gains in the Traditionally Christian
Nineteenth-Century Immigration

The denominations whose membership was chiefly from the older American stock put forth efforts to reach the nineteenth-century immigration. The barriers to success were many. In the first generation, language was an obstacle, for the new-comers from non-English-speaking countries were slow to acquire English, and only a minority among the older stock, and they mostly Germans, spoke anything but English. Much religious indifference existed among the millions who were engrossed in making a livelihood and who were now in a land where conformity to the rites of the Christian faith was not required, as in the old country, by law or by social convention. Those amenable to a church connexion preferred a form with which they were already familiar, whether Protestant, Roman Catholic, or Orthodox, and where they would hear their own tongue and meet others of their background. To most of them the Protestantism of the older stock seemed alien and, on the part of Roman Catholics, heretical. Yet some progress was made, especially among immigrants of Protestant ancestry.

The gains by the Protestant bodies which had been in the United States before 1815 were by a variety of means. In language, doctrine and forms of worship immigrants from England, Scotland, and the North of Ireland usually found themselves at home in the existing churches. Whether Anglicans, Presbyterians, Methodists, Congregationalists, or Baptists by rearing, they discovered denominations with which they were already familiar and were easily assimilated. For non-Anglo-Saxons more difficulty was encountered. Much was accomplished by individual congregations and their pastors for which no record survived.

Methodists and Baptists had some success in reaching non-Anglo-Saxon immigrants of Protestant antecedents. As we have seen, they had had a phenomenal growth among what might be called the proletariat of the older American stock—those of lower incomes and scanty education. Since most of the new immigration were from similar economic and educational levels, they were more inclined to respond to the Methodists and Baptists than to denominations which ministered to the middle- and upper-income groups.

On the eve of 1815 two denominations of Methodist polity and spirit, the United Brethren in Christ and the Evangelical Association, had sprung up among the older German stock.[72] Using German in their preaching and public worship, they were able to reach many of the German immigration. In the Methodist Episcopal Church German congregations, German districts (1844), and eventually (1864) a German conference arose. A pioneer in laying their foundations was Henry Boehm (1775-1875), who for a time travelled with As-

---

[72] Volume I, pp. 192, 193.

bury.[73] William Nast (1807-1899) was more prominent. Born and educated in Germany, he came to the United States, after a spiritual pilgrimage was ordained a Methodist preacher, and was the chief founder of German Methodism in that country.[74] By 1907, moreover, the Methodists had gathered about five thousand into a Danish-Norwegian Conference and in that same year had about eighteen thousand in Swedish congregations.[75]

The American Baptist Home Mission Society and Baptist state conventions assisted what was in part a spontaneous movement among Germans to form Baptist congregations. The Home Mission Board of the Southern Baptist Convention had missions among the Germans in Texas, Missouri, and Kentucky. About 1859 the General Conference of German Baptist Churches in America was organized.[76] A seminary for the training of clergy for German Baptist churches was begun in Rochester, New York, in close coöperation with the Baptist seminary in that city. Here taught Augustus Rauschenbusch, father of the more distinguished Walter Rauschenbusch, and whom we have already met in Germany.[77] In the 1840's and 1850's the initial Norwegian, Swedish, and Danish Baptist churches were organized. They soon formed associations and conferences, sometimes including all Scandinavians, more often separately for the three nationalities. Assistance was given by the American Baptist Home Mission Society and Baptist state conventions. A few Finns also became Baptists. The largest of the Scandinavian Baptist groups was Swedish. In 1913 it had about 28,000 members, only slightly less than the German Baptist movement.[78] From it after 1914 were to come some of the outstanding leaders of the Baptists in the North.

Other denominations of the older American stock did not neglect the new arrivals. The American Home Missionary Society was active in supporting missionaries. Congregations were gathered from the Germans, largely those from Russia. By 1911 about thirteen thousand were in them.[79] In 1883 the Society

[73] *Dictionary of American Biography*, Vol. II, pp. 403, 404.

[74] *Ibid.*, Vol. XIII, p. 393; Paul F. Douglass, *The Story of German Methodism. Biography of an Immigrant Soul* (Cincinnati, The Methodist Book Concern, 1939, pp. xviii, 297, 64), *passim*.

[75] *The Methodist Forward Movement in the United States. Annual Report of the Board of Home Missions and Church Extension of the Methodist Episcopal Church for the Year 1907-1908*, pp. 27-30.

[76] Torbet, *A History of the Baptists*, p. 396; O. E. Krueger in *The Chronicle*, Vol. II, pp. 98-110; John A. Held, *European Missions in Texas* (Nashville, Broadman Press, 1936, pp. 136), pp. 49 ff.

[77] Volume II, Chapter V; *Leben und Wirken von August Rauschenbusch*, begun by himself and completed by Walter Rauschenbusch (Cleveland, Peter Ritter, 1901, pp. xii, 274), *passim*.

[78] R. A. Arlander in *The Chronicle*, Vol. II, pp. 114-117; Stephenson, *The Religious Aspects of Swedish Immigration*, pp. 249, 253, 254; P. Stiansen, *History of the Baptists in Norway* (Chicago, The Blessing Press, 1933, pp. xi, 476); Padelford, *The Commonwealths and the Kingdom*, p. 154; *Eighty-First Annual Report of the American Baptist Home Mission Society*, 1913, p. 34. For correspondence of Swedish Baptists to and from the United States see Gunnar Westin, editor, *Ur den Svenska Folkväckelsens Historia och Tankevärld. III: 2. Brev från och till den Svenska Baptismens babrytare 1850-1855* (Stockholm, B.-Mis Bökförlags A.-B., 1934, pp. 288), *passim*.

[79] George J. Eisenach, *A History of the German Congregational Churches in the United States*

organized a department for the Scandinavians. A number of the Swedes were continuing the free church tradition then flourishing in the mother country and were organizing Free Churches and Free Mission Churches which were Pietist in temper and akin to the Evangelicalism at that time strong in the Congregationalism of the United States.[80] Presbyterians were active among Bohemians, Slovaks, and Hungarians, chiefly of the Reformed tradition.[81] Since the Church of Sweden was episcopally governed by bishops who were regarded by Anglicans as in the apostolic succession, in 1856 the Protestant Episcopal Church constituted a committee on friendly relations with that church. To prevent a leakage of Swedish Lutherans from a church connexion it suggested that before leaving their mother country they be given letters of dismissal to Episcopal congregations in communities where no Swedish Lutheran congregations existed, and proposed to consecrate a bishop for the Swedish Americans. No bishop was consecrated, but by 1900 about a dozen Swedish congregations had arisen in the Episcopal Church with about two thousand communicants.[82]

Protestant efforts to win immigrants of Roman Catholic profession or ancestry were numerous but in the nineteenth century met with only slight numerical success. Not until the twentieth century was a large influx seen of Roman Catholics into Protestant churches, and little of this was through efforts put forth directly to that end but came about in other ways—largely, but by no means entirely, intermarriage.

A few of the nineteenth-century attempts by the older denominations to convert Roman Catholics may serve as samples of what a complete story would include. The American and Foreign Christian Union was formed in 1849, as a fusion of the American Protestant Society, the Foreign Evangelical Society, and the Christian Alliance. Its declared purpose was "the diffusion of evangelical truth wherever a corrupt Christianity exists, at home or abroad." The first annual report of the society announced missions in the United States among Roman Catholic French, Germans, Italians, Irish, Spaniards, and Portuguese, and from Texas and New Orleans to New England.[83] The Presbyterians were active through local congregations, presbyteries, synods, and their national home missionary societies.[84] Northern Baptists maintained missions for several Roman

---

(Yankton, S.D., The Pioneer Press, 1938, pp. xvi, 315), *passim;* George J. Eisenach, *Pietism and the Russian Germans in the United States* (Berne, Ind., The Berne Publishers, 1946, pp. 218), *passim.*

[80] Clark, *Leavening the Nation,* pp. 273–275.

[81] *One Hundred Twelfth Annual Report, Board of Home Missions of the Presbyterian Church in the U.S.A.,* 1914, pp. 15, 16.

[82] Stephenson, *op. cit.,* pp. 210 ff.

[83] *The American and Foreign Christian Union* (New York, the American and Foreign Christian Union, 1850 ff.), Vol. I, pp. 1, 252–273.

[84] *One Hundred Twelfth Annual Report, Board of Home Missions of the Presbyterian Church in the U.S.A.,* p. 383.

Catholic national groups.[85] The Methodists had missions among Roman Catholics, some of them for the Spanish-speaking in New Mexico.[86] However, only an inconsiderable fraction of the Roman Catholic immigration were drawn into Protestant congregations especially designed for them and using their mother tongues. How many were assimilated to English-speaking congregations we have no way of knowing.

A very substantial proportion, possibly most, of the nineteenth-century immigrants from the Continent of Europe of Protestant background were gathered into churches which continued the traditions, language, and liturgies with which they had been familiar. Several factors contributed to this achievement. Small minorities gathered into communities which sought in the New World freedom to realize the ideals to which they believed the Christian faith called them. For the overwhelming majority the attraction was an institution which they had known in the fatherland and in which, in an alien environment, they could meet others of their kind and hear and use their native speech. The essential impetus and leadership were given by clergy, at the outset many of them from Europe and the mother churches.

Practically all the varieties in the theology and churchmanship of the Protestantism from which the immigrants came were represented. In the main, however, theological conservatism, whether in the Lutheran or Reformed, was relatively more prominent than in Europe, partly because some of the migration was to escape persecution but chiefly because the theologically conservative had greater zeal and sent more missionaries than the theologically liberal. Many societies in Germany and German-speaking Switzerland sought to hold the German immigrants to the faith. Some, such as the *Berliner Gesellschaft,* were organized with that as their specific purpose. Others, among them Barmen and Basel, had it as only one of their objectives. Numbers of missionaries embodied a combination of Pietism and theological conservatism. As a consequence, most of the Protestant churches which arose from the nineteenth-century immigration were more resistant to the intellectual currents of the revolutionary age than were the mother bodies in Europe. Conservatism was heightened by the understandable unwillingness to conform to the new environment—the effort to perpetuate the native tongue and transmitted beliefs against the corrosive forces making for assimilation to the American scene.

We need not attempt a complete list of the groups which sought refuge in the United States either to take the opportunity to enjoy religious liberty or to set up an idealistic community in a new country. A few will serve as exam-

---

[85] Padelford, *op. cit.,* pp. 156–161; J. Rzepecki in *The Chronicle,* Vol. II, pp. 139, 140; V. P. Stupka in *The Chronicle,* Vol. II, p. 122.

[86] *The Methodist Forward Movement in the United States. Annual Report of the Board of Home Missions and Church Extension of the Methodist Episcopal Church for the Year 1907–1908,* pp. 73–75.

ples. The Rappites, following Johann Georg Rapp (1757-1847), came from Württemberg in 1803. Practising celibacy and never numbering many more than four hundred, they established a colony in Harmony in Pennsylvania in 1805. They removed to New Harmony, Indiana, in 1815, and in 1824 sold their lands there to Robert Owen[87] and settled in Economy, Pennsylvania.[88] The Zoarites, from Swabia, found a home in Tuscarawas County, Ohio, in 1817.[89] Much more numerous were the Mennonites. Attracted by the religious liberty offered in Pennsylvania, a few settled there between 1760 and 1820. After the latter year more began to arrive, and took refuge in several states. They were largely farmers, tended to form tightly knit settlements and so far as possible to keep aloof from the world about them, cultivating a community life which they aspired to make fully Christian. Many were from Germany, France, Switzerland, and Holland. Not far from 1870 the Russian Government withdrew the exemption from military service and other privileges which had been earlier guaranteed the Mennonites to attract them, with their industry and thrift, in an effort to improve the economic life of the tsar's domains. In the 1870's hundreds fled to the United States. The Mennonites divided into many groups, some of European and some of American origin. Among them were the Amish and Hutterian Brethren. In 1860 the General Conference was instituted in an effort to bring them all together. In 1906, in spite of a substantial natural increase, the total in all branches was said to be only 54,789.[90]

What became in time the second largest Lutheran body in the United States, usually called the Missouri Synod, arose out of an immigrant company of 612 which in 1838 and early in 1839 found homes in St. Louis and in Perry County, Missouri, south of that city. The leader was Martin Stephan. A powerful preacher, while a pastor in Dresden, embarrassed by restrictions from the civil and ecclesiastical authorities, professing to be loyal to the symbolical books of Lutheranism, he sought freedom on the frontier of the United States. Arrived in America, Stephan proved to be dictatorial and sexually irregular, and soon after the colony reached Missouri he was expelled from its fellowship. The leadership now passed to Carl Ferdinand Wilhelm Walther (1811-1887). Wal-

[87] Volume II, Chapter XXVIII.

[88] John A. Bole, *The Harmony Society: A Chapter in German-American Culture History,* in *German American Annals* (Philadelphia, The German American Historical Society, 1904), pp. 274–308, 339–366, 403–434, 467–481, 571–581, 597, 628, 665–677; Faust, *The German Element in the United States,* Vol. I, pp. 445, 456; *Dictionary of American Biography,* Vol. XV, pp. 383, 384.

[89] Faust, *op. cit.,* Vol. I, p. 421.

[90] C. Henry Smith, *The Mennonites in America* (Scottdale, Pa., Mennonite Publishing House, 1909, pp. 484), *passim;* Cornelius Krahn, editor, *From the Steppes to the Prairies (1874-1949)* (Newton, Kan., Mennonite Publication Office, 1949, pp. viii, 115), *passim;* C. Henry Smith, *The Coming of the Russian Mennonites. An Episode in the Settling of the Last Frontier 1874-1884* (Berne, Ind., Mennonite Book Concern, 1927, pp. 296), *passim;* H. P. Krehbiel, *The History of the General Conference of the Mennonites of North America* (The Author, 1898, pp. xx, 504), *passim;* Alice K. Gingerich, *Life and Times of Daniel Kauffman* (Scottdale, Pa., Herald Press, 1954, pp. 160), *passim;* U.S. Department of Commerce, Bureau of the Census, *Religious Bodies: 1926,* Vol. II, p. 846.

ther was chiefly responsible for the emergence from the small company, dismayed by the disclosed unworthiness of Stephan, of a numerous, theologically conservative, and powerful ecclesiastical body. In his teens more interested in music than religion, under pressure from his father, a clergyman and the son of a clergyman, he had enrolled in the University of Leipzig as a student of theology. There he suffered from doubts, came in touch with Pietists, had a Pietist conversion, was a diligent student of Luther's writings, and after leaving the university became a pastor. He was with an early contingent of Stephan's followers. Walther founded a school from which grew Concordia Theological Seminary. As pastor of a church in St. Louis he won fame as a preacher. He edited a weekly journal, *Der Lutheraner,* and a monthly, *Lehre und Wehre.* In them he vigorously set forth what he believed to be true Lutheranism and denounced what he regarded as error. They were welcomed by conservative Lutheran pastors elsewhere in the Mississippi Valley. In 1847 Walther brought about the organization of "the German Evangelical Lutheran Synod of Missouri, Ohio, and Other States," usually more briefly known as the Missouri Synod. He was the first president and held the post to 1850, and again from 1864 to 1878. Beginning with twelve congregations and twenty-two pastors, by the time of Walther's death the synod had swelled to about fifteen hundred congregations and nearly a thousand clergymen. For this growth Walther was to no small degree responsible. A winning speaker, a formidable debater, skilled in theological controversy, yet with a gift for friendship, singularly free from self-seeking, and an able organizer, Walther had the satisfaction of seeing the Missouri Synod attain large proportions.[91] An important factor in the growth was the creation of a system of parochial schools, by far the most extensive of any Protestant church in the United States.

We have seen the close kinship to the Lutheran revival led by Löhe and the assistance given by him to the Missouri Synod in its early years. Yet we have also called attention to the separation of the two movements over issues of doctrine and organization.[92] In a reaction against the autocratic rule of Stephan, after his expulsion the Missouri Lutherans stressed a congregational form of government, and to this Löhe objected.

Walther did not see his dream fulfilled of a single united Evangelical Lutheran Church in North America. A major obstacle was the doctrine of predestination. Walther and his colleagues held that a man cannot have saving faith in Christ

[91] *Dictionary of American Biography,* Vol. XIX, pp. 402, 403; Wentz, *A Basic History of Lutheranism in America,* pp. 116–119; Walter O. Forster, *Zion on the Mississippi: the Settlement of the Saxon Lutherans in Missouri 1839–1841* (St. Louis, Concordia Publishing House, 1953, pp. xiv, 606), *passim;* Baepler, *A Century of Grace,* pp. 15–207.

[92] Volume II, Chapter V. On assistance from Löhe to the Missouri Synod, see Theodore Graebner, *Church Bells in the Forest. A Study of Lutheran Pioneer Work on the Michigan Frontier 1840–1850* (St. Louis, Concordia Publishing House, 1944, pp. viii, 98), *passim;* Schmidt, *Wort Gottes und Fremdlingschaft,* pp. 45 ff.

unless God moves him to that step. Some other Lutheran synods maintained that a man can of himself have faith and that God elects a man to salvation "in view of his faith."[93]

In addition to Walther, two outstanding early leaders of the Missouri Synod were F. C. D. Wyneken (1810–1876), who came as a missionary to the Germans in 1838 and a few years later joined the Missouri group, and Wilhelm Sihler (1801–1885), also German born, who arrived in 1843 in response to an appeal by Wyneken.[94]

Another colony impelled by conscience was made up of "Old Lutherans," who, persecuted in Prussia for their opposition to the enforced union of the Lutherans and Reformed, sought refuge in the United States. The first company arrived in 1839, led by J. A. A. Grabau, and settled in and near Buffalo, New York, and Milwaukee, Wisconsin. Hope of union with the Missouri Lutherans was shattered by a sharp controversy over the nature of the ministry and the Church. The Buffalo Synod was organized in 1845.[95]

Although a minority of the traditionally Protestant population from the Continent of Europe was held to the faith through colonies of earnestly religious folk, the majority owed their church connexion to the initiative of clergymen, numbers of them missionaries from the Old World, and to laymen who coöperated with them. Out of their efforts arose ecclesiastical bodies, some large, others small. They reflected the national origins of their constituencies, but the doctrinal convictions which they brought with them not infrequently divided immigrants from the same country. We can take the space merely for brief mention of a few of the bodies, and for the most part only the largest.

Before 1815 and the fresh influx from Germany, the older Lutheranism of the United States was spreading. It was organized into ministeriums, of which the first was that of Pennsylvania. In 1786 the Ministerium of New York was begun, followed in 1803 by the Synod of the South. Soon after 1815 other synods were organized—that of Ohio and Adjacent States in 1818, that of Maryland and Virginia in 1820, that of Tennessee, also in 1820, that of South Carolina in 1824, that of West Pennsylvania in 1825, and the separate Virginia Synod in 1829. Eighteenth-century rationalism affected some of the synods, and here and there a trend existed towards union with the Reformed or the Episcopalians. In 1820 representatives of four synods organized a General Synod. The new body was opposed to rationalism and to union with other denominations. It was saved from early dissolution by Samuel S. Schmucker (1799–1873), and through him a seminary was begun (1826) in Gettysburg, Pennsylvania, for the training of the ministry.[96] Under several of these synods and the General Synod

[93] Wentz, *op. cit.*, pp. 212, 213.
[94] Baepler, *op. cit.*, pp. 53, 64, 75–82, 211, 212; Schmidt, *op. cit.*, p. 72.
[95] Wentz, *op. cit.*, pp. 119, 120.
[96] Jacobs, *A History of the Evangelical Lutheran Church in the United States*, p. 309; Wentz,

missionaries were sent to the Germans in the West.[97]

Out of the vast immigration from Germany, and especially in the first five decades after 1815, came a marked growth of American Lutheranism, conflicts with and in the older Lutheranism, and a number of new bodies. Between 1830 and 1870 Lutheran membership increased to about 400,000, or nine-fold, and made Lutheranism the fourth in size of the Protestant denominational families.[98] Much but not all of the growth was west of the Appalachians. Among many of the clergy and some of the laity in this immigration the reaction was pronounced against the union of Lutherans and Reformed then current in Germany and especially in Prussia. That reaction was reinforced and compounded by the swing away from eighteenth-century rationalism and by some of the nineteenth-century developments in German theology towards a staunch Lutheran confessionalism.[99] The revived Lutheranism was potent in the Lutheran churches which gathered the new immigration into their fold. It was critical of the kind of Pietism which, through Henry M. Mühlenberg and those coöperating with him, was strong in the older American Lutheranism. Lutheran conservatism was also buttressed by adherence to the German language in instruction, preaching, and liturgy. Many among the immigrants tended to resist assimilation to the surrounding culture, and to do so held to their mother tongue in their church life and stressed adherence to Lutheranism as expressed in the Augsburg Confession and the symbolical books.[100]

The Synod of Iowa and Other States, organized in 1854, arose primarily from missionaries sent by Löhe from Neuendettelsau. As might have been expected from its connexion with Löhe, it was staunchly Lutheran. But it feared the extreme congregationalism of the Missouri Synod and what it deemed the latter's "legalistic misuse of the symbols" and regarded the Buffalo Synod as too hierarchical.[101] Aided by funds from Neuendettelsau, the Synod of Iowa extended its activities very widely and eventually had congregations in every state west of the Mississippi except Arizona and New Mexico. The Lutheran Evangelical Synod of Texas, inaugurated in 1851, which eventually joined it, was deeply indebted to missionaries sent by C. F. Spittler, founder of the Pilgrim Mission of St. Chrischona.[102]

The Joint Synod of Wisconsin, Minnesota, Michigan and Other States was

---

op. cit., pp. 68 ff.; Ferm, *The Crisis in American Lutheran Theology*, pp. 15-116; Wolf, *The Lutherans in America*, pp. 271-405.

[97] Schneider, *The German Church on the American Frontier*, pp. 42-47; Wentz, *op. cit.*, pp. 68-70.

[98] Wentz, *op. cit.*, p. 115.

[99] Volume II, Chapters III, V.

[100] Jacobs, *op. cit.*, pp. 394, 395; Wentz, *op. cit.*, pp. 119, 120.

[101] Johannes Deindorfer, *Geschichte der Evang.-Luth. Synode von Iowa und anderen Staaten* (Chicago, Wartburg Publishing House, 1897, pp. x, 385), *passim*; Wentz, *op. cit.*, p. 120.

[102] G. J. Zeilinger, *A Missionary Synod with a Mission. A Memoir of the Seventy-Fifth Anniversary of the Evangelical Lutheran Synod of Iowa and Other States* (Chicago, Wartburg Publishing House, 1929, pp. 115), pp. 53-59.

the outgrowth of several movements among and for the immigrants. In the 1830's, between 1840 and 1854, and between 1881 and 1884 large numbers of Germans came to Wisconsin, Michigan, and Minnesota, in part because of dissatisfaction with political conditions in the fatherland. In 1833 a missionary from Basel organized a congregation near Ann Arbor, Michigan. In 1850 the First Evangelical Lutheran Synod of Wisconsin was formed, at the instance of John Muehlhauser, who had been trained in Basel and Barmen and sent by the Langenberg Society, an organization in the Prussian Rhineland having as its purpose the dispatching of pastors to the Germans in America. In the 1850's and 1860's, owing largely to missionaries from Germany, the Wisconsin Synod moved in the direction of strict Lutheranism. The Michigan Synod, begun in 1860, mainly by pastors sent by the Basel Missionary Society, also progressively adopted a position of stalwart Lutheran orthodoxy. So did the Synod of Minnesota, organized in 1860. In 1892 the three synods entered into a federation which bore the name that heads this paragraph and was sometimes called the General Synod of Wisconsin or the Synod of the Northwest.[103]

Many conservative Lutherans from Germany, instead of founding new synods, became members of existing synods, where they helped to stiffen confessional loyalties. Their influence was especially marked in the Pennsylvania Ministerium, the New York Ministerium, and the General Synod.[104]

Not all the nineteenth-century German immigration was attracted to churches which stood for a revived Lutheranism: many thousands became members of the German Reformed Church (later the Reformed Church in the United States) and the Evangelical Synod of North America.

The German Reformed Church, organized before 1815 among the pre-nineteenth-century German immigrants, reached out to the Ohio frontier. In 1820 the Classis of Ohio was formed, succeeded in 1824 by the Evangelical Reformed Synod of Ohio. Some of its pastors preached in German to the nineteenth-century arrivals, and several pastors who had been born in Germany reinforced the Ohio Synod. In 1844 the Ohio Synod, often known as the Western Synod, sent delegates to a Triennial Convention, in which the mother body, the Synod of the Reformed Church in the United States, usually referred to as the Eastern Synod, and the Dutch Reformed Church were represented. After a few years the Dutch Reformed Church withdrew and in 1863 the two German synods joined in organizing the General Synod.[105] In 1859 the decision was made to begin a mission house to prepare German ministers for service in the United States. It was located in Wisconsin in a colony which had fled from Lippe to obtain freedom to teach their children the Heidelberg Catechism rather than the one prescribed by the state. In it hundreds of young men were educated.[106]

[103] Wentz, *op. cit.*, pp. 272–276.
[104] *Ibid.*, p. 122.
[105] Dubbs in *American Church History*, Vol. VIII, pp. 382–388.
[106] *Ibid.*, pp. 404, 405.

In the second half of the century a number of additional synods were organized, some of them frankly German for the new immigration and others for English-speaking constituencies.[107] The German Reformed Church was growing.

The Evangelical Synod of North America sprang from a number of movements which brought together Lutherans and Reformed among the German immigrants. Some congregations arose from the background of the union churches in the various states of Germany. Others came out of a desire to present a united Protestant witness against the de-Christianizing tendencies and the militantly anti-Christian attitudes among German immigrants. The major nucleus around which the Evangelical Synod gathered was the *Kirchenverein des Westens,* formed in 1840 in Missouri. It was quite independent of any ecclesiastical connexions in Europe or America and was created to meet the socio-religious conditions among the Germans in the West. Although it was controlled by no other organization, it was indebted to the L.U.P.O.S. (Looking Upward, Press Onward Society). The L.U.P.O.S. had been formed by Congregationalists in Hartford, Connecticut, in the 1830's to offset what was deemed the threat presented by the *Leopoldinen-Stiftung,* a society with its seat in Bavaria and having as its purpose the winning to the Roman Catholic Church of the German immigrants in the United States. The L.U.P.O.S. appealed to the Basel Missionary Society to send young men to America and offered to provide for their financial support. In 1836 two arrived and soon went West, one to St. Louis and the other as an itinerant preacher, chiefly in Illinois. Other missionaries also came early from the Rhenish Missionary Society, Bremen, and Strassburg. Additional missionaries were sent by the Basel society, and the American Home Missionary Society gave financial assistance. Requirements for church membership were stiffened as against the ones inherited from Germany, where baptism was a social convention and no stringent moral standards were maintained.[108] In its early days the *Kirchenverein* met vigorous criticism, on the one hand from leaders of rationalistic German congregations, and on the other hand from the Missouri Lutherans and Grabau of the Buffalo Synod.[109] Yet the *Kirchenverein* persisted and grew.

Other German Evangelical churches arose in various parts of the country and formed themselves into synods. Among the latter were one organized in Cincinnati in 1844, another in Buffalo in 1854, and still another in Ohio in 1850. Several of them came together and by successive steps constituted the German Evangelical Synod of the West. In it the *Kirchenverein* joined. The culminating date was 1877 and the resulting body was known as the German Evangelical Synod of North America or, eventually, the Evangelical Synod of North America.[110] In 1934 the Evangelical Synod of North America united with the (Ger-

---

[107] *Ibid.,* p. 406.
[108] Schneider, *op. cit.,* pp. 42–106, 238 ff.
[109] *Ibid.,* pp. 113–132, 372–374.
[110] *Ibid.,* pp. 387–396.

man) Reformed Church in the United States, the latter by that time augmented by union with the Hungarian Reformed Church (1924), to form the Evangelical and Reformed Church.[111]

The Scandinavian immigration found a home chiefly in Minnesota but was also numerous in the neighbouring states—the Dakotas, Wisconsin, Michigan, Illinois, and Iowa. At the outset it was predominantly of farmers. Later some skilled workmen, mainly Swedes, came to the industrial cities of the East. The motive of immigration was overwhelmingly economic. Engrossed in making a living and released from the compulsory membership to which they had been accustomed in the state churches of their motherlands, of those who arrived in the latter part of the century it is estimated that only 7 per cent. of the Danes, not more than a fifth of the Swedes, and somewhat less than a third of the Norwegians joined any church.[112]

In the early days of the nineteenth-century immigration from Sweden, the awakenings in that country were in full course and the foundations of the churches which served the Swedes in the United States were laid by men who were committed to them.

The body which gathered more Swedes into its fellowship than any other was the Evangelical Lutheran Synod of North America, known briefly as the Augustana Synod. It owed its establishment chiefly to two men who had been pastors of the Church of Sweden, Lars Paul Esbjörn (1808–1870) and Tuve Nilsson Hasselquist (1816–1891). Esbjörn[113] had been ordained in the Church of Sweden. He early came under the influence of Pietism, partly through the Methodist George Scott, and of the temperance movement through Peter Wieselgren.[114] Blocked from promotion by these views and longing for opportunity for a free church, in 1849 he led a party of sympathizers to the United States. He first settled in Andover, Illinois. Financial aid came from the American Home Missionary Society. Partly as a condition of that aid, for it could be given only to one having an ecclesiastical connexion in the United States, he joined the Lutheran Synod of Northern Illinois. He moved more and more towards loyalty to the Lutheran symbolical books. In 1860 he and other Scandinavians, dissatisfied with what they regarded as doctrinal laxity, left the Synod of Northern Illinois and organized the Scandinavian Evangelical Lutheran Augustana Synod of North America. The new body, as might have been guessed from the deliberately chosen designation Augustana, held firmly to "the unaltered Augsburg Confession as a short and correct summary of the principal Christian doctrines, understood as developed and explained in the

---

[111] Sweet, *The Story of Religion in America,* p. 425.

[112] Wentz, *op. cit.,* p. 186.

[113] Sam Ronnegård, *Prairie Shepherd. Lars Paul Esbjörn and the Beginnings of the Augustana Lutheran Church,* translated by G. E. Arden (Rock Island, Ill., Augustana Book Concern, 1952, pp. xii, 308), *passim; Dictionary of American Biography,* Vol. VI, pp. 182, 183.

[114] Volume II, Chapter XVI.

other symbolical books of the Lutheran Church." To provide pastors, it opened a college and seminary in Chicago with Esbjörn as the first president. In 1863 Esbjörn returned to Sweden as pastor of his former parish. Warmhearted, generous, free from conceit, impulsive, he left in America a heritage of devoted Christian faith and life.

Hasselquist, son of a prosperous farmer, educated in Lund, a man of powerful build and a forceful preacher, was a Pietist and a pronounced critic of the tie between Church and state. An appeal from Esbjörn brought him to the United States (1852).[115] There he became the first president of the Augustana Synod (1860–1870) and, after Esbjörn left for Sweden, from 1863 to 1891 succeeded him as president of the college and seminary. He favoured a centralized organization of the church and as rapid a transition as possible from Swedish to English. A staunch Lutheran in his theology, he was often informal in his conduct of church services. In 1870 the Norwegians withdrew from the Augustana Synod and the latter became purely Swedish. In its liturgical practice it held to the form of service in use in the Church of Sweden. In 1894 the word "Scandinavian" was dropped from the title.[116] By the year 1914 it had about 200,000 members, approximately a fourth of them in Minnesota and a third in Illinois, Michigan, and Iowa, but it was represented in at least twenty-six other states.[117]

The church connexions of the Swedes were not confined to the Augustana Synod. That synod enrolled more than half of the people who were in distinctively Swedish churches, but a substantial proportion of those of Swedish origin and immediate ancestry were distributed in a number of other bodies. We have already noted the Swedish Baptist churches, those with Congregational affiliations, and the friendly approach of the Episcopalians. Some Swedes were Methodists. Eric Janson (1808–1850), of peasant stock, who experienced a striking conversion in 1830, gathered around him a group of followers, met with violence, ran afoul of the officers of the law, in 1846 led a company to the United States, was followed by others, and founded a theocratic communistic colony at Bishop Hill in Illinois. Janson was killed in 1850, and the experiment ended in 1860, followed by extended and disastrous litigation.[118]

Much larger repercussions in the United States came from the *Svenska Missionsförbundet* ("Swedish Mission Covenant"), which sprang from the awak-

[115] *Dictionary of American Biography*, Vol. VIII, pp. 384, 385. See an extensive correspondence, mostly to and from Hasselquist, in Gunnar Westin, editor, *Emigranterna och Kyrkan. Brev från och till Svenskar i Amerika, 1849–1892* (Stockholm, Svenska Kyrkans Diakonistyrelses Bokförlag, 1932, pp. 612), *passim*.

[116] The standard history is Oscar N. Olson, *The Augustana Lutheran Church in America* (Rock Island, Ill., Augustana Book Concern, 2 vols., 1950–1956), *passim*. See also Stephenson, *The Religious Aspects of Swedish Immigration*, pp. 147–195, 310–371; Wentz, *op. cit.*, pp. 128–132, 198–206.

[117] U. S. Department of Commerce, Bureau of the Census, *Religious Bodies: 1926*, Vol. II, p. 723.

[118] Stephenson, *op. cit.*, pp. 49–73.

enings led by Rosenius and Waldenström and was organized in 1878.[119] A large proportion of the Swedish immigration of the 1870's and 1880's was from the region of Jönköping, which had been most affected by the awakened *Läsare* ("Readers").[120] The Swedish Evangelical Mission Covenant was organized in America. The disciples of Rosenius among the immigrants found the Augustana Synod and the Baptists too institutional for their taste, and by 1868 the Mission Friend movement, made up of ardent Evangelicals, had assumed substantial proportions. It was stimulated by E. August Skogsbergh, who came in 1876 at the invitation of a Mission Friend congregation in Chicago and eventually was dubbed the "Swedish Moody." For some years he was a pastor in Minneapolis and Seattle, spent much of his time as an itinerant evangelist, and, the greatest popular preacher among the Swedish Americans, attracted large congregations. He also established schools and edited papers. In the 1870's Swedish Lutherans with Pietist leanings formed the Swedish Evangelical Lutheran Synod and the Swedish Evangelical Lutheran Ansgarius Synod. Both adopted the Augsburg Confession. In 1885 they merged in the Swedish Evangelical Covenant Mission. The new body did not adopt a formal creed, not even the Augsburg Confession, but accepted the Word of God and the Old and New Testaments as the only rule of faith, doctrine, and conduct. Yet it was conservative theologically. Relations between it and the Augustana Synod were occasionally strained and even stormy, but in time the tensions lessened.[121]

In 1908 a much smaller movement, also with a Pietist-Evangelical complexion, the Swedish Evangelical Free Church, was formally incorporated in Minnesota.[122] Frederick Franson (1852–1908), who was associated with it and the Mission Friends, as an itinerant evangelist traversed much of the United States, Western Europe, Asia, South Africa, South America, and the West Indies, preaching the early second coming of Christ and repentance. He organized the Scandinavian Alliance Mission with headquarters in Chicago and a Swedish branch of the Christian and Missionary Alliance.[123]

Because of these many movements the trend towards de-Christianization among the Swedish emigrants was in part checked. Even though only a minority were brought to a church connexion, from that minority issued vigorous

---

[119] Volume II, Chapter XVI.

[120] Stephenson, *op. cit.*, p. 103.

[121] *Ibid.*, pp. 264–288; David Nyvall and Karl A. Olsson, *The Evangelical Covenant Church* (Chicago, Covenant Press, 1954, pp. 191), *passim;* C. V. Bowman, *Missionsvännerna i Amerika. En återblick på-deras uppkomst och första verksamhestid* (Minneapolis, Minneapolis Veckoblad Publ. Co., 1907, pp. 277), *passim.* For letters from Rosenius to friends in the United States see Gunnar Westin, editor, *Ur den Svenska Folkväckelsens Historia och Tankevärld. II. Brev från C. O. Rosenius till hans Vänner in Amerika* (Stockholm, Evangeliska Fosterlands-Stiftelsens Bokförlag, 1931, pp. 229), *passim.*

[122] Stephenson, *op. cit.*, p. 288.

[123] Josephine Princell, *Frederick Franson, World Missionary* (Chicago, Chicago-Bladet Publishing Co., no date, pp. 156), *passim;* Stephenson, *op. cit.*, pp. 126–128.

ecclesiastical bodies which sought to win the Swedish Americans and reached out in missions to other lands.

Norwegians were not quite as numerous as Swedes, but of the million and a quarter in the United States in 1910 who had been born in Scandinavia about a third were from Norway as against a half from Sweden.[124] That meant that a larger proportion of the population of the former country than of the latter had gone to America. One estimate declares that in 1925 about two and a half million people in the United States were of Norwegian descent.[125]

The somewhat larger minority of the Norwegians than of Danes or Swedes who established church ties in their new homes were gathered into a variety of synods and churches, the largest of which eventually coalesced. A small group, mainly Quakers who came from Stavanger to northern New York in 1825 to escape persecution, had only slight if any continuing effect.[126] Nor did a colony of Moravians in Door County, Wisconsin.[127] In the mid-1930's a number of Haugeans established themselves on Fox River, in La Salle County, Illinois. In 1839 Elling Eielsen (1804–1883) came to the Fox River settlement and for some years made it his home. Of rural stock, after deep depression and inward struggle, he had come into a warm religious experience while still in Bergen and under friendly Haugean influence. As a lay preacher he had traversed much of Norway, largely on foot. He was outspoken in his criticism of the clergy of the state church. In the United States he combined settled residence with itinerant evangelism, chiefly among Norwegians. In 1846, in Wisconsin, he organized the Evangelical Lutheran Church of North America, the first synod among Norwegian Americans and often known as the Eielsen Synod. Some members of the Eielsen Synod withdrew and united with the Scandinavian Lutheran Augustana Synod. Other secessions occurred. One, in 1856, left only five ordained ministers in the Eielsen Synod, then renamed the Evangelical Lutheran Church in America. The other, in 1876, issued in Hauge's Norwegian Evangelical Lutheran Synod in America.[128]

In 1853 the Norwegian Evangelical Lutheran Church of America came into being. It was also called the Norwegian Synod. At the outset all its pastors had been ordained in the Church of Norway, but it was fully autonomous. The foundations had been laid by C. L. Clausen and J. W. Dietrichson, both Grundtvigians. Dietrichson, a masterly person, had been ordained by the Bishop

[124] Frank Julian Warne, *The Immigrant Invasion* (New York, Dodd, Mead and Co., 1913, pp. 336), pp. 18, 19.

[125] Norlie, *History of the Norwegian People in America*, p. 313.

[126] *Ibid.*, pp. 112–135; H. J. Cadbury, "The Norwegian Quakers of 1826," in *The Norwegian-American Historical Association Studies and Records*, Vol. I, pp. 60–94.

[127] Theodore C. Blegen, *Norwegian Migration to America 1825–1860* (Northfield, Minn., The Norwegian American Historical Association, 1931, pp. xi, 413), pp. 335, 336.

[128] *Dictionary of National Biography*, Vol. VI, pp. 61, 62; Wentz, *op. cit.*, pp. 125, 126; Rohne, *Norwegian American Lutheranism*, pp. 39–41, 48–50, 89–111, 148–157, 185–190, 241–243.

of Christiania (Oslo) for work among the Norwegians in the United States and was in that country most of the time from 1844 to 1850. He organized congregations and recruited pastors from Norway.[129] The first president of the church was Adolph Carl Preus (1814–1878), a brother-in-law of Dietrichson, who came to America in response to the latter's appeal and was there until 1862. While in the United States he organized twenty congregations.[130] Largely through Herman Amberg Preus and some other pastors who before coming to the United States had been under the influence of Gisle Johnson[131] and his anti-Grundtvigianism, the Grundtvigian elements in the proposed constitution of the Norwegian Evangelical Lutheran Church of America were excised. H. A. Preus was also vigorously against Haugeanism.[132] Coöperation in theological education was arranged with the Missouri Synod and more than a hundred of the Norwegian Synod's pastors received their theological training in Concordia Theological Seminary. The trend was against Grundtvigianism and Haugeanism, and eventually Walther was esteemed even above Gisle Johnson and Caspari.[133]

Further divisions occurred in the ranks of the Norwegian Lutherans. In 1870 the Norwegian-Danish Augustana Synod, later the Norwegian Augustana Synod, and the Conference for the Norwegian-Danish Evangelical Lutheran Church in America were formed, the latter from congregations which had withdrawn from the Augustana Synod and others which separated from the Norwegian Synod.[134] In 1888 out of a controversy over the doctrine of election those in the Norwegian Synod who opposed the position of the Missouri Synod joined with the Norwegian Augustana Synod and the Conference in organizing the United Norwegian Lutheran Church. This then became the largest Norwegian Lutheran body in the United States.[135] In 1897 the "Friends of Augsburg" (Seminary), who had separated from the United Norwegian Lutheran Church, took the name of the Lutheran Free Church. A small body, they emphasized congregational autonomy and, while adhering to Luther's smaller catechism and the Augsburg Confession, allowed much latitude in doctrine.[136] An even smaller body, the Lutheran Brethren of America, also known as the Church of the Lutheran Brethren of America, stressing the strict discipline of its members, was organized in 1900.[137]

The Danes did not begin coming to the United States in large numbers until

---

129 Rohne, *op. cit.*, pp. 64–88, 91–94, 112–123.
130 *Ibid.*, pp. 114–135.
131 Volume II, Chapter XV.
132 Wentz, *op. cit.*, pp. 119–124.
133 Rohne, *op. cit.*, pp. 194–197; Wentz, *op. cit.*, p. 124.
134 Ylvisaker, Anderson, and Lillegard, *Grace for Grace*, p. 49; Rohne, *op. cit.*, pp. 234–240.
135 Ylvisaker, Anderson, and Lillegard, *op. cit.*, pp. 49, 50.
136 Mayer, *The Religious Bodies of America*, p. 184; Bureau of the Census, *Religious Bodies, 1916*, Vol. II, p. 403.
137 Mayer, *op. cit.*, p. 185; Bureau of the Census, *Religious Bodies, 1916*, Vol. II, pp. 412, 413.

the 1860's. Their totals never approached in size those of the Swedes and Norwegians, and in 1914 the two Lutheran bodies which served them together enrolled only about thirty thousand members. The older, the Danish Evangelical Lutheran Church in America, was organized in 1872 by pastors sent by the Church of Denmark to minister to the immigrants. At first the high church, Grundtvigian, and Inner Mission elements coöperated. In 1894 a number withdrew to form the Danish Evangelical Lutheran Church in North America. Two years later the latter body joined with the Danish Evangelical Lutheran Church Association (which in 1883 had been formed of those who separated from the Norwegian-Danish Conference) to organize the United Danish Evangelical Lutheran Church in America. The Danish Evangelical Lutheran Church in America, somewhat smaller than the new united body, continued close ties with the Church of Denmark, was strongly congregational and democratic in polity, tended to be Grundtvigian, and emphasized education.[138]

About half as many Finns as Danes were gathered into Lutheran churches using the mother tongue. They were in three bodies. The largest, enrolling about half the Finnish church members, was the Suomi Synod, or the Finnish Evangelical Lutheran Church of America, organized in 1890 and having the majority of its members in Michigan. The Finnish Evangelical Lutheran National Church, which had its membership chiefly in Minnesota and Michigan and embodied more congregational autonomy than the older body, was also formed in 1890. In time it was loosely affiliated with the Missouri Synod. The Finnish Apostolic Lutheran Church, or Apostolic Lutheran Church (Finnish), arose in the 1870's from the followers of Lars Levi Laestadius,[139] the Swedish leader of a distinctive form of awakening.[140]

The Icelandic Evangelical Lutheran Synod in North America, organized in 1885, included settlements of Icelanders in the United States and Canada. Its congregations were largely rural and widely scattered, but in 1893 it employed a man to give full time to travelling among the Icelanders and later a board of home missions was established.[141]

The Slovaks began coming in force in the 1880's. Some of their pastors were trained in Concordia Seminary. For them two bodies arose—the Slovak Evangelical Union (1893) and the Slovak Lutheran Church (1902).[142]

The large Hungarian immigration included many who in their native land were members of the Reformed Church. Congregations for them were organized by the Reformed Church in the United States and the Presbyterian Church

---

138 Mayer, *op. cit.*, p. 185; Bureau of the Census, *Religious Bodies, 1916,* Vol. II, pp. 394–396, 406–408.

139 Volume II, Chapter XVI.

140 Bureau of the Census, *Religious Bodies, 1916,* Vol. II, pp. 401, 402, 409–412.

141 *Ibid.*, pp. 398, 399.

142 Geork Doldk, *A History of the Slovak Evangelical Church in the United States of America, 1902–1927* (St. Louis, Concordia Publishing House, 1955, pp. xii, 207), *passim.*

in the U.S.A., and some were drawn into the Baptist, Congregational, and other denominations. On invitation, the Reformed Church in Hungary sent a representative to America, and in 1904 the Hungarian Reformed Church in America was inaugurated. It was under the supervision of the Reformed Church in Hungary and received ministers and financial aid from that body.[143]

Numbers of Reformed came from Holland in the nineteenth century. Their motives for immigration were predominantly social and economic, but religion played a large part. Much of the Protestant emigration from Holland was from the religious awakenings which we have noted.[144] In 1847 a group from the *Christijke Gereformeerde Kerk* ("Christian Reformed Church"), an outgrowth of the *réveil*, founded Holland, in Michigan. The potato blight which brought disaster to Ireland and to some sections of the Continent of Europe devastated the Netherlands in 1845. Some of the farmers hard hit by it were also being persecuted for withdrawing from the Dutch Reformed Church. It was they who formed the nucleus of the settlement in Michigan. Around that settlement a strong centre of the Dutch Reformed Church developed, reinforced by the coming of others who held to the same convictions. Also in 1847, Pella, in Marion County, Iowa, was begun by a similarly minded group. As the decades passed, more immigrants came from the Netherlands, by no means all of them from religious motives, and scattered widely through the country. Most of those who arrived in 1847 and later were drawn into affiliation with the Dutch Reformed Church, which had been in the country since colonial days and eventually was known as the Reformed Church in America. Commissioners were sent by that church to invite the colonists to membership. The majority complied, but a substantial minority remained true to the *Christlijke Gereformeerde Kerk*. They were augmented by others who seceded from the Dutch Reformed Church, some on the ground that it was compromising Reformed doctrine and others because they held that the church should not permit its members to become Freemasons or join other oathbound secret societies.[145]

ROMAN CATHOLIC GAINS AMONG THE TRADITIONALLY CHRISTIAN NINETEENTH-CENTURY IMMIGRATION

As we have suggested, the nineteenth century witnessed the coming to the United States of millions who had Roman Catholic ancestry. Before their arrival, the country had been overwhelmingly Protestant by tradition. Even though only a small minority were members of churches, the European background of the vast majority was Protestant. The Roman Catholic Church was represented historically by a minority in Maryland and also by some in Phila-

[143] Bureau of the Census, *Religious Bodies, 1916*, Vol. II, pp. 639, 640.
[144] Volume II, Chapter XXV.
[145] Corwin, *History of the Reformed Church, Dutch*, pp. 211, 212; Lucas, *Netherlanders in America*, pp. 42–195 and *passim*.

delphia, New York, Boston, and other cities. In 1790, as we have seen, John Carroll, an ex-Jesuit, of an old Maryland Roman Catholic family, was consecrated the first bishop in the United States. He died in 1815, but before his death he had been made archbishop, with his seat in Baltimore, other episcopal sees had been created, and several orders and congregations had entered the country.[146]

The challenge which the Roman Catholic Church faced in the United States in the nineteenth century was prodigious. Of the thirteen and a half million foreign born in the country in 1910 at least seven and a half million, or 60 per cent., had been baptized in her faith.[147] That total did not include those born in America or the numbers who had died. Many were from countries where anti-clericalism was strong and so would be inclined to be either hostile or indifferent. For millions the connexion was only conventional and would not automatically be retained. The overwhelming majority were poverty-stricken and had come from economic, not religious motives. The struggle for a livelihood was primary, and in a land where no religion was established by law the duties obligatory on a Roman Catholic could easily be disregarded.

The challenge was the more urgent because of the hostility of large elements in the older American stock. The vast influx from abroad was viewed as a threat to existing customs and institutions. Antagonism to Protestant immigrants from the Continent of Europe was not uncommon. It was more acute against Roman Catholics and from time to time broke out 'in organized opposition and even in open and on occasion violent persecution. It was akin to the anti-clericalism in Europe and was compounded of a dislike of aliens and the fear that democracy would be undermined and the nation dominated by a hierarchical structure headed by a non-American in the Vatican. "Nativism" became marked in the 1830's and 1840's and mounted to a crescendo in the 1850's. In the Know-Nothing movement it had political as well as non-political expressions. In 1834 a mob wrecked a convent in Boston. The outrage was quickly denounced publicly by many Protestants. But S. F. B. Morse, the inventor of the electric telegraph, came out with *A Foreign Conspiracy against the Liberties of the United States,* which had a wide circulation. In 1837 the Native American Party was organized and soon became frankly anti-Roman Catholic. May and July, 1844, saw anti-Catholic riots in Philadelphia and the burning of some Roman Catholic churches and residences. In that year similar riots in New York City were narrowly averted by the measures of the mayor and the arming of the churches by the bishop. Ten years later some churches in Massachusetts and New Hampshire were destroyed. The Know-Nothing movement became a factor in national politics, elected a few congressmen, and was potent in some states and

---

[146] Volume I, p. 160.
[147] Based on the table in Shaughnessy, *Has the Immigrant Kept the Faith?*, p. 175.

cities.[148] During the Civil War anti-Roman Catholic agitation died down, but with the continued influx of Roman Catholic immigrants it revived. It found focus in the American Protective Association, organized in 1887 in Iowa, and swelled to national proportions. One of the continuing issues was the school question—the existence of Roman Catholic parochial schools, the unwillingness of most of the hierarchy to have Roman Catholic children in the public schools, where instruction in the Roman Catholic faith could not be given, and Roman Catholic insistence that the parochial schools be accorded financial support through public taxation.[149]

In spite of the difficulties and the opposition, the number of Roman Catholics in the United States mounted rapidly—from 1,606,000 in 1850 to 12,041,000 in 1900,[150] to 14,210,000 in 1906, and to 15,721,000 in 1916.[151] Although Roman Catholics were still a minority and much less numerous than Protestants, at the close of the nineteenth century the Roman Catholic Church was the largest ecclesiastical body in the country and had a nation-wide organization. The overwhelming majority—about 85 per cent.—were believed to be immigrants or descendants of immigrants of Roman Catholic faith who had come to the country after 1820. In the main, in the opening years of the twentieth century the Roman Catholic Church had succeeded in retaining, at least in formal connexion, by far the larger proportion of those who by ancestry were her children. Because the industrialization of the country proceeded more rapidly in the North-east than elsewhere, and since most of the Roman Catholic immigration found employment as unskilled labourers in the cities and mining centres of that region, the Roman Catholic Church was predominantly urban—in factory and mining towns and cities, and until after 1914 mainly in the inner-city sections. The older American stock, mostly Protestant by heritage, tended to leave the hearts of the cities, less attractive as they were, for the suburbs. Not until after 1914 did the descendants of the nineteenth-century Roman Catholic immigration share sufficiently in the prosperity of the country to begin to find homes in substantial numbers in the suburbs. Some Roman Catholics, especially Germans, were on farms in the West. Because of the competition of Negro labour and the prevailingly agricultural character of the region, the nineteenth-century immigration mostly shunned the South, and that section remained Protestant. But in Louisiana, long in Spanish and French hands, the Roman Catholic Church was strong.[152]

[148] Weigle, *American Idealism*, p. 169; Reuben Maury, *The Wars of the Godly* (New York, Robert M. McBride & Co., 1928), pp. 53–168; O'Gorman, *A History of the Roman Catholic Church in the United States*, pp. 356–359, 375; Ellis, *American Catholicism*, pp. 60–68.

[149] Ellis, *op. cit.*, pp. 106–108; O'Gorman, *op. cit.*, pp. 371, 372; Maury, *op. cit.*, pp. 189 ff.

[150] Ellis, *op. cit.*, p. 86.

[151] Bureau of the Census, *Religious Bodies, 1916*, Vol. II, p. 653.

[152] Shaughnessy, *op. cit.*, *passim*. See also a chart in Weigle, *op. cit.*, p. 168, based upon the latter.

The success of the Roman Catholic Church in holding its hereditary constituency was due to a variety of factors. As for Protestant immigrants, the church was something familiar in a foreign land. Here the mother tongue could be heard in the sermon; here was a social centre for meeting one's own kind; here, too, the services were those to which the immigrant had been accustomed. The fact that in the first half of the century most of the Roman Catholic immigration was from Ireland and Germany proved fortunate. For the Irish the Roman Catholic Church had long been a symbol and bond of their identity as against their English rulers. Except for some slight assistance from the crown, its financial support had come from its parishioners. The Irish, therefore, were prepared to pay from their poverty for the maintenance of their church in a land in which it was not established. The Roman Catholic Church in Germany experienced a decided revival in the nineteenth century and a large proportion of its children from that country would be predisposed to respond to efforts to hold them to the faith of their fathers. Substantial assistance came from Europe in personnel and funds. Able leadership was not long in emerging in the United States itself. A rapidly mounting proportion of the bishops, clergy, and members of orders and congregations were from the immigrants and their children. Most of the money which made possible the erection of churches, schools, and other institutions was from the immigrants. The parochial schools, often maintained at great sacrifice, nurtured the young in the faith and were favorable to vocations to the priesthood and to the orders and congregations of men and women. Among the clergy and in the episcopate were many able and devoted men. Rome took an active interest and was a centre to which disputes between the several national groups, between powerful bishops, and between advocates of conflicting policies could be referred for authoritative decision.

Assistance from Europe took various forms and was especially important in the earlier decades. Although the immigration from France was inconsiderable, in the fore part of the century many clergy and members of orders and congregations were from that country. Some were *émigrés* seeking refuge from the Revolution. Of the thirty-four bishops between 1820 and 1840, thirteen were French as against nine natives of Ireland, two Belgians, one Englishman, one German, one Spaniard, and one Italian.[153] After peace had been restored (1815), the bishops of French origin continued to ask French Roman Catholics for missionaries. Among those who responded were the sisters of the Society of the Sacred Heart. The initial contingent arrived in 1818. The congregation spread widely and was in charge of schools and orphanages.[154] However, most of the Roman Catholics of French blood were from Canada and preferred clergy and religious from that background. Priests from France experienced

---

[153] Guilday, *The Life and Times of John England*, Vol. I, p. 475, n. 1.

[154] Louise Callan, *The Society of the Sacred Heart in North America* (New York, Longmans, Green and Co., 1937, pp. xvii, 809), *passim.*

difficulty in adjusting themselves to the American scene and to nationalities other than their own. In spite of the fact that from France in the nineteenth century more Roman Catholic missionaries went to other lands than from any other one country, a decreasing number came to the United States. Yet the Society for the Propagation of the Faith, of French origin and until 1922 directed from France and a major source of funds for Roman Catholic missions, came into being through an appeal from Bishop Du Bourg of New Orleans. By the year 1914 the Society had contributed more than six million dollars to the several dioceses.[155]

The French Canadians, very clannish, loyally Roman Catholic, and mostly in New England, were served mainly by French Canadian priests and sisters.[156] Indeed, the French Canadians constituted an enclave which was resistant to integration in the comprehensive structure of the Roman Catholic Church in the United States.

Both before and after 1830 (the year of its independence), Belgium contributed largely to the Roman Catholic Church in the United States. In that country John Carroll had part of his education. The American-born Edward Dominic Fenwick, the first Bishop of Cincinnati, was educated at a college of the English Dominicans in Belgium and was there admitted to the Order of Preachers. It was he who introduced the Dominicans to the United States.[157] A Belgian headed a party of Jesuits who in 1823 began the enterprise of the Society on the frontier near St. Louis which was to serve both Indians and whites in that vast region.[158] Charles Nerinckx, a Belgian, a pioneer in Kentucky, attracted at least two contingents from his mother country who reinforced the Jesuits in the United States.[159] Belgium was the source of Poor Clares and Beguines and of Xaverian Brothers.[160] In 1840 a contingent of Sisters of Notre Dame de Namur arrived to lay the foundations of their congregation in the United States, preliminary to convents from the Atlantic to the Pacific which were to be of great assistance in teaching.[161] The year 1857 witnessed the

[155] Edward John Hickey, *The Society for the Propagation of the Faith. Its Foundation, Organization and success (1822–1922)* (Washington, The Catholic University of America *Studies in American Church History*, Vol. III, 1922, pp. x, 195), pp. 18 ff., 153; Joseph Freri, *The Society for the Propagation of the Faith and Foreign Missions* (New York, Press of the Society for the Propagation of the Faith, 1912, pp. 40), pp. 27–29.

[156] Bracq, *The Evolution of French Canada*, pp. 215–217.

[157] V. F. O'Daniel, *The Right Rev. Edward Dominic Fenwick, O. P., Founder of the Dominicans in the United States* (Washington, The Dominicans, 1920, pp. xiv, 483), pp. 33–40.

[158] Garraghan, *The Jesuits of the Middle United States*, Vol. I, pp. 45 ff.

[159] Griffin, *The Contribution of Belgium to the Catholic Church in America (1523–1857)*, pp. 97 ff.; Maes, *The Life of Rev. Charles Nerinckx*, pp. 130–148, 196–214; Garraghan, *op. cit.*, Vol. I, pp. 13–22.

[160] Griffin, *op. cit.*, pp. 142, 165, 187, 188.

[161] *Ibid.*, pp. 181–196; Helen Louise Nugent, *Sister Louise (Josephine van der Schrieck) (1813–1886), American Foundress of the Sisters of Notre Dame de Namur* (Washington, The Catholic University of America *Studies in American Church History*, Vol. X, 1931, pp. ix, 352), *passim;* F. de Chantal, *Julie Billiart and Her Institute* (London, Longmans, Green and Co., 1938, pp. x, 280), pp. 206 ff.

founding in Louvain of the American College of the Immaculate Conception of the Virgin Mary for training American-born students for service in their own country and for preparing Europeans for dioceses in the United States. During its first three-quarters of a century it educated over a thousand.[162]

Irish immigrants and Americans of Irish birth or descent provided a very large proportion of the personnel of the Roman Catholic Church in the United States. Since Ireland was English-speaking and the Roman Catholic Church in that country often produced more priests than it needed, and since so large a proportion of the immigration to the United States was from Ireland, Rome and the American bishops sought in that land for clergy and not unsuccessfully. Thus John England (1786-1842), after a promising record as a courageous, zealous, and eloquent priest in his native Ireland, was appointed in 1820 as the first Bishop of Charleston, South Carolina, and served there with distinction.[163] From Ireland came Ursulines and the first head of the seminary which England founded for the training of the clergy.[164] John Hughes (1797-1864), Bishop and then the first Archbishop of New York, was born in Ireland but was educated in the United States. A vigorous organizer and administrator, courageous and creative, he left a profound impress upon his church in that growing city and was one of the most prominent American bishops of his day.[165] James Gibbons (1834-1921), Archbishop of Baltimore and the second from the United States to be created cardinal, was born in Baltimore of Irish parents but as a child was taken by them to Ireland and did not return to America until his nineteenth year.[166] John Ireland (1838-1918), Bishop and then Archbishop of St. Paul, outstanding in the life of his church, as a child was brought by his parents from his native Ireland to the United States and was reared in the city with which his name was to be associated.[167] Many others of Irish birth or Irish ancestry became bishops of the Roman Catholic Church in the United States.[168]

From Germany, sharing with Ireland the distinction of being the chief source of the immigrants in the fore part of the century and in the second half of the century ranking only after Italy and Austria-Hungary as the fatherland of the largest number of Roman Catholic arrivals, and with a pulsing life in the Roman Catholic Church within its borders, came not only personnel but also funds to assist in holding the immigrants to their ancestral faith. Aid also was given

[162] Griffin, *op. cit.*, pp. 219 ff.; J. van der Heyden, *The Louvain American College, 1857-1907* (Louvain, F. and R. Ceuterick, 1909, pp. x, 412), *passim;* Roger Aubert, "Le College Americain de Louvain (1857-1957)," in *Ephemerides Theologicae Lovanienses,* Vol. XXXIII, 1957, pp. 713-728 (Bruges, Ch. Beyaert), *passim.*

[163] O'Brien, *John England, passim;* Guilday, *op. cit., passim.*

[164] Guilday, *op. cit.*, Vol. I, p. 498, Vol. II, pp. 143 ff.

[165] O'Gorman, *op. cit.*, pp. 367 ff.; *Dictionary of American Biography,* Vol. IX, pp. 352-355.

[166] Ellis, *The Life of James Cardinal Gibbons,* Vol. I, pp. 3-26.

[167] Moynihan, *The Life of Archbishop John Ireland,* pp. 1-6.

[168] For some of these see O'Donnell, *The Catholic Hierarchy of the United States, 1790-1922,* pp. 6, 13, 19, 23, 40, 42, 47, 59, 84, 130-132, 146, 152, 154, 156, 157.

from the German portions of Switzerland and from Austria. Many of the German immigrants found homes in the West. Cincinnati and St. Louis early became strong German centres and German Roman Catholics were scattered widely in cities and farms in the upper part of the basin of the Mississippi.[169] The *Leopoldinen-Stiftung* ("Leopoldine Society") was founded in Austria in 1829 for the purpose of aiding missions in America.[170] The *Ludwig-Missionsverein* arose, like the *Leopoldinen-Stiftung,* from an appeal for help from Frederick Rese, Vicar-General of the see of Cincinnati. Its base was Bavaria. Its foundations dated from 1828, but it was not formally organized until 1838. Neither society confined its assistance to the United States but, like the Society for the Propagation of the Faith, extended its contributions to other areas as well.[171] Several orders and congregations owed either their introduction or their reinforcement to Germans from the Old World. Thus in their early years in the United States the Redemptorists were largely of German origin.[172] The Congregation of the Fathers of the Precious Blood had its first post in the United States in Ohio in 1843, and its labours, largely in the Middle West, were directed mainly to the care of German immigrants.[173] A Franciscan from Bavaria responded to a call from Bishop Purcell of Cincinnati during his visit to Europe in 1839 and when the Bavarian province found itself unable to spare more of its members, Brothers Minor came from other German or German Swiss provinces of the order. From them arose what in time (1885) became the Franciscan Province of St. John the Baptist. It expanded its field to several states in the Mississippi Valley and to Canada. It directed its efforts chiefly to German Congregations but also served English, French, and Polish elements.[174] The foundations of the Franciscan Province of the Sacred Heart were laid in 1858 in Illinois by a contingent of seven from Westphalia. That province was to extend its services—to Ohio, Missouri, and Tennessee.[175] In 1846 Benedictines from Bavaria arrived and established a centre in Pennsylvania which in time became an abbey. Boniface Wimmer, a member of the original contingent, was the founder of the order in the United States. Benedictine congregations multiplied in several states. Some congregations of women were also introduced from Germany. Among them came the School Sisters of Notre Dame (the initial contingent from Munich in 1847), Benedictine sisters from Eichstadt (1852), Dominican sisters from Bavaria (1853), and the Poor Sisters of St. Francis from

[169] Rothan, *The German Catholic Immigrant in the United States (1830–1860),* pp. 1–76; Barry, *The Catholic Church and German Americans,* pp. 3–10.

[170] Rothan, *op. cit.,* p. 80; Benjamin J. Blied, *Austrian Aid to American Catholics* (Milwaukee, no publisher given, 1944, pp. 204), *passim.*

[171] Theodore Roemer, *The Ludwig-Missionsverein and the Church in the United States (1838–1918)* (Washington, The Catholic University of America Press, 1933, pp. xii, 161), pp. 2, 3.

[172] Rothan, *op. cit.,* pp. 82, 83.

[173] *Ibid.,* p. 83.

[174] *Ibid.,* pp. 83, 84.

[175] *Ibid.,* pp. 84, 85.

Aachen (1858), all devoting themselves to teaching or the care of the sick.[176]

Planted in the United States, these various orders and congregations grew chiefly by recruiting members from the immigrants and their children. They became part of the American scene.

To the regulars from Germany were added many seculars. Their totals ran into the hundreds. Some were assigned to circuits, Roman Catholic parallels to the device employed by the Methodists in reaching the settlers on the frontiers. German priests served primarily the immigrants of German speech, but many of them ministered to parishes in which those of their faith were from more than one language group.[177]

Several of the early bishops of the Roman Catholic Church in the United States were German, either from Germany itself or from other countries. The first was Frederick Rese (1791–1871). Educated in Rome and for a few years a pastor in Germany, in 1829 he came to America and in 1833 was appointed the first Bishop of Detroit.[178]

While the major part of the assistance in holding the Roman Catholic immigrants to the faith was from France, Belgium, Ireland, and Germany, some was from other countries. Thus in 1887 Bishop Scalabrini of Piacenza founded the Congregation of the Missionaries of St. Charles Borromeo to prepare missionaries for the Italians in the New World. He had been moved by the plight of emigrants in a railway station and determined to do something for them. Very soon representatives were going both to the United States and to Brazil.[179] The initial contingent of Pallottine Sisters arrived in 1889 and devoted themselves to the Italians on the East Side of New York.[180] They later spread widely. Italian Franciscans also served in the United States.[181] Whitefield, the fourth Bishop of Baltimore, was of English birth and education. At least one other bishop had been born and educated in Holland. Still another was a Pole.[182]

Here and there, as with Protestants, were Roman Catholics who came to the United States with the purpose of founding a Christian community. Thus in 1854 a group from Baden led by a priest arrived in Wisconsin, purchased a tract of land, and planned to lead a communal life. The unmarried men and women were to dwell in separate houses and devote themselves to the religious life. The colony was incorporated as the Roman Catholic Religious Society of St. Nazianz. In 1896 the survivors joined the Salvatorians.[183]

[176] *Ibid.*, pp. 85–89; Colman J. Barry, *Worship and Work, Saint John's Abbey and University, 1856–1956* (Collegeville, Minn., Saint John's Abbey, 1956, pp. 447), pp. 7–9.

[177] Rothan, *op. cit.*, pp. 89–91.

[178] *Ibid.*, pp. 91–93.

[179] *The Catholic Encyclopedia*, Vol. X, p. 368.

[180] Thomas F. Cullen, *The Catholic Church in Rhode Island* (North Providence, R. I., The Franciscan Missionaries of Mary, 1936, pp. 482), p. 407.

[181] Callahan, *Medieval Francis in Modern America*, pp. 61–70.

[182] O'Donnell, *op. cit.*, pp. 5, 65, 169.

[183] Rothan, *op. cit.*, pp. 64, 65.

We also hear of a number of projects in which colonies of Roman Catholics settled together, sometimes on the initiative of ecclesiastical authorities, buying land and centring their life around a church and school. Prince Demetrius Augustine Gallatzin (1770–1840), baptized in the Russian Orthodox Church, converted in his teens, prepared for the priesthood in Baltimore, ordained (1795) and preferring to be known as "Mr. Smith," bought a tract of land at Loretto, in western Pennsylvania, then on the frontier. He resold it to Roman Catholic colonists and erected a tannery, a flour mill, and a sawmill for them. He was aided by gifts from various sources, including his boyhood friend, the King of Holland.[184] We know of two settlements in Missouri.[185]

Attempts were made to attract Irish Roman Catholics to the vacant lands of the West. Coming as they did from rural life in Ireland, presumably they would prosper more on the soil than in the crowded and often fetid city slums where they tended to congregate. Efforts towards this end were put forth in the 1850's. In 1864 the Minnesota Irish Emigration Society was begun in St. Paul. In the next decade the energetic Bishop Ireland of St. Paul revived the project, set up the Catholic Colonization Bureau of Minnesota, and in 1877 stimulated the organization of the Catholic Colonization Company. The project envisioned the purchase from the railroads of some of the vast lands that had been granted them by the federal government as a means of subsidizing their construction, and to settle Roman Catholic colonies on them, or to have the colonists take up government land under a homestead law. Each colony was to have a church and a school. Thousands of acres were acquired from the railroads and sold to the settlers. Bishop Ireland also gave his support to the Irish Catholic Colonization Association, which dated from 1879. More than one bishop, including Spalding of Pretoria, shared in promoting the organization.[186]

Roman Catholic schools and especially the extensive system of parochial schools were of major importance in holding the children of the immigrants to the faith. A basic conviction fostered by the Popes was that instruction in religion must be an integral part of education. In the United States public education early became the rule, in principle available for all children on the elementary level. Because of the large variety of religions, both Christian and non-Christian, instruction in the public schools in the tenets of any one church was impossible. This stricture was not imposed out of hostility to religion, but because as between the numerous faiths the state must be neutral. In many schools the Bible was read without comment and the Lord's Prayer repeated as part of the daily

[184] Maynard, *The Story of American Catholicism*, pp. 272–275; *Dictionary of American Biography*, Vol. VII, pp. 113–115; *The Catholic Encyclopedia*, Vol. VI, pp. 367–369.

[185] Rothan, *op. cit.*, pp. 49–51.

[186] Moynihan, *op. cit.*, pp. 20–32; Ellis, *Documents of American Catholic History*, pp. 575–581; Mary Evangela Henthorne, *The Career of the Right Reverend John Lancaster Spalding of Pretoria, as President of the Irish Catholic Association of the United States, 1879–1892* (Champaign, Ill., The Twin City Printing Co., 1932, pp. 191), *passim.*

routine, but in large numbers, because of the criticism that these practices were sectarian, they were omitted. Under such conditions, the Roman Catholic hierarchy believed that schools must be maintained by their church, particularly on the parish and elementary level, and also of secondary and higher grades.

Roman Catholic schools, necessarily on a small scale, began in various places in the United States before 1815. They were expanded after that year. A French *émigré* priest, Gabriel Richard (1767-1832), laid foundations in Detroit which had repercussions through much of Michigan.[187] Shortly before 1815 beginnings were made in Georgetown in the District of Columbia for the training of teaching sisters. In 1816 these sisters were constituted a convent of the Sisters of the Visitation and by 1850 six branches had been established elsewhere.[188] The second women's community was the Sisters of Charity, founded by a convert from Protestantism, Elizabeth A. Seton (1774-1821). Largely at the instance and with the encouragement of Du Bourg, later Bishop of New Orleans, in 1808 she began a school for girls in Baltimore. From it came a community of religious, first called the Sisters of St. Joseph but later (1812) adopting the rules of Vincent de Paul for the Daughters of Charity. They gave themselves to teaching and in a little over a decade had founded eight schools.[189] Charles Nerinckx (1791-1824), a Belgian *émigré* priest who came to America in 1805, was assigned by Carroll to Kentucky and spent much of his time in the saddle, organizing congregations and ministering to his widely scattered flock. He was rightly known as the apostle of that state. He stimulated the founding of the sisters of Loretto, who gave themselves to teaching. The institute received Papal approval in 1816.[190] Almost contemporaneously, also in Kentucky, the Sisters of Charity of Nazareth, who adopted the rule of Vincent de Paul for his Daughters of Charity, came into being (1813), with Catherine Spalding as mother superior. Their schools were in Kentucky, Indiana, and Tennessee.[191] In 1822 the beginnings were made in Kentucky of a mother house of Dominican Sisters which had daughter houses in several places in the West that were centres of educational activity.[192] In diocese after diocese in the fore part of the nineteenth century, both on the Atlantic seaboard and in the West, schools were begun, most of them of elementary but some of secondary grade, and here and there one for higher education.[193]

A struggle famous in the annals of the parochial schools was waged in New

---

[187] Burns, *The Principles, Origin and Establishment of the Catholic School System in the United States*, pp. 180-186.

[188] *Ibid.*, pp. 204-207.

[189] *Ibid.*, pp. 207-221; *The Catholic Encyclopedia*, Vol. XIII, pp. 739, 740; Katherine Burton, *His Dear Persuasion. The Life of Elizabeth Ann Seton* (New York, Longmans, Green and Co., 1940, pp. 304), *passim*.

[190] Burns, *op. cit.*, pp. 224-235; *The Catholic Encyclopedia*, Vol. X, p. 752.

[191] Burns, *op. cit.*, pp. 235-243.

[192] *Ibid.*, pp. 243-246.

[193] *Ibid.*, pp. 247-258.

York in 1840 and 1841 by Bishop John Hughes. The Public School Society, an organization with a Protestant slant, was operating undenominational schools in New York and through it the public funds appropriated for education were administered. In 1824 grants to denominational schools had been discontinued. But in 1840 the Roman Catholics asked for a share in the common school fund for their schools. The civil authorities of New York denied the request. Bishop Hughes, with his accustomed vigour, took the leadership of the Roman Catholic forces and fought for a division of the funds on a programme which he outlined. The outcome was the dislodging of the Public School Society from its control of public funds and the extension to New York City of the state legislation for the schools, with no appropriation by the state to the Public School Society or to Roman Catholic schools. Hughes therefore directed his energies to the development of a system of schools supported by the Roman Catholics.[194]

The bishops took collective action to further Roman Catholic schools. The first provincial council of Baltimore, in 1829, declared it to be "absolutely necessary that schools should be established, in which the young may be taught the principles of faith and morality, while being instructed in letters," and the second provincial council, in 1833, took steps towards the preparation of suitable textbooks.[195] The first plenary council of the bishops of the United States (1852) came out emphatically for parochial schools, and in 1884 the third plenary council decreed the establishment of a parochial school in every parish in the next two years except where the bishop permitted otherwise.[196]

Some of the parochial schools carried on instruction in the language of the fatherland. German schools were especially numerous. One reason given for them was that where the Germans had German schools and spoke only German they would be true to their ancestral faith, and that where English supplanted German religious loyalty was shaken.[197]

Here and there support was obtained for parochial schools from public funds. For instance, for the sixteen years before 1852 this was true of Roman Catholic schools in Lowell, Massachusetts. Compromise arrangements were reached in Savannah, Georgia, St. Augustine, Florida, and Poughkeepsie, New York.[198] In the 1890's, what was called the Faribault plan, proposed by Archbishop Ireland of St. Paul, seemed to offer a satisfactory *via media*, but it provoked much controversy and was discontinued—although in some places it was in part kept up.[199]

In spite of the fact that, with a few exceptions, they were without aid from public funds and that property-owning Roman Catholics were taxed to support

[194] *Ibid.*, pp. 359–375.
[195] *Ibid.*, pp. 248–250.
[196] Ellis, *American Catholicism*, p. 80; *The Catholic Encyclopedia*, Vol. XIII, pp. 560–562.
[197] Rothan, *op. cit.*, pp. 123–138.
[198] *The Catholic Encyclopedia*, Vol. XIII, pp. 560–562.
[199] *Ibid.*; Moynihan, *op. cit.*, pp. 79–103.

the state schools, the parochial schools attained large dimensions. On the eve of 1914 they enrolled over a million pupils, had over twenty thousand teachers, and cost over fifteen million dollars a year.[200] Obviously they were a major means, maintained at great sacrifice on the part of the faithful, of instructing the young in Roman Catholic doctrine, practices, and morals as an integral part of the educational process. Yet a very large proportion, probably the majority, of the children of Roman Catholic parents were not in them but in the public schools. If they were to be reared in the faith, it would have to be by other means. For them catechetical classes were widely employed.

ROMAN CATHOLIC CONVERTS FROM PROTESTANTISM

Roman Catholic leaders were not content with holding the allegiance of the immigrants who were traditionally of their branch of the faith. They also sought to win Protestants, both of the older stock and of the nineteenth-century arrivals. How successful they were in point of numbers is not clear: whether more or less so than Protestants in attracting Roman Catholics is not certain. Some conversions, as by Protestants, were through intermarriage. As the century wore on, and especially in the twentieth century, the movement both ways across confessional lines increased; with the passage of time and the blurring of hereditary barriers of nationality, and with English the common language, differences in religion presented a less serious obstacle to marriage than formerly, and often, although not always, the husband and wife agreed to have a common church membership.

In the nineteenth century a large proportion, apparently the majority, of the more notable conversions from Protestantism to the Roman Catholic Church were by way of the Anglo-Catholic movement in the Protestant Episcopal Church. In the United States, as in England, a number of clergy and laity followed this path from Anglicanism to the Roman Catholic faith. Thus Levi Silliman Ives (1797–1876), the first Episcopal Bishop of North Carolina, in his youth a Presbyterian, then moving into the Episcopal Church and marrying the daughter of Bishop Hobart of New York, had increasingly high-church convictions and in his mid-fifties was received into the Roman Catholic Church. In his new affiliation he founded the Society for the Protection of Destitute Catholic Children in New York.[201] James Kent Stone (1840–1921), an Episcopal clergyman, successively president of Kenyon College in Ohio and Hobart College in New York, moved from Anglo-Catholicism to Roman Catholicism, joined the Paulists—of whom more in a moment—then the Passionists, and as Father Fidelis of the Cross helped lay foundations for that congregation in the

[200] *The Catholic Encyclopedia*, Vol. XIII, p. 560.
[201] Burton, *In No Strange Land*, pp. 1–11.

United States, Latin America, and Brazil.[202] Lewis Thomas Wattson (1863–1938), son of an Episcopal clergyman and himself ordained in that communion, founded the Society of Atonement with Franciscan ideals, its headquarters on Graymoor Mountain near the Hudson River. It was in the Episcopal Church, but he hoped through it to effect a reconciliation of Anglicanism with the Pope. In 1910 he and his entire society crossed the gap, by that time narrow, into the Roman Catholic Church. The preceding year Henry Sargent, head of the (Episcopal) Order of the Holy Cross, had taken the same step, but without bringing his brothers with him.[203]

Several women with outstanding social connexions were among the converts. In addition to Elizabeth A. Seton, they included Rose Hawthorne Lathrop, daughter of National Hawthorne. After her conversion she gave herself to the indigent sick in New York City, especially those suffering from cancer. Eventually, with a group of her fellow workers, she joined the Dominicans.[204]

Orestes Augustus Brownson (1803–1876) was a convert who came out of an unusual spiritual pilgrimage. A native of Vermont, from an old Connecticut family, deeply religious from childhood, in his late teens he joined a Presbyterian church in New York State. But he found some of its doctrines repellent, became a Universalist, for a time was a Universalist minister, then moved into a liberalism which put him in sympathy with social movements such as those of Robert Owen and was briefly, in an agony of doubt, an agnostic. Abandoning agnosticism, he became a Unitarian minister and continued to be interested in social reform. In Boston, in his Unitarian period, he sought to pioneer in the Church of the Future through a Society for Christian Union and Progress which would make for more intellectual freedom, social improvement, and spiritual morality, and found his audience chiefly among the working class. He was disturbed over the problems brought by the rising industrialism and by capitalism and sought to formulate a solution. He came under the influence of the philosophy of Victor Cousin, then popular in some circles in Europe. Several of his close friends were in the Transcendentalist Brook Farm and he sent his son there. As a journalist, author, and speaker he was a national figure. In 1844 he joined the Roman Catholic Church and became its vigorous advocate. He remained true to that faith, but his later years were troubled by bodily infirmities and for the most part were unhappy.[205]

A younger contemporary and friend of Brownson, Isaac Thomas Hecker (1819–1888), had a quite different career. He was born in New York City, the

---

[202] *Ibid.*, pp. 109–124.

[203] *Ibid.*, pp. 185–200; David Gannon, *Father Paul of Graymoor* (New York, The Macmillan Co., 1954, pp. x, 372), *passim.*

[204] Burton, *In No Strange Land,* pp. 173–184.

[205] Arthur M. Schlesinger, Jr., *Orestes A. Brownson. A Pilgrim's Progress* (Boston, Little, Brown and Co., 1939, pp. 320), *passim;* Theodore Maynard, *Orestes Brownson, Yankee, Radical, Catholic* (New York, The Macmillan Co., 1943, pp. xvi, 456), *passim.*

son of German immigrants, where he knew poverty. With his brothers he joined various reform movements. Through them he made the acquaintance of Brownson and at the latter's advice lived for a time at Brook Farm. Always religious, he groped for an answer to his questions. Partly through the influence of Brownson he became a Roman Catholic (1844). Gripped by a deep desire for the conversion of America, he joined the Redemptorists and formed friendships with some other converts, former Anglo-Catholics. He and they conducted missions in a number of cities, preaching, teaching, and hearing confessions. They did most of their work in English. They wished to found a house for English-speaking Redemptorists the better to effect their purpose. Although Archbishop Hughes of New York and the Bishop of New Jersey approved, their Redemptorist superiors refused permission. Hecker went to Rome, there to appeal to the head of the congregation. For this step, alleged to have been a violation of his vows of poverty and obedience, he was expelled from the Redemptorists. However, in 1858 Pope Pius IX dispensed from their vows Hecker and four other Redemptorist converts and encouraged them to continue their efforts for the "eternal salvation of souls." Returning to the United States, Hecker set about forming, with these friends, the Missionary Society of St. Paul the Apostle (July, 1858), the first strictly American congregation of men. It was committed to the personal perfection of its members and to the conversion of the country to the Catholic faith. It received at once the approval of Archbishop Hughes. Headquarters were established in New York City, and eventually houses were opened in other cities. Although ordinary parish work was undertaken, much attention was paid to reaching Protestants by preaching and literature. Missions were held in many centres to raise the quality of life of Roman Catholics, to promote temperance, and to win non-Catholics. Beginning in 1894, a programme was begun of enlisting and training diocesan clergy to carry on missions. To this end the Catholic Missionary Union was inaugurated and the Apostolic Mission House was opened in connexion with the Catholic University of America. The Paulists (as the members of the congregation were known) extended their activity to England and Australia. Yet by 1914 their membership was only about one hundred.

While emphatically orthodox in doctrine, Hecker believed that if the purpose of converting the United States was to be attained methods consonant with the American temper and way of life must be employed. Later, as we are to see, this led to the accusation in some Roman Catholic circles in Europe that the church in the United States was threatened with heresy in the form of Americanism.[206]

[206] Katherine Burton, *Celestial Homespun: the Life of Isaac Thomas Hecker* (New York, Longmans, Green and Co., 1943, pp. 393), *passim;* Joseph McSorley, *Father Hecker and His Friends: Studies and Reminiscences* (St. Louis, B. Herder Book Co., 1953, pp. xv, 304), *passim;* Vincent F. Holden, *The Early Years of Isaac Thomas Hecker (1819–1844)* (Washington, The Catholic Uni-

ROMAN CATHOLIC WORSHIP AND DEVOTIONAL PRACTICES

What was the status of public worship and the devotional life in the Roman Catholic Church in the United States in the nineteenth century? Because the Roman Catholic Church was in the brick and mortar stage, engrossed in caring for the vast flood of immigration of its professed children, in raising up and educating a clergy, in founding and developing institutions, and in creating a system of parochial schools with the erection of buildings and the training of teachers, and because it was embedded in a rapidly growing society which was engaged in mastering a vast territory, its activist character was prominent. The mobile nature of its constituency and the difficulty of preparing priests in sufficient numbers to care for the mounting flood frequently made impossible the kind of cure of souls envisioned by the Council of Trent, in which the pastor knew personally each member of his flock. These factors combined with a near approach to religious illiteracy, the merely formal connexion with the church of their fathers which a large proportion of the professed Roman Catholics brought with them, and their struggle to establish themselves in their new homes contributed to a low level of devotional life.[207] The fact that by the middle of the twentieth century only one Roman Catholic who had been a resident of the United States had been canonized and that she had been born and reared in Italy appears to be significant. While some of nineteenth-century American birth might eventually be officially judged to have attained the standards of sanctity deemed by their church to warrant canonization, the fact that a number of their European contemporaries had been so recognized before them appears to indicate that from the standpoint of Rome the Catholic Church in the United States was unpromising as a source of ideal Christian character.

During most of the nineteenth century conditions left much to be desired. Until well on in the century some collections of hymns issued for use by Roman Catholics contained numbers of Protestant origin.[208] The argument from silence is notoriously inconclusive, but the fact that little material has been found on the inner life of the Roman Catholic Church in the United States in the nineteenth century[209]—in contrast with the abundance of it for Europe—may indicate that the level of the devotional life was far below that attained in Europe in the awakenings of that period. The Liturgical Movement did not make itself felt in the United States until after 1914, fully a generation after it had sprung up on the other side of the Atlantic. By and large the laity did not intelligently

versity of America Press, 1939, pp. ix, 257), *passim; The Catholic Encyclopedia,* Vol. X, pp. 368, 369; Vincent F. Holden, *The Yankee Paul. Isaac Thomas Hecker* (Milwaukee, The Bruce Publishing Co., 1958, pp. xx, 508), *passim.*

[207] Ernest Benjamin Koenker, *The Liturgical Renaissance in the Roman Catholic Church* (University of Chicago Press, 1954, pp. xi, 272), pp. 39, 40.

[208] Erwin Esser Nemmers, *Twenty Centuries of Catholic Church Music* (Milwaukee, The Bruce Publishing Co., 1949, pp. xvii, 213), p. 166.

[209] Ellis, *Documents of American Catholic History,* p. 644.

participate in the mass but spent their time during its celebration in the recitation of the rosary and reading certain types of prayer books.[210] International Eucharistic congresses began in Europe in the 1880's, but it was not until 1926 that one was held in the United States.[211]

The American hierarchy were not unmindful of the problem and again and again addressed themselves to it. Thus in his initial pastoral letter Carroll urged parents to teach their children the practice of morning and evening prayer and to frequent the sacraments.[212] The first provincial council of Baltimore (1829) in its pastoral letter to the clergy bewailed the neglect of the sacraments by the laity and ascribed it in part to the attitudes and even the misconduct of some priests.[213] In the second plenary council (1866) the bishops in their pastoral letter deplored the fact that even laymen who were faithful in hearing mass, too often for years did not avail themselves of the sacraments.[214] In their pastoral letter of 1919 the bishops sought to encourage the custom of family prayers.[215]

In the latter part of the century conditions seem to have improved. Thus we hear of active participation from the United States in the international Eucharistic congresses in London in 1908 and in Montreal two years later.[216] Moreover, with the checking of the flood of immigration after 1914 the Roman Catholic Church was better able to catch up with its task of assimilation, and the devotional life improved. Even as early as 1919 the bishops could rejoice in the increased number who were daily coming to Mass.[217]

PROGRESS AMONG THE INDIANS

The Indians presented a major challenge to Christianity. To the aboriginal inhabitants, the coming of the white man and the rapid westward movement of his settlements brought a basic revolution in culture. Here was a phase of the global changes wrought by the revolution which issued from Western Christendom and which were especially sweeping among peoples of "primitive" cultures. The settlers coveted the lands of the Indians and encroached upon them, often with bloodshed. The Government of the United States vacillated in its policies. In the main, it sought to protect the Indians from exploitation, entered into treaties with the various tribes, guaranteed the integrity of the extensive lands reserved for them, and adopted an attitude of benevolent paternalism. But often government agents were inefficient or even corrupt and treaties were violated. The basic and inevitable adjustment of the hunting, tribal, and semi-

[210] Ellis, *American Catholicism*, p. 134.
[211] *Ibid.*, pp. 130, 131.
[212] Guilday, *The National Pastorals of the American Hierarchy (1792–1919)*, p. 3.
[213] *Ibid.*, pp. 49–51.
[214] *Ibid.*, pp. 218, 219.
[215] *Ibid.*, p. 277.
[216] Ellis, *The Life of James Cardinal Gibbons*, Vol. II, pp. 320–323.
[217] Guilday, *The National Pastorals of the American Hierarchy (1792–1919)*, p. 278.

agricultural economy to the white man's encompassing civilization meant the disintegration of the traditional cultures with disastrous physical and moral results for many thousands. The white man's "fire water" and diseases worked havoc. Could Christianity win the Indians and help to make the transition constructive rather than destructive? The problem was complicated by the division of the Indians into many tribes, each with its distinctive language and customs. The numbers involved were not large. The census of 1910 showed a total of 291,014 in the country, including 25,331 in Alaska. This was an increase from 1890, but possibly a decrease from 1870 and still earlier in the century.[218] Yet scattered as the Indians were in all the states and territories and fragmented into many units, any mass conversion such as that accomplished by Roman Catholics among the pre-Columbian civilized peoples in Mexico and Northwestern South America was out of the question. The approach would have to be tribe by tribe. Protestants, Roman Catholics, and Russian Orthodox were active. The federal government long gave substantial assistance by subsidizing mission schools. It gradually reduced these appropriations, placing the schools directly under the Indian Service rather than missions, and for a time after 1900 discontinued all financial aid to mission schools. Subventions were continued in other forms, especially beginning in 1905. For a time after 1869 the nomination of government agents among the Indians was delegated to the various religious bodies having missions among them. However, this practice was progressively abandoned.[219]

To give even a summary of Protestant, Roman Catholic, and Orthodox missions to the Indians would entail a longer account than the scope of our survey rightly permits.[220] We must content ourselves with a few concrete instances which illustrate the impact of the revolutionary age upon the Indians and Christian effort in response to it, and some comprehensive generalizations.

A story compounded of callous cruelty, tragic suffering, and high heroism is connected with the Cherokees. At the outset of the nineteenth century, these people, said to number about twelve thousand, were occupying their ancestral lands in a piedmont and mountain region in Alabama, Georgia, Tennessee, South Carolina, North Carolina, and Virginia. They had made some advance towards adjustment to the paleface's civilization and one of them had devised a syllabary for their language. Missionaries entered the territory, representing Moravians, Presbyterians, Baptists, and notably the American Board of Com-

---

[218] U. S. Department of Commerce, Bureau of the Census, *Indian Population in the United States and Alaska, 1910*, p. 10.

[219] Schmeckbier, *The Office of Indian Affairs*, pp. 2–11, 39, 40, 54, 55, 77, 78, 81, 212, 269, 438, 483.

[220] A comprehensive narrative has never been written, either of Protestant or of Roman Catholic missions to the Indians of the United States. A brief summary, with bibliographical references, is in Latourette, *A History of the Expansion of Christianity*, Vol. IV, pp. 299–324. On one phase of Roman Catholic effort see Peter J. Rahill, *The Catholic Indian Missions and Grant's Peace Policy, 1870–1884* (Washington, The Catholic University of America Press, 1953, pp. xx, 396).

missioners for Foreign Missions. Land-hungry whites, covetous of the Cherokee lands, forced the removal of the Cherokees beyond the Mississippi. In its determination to oust the Cherokees, the state of Georgia attempted to keep out the missionaries, imprisoned two of them, and defied the federal government and the latter's Supreme Court. Some of the missionaries accompanied the Cherokees on their painful trek (1838) to their new lands, and among the Cherokee Christians were leaders who helped their people to avoid complete demoralization on the journey and in their new homes. The faith made such headway that in 1860 the American Board of Commissioners for Foreign Missions decided that its assistance was no longer necessary.[221]

Far-reaching efforts, both by Protestants and by Roman Catholics, were stimulated by a striking incident in 1831. That autumn a party of four Indians came to St. Louis, then the main western outpost of the white man's advance, asking for information about the paleface's religion. They were from beyond the Rocky Mountains, probably from the Nez Perces and Flatheads in the Pacific Northwest. Some knowledge of Christianity had filtered in to them, presumably from a variety of sources. Two of the four died in St. Louis and while ill were baptized as Roman Catholics.[222]

The publication of the news of the mission aroused much interest in Protestant circles. The Methodists responded with a mission headed by Jason Lee (1803–1845). Lee reached Oregon in 1834. Centres were established in several places in the Pacific North-west, notably the fertile Willamette Valley. But the Indian tribes were being rapidly decimated by disease, and the Methodists soon devoted most of their energy to the white settlers who were pouring into the country.[223] The American Board of Commissioners for Foreign Missions had been exploring the possibility of a mission to the north-west coast, and the news of the Indian delegation of 1831 spurred it to action. Under it Samuel Parker

---

[221] Robert Sparks Walker, *Torchlights of the Cherokees. The Brainerd Mission* (New York, The Macmillan Co., 1931, pp. xl, 339), *passim;* Ralph H. Gabriel, *Elias Boudinot, Cherokee, and His America* (Norman, University of Oklahoma Press, 1941, pp. xv, 190), *passim;* Edmund Schwarze, *History of the Moravian Missions among Southern Indian Tribes of the United States* (Bethlehem, Pa., Times Publishing Co., 1923, pp. xvii, 331), *passim;* Joseph Tracy, *History of the American Board of Commissioners for Foreign Missions* (New York, M. W. Dodd, 2nd ed., 1842, pp. viii, 452), pp. 68, 69, 249–254; William Ellsworth Strong, *The Story of the American Board* (Boston, The Pilgrim Press, 1910, pp. xii, 713), pp. 46–186; R. S. Cotterill, *The Southern Indians: The Story of the Civilized Tribes before Removal* (Norman, University of Oklahoma Press, 1954, pp. xiii, 255), *passim.*

[222] Clifford Merrill Drury, *Henry Harmon Spalding* (Caldwell, Ida., The Caxton Printers, 1936, pp. 438), pp. 72–90; Cornelius J. Brosnan, *Jason Lee, Prophet of the New Oregon* (New York, The Macmillan Co., 1932, pp. x, 348), pp. 2–10; Bishop Rosati, letter, Dec. 31, 1831, in *Annales de l'Association de la Propagation de la Foi* (Lyon, 1837 ff.), Vol. V, pp. 599, 600.

[223] Brosnan, *op. cit., passim;* H. K. Hines, *Missionary History of the Pacific Northwest* (Portland, Ore., H. K. Hines, 1899, pp. 510), *passim;* D. Lee and J. H. Frost, *Ten Years in Oregon* (New York, J. Collord, 1844, pp. 344), *passim;* James W. Bashford, *The Oregon Missions* (New York, Abingdon Press, 1918, pp. 311), *passim;* Archer Butler Hulbert and Dorothy Printup Hulbert, editors, *The Oregon Crusade: Across Land Sea to Oregon* (Denver, The Stewart Commission of Colorado College and the Denver Public Library, 1935, pp. xvi, 301), pp. 133–204.

(1779–1855), a Congregational clergyman, raised funds, found recruits, and went to the west coast (1835) to survey the situation. In 1836 one of his recruits, Marcus Whitman, took his bride to the Cayuses in what was eventually south-eastern Washington, and Henry H. Spalding and his wife and W. H. Gray went to the Nez Percés, not far from the later Lewiston, Idaho. Although the Whitmans were massacred in 1847, the missions continued, and enduring congregations, largely Presbyterian, were founded.[224]

In 1840 Pierre-Jean De Smet (1801–1873), a Belgian Jesuit, of the mission which we have already noted as having been established near St. Louis, made an extended journey to the Flatheads. He went in response to invitations from four successive deputations asking for missionaries, of which the first had been that of 1831. In succeeding years he inaugurated missions among several tribes in the Pacific North-west, then known as the Oregon Country. Again and again he made the arduous journey across the plains and mountains west of the Missouri River. In his trail, largely at his instance, continuing enterprises sprang up. More than once he helped to make peace between Indians and whites.[225]

De Smet's efforts in the Pacific North-west contributed to the development of Roman Catholic missions in that region which were undertaken from another source. In 1838, two years before his first memorable journey, two priests had arrived from the diocese of Quebec, François Norbert Blanchet (1795–1883) and Modeste Demers. They had been sent at the request of John McLoughlin, the ranking resident official of the Hudson's Bay Company, then the dominant white authority in that area. McLoughlin wished them to care for the Roman Catholic employees and former employees of the Company, largely French Canadians, who were in the region. After arriving, Blanchet and Demers also sought to evangelize the Indians. De Smet entered into correspondence with them. On his second journey they met (1842) at Fort Vancouver on the lower Columbia, and De Smet resolved to recommend to his superiors the fixing of headquarters of the Jesuit mission in Oregon in the Willamette Valley. He also urged the creation of a bishopric for the region. De Smet might have been appointed to the post had he not demurred and had Roothan, the General of the Jesuits, not refused the honour for him. Instead, Blanchet was

224 Of the extensive bibliography on this mission the following are among the important books: Clifford Merrill Drury, *Marcus Whitman, M.D., Pioneer and Martyr* (Caldwell, Ida., The Caxton Printers, 1937, pp. 473); Drury, *Henry Harmon Spalding; M. Eells, Ten Years of Missionary Work among the Indians at Skokokmish, Washington Territory, 1874–1884* (Boston, Congregational Sunday-School and Publishing Society, 1886, pp. 271); Archer Butler Hulbert and Dorothy Printup Hulbert, Editors, *Marcus Whitman, Crusader* (Denver, The Stewart Commission of Colorado College and the Denver Public Library, 3 vols., 1936–1941).

225 E. Laveille, *The Life of Father De Smet, S.J. (1801–1873)*, translated by Marian Lindsay (New York, P. J. Kenedy & Sons, 1915, pp. xxii, 400); Helene Margaret, *Father De Smet, Pioneer Priest of the Rockies* (New York, Farrar & Rinehart, 1940, pp. 371); Garraghan, *The Jesuits of the Middle United States*, Vol. II, pp. 236 ff., 442 ff., Vol. III, pp. 66 ff.; L. B. Palladius, *Indian and White in the Northwest, or, a History of Catholicity in Montana* (Baltimore, John Murphy & Co., 1894, pp. xxv, 411), *passim*.

chosen and in 1846 was made Archbishop of Oregon City, the second archiepiscopal see to be created in the United States and with jurisdiction over a vast territory. The dream was an ecclesiastical structure through which comprehensive planning and action could be carried through for missions not only to the Indians but also to the white immigration which was already presaging the future importance of the region.[226]

We must note that the Roman Catholics of the United States were not content to leave to missionaries from Europe or Canada the full responsibility for the evangelization of the Indians. For example, in 1889 Katherine Drexel, from a wealthy Roman Catholic family, founded the Sisters of the Blessed Sacrament for missions among the Indians and Negroes of the country.[227]

In another section of the country the Protestant Episcopal Church had strikingly successful missions to the Indians. He who was called the Apostle to the Sioux was William Hobart Hare (1838–1909). Grandson of a distinguished Bishop of New York, through a journey which he took because of his wife's health he became interested in the tribe. In 1872 he was appointed missionary bishop, with the Sioux as his chief responsibility. Under his vigorous leadership, by the time of his death about ten thousand had been baptized.[228]

Alaska, Russian territory from late in the eighteenth century until 1867, when it was sold to the United States, was the scene of Russian Orthodox missions among the Eskimos and Indians. The outstanding missionary was John Veniaminoff, who arrived in 1824 after his church had been represented for nearly a generation. He set himself to raise the moral tone of the nominal Christians, conducted schools, prepared a catechism, and translated portions of the New Testament into the native tongue. Eventually he was made bishop of a see which embraced Kamchatka, the Kuriles, the Aleutians, and later Yakutsk. He therefore moved his residence from Alaska. In 1872 the Holy Synod created an independent diocese which included Alaska. In 1903 the membership of the Orthodox Church in Alaska was put at 10,225, of whom 320 were Russians and 2,110 of mixed blood.[229]

As a result of the missions of the several churches, in 1921 the number of Roman Catholics among the Indians was said to be 61,456, and to have seen a marked increase during the preceding decade.[230] In 1913 the number of Protestant communicants was reported as 31,815 and of other adherents as about 35,-

[226] Garraghan, *op. cit.*, Vol. II, pp. 271 ff.

[227] *The Catholic Encyclopedia*, Vol. II, p. 599.

[228] M. A. DeWolfe Howe, *The Life and Labors of Bishop Hare, Apostle to the Sioux* (New York, Sturgis & Walton, 1911, pp. 417), *passim*.

[229] Konrad Lübeck, *Die Christienisierung Russlands* (Aachen, Xavierius Verlagsbuchhandlung, 1922, pp. 118), pp. 48–52.

[230] G. E. E. Lindquist, *The Red Man in the United States. An Intimate Study of the Social, Economic and Religious Life of the American Indian* (New York, George H. Doran Co., 1923, pp. 461), p. 430.

000.[231] If correct, these figures indicate that in 1914 the numbers of Roman Catholics and Protestants were about equal, and that about two-fifths of the Indians were Christians. This was approximately the same proportion as that of church members in the population of the country as a whole. Clergy were being trained, self-supporting congregations were coming into being, and the Bible had been translated in whole or in part into several Indian tongues. Fully as significant was the contribution which Christianity had made through schools and other means in assisting the Indians to adjust to the revolutionary age into which they were being hurtled.

In addition to what it was accomplishing through missionaries, Christianity was impelling many to action on the Indians' behalf. Thus beginning in 1883 Albert Keith Smiley (1828–1912), a Quaker, held annual conferences at Lake Mohonk at which measures on behalf of the red men were discussed by those in a position to take action.[232] Many with strong Christian motivation were members of the Indian Rights Association.[233]

The Faith Spreads Among the Negroes

The Negroes constituted a much larger challenge numerically than did the Indians. In 1790 they were said to total 757,208, or 19.3 per cent. of the population, and in 1910, 9,827,763, or 10.7 per cent. of the population.[234] The proportion with white blood was mounting—from about 11.2 per cent. in 1850 to about 20.9 per cent. in 1910.[235] Until after 1914 the Negroes were largely massed in the South. In 1910, 89 per cent. were in that section of the country.[236] This meant that they were far more exposed to Protestantism, and to the Protestantism of the older American stock, than to the Roman Catholic form of the faith or to the Protestantism of the nineteenth-century immigration, for, as we have seen, because of the competition of Negro labour most of the nineteenth-century immigrants kept aloof from the South. Here was an important aspect of the challenge brought by the revolutionary age.

A number of factors facilitated the spread of Christianity among the Negroes. With rare exceptions, in their compulsory distribution under the slavery through which they had been brought to America, the Negroes had lost their tribal solidarity and their communal customs and traditions. Immersed as they were in the surrounding white population and subject to white masters, they tended to

---

[231] Thomas C. Moffett, *The American Indian on the New Trail* (New York, Missionary Education Movement of the United States and Canada, 1914, pp. xiii, 302), p. 289.

[232] *Proceedings of the Annual Meetings of the Lake Mohonk Conference of Friends of the Indians*, 1883 ff.; *Dictionary of American Biography*, Vol. XVII, pp. 230, 231.

[233] *Annual Reports of the Executive Committee of the Indian Rights Association* (Philadelphia, 1884 ff.).

[234] U. S. Department of Commerce, Bureau of the Census, *Negro Population 1790–1915*, p. 25.

[235] *Ibid.*, p. 208.

[236] *Ibid.*, p. 33.

conform to the white man's culture and adopted his language. With English they absorbed the ideas carried by that tongue. As the importation of slaves became more difficult and when, with the Civil War and emancipation, the influx from Africa abruptly ceased, assimilation to the dominant culture became more rapid. Throughout the century revivals with an accompanying growth in church membership were fairly constant in the encompassing white population. They could not but prove contagious among the Negroes. Presumably, too, they would be predominantly from those forms of Protestantism, chiefly Methodist and Baptist, that were the means through which Christianity had spread among the elements in the white population to whose economic and cultural level the Negroes most nearly approximated.

Before emancipation the process of conversion had begun, but it had not proceeded as far as the increase of church membership among the whites. In 1860 the number of Negro church members seems to have been about 520,000, six times that of 1798, and 11.7 per cent. of the Negro population, as against the 22.7 per cent. of the whites who were church members.[237]

The growth was through several channels. In their enthusiasm for giving the Gospel to the masses, both Methodists and Baptists early reached out to the Negroes. As early as 1787 the Methodist General Conference urged that special attention be paid to the slaves,[238] and in 1800 the bishops were authorized to ordain Negroes as deacons.[239] Not far from 1829, William Capers, later to be a bishop, began to be prominent in efforts to reach the slaves. When he died (1855) the South Carolina Methodists had twenty-six missions and thirty-two preachers caring for 11,546 coloured communicants.[240] In 1851 the Methodist Episcopal Church, South, had ninety-nine missionaries to the slaves,[241] and in 1860 its Negro membership was not far from 200,000.[242] Several exclusively Negro Methodist bodies came into being at the instance of Negroes. Of them the two largest were the African Methodist Episcopal Church, whose moving spirit was Richard Allen (1760–1831) and which arose in Philadelphia in 1816,[243] and the African Methodist Episcopal Zion Church which began as a single congregation in New York City in 1796 and in 1821 joined with other congregeto form a national body.[244] Baptist churches for Negroes were appearing well before 1815. They multiplied in both South and North. In some places, because

<hr/>

[237] For the details leading to this estimate, see Latourette, *A History of the Expansion of Christianity*, Vol. IV, pp. 341, 342.

[238] *Minutes of the Annual Conferences of the Methodist Episcopal Church*, Vol. I, p. 28.

[239] *Ibid.*, p. 44.

[240] C. G. Woodson, *The Education of the Negro Prior to 1861* (New York, G. P. Putnam's Sons, 1915, pp. v, 454), pp. 189–191.

[241] J. M. Batten in *Church History*, Vol. VII, p. 234.

[242] U. S. Department of Commerce, Bureau of the Census, *Religious Bodies: 1926*, Vol. II, p. 1030.

[243] Charles H. Wesley, *Richard Allen, Apostle of Freedom* (Washington, The Associated Publishers, 1935, pp. xi, 300), *passim*.

[244] Woodson, *The History of the Negro Church*, pp. 78–85.

the state law did not permit separate Negro churches, they were interracial, but often with Negroes predominating.[245] Presbyterians, Episcopalians, and Congregationalists concerned themselves with the Negroes, but did not make extensive headway among them.[246] Numbers of white masters and mistresses had the religious interests of their slaves at heart. In many white congregations Negroes were in attendance in galleries reserved for them. For the most part, Christianity spread from Negro to Negro and often through Negro preachers. Although out of fear that they would foment unrest and even revolt some Southern states attempted to prevent Negroes from preaching, in practice it was usually possible for a Negro to preach if a white person of standing would vouch for him. Before emancipation, the Christian ministry was the only channel in most of the South through which a Negro could achieve leadership.[247]

The drastic changes which emancipation wrought in the status of the Negroes were accompanied by striking developments in their religious life. In the new day into which they were ushered and, after the brief stormy years of reconstruction, in practice disfranchised, the Negroes found in their churches the one institution which was exclusively theirs. To ensure their complete independence they tended to withdraw from white churches. The African Methodist Episcopal Church and the African Methodist Episcopal Zion Church expanded southward and grew rapidly. The Methodist Episcopal Church, South, lost more than half its Negro members and to make provision for the greater autonomy of those who remained adopted a plan for separate Negro congregations and conferences and in 1870 encouraged the formation of the Coloured Methodist Episcopal Church.[248] Negro Baptist churches multiplied and organized themselves into district, state, regional, and national conventions.[249] Through their churches the Negroes found emotional outlet and intellectual development.[250] In the half-century between emancipation and 1914 proportionately the Negro churches grew more rapidly than the white churches. Whereas in 1860 the percentage of Negroes who were members of churches was only about half that of the whites, in 1916 it was slightly larger—44.2 per cent. as against 43.4 per cent. in the population of the country as a whole.[251]

A major development in Negro Protestant Christianity was the "spirituals." They were a type of folk music deeply indebted to similar "spirituals" which arose among the whites, partly from the camp-meetings. However, many of them were original. Some became very popular among the whites.[252]

---

[245] *Ibid.*, pp. 41–56, 85–91, 108–122.

[246] Latourette, *op. cit.*, Vol. IV, pp. 334, 335.

[247] J. M. Batten in *Church History*, Vol. VII, p. 234.

[248] U. S. Department of Commerce, Bureau of the Census, *Religious Bodies: 1926*, Vol. II, pp. 1003, 1013, 1030–1032.

[249] Woodson, *The History of the Negro Church*, pp. 196–201.

[250] Mays and Nicholson, *The Negro's Church*, pp. 279 ff.

[251] Bureau of the Census, *Religious Bodies, 1916*, Vol. I, p. 544; Weber, *1933 Yearbook of the American Churches*, p. 299.

[252] George Pullen Jackson, *White Spirituals in the Southern Uplands. The Story of the Fasola*

Later we will have something to say of the fashion in which the churches, both white and coloured, helped in the remarkable advances in education made by the Negroes in the decades after emancipation.

Although the overwhelming majority of the Negroes who became Christians had their membership in denominations akin to those of the older white American stock, mainly Baptist and Methodist, the Roman Catholics did not neglect the Negroes. In Maryland and the District of Columbia Roman Catholic clergy and sisters ministered to them. In Louisiana in the days of French rule many Negroes had been won to the Roman Catholic faith, and their numbers were reinforced by those fleeing from the revolt in San Domingo. In several of the other Southern states Roman Catholic Negroes were found.[253] Immediately after emancipation, thousands of Negroes left the Roman Catholic Church. It is said that in Louisiana alone 65,000 fell away. The reason seems to have been the desire for full independence of white control and the attraction of the Baptist and Methodist churches with their emotional appeal and their autonomy.[254] However, in the four decades before 1914 some progress was made in regaining lost ground and here and there advances were registered. Several congregations and orders undertook special work for the Negroes. As an outgrowth of the third plenary council (1884) the hierarchy set up the Commission for Catholic Missions among the Coloured People and Indians, and in 1907 the Catholic Board for Mission Work among the Coloured People was instituted. The official count by the church gave the number of Negro Roman Catholics as 138,312 in 1888 and 152,692 in 1892.[255]

Christianity and the Jewish Immigration

The number of Jews in the United States rose sharply, but no large-scale attempt was made to convert them. The Jews in the country increased from about three thousand in 1818 to nearly three million in 1914.[256] However, only slight attention was paid by either Roman Catholics or Protestants to missions to the Jews. Here and there a Jew became a Roman Catholic, through attendance at a Roman Catholic school, through acquaintance with Roman Catholics, or through being a patient in a Roman Catholic hospital.[257] A few organiza-

---

Folk, Their Songs, Singing, and "Buckwheat Notes" (Chapel Hill, University of North Carolina Press, 1933, pp. xv, 444), pp. 274–302; E. A. McIlhenny, *Befo' de War Spirituals. Words and Melodies* (Boston, The Christopher Publishing House, 1933, pp. 255), *passim;* R. Nathaniel Dett, editor, *Religious Folk-Songs of the Negro as Sung at Hampton Institute* (Hampton, Va., Hampton Institute Press, 1927, pp. xxvii, 236, XIII), *passim.*

[253] Gillard, *The Catholic Church and the American Negro,* pp. 14–51.

[254] *Ibid.,* pp. 258 ff.

[255] *Ibid.,* pp. 1, 39–45.

[256] *Christians and Jews. A Report of the Conference on the Christian Approach to the Jews, Atlantic City, New Jersey, May 12–15, 1931* (New York, International Missionary Council, 1931, pp. 155), Appendix I.

[257] Rosalie Marie Levy, *Why Jews Become Catholics. Authentic Narratives* (New York, published by the author, 1924, pp. v, 203), *passim.*

tions, all small, were formed by Protestants for the purpose of reaching the Jews; some were denominational, others undenominational. Now and then a pastor of an individual congregation interested himself in the Jews. Occasionally a Jew became a Christian through personal contacts with Protestants.[258] Yet here was the only element in the population in which Christianity was not making substantial numerical gains.

THE SPREAD OF CHRISTIANITY AMONG IMMIGRANTS FROM EAST AND SOUTH ASIA

Immigrants from East and South Asia were only a small proportion of the population, but Christians, especially Protestants, sought to win them to the faith. For a time it seemed that from the teeming nations of East Asia a flood of immigration would swamp the west coast, but restrictive legislative and other measures kept the numbers to small minorities outside Hawaii—Chinese to a maximum of slightly over a hundred thousand in 1890, a number which then declined, and of Japanese to less than that number. Koreans and Filipinos were much fewer and arrivals from South-east and South Asia were still smaller minorities. Protestants of several denominations conducted missions for Chinese and Japanese, but only a small proportion of either nationality became Christians.[259]

BY WAY OF SUMMARY

In no other country did Christianity, challenged by the forces of the revolutionary age which made for de-Christianization, register such large numerical gains in church membership as it did in the United States. In the face of the rapid growth in population and the vast movements from East to West, from rural sections to cities, and from Europe to the New World, all of which threatened existing church connexions, the percentage who held membership in churches rose fairly steadily. The one period in which no gain was seen was the Civil War years—an exception which in view of the demoralization brought by that conflict was not surprising. Exact statistics are not obtainable, but what seem to be the best estimates give the percentages of church membership to the total population as follows: 1800—6.9; 1810—8.6; 1820—11.2; 1830—13.3; 1840—14.4; 1850—15.5; 1860—22.7; 1870—17.5; 1880—20.4; 1890—22.2; 1900—35.7; 1910—43.4.[260] For several denominations the figures do not include children. Nor do they take account of the many, also amounting to millions, who were once on church rolls but were dropped as inactive.

The gains were chiefly by Protestants and were from the older stock, the nineteenth-century immigration, the Indians, the Negroes, and the Orientals.

---

[258] See a number of examples, with footnote references, in Latourette, *A History of the Expansion of Christianity*, Vol. IV, pp. 293, 294.

[259] Latourette, *op. cit.*, Vol. IV, pp. 294–296, gives the appropriate references.

[260] Weber, *op. cit.*, p. 299.

They were part of that extensive geographic growth of Protestantism which was one of the marked features of the nineteenth and twentieth centuries. The Roman Catholic Church also grew, mainly through holding to the faith its children among the nineteenth-century immigration, but also through a few conversions from the older stock and some tens of thousands from the Indians and the Negroes. The growth of the Eastern Churches was as yet inconsiderable. Such as was achieved was through immigration and to a less extent among the Alaskan Indians and Eskimos.

To what extent the numerical increase indicated an augmentation of Christian character in the population as a whole would be impossible to determine. That some, especially among the nineteenth-century immigration, was from other than purely religious motives was clear. The adherence of the immigrants was predominantly to the churches with which they or their parents had been connected in the countries from which they came: it was a continuation of hereditary ties and to no small degree arose from loyalty to the group and language and the desire for fellowship in an alien environment. Yet it would not have been effected without deep religious conviction on the part of the clergy who gathered the immigrants into the churches.

Significant, too, were the large numbers from non-Christian ancestry who were won to the Christian faith—Indians, Negroes, and, to a less extent, immigrants from East Asia. Converts from the Indians were about equally divided between Protestants and Roman Catholics, but those among the Negroes were overwhelmingly Protestant. The conversions came about partly because these non-Christian peoples were immersed in a culture which had strong Christian ingredients and were in a white population in which the percentage of church membership was rapidly mounting. Yet they were accomplished largely by the efforts of devoted men and women.

Fully as important as the increase in church membership were the kinds of Christianity through which the growth came about. The spread of the faith among the older stock was mainly through Protestantism of the Evangelical tradition—akin to the Evangelical and Pietist awakenings on the other side of the Atlantic. In no country in Europe, with the possible exception of Wales, was that Evangelicalism as prominent and as permeating as in the United States. It prevailed in the Protestantism of the pre-nineteenth century-stock. It was spread through revivalism—in camp-meetings, by itinerant evangelists, by resident ministers who employed the methods of the evangelists, and through Sunday Schools. It assumed belief in the Bible as the Word of God, in the basic sinfulness of man, and in conversion through faith in the redemption wrought by God through Christ. Except for repercussions from the Enlightenment and Deism, the majority of the Protestants of the older stock were as yet untroubled by the intellectual challenges which were issuing in Europe from the revolution. These challenges were beginning, but their full force was not felt until late in the nineteenth century and in the fore part of the twentieth century.

The main emphasis in the Protestantism which held to the faith the nineteenth-century immigration of Protestant antecedents was conservative—resurgent Lutheran confessionalism, Pietism combined with theological orthodoxy issuing from the awakenings in Scandinavia and from such centres as Basel, and among the Dutch the renewed Reformed conservatism born of the *réveil*. For the most part it was resistant to the currents which were flooding Europe. Indeed, some of it had arisen in conscious reaction against them.

The Roman Catholic Church also depended for its success in holding the allegiance of its children among the nineteenth-century immigration upon elements which were affected little or not at all by questions being hurled at Christianity by the revolutionary age. The Irish were important, and they were so engrossed in the struggle with their English overlords that they paid scant attention to the issues that were troubling many Roman Catholics on the Continent. Even more prominent in building up the Roman Catholic Church in the United States were the orders and congregations which had been reinvigorated by the awakenings of the nineteenth century and the new congregations which were born of the awakenings.

Both the Protestant and the Roman Catholic gains were the fruit of the fresh surges of life characterizing the Christianity of the nineteenth century. The surges had taken a variety of forms, but each was in accord with the genius of the particular branch of the faith in which it was seen. In the United States their expressions were peculiar to that country, and in many respects the resulting Christianity was different from that of Europe. Yet in most of its many manifestations the Christianity of the United States had a distinct family likeness to that of Europe.

CHAPTER IV

The United States of America: The Development of Ecclesiastical Organization and Leadership

WHAT developments were seen in the United States of America in the nineteenth century in the ecclesiastical structure and leadership of the churches through which Christianity found expression? In the multiform denominational picture presented in that country were any common patterns discernible? Freed as they were from control by the state such as existed in Europe, how far if at all did the churches conform to features of the society in which they were enmeshed? What provision did they make for recruiting and training their leaders, especially their clergy? What efforts were put forth to achieve unity in the Christianity of the country, more varied as it was than in any other land in the entire history of the faith? With what success did they meet?

To give a complete answer to these questions would necessitate expanding this chapter to a number of volumes. That, obviously, we must not do. We must content ourselves with summaries and generalizations, illustrated by a few specific examples which will serve to illuminate them.

First we must note that the absence of state control and the general atmosphere of adventure in creativity—the *novus ordo seclorum* of which the great seal of the United States spoke—encouraged attempts at organization which would not be bound slavishly to the European inheritance.

Yet, in the second place, we must hasten to say that organizationally much of conservatism existed, with an adherence to forms derived from the European background.

Third, we do well to observe that, in accord with the throbbing nationalism which was a feature of the revolutionary age and which was mounting and welding together in one inclusive unity the vast and expanding area embraced by the United States, the tendency was marked to create for each denomination a structure that would knit together all its members within the borders of the country. Dreams were also fostered of seeking a visible unity bringing to fruition the prayer cherished since the beginning of the faith "that they all"—all who believe in Christ through the witness of the Apostles—"might be one."

But, in the fourth place, a number of stubborn facts stood in the way of the realization of the dream of unity. Some of them arose out of the long history of the faith; others were peculiar to the American scene and were concomitants of the processes through which, in the changing age, the nation was being built. Among these facts were the denominational differences transmitted from the Old World. Basic were the gulfs separating Protestantism from the Roman Catholic Church, the several Protestant denominations from one another, and the Northern churches from those of the South.

The gulfs were widened and deepened by the difference in dates between the arrivals in strength of the various denominations. The faith of the large majority of the "older stock"—those and their children who had come to America before the nineteenth century and who had a church membership—was Protestant. That faith expressed itself in particular denominations, largely of British origin with Non-conformity predominant. It had spread, mainly through "revivalism" and more through Baptists and Methodists than through other ecclesiastical families. Within itself it was divided, partly by the economic and educational strata. Most of the Protestants of the nineteenth-century immigration from the Continent of Europe were gathered into churches, chiefly Lutheran, which tended to keep apart from the Protestant churches of the older stock. The barrier was in some degree linguistic and cultural, but it was also doctrinal and in forms of worship and organization. Roman Catholics were overwhelmingly from the nineteenth-century immigration and at the outset poverty-stricken. Repeatedly persecuted by elements in the older stock, they tended, quite understandably, to be resentful and to constitute a cultural enclave, until well along in the twentieth century a self-conscious large minority. They were on a lower educational and economic level than the culturally Anglo-Saxon Protestant majority and felt themselves a distinct and partially alien element.

Added to the other divisive factors was sectionalism. The difference between the North and the South was especially marked. It was due partly to Negro slavery and the economic and social patterns associated with slavery. The South was agricultural, with a major emphasis upon raising cotton for the factories in Great Britain and the North. Although the majority of the Southern whites were small farmers and did not own slaves, the plantations of the minority, cultivated by Negro slaves, set much of the pattern for Southern society. The North, especially the North-east, was being rapidly industrialized and was becoming urban and the West was moving in that direction. The contrast between North and South was accentuated by the Civil War, with the impoverishment of the defeated South and the bitterness and regional solidarity born of that struggle and the ensuing reconstruction.[1]

---

[1] On some of these differences associated with social and historic patterns, see H. Richard Nie-

STRUCTURAL DEVELOPMENTS WITHIN THE PROTESTANTISM OF THE OLDER STOCK

We have seen[2] a little of the development of inclusive denominational structures following the independence of the United States and prior to 1815. We noted the creation of the Protestant Episcopal Church, the formation of the Methodist Episcopal Church (1784) and of the Presbyterian Church in the United States of America (1788), the close association of Congregationalists with Presbyterians through representation of a large proportion of New England Congregationalists in the General Assembly of the Presbyterian Church and through the Plan of Union adopted in 1801 for coöperation in meeting the challenge of the Western frontier, and the inauguration of the Missionary Convention of the Baptist Denomination in the United States of America (more briefly called the Triennial Convention) in 1814. We remarked that in 1789 the largest denomination, in point of numbers of congregations, was Congregational, followed second by the Presbyterians, third by the Baptists, fourth by the Episcopalians, and then, all of them much smaller, by the Quakers, German and Dutch Reformed, Lutherans, and Roman Catholics in descending order. By 1815, so we reported,[3] the revivals, operating in part through camp-meetings, had brought into being the United Brethren in Christ, the Evangelical Association, the Christians and Disciples of Christ, and the Cumberland Presbyterians. They had also contributed to the very remarkable growth of the Methodists and the Baptists.

In the course of the nineteenth century further developments occurred in the structures of the denominations which recruited their members chiefly from the older stock. A few of them must serve as samples of what a complete story would disclose.

The Congregationalists soon began to be more conscious of their distinctive characteristics and to draw apart from the Presbyterians. In the 1830's and 1840's they gathered into associations and state conventions on the Western frontier. In 1852 a national council or synod representative of Congregationalism met in Albany, New York, by unanimous vote withdrew from the Plan of Union, and took steps towards the extension of Congregationalism. In 1864 a national council convened in Boston, more widely representative than the Albany council and the predecessor of other similar gatherings at regular intervals.[4]

Not all Presbyterians had been happy over the Plan of Union. The critics, chiefly of Scotch-Irish stock, regarded the congregations which arose through it as compromising Presbyterian doctrine and practice. The congregations which

---

buhr, *The Social Sources of Denominationalism* (New York, Henry Holt and Co., 1929, pp. viii, 304), *passim*.

[2] Volume I, pp. 188–191.

[3] Volume I, pp. 192–194.

[4] Walker, *A History of the Congregational Churches in the United States*, pp. 370 ff.

had sprung up from the Plan of Union, the "New School" Presbyterians, were made up mainly of New Englanders and their descendants. The critics, the "Old School" Presbyterians, were in control of the General Assembly of 1837 and expelled four "New School" synods—one in the Western Reserve in Ohio and three in New York State. The "New School" men protested the action and attempted to seat the representatives of their presbyteries in the General Assembly of 1838. When they did not succeed, their delegates withdrew and constituted a General Assembly which they claimed to be the only legal one.[5] They continued to coöperate with the Congregationalists in the American Board of Commissioners for Foreign Missions. In 1861, with the outbreak of the Civil War, the Presbyterians in the South formed the Presbyterian Church in the Confederate States of America and after the war remained apart under the designation "The Presbyterian Church in the United States."[6] In 1869, with only small minorities dissenting, the Old School and New School General Assemblies voted for reunion, and the consummating act was carried through the following year as the Presbyterian Church in the United States of America.[7]

Of the larger denominations, the Episcopalians, Congregationalists, and Presbyterians stressed more than the others an educated ministry. Partly for this reason they were predominantly of those to whom such a ministry appealed and, accordingly, in the main drew their members from the upper educational and economic levels of the population.

With their form of evangelism and, with notable exceptions, a ministry which for much of the century was not as highly educated as that of the Episcopalians, Congregationalists, and Presbyterians, more than these denominations the Methodists attracted members from the millions with a limited education and of a lower economic level. By 1914 they included in their several branches about seven million members, of whom about six million were white—more than any other denominational family of Protestants in the country. A little over a million Methodists were Negroes, about half in the African Methodist Episcopal Church and the other half divided almost equally between the African Methodist Episcopal Zion Church and the Colored Methodist Episcopal Church. In 1916 the Methodist Episcopal Church, predominantly white, reported 3,717,785 members, the Methodist Episcopal Church, South, 2,144,479 members, and the Methodist Protestant Church, the only other large Methodist prevailingly white body, 186,908 members.[8] The Methodist Protestant Church came into being in 1830 as the result of prolonged controversy. The "reformers" who withdrew from the Methodist Episcopal Church and created it insisted upon a larger participation by the laity—their representation in the Annual and

[5] Thompson, *A History of the Presbyterian Churches in the United States*, pp. 102 ff.
[6] *Ibid.*, pp. 150 ff.
[7] *Ibid.*, pp. 172 ff.
[8] Bureau of the Census, *Religious Bodies, 1916*, Vol. I, p. 21.

General Conferences—and were against the institutions of the episcopacy and the presiding eldership.[9] In 1858 the Methodist Protestant Church divided on the issue of the admission of Negroes to suffrage and to office, but reunited in 1877.[10]

The existence of the Methodist Episcopal Church, South, was due to slavery. From its inception the Methodist Episcopal Church had opposed slavery and in 1816 its General Conference had ordered that no owner of slaves should be appointed to any official position in the church if the laws of the state in which he lived made it possible for him to free them. In the General Conference of 1844 it appeared that Bishop James O. Andrew of Georgia who when elected held no slaves had by inheritance and marriage become an unwilling owner of some, and in a state which did not permit their manumission. After prolonged debate the General Conference by a close sectional vote gave as its opinion that Bishop Andrew should "desist from the exercise of his office as long as this impediment remains." This he and the Southern delegates regarded as suspending him, and as a flagrant violation of the constitution of the church. Accordingly, in 1845 representatives of the Southern conferences voted for separation and in 1846 the first General Conference of the Methodist Episcopal Church, South, was held. At the outset its membership was nearly half a million, of whom about a fourth were Negroes. By the outbreak of the Civil War the membership had increased to about three-quarters of a million.[11] The Civil War impoverished the Southern church, brought a loss in membership, and was followed by the withdrawal of most of its Negro members into other Methodist bodies. During the reconstruction years the Methodist Episcopal Church moved into the South, expanding its operations, to the distress of the Southern church.[12] Not until after World War I was the breach healed.

By 1914 Baptists were approximately as numerous as the Methodists, but since nearly half were in the National Baptist Convention, made up of Negro churches, they enrolled fewer whites than did the Methodists. Yet they had more white members than any other Protestant denominational family except the Methodists. If all of their branches be included, Methodists and Baptists together claimed about the same number of members as the Roman Catholic Church. However, since the Baptists did not baptize infants or count them in their statistics, their constituency probably outnumbered that of the Methodists, and the Baptist and Methodist constituencies jointly totalled more than the Roman Catholics.[13]

If to those bodies which bore the name of Methodist the denominations be

---

[9] Buckley, *A History of Methodists in the United States*, pp. 364–368.

[10] Bureau of the Census, *Religious Bodies, 1916*, Vol. II, p. 463.

[11] *Ibid.*, pp. 475, 476; Buckley, *op. cit.*, pp. 407 ff.

[12] Robert D. Clark, *The Life of Matthew Simpson* (New York, The Macmillan Co., 1956, pp. xi, 344), pp. 245 ff.

[13] Bureau of the Census, *Religious Bodies, 1916*, Vol. I, pp. 19–21.

added which were Methodist in polity and spirit, notably the United Brethren and the Evangelical Association, and if with the Baptists were included bodies closely akin to them in many beliefs and in temper, especially the Disciples of Christ and the Churches of Christ and, not so closely resembling them but having features in common, the Church of the Brethren, the Plymouth Brethren (six small bodies in 1916), and the Mennonites, the Roman Catholics would be seen to be greatly outnumbered and the bodies nourished by revivalism to constitute the large majority of the Protestants of the United States. Here was a fact of major significance in the response of the Protestantism of that country to the challenge of the revolutionary age and especially of its intellectual and social phases.

In general, the Baptists drew from slightly lower educational and income levels of the population than did the Methodists. They multiplied largely through revivals, and a very large proportion of their clergy had scanty education. Like the Methodists, the Baptists were divided into many bodies, but even more than the Methodists, on the eve of 1914 the majority were concentrated under a few large bodies—the Northern Baptist Convention, the Southern Baptist Convention, and the National Baptist Convention.

The Northern Baptist Convention was not organized until 1907. But it was the lineal successor of earlier organs of coöperation. The Triennial Convention, originally for foreign missions, soon embraced home missions. In 1845 it was succeeded by the American Baptist Missionary Union, renamed (1910) the American Baptist Foreign Mission Society. The American Baptist Tract Society, later called the American Baptist Publication Society, came into being in 1824. The American Baptist Home Mission Society was formed in 1832. Women's societies for home and foreign missions sprang up, eventually to be coördinated nationally.[14] The Northern Baptist Convention was a means of bringing these various agencies into closer coöperation. In it were merged in 1911 the Freewill Baptist churches, which, embodying Arminian principles, had sprung up as an independent revivalistic movement late in the eighteenth century.[15]

The Southern Baptist Convention, eventually to be by far the largest of the Baptist conventions and, next to the Methodist Church, the most numerous Protestant ecclesiastical body in the United States, came into being in 1845. As with the Presbyterians and the Methodists, the cause of its separate existence was slavery. The abolitionist tide was running strong among Baptists in the North, and both the American Baptist Home Mission Society and the Board of Managers of the Triennial Convention had made it clear that they would not appoint as missionaries any who owned slaves. Delegates from Southern churches met in May, 1845, at Augusta, Georgia, and organized the Southern Baptist Convention. From the beginning it operated through boards for mis-

---

[14] Torbet, *A History of the Baptists,* pp. 318, 354, 382, 404, 405.
[15] *Ibid.,* pp. 274–276.

sions and other purposes, which were subordinate to it.[16]

The Southern Baptist Convention did not succeed in drawing together all the Baptists in the South and from time to time was threatened with disruption in its own ranks. From the outset Baptists in the South who because of their strict adherence to the doctrines of predestination and election were opposed to missions held aloof. They were sometimes known as Primitive or "Hardshell" Baptists. Some Southern Baptists so emphasized the autonomy of the local church that they were reluctant to share in the support of a mission board or society on the ground that it compromised that autonomy and was without precedent in the New Testament. Others, often called "Landmarkers," cherished convictions paralleling the high-church views in some other denominations. They maintained that the churches of the New Testament were Baptist churches, that only such churches were Christian churches, and that an historical continuity could be demonstrated between contemporary Baptist churches and those of the New Testament. They, too, stressed the local church. They held that the Communion was purely a function of the local church and that the Christian must take it only in the local church in which he held membership. They believed true baptism to be for believers only and only by immersion. They maintained that immersion administered by one who was not a Baptist was "alien" and not valid. They denied their pulpits to non-Baptist ministers. The Landmark positions were not entirely uniform, nor were they espoused by all the Southern churches, but they were widely influential.[17]

As to the Southern Methodists, the Civil War and Reconstruction brought impoverishment to Southern Baptists. The American Baptist Home Mission Society, now Northern in its constituency, extended its operations into the South, particularly in schools for the Negroes, and some talk was heard of reunion.[18] But the Southern Baptist Convention continued, revived, and in the twentieth century had a phenomenal expansion, not only in the South but also in the North and West and in many other countries. By the mid-twentieth century Baptists were by far the most numerous denomination in the South, outnumbering both other Protestants and Roman Catholics. They had become a kind of "folk church" of that section.

In 1886 the National Baptist Convention, made up of Negro churches, was organized. Conventions, some state and some national, of Negro Baptist churches had multiplied after the Civil War and emancipation. It was not until 1895 that several of them consolidated their efforts in an augmented National Baptist Convention. In 1916 this was the largest of the Baptist conventions—

[16] *Ibid.*, pp. 299 ff.; Barnes, *The Southern Baptist Convention, 1845–1953*, pp. 12 ff. On the Southern Baptists before the formation of the Southern Baptist Convention see W. B. Posey, *The Baptist Churches in the Lower Mississippi Valley, 1776–1845* (Lexington, University of Kentucky Press, 1957, pp. viii, 166).

[17] Torbet, *op. cit.*, pp. 298, 299; Barnes, *op. cit.*, pp. 103–113.

[18] Barnes, *op. cit.*, pp. 74 ff.

reporting 2,938,579 members as against 2,708,870 members claimed by the Southern Baptist Convention and 1,232,135 by the Northern Baptist Convention.[19]

STRUCTURAL DEVELOPMENTS WITHIN THE PROTESTANTISM OF THE NINETEENTH-CENTURY IMMIGRATION

We have already spoken of the fashion in which a substantial proportion of the nineteenth-century immigration of Protestant ancestry was held to the faith of their fathers.[20] We noted that those from the British Isles were for the most part absorbed by the denominations of the older American stock, for, with the exception of the Reformed and the Lutheran minorities, the latter were of British provenance. We saw that Protestants from the Continent of Europe tended to group themselves according to their national origins, keeping in their services the languages of their fatherlands, and were further divided by doctrinal differences.

We must now summarize the attempts to bring into inclusive national structures all those of a particular confession. With some exceptions, before 1914 the efforts were largely confined to drawing together only those of one national background. We have called attention to the success of the Reformed Church in America, which arose out of pre-nineteenth-century Dutch arrivals, in incorporating the majority of the nineteenth-century immigration from the Netherlands who held to the Dutch Reformed Church. As we also saw, the Reformed Church in the United States, with its core of pre-nineteenth-century German Reformed, brought into its fellowship many from the nineteenth-century influx of Germans who were by tradition of that communion.

Some among the Lutherans early dreamed of an ecclesiastical body which would include all of their confession in the United States. That dream lay behind the creation of the General Synod, organized in 1820. For years its chief figure, although not its creator, was Samuel Simon Schmucker (1799–1873). Educated in the University of Pennsylvania and Princeton Theological Seminary, he was said to have been the best-trained man in his church. He saved the General Synod from dissolution and was the main promoter of the formation of Gettysburg Theological Seminary and the first professor in that institution.[21] As we have recorded, the vast influx of Germans and Scandinavians of Lutheran background was followed by the emergence of a number of Lutheran bodies, aligned partly by national origins and partly by doctrinal differences. The general trend in the new synods was towards conservative Lutheranism. On the other hand, a number of men in the General Synod, of whom Schmucker was one, advocated what was known as "American Lutheranism," namely, an

---

[19] Bureau of the Census, *Religious Bodies, 1916*, Vol. I, p. 19, Vol. II, p. 97.
[20] This volume, Chapter III.
[21] Anstadt, *Life and Times of Rev. S. S. Schmucker*, pp. 1–213.

adaptation to the American scene and the incorporation of some of the features of the Protestantism about them, with its revivalism, its emphasis on personal piety, and its informality in worship. Although Schmucker had taken the initiative in having the Gettysburg Seminary adopt the Augsburg Confession, he later suggested some modifications in that symbol. As the General Synod grew, the use of English in its public services rapidly increased and it tended to be less rigid doctrinally than some of the other bodies. By the time of the outbreak of the Civil War it embraced about two-thirds of the Lutheran communicants in the country. But on the eve of that struggle the Swedes and Norwegians left one of its member synods, that of Illinois, and formed the Augustana Synod. The Civil War brought the withdrawal of several synods to form the General Synod of the Evangelical Lutheran Church in the Confederate States of America. After the war the name was changed to the Evangelical Lutheran General Synod, South, and in 1886, after the adhesion of some other synods, the designation became the United Synod of the Evangelical Lutheran Church in the South. In the meantime, in protest against the liberalism of the General Synod, the Ministerium of Pennsylvania withdrew from that body, really although not officially in 1864. The complete break came in 1866. In 1864 Schmucker resigned from the Gettysburg faculty and was succeeded by a conservative. Schmucker's leadership had been repudiated[22] and the dream of a united Lutheranism in the United States was effectively shattered, at least for the time being.

On its withdrawal from the General Synod, the Pennsylvania Ministerium invited all synods holding the unaltered Augsburg Confession to form a new general body. Representatives of thirteen synods met in December, 1866, and in November, 1867, delegates from eleven synods organized the General Council of the Evangelical Lutheran Church in North America. At the outset it was four-fifths the size of the General Synod and in a few years outstripped it.[23]

In 1872 the Missouri Synod, which had been represented at the conference preliminary to the formation of the General Council but had declined to join, took the initiative in creating the Evangelical Lutheran Synodical Conference of North America. Several other synods became members and in 1914 the Synodical Conference was the largest of the Lutheran bodies in the United States. In it the Missouri Synod was by far the strongest element.[24]

The General Synod, the United Synod, and the General Council had much in common. Increasingly they employed English in their public worship. In 1876 the United Synod proposed to the other two that they collaborate in preparing "one common service for all English-speaking Lutherans in the United States." After some years the other two assented, a joint committee set to work, and in 1888 it completed what was known as the Common Service. The Com-

[22] Wentz, *A Basic History of Lutheranism in America*, pp. 133–152.
[23] *Ibid.*, pp. 153, 154.
[24] Bureau of the Census, *Religious Bodies, 1916*, Vol. I. p. 20, Vol. II, p. 367.

mon Service was based upon the Lutheran liturgies of the sixteenth century and they in turn continued the liturgical tradition of the pre-Reformation church of the West, which traced *its* development to the liturgies of the early Christian centuries. Of the three, the General Synod tended to be the least inflexible in doctrine and to be more coöperative with other Protestants. The three drew more and more closely together and in 1918 joined to form the United Lutheran Church in America. That church then became the largest Lutheran body outside of Europe.[25]

The United Lutheran Church was an important step towards bringing together the Lutherans of the United States, but it was only one of several stages. Its members were overwhelmingly of German birth or ancestry. In 1917 three bodies of Norwegian antecedents joined in the Norwegian Lutheran Church of America, later to be known as the Evangelical Lutheran Church. Other mergers came after 1914. Subsequent to World War I, largely in consequence of coöperation during that struggle, the National Lutheran Council came into being. But we are getting ahead of our story.

TRAINING THE PROTESTANT CLERGY

How were the clergy trained for the Protestant churches? The winning of the unchurched and the staffing of the rapidly growing churches, of both the older and the newer stock, required the recruiting and preparation of thousands each year. Most of them had to be found in the United States. A few came from Europe, especially in the early days of the churches which arose to care for the nineteenth-century immigration. However, the overwhelming majority of the clergy, even of the churches of the nineteenth-century immigration, were born in the United States. Here was one of the many evidences that in the United States, so largely a product of the revolutionary age, Christianity was displaying abounding vitality. An intimately related question was the quality and training of ministers. Were they of such a character that the churches would be prepared to meet the challenge of the complex and kaleidoscopic social, economic, and intellectual forces of the age? The large part played by the laity, particularly in the denominations of the older stock, in contrast with the picture in much of Europe and especially on the Continent, tended to make the clergy less central than in the Old World. Yet the freedom of the churches from the control of the state placed more responsibility on the ecclesiastical structure and so on the clergy than in the older Christendom.

The amount of formal education of the ministry varied from denomination to denomination. By long tradition, in the Protestant Episcopal Church, and in the Congregational, Reformed, and Lutheran churches—most of them confessions that east of the Atlantic were established—the standards were high. Among the early Methodists the educational requirements for the ministry were low

[25] Wentz, *op. cit.,* pp. 232, 233, 279.

but increased as the century progressed. For the Baptists, Disciples of Christ, and some of the smaller bodies which flourished on evangelism they were also low but in general tended to be raised with the passing years. Among the Negro churches the educational qualifications were much below those of the majority of white churches.[26]

Before the independence of the United States, preparation for the ministry was chiefly in the existing colleges and by individual ministers. Most of the colleges had been founded with the education of candidates for the ministry as one of their leading objectives. The oldest, Harvard, furthered this purpose by creating a professorship of divinity in 1721 and the third oldest, Yale, by a similar professorship in 1755.[27] Individual pastors took candidates for the ministry, some of them college graduates, into their homes or in houses adjoining their homes, to guide them in their reading of theology and related subjects. Such was the "Log College" begun by William Tennent in Pennsylvania in 1716, followed by other schools established on its model.[28] Such, too, were what were popularly called "the schools of the prophets" conducted by pastors in New England.[29] Thus Joseph Bellamy, a Yale graduate, in a little less than half a century (1742–1790) had about a hundred students in his home, and Nathanael Emmons, also from Yale, had between eighty and ninety under his tuition.[30] This kind of training, by a man in the active pursuit of his calling, was also that of the other two learned professions, law and medicine.

Before 1815 specialized schools were emerging for the preparation of ministers, partly because, with independence, the supply from Europe dwindled or disappeared, partly because of the increased demand for clergy arising from the growth in population and especially from the increase in church membership through the revivals, and partly from the desire to safeguard the ministry from what were regarded as unsound doctrines. What is said to have been the first theological faculty in the United States was the appointment in 1784 of John H. Livingstone, pastor of the Collegiate Church in New York City, to be professor of divinity for the Dutch Reformed Church. He was later given a colleague. Instruction was begun at Flat Bush, Long Island, near New York City, and a continuing centre was established in 1810 in New Brunswick, New Jersey, for what became the New Brunswick Theological Seminary. In 1794 the United Presbyterians founded a seminary in Pennsylvania, which was later moved to Xenia, Ohio. In 1807 the Moravians started a seminary in Bethlehem, Pennsylvania. In 1808 the orthodox Congregationalists of New England instituted Andover Theological Seminary, in some degree in protest against the appointment of an avowed Unitarian as professor of divinity in Harvard. The year 1810 saw

26 *The Education of American Ministers*, Vol. I, pp. 34 ff.
27 *Ibid.*, p. 75.
28 Weigle, *American Idealism*, p. 115; Sweet, *The Story of Religion in America*, pp. 144, 145.
29 Bainton, *Yale and the Ministry*, pp. 49 ff.
30 W. W. Sweet in *Church History*, Vol. VI, pp. 260 ff.; Bainton, *op. cit.*, p. 59.

the beginning of a seminary in Cedarville, Ohio, by the Reformed Presbyterians. After some years of discussion, in 1812 the Presbyterian Church in the U.S.A. inaugurated the Princeton Theological Seminary, in the same village as the College of New Jersey, later Princeton University, but quite distinct from that institution.[31]

Following 1815 theological seminaries multiplied. In the next sixteen years at least fifteen came into being. Two, at Harvard in 1818 (various dates are given for the inception of the Harvard Divinity School; one places it in 1811 with the provision for systematic guidance for students of theology), and at Yale in 1822, were faculties in connexion with colleges which from their beginning had had the training of the ministry as a purpose. They now pursued it with enlarged staffs and on a graduate level. Most of the seminaries were independent of existing colleges and geographically separated from them. The tendency was to segregate the training for the ministry from the inclusive academic environment and to have it under denominational auspices. Significantly, most of the new institutions, like their predecessors, were founded by Congregationalists, Presbyterians, Episcopalians, and Lutherans. Methodists and Baptists, although growing rapidly through the revivals, for the most part had ministers without much formal education. Disciples of Christ fell into a similar pattern. In addition to the Harvard and Yale Divinity Schools the sixteen-year period witnessed the founding of a Congregational seminary at Bangor, Maine (1816); the opening of three Episcopalian institutions, General Theological Seminary in New York City (1819), another in Alexandria, Virginia (1823), and a third at Gambier, Ohio, as part of Kenyon College and later to be Bexley Hall; and the beginning of two by Presbyterians, Auburn in central New York State (1818) and Union in Richmond, Virginia (1823). The Lutherans had Hartwick in New York State (1816), at the outset based on a school for Indians, and Gettysburg (1826). The Baptists opened one in Hamilton, New York (1817), and another in Newton, Massachusetts (1824); and the German Reformed began one in Lancaster, Pennsylvania (1825).[32]

Between 1839 and 1869 thirty-seven institutions were founded which had as their primary purpose training men for the Protestant ministry. Of these, the Lutherans, now multiplying through immigration, were responsible for eight, the Episcopalians for six, the Presbyterians, Methodists, and Baptists for four each, and the Reformed for three. They were in addition to the colleges which were being rapidly founded under church auspices and which had preparation for the ministry as one of their purposes.[33]

Still more theological seminaries were founded in the second half of the

---

[31] *The Education of American Ministers*, Vol. I, pp. 75, 76.
[32] *Ibid.*, pp. 76, 79; Robert L. Kelley, *Theological Education in America* (New York, George H. Doran Co., 1924, pp. 456), p. 25.
[33] *The Education of American Ministers*, Vol. I, pp. 79, 80.

century. In addition, the fore part of the century saw numerous education societies spring into existence which had as their purpose financial assistance to young men studying for the ministry.[34]

In spite of the multiplication of church-connected colleges and theological seminaries, in the early twentieth century by no means all the Protestant clergy had an extended academic preparation. Early in the 1930's, in the nineteen major white denominations slightly less than a fourth were graduates of both a college and a seminary and nearly half had not graduated from either a college or a seminary. As in the earlier decades of the nineteenth century, the highest proportion of the clergy with both college and seminary preparation were Lutherans, Reformed, Presbyterians, Episcopalians, and Congregationalists. The smallest percentages were among the Methodists, Baptists, and Disciples of Christ—namely, those serving the elements in the population in the lower income and educational brackets. As might have been expected because of the depressed economic and educational level of their constituencies, the Negro churches, in which Methodists and Baptists predominated, had a still smaller percentage of clergy with training in both college and seminary and an overwhelming majority without preparation in either.[35]

Coöperation Among Protestants

How far and in what ways did the Protestants of the United States coöperate?

Against coöperation were the multiplicity of denominations, their diverse national antecedents, their basic differences in traditions, structures, and doctrines, sectional barriers, and the absence of any compulsion from the state to bring uniformity.

Yet some factors made for coöperation. The Evangelical ethos expressing itself in revivalism characterized most of the Protestantism of the older stock. It stressed conversion. Back of it were basic convictions about the Gospel which several denominations had in common. As was true of the British Evangelicalism from which it sprang and with which it still kept sympathetic connexions, the Evangelicalism of the United States gave birth to movements for the elimination of collective ills and for the improvement of human society.

Coöperation began early and took many forms. At the outset it was confined chiefly to the denominations which had been in the country before the nineteenth century and which, therefore, shared in the pervasive pattern. In the next century most of the denominations which enrolled the nineteenth-century immigration were drawn into it. But in none of its forms was coöperation all-inclusive: no unified structure emerged which embraced all the Protestantism of the United States. Yet coöperation mounted on the local and national levels

---

[34] S. E. Mead in H. R. Niebuhr and D. D. Williams, editors, *The Ministry in Historical Perspective* (New York, Harper & Brothers, 1956, pp. xi, 331), p. 234.

[35] *The Education of American Ministers*, Vol. II, pp. 14–17.

and in the next century continued to grow.

We have already seen some of the expressions of coöperation—especially through the Sunday Schools and the Plan of Union of Presbyterians and Congregationalists. We are to note it in the Young Men's and Young Women's Christian Associations and the Young People's Society of Christian Endeavour. We must now give an account, necessarily only in brief summary, of some of the other forms.

A phase of coöperation early in the century was societies which had as members men and women of several denominations who joined as individuals and in so doing did not commit their respective churches. Such were the American Bible Society, inaugurated in 1816, the American Tract Society, organized in 1825, the American Society for the Promotion of Temperance, whose founding date was 1826, the American Peace Society initiated in 1828 and coördinating on a national scale efforts begun locally soon after the Napoleonic Wars, and the American Anti-slavery Society, born (1833) of the rising anti-slavery tide.[36]

Growing out of the same impulse were societies in which churches as well as individuals coöperated. Outstanding were the American Board of Commissioners for Foreign Missions, begun in 1810, the American Education Society, inaugurated in 1815 to aid in the preparation of ministers, and the American Home Missionary Society, organized in 1826. In them Congregationalists, still from their stronghold in New England a leading force in Protestantism, were outstanding.[37]

Several denominations sought to bring about unity among Christians by a return to the New Testament Church. Prominent among them were the Disciples of Christ. All, however, issued not in unity but in fresh denominations.

Out of the Lutherans of pre-nineteenth-century stock came proposals for effecting the union of existing denominations. The tercentenary of the Reformation and the accompanying Prussian Plan of Union (1817) inspired dreams of the union of all denominations and suggestions for the union of the Lutherans and Reformed. They provoked debates in some of the synods but without immediate concrete achievements.[38] Samuel Simon Schmucker attracted much more attention by the publication in 1838 of his *Fraternal Appeal to the American Churches. With a Plan for Catholic Union, on Apostolic Principles.* It went through several editions. Schmucker proposed what he called the Apostolic Protestant Church, suggesting a united confession embodying the Protestant doctrines common to all creeds. His united church would be a federation in which the existing churches would continue their ways of worship and their respective creeds, but within it a free interchange of ministries would be the rule and the Communion would be open to all members. On the local level

---

[36] Rouse and Neill, *A History of the Ecumenical Movement 1517–1948*, p. 235.
[37] *Ibid.*
[38] *Ibid.*, pp. 242, 243; Anstadt, *Life and Times of Rev. S. S. Schmucker*, pp. 131 ff.

joint annual Communion services would be held.[39] Although his programme was not adopted, Schmucker, undiscouraged, near the end of his life issued it again in modified form.[40]

The nineteenth-century flood of immigration with its conservative Lutheranism led to the rejection of the "American Lutheranism" of Schmucker and his friends. The resistance of other ecclesiastical bodies contributed to the lack of acceptance of Schmucker's *Appeal*. Not even in the first half of the twentieth century was it realised. Yet, although independently of Schmucker's proposal, the Evangelical Synod of North America arose as a union of Lutherans and Reformed in the German nineteenth-century immigration.

The current set towards greater coöperation among Protestants and increasingly had concrete expressions. One was American participation in the Evangelical Alliance. Schmucker looked hopefully to it and laboured for it as a means for the federation of all Protestant denominations the world over. It is said that his *Appeal,* circulated on the other side of the Atlantic, was in part responsible for the formation of the Evangelical Alliance (1846). He was present at the first meeting of the Alliance and was hailed in a public address as its father.[41] However, the Alliance was not a federation of churches, as his plan would have made it, but was composed of individuals.

The Evangelical Alliance had its main centre in Europe, but it had important repercussions in the United States. Because of division as to whether the Alliance should admit slave-owners as members, no branch of it was formed until 1867, after the Civil War and emancipation. In 1873 the American branch was host to the General Conference of the world body, and other significant meetings were held, in Washington in 1887 and in Boston in 1889.[42]

A moving spirit in the earlier stages of the Evangelical Alliance in the United States was Philip Schaff (1819–1893). Schaff, the son of a Swiss carpenter, had a brilliant student career in Tübingen, Halle, and Berlin and was on his way to a promising academic future in Germany when, partly through the suggestion of Tholuck and Neander, he was invited to the faculty of the theological seminary of the German Reformed Church in Mercersburg, Pennsylvania. He accepted (1844) and had a major share in the formulation of what came to be known as the Mercersburg theology, to which we are to recur. A phase of the Mercersburg theology was emphasis upon the continuity of the historic Christian tradition in the Reformation and a desire to stress it and its liturgy as a way to Christian unity. Irenic, a bridge between German scholarship and American

[39] Rouse and Neill, *op. cit.,* pp. 244, 245; Anstadt, *op. cit.,* pp. 296 ff.

[40] S. S. Schmucker, *The True Unity of Christ's Church: Being a Renewed Appeal to the Friends of the Redeemer, on Primitive Christian Union, and the History of Its Corruption. To which is now added a Modified Plan for the Re-union of All Evangelical Churches; Embracing as Integral Parts, The World's Evangelical Alliance, with All Its National Branches* (New York, Anson D. F. Randolph & Co., 1870, pp. 262), *passim.*

[41] Anstadt, *op. cit.,* pp. 298–300.

[42] Weigle, *op. cit.,* p. 214.

Protestantism, Schaff contributed both by his writings, especially *The Creeds of Christendom,* a collection of the statements of faith of the various confessions, and by his leadership in the Evangelical Alliance. He participated in the founding of the American branch and to his organizing ability was chiefly due the success of the meeting of 1873.[43]

Others also shared in the American branch of the Evangelical Alliance. William E. Dodge (1805–1883), a wealthy New York business man, was president from its inception to his death.[44] A Presbyterian clergyman, Samuel Irenaeus Prime (1812–1885), for thirty-four years editor of the influential *New York Observer,* was a warm advocate.[45] From 1885 to 1898 a Congregational clergyman, Josiah Strong (1847–1916), of whom we are to hear more in connexion with the social gospel, was general secretary. He toured the country organizing branch units of the Alliance and conducted religious censuses in an effort to reach the unchurched. Strong came to the conviction that the Evangelical Alliance was too Pietistic. Restive under a conservative board of directors who would not approve his social emphasis, he resigned (1898). While on paper the Alliance continued until 1944, with Strong's departure it languished.[46]

In the meantime a movement towards Christian unity was developing within the Protestant Episcopal Church. William Reed Huntington (1838–1909) came out in 1870 with a strong plea for a programme for union which advocated that that church invite all other churches to join it in a simplified Anglicanism later put forward in the Lambeth Quadrilateral and which outlined what he believed to be the minimum condition of agreement. It was (1) acknowledgement of the Holy Scriptures as the Word of God, (2) the primitive creeds as the rule of faith, (3) the two sacraments, baptism and the Lord's Supper, as ordained by Christ, and (4) acceptance of the historic episcopate as essential to governmental unity. In 1898 Huntington abandoned his plan of making Anglicanism the basis of a national American church and proposed instead a structure which would consist of local churches coördinated by counties, state councils, and a bicameral national assembly meeting at least once in ten years.[47]

The Federal Council of the Churches of Christ in America had a constitution drawn up by an inter-church conference held in 1905. It came formally into being in 1908 when the constituent churches had adopted that document. Its chief creator was a Congregationalist, Elias B. Sanford (1843–1932). The Federal Council went beyond the Evangelical Alliance in having churches, not individuals, as members, but it did not go as far as Huntington had advocated

---

[43] Schaff, *The Life of Philip Schaff, passim,* especially pp. 252 ff.

[44] *Dictionary of American Biography,* Vol. V, pp. 352, 353.

[45] Rouse and Neill, *op. cit.,* p. 255; *Dictionary of American Biography,* Vol. XV, p. 228.

[46] Rouse and Neill, *op. cit.,* pp. 255, 256; *Dictionary of American Biography,* Vol. XVIII, pp. 150, 151.

[47] Rouse and Neill, *op. cit.,* pp. 250–252; *Dictionary of American Biography,* Vol. IX, pp. 420, 421.

in creating a unified ecclesiastical structure. In the course of time the Federal Council drew into its membership churches which embraced a majority of the Protestants of the United States and Canada. At the outset it was made up almost entirely of Protestant churches of the older stock. Yet not all of them joined it. For example, the Southern Baptist Convention held aloof. City and state federations of churches were also organized, some of them before the Federal Council. They and the national body were quite independent of one another.[48]

EMERGING COMMON PATTERNS IN PROTESTANTISM

In other ways than coöperation through organizations the Protestantism of the United States of America was developing a kind of unity. It was especially seen in the Protestantism of the older stock, but here and there it was beginning to appear in the Protestant bodies of the nineteenth-century immigration. The prevalence of revivalism which overpassed denominational borders and increasing collaboration in evangelistic campaigns such as those of Moody and Sunday were a contributing factor. Mid-week meetings in one or another form, usually that of prayer meetings, and morning and evening Sunday services of much the same kind were widespread among many denominations. Numerous hymnals, such as the collections under the names of Moody and Sankey, were used by congregations of more than one denomination. Often denominational hymnals contained both music and words from many ecclesiastical backgrounds. The Common Service, prepared as we have seen in the 1880's for use in English-speaking congregations, was adopted by several Lutheran synods.

THE ROMAN CATHOLIC CHURCH ACHIEVES A NATIONAL STRUCTURE

At the outset of the nineteenth century the achievement of a nation-wide structure of the Roman Catholic Church was not a foregone conclusion. The task was not as difficult as for Protestants. By its very nature and its long tradition Protestantism was divided and was without a recognized centre of visible unity. In contrast, the Roman Catholic Church had in the Papacy an institution making for cohesion. In the nineteenth century the effective administrative authority of the Popes was markedly enhanced. However, in the United States several formidable obstacles stood in the way of the attainment of a unified national structure. Few seriously questioned the authority of the Pope, but Rome was on the other side of a wide ocean. On the local level, in accordance with the democratic spirit of the new nation and the practice in American Protestantism, lay trustees sought to control the property of the worshipping congregations and

---

[48] Elias B. Sanford, *Origin and History of the Federal Council of the Churches of Christ in America* (Hartford, Conn., S. S. Scranton Co., 1916, pp. xii, 528), *passim;* Rouse and Neill, *op. cit.*, pp. 256, 257.

the appointment of pastors. Were they to succeed, the authority of the hierarchy would be badly compromised. The vast influx of Roman Catholics from the several countries of Europe, with their differing languages and traditions, posed a highly difficult problem. Should those of one nationality be served only by clergy and supervised only by bishops of their background? Should the national differences be perpetuated and reciprocally independent Catholic churches emerge, as in the Lutheranism of the United States distinguished by the country of origin, but, in contrast with Protestantism, acknowledging Rome as a centre of unity? On the other extreme, in its effort to shed what many of its critics and even of its friends regarded as its alien character, should the Roman Catholic Church seek to adapt itself to the American ethos and in so doing run the risk of a basic rift in its supra-nationalism? The problem was further complicated by the presence of strong personalities, numbers of them bishops, who tended to clash.

Trusteeism, as it was called, for many years threatened the unity of the Roman Catholic Church and the authority of the bishops. Under the laws of at least some of the states, the property of the parish was held by trustees elected by the members. This was the practice in most Protestant churches. The Council of Trent had given some ground for Roman Catholic laity to claim precedent in canon law for a similar procedure. A major source of friction arose when the trustees insisted on selecting their own pastors. To this the bishops would not consent and in that position were supported by Rome. The issue was complicated by other factors. Rome had confirmed the choice of the first three American bishops by the clergy. Why, said the laity, should they not enjoy the same privilege in the placing of pastors? Stresses arose from the complex national composition of the Roman Catholic Church in the United States. On more than one occasion Irish objected to having as pastors French priests, and for a time the latter were numerous, refugees from revolutionary France. Now and again Germans insisted upon a pastor of their own nation. Moreover, the anti-Catholic agitation—Nativism and the Know-Nothing movement—saw in the appointment of pastors by bishops who were appointed by Rome and in the control of the Roman Catholic Church in the United States through the Propaganda the intrusion of a foreign power into American affairs and a threat to American independence.

Again and again and at several centres trusteeism exploded into open conflict. Carroll was plagued by it. In Philadelphia the trustees insisted upon naming the clergy of the cathedral. For a time open schism resulted and on one occasion the bishop placed the trustee-dominated cathedral under an interdict. In New Orleans the trustees of the cathedral were abetted by a Spanish friar in their insistence on naming the clergy for that edifice. Incidents developed in Charleston, Norfolk, and Buffalo. Under pressure from the Know-Nothing agitators in

1855 the New York legislature put on the statute books a law, not repealed until 1863, which required lay ownership of all church property and forbade a clergyman to hold property in his own name. In New York City early in his episcopate the vigorous John Hughes scotched trusteeism by an appeal to the constituency which resulted in the election of men who supported him. By the second half of the century the bishops had won. They were uncompromising in their pronouncement in 1884 in the Synod of Baltimore. Rome emphatically supported them. Depending on the laws of each state, the physical properties of the parishes were legally in the name either of the bishop or of trustees, but if the latter, in such fashion that the authority of the bishops over the appointment, transfer, or dismissal of the parish clergy was not impaired.[49]

Of longer duration than trusteeism was the problem posed by the varied national origins of the Roman Catholics. Coming from so many countries and with so many languages, could the Roman Catholics be welded into one ecclesiastical structure? The issue was especially acute between the Irish and the Germans. They made up the majority of the Roman Catholic immigration in the fore part of the century and continued to be outstanding in its leadership. Temperamentally they differed. The Irish tended to be volatile and mercurial, the Germans to be phlegmatic. With English as their mother tongue, the Irish were more quickly Americanized than the Germans. The latter tended to cling tenaciously to their language in church, parish schools, societies, and periodical press. Prelates of Irish blood, such as John Ireland, were outspoken temperance advocates and the Germans, committed to the brewing and drinking of beer, were resentful. Germans early demanded a separate parish in Baltimore and a bishop for themselves and took the position that Carroll had authority only over English-speaking Catholics.[50] In 1847 the Propaganda so far took account of the situation that it directed the Sixth Provincial Council of Baltimore to see to it that bishops appointed to dioceses with a German population be well acquainted with their language and that in these dioceses priests be familiar with that tongue.

This was the more important in view of the predominant position in the American hierarchy occupied by men of Irish birth or ancestry. In 1886, of the sixty-nine bishops in the United States thirty-five were of Irish extraction, fifteen of German blood (including Austrian and Swiss), eleven of French origin, five of English provenance, and one each of Dutch, Scottish, and Spanish back-

---

[49] Lord, Sexton, and Harrington, *History of the Archdiocese of Boston*, Vol. III, p. 339; Ellis, *American Catholicism*, pp. 43–48; Maynard, *The Story of American Catholicism*, pp. 187–195; O'Gorman, *A History of the Roman Catholic Church in the United States*, pp. 269, 270, 279, 280, 317–323, 352, 353, 367–369, 399, 400; Guilday, *The National Pastorals of the American Hierarchy* (1792–1919), p. 242; Ellis, *Documents of American Catholic History*, pp. 225–231; Patrick J. Dignan, *A History of the Legal Incorporation of Catholic Church Property in the United States* (1784–1932) (Washington, The Catholic University of America Press, 1933, pp. 289), *passim*.

[50] Maynard, *op. cit.*, p. 506; Ellis, *The Life of James Cardinal Gibbons*, Vol. I, pp. 331–334.

ground. By the middle of the twentieth century over a hundred of the bishops had been born in Ireland, at least twice that number had been of Irish blood, and most of the important sees had had incumbents of Irish stock. With one exception, New York City as diocese and archdiocese had always been served by an Irishman, with two exceptions the same was true of Boston, with some exceptions Baltimore was long an Irish preserve, and much the same was true of several of the important Western posts.[51]

In the second half of the century the German-Irish issue became especially acute. It was brought sharply to a head in 1891 when the St. Raphael Society, with Peter Paul Cahensly as its secretary, in a memorial to the Pope declared that in the United States the Roman Catholic Church had lost ten million of her children, mainly through the failure to provide them with priests of their own nationality. As a remedy the memorial advocated that each of the nationalities have its own churches and parochial schools and bishops who spoke their tongue. Cahensly was a German merchant who had been largely responsible for the organization of the St. Raphael Society, which had as its object aid to German Roman Catholic emigrants.[52] The memorial was a climax to a controversy that had been mounting in the 1880's in which Germans on more than one occasion had complained to Rome of what they believed to be discrimination against them by the Irish clergy and had brought pressure to have men of German stock and language appointed to specific dioceses. Ireland, with his fiery Irish temperament, had been pronounced in his opposition, and Gibbons, as the ranking American prelate, although Irish, had attempted to pour oil on the troubled waters.[53] He insisted that in the United States Roman Catholics should be loyal Americans and not perpetuate their European national divisions. In Rome Rampolla, the Papal Secretary of State, and Leo XIII himself were emphatic in denouncing the suggestion of national bishops in the American church.[54] Cahensly was not entirely quieted. On a visit to Canada and the United States in 1910 he spoke out in advocacy of immigrants' preserving their mother tongue and of priests' caring for immigrants in their native language.[55]

Germans were not the only national group which asked for special treatment. Among the Poles the issue led to a continuing break and the emergence of a distinct ecclesiastical body, the Polish National Catholic Church. In the 1880's, with the rapid rise of Polish immigration, demands began to be heard for a

---

[51] Maynard, *op. cit.*, p. 506; Ellis, *The Life of James Cardinal Gibbons*, Vol. I, p. 334.

[52] Maynard, *op. cit.*, p. 509; Ellis, *The Life of James Cardinal Gibbons*, Vol. I, pp. 367, 368.

[53] Ellis, *The Life of James Cardinal Gibbons*, Vol. I, pp. 334–370; Moynihan, *The Life of Archbishop John Ireland*, pp. 54 ff.

[54] Ellis, *The Life of James Cardinal Gibbons*, Vol. I, pp. 368–382.

[55] For a sympathetic account of Cahensly and of the German American position, especially important for the documents in the appendices, see Barry, *The Catholic Church and German Americans, passim*. For a comprehensive survey of the entire range of the German Roman Catholics in the United States, also sympathetic, see Georg Timpe, editor, *Katholisches Deutschtum in den Vereinigten Staaten von Amerika*.

separate diocese of Catholics of Slavic extraction.[56] Separation came over a phase of trusteeism combined with Polish nationalism. In several cities Polish laymen insisted on sharing in the choice of a pastor and objected to the appointment of non-Polish priests to parishes made up of Poles, or revolted against unpopular Polish priests. In at least one instance they protested against the removal of a Polish priest and, when their claim to the ownership of the church property was disallowed by the courts, put up a building of their own.

The leader in the organization of the Polish National Catholic Church was a priest, Francis Hodur. At the invitation of its parishioners, he accepted the pastorate of a congregation in Scranton, Pennsylvania, for which they had erected an edifice when they were shut out of a church after protesting to the bishop, in vain, against the incumbent. Hodur went to Rome at the request of his and several other congregations with a petition that the title of church property be lodged in a parish committee chosen by the parishioners without interference of priest or bishop, and that the parishioners have a voice in the choice of their pastors. Consistently with its announced policy, through the Prefect of the Propaganda Rome categorically denied the request. Hodur's congregation backed him in his refusal to abide by the decision and he and they were excommunicated. At his invitation delegates from congregations in five states who shared his convictions met (1904), formed themselves into a church, and elected him as bishop. He received consecration from Old Catholic bishops in Holland. In the 1890's a similar movement sprang up in the Middle West, headed by Anthony Kozlowski, a priest, who was elected bishop by his followers and consecrated by an Old Catholic bishop. The movements coalesced to form the Polish National Catholic Church in America. In 1916 it reported a membership of 28,245. While preserving some of the forms of worship of the Roman Catholic Church, it differed in doctrine. It rejected papal infallibility and stood for the right of all men to interpret the Bible according to their convictions.[57] The large majority of Polish immigrants did not go along with the dissidents but remained in the Roman Catholic Church.[58]

Italians were also a source of trouble. Latecomers, they found the Irish dominant in the hierarchy and struggled for control, almost parish by parish.[59]

Although the pressures for administering the Roman Catholic Church in the United States through dioceses arranged according to the national origins of the faithful were successfully resisted and thus a comprehensive national structure was assured, frequently parishes were arranged for those of one nationality

---

[56] Ellis, *The Life of James Cardinal Gibbons*, Vol. I, pp. 362, 363, 272.

[57] Paul Fox, *The Polish National Catholic Church* (Scranton, Pa., School of Christian Living, no date, pp. 146), *passim;* Bureau of the Census, *Religious Bodies,* 1916, Vol. II, pp. 546, 547; Ellis, *The Life of James Cardinal Gibbons,* Vol. I, p. 384; Theodore Andrews, *The Polish National Catholic Church in America and Poland* (London, S.P.C.K., 1953, pp. ix, 117), pp. 15–80.

[58] As in the Baltimore archdiocese. Ellis, *The Life of James Cardinal Gibbons,* Vol. II, p. 464.

[59] Handlin, *The Uprooted,* pp. 135–137.

and language. Thus in 1881 Gibbons dedicated a church in Baltimore for the Italians; in 1897 that city had six parishes for the Germans, two for the Poles, and one each for the Bohemians and Lithuanians; and in 1912 Gibbons reported that under his jurisdiction separate parishes, parochial schools, and priests were provided for Poles, Bohemians, and Lithuanians.[60] Yet ultimately this arrangement required special authorization from Rome, for canon law decreed (1918) that without special permission from the Holy See "parishes may not be established that are not divided by territory but by the difference of language of the people in the same town or city."[61]

Moreover, true to its purpose of being inclusive of many national traditions, the Roman Catholic Church was careful to preserve in the United States as elsewhere rites other than Latin which belonged to the several racial groups. For example, in 1907 a Greek bishop was appointed for the Galician Uniates. In some instances priests were appointed for one or another of the Oriental rites but under the jurisdiction of bishops of the Latin rite.[62]

In a variety of ways provision was made for the administration as a unit of the Roman Catholic Church in the United States. Councils of all the bishops within the nation convened from time to time. Between 1829 and 1849 seven provincial councils were held in Baltimore, but since until 1846 the Archbishop of Baltimore was the only metropolitan in the United States and was conceded quasi-primatial honours by the other prelates, they were generally regarded as national in scope and authority. What were officially known as national or plenary councils of the American church were held in Baltimore in 1852, 1866, and 1884—the only ones before 1919.[63]

In 1893 an Apostolic Delegation was established in Washington. The step met with decided opposition from a large proportion of the hierarchy of the United States, including Gibbons. Among other reasons for the reluctance was fear that the step would be interpreted by the American public as evidence for the truth of the accusation often made by critics that the Roman Catholics in the United States were subjects of a foreign power and not loyal Americans. Yet Ireland supported the step, and the measure was an indication of the conviction in Rome that the Roman Catholic Church in the United States was coming of age.[64]

The recognition by Rome of the maturity of the Catholic Church in the United States was demonstrated conclusively when, in 1908, the American bishops, along with those of Canada and Newfoundland, were freed from the control of the Propaganda. Hitherto in Rome the United States had officially been regarded as a mission field and the Roman Catholic Church within its borders

---

[60] Ellis, *The Life of James Cardinal Gibbons*, Vol. I, pp. 335, 339, Vol. II, p. 464.
[61] Moynihan, *op. cit.*, p. 77.
[62] Maynard, *op. cit.*, pp. 508, 509.
[63] Guilday, *op. cit.*, p. xi.
[64] Ellis, *The Life of James Cardinal Gibbons*, Vol. I, pp. 595 ff.; Moynihan, *op. cit.*, pp. 296 ff.

as not on an equality with the older churches. Now it was accorded the same status as they.[65]

Would the Roman Catholic Church as it came of age in the United States adopt methods and attitudes which would domesticate it in the American scene? Would it become a national church with distinctive characteristics—as it had in countries such as Spain, France, and Germany? If so, in the process would it compromise the faith of the church? The danger might be real, for in the United States the church was immersed in a culture which, so far as it had been shaped by Christianity, was prevailingly Protestant and of the Puritan-Evangelical tradition. The issue became acute in the 1890's and was accompanied by heated differences in the American hierarchy and accusations on the other side of the Atlantic that in its "Americanism" the Roman Catholic Church in the United States was verging on heresy.

Within the American hierarchy sharp dissension arose over the attitude to be taken towards American institutions. On one side were the ranking prelate, Gibbons, the doughty Ireland of St. Paul, and John Joseph Keane (1839–1918), successively Bishop of Richmond, the first rector of the Catholic University of America, and Archbishop of Dubuque. They did not always agree with one another, but in general they favoured democracy as it operated in the United States, believed the ban by Rome on the Odd Fellows, the Knights of Pythias, and the Sons of Temperance to be a mistake, were sympathetic with organized labour, notably in the form of the highly controversial Knights of Labour, were inclined to work out a compromise on the public schools, and were not averse to participating in the World's Parliament of Religions held in Chicago in 1893 in connexion with the World's Fair. On the other side were men like Bernard John McQuaid (1823–1909), the first Bishop of Rochester, a strict disciplinarian who insisted that Catholics send their children to parochial schools, and was opposed to the Knights of Labour, and his close friend, Michael Augustine Corrigan (1839–1902), Archbishop of New York, who firmly forbade Roman Catholic membership in any of the secret societies, was cool even to the Ancient Order of Hibernians, disagreed with Ireland on the latter's attitude towards the public schools, and was outspoken in his opposition to McGlynn, who, as we are to see, was a warm advocate of Henry George and the latter's single-tax programme.

The debate extended to Europe and became even more acute than in the United States, partly because of the situation in France. There Roman Catholics who wished reconciliation with the Third Republic believed that they saw in the rapid growth of their church in the United States proof that the faith could prosper in a democracy. On the other hand, their opponents, rigorously intransigent in their hostility to the existing government, maintained that the numerical success of Roman Catholicism in the United States was being achieved

65 Maynard, *op. cit.*, pp. 496, 497.

at the price of compromising essential doctrines. Fuel was added to the flames by the publication of 1897 of a French translation of Walter Elliott's *Life of Father Hecker*. It quickly passed through seven editions. In the programme which it set forth as Hecker's for the conversion of the United States the critics declared that their worst suspicions were confirmed. They denounced it as semi-heretical and schismatic. On the other hand, Catholics who favoured the republic hailed it as a way of furthering the faith under the forms of government which were emerging in the revolutionary age. Were Hecker and in a less bold way Gibbons, Ireland, Keane, and others like them pointing the way to the peaceful coëxistence and even coöperation of the Roman Catholic Church with the revolutionary forces of the day or were they advocating heresy?

So serious was the issue that Rome believed it must not be ignored. On January 22, 1899, Leo XIII signed a letter, *Testem benevolentiae,* directed to Gibbons and soon made public. Gibbons had sought to prevent its composition and was unhappy that it was being given out for circulation. It had been first prepared by other hands than the Pope's. Before sending it to Gibbons Leo XIII had softened it with words of appreciation of the American bishops and people and without directly charging any one with holding the teachings which it condemned. He declared that he was simply moved by the desire to put an end to the contentions that were disturbing the peace of the church. To this end he would make clear his stand on some positions which had been ascribed to Hecker. He condemned the view that, the more easily to bring over to the Catholic faith those who dissented from it, the church should adapt itself to "our advanced civilization," relaxing its ancient rigour not only in regard to the rule of life but also to the doctrines in which the deposit of faith was contained. He also forbade the omission or suppression of "certain principles of Catholic doctrine" in seeking to win converts. While calling attention to the historic willingness of the church to modify its rule of life to take account of the manners and customs of the nations which it embraced, he said that the church must maintain its authority in an age of license and that it could not approve opinions which he specifically named and which he said "some comprise under the name of Americanism."

After waiting for several weeks, Gibbons replied, courteously but firmly, saying that "this Americanism, as it has been called, has nothing in common with the views, aspirations, doctrine, and conduct of Americans," that he knew in the entire country of no bishop, priest, or "even a layman with a knowledge of his religion who has ever uttered such enormities. No, that is not—it never has been and never will be—our Americanism."

For a time echoes of the controversy continued to be heard, but before long they died down. Rome had spoken in accord with the position which it had repeatedly taken towards the revolutionary currents of the age. Gibbons, as the ranking ecclesiastic in the United States, was emphatic that the Roman Catholic Church in his country was loyal to the faith. He and others were aggrieved that Rome had so little understood the American scene.[66]

Tensions in the Roman Catholic Church in the United States were again and again heightened by disagreements among strong-minded men. They were especially noticeable when the men were bishops. If they were parish clergy, under the rule of holy obedience their bishop could command them either to compose their differences or to keep silent. In a young and growing church such as was the Roman Catholic communion in the United States, faced with the problem of holding and assimilating the vast immigration and building physical structures and institutions of many kinds, a bishop, if he was to be a success, must be a forceful leader, promoter, and executive. The vitality of the Roman Catholice Church in the United States was in part demonstrated by the number of bishops of that calibre which it produced. Several were foreign born and either came to America in their early maturity or were brought by their immigrant parents in infancy or boyhood. An increasing number were born and educated in the United States.[67] Having to rule as they did in their respective dioceses, the greatest of the bishops as well as those of lesser note held strong convictions and in them not infrequently clashed with their fellows. We have seen a few instances. They could be multiplied. From time to time the archbishops met to seek agreement. Less frequently, as in provincial councils and plenary councils, all the bishops came together. Always Rome was in the background as a centre of authority—authority which in the nineteenth century was heightened in practice even though not in theory.

Although it had disproved the charge of heresy which misunderstanding had led critics in Europe and Rome to scent under the guise of Americanism, and in spite of tensions between the nationalities from which it was gathered and repeated disagreements among its hierarchy, in the United States the Roman Catholic Church had a distinctive ethos with a character all of its own and a kind of unity that was more than structural. The fact that it was a minority, although a growing minority, in an environment in which large elements were suspicious and at times hostile helped to tie it together for common defense. The

[66] Of the large literature on the "Americanism" controversy, see Emmanuel Barbier, *Histoire du Catholicisme Liberal et du Catholicisme Social en France du Concile du Vatican a l'Avenement de S. S. Benoit XV (1870–1914)* (Bordeaux, Y. Cadoret, 6 vols., 1924), Vol. II, pp. 242 ff.; Felix Klein, *Americanism: A Phantom Heresy* (Atchison, Kan., Aquin Book Shop, 1951, pp. xxx, 345) which with its introduction by Archbishop John Ireland and its title clearly shows its slant; Thomas T. McAvoy, *The Great Crisis in American Catholic History 1895–1900* (Chicago, Henry Regnery Co. 1957, pp. xi, 402), with ecclesiastical imprimatur; Ellis, *The Life of James Cardinal Gibbons*, Vol. II, pp. 1–80, well-informed, frank, and favourable to Gibbons; Moynihan, *The Life of Archbishop John Ireland*, pp. 104–135, favourable to Ireland; Cross, *The Emergence of Liberal Catholicism in America*, pp. 182 ff.

[67] A list with brief biographical sketches is in O'Donnell, *The Catholic Hierarchy of the United States, 1790–1922.*

martyr mind in the face of latent or open persecution, elsewhere also a feature of Roman Catholic mentality, was combined with a conviction of destiny deepened by rapid growth in numbers, institutions, and wealth. Like much of the Protestantism of the country, in the United States the Roman Catholic Church was activistic and outstanding in its genius for organization. In this it was in accord with the temper of the country. Here was its real Americanism. Moreover, painfully conscious that it was again and again denounced as un-American, its leaders emphatically protested their loyalty to American ideals and institutions. Here it was in contrast with the attitude taken by many of the faithful towards their respective governments in country after country in Europe.

THE EMERGENCE OF ROMAN CATHOLIC CLERGY

In the United States the Roman Catholic Church was strikingly successful in recruiting and educating a large body of clergy. In this respect it was like the Roman Catholic Church in Canada but in notable contrast with that in Latin America. In the early decades of the nineteenth century a large proportion of the priests came from Europe. As the century wore on, a mounting proportion of the clergy were born in the United States.

The bishops stressed the importance of encouraging vocations to the priesthood and of financial support for theological seminaries. Again and again in their pastoral letters the hierarchy recurred to the subject.[68] In one, in 1866, while rejoicing in the number of vocations in some sections they lamented the paucity of them in others.[69]

The growth of theological education was marked. In 1791 Sulpicians from France opened a seminary in Baltimore. It had a hard struggle, but by 1815 thirty of its former students had been ordained priests.[70] By 1854 it is said that at that time priests, regular and secular, in the country totalled 1,604, many of whom had been educated abroad.[71] In 1859 the North American College was opened in Rome.[72] In several dioceses seminaries were begun and grew. Thus in the Archdiocese of Boston one was started in the 1880's and instructors for it were obtained from the Sulpicians in Paris.[73] Earlier in the century, before 1820, in and near Bardstown, a pioneer cathedral town in Kentucky, a *petit seminaire* and a major seminary were maintained.[74] In 1824 John England, the famous Bishop of Charleston, opened a theological seminary, and although it

[68] Guilday, *op. cit.*, pp. 74, 136, 159, 187, 240, 289, 290.

[69] *Ibid.*, p. 217.

[70] Power, *A History of Catholic Higher Education in the United States*, p. 43; Ellis, *Documents of American Catholic History*, p. 180; Joseph William Ruane, *The Beginnings. The Society of St. Sulpice in the United States* (1791–1829) (Washington, The Catholic University of America Press, 1935, pp. x, 266), *passim*.

[71] Ellis, *Documents of American Catholic History*, p. 343.

[72] *Ibid.*, p. 344.

[73] Lord, Sexton, and Harrington, *History of the Archdiocese of Boston*, Vol. III, pp. 58–61.

[74] Maes, *Life of Rev. Charles Nerinckx*, pp. 393–395.

was closed in 1851, during its existence it produced about sixty priests, four of whom became bishops.[75] The year 1843 saw the opening of a diocesan seminary on the outskirts of St. Louis.[76] Early in the 1850's a seminary was inaugurated in the diocese of Cleveland. For many years most of its instructors were from Europe.[77] The redoubtable Bishop McQuaid of Rochester took great pride in his theological seminary—including its well stocked wine-cellar—and spent many years in planning and building it. It drew students from other dioceses as well as his own.[78]

The Roman Catholic Church maintained high standards for the education of its clergy. In the mid-1920's two-thirds of its priests had both college and seminary training and only a fifth had merely a seminary preparation. In this respect it did not rank as high as the Reformed Church and some of the Lutheran bodies, but it was about on a par with the Northern and Southern Presbyterians, better than the Episcopalians and the Congregationalists, and much ahead of the Methodists and Baptists.[79]

THE EASTERN CHURCHES

In the nineteenth century the Eastern Orthodox Churches were but slimly represented in the United States. In 1906 they reported only about 125,000 members. Of these about two-thirds were Greek Orthodox and the others were Russian, Serbian, and Syrian. Ten years later they had about doubled: the largest numbers were still of the Greek Orthodox Church with about half the whole, but the Russian Orthodox were not far behind, with nearly two-fifths of the total. In addition, in 1916 the Serbians, Syrians, Albanians, Bulgarians, and Rumanians were represented, but none of the three with as many as two thousand members. Of the Orthodox, only the Russians had an inclusive national organization. Even the Greek priests were without a resident bishop:[80] they were subject to the Holy Synod of Greece.

SUMMARY

In the course of the nineteenth century the general trend among most denominations was to coalesce in a nation-wide ecclesiastical structure. In Protestantism various factors conspired to prevent a complete attainment of the goal. Some were doctrinal. Others were sectional, particularly the sharp division between the North and the South. Still others arose from differences in national origin and in language.

---

[75] O'Brien, *John England*, pp. 37–43.
[76] Rothensteiner, *History of the Archdiocese of St. Louis*, Vol. I, p. 837.
[77] Hynes, *History of the Diocese of Cleveland*, pp. 95–99.
[78] Ellis, *Documents of American Catholic History*, pp. 567–569.
[79] *The Education of American Ministers*, Vol. II, p. 17.
[80] Bureau of the Census, *Religious Bodies, 1916*, Vol. II, pp. 250–264.

In spite of the divisive forces, increasingly and in a variety of ways Protestants coöperated across denominational lines, and proposals were made for an all-embracing unity. The coöperation was chiefly among Protestants of the pre-nineteenth-century stock and of the Evangelical tradition. It found expression in such organizations as the Sunday Schools, the Young Men's and Young Women's Christian Association, Christian Endeavour, the Evangelical Alliance, and on the eve of 1914 in the Federal Council of the Churches of Christ in America.

Progress was made by Protestants in recruiting and training clergy for the rapidly growing membership. The level of education varied with the denomination and in general was highest in those bodies which were continuations of the state churches of Europe and which drew their members from the families of higher than average incomes.

The Roman Catholic Church in the United States from the beginning of the century had an inclusive national structure. It maintained and developed it, and that in spite of obstacles which from time to time threatened to disrupt it. Although long dependent on clergy from Europe, increasingly it recruited and trained a native priesthood. Shortly after 1900 Rome recognized its growing maturity by withdrawing it from the supervision of the Propaganda.

The Eastern Churches came to the eve of 1914 with relatively small constituencies and with only one nation-embracing structure—that of the Russian Orthodox Church.

CHAPTER V

The United States of America: Movements Emerging from Christianity

To WHAT extent in what forms did the Christianity of the United States of America give rise to new movements or adopt and develop movements which came from Europe? Did it display creative vitality in giving birth to fresh efforts to meet the challenges of the revolutionary situation with which the nineteenth century confronted it? The vigour demonstrated by Christianity in countering the threats of de-Christianization of its hereditary adherents and in winning those who by ancestry were non-Christian was paralleled by a variety of ecclesiastical bodies and organizations which, as we have seen, were also evidence of abounding life. Many were continuations of what had been transmitted from Europe but in ways which showed adaptations to the American scene. In the present chapter we will deal with the new kinds of denominations arising from Protestantism, the movements through which Protestants sought to solve the problems brought by the new day, and the organizations which emerged within the broad bosom of the Roman Catholic Church.

NEW DENOMINATIONS EMERGE FROM PROTESTANTISM

A striking feature of the nineteenth-century Protestantism of the United States was the quite new kinds of denominations which sprang from it. They were evidence of the fashion in which the creative impulse inherent within Protestantism found fresh and often novel expression in the fluidity and freedom characteristic of the United States in the nineteenth century. However, even when taken together, the total membership in these bodies constituted only a minority, although a substantial minority, of the Protestant Church membership: the majority of Protestants were affiliated with one or another of the denominations having a European background.

To the beginnings of these bodies which had their origins on the eve of 1815 we have already called attention.[1] We have seen that several were the fruit of

[1] Volume I, pp. 192–195.

the awakenings widespread shortly before and after 1800. Two, the United Brethren in Christ and the Evangelical Association, in temper and structure were Methodist but ministered chiefly to the German elements of the pre-nineteenth-century immigration. In 1916 the former, by that time divided into two bodies of unequal size, numbered 367,034, the latter 120,756.[2] By far the largest, and, indeed, throughout the period covered by these volumes the largest of all the bodies of purely American birth, was the Disciples of Christ. As we have recorded, it had its beginnings in movements led respectively by Alexander Campbell and Barton W. Stone. It was an effort at a new reformation and sought to escape the inherited denominational divisions by finding its pattern in the New Testament and by taking, instead of the current denominational designations, the simple name Christian or Disciples of Christ. The followers of Campbell early separated from the Baptists, with whom they had much in common. That union of the bodies led by Campbell and Stone was consummated in 1832. The first national convention of the movement was held in Cincinnati in 1849. Not all the local congregations which chose to be called Christian affiliated themselves with this group. Some later found fellowship with the Congregationalists. Still earlier others separated themselves as the Churches of Christ. However, in 1916 the Disciples of Christ numbered 1,226,028 and their major offshoot, the radically conservative anti-missionary society Churches of Christ, reported a membership of 317,937.[3]

Of the denominations of purely American origin, the one next to the Disciples of Christ in numerical strength at the close of the century was the Church of Jesus Christ of Latter Day Saints, usually called more briefly the Mormons. Like the Disciples of Christ, it had its beginning on the frontier. Its founder, Joseph Smith (1805–1844), was born in Vermont of old New England stock. So far as the family had a religious background it was Puritan. He was from the floating, semi-illiterate, poverty-stricken class which was common on or near the frontier. As a lad he went with his parents to western New York, then not far removed from pioneer conditions. It had been frequently swept by revivals and was sometimes for that reason called the "burned-over" district. Troubled by the existing differences between denominations, eager to know which church was right, Smith believed that when he was in his fifteenth year in a vision of God the Father and God the Son it had been revealed to him that no existing ecclesiastical body had the full Gospel. Three years later, so he said, he was told in visions that God had commissioned him to restore the true Church. He maintained that in a further vision he was directed to the discovery of ancient records buried in a hill and engraved on plates which had the appearance of gold. He declared that the plates were inscribed in what he called "reformed

[2] Bureau of the Census, *Religious Bodies, 1916*, Vol. I, pp. 20, 21.

[3] *Ibid.*, p. 20; Winfred Ernest Garrison, *Religion Follows the Frontier. A History of the Disciples of Christ* (New York, Harper & Brothers, 1931, pp. xiv, 317), *passim.*

Egyptian" and that with supernatural assistance he was enabled to translate them. He dictated the translation to others, who wrote it down. The result was *The Book of Mormon,* published in 1830. It contained extensive portions of the Old and New Testaments, slightly altered from the King James Version, together with what purported to be a history of migrations from Asia to America, one of them of a family which fled from Jerusalem before its fall to the Babylonians, and of what followed in America. It reported that Christ had visited America after his resurrection and ascension and had taught its peoples, repeating much of what he had given in the days of his flesh. Some centuries later, so *The Book of Mormon* went on to narrate, civil wars destroyed most of the inhabitants.

In 1830 Smith organized the Church of Jesus Christ of Latter Day Saints, at Fayette, Seneca County, in New York State, based upon *Articles and Covenants* which were said to have been given to him by revelation. These documents declared Smith to be acting under the commission of God, set forth the doctrines of the church, and prescribed its organization and its ordinances. Later, laws and regulations were added, also professedly through revelation, and the whole was incorporated in *Doctrine and Covenants,* which remained authoritative in the church. Missionaries were sent out, some of them to Europe. Converts were gathered and centres were begun—in Missouri, in Kirkland, Ohio, again in Missouri, and then in Nauvoo, Illinois. Smith continued to have what he declared to be revelations. He made a sharp distinction between the "Saints," the members of the church, and "Gentiles," the non-members. From time to time internal discord punctuated the life of the church. Persecution by the Gentiles, often with violence, attended the course of the infant church. In June, 1844, Joseph Smith and his brother Hyrum were killed by a mob at Carthage, Illinois.[4]

The death of Smith did not end the Church of Jesus Christ of Latter Day Saints. Some of its members gathered around James Jesse Strang·(1813-1856), who, reared a Baptist but becoming a sceptic, was converted in 1844. He led a group first to Wisconsin, then to northern Michigan, where he established a New Zion, was its autocratic king, had revelations, professed to translate plates, and for a time served in the state legislature. He was assassinated by a mob incited by those who had left the church.[5]

---

[4] Of the large and much of it controversial and conflicting literature on Joseph Smith and the Church of Jesus Christ of Latter Day Saints the following are samples: Fawn K. Brodie, *No Man Knows My History: The Life of Joseph Smith, the Mormon Prophet* (New York, Alfred A. Knopf, 1945, pp. ix, 476, xvii), based on extensive research, attempts to be objective but is decidedly critical; John A. Widstoe, *Joseph Smith, Seeker after Truth, Prophet of God* (Salt Lake City, Deseret News Service, 1952, pp. x, 385), is a semi-official biography, laudatory; Harry M. Beardsley, *Joseph Smith and His Mormon Empire* (Boston, Houghton Mifflin Co., 1931, pp. xii, 421), is critical of Smith; G. Homer Durham, editor, *Joseph Smith, Prophet-statesman* (Salt Lake City, The Bookcraft Co., 1944, pp. xiv, 225), sympathetically edited, is made up of excerpts from the *Book of Mormon, Doctrine and Covenants,* and various writings by Smith or reflecting his views.

[5] *Dictionary of American Biography,* Vol. XVIII, pp. 123-125.

Eventually most of the Mormons in the Middle West were in what was called the Reorganized Church of Jesus Christ of Latter Day Saints. As its head they elected Joseph Smith (1832–1914), a son of the founder. He insisted that his father had never practised polygamy, as the majority who went to Utah claimed, and he also rejected some others of the doctrines which the Utah branch of the church promulgated—among them the assertion that as man now is God was, and as God now is man is to be. Impressive physically, he was the dominant figure even into his extreme old age.[6]

What became by far the largest wing of the Church of Jesus Christ of Latter Day Saints had as its major organizer and long-time autocratic head Brigham Young (1801–1877). In 1916 it reported 403,388 members as against 58,941 claimed by the Reorganized Church.[7] Like Joseph Smith, Young was born in Vermont in the restless, drifting element which was common on the frontier and as a child was taken to the "burned-over" region. In his early twenties he became a Methodist. Then, in 1832, he was converted to Mormonism and, practical-minded, seems never to have been troubled by doubts. He had been an effective missionary in the United States and England when the news of Smith's assassination brought him hurrying back to Nauvoo. He rallied the majority to the support of the twelve apostles, of whom he was the head, and in 1847 was elected president of the church. That same year he led over two thousand families on the long covered-wagon journey to the valley of the Great Salt Lake. Here he hoped, remote from other white settlement, to enable the Saints to lead their lives untroubled by the Gentiles. The annexation of California by the United States in 1848, the discovery of gold, the swarming of miners across the continent, and the building of the trans-continental Union Pacific Railway in the 1860's quickly broke in on the hoped-for isolation. But under Brigham Young the Mormons not only survived but also created a notable community. The fertile valleys were occupied, irrigation was developed, and coöperative industries and business enterprises were built up. Missionaries recruited converts in the United States and Europe, largely from tenant farmers and the urban unemployed. Between 1840 and 1877, 85,220 came from Europe to the Mormon settlements in the West, and of these 43,356 were from the British Isles. To aid the movement the Perpetual Emigration Fund was begun. Partly through polygamy, which Young insisted that Joseph Smith had commanded and practised, the membership of the church was further and rapidly augmented. Although he himself had had only a few weeks of formal education, Young built up a comprehensive system of schools. An extraordinarily able executive, he had little interest in the supernatural and discountenanced prophecy, speaking with tongues, and the interpretation of dreams. He himself claimed few revelations.

[6] *Ibid.*, Vol. XVII, pp. 312, 313.
[7] Bureau of the Census, *Religious Bodies, 1916*, Vol. I, p. 20.

We must not take the time to go into the distinctive theological beliefs and social practices of the Mormons which set them aside from the main stream of Protestantism. Indeed, the Mormons would not call themselves Protestants but thought of themselves as a distinct movement, representing the Gospel in its purity interpreted by revelations peculiar to their church. Through Brigham Young especially, but also through other capable leaders, they became a community closely knit by religious, economic, and social ties.[8]

Slightly earlier than the Church of Latter Day Saints, like it emerging from the revival movements in the fore part of the nineteenth century but keeping more closely to the tradition of the Evangelical-Pietist stream of Protestantism, was the General Eldership of the Churches of God in North America. It arose primarily in the German Reformed Church (later called the Reformed Church in the United States), and mainly among those of German descent in Pennsylvania, but it also spread into the Western states. Its founder was John Winebrenner (1797–1860). The son of a prosperous German farmer in Pennsylvania, he was reared in the Reformed Church and became a minister in that body. During his student days, at the age of twenty, he had a deep religious experience of the Pietist kind, and under his preaching revivals broke out. He felt impelled to leave the Reformed Church and to help nourish congregations of those who had been born again. Like those in the awakenings who adopted the simple name of Christian or Disciples of Christ, he wished to restore primitive Christianity. To this end he and his followers adopted for their congregations the designation "Church of God," because they found it repeatedly in the New Testament, and a presbyterian form of church government, for which they believed New Testament precedent also existed. In theology the Churches of God were Arminian rather than Calvinistic. They believed three ordinances to be commanded in the New Testament—the baptism of believers only and by immersion only, the Lord's Supper, and the washing of feet. The latter two were always observed together and in the evening. Through the evangelistic preaching of Winebrenner and his co-labourers the Churches of God multiplied, especially in Maryland and Pennsylvania and then in the Middle West. In 1845, at the instance of Winebrenner, what was known as the General Eldership was constituted, a national representative body which met triennially and

---

[8] Susa Young Gates (one of his daughters) in collaboration with Leah D. Widstoe, *The Life Story of Brigham Young* (New York, The Macmillan Co., 1930, pp. xviii, 388), sympathetic; M. R. Werner, *Brigham Young* (New York, Harcourt, Brace and Co., 1925, pp. xvi, 478), with an effort at objectivity; Ray B. West, Jr., *Kingdom of the Saints. The Story of Brigham Young and the Mormons* (New York, The Viking Press, 1957, pp. xxii, 389), by a former Mormon, sympathetically objective; Gustave O. Larson, *Prelude to the Kingdom: Mormon Desert Conquest: a Chapter in American Coöperative Experience* (Francestown, N.H., Marshall Jones Co., 1947, pp. xiv, 327), especially good on Mormon missionary effort in Europe and the emigration to Utah; M. H. Cannon in *The American Historical Review*, Vol. LVII, pp. 893–908; Robert Glass Cleland and Juanita Brooks, editors, *A Mormon Chronicle: the Diaries of John D. Lee, 1848–1876* (San Marino, Cal., Huntington Library, 2 vols., 1955); William Mulder, *Homeward to Zion. The Mormon Migration from Scandinavia* (Minneapolis, University of Minnesota Press, 1957, pp. xii, 375).

was composed of delegates from each of the annual elderships, regional bodies. The General Eldership of the Churches of God in North America was not large; in 1916 it reported 28,376 members.[9]

In the 1870's a division occurred in the General Eldership of the Churches of God. It was led by D. S. Warner, who was expelled from that body for what it deemed heretical views. He taught entire sanctification as a second work of grace, divine healing, and extreme asceticism. Those who followed him rejected all creeds, recognized "the Lord's people" in all denominations, and sought to bring about the identity, or at least the possible identity, of the visible and the invisible church. The Churches of God which arose from Warner's movement had their headquarters at Anderson, Indiana, and this was generally used to differentiate them from the others bearing that name.[10]

Another of the several bodies bearing the name of Church of God sprang up in the 1880's in the mountains of Tennessee, where frontier conditions persisted which were congenial to the kind of revivalism characteristic of pioneer communities. Its first leader was Richard G. Spurling, Jr. In 1903 A. J. Tomlinson joined the movement, then still small, and in 1909 became its first General Overseer. The name was successively changed from the Christian Union to the Holiness Church and then to the Holiness Church of God. It was part of the holiness or pentecostal movement which arose, largely from Methodism, in the second half of the nineteenth century. In 1914 it numbered only 4,568 members but had begun to send missionaries to other lands. It spread widely after that year—to most of the states and to a number of foreign countries. The majority of its congregations continued to be in the mountains and piedmont regions of the Southern states.[11]

The national holiness movement, of which the Church of God mentioned in the last paragraph was an offshoot, began soon after the Civil War, in part as a reaction against the secularism, immorality, and religious indifference which were accentuated by that struggle. It was one expression of the vitality in Protestantism of the Pietist-Evangelical tradition which responded to the challenge of the revolutionary age. Its spread was chiefly among humble folk of the lower income and educational levels. The first general holiness camp-meeting was held in 1867 in Vineland, New Jersey. At its outset the movement was largely within Methodism, but it soon broke away into groups, which denounced the older churches as cold and apostate. It made much of Christian

---

[9] C. H. Forney, *History of the Churches of God in the United States of North America* (Harrisburg, Publishing House of the Churches of God, 1914, pp. xiv, 933), *passim;* S. G. Yahn, *History of the Churches of God in North America* (Harrisburg, Central Publishing House, 1926, pp. 149), *passim;* Bureau of the Census, *Religious Bodies, 1916,* Vol. I, p. 20, Vol. II, pp. 212, 213.

[10] Mayer, *The Religious Bodies of America,* pp. 331–333; Charles Ewing Brown, *When the Trumpet Sounded. A History of the Church of God Reformation Movement* (Anderson, Ind., The Warner Press, 1951, pp. 402), *passim.*

[11] Charles W. Conn, *Like a Mighty Army Moves the Church of God 1886–1955* (Cleveland, Tenn., Church of God Publishing House, 1955, pp. xxiv, 380), *passim.*

perfection and held it to be attained through an experience known as "the second blessing." Numbers of its adherents "spoke with tongues" and believed in divine healing and the early second coming of Christ.

The largest of the religious bodies emerging from the holiness movement was the Church of the Nazarene. The first church by that name was organized in Los Angeles in 1895. In 1907 the Church of the Nazarene combined with the Association of Pentecostal Churches of America to form the Pentecostal Church of the Nazarene. The Holiness Church of Christ was added in 1908 and the Pentecostal Mission in 1915. In 1919 the word "Pentecostal" was dropped and the denomination became the Church of the Nazarene. It borrowed extensively from Methodism and claimed to be a revival of the original Wesleyan movement. It discountenanced speaking with tongues—a reason for discarding "Pentecostal" from its name.[12]

What was eventually one of the largest of the denominations of American origin, with a nearly world-wide spread and a phenomenal growth, chiefly after 1914, was that of the Seventh Day Adventists. It sprang out of the preaching of William Miller and was a phase of the revivalism which characterized the Evangelical strain pervading the Protestantism of the United States. William Miller (1782–1849) was reared and came to maturity under almost frontier conditions. He was born in Litchfield County, Connecticut, grew up in New York State, became a farmer in Vermont, and then was a farmer in New York not far from the Vermont boundary. He was an avid reader, was converted after a severe inward struggle, and from his study of the Bible became convinced that Christ would return in 1843. In view of their imminence, he urged all to prepare for the second coming and the end of the world. Baptist, Methodist, and Congregational ministers welcomed him to their pulpits and hundreds of his hearers were converted. He was joined by Joshua Vaughan Hines (1805–1895), who, convinced of the truth of his message, helped him to gain a hearing. Miller preached in great tents to perhaps half a million people. He discouraged hysteria and speaking with tongues. When the year 1843 passed without the prophesied advent, Miller reviewed his calculations, decided that he had been in error, and set October 22, 1844, as the date. In many places excitement ran high.[13]

When the day again passed without the expected return of Christ, the movement to which Miller's preaching had given rise did not evaporate. Advent congregations had sprung up in many places and in 1845 a conference was held

---

[12] Clark, *The Small Sects in America*, pp. 92–96; Clarence Eugene Cowen, *A History of the Church of God (Holiness)* (Overland Park, Kan., Herald and Banner Press, 1949, pp. 233), *passim*.

[13] *Dictionary of American Biography*, Vol. IX, p. 60, Vol. XII, pp. 641–643; Clara Endicott Sears, *Days of Delusion* (Boston, Houghton Mifflin Co., 1924, pp. xvi, 262), *passim;* Froom, *The Prophetic Faith of Our Fathers*, Vol. IV, pp. 429 ff.; Nichol, *The Midnight Cry*, pp. 1–260; Francis D. Nichol, "The Growth of the Millerite Legend," in *Church History*, December, 1952.

at which Miller was present and which sought to define the position of his adherents. More than one denomination eventually emerged. The largest were the Advent Christian Church, with 30,597 members reported in 1916,[14] and the Seventh Day Adventists, a much larger body, which in 1916 claimed 79,355 members in the United States.[15]

The Seventh Day Adventists believed that no mistake had been made in regarding 1844 as the predicted date, but that the nature of the event had been misunderstood—that then had come the cleansing of the sanctuary in heaven which was to precede the second advent of Christ. They held the second coming of Christ to be near but did not set a date for it. They were also convinced that the Ten Commandments were binding, the basis of the "investigative judgement" then in progress, and that the fourth commandment enjoined the keeping of the seventh day as the Sabbath. They held that after the second advent and the millennial reign of Christ the final judgement would come, together with the destruction of Satan and his followers, and that sin would be banished from the earth and the righteous dwell there forever. The Seventh Day Adventists observed the Lord's Supper, believer's baptism by immersion, and foot-washing. Negatively they rejected the use of alcohol and tobacco; positively they made much of measures to promote physical health and founded and maintained many sanitariums and hospitals. Tithing was obligatory on their members, and giving to the purposes of the church was encouraged beyond the tithe. The Seventh Day Adventists were ardently missionary and by the close of 1916 were active in ninety-two other countries and in them had already gathered 65,178 members, or only about 14,000 less than in the United States. The church was organized in a fashion which, while respecting the autonomy of the local congregation, made for efficient and united action.[16]

A movement roughly contemporary with the rise of the Seventh Day Adventists but much further from historical Christianity was Spiritualism. Indeed, we would scarcely include it if it had not displayed some religious features, come largely out of a Protestant background, attracted some Protestant clergymen, and given birth to what called themselves churches. It sprang up in the 1840's, flourished in the 1850's, and then, while not disappearing, subsided. Its chief distinguishing feature was its professed communication with the dead. Prominent in it were the sisters, Margaret and Kate Fox (Margaret eventually became

---

[14] Nichol, *The Midnight Cry*, pp. 261 ff.; Bureau of the Census, *Religious Bodies, 1916*, Vol. I, p. 19, Vol. II, pp. 12–17.

[15] Bureau of the Census, *Religious Bodies, 1916*, Vol. I, p. 19.

[16] *Ibid.*, Vol. II, pp. 20–27; Froom, *op. cit.*, Vol. IV, pp. 855 ff.; Matilda Erickson Andross, *Story of the Advent Message* (Washington, Review and Herald Publishing Co., 1926, pp. 352), *passim;* M. Ellsworth Olsen, *A History of the Origin and Progress of Seventh-Day Adventists* (Washington, Review and Herald Publishing Co., 1925, pp. 768), *passim;* Clark, *op. cit.*, pp. 50–56; *Seventh-day Adventists Answer Questions on Doctrine. An Explanation of Certain Major Aspects of Seventh-day Adventist Belief* (Washington, Review and Herald Publishing Co., 1957, pp. 720), *passim.*

a Roman Catholic), Ira Erastus Davenport, and Andrew Jackson Davis. It crossed the Atlantic and had adherents in England.[17] It had likenesses to what appeared in Latin America and reached its crest in the twentieth century, chiefly among nominal Roman Catholics.

A quite different movement but, like the Mormons and the Adventists, out of a New England background was Christian Science, organized in the Church of Christ, Scientist. Its founder was Mary Baker Eddy (1821–1910), whose writings, especially *Science and Health with Key to the Scriptures,* were regarded as authoritative. She was the youngest child of a New Hampshire farmer, was reared in a devout home, and in her teens joined a Congregational church. As a child and young woman she suffered much from what seem to have been nervous disorders and hysteria. Her formal education was very desultory. Her first marriage was ended by the early death of her husband and her second marriage by divorce. Unhappiness, poverty, and invalidism attended most of her first matrimonial years. What she regarded as health came through Phineas Parkhurst Quimby (1802–1866). Also of New England birth and rearing, he had treated disease by mesmerism, then had come to believe that all disease was of mental origin and had worked out a way of dealing with it which he sometimes called Science or Christian Science. Healed, as she believed, for a time she who was later Mrs. Eddy taught his system. Eventually she became independent of him, although always indebted to him for many of her ideas. In 1875 she brought out *Science and Health.* Subsequently she produced many revised editions. In it she maintained that Eternal Mind is the source of all being, that matter is non-existent, that disease is caused by mind alone, and that Eternal Mind was revealed through Jesus Christ, who taught the power to overcome the illusion of sin, sickness, and death. Hence the designation "Christian Science." In 1877 she married Asa Gilbert Eddy, a simple soul of humble origin who adored her. In 1876 she organized the Christian Science Association, followed, in 1879, by the Church of Christ, Scientist. In 1886 the National Christian Science Association was formed and in 1892 Mrs. Eddy founded in Boston the "First Church of Christ, Scientist," known as "the Mother Church." She established schools for training practitioners and taught in the head one. In 1889 she retired to Concord, New Hampshire, but continued to direct the church which she had initiated. Her system gained wide attention and by the time of her death the Church of Christ, Scientist, in its many local units, may have numbered a hundred thousand members. After her death it continued to grow under the direction of the board which succeeded to her power and which exerted its control through the Mother Church.[18]

---

[17] Joseph McCabe, *Spiritualism. A Popular History from 1847* (New York, Dodd, Mead and Co., 1920, pp. 242), *passim;* Arthur Conan Doyle, *The History of Spiritualism* (New York, George H. Doran Co., 2 vols., 1926), Vol. I, pp. 42 ff.; *Dictionary of American Biography,* Vol. V, pp. 84, 105, Vol. VI, pp. 570, 571.

[18] Like a number of others mentioned in the preceding paragraphs, Mary Baker Eddy was a

Divisions developed in the ranks of the Christian Scientists. An outstanding controversial figure was Augusta Emma Simmons Stetson (1842–1928). One of Mrs. Eddy's students, she was commissioned by her to introduce Christian Science to New York City. This she did with such success that First Church in that city erected a great structure and her admirers gave her a palatial residence. She began teaching doctrines, among them celibacy, which Mrs. Eddy and the directors of the Mother Church deemed heretical, her name was stricken from the rolls, and after an adverse vote of the members of First Church in New York City she resigned from that body. Yet she insisted that she was loyal to Mrs. Eddy and *Science and Health,* declared that the directors of the Mother Church were perverting Christian Science, held that Mrs. Eddy would rise again, employed advertising in the newspapers and later radio to publicize her teachings, organized a great chorus to sing what she called spiritual songs, announced her belief in the imminent second coming of Christ, and vigorously attacked the Roman Catholic Church. She had many followers.[19] Mrs. Annie C. Beel, daughter of a clergyman of the Church of England, a convert to Christian Science, differed from the teachings of the existing churches of the movement in England, claimed that she had the true interpretation of Christian Science, and in 1913 founded in London what she called the Central Assembly of the Individual and Universal Church of Christian Science. She held that the Central

---

highly controversial figure. An official life, giving the version of her admirers, is Sibyl Wilbur, *The Life of Mary Baker Eddy* (New York, Concord Publishing Co., 1908, pp. xvi, 425). Another biography with official imprimatur is Lyman P. Powell, *Mary Baker Eddy. A Life Size Portrait* (Boston, The Christian Science Publishing Society, 1950, pp. 350). A critical account, attempting objectivity and based on extensive research, is Ernest Sutherland Bates and John V. Dittemore, *Mary Baker Eddy. The Truth and the Tradition* (New York, Alfred A. Knopf, 1932, pp. 476, xxxiv). Slightly earlier and of a somewhat similar character is Edwin Franden Dakin, *Mrs. Eddy. The Biography of a Virginal Mind* (New York, Charles Scribner's Sons, 1930, pp. x, 563). A careful, critical account is in the *Dictionary of American Biography,* Vol. VI, pp. 7–14. For a late edition of the standard book see Mary Baker Eddy, *Science and Health with Key to the Scriptures* (Boston, Trustees under the Will of Mary Baker G. Eddy, 1906, pp. xii, 700). For a sympathetic study of Christian Science, see Henry W. Steiger, *Christian Science and Philosophy* (New York, Philosophical Library, 1948, pp. xi, 233). Sympathetic accounts of Mrs. Eddy are Irving C. Tomlinson, *Twelve Years with Mary Baker Eddy. Recollections and Experiences* (Boston, The Christian Science Publishing Society, 1945, pp. 227), and William Dana Orcutt, *Mary Baker Eddy and Her Books* (Boston, The Christian Science Publishing Society, 1950, pp. 198). Another favourable account, containing many documents, is Norman Beazley, *The Cross and the Crown. The History of Christian Science* (New York, Duell, Sloan and Pearce, 1952, pp. xi, 664). See also an official publication, Clifford P. Smith, *Historical Sketches from the Life of Mary Baker Eddy and the History of Christian Science* (Boston, The Christian Science Publishing Society, 1941, pp. ix, 268). For a sketch of Phineas Parkhurst Quimby see *Dictionary of American Biography,* Vol. XV, pp. 304, 305. For a brief objective summary of Mrs. Eddy's life based on extensive research, see Charles Braden, *Christian Science Today: Power, Policy, Practice* (Dallas, Southern Methodist University Press, 1958, pp. xvi, 432), pp. 11–41. A sympathetic account, relating Mrs. Eddy to Transcendentalism, especially to Bronson Alcott, is Robert Peel, *Christian Science. Its Encounter with American Culture* (New York, Henry Holt and Co., 1958, pp. xiv, 239).

[19] *Dictionary of American Biography,* Vol. XVII, pp. 595, 596; Augusta E. Stetson, *Reminiscences, Sermons, and Correspondence Proving Adherence to the Principle of Christian Science as Taught by Mary Baker Eddy* (New York, G. P. Putnam's Sons, 1914, pp. xx, 1214), *passim;* Swihart, *Since Mrs. Eddy,* pp. 1–182.

Assembly had the sole right to all the authorized titles and publications of the Mother Church in Boston. Going to the United States, she took advantage of a rift between the board of directors of the Mother Church and the trustees of the Publishing Society (1920-1921) and organized the new Christian Science Parent Church in America.[20]

Other movements arose which were partly from Protestantism and which, like Christian Science, sought freedom from pain and disease and departed more or less widely from historic Christianity. Among them were New Thought, Divine Scientists, and the Unity School of Christianity.[21] Unity began in 1892 when healing came to a man and his wife in Kansas City. Its chief spread was after 1914. It eventually propagated its message through scores of centres and fifty radio stations and with literature in many foreign languages. Its headquarters continued to be in and near Kansas City.[22]

A movement which sprang from the Protestantism of the United States in the nineteenth century and had a phenomenal growth in the twentieth century was Jehovah's Witnesses. The founder was Charles Taze Russell (1852-1916). In his young manhood he was a successful business man. He was reared a Presbyterian and was later a member of a Congregational church and the Young Men's Christian Association. For a time he suffered from doubts and then arrived at the conviction that all of the creeds had elements of truth but also contained error. He came in contact with the Adventists, and out of a study of the Bible arrived at conclusions about human history found, he believed, in that book and confirmed by the Great Pyramid, a structure which he was persuaded was of divine origin, "a miracle in stone." He held that the differences between the teachings of the various denominations could be resolved by a study of the Bible and that he had discovered the clue. He saw in the Bible what he viewed as God's "plan of the ages," centring around man's creation, his redemption in Christ, and the culmination of history. He taught that Christ's invisible second coming had been in 1875 and "the time of the Gentiles" was to end in 1914, and he set forth the dates of other events which he believed a careful study of the Scriptures had enabled him to discern.

Russell first gathered about him a small group in Allegheny, Pennsylvania (1872), which in 1884 organized themselves into a corporation called the Zion Watch Tower Society. In 1909 headquarters were moved to Brooklyn under the designation of the People's Pulpit Association. In England the movement was incorporated as the International Bible Students' Association. In the United States it eventually bore the legal name of the Watch Tower Bible and Tract Society. Through extensive travel, lectures, sermons, and publications Russell spread his message. The writings of the movement were translated into many

[20] Swihart, *op. cit.*, pp. 185 ff.
[21] Clark, *op. cit.*, p. 28.
[22] Marcus Bach in *The Christian Century*, Vol. LXIV, pp. 357-359.

languages. By 1914 the membership seems to have been less than a hundred thousand. Although never formally ordained by any ecclesiastical body, Russell was elected "pastor" of groups which followed his teachings. On his death the leadership of the movement passed to Joseph Franklin Rutherford (1869–1942), a lawyer whom the Witnesses called judge and who earlier in his career seems to have served in that capacity.[23]

An ephemeral movement but one which for some years attracted wide public attention was associated with the name of John Alexander Dowie (1847–1907). Born in Edinburgh and reared in Australia, Dowie had already acquired some fame as a virulent opponent of alcohol and tobacco and a faith healer when in 1888 he came to the United States. In 1896 he organized the Christian Catholic Church in Zion. He and his followers built Zion City, a town of about five thousand, forty-two miles from Chicago. It had no drug stores, physicians' offices, theatres, or dance halls. The community had already run into financial difficulties, internal dissensions, and litigation when death removed the founder from the scene.[24]

Several of the movements which we have mentioned had a very large growth in the twentieth century. Yet, as we have suggested, if all are taken together, in 1914 they constituted only a minority of the Protestants of the United States. Even after their rapid increase subsequent to 1914, by mid-century they still were merely a fraction, although a substantial fraction, of those in America who had connexions with Protestant churches. The fact that they were indigenous, that they had their origin in the nineteenth century, and that most of them continued to grow was evidence of vitality in Christianity. To those familiar with the history of that faith, about them was something reminiscent of the movements in the Middle Ages and during the period of the Protestant and Catholic Reformations which arose from the abounding vigour in Christianity—some of which remained with the Catholic Church and some of which Rome branded as heresies.

New Religious Movements, for the Most Part Undenominational, Emerge from Protestantism

Not only did new denominations emerge from the Protestantism of the United States, but other movements also developed, most of them to meet special aspects of the challenge of the revolutionary age. Some had their origin

[23] Milton Stacey Czatt, *The International Bible Students: Jehovah's Witnesses* (Scottdale, Pa., Mennonite Press, 1933, pp. 44), *passim;* Herbert Hewitt Stroup, *The Jehovah's Witnesses* (New York, Columbia University Press, 1945, pp. vii, 180), *passim;* Marley Cole, *Jehovah's Witnesses: The New World Society* (New York, Vantage Press, 1955, pp. 229), *passim,* especially the appendices. In Cole, *op. cit.,* pp. 189 ff., see the documentary evidence that President Dwight D. Eisenhower's parents were once River Brethren and then became Jehovah's Witnesses.

[24] Arthur Newcomb, *Dowie. Anointed of the Lord* (New York, The Century Co., 1930, pp. 403), *passim; Dictionary of American Biography,* Vol. V, pp. 413, 414.

on the other side of the Atlantic but took on major dimensions in the United States. Others rose in the United States.

Among those which had their beginnings in Europe were the Sunday School, the Salvation Army, the Young Men's Christian Association, and the Young Women's Christian Association. We have already spoken of the great expansion of the Sunday Schools and of their important share in the Protestantism of the United States, especially that of the older American stock.

The Salvation Army, begun in London in 1865 by William Booth, was not introduced to the United States until 1880. It then came through a group from England. It was first in New York City and quickly expanded to Philadelphia and Newark, New Jersey. The year before, a family of English immigrants who had been committed to the Army before coming to America had begun work in Philadelphia after the manner of the Salvation Army and asked Booth for official recognition and support. Booth felt that the resources of the Army were as yet inadequate for the clamant needs in England and that foreign undertakings would spread them too thin. But if the movement was being inaugurated in the United States, he believed it imperative to keep it under his direction. The opening in the growing cities for an enterprise such as the Salvation Army was clear. The classes to which the Army appealed were not being reached by the churches. Here and there were rescue missions which sought to grapple with the problem, but not by the methods Booth was employing.

The Salvation Army had a rapid expansion in the United States. Many Americans offered themselves as officers and by February, 1882, they equalled in numbers those sent from England. As in England, opposition was encountered. Buckets of water, rotten eggs, and dead cats were thrown at the Salvationists in their street meetings and parades. Now and again members of the Army were haled into court for their street preaching.

Early a schism arose in the effort to make the Salvation Army in the United States independent of Booth and purely American. Booth countered by sending his son Ballington to take command, together with Ballington's wife Maud. Ballington became estranged from his father in 1896, resigned, and with his wife organized the Volunteers of America. Yet for nearly fifty years the branch of the Salvation Army in the United States was under the command of one or another of William Booth's children.

In time opposition was overcome. The Army branched out in a number of directions and in many cities and became a recognized and important feature of the American religious scene, partly in evangelism and partly in social services among the urban underprivileged.[25]

[25] U. S. Department of Commerce, Bureau of the Census, *Religious Bodies: 1926,* Vol. II, pp. 1390, 1391; Herbert A. Wisbey, Jr., *Soldiers without Swords: A History of the Salvation Army*

It was in the United States that the Young Men's Christian Association had its most extensive development. As we have seen,[26] the first Young Men's Christian Association was organized in London in 1844. One of the fruits of the Evangelical movement, it sought the spiritual, social, and intellectual welfare of the young men of white-collar, middle- or lower-middle-class status who were being employed, largely as clerks, in a city which was burgeoning through the Industrial Revolution. Knowledge of the new movement spread to the United States, partly through visitors to the World's Fair of 1851 in the Crystal Palace in London. Early in 1852 Young Men's Christian Associations sprang up, first in Boston and then in several other cities, notably New York and Washington. Almost simultaneously Associations appeared in Canada. In 1854 a convention gathered in Buffalo in which the Confederation of Young Men's Christian Associations of the United States and the British Provinces was formed. Conventions met annually until 1877 and then biennially until 1901. An International Committee developed, with an Executive Committee. The latter's headquarters were soon established in New York City. Its first employed secretary was Robert Weidensall (1836–1922) and its second employed secretary and its first general secretary was Richard Cary Morse (1841–1926), a nephew of the inventor of the electric telegraph. Each remained with the International Committee for a long lifetime. By 1894, 1,400 Associations were in existence in the United States and Canada, with more than a quarter-million members, 1,200 general secretaries (secretary being the name given to the employed officers), 297 buildings, and property value at $14,694,400. The challenge which the Associations endeavoured to meet was urgent. In 1886 it was said that only 5 per cent. of the young men were church members, that perhaps 15 per cent. regularly attended church, and that 75 per cent. never attended church.[27]

The Young Men's Christian Association in the United States was primarily a lay institution, representing the Evangelical tradition of the Protestantism of the older American stock. Both Weidensall and Morse had been trained in college and theological seminary, but neither was ordained. While clergy were active in the Associations, the direction was in the hands of laymen, largely business and professional men. Voting was limited to members of Evangelical churches. The Associations were in no sense a new denomination. In this respect they differed from the Salvation Army, which in effect became an ecclesiastical body. They sought to win young men to membership in the churches and to enable Protestants to collaborate in meeting the needs of youth. They drew their membership from many different denominations. Debates on doctrinal issues were discouraged. The direction was mainly by men closely allied to the business and

in the United States (New York, The Macmillan Co., 1955, pp. viii, 242), *passim;* Abell, *The Urban Impact on American Protestantism 1865–1900*, pp. 118–136.

26 Volume II, Chapter XXVIII.

27 *Christian Union*, December 16, 1886, quoted in S. Wirt Wiley, *History of Y.M.C.A.-Church Relations in the United States* (New York, Association Press, 1944, pp. xii, 227), p. 20.

industrial interests of the day, and the YMCA drew its financial support mostly from men, many of them wealthy, whose incomes were from the economic system that arose from the Industrial Revolution and the *laissez-faire* "free enterprise" principle. On social and economic issues the YMCA tended to be conservative.

The programme of the YMCA had a striking development. At the outset it was primarily evangelistic and for years emphasized conversion of an Evangelical type. As we have seen, Dwight L. Moody was an officer of the Chicago YMCA. He also responded to appeals to help elsewhere, giving evangelistic addresses in state and international conventions and raising money for buildings. Early, with the New York YMCA as the creative and radiating centre, what was called the four-fold programme was devised, with buildings designed to carry it out. The YMCA was conceived as a "home away from home" for the young men flooding into the cities that were growing as a phase of the revolutionary age. The programme was intended to develop the spiritual, physical, social, and intellectual aspects of well-rounded manhood. Eventually the symbol was adopted of an inverted triangle, with spirit at the top, supported by the other two legs, mind and body. For the "spiritual" side, evangelistic and other religious meetings were held and Bible classes were conducted. On the physical side buildings containing gymnasiums were erected, wholesome sports and physical education were promoted, and basket ball and volley ball, the former especially soon to have world-wide popularity, were invented. On the social side provision was made for fellowship, sex education was undertaken, and the buildings had rooms and restaurants for residents and transients. To further the intellectual interests, reading rooms and libraries were maintained and educational classes multiplied, largely in the evenings for young men and boys employed during the day.

The Young Men's Christian Associations branched out into a number of fields. They made much of work for boys and conducted summer camps for them, with "wholesome recreation without temptation" as their object. They promoted the Boy Scout movement. Associations were organized among Indians and more extensively among Negroes. During the Civil War and the Spanish-American War men under arms were cared for. After the latter conflict the International Committee inaugurated an army and navy department, and in scores of places in the United States and overseas centres were maintained for the men in uniform. Associations multiplied for men employed by the railroads and were equipped with suitable buildings: by 1911 they numbered 230 with 518 secretaries. Special programmes and facilities were created for men in industry. The effort was made to extend the YMCA to towns and rural areas.[28]

[28] For the history of the YMCA in the United States the authoritative, official account, based on careful and objective research, is Hopkins, *History of the Y.M.C.A. in North America.* See also,

A phase of the YMCA which was to have far-reaching effects was the Student Department of the International Committee. Associations were early formed on the campuses of a number of colleges and universities, and in 1877 the Student Department was set up. Its first secretary was Luther D. Wishard (1854–1925), but its chief creator was John Raleigh Mott (1865–1955). Born in the state of New York, Mott was reared in a small town in Iowa. In Cornell University he was profoundly moved by J. E. K. Studd, who, as we have said, deeply impressed by Moody, had been induced to travel among the colleges and universities in the United States. While at Cornell, Mott was president of the Association and attended the first student conference held (1886) at the instance of the Student Department on the campus of Moody's school at Mt. Hermon, Massachusetts. He was the major organizer and promoter of the Foreign Work of the International Committee and eventually was general secretary of the International Committee, general secretary of the National Council of YMCA's and in his later years honorary life president of the World's Committee and World's Alliance of the YMCA's. A prodigious traveller, he was an evangelist to students in many lands. Mott was chiefly responsible for the formation of the World's Student Christian Federation (1895), was its first general secretary and then its chairman, was the creator and first chairman of the International Missionary Council, and was the first honorary president of the World Council of Churches. He was also long chairman of the executive committee of the Student Volunteer Movement for Foreign Missions, which arose from the memorable conference at Mt. Hermon. An extraordinarily able administrator, with a commanding platform presence as presiding officer and in public address, Mott planned and dreamed in terms of the conquest of the world, not by the United States, the Occident, the YMCA, or any one church, but by and for Christ. To that end he sought to win students to a Christian commitment, for in them he thought that he saw the future leaders of the nations. A friend of statesmen, men of affairs, and ecclesiastics of many lands, he had as his single aim the spread of the Christian faith and sought to unite Christians of many denominations and confessions in the achievement of his mankind-embracing vision. Although widely read, he was not a profound scholar or theologian. He had a simple Christian faith, believed implicitly in prayer, and was a constant student of the Bible. An activist, he was representative of the American Protestant layman of his day at his best and as such had the confidence of his fellow laymen.[29]

Partly under Mott's leadership, for the generation which spanned the closing years of the nineteenth century the Student YMCA's provided the chief channels

---

of the very extensive literature, Richard C. Morse, *My Life with Young Men. Fifty Years in the Young Men's Christian Association* (New York, Association Press, 1918, pp. xiv, 547).

[29] Mathews, *John R. Mott, World Citizen, passim; The Papers and Addresses of John R. Mott, passim.*

for voluntary Protestant activities by men on the college and university campuses of the United States and Canada. Under them religious meetings were held, Bible study classes carried on, service rendered on the campuses and in the surrounding communities, and summer conferences for students conducted.[30]

The YMCA's of the United States, in collaboration with those of Canada, had world-wide repercussions. Largely through men recruited in the Student Associations, they stimulated the creation and growth of YMCA's in many lands in Asia, Africa, Latin America, and Europe which were self-governing, mainly self-propagating, and increasingly self-supporting.[31] The Mt. Hermon conference (1886) was the birthplace of the Student Volunteer Movement for Foreign Missions. That movement recruited thousands of young men and women for service overseas under numbers of Protestant denominations and was responsible for the birth of similar movements on the other side of the Atlantic and in at least two countries in Asia.[32] Through students who came to their conferences from many lands and through their part in bringing into being the World's Student Christian Federation (1895) the Student YMCA's made contributions to the Ecumenical Movement which became especially notable in the twentieth century.

The Young Women's Christian Association, like the Young Men's Christian Association born in England of the Evangelical spirit, while not numerically or financially as strong as the brother movement, also attained its largest dimensions in the United States. There it arose out of the "prayer-meeting revival" of 1857–1858 in New York City. In 1858 a Ladies' Christian Association was organized in the chapel of New York University. From the beginning, its purpose was to "seek out especially young women of the operative class," namely, those employed in the business and industries of the growing cities, to aid them in finding employment and suitable rooming places, to gather them into Bible classes, and to "surround them with Christian influences." In other words, it endeavoured to do for young women what the YMCA was doing for young men. It was incorporated in 1866 as the Ladies' Christian Union. The first organization in the United States to bear the name of the Young Women's Christian Association came into being in Boston in 1866, consciously inspired by the example of the Young Men's Christian Association. In succeeding years what were usually called Young Women's Christian Associations sprang up in a number of cities. Boarding homes were an early major concern of the Association and Bible classes were stressed. Reading rooms and libraries were

[30] Shedd, *Two Centuries of Student Christian Movements*, pp. 103–186, 238 ff.

[31] Latourette, *World Service, passim.*

[32] Shedd, *op. cit.*, pp. 253–276; Mott, *Papers and Addresses*, Vol. I, *passim*; Ruth Wilder Braisted, *In This Generation. The Story of Robert P. Wilder* (New York, The Friendship Press, 1941, pp. xvi, 205), *passim*; Robert P. Wilder, *The Great Commission. The Missionary Response of the Student Volunteer Movements in North America and Europe: Some Personal Reminiscences* (London, Oliphants, c. 1936, pp. 115), *passim*.

also common. In the 1880's gymnasiums were introduced. That same decade saw the beginnings of travelers' aid departments, in part suggested by an earlier English example. Student YWCA's paralleled Student YMCA's: in the early stages some were assisted by Wishard. In 1886 the National Association of Young Women's Christian Associations was organized for the promotion of the social, physical, intellectual, and spiritual life of young women—the four-fold programme already formulated by the Young Men's Christian Associations. The World's Young Women's Christian Association was formed in 1894 with headquarters in London. What was accounted the first convention of Young Women's Christian Associations of the United States of America convened in 1906. The connexions between the men's and the women's movements were close. Thus adjoining buildings for the two were often erected; Mrs. John V. Farwell, Jr., the first president of the National Association, was of a family prominent in the Chicago YMCA; Annie M. Reynolds, the first secretary of the World's YWCA, was the sister of James M. Reynolds, who had been active in the Student YMCA; Rebecca F. Morse, of the national organization, was a sister of Richard C. Morse; and Grace H. Dodge, outstanding in the National YWCA, was from a family that for three generations was a mainstay of the YMCA in New York City and on the national scene.[33]

A set of movements which, like the Salvation Army and the Young Men's and Young Women's Christian Associations, were sprung from the Evangelical wing of Protestantism and directed their efforts to the challenge presented by the growing cities were city missions and rescue missions. Like the Salvation Army but unlike the YMCA and the YWCA, they sought to reach the flotsam and jetsam and to prevent human wreckage among the lowest-income classes of the inner cities. Unlike the other movements, they were not closely coördinated in national organizations but at best were loosely associated with one another and then not on any inclusive basis. They had parallels on the other side of the Atlantic, but for the most part they issued spontaneously from the Evangelical tide. Any comprehensive account or even summary would prolong our pages unduly, and it is doubtful whether the sources could be uncovered for a complete story. We must content ourselves with a few examples.

As we have seen,[34] city missions for the underprivileged in the slums of the great cities were deeply indebted to David Nasmith (1799–1839). How far the various city missions in the United States were due directly to him we do not know. We hear of city mission societies in New York and Brooklyn.[35] One

[33] Elizabeth Wilson, *Fifty Years of Work among Young Women, 1866–1916. A History of Young Women's Christian Associations in the United States of America* (New York, National Board of the Young Women's Christian Associations of the United States of America, 1916, pp. 402), *passim;* Mary S. Sims, *The Natural History of a Social Institution—the Young Women's Christian Association* (New York, The Woman's Press, 1936, pp. x, 251), *passim;* Shedd, *op. cit.,* pp. 187 ff.

[34] Volume II, Chapters XXVIII, XXXI.

[35] A. H. McKinney, *Triumphant Christianity. The Life and Work of Lucy Seaman Bainbridge*

began in Boston in 1816 as the Boston Society for the Moral and Religious Instruction of the Poor and in a few years became the Boston City Mission Society. By 1878 it had divided the city into districts and was employing twenty missionaries. It reported conversions and the gathering of children into Sunday Schools.[36]

Of the rescue missions we can take the time to mention only three. Of these Jerry McAuley (1839–1884) was the founder of two. A native of Ireland, reared a Roman Catholic, he had an unfortunate home background, came to the United States at the age of thirteen, lived in New York City, became a river thief, and at nineteen was sentenced to fifteen years in Sing-Sing for a crime of which he was innocent. While in prison he was converted in an Evangelical fashion, was pardoned, on being discharged reëntered the world without friends, and fell again into evil ways as an alcoholic, as a passer of counterfeit money, and once more as a river thief. But renewing his Christian faith, partly through the New York City Mission and Tract Society, after other relapses and restorations, he began (1872) a mission on Water Street in one of the most vice-ridden sections of the city. Later he started an additional mission, Cremorne, in another sodden part of the metropolis. After his early death, from tuberculosis, the missions were continued. Samuel H. Hadley (1842–1906), an alcoholic, converted in the McAuley Cremorne Mission, for twenty years (1886–1906) was superintendent of the Water Street Mission, travelled widely on evangelistic trips, and won his brother, H. H. Hadley. The latter began sixty-two rescue missions and founded the Blue Button Army for total abstinence "for Christ's sake" which enrolled over 600,000 members.[37] The Pacific Garden Mission, said to have been the first rescue mission in the West, was begun in 1877 in one of the worst districts of Chicago. Its founders, Colonel and Mrs. George R. Clarke, were highly educated, moved in the "best" social circles, but felt constrained by their Christian faith to give themselves to the human wreckage in the rapidly growing chief city of the Middle West. Among the converts of the mission was Billy Sunday.[38]

A quite different movement was the Young People's Society of Christian Endeavour, founded by Francis E. Clark (1851–1927). Of old New England stock, Clark became pastor of a mission in Portland, Maine, and built it up to a large Congregational church. While there, in 1881 he began, as a way of

(New York, Fleming H. Revell Co., 1932, pp. 206), *passim*, and especially p. 53 ff.; *Dave Ranney, or Thirty Years on the Bowery. An Autobiography* (New York, American Tract Society, 1910, pp. 205), *passim*.

[36] *Annual Reports of the City Mission Society of Boston*, earlier *The Boston Society for the Moral and Religious Instruction of the Poor*, 1817 ff.

[37] R. M. Offord, editor, *Jerry McAuley, An Apostle to the Lost* (New York, American Tract Society, 7th ed., 1907, pp. x, 304), *passim*; Samuel H. Hadley, *Down on Water Street. A Story of Sixteen Years Life and Work in Water Street Mission, a Sequel to the Life of Jerry McAuley* (Chicago, Fleming H. Revell Co., 1906, pp. 254), *passim*.

[38] Carl F. H. Henry, *The Pacific Garden Mission. A Doorway to Heaven* (Grand Rapids, Mich., Zondervan Publishing House, 3rd ed., 1942, pp. 144), *passim*.

enlisting youth, the Young People's Society of Christian Endeavour. It had been partly inspired by slightly earlier movements to attract young people, notably a Young People's Association in a Presbyterian church in Brooklyn. Clark's example was contagious. Within a year six other societies were formed and a convention was held. A year later 53 societies were counted with more than 2,600 members. The movement met an obvious need. It spread to many denominations and in a single year as many as 5,000 societies and 250,000 members were added. In 1887 a society was organized in England and in 1888 one in Australia. By 1914 Christian Endeavour was found in several countries in Europe, Asia, and Africa and was said to have 5,000,000 members in more than 100,000 societies. It was mainly in denominations of British provenance and in the United States, chiefly in those which served the older stock.

Christian Endeavour had as its guiding principles "confession of Christ, service for Christ, fellowship with Christ's people, and loyalty to Christ's church." The members covenanted to strive to do whatever Christ would have them do, to pray and read the Bible every day, to be loyal to the Church, attending her regular Sunday and week-day services, and to be present at every Christian Endeavour prayer meeting and to take some part aside from singing.

Various forms of activity sprang from Christian Endeavour—such as "life-work recruits" for full-time service with the churches, "fresh-air" summer camps for women and children in the cities, religious services and Bible classes in hospitals, prisons, and on ships, campaigns for temperance and against vice, and the "Tenth Legion" of those who pledged themselves to give not less than a tithe of their income to "Christian work." Officers and committees gave organized form to the activities, and conventions were held—county, state, national, and international. To coördinate the whole, the United Society of Christian Endeavour was formed for the United States (1885) and in 1895 the World's Christian Endeavour Union was created, both with Clark as the president.[39]

Here was an expression of the strain of Evangelicalism which was strong in the Protestantism of the older stock in the United States and of English Nonconformity. The rapid growth of Christian Endeavour was among those who were moulded by that Evangelicalism in the form in which it existed in the latter part of the nineteenth century.

Christian Endeavour continued into the twentieth century, but by 1914 it had passed its peak, and other movements, largely denominational, partly inspired by it, were carrying on the vision which had given it birth, and, when taken together, in larger dimensions. What was said to have been the most successful of the denominational movements in enlisting young people was the

[39] Weigle, *American Idealism*, p. 204; Francis Edward Clark, *The Christian Endeavour Manual* (Boston, United Society of Christian Endeavor, rev. ed., 1925, pp. 284), *passim;* Eugene Francis Clark, *A Son's Portrait of Dr. Francis E. Clark* (Boston, The Williston Press, 1930, pp. xix, 255), *passim;* R. P. Anderson, *The Story of Christian Endeavor* (Boston, United Society of Christian Endeavor, c. 1914, pp. 48), *passim.*

Epworth League, of the Methodist Episcopal Church. It came into being in 1889 and arose from the amalgamation of several movements within that church which had been begun earlier in the decade and which were preceded by at least one effort in the 1870's. Its local units maintained weekly prayer meetings and furthered private prayer, religious meditation, the study of the Bible, and various forms of philanthropic service. It was closely associated with the growth of the deaconess movement in the Methodist Episcopal Church.[40] The Luther League of America, organized in 1895, for a time embraced youth from most of the Lutheran churches. However, although when meeting in conferences its members wished a comprehensive ecclesiastical body which would embrace all the Lutherans in the United States, several Lutheran churches withdrew and formed their own youth leagues. Thereupon the Luther League of America became an organ solely of the United Lutheran Church.[41] In 1893, before the formation of the Luther League of America, the Walther League had been organized in the Missouri Synod. It had been preceded by organizations for young men and young women, some of which began in the 1840's and 1850's. Its growth was slow: in 1917 its local societies numbered less than three hundred. But after that year it had a rapid expansion.[42]

MOVEMENTS AND ORGANIZATIONS DEVELOP IN THE ROMAN CATHOLIC CHURCH

A striking feature of the record of Christianity in the United States was the number of organizations and movements which flourished within the Roman Catholic Church. Some were of European provenance—orders and congregations which were introduced and took root. Others were of American origin, some of them congregations of a traditional kind and others quite novel and adapted to the American scene. While many of them were initiated by immigrants, the fact that they grew, some of them luxuriantly, and that others were created by native Americans was evidence of abounding vitality. This was the more remarkable in view of the poverty of the large majority of the Roman Catholics and the struggle they were having in establishing themselves and making a living in the land in which they were new arrivals.

The proliferation of movements within the Roman Catholic Church in the United States was paralleled, as we have seen,[43] by what was taking place in several countries in Europe, especially in France, Italy, Belgium, and Germany. But, as we have also seen, Spain and Portugal were relatively lacking in them, and, as we are to note in a later chapter, the Roman Catholic Church in Latin America presented a striking dearth of either a revival of old orders and

---

[40] Dan B. Brummitt, *Epworth League Methods* (Cincinnati, Jennings and Graham, 1906, pp. 463), *passim*.

[41] *Golden Jubilee. The Luther League of America. An Historical Sketch 1895–1945* (Philadelphia, Muhlenberg Press, 1945, pp. 64), *passim*.

[42] Baepler, *A Century of Grace*, p. 210.

[43] Volume I, Chapter VIII.

congregations or the appearance of new congregations and movements.

So numerous were the orders and congregations which found fertile soil, and so many were the new congregations and movements which sprang up in the Roman Catholic Church in the United States, that we must not take the space even to name them all. Several have already been mentioned. We will attempt a comprehensive picture and will single out a few, partly although not entirely at random, and will include among them some to which we have already called attention.

Of the orders and congregations of men (not including the congregations of lay brothers) at least forty-one had established themselves in the United States before 1914. Only four appear to have been of American origin—the Paulist Fathers, St. Joseph's Society of the Sacred Heart (for missions among the Negroes), the Maryknoll Fathers (the Catholic Foreign Mission Society of America), and the Society of the Atonement. Of the four, St. Joseph's Society of the Sacred Heart was begun (1871) by members of a foreign congregation, the Mill Hill fathers. Not until 1892 did it become independent of Mill Hill.[44] The Society of the Atonement, as we have suggested, was begun in the Protestant Episcopal Church by Lewis Wattson. In 1909 he and his society, with their seat at Graymoor, were received into the Roman Catholic Church.

The others had their origin in one or another of the countries of Europe. As might have been expected, the largest were the Benedictine order (its oldest congregation, the Cassinese, with its first arch-abbey at Latrobe, Pennsylvania, founded in 1855 and with abbeys in twelve other states by 1914); the several branches of the Franciscans (one of them with at least seven provinces in various parts of the country before 1914, with the Conventuals represented by two provinces before that year and the Third Order with a province founded in 1910); the Jesuits (with three provinces before 1914); the Oblates of Mary Immaculate (with two provinces before 1914); the Vincentians (Congregation of the Mission or Lazarists, with two provinces and a vice-province before 1914); the Dominicans (with three provinces before 1914); and the Redemptorists (with two provinces before that year).[45] In 1848 the first permanent Trappist foundation was made, in Kentucky, by French members of the order.[46]

The first continuing Franciscan foundation in the Eastern states was due to the munificence of Nicholas Devereux (1791–1855). He came to the United States in his teens, acquired wealth, and made possible the initial party (1855), all Italians. On a tract of land near Allegheny, sixty miles from Buffalo, they established a monastery, church, and seminary and from that centre carried on

[44] *The Catholic Encyclopedia*, Vol. VIII, p. 521.
[45] *The Official Catholic Directory, 1940*, pp. 721–734. On the beginnings of the Cassinese congregation see Colman J. Barry in *The Catholic Historical Review*, Vol. XLI, pp. 272–296. See also in this connexion Ellis, *Documents of American Catholic History*, pp. 286 ff.
[46] Ellis, *American Catholicism*, pp. 132, 133; Ellis, *Documents of American Catholic History*, pp. 301, 302.

extensive missionary activities. A Hungarian Franciscan had already (1844) opened a church in New York City. Expelled as a stage in the *Kulturkampf,* German Franciscans came (1875) from Fulda and after several vicissitudes found homes in Paterson, New Jersey, and in New York State in the foothills of the Adirondacks.[47]

Something of the early course of the Dominicans is seen in the record of Matthew A. O'Brien (1804–1871). A native of Ireland, O'Brien came to the United States in 1826, studied for the priesthood in Kentucky, was admitted to the Order of Preachers, served first in Kentucky, then in Ohio, where he became provincial, and later was transferred to London, Ontario, to inaugurate his order there and to help care for a pioneer field of his church.[48]

By 1914 the congregations of brothers (as distinguished from the orders and congregations which included priests), most of whom devoted themselves to teaching, numbered at least seven, all but three of foreign origin. The largest were the Brothers of Christian Instruction, the Brothers of St. Francis Xavier, the Brothers of the Sacred Heart, the Marist Brothers, and the Brothers of Christian Schools.[49] The Brothers of Christian Schools, or Christian Brothers, were founded in France by John Baptist de Salle in the seventeenth century. Their pioneer contingent arrived in 1817 at the invitation of Bishop Du Bourg of New Orleans. They had their initial headquarters and their first school south of St. Louis. However, the enterprise ran into difficulties and disintegrated. In 1837 the Christian Brothers established themselves in Montreal. It was from Canada that the contingent came, in 1846, which began the continuing life of their congregation in the United States. They opened a school in Baltimore in 1848. From that humble beginning they expanded and in 1948 had 1,582 brothers teaching 43,000 youths in 90 schools from New York to San Francisco.[50] The three of American origin were the Franciscan Brothers of Brooklyn, founded in 1858, the Maryknoll Missioners of the Catholic Foreign Mission Society of America, and the Brothers of the Holy Infancy and Youth of Jesus, founded in 1853 by John Timan, the first Bishop of Buffalo, to care for destitute and wayward boys and succeeded by the Society of Our Lady of Victory, founded by Nelson H. Baker in 1882 to serve destitute Roman Catholic children.[51]

Congregations of women were much more numerous than orders and congregations of men. As was true of those of men, the majority had their origin in Europe and were introduced by foreigners. Some began in Canada. Most of

[47] Callahan, *Medieval Francis in Modern America, passim.*

[48] Victor F. O'Daniel, *An American Apostle. The Very Reverend Matthew Anthony O'Brien, O.P.* (Washington, The Dominicana, 1928, pp. xvi, 341), *passim.*

[49] *The Official Catholic Directory, 1940,* pp. 735, 736.

[50] Angelus Gabriel, *The Christian Brothers in the United States 1848–1948* (New York, The Declan X. McMullen Co., 1948, pp. xviii, 700), *passim.*

[51] On the last of these congregations, see *The Catholic Encyclopedia,* Vol. VII, p. 418.

them were occupied either in teaching or the care of the sick, or both. Some were for the protection or restoration of girls in distress. A few were of cloistered nuns who gave themselves to prayer and the perpetual adoration of the Blessed Sacrament. By the year 1914 at least a hundred congregations were in existence which had been introduced from abroad and at least fifty had been organized in the United States.[52]

Of the women's congregations of foreign origin, one of the earliest to branch out into the United States was the Discalced Carmelites. Its mother house was instituted in Baltimore in 1790 and was followed by many others.[53] The Sisters of Charity of Refuge, also called the Good Shepherd, founded in France for the preservation and reclamation of young girls, was introduced to the United States in 1855.[54] The Sisters of the Presentation of the Blessed Virgin Mary originated in Ireland in 1777, sent their first contingent to San Francisco in 1854, and spread very widely.[55] The Sisters of the Third Order of St. Dominic were introduced to the United States in 1822. In time they had a number of mother houses and general mother houses, chiefly from the Middle West to the west coast.[56] The Ursulines, for the education of girls, were first in New Orleans in 1727 and were later represented from the east to the west coast.[57] The Visitation Nuns, founded by Francis de Sales, with a combination of moderation in physical discipline and the intense cultivation of the spiritual life, were contemplatives, giving themselves to prayer. They also engaged in teaching. Their first foundation in the United States was in Georgetown, in 1799. In the twentieth century they, too, were to be found from the east to the west coast, some cloistered and others as teachers.[58] The Sisters of Mercy were begun by Catherine McAuley in Dublin about 1827 or 1831 to minister to the poor in Ireland and to the poverty-stricken Irish in the urban slums of England and Scotland. They early spread to the United States and before they had seen a century were established in many centres, mostly in the North-east, but also as far west as San Francisco. They had schools and orphanages and served in hospitals. They were divided into diocesan groups, but in 1905 Pius X had expressed the wish to have them brought together under a general administration. This was not accomplished until 1929: in that year the thirty-nine mother houses in the United States were joined in a union.[59] A smaller enterprise was

[52] *The Official Catholic Directory, 1940*, pp. 737–768.
[53] *Ibid.*, p. 739.
[54] *Ibid.*, p. 742.
[55] *Ibid.*, p. 752.
[56] *Ibid.*, p. 760.
[57] *Ibid.*, p. 767; *The Catholic Encyclopedia*, Vol. XV, pp. 228, 229.
[58] *The Official Catholic Directory, 1940*, p. 767; *The Catholic Encyclopedia*, Vol. XV, pp. 481–483.
[59] *The Official Catholic Directory, 1940*, pp. 753–755; Mary Loretto Costello, *The Sisters of Mercy of Maryland 1855–1930* (St. Louis, B. Herder Book Co., 1931, pp. xvi, 249), *passim;* Mary Eulalia Herron, *The Sisters of Mercy in the United States 1843–1928* (New York, The Macmillan Co., 1929, pp. xvii, 434), *passim.*

that of the Religious of the Sacred Heart of Mary, begun in France in 1849, at Béziers. Devoted to teaching, the congregation was introduced to the United States in 1877. At first its growth was slow, but in 1903 Johanna Butler (1860–1940), Marie Joseph in religion, was sent to take charge. A native of Ireland, after having her novitiate at Béziers she was assigned to Portugal and then transferred to the United States. In the latter country she developed a school on the Hudson at Marymount. Eventually she was made the superior general of the entire congregation.[60]

Of the numerous congregations of women which sprang up in the United States the oldest was founded by that remarkable convert, Elizabeth Ann Seton (1774–1821). Reared by a wise and distinguished father—for her mother died when she was three—she was happily married, had several children, and, while still a Protestant, living in New York City, had led in the formation of the Society for the Relief of Poor Widows and Children (1797). Widowed, she became a Roman Catholic. Although now in straitened financial circumstances, she opened a school for girls in Baltimore (1808) and founded the Sisters of St. Joseph (1809), with headquarters at Emmitsburg. In 1812 she adopted the rule of Vincent de Paul, and the congregation became known as the Sisters of Charity of St. Joseph. Through it she inaugurated the first Roman Catholic orphanage, the first Roman Catholic hospital, the first Roman Catholic maternity hospital, and the first parish school in the country. At the invitation of bishops she sent the sisters to many parts of the land to conduct parish schools and was the real foundress of the parochial schools in the United States. Yet in spite of her prodigious labours and a heavy correspondence she took time to lead a life of recollection and prayer—in this combination resembling many other women of outstanding sanctity in both the Roman Catholic Church and Protestantism.[61]

Rose Hawthorne Lathrop, daughter of Nathanial Hawthorne, whose conversion we have already noted, founded the Servants of Relief for Incurable Cancer of the Third Order of St. Dominic. She began in a small way caring for the desperately poor who were in advanced stages of the dread disease. Her first house was in New York City, on Water Street, in the neighbourhood of Jerry McAuley's mission. In 1899 she became a Dominican tertiate. That year she acquired more suitable quarters in another part of the city and called it St. Rose's Free Home for Incurable Cancer, naming it for the first American saint, Rose of Lima. In 1907 better property was obtained, Rosary Hill.[62]

[60] Katherine Burton, *Mother Butler of Marymount* (New York, Longmans, Green and Co., 1944, pp. xi, 290).

[61] Katherine Burton, *His Dear Persuasion. The Life of Elizabeth Ann Seton* (London, Longmans, Green and Co., 1940, pp. xi, 304), *passim; Dictionary of American Biography,* Vol. XVI, p. 596; Ellis, *Documents of American Catholic History,* pp. 193, 194.

[62] James J. Walsh, *Mother Alphonsa Rose Hawthorne Lathrop* (New York, The Macmillan Co., 1930, pp. 275), *passim.*

Many organizations of laity sprang up, with clerical approval and usually with clerical supervision. Confraternities existed for various purposes—for example, one of women to teach the catechism to children attending the public schools.[63] We hear of Catholic city federations of laymen for common action on matters of general concern, such as the better public observance of Sunday, protesting against the anti-clerical legislation in France, raising funds for particular objects, and finding homes for dependent Catholic children.[64] Catholic Ladies Aid Societies paralleled similar organizations in Protestant churches, and one of them made itself responsible for a home for girls temporarily out of employment, to train them in domestic arts.[65] We must also remind ourselves of the several organizations which were formed to promote Roman Catholic settlement on the land.

Fraternal organizations came into being, often with insurance and mutual-aid features. They were especially important since the Roman Catholic Church forbade its members to join such secret societies as the Masons, the Odd Fellows, the Knights of Pythias, and the Sons of Temperance. Thus the Catholic Knights of America was formed in 1877 as a fraternal life insurance company.[66] The Ancient Order of Hibernians had its roots in Ireland where it had been a protective organization against the hardships and persecutions from which Roman Catholics suffered in the Emerald Isle. Not far from 1836 a branch was established in the United States. Factions developed and in 1898 in an effort to transcend them a union was achieved under the name of the Ancient Order of Hibernians. The announced purpose was to promote friendship, unity, and Christian charity and to aid sick, aged, and disabled members. Each local unit was to have a chaplain appointed by the ordinary of the diocese, and only practising Catholics could join. In 1908 the membership in the United States and Canada was said to be 127,254.[67] The Knights of Columbus enrolled a somewhat larger number of members. It was founded in New Haven, Connecticut, in 1882. Its declared objectives were the development of a practical Catholicity among its members, the promotion of Catholic education and charity, and through its insurance department the aiding of families of deceased members. It spread to every state and territory in the United States, to every province in Canada, and to the Philippines, Mexico, Cuba, and Panama. In 1910 it claimed 74,909 insured members and 160,703 associate (non-insured) members. It provided homes for Catholic orphans, endowed hospital beds, gave scholarships in Catholic colleges, maintained employment bureaus, and supported lectures on Catholic doctrine to non-Catholics.[68] The Irish Catholic

---

[63] Hynes, *History of the Diocese of Cleveland*, p. 289.
[64] *Ibid.*, pp. 213, 214.
[65] *Ibid.*, pp. 225, 226.
[66] *The Catholic Encyclopedia*, Vol. III, p. 453.
[67] *Ibid.*, Vol. VIII, pp. 144, 320, 321; Hynes, *op. cit.*, pp. 172, 173.
[68] *The Catholic Encyclopedia*, Vol. VIII, pp. 670, 671.

Benevolent Union was founded in 1896.[69] In 1901 at the instance of the Knights of St. John in an effort to bring together the many lay organizations under the guidance of the hierarchy, the American Federation of Catholic Societies was formed. It proposed to encourage the Catholic education of youth, to counter bigotry, and to strive for the infusion of Christian principles into social and public life by combatting divorce, dishonesty in business, and corruption in politics.[70]

SUMMARY

In the onrush of the revolutionary age in the rapidly growing United States with the accompanying danger of abandoning whatever of the faith had been inherited from Europe, Christianity gave ample evidence of abounding vitality. This it did partly in winning a mounting proportion of the older elements in the population to membership in the churches, in holding the allegiance of a substantial percentage of the immigration, and in making marked advances among the Indians and Negroes, hereditary non-Christians. It also gave birth to many fresh movements and adopted and adapted to the situation which it found in the United States movements and institutions that had their origin in Europe. This was true both of Protestantism and of the Roman Catholic Church.

In Protestantism the new movements were chiefly from the older American stock and from the kind of Evangelicalism which characterized it. Some were new denominations. The largest was the Christians or Disciples of Christ—a fruit of the awakenings on the frontier in the fore part of the century. Also from the revival movement and in the Evangelical-Pietist tradition were the Churches of God, the Church of the Nazarene, and the Seventh Day Adventists. Further from historic Protestantism and the Evangelical tradition but emerging from the background of the Evangelical revivals were the Church of Jesus Christ of Latter Day Saints (the Mormons), the Church of Christ, Scientist (the Christian Scientists), and Jehovah's Witnesses. Arising from contagion from the Evangelical forces in England, but having a still larger development in the United States, mainly under the leadership of those of the older stock who were deeply moved by the Evangelical awakenings, were the Sunday Schools, the Salvation Army, the Young Men's and Young Women's Christian Associations, and possibly the city missions. Purely indigenous were the rescue missions, the Young People's Society of Christian Endeavour, and the various denominational young people's movements. Such movements were almost entirely absent in the denominations which arose from the nineteenth-century Protestant immigration. When they appeared it was mainly by contagion or conscious copying of those of the older stock.

[69] *Ibid.*, p. 144.
[70] *Ibid.*, Vol. XIV, p. 71.

In the Roman Catholic Church the vitality which had brought about the revival of pre-nineteenth-century orders and congregations and had given rise to more new congregations than in any preceding century had repercussions in the United States. Scores of orders and congregations were introduced and flourished. Although, almost inevitably, they were planted by foreigners, the large majority quickly recruited members from immigrants and the children of immigrants. A number of new congregations emerged on American soil, some of them from the vision and will of converts from Protestantism.

Here was a vigour in stark contrast to the forces which threatened Christianity. While the churches and their affiliated movements did not capture all the population—or even a majority of it—they and the faith of which they were expressions were making themselves increasingly felt.

CHAPTER VI

The United States of America: Christiantity and Education

How FAR did Christianity shape the educational structure of the United States in the nineteenth century? Here was a nation which was largely the product of the revolutionary age. Even before the outset of the century it was leading in some of the political phases of the revolution. During the century it was to feel the impact of the Industrial Revolution and was to take the initiative in some of the mechanical inventions which were profoundly to alter the life of mankind—as in the electric telegraph, the telephone, the incandescent electric light, the electric railway, and the automobile. Obviously these innovations would be accompanied by equally revolutionary changes in the schools. The masses would require elementary education to fit them to be citizens in a democracy and to utilize the mechanical devices of the new age. Secondary and higher education would need to take account of the intellectual currents of the day and to share in the discovery and utilization of the expanding knowledge of the revolutionary century. In meeting the challenge Christianity had a wide and a profound effect. Some was through the churches. Some was by individuals and organizations which in large although not easily measurable degree owed to Christianity their vision and their impelling motives.

PROTESTANTISM AND EDUCATION

In the elementary stages of education Protestant churches as such had a declining share. At the outset of the century much of the elementary education was through schools directed or closely connected with them. Thus most Lutheran congregations had schools.[1] And in the middle of the century the Old School Presbyterians conducted an extensive system of parochial schools.[2] However, as the public school system developed, Protestant churches more and more ceased to operate parish schools. The reading of the Bible without comment and the repetition of the Lord's Prayer long constituted a part of the

[1] Wentz, *A Basic History of Lutheranism in America*, p. 90.
[2] Lewis Joseph Sherrill, *Presbyterian Parochial Schools, 1846–1870* (New Haven, Conn., Yale University Press, 1932, pp. xv, 261), *passim*.

daily programme of many public schools, but with some exceptions all sectarian teaching was forbidden, and on the ground that they partook of that character even the reading of the Bible and the Lord's Prayer progressively disappeared.

But in the founding and development of the public schools a number of the pioneers were deeply indebted to Protestant Christianity. A full roster would carry us far beyond all proper limits. We can take the space to mention only a few of the outstanding figures.

Horace Mann (1796–1859) gave up a lucrative practice of law and a promising political career to become the first president of the board of education of Massachusetts, created in 1837. In that office he imparted to the public schools of the state a marked impetus, and posterity regarded him as the greatest of the builders of the American system of free schools. He sought to instill in the mind and conscience of the nation the conviction that education should be universal, non-sectarian, and free, and that its object should be social efficiency, good citizenship, and moral character. Reared under the preaching of Nathanael Emmons, a Calvinist of the Hopkinsian school, Mann reacted against the doctrines of election and reprobation and became a Unitarian. However, as is clear from sermons which he preached late in life, he believed profoundly in God, that God sent His Son to be an example, and that the foundation of human duty is in the being and attributes of God. Clearly it was this faith which led him early to resolve to devote himself to the service of humanity.[3] Mann's efforts were reinforced by Charles Brooks (1795–1872), a Unitarian clergyman who travelled extensively through Massachusetts in 1835–1838, discussing educational principles with interested groups and telling of the methods which he had observed in Europe.[4]

Henry Barnard (1811–1900), Connecticut born and reared, a graduate of Yale, was credited with being next to Horace Mann in the promotion and shaping of universal primary public school education. He was active first in his native state, then in Rhode Island, and later in the nation at large. He was deeply religious, but it is not certain that he was ever a member of a church.[5]

John D. Pierce (1797–1882), a pioneer Congregational clergyman in Michigan, was the first superintendent of public instruction in that state (1836–1841). While in that office he formulated a plan for the public school system beginning with the primary grades and culminating in the state university which in its main outlines was followed for many years.[6]

Samuel Lewis (1799–1854), a lawyer and Methodist local preacher, as the

---

[3] *Dictionary of American Biography*, Vol. XII, pp. 240–242; Raymond B. Culver, *Horace Mann and Religion in the Massachusetts Public Schools* (New Haven, Conn., Yale University Press, 1929, pp. x, 301), pp. 224–229; Horace Mann, *Twelve Sermons Delivered at Antioch College* (Boston, Ticknor and Fields, 1861, pp. 314), pp. 12, 28–30.

[4] Weigle, *American Idealism*, p. 281; *Dictionary of American Biography*, Vol. III, pp. 74, 75.

[5] *Dictionary of American Biography*, Vol. I, pp. 121–125.

[6] *Ibid.*, Vol. XIV, p. 583.

first superintendent of common schools in Ohio (1837–1840) placed the public schools of that state on a firm basis.[7] The year before Lewis's office was created, Calvin E. Stowe (1802–1886), professor in Lane Theological Seminary in Cincinnati, spent some time in Europe studying the schools and, returning, made a report which was circulated not only by the Ohio legislature but also by the legislatures of five other states.[8]

In the next decade Robert Jefferson Breckinridge (1800–1871), who in his young manhood through personal tragedy had come into a deep religious experience and had become a Presbyterian minister, as superintendent of public instruction in Kentucky saved the public schools of that state and placed them on a sound basis. Before he took office a third of the adult population, so it is said, were illiterate and half the children had never attended school. A vigorous advocate and debater who had been one of the leaders of the Old School Presbyterians in the controversy which led to the separation of the New School, Breckinridge brought to the cause of public education in Kentucky the invincible campaigning temper which had made him a power in his church.[9]

Calvin H. Wiley (1819–1887), a deeply religious lawyer who sought to apply Christian principles to all life, in his middle years ordained to the Presbyterian ministry, during his thirteen years as the first superintendent of common schools in North Carolina had achievements which paralleled those of Mann in Massachusetts and Barnard in Connecticut and Rhode Island.[10]

In neighbouring Virginia lived a Presbyterian minister, William H. Ruffner (1824–1908), who after he entered politics formally demitted the ministry but not his faith. During the years of reconstruction that followed the Civil War, in the face of strong opposition, he obtained the enactment of a law ensuring universal education for both whites and Negroes which became a model for several other Southern states.[11]

Joseph Ward (1838–1889), "the father of Congregationalism in the Dakotas," was the chief author of the education law of South Dakota and was influential in keeping the school lands of the territory out of the hands of Eastern speculators.[12]

George H. Atkinson (1819–1889), outstanding as a Congregational home missionary in Oregon, had an important role in the inception of public education in that state.[13]

This impressive list of men who out of Christian conviction derived from their Protestant rearing championed successfully the ideal of public education

7 Weigle, *op. cit.*, p. 283; *Dictionary of American Biography*, Vol. XI, pp. 223, 224.
8 Weigle, *op. cit.*, p. 283.
9 *Dictionary of National Biography*, Vol. III, pp. 10, 11.
10 *Ibid.*, Vol. XX, p. 213; Weigle, *op. cit.*, p. 285.
11 *Dictionary of American Biography*, Vol. XVI, pp. 218, 219.
12 *Ibid.*, Vol. XIX, pp. 429, 430.
13 *Ibid.*, Vol. I, pp. 408, 409.

for all on a non-sectarian basis could be greatly lengthened.

In the nineteenth century Protestant churches in the United States, as churches, made their major contribution to education through establishing colleges and universities. Often, before public high schools attained their later dimensions, secondary education was also undertaken, in the older states through academies and west of the Appalachians through academies generally but not exclusively attached to colleges.

In the colonial period almost all the colleges were founded as frankly Christian institutions, usually in close association with the churches. In the nineteenth century several of them expanded their programmes and became universities. In that capacity some continued to be outstanding in the higher education of the country—notably Harvard, Yale, Columbia, and Princeton.

The Protestant colleges were often pioneers in higher education in their respective states and territories. In some areas they antedated the state universities. In several others they offered a better education than did the latter in their early years. Here and there a state institution grew out of one or another of them. In other words, they helped prepare for the youthful and growing nation a leadership familiar with the heritage of the Occident and trained in the intellectual disciplines and the sciences of the revolutionary age. Again and again in the first half of the century many of the colleges were swept by revivals and through them contributed to the vigour and spread of the faith at home and abroad.

By 1860 about 166 colleges which had an enduring life had been founded under Protestant denominational auspices.[14] Indicative of the emphasis on education by the various denominations was the fact that Presbyterians led in the number of colleges begun, and that in proportion to their numerical strength they and the Congregationalists outdistanced all the others, with the Episcopalians a bad third.[15] It is also significant that, while proportionately behind these three, Methodists, Baptists, Disciples of Christ, and Lutherans were inaugurating colleges which survived.[16] This meant that the Methodists, Baptists, and Disciples of Christ, drawing as they did from the lower-income levels of the population on the frontier, were beginning to educate their constituencies, and that the Lutherans, the largest of the denominational families arising from the nineteenth-century immigration, were making a similar provision.

In the latter part of the century colleges with Protestant church affiliation continued to mount. In 1900, of 664 institutions in the country of college and university grade, 403, or more than half, were under Protestant auspices.[17] State institutions multiplied and, being able as they were to obtain support from

---

[14] Tewksbury, *The Founding of American Colleges and Universities Before the Civil War*, p. 69.
[15] *Ibid.*
[16] *Ibid.*
[17] F. W. Padelford in *Christian Education*, Vol. XIX, pp. 210 ff.

public taxation, in equipment, staff, and student bodies forged ahead of most of the colleges and universities which depended on private benefaction and church aid. However, several universities that were officially Christian, notably Harvard, Yale, Columbia, and Princton, continued to be eminent in the intellectual world, and some of nineteenth-century founding, among them New York University and the University of Pittsburgh, both Presbyterian in their origin, and Western Reserve University, with a Yale and Plan of Union background, became prominent in the urban environment in which they found themselves. The two great universities of the metropolis of the Middle West, Northwestern and the University of Chicago, the one a Methodist and the other a Baptist creation, were evidence of the fashion in which the two denominations that had led in winning to Protestant church membership the less educated of the older American stock in the frontier days of the Mississippi Valley were contributing to the higher education of that region.

Protestants were also pioneering in higher education for women. Among the institutions which led were Mt. Holyoke Seminary, created by Mary Lyon and a path-breaker in college training for women;[18] Wellesley College, founded by the devotedly Christian Henry F. Durant—he wished all its teachers to be earnest Christians—to give the same opportunities to women offered by Harvard to men;[19] and Oberlin, in that idealistic Christian colony in Ohio, which in the very first circular of its "collegiate institute" announced the purpose of offering the same privileges to women as to men, a promise resolutely kept.[20]

Protestants were responsible for a form of popular education associated with the name of Chautauqua. On Chautauqua Lake in New York State was a site for camp-meetings. In 1874 John H. Vincent (1832–1920), for twenty-four years the first chairman of the International Sunday School Lesson Committee and in 1888 elected a bishop of the Methodist Episcopal Church, began there a summer assembly for the training of Sunday School teachers. Four years later he expanded it into the Chautauqua Literary and Scientific Circle for popular education through home reading. In 1879 in connexion with this programme a summer school was begun at Chautauqua. It was given great impetus through the organizing ability and enthusiasm of William Rainey Harper (1856–1906), later to be the first president of the University of Chicago. The idea spread and in many parts of the country Chautauqua summer assemblies multiplied. They contributed markedly to a movement in education which utilized summer

---

[18] Edward Hitchcock, compiler, *The Power of Christian Benevolence, Illustrated in the Life and Labors of Mary Lyon* (Northampton, Mass., Hopkins, Bridgman and Co., 1852, pp. viii, 486), *passim;* Beth Bradford Gilchrist, *The Life of Mary Lyon* (Boston, Houghton Mifflin Co., 1910, pp. x, 462), *passim.*

[19] William R. Moody, *D. L. Moody* (New York, The Macmillan Co., 1931, pp. 556), p. 305.

[20] Frances Juliette Hosford, *Father Shipherd's Magna Carta. A Century of Coeducation in Oberlin College* (Boston, Marshall Jones Co., 1937, pp. ix, 180), p. 5.

schools in colleges and universities, summer assemblies, conferences, and training centres.[21]

PROTESTANTS AND THE EDUCATION OF NEGROES

A major aspect of Protestantism in the United States was the contribution to the education of the Negroes. Much of this was by whites and much by Negroes.

Before the Civil War and the national emancipation of the slaves white Protestants had begun several schools for Negroes. Thus in the 1850's Presbyterians founded for Negroes Asmun Institute, later called Lincoln University, which had a long and honourable record.[22] John G. Fee of Kentucky, the son of a slave-holder, was disowned by his father for coming out against slavery, became a clergyman, and with others of like mind founded Berea College (opened 1859) for the coëducation of Negroes and whites. A pacifist, never carrying arms, he prayed for his enemies among the pro-slavery elements while they were mobbing him.[23] In 1856 the Methodists incorporated Wilberforce University, in Ohio, for Negroes.[24] In the last few decades before the Civil War, in several Southern states legislation was enacted to prevent the education of the Negro out of fear that it might lead to revolts. Since efforts by Southern churches were discouraged, Negro education tended to be confined to the North.[25]

After the Civil War white Protestants inaugurated many institutions for the education of the freedmen. Most of them were begun by Northerners, because they felt a special obligation for those whom they had helped liberate and because for the first few decades after the war the Southern whites and their churches were too impoverished to enter upon major undertakings. The American Missionary Association, which, emphatically anti-slavery, had been organized before the war and drew its chief support from Congregationalists, founded colleges for Negroes in several of the Southern states—among them Hampton Institute in Virginia, Fisk University in Tennessee, and Atlanta University in Georgia.[26] In 1913 it was aiding sixty-five schools which had an

[21] Arthur Eugene Bestor, *Chautauqua Publications. An Historical and Bibliographical Guide* (Chautauqua, N.Y., Chautauqua Press, 1934, pp. 67), pp. 1–10; Jesse Lyman Hurlburt, *The Story of Chautauqua* (New York, G. P. Putnam's Sons, 1921, pp. xxv, 429), *passim;* John H. Vincent, *The Chautauqua Movement* (Boston, Chautauqua Press, 1886, pp. ix, 308), *passim;* Leon H. Vincent, *John Heyl Vincent. A Biographical Sketch* (New York, The Macmillan Co., 1925, pp. 319), pp. 115–157; Weigle, *op. cit.,* pp. 200, 201.

[22] Woodson, *The Education of the Negro Prior to 1861,* p. 270.

[23] Edwin R. Embree, *Brown America* (New York, The Viking Press, 1931, pp. vi, 311), pp. 59–88.

[24] Woodson, *op. cit.,* p. 272.

[25] *Ibid.,* pp. 180, 182, 186.

[26] *Twenty-Ninth Annual Report of the American Missionary Association* (1875), p. 76; *Fifty-sixth Annual Report of the American Missionary Association* (1902), p. 15; Beard, *A Crusade of Brotherhood,* pp. 121–128. On Hampton Institute see Francis Greenwood Peabody, *Education for*

enrollment of over twelve thousand students.[27] Episcopalians conducted several institutions, among them Bishop Payne Divinity School.[28] The Friends had schools for freedmen, including Penn School on St. Helena Island off the coast of South Carolina.[29] The Methodist Episcopal Church through its Freedmen's Aid Society supported twenty-six schools for Negroes and through its women sixteen homes for training girls in domestic science and other arts and occupations.[30] The American Baptist Home Mission Society founded a number of schools, among them colleges, and together with the Woman's American Baptist Home Mission Society aided Spelman College, in time the most noted institution for the higher education of Negro girls.[31] The Presbyterian Church in the United States of America had a Board of Missions for Freedmen which in 1914 assisted 136 schools.[32] Howard University, founded in Washington, D.C., in 1866 in a prayer meeting in the First Congregational Church of that city, received aid from the federal government through the Freedmen's Bureau. When the panic of 1873 placed it in dire straits it was rescued by a clergyman, W. W. Patton, who reorganized it. Much of the money for its support came from Congregationalists.[33]

Out of their post-war poverty, Southern churches assisted in the education of the Negroes. Thus in 1885 the Home Mission Board of the Southern Baptist Convention reported the holding of institutes in Georgia for the coloured ministry.[34] The Methodist Episcopal Church, South, aided a number of colleges for Negroes, notably Paine College, in Georgia, a joint enterprise with the Coloured Methodist Episcopal Church.[35]

Several foundations begun by Protestants under the impulse of their faith did much for the education of the Negroes. The John F. Slater Fund was instituted in 1882 for the purpose of conferring on the Negroes of the South "the blessings

---

Life. The Story of Hampton Institute (Garden City, N.Y., Doubleday, Page & Co., 1918, pp. xxiv, 393), *passim*, and Edith Armstrong Talbot, *Samuel Chapman Armstrong, A Biographical Study* (New York, Doubleday, Page & Co., 1904, pp. vi, 301), *passim*.

[27] *Sixty-Seventh Annual Report of the American Missionary Association* (1913), p. 9.

[28] James Thayer Addison, *Our Expanding Church* (New York, National Council of the Protestant Episcopal Church, 1930, pp. ix, 117), p. 83.

[29] Jones, *A Study of the Private and Higher Schools for Colored People in the United States*, Vol. I, p. 253; Rosa B. Cooley, *School Acres. An Adventure in Rural Education* (New Haven, Conn., Yale University Press, 1930, pp. xxii, 166), *passim*.

[30] *The Methodist Forward Movement in the United States. Annual of the Board of Home Missions and Church Extension of the Methodist Episcopal Church for the Year 1907–1908*, p. 11. See also Ralph E. Morrow, *Northern Methodism and Reconstruction* (East Lansing, Mich., Michigan State University Press, 1956, pp. ix, 269), pp. 153–176.

[31] White, *A Century of Faith*, pp. 102–119; Phila A. Whipple, *Negro Neighbors Bond and Free* (Boston, Woman's American Baptist Home Mission Society, 1907, pp. 143), pp. 122 ff.

[32] Monroe N. Work, editor, *Negro Work Book. An Annual Encyclopedia of the Negro* (Tuskegee Institute, The Negro Year Book Publishing Co., 1914 ff.), 1914–1915, p. 215.

[33] Embree, *op. cit.*, pp. 103–107; D. O. W. Holmes in *The Journal of Negro History*, Vol. III, pp. 131 ff.

[34] *Proceedings of the Southern Baptist Convention 1885. Report of the Home Mission Board*, p. vii.

[35] *Missionary Yearbook of the Methodist Episcopal Church, South, 1936*, p. 24.

of Christian education." Its creator was John Fox Slater (1815–1884), a devout Congregational Connecticut textile manufacturer whose initial gift of a million dollars (1882), wisely administered, had by 1935 expended about four times that sum, chiefly for the training of Negro teachers.[36] Anna T. Jeanes, of a Quaker family, established the Jeanes Fund for the aid of rural schools for Negroes, and its first directing head was a deeply religious Virginian Episcopalian, James Hardy Dillard.[37] The General Education Board (incorporated in 1903), endowed by John D. Rockefeller, continued the donor's assistance to Negro colleges made through Baptist home mission societies. It was undenominational and gave millions of dollars for the education of the Negro.[38]

Negro Protestants did much for the education of their own race. Out of their poverty, Negro churches early began to establish schools. They were often assisted by funds from white givers, but the initiative was theirs. By 1917 Negro church boards controlled 153 schools, of which 60 were said to have sufficient equipment and income to render valuable service.[39] The outstanding Negro educator of the latter part of the nineteenth century was Booker T. Washington (1856–1915). Born a slave, the son of an unknown white father and a coloured mother, he was a graduate of Hampton Institute and was largely shaped by it. He became the best-known leader of his race of his generation. Under the inspiration of what he had received at Hampton he built up in Tuskegee, Alabama, what at the outset was a normal school but in time had an even wider programme.[40]

THE ROMAN CATHOLIC CHURCH AND EDUCATION

The Roman Catholic Church built a much more extensive educational system than did any of the other churches of the United States. As we have suggested, the chief emphasis was on parish schools on the elementary level. While other churches acquiesced in non-sectarian public education, for the most part the Roman Catholic hierarchy believed that if the young were to be reared in the faith and not fall victim to the secularism which characterized the revolutionary age their church must have or control schools in which religion was taught along with other subjects. In this they were in accord with the policy of the Roman Catholic Church in other countries as set forth by the Popes. They insisted, moreover, that the state share in the expense. They held it to be unjust

---

[36] *Dictionary of American Biography,* Vol. XVII, p. 205.

[37] Benjamin Brawley, *Doctor Dillard of the Jeanes Fund* (New York, Fleming H. Revell Co., 1930, pp. 151), *passim.*

[38] Horace Mann Bond, *The Education of the Negro in the American Social Order* (New York, Prentice-Hall, 1934, pp. xx, 501), p. 137; *The General Education Board. An Account of Its Activities 1902–1914* (New York, General Education Board, 1915, pp. xv, 240), *passim.*

[39] Jones, *op. cit.,* Vol. I, pp. 149–152, 254.

[40] *Booker T. Washington's Own Story of His Life and Work* (Naperville, Ill., J. L. Nichols & Co., 1916, pp. 510), *passim;* Booker T. Washington, *Up From Slavery. An Autobiography* (New York, Doubleday, Page and Co., 1901, pp. ix, 330), *passim.*

that Roman Catholics were taxed to support public schools and at the same time, for conscience' sake, taxed themselves to maintain schools to give their children the kind of education in which they believed.

Recognizing the difficulties presented by that policy, here and there a bishop favoured an arrangement which, while not compromising the essential principle, would make for an accommodation with the state. One of these was the so-called Faribault plan sponsored by the influential Archbishop Ireland of St. Paul. Ireland, an ardent American, addressing the National Education Association in 1890, came out emphatically for compulsory primary education and the public school. At the same time he was equally insistent that it was disastrous to have religious instruction excluded from these schools. As one possible solution he suggested that the state pay for instruction in secular subjects in denominational schools and as another a plan in use in several cities and bearing the name of Poughkeepsie by which the school board rented parochial schools during school hours, paid the salaries of the teachers, and conducted examinations of teachers and pupils. In accordance with Ireland's idea, in Faribault and Stillwater, Minnesota, within his archdiocese, the public school board rented for a dollar a year the parochial school building during the hours devoted to secular knowledge, paid the teachers, and maintained the building, but before and after school hours the institution remained parochial. Ireland's plan was vigorously attacked, both by conservatives among the bishops, notably McQuaid and Corrigan, and in Roman Catholic circles in Europe, and by Protestants and others outside his church. The one group contended that he was endangering the religious character of the parish schools and the other that he was paving the way for the absorption of the public schools by the Roman Catholic Church. Rome approved Ireland's solution (1892). In the end, the public schools in both Faribault and Stillwater terminated the arrangement. But the issue of the relation of the state to the parish schools the country over remained controversial.[41]

As was to be expected, the Roman Catholic Church not only maintained parochial schools on the principle that each parish should have one but also had many secondary schools, colleges, and universities. Even before the Civil War, when the Roman Catholic population was not as large as it later became and the poverty of most of the constituency was extreme, the Roman Catholic Church had founded fourteen colleges which had a continuing life—in proportion to its numerical strength more than either Methodists or Baptists.[42] In 1900, of the 664 colleges and universities in the country, 403 were under Protestant and 63 under Roman Catholic auspices.[43]

[41] Moynihan, *The Life of Archbishop Ireland*, pp. 79–103; Maynard, *The Story of American Catholicism*, pp. 466–470; Zwierlein, *Life and Letters of Bishop McQuaid*, Vol. III, pp. 160 ff.; Daniel Flavian Reilly, *The School Controversy (1891–1893)* (Washington, The Catholic University of America Press, 1943, pp. x, 302), *passim*.

[42] Tewksbury, *op. cit.*, p. 69.

[43] F. W. Padelford in *Christian Education*, Vol. XIX, pp. 210 ff. See also Power, *A History of Catholic Higher Education in the United States*, pp. 152, 275, 315.

Of the Roman Catholic universities the most famous was the Catholic University of America, opened in Washington in 1889. A number of Roman Catholics had long regretted the low educational level of the masses of their fellow believers in the United States and the lack of leadership in the intellectual life of the country. Some desired, too, an institution where the clergy, both before and after ordination, could be given a broader academic preparation than that obtainable in theological seminaries. The Second Plenary Council, held in Baltimore in 1866, expressed the hope that such a university would be established. Its presiding officer, Archbishop Martin John Spalding (1810–1872), of old American stock, had been active in promoting the American College in Louvain and the American college in Rome and strongly favoured the project.[44] It was his nephew, John Lancaster Spalding (1840–1916), who more than any other one man was responsible for bringing the dream to reality. Educated in the American College in Louvain and the American College in Rome, consecrated Bishop of Peoria in 1877, he became a strong advocate. John Joseph Keane (1839–1918) resigned the see of Richmond to become the first rector and did much through his own scholarly character and through raising the needed funds to launch the university. Leo XIII endorsed it and granted it the right to confer degrees. The institution quickly ran into heavy weather. At the very outset the powerful Bishop McQuaid opposed it, criticizing it among other counts as being too Southern.[45] It early became involved in the controversy over Ireland's attitude towards the public schools and then in the "Americanism" storm. In 1896 Keane was removed from his rectorship by direct Papal action, apparently because of complaints of his "liberalism," and McQuaid exulted in what he deemed the failure of the university and the slap at Gibbons, Ireland, and Keane.[46] Yet the university survived and prospered. Gibbons proved a loyal friend. While the majority of its faculty were laymen or secular priests, on its teaching staff were members of several orders and congregations, and many of the religious orders sent students to it to be trained for the higher degrees.[47]

THE THREAT OF DE-CHRISTIANIZATION OF EDUCATIONAL INSTITUTIONS ON CHRISTIAN FOUNDATIONS

Would the colleges and universities founded by churches or under frankly Christian auspices deserve the name "Christian"? As the multiform intellectual currents of the revolutionary age played upon them, would they close their doors to them, or would they welcome them? Immersed as they were in a

---

[44] *Dictionary of American Biography*, Vol. XVII, pp. 424–426.

[45] Zwierlein, *op. cit.*, Vol. III, pp. 391 ff.; Patrick Henry Ahern, *The Life of John J. Keane, Educator and Archbishop, 1839–1918* (Milwaukee, The Bruce Publishing Co., 1955, pp. xi, 396), *passim;* Power, *op. cit.*, pp. 223–245.

[46] Maynard, *op. cit.*, pp. 482–486, 518, 519; Cross, *The Emergence of Liberal Catholicism in America*, pp. 156 ff.

[47] Maynard, *op. cit.*, pp. 486, 487.

society becoming increasingly industrialized and urbanized, would they succumb to the materialistic pressures about them and the standards of success set by a culture in which many non-Christian and even anti-Christian forces were at work? State institutions were multiplying and enrolling a mounting proportion of the college and university students. Like the public elementary and secondary schools, they were perforce non-sectarian and religiously neutral. Would the professedly Christian colleges and universities conform?

In general, the trend was towards the secularization of higher education. Not only were state universities becoming more prominent, but private munificence was inaugurating universities which were frankly non-sectarian. Thus in founding the university which bore his name, Ezra Cornell declared that it would be "our aim and our constant effort to make true Christian men, without dwarfing or paring them down to fit the narrow gauge of any sect," and the charter of the university stated that "persons of every religious denomination or of no religious denomination shall be equally eligible to all offices and appointments."[48] Johns Hopkins University, which was among the trail-blazers in graduate work and so in adopting the methods for advancing human knowledge typical of the day, took a similar attitude. Such well-established universities as Harvard, Yale, and Princeton in one way or another insisted on their independence of ecclesiastical opinion and stood for freedom of thought and teaching, even when that entailed having on their staffs men who were clearly not orthodox when judged by historic Christian doctrines. In many institutions the purpose seemed to be to prepare their students for personal advancement in a technological society rather than the arousing of intellectual interest or the development of character.[49] Increasingly students enrolled in the more respected colleges and universities of Christian foundation in the hope of financial success and social prestige in a highly competitive world dominated by economic factors. Early in the century, out of 2,163 students enrolled in eleven New England colleges, 745, or slightly more than a third, were preparing for the Protestant ministry.[50] At the end of the century the total of those headed for the ministry in the same colleges was much smaller and in proportion to the student bodies the decline was even more striking. Not all colleges and universities succumbed to the secularizing forces. But the pressures were strong and often came in subtly disguised forms.

SUMMARY

At the outset of the nineteenth century most of such formal education as existed had as an integral feature instruction in the Christian religion. In the

---

[48] Hofstadter and Hardy, *The Development and Scope of Higher Education in the United States,* p. 34.

[49] *Ibid.,* pp. 34 ff.

[50] Shedd, *Two Centuries of Student Christian Movements,* p. 12.

rapid development in education which marked the century the churches and men and women whose impelling motive was from the Christian faith were pioneers, especially in the early decades. Protestants, several of them clergymen, led in the adoption of universal primary public education and the promotion of better teaching methods and physical equipment, sometimes on the national and sometimes on the state level. Roman Catholics greatly expanded their parochial schools. In the realm of higher education, churches, both Protestant and Roman Catholic, founded many colleges and universities.

As the years passed, the trend towards secularization was strong. Largely because of pressures from rival religious bodies, religious instruction and even the reading of the Scriptures and the repetition of the Lord's Prayer without comment gradually faded from the public schools. In colleges and universities the Christian purpose tended either to be absent or to wane. This was partly because religiously neutral state institutions multiplied and enrolled an increasing proportion of the students of that grade, partly under the conviction of the importance of freedom of research and teaching, partly because of the mounting pressures of the industrialization and urbanization of society. Here and there an institution sought to resist the trend and to combine high scholarly standards and intellectual freedom with the Christian faith. Increasingly voluntary associations of students and teachers nurtured the Christian life on the campuses. Indeed, never had this voluntary activity of avowed Christians on the campuses of the United States been as vigorous as it was on the eve of 1914. In the latter part of the nineteenth century it came chiefly through the Young Men's and Young Women's Christian Associations. In the twentieth century denominational student Christian movements multiplied and taken together were stronger than the YMCA's and the YWCA's had been, even late in the nineteenth century. Here, as in so much of the nineteenth-century Occident, two contrary currents were seen—one towards de-Christianizing the historic Christendom and the other towards propagating and strengthening the Christian faith and towards permeating a progressively secular world with the Gospel.

CHAPTER VII

The United States of America: The Response of Christianity to Intellectual Currents

WHAT response did the Christianity of the United States of America make to the intellectual currents of the revolutionary age? We have seen in the two preceding volumes something of those currents as they issued from Western Christendom. In them we attempted to sketch the responses of the Christianity of Europe. We have just now hinted at the effects of these currents on the educational structure of the United States. We must attempt to enquire into the fashion in which the Christian forces and particularly the churches dealt with the currents as they impinged upon them and their constituencies.

The intellectual currents had two geographical sources. One was Western Europe. From there came much of the science and religious questioning and scepticism which we have repeatedly noted. Eighteenth-century rationalism still aroused echoes which, if they died away, did so only belatedly. Darwin and those who followed him in formulating the hypotheses associated with his name were having widening repercussions. The theology and the Biblical studies which were arising from the ferment in Protestantism on the other side of the Atlantic and especially in Germany were beginning to circulate in the United States. One medium for their dissemination was books, both in the original language and in English translation. Another was the students who went abroad, mostly to the universities of Germany, to drink of the heady new waters at their sources. Still another, although less important, was the scholars, like Philip Schaff, who cast in their lot with the new nation. Further, as we have again and again reminded ourselves, the United States was itself one of the springs from which the currents issued.

The intellectual currents made themselves felt in ways reflecting the characteristics of the various religious communities upon which they impinged. In general they were more potent in Protestant than in Roman Catholic circles. In Protestantism the responses fell in the main into three groups. One was of denominations with a high educational level of clergy and laity and recruited chiefly from the pre-nineteenth-century stock. Here the major developments were among the Congregationalists, Presbyterians, German Reformed, and Episcopalians. A second was of denominations which flourished on revivalism and among those of lower educational and economic status who constituted the majority of the pre-nineteenth-century stock. The third was of the denominations whose membership was predominantly from the nineteenth-century immigration.

THE RESPONSE OF PROTESTANT DENOMINATIONS OF THE EDUCATIONAL AND ECONOMIC ELITE OF THE PRE-NINETEENTH-CENTURY STOCK

We have already seen the beginnings of the response to the intellectual currents of the revolutionary age in the denominations whose stronghold was in the pre-nineteenth-century stock with a highly educated clergy.[1] We noted the developments in Congregationalism, at the outset of the century numerically the strongest and geographically the most nearly compact denomination in the country. We remarked the fashion in which Congregationalism was penetrated by the Great Awakening and the awakenings around the turn of the century. We briefly recorded the rise of Unitarianism, mainly in and near the chief New England city, Boston, among the educated and economic elite in opposition to the revivals and with rationalistic reactions from the Calvinistic theology which had heretofore prevailed. We also mentioned the beginnings of Universalism, similarly as a protest against Calvinism.[2] We summarized the beginnings of the New England theology, one stream of which is usually traced to Jonathan Edwards and the other, which issued in Unitarianism, having Charles Chauncy as its outstanding early figure. We pointed out a further development of the Edwardsian strain in Samuel Hopkins and through other Yale graduates, notably Timothy Dwight and Nathanael Emmons. We called attention to the founding of Andover Theological Seminary (1808) by the Hopkinsians and the Old Calvinists in protest against the commitment of Harvard to Unitarianism.

THE RESPONSE OF CONGREGATIONALISM: UNITARIANISM

We must now sketch the developments which issued from Congregationalism. It seems wise first to trace those associated with Unitarianism and Universalism and then to go on with the Congregationalism which held more nearly to historic Christianity. The latter enrolled a very much larger number than did Unitarianism, Universalism, and their associated movements.

Unitarianism was more prominent than Universalism. The difference was briefly and not inaptly expressed in the aphorism: "Unitarianism believed that man was too good to be damned; Universalism that God was too good to damn

[1] Volume I, pp. 195–198.
[2] On the beginnings of Unitarianism and also of Universalism in the second half of the eighteenth century, see Conrad Wright, *The Beginnings of Unitarianism in America* (Boston, Starr King Press, 1955, pp. 305), *passim*.

man." The sharp division between the Unitarian and the Trinitarian Congregationalists was accentuated when in the Dedham case (1820) the Massachusetts Supreme Court ruled that the church property belonged to the majority of the voters in the parish who through taxes supported the church and not to the communicants.[3] This was in the day when the Congregational churches were still established and when the church, composed of those who gave evidence of conversion and had made a formal profession of faith, was distinct from the parish. As a result, since in most churches the majority of the communicants were orthodox, they withdrew, had a pastor who was in accord with their convictions, and erected their own meetinghouses. In many towns, mostly in eastern Massachusetts, two Congregational churches came into being, the one Unitarian and the other Trinitarian. The Orthodox refused to exchange pulpits with the Unitarians. The Unitarians tended to attract the well-to-do, socially prominent, and better-educated elements.[4]

In the fore part of the nineteenth century the outstanding spokesman for Unitarianism was William Ellery Channing (1780–1842).[5] Born and reared in Newport, Rhode Island, Channing knew and revered Ezra Stiles, a moderate Calvinist of broad sympathies, later president of Yale. He went to Harvard and there read Locke, Berkeley, Hume, Priestley, and the "moderate" Scottish theologians and philosophers Reid and Hutcheson. Thus he was in touch with some of the currents of thought which arose from an early stage of the revolutionary age. He was impressed with Hutcheson's teaching that the promotion of happiness for others is the standard of virtue. He sat under the preaching of Samuel Hopkins in Newport and was profoundly moved by his doctrine of universal disinterested benevolence but rejected much of his Calvinism. In 1803 he became pastor of the Federal Street Church in Boston and although in later years, physically frail, he devoted most of his time to writing, he held that post until his death. A sermon which he preached in Baltimore in 1819 marked him as a leader in the Unitarian movement. Although he deplored the division among Christians, he consented to the formation of the American Unitarian Association (1825). He was elected its first president but declined on the ground of health. He was long the permeating spirit of the movement, and the main current in it was known as "Channing Unitarianism." He took the Bible as his authoritative guide. He held Christ in great reverence and regarded him as perfect man and his teachings as standard. Yet he insisted that the Scriptures gave no ground for the doctrine of the Trinity, that the New Testament

---

[3] Allen, *Historical Sketch of the Unitarian Movement since the Reformation,* pp. 193, 194.
[4] *Ibid.,* pp. 194, 200.
[5] Of the many writings by and about Channing see *The Works of William E. Channing* (Boston, George G. Channing, 6 vols., 1849); *Memoir of William Ellery Channing* (Boston, Wm. Crosby & H. P. Nichols, 5th ed., 3 vols., 1851); John White Chadwick, *William Ellery Channing, Minister of Religion* (Boston, Houghton Mifflin Co., 1903, pp. xiv, 463); David P. Edgell, *William Ellery Channing. An Intellectual Portrait* (Boston, Beacon Press, 1955, pp. xv, 264); Robert Leet Patterson, *The Philosophy of William Ellery Channing* (New York, Bookman Associates, 1952, pp. 298).

designation of God was Father, and that Jesus was subordinate to Him. He repudiated the doctrine of original sin and the total depravity of man as inconsistent with the Fatherhood of God and as dishonouring the Creator. He held to the goodness of God, the perfectibility of man, freedom of the will, and the responsibility of men for their actions. He was much interested in literature and was familiar with German, French, and English thought. His influence was more through the printed page than through his preaching. He opposed slavery and war, and, although he was not a thoroughgoing pacifist, the Massachusetts Peace Society was organized in his study. He exerted an influence on many New England men of letters, among them Emerson, Bryant, Longfellow, Lowell, and Holmes.

While for years the main stream of Unitarianism was essentially that of Channing, it had many variants. Some remained close to it. Others departed widely from it, so far, indeed, that they could not be regarded as in its fellowship.

James Freeman Clarke (1810–1888), the founder of the Church of the Disciples in Boston, was looked at askance by some of the more conservative but was also disliked by radicals and was really moderate.[6] A loyal Unitarian and a devout Christian as he understood those terms, he had warm sympathy with other denominations, believed in the universality of truth and goodness among men, and sought to discern them in all persons, sects, and religions. He was called the father of comparative religion in America.

Andrews Norton (1786–1853), long on the faculty of the Harvard Divinity School, was so powerful in shaping Unitarian thought that Carlyle called him "the Unitarian Pope" and Emerson dubbed him "the embodiment of the Cambridge Parnassus." Although rejecting the theory of verbal inspiration of the Scriptures, he held to a form of inspiration and supported the genuineness of the Gospels as contrasted with the views that they were compiled from earlier sources, since lost.[7]

Theodore Parker (1810–1860), out of a youthful struggle with poverty, managed to obtain a Harvard education, both in the arts and in theology. He had been reared in a devout Unitarian home where his father, a farmer, a prodigious reader, had instilled in him a love of fearless thinking. An amazing linguist, he read extensively in European contemporaries, including Cousin, Coleridge, Strauss, and De Wette. He translated De Wette's *Introduction to the Old Testament* with some additions of his own. Yet he also read John Woolman's journal and was deeply moved by it. He belonged to what was

---

[6] Edward Everett Hale, editor, *James Freeman Clarke. Autobiography, Diary and Correspondence* (Boston, Houghton Mifflin Co., 1891, pp. 430), *passim; Dictionary of American Biography,* Vol. IV, pp. 153, 154; Arthur S. Bolster, *James Freeman Clarke, Disciple to Advancing Truth* (Boston, Beacon Press, 1954, pp. xii, 373).

[7] *Dictionary of American Biography,* Vol. XIII, pp. 568, 569; George H. Williams, editor, *The Harvard Divinity School* (Boston, Beacon Press, 1954, pp. xvi, 366), pp. 46–49.

coming to be known as the "new school" of Unitarianism, which took a rationalistic view of religion and, while not denying the miracles, regarded them as adding no authority to things morally true. He was ordained and had Unitarian parishes, near and in Boston, but became too radical for many of the old school. Norton sharply differed from him. Yet he was akin to the mediating school in Germany, regarded Jesus as the highest known representative of God, and was critical of Deism and of extreme Transcendentalism and of Emerson. He was outspoken in his denunciation of slavery and suffered imprisonment for adding deeds to his convictions.[8]

Ralph Waldo Emerson (1803–1882) was in some respects still more radical and more widely influential. From a long line of New England ministers and the son of William Emerson, the Minister of Boston's First Church, he went dutifully to Harvard, floundered around for a few years trying to find himself, then studied theology at Harvard and for a time was pastor in a Unitarian parish in Boston. But he felt out of place in that post and resigned. Occasionally thereafter he preached, but he was best known as a writer and lecturer. In 1838 in an address at the Harvard Divinity School he shocked the authorities by declaring that the Church as then constituted was dead and helpless and was no place for scholars and prophets. He urged the members of the graduating class to seek a new revelation adapted to the times. He spoke of the Over-Soul as pervading all and of the potential nobility of man. He admired Coleridge, Wordsworth, and Carlyle. He spoke to the youth of America and youth listened, spellbound if not always comprehending. His was a message of emancipating individualism which appealed to the American temper of the day. But what he said was far from historic Christianity.[9]

Out of the stream from which Unitarianism issued came another movement, Transcendentalism. It did not enlist large numbers and had a relatively brief life, but because of the eminence of some of its exponents it attracted wide attention.[10] The Transcendentalists were at the outset a group of young New England intellectuals who began meeting about 1836 in Concord, Massachusetts, often in Emerson's study, to discuss new developments in philosophy, theology, and literature. They were profoundly influenced by German writers at a time

[8] John Weiss, *Life and Correspondence of Theodore Parker* (New York, D. Appleton and Co., 2 vols., 1864); Henry Steele Commager, *Theodore Parker* (Boston, Little Brown and Co., 1936, pp. ix, 339); John Edward Dirks, *The Critical Theology of Theodore Parker* (New York, Columbia University Press, 1948, pp. viii, 1–73).

[9] Of the extensive writings by and on Emerson see Ralph L. Rusk, *The Life of Ralph Waldo Emerson* (New York, Charles Scribner's Sons, 1949, pp. ix, 592), and Van Wyck Brooks, *The Life of Emerson* (New York, E. P. Dutton and Co., 1932, pp. 315).

[10] George F. Whicher, editor, *The Transcendentalist Revolt against Materialism* (Boston, D. C. Heath and Co., 1949, pp. ix, 107); Perry Miller, *The Transcendentalists, an Anthology* (Cambridge, Mass., Harvard University Press, 1950, pp. xv, 521); Stanley M. Vogel, *German Literary Influences on the Transcendentalists* (New Haven, Conn., Yale University Press, 1955, pp. xvii, 196); Octavius Brooks Frothingham, *Transcendentalism in New England* (New York, G. P. Putnam's Sons, 1897, pp. ix, 394).

when the prevailing thought in Germany was at its metaphysical and romantic height. Some German thought came by direct study, especially of Herder, Wieland, Schiller, and Goethe rather than Kant, Fichte, and Schelling, and some through English intermediaries, particularly Coleridge and Carlyle. The name Transcendental Club, given by neighbours in derision, came from Kantian philosophy. The Transcendentalists were disturbed by the sweep of materialism in the rapidly developing United States. They wished to match it by progress in higher values and laboured for what was akin to a religious revival. Some of the Transcendentalists hoped for the attainment of their objective by the renovation of man's nature and others by reforming human institutions. Brook Farm, their brief creation, was an attempt to give to the world an example of a perfect human society. In that respect it was akin to the many idealistic communities which arose in the United States in the nineteenth century from the dream of creating in the new nation groups that would fully embody Christian standards and be radiating centres of a fresh birth of humanity. It also was part of the continuing stream for social and moral reform which went back to the purposes that had entered into the founding of New England, Pennsylvania, and Georgia, and which in the next chapter we shall see as a major and continuing contribution to the United States from Christianity, chiefly from Protestantism of the Puritan-Pietist-Evangelical tradition. Nathaniel Hawthorne (1804–1864) for a time was a member of the Brook Farm Community but did not hold to its view of human nature.

To Herman Melville (1819–1891) the idealism represented by the Transcendentalists dodged the central problems of the nature of man—as did Calvinism, Unitarianism, and Emerson. He expressed what was in the minds of some other thoughtful souls of the revolutionary age as in his novels he struggled with the contrast in the dual nature of man and in the character of the universe of which man is a part.[11]

THE RESPONSE OF THE CONGREGATIONAL MAJORITY

The majority wing of Congregationalism was affected by the intellectual currents of the revolutionary age but responded in ways which differed from those of the Unitarian minority.

Andover Theological Seminary, founded (1808) against Harvard's commitment to Unitarianism, was long a major centre of theological thought and of training for the Congregational ministry. Begun by the Hopkinsians and the Old Calvinists, it opposed the Unitarian doctrine of God and man.

For many years Andover Theological Seminary remained true to the creed to which the members of its faculty were required to subscribe publicly every five years. It was also a well-spring from which men went out committed to revivals

[11] Stewart, *American Literature and Christian Doctrine*, pp. 73 ff.; Gabriel, *The Course of American Democratic Thought*, pp. 67–77; Matthiessen, *American Renaissance*, pp. 371–516.

and from which issued many missionary movements and missionaries. Along with this strong Evangelicalism was a growing awareness of the currents of thought which were pulsing on the other side of the Atlantic. Thus Moses Stuart (1780–1852), a brilliant Yale graduate who under the influence of Timothy Dwight entered the ministry and went from a successful pastorate in New Haven to become professor of Biblical literature in Andover and was on the faculty from 1810 to 1848, argued stoutly for Trinitarianism against Channing. He knew contemporary German Biblical scholarship. It was meat and drink to him, but he remained conservative and rejected many of its positions. He was also familiar with Lyell's newly published *The Principles of Geology* and, holding firmly to the creation of the world in six days of twenty-four hours each, made lively entrance into discussions of the theological implications of the new geology. A great teacher and a prodigious author, he had a wide influence through his students and forty or more books.[12] Stuart's successor was Calvin Ellis Stowe (1802–1886). Husband of the more famous Harriet Beecher Stowe, daughter of Lyman Beecher, he was a remarkable linguist who was familiar with European scholarship and was regarded in his generation as the outstanding American expert on the Old Testament. In his inaugural address at Andover he sought to refute Strauss and the Tübingen school of Baur.[13] Edwards Amasa Park (1808–1900), a graduate of Brown and Andover, a great preacher and orator, and on the Andover faculty for over half a century (1836–1881), had studied in Germany and was committed to the "common sense" philosophy of the Scottish "moderates" Thomas Reid and Dugald Stewart. Yet this did not keep him from remaining a convinced Hopkinsian and a powerful preacher of revivals. His students remembered him and his colleagues as stressing the freedom of the will—which was moving far from the earlier Calvinism but was essential to revivalism. In his later years the stream of theological thought had so far passed beyond Park that he did not publish the work on systematic theology on which he had been labouring for years and whose outlook he had sought to instill in his students.[14]

In the latter half of the century the Andover faculty were influenced by the contemporary currents of thought to such a degree that, while regarding themselves as "evangelical liberals" and their thought as "progressive orthodoxy," they moved far from the positions of their predecessors. In this they paralleled the developments which were taking place in numbers of Protestant churches on the Continent of Europe and in the British Isles. In the 1880's a sharp break came. In 1880 William J. Tucker in coming on the faculty qualified

[12] Williams, *The Andover Liberals*, pp. 17, 18; *Dictionary of American Biography*, Vol. XVIII, pp. 174, 175; Bainton, *Yale and the Ministry*, pp. 90–92.

[13] *Dictionary of American Biography*, Vol. XVIII, p. 115; Williams, *op. cit.*, p. 18.

[14] Foster, *A Genetic History of the New England Theology*, pp. 471 ff.; *Dictionary of American Biography*, Vol. XIV, pp. 204, 205; Williams, *op. cit.*, pp. 19–22; Tucker, *My Generation*, p. 56; S. E. Ahlstrom in *Church History*, Vol. XXIV, pp. 264, 265.

his subscription to the creed framed by the founders. Two years later Charles M. Mead and Joseph H. Thayer, who had studied in Germany and were beginning to use the historical-critical approach to the Bible, resigned, giving as their reason that they had conscientious scruples against repeating their endorsement of the creed every five years. When Park retired (1881), Newman Smyth, named as his successor and willing to assent to the creed, was rejected by an official body known as the Visitors because he had attacked Old Calvinism and held to the possibility of "future probation." "Future probation" meant that those who in this life had not had opportunity to hear of the Christian faith or to come under the influence of Christian motives to repentance and faith might be given such an opportunity. Smyth then declined the offer of a new chair in Christian apologetics. George Harris, who was inducted into Park's Chair, pled for putting faith on a rational basis and declared his belief in progress and in the Kingdom of God as a new social order on earth. The other members of the faculty appointed in the 1880's had much the same attitude and expressed it through *The Andover Review,* which they founded in 1884. Conservatives attacked them in the religious press and elsewhere. In 1886 they were formally accused to the Board of Visitors of heresy. A public trial followed before the Visitors with the result that one of the five defendants, Egbert C. Smyth, was ordered removed from his chair and the others, holding substantially the same convictions, were acquitted. The case was carried to the Supreme Court of Massachusetts and Smyth was reinstated. On the ground that the Chief Justice had dissented, the case was renewed before the Board of Visitors and the latter, now with its membership altered by deaths, ordered it dismissed (1892). The "Andover case" had dragged on for six years, preceded by two years of controversy. Its outcome was hailed in liberal circles as a victory for freedom of thought and teaching.[15]

In the meantime a parallel but somewhat different development was seen in Yale. From its founding, Yale had been more conservative theologically than Harvard.[16] In the eighteenth century its most distinguished graduate and for a short time a junior member of its faculty was Jonathan Edwards. A grandson of Edwards, Timothy Dwight, was president from 1795 to 1817 and under his preaching the college was profoundly moved by the Second Awakening. A man of broad educational vision, Dwight introduced the study of science and prepared the way for the professional schools. Five years after his death, in 1822,

---

[15] Williams, *op. cit.,* pp. 26 ff.; Tucker, *op. cit.,* pp. 125–221; *The Andover Case: with an Introductory Historical Statement; a Careful Summary of the Arguments of the Respondent Professors; and the Full Text of the Arguments of the Complainants and Their Counsel, together with the Decision of the Board of Visitors: Furnishing the Nearest Available Approach to a Complete History of the Whole Matter* (Boston, Stanley and Usher, 1887, pp. xxix, 194), *passim;* Newman Smyth, *Recollections and Reflections* (New York, Charles Scribner's Sons, 1936, pp. 244); pp. 104–109.

[16] Bainton, *op. cit.,* p. 1.

the Divinity School was begun to carry on in more specialized fashion the training for the ministry which from the beginning had been a major purpose of the college. Its first professor of theology and its most dynamic figure in its early years was Nathaniel William Taylor (1786–1858).[17] From the founding of the Yale Divinity School until his death—more than a third of a century—Taylor sent out a succession of ministers who had been deeply impressed by his theology. As an ardent participant in the revivals, he was constrained to find theological justification for urging men to repent. In doing so he departed somewhat from the earlier Yale graduates, Edwards, Hopkins, Bellamy, and Dwight, who had had a large share in preparing men for the ministry. He denied that our consciousness of freedom is an illusion, held to the reality of freedom of choice, declared that man is not born totally depraved, and taught that an appeal must be made to man's desire for happiness—his "self-love"—and that in a regenerated person this becomes the unselfish love of God. Yet he was in the current of thought of these predecessors, believed that he held true to the essentials of the Calvinistic theology which had prevailed in New England, and attempted boldly to state it in ways that would both be logically consistent and permit revivalism with its appeal to all to repent.

In contrast with the Unitarians Taylor held that man is corrupt and needs to be converted. But also in contrast with some in the Calvinist ranks he insisted that man can respond to God's pleas. Here he was among those who sought intellectual justification for the departure from the inherited Reformed theology with its doctrines of predestination and irresistible grace. He wished to establish an underlying assumption of the revivalism through which Protestant Christianity was spreading among the unchurched of the older stock, namely, the ability of men to repent and accept God's grace. Taylor's version was sometimes called "the new divinity," sometimes "Taylorism," at other times "New Haven theology," and at still other times "Beecherism." Taylor and Beecher were in substantial agreement. Taylor not only was intimately familiar with the writings of Calvin and of the New England theologians but also knew the arguments of the Scottish "moderates" Reid and Stewart, with their "common sense" theology, who like him stood for freedom of the will against the "doctrine of inability." Indeed, Stewart and then Reid were required reading for Yale undergraduates.[18]

Taylor's vigorous formulation of his convictions, his exposition of them to his students and in his preaching—for he preached somewhere nearly every Sunday—and his presentation of them in his writings aroused controversy. He tilted with the Unitarians of Boston—for he was staunchly against their views

[17] Mead, *Nathaniel William Taylor, passim;* Bainton, *op. cit.,* pp. 81–83, 96 ff.; Nathaniel W. Taylor, *Lectures on the Moral Government of God* (New York, Clark, Austin and Smith, 2 vols., 1859); *Dictionary of American Biography,* Vol. XVIII, pp. 338, 339.
[18] S. E. Ahlstrom in *Church History,* Vol. XXIV, p. 264; Mead, *op. cit., passim;* Bainton, *op. cit.,* pp. 97, 98; Gabriel, *Religion and Learning at Yale,* p. 135.

and few if any Unitarians existed in Connecticut. Opposition arose among the orthodox Congregationalists. It was led by Bennet Tyler (1783-1858). A graduate of Yale, Tyler was pastor in Portland, Maine, when periodical articles by Taylor in 1829 precipitated a warm debate between supporters of the "new divinity" and the Calvinists who could not agree with it. In 1834 to counter Taylor's influence the Theological Institute of Connecticut was founded, later to be the Hartford Theological Seminary. Tyler was its president from its beginning to 1857.[19]

Taylor's views contributed to the split between the Old School and the New School Presbyterians. For years New England Congregational influence had been strong in the Presbyterian churches on Long Island and in New Jersey. The Plan of Union between Congregationalists and Presbyterians strengthened that influence in the churches which were arising from the westward migration. Many students who had been trained at Yale under Taylor occupied Presbyterian pulpits, especially in New York, both city and state. When Lane Seminary was begun by Presbyterians in Cincinnati (1832), Lyman Beecher was called to its professorship of theology and accepted. Congregationalists and Presbytarians joined in founding Union Theological Seminary in New York City in 1836. As Hopkinsianism and Taylorism began to penetrate the Presbyterian Church through these channels, alarm developed among the Presbyterians who represented the Scotch-Irish tradition and had their theological seminary in Princeton. As we have seen, the separation of the New School from the Old School Presbyterians came in 1838. For it the teachings of Taylor were in part accountable.[20]

Before the break occurred, three men had been arraigned before the Presbytery of Illinois (1833) for teaching the New Haven theology and Lyman Beecher had been prosecuted for heresy before the Presbytery and the Synod of Cincinnati (1835). All four of the accused were acquitted.[21]

Another voice from Yale and Connecticut, but of a quite different kind, was that of Horace Bushnell.[22] Horace Bushnell (1802-1876) was born and reared on a Connecticut farm. He united with a Congregational church when he was nineteen and graduated from Yale in 1827. Religious doubts kept him from preparing for the ministry as he had once intended and he was headed for law. Then, as a tutor at Yale in 1831 he was caught up in a revival which was

---

[19] *Dictionary of National Biography*, Vol. XIX, p. 85; Foster, *op. cit.*, pp. 381 ff.; Bainton, *op. cit.*, pp. 96 ff.; Bacon, *Leonard Bacon*, pp. 117–143.

[20] Foster, *op. cit.*, pp. 430 ff.

[21] Thompson, *A History of the Presbyterian Churches in the United States*, p. 108; Bainton, *op. cit.*, pp. 103, 104.

[22] Mrs. Mary A. (Bushnell) Cheney, editor, *Life and Letters of Horace Bushnell* (New York, Harper & Brothers, 1880, pp. x, 579), *passim; Dictionary of American Biography*, Vol. III, pp. 350–354; Bainton, *op. cit.*, p. 113 ff.; E. C. Gardner in *Theology Today*, Vol. XII, pp. 10 ff.; Barbara M. Cross, *Horace Bushnell, Minister to a Changing America* (University of Chicago Press, pp. XV, 201), *passim.*

sweeping the campus. He entered the Yale Divinity School and there was under the teaching of Taylor. While he greatly respected the older man, he reacted against both his methods and his conclusions. He turned to Coleridge, and especially to the latter's *Aids to Reflexion*. In his attitude towards religion he had kinship with Schleiermacher, Neander, Coleridge, J. F. D. Maurice, and F. W. Robertson and was influenced by the Scottish "Common Sense" philosophy. He had more of feeling than of the kind of logic employed by Taylor and the Calvinists. From 1833 to 1861 he was pastor of a Congregational church in Hartford in his home state. When in mid-stream in his service in that church and after much inner searching and struggle he had a sudden experience which he felt was a vision of truth that gave him perfect freedom. It was followed by his *God in Christ* (1849).[23] He wrote extensively and was widely read. Rejecting the belief current in the Congregationalism of his day that the individual must have reached maturity and have had the experience of the new birth before becoming a Christian, he held, in his treatise *Christian Nurture,* that "the child is to grow up as a Christian and never know himself as being otherwise."[24]

Bushnell came out firmly as a Trinitarian. He held that although many Unitarians earnestly maintained the authenticity of miracles, by denying human depravity they abandoned the recognition of the need for supernatural grace and set forth a religion of ethics and of self-culture rather than one of faith and regeneration. He recognized, as did others, that the debate between the Unitarians and the Orthodox centred around convictions concerning the nature of man. Fully cognizant of sceptical views on the other side of the Atlantic, including those of Strauss and Renan, he stoutly maintained the authenticity of the miracles of Jesus. Vividly aware of the emphasis in the revolutionary age on nature and natural laws to the seeming exclusion of the supernatural, he held that Christianity "is supernatural, not because it works through the laws of nature, limited by and doing the works of the laws, but because it acts regeneratively and new-creatively to repair the damage which those laws, in their penal action, would otherwise perpetuate." He maintained that both nature and the supernatural are of God and in the divine purpose.[25]

Some of Bushnell's views, including those on the atonement, akin as they were to the "moral influence" theory, were looked upon by many as heretical, but he was never brought to trial for heresy. To many thoughtful souls, both within Congregationalism and outside it, troubled by the issues raised by the intellectual currents of the day and unsatisfied by the inherited theology, Bushnell came as a breath of fresh air and seemed to them to answer their deepest

---

[23] Horace Bushnell, *God in Christ* (Hartford, Brown and Parsons, 1849, pp. 356).
[24] Horace Bushnell, *Christian Nurture* (New York, Charles Scribner's Sons, 1861, pp. 407), p. 10.
[25] Horace Bushnell, *Nature and the Supernatural as together Constituting the One System of God* (New York, Charles Scribner's Sons, 2nd ed., 1877, pp. 528), especially pp. 22, 24, 42.

questions. His combination of thought with feeling was a welcome relief to New Englanders who had reacted from the closely knit logic of the sermons on which they had been reared.

Yale and its Divinity School and graduates continued to be a centre of adjustment to the challenges posed by the scholarship of the day. But, in spite of the dissent represented by Tyler and the Old School Presbyterians, it was not brought as spectacularly into the public eye as was Andover Theological Seminary with its prolonged heresy trial. In the second half of the century it had on its faculty men who had studied in Germany and who were committed to the historical approach to the Scriptures and theology, but in the main it could be compared to the mediating school in German nineteenth-century Protestantism. Yale's initial leading scientists, notably Benjamin Silliman and James Dwight Dana, the latter making the university the foremost centre in America for the study of geology, were devout Christians.[26]

Another radiating centre of theological thought in nineteenth-century American Congregationalism was Oberlin. Its chief early figure was Finney. Like the Yale Divinity School it bore the strong impress of revivalism. Moreover, Finney was much influenced by Taylor. Yet Oberlin was even more a child of revivalism than was the Yale Divinity School, for in Yale's setting remnants of the anti-revivalistic attitude of the Old Lights and Old Calvinists persisted. Oberlin was an idealistic community which in the nineteenth-century context attempted what the founders of New Haven had endeavoured to do in the seventeenth century: build a perfect Christian community in the New World. But in the conditions in which it was set the expressions of that idealism differed from those of an earlier day. For example, it stood for equal opportunity for the sexes and in its early days its trend was towards a belief that through the grace of God Christian perfection in this life was both desirable and attainable.[27]

Around the turn of the century a different emphasis in Oberlin was represented and in part shaped by Henry Churchill King (1858–1934).[28] A graduate of Oberlin, during student days in Berlin King was much influenced by the philosophy of Lotze and the theology of Ritschl. He was professor of theology at Oberlin from 1897 to 1925 and president of the college from 1902 to his retirement. He sought to make Oberlin a "character-begetting power." A religious philosopher of the idealistic school and in part a Ritschlian, thus representing the "social gospel" trend of his day, he was a liberal evangelical, accepted biological evolution and the current methods of Biblical criticism, and was fervently loyal to the Christian faith.[29] He was widely influential in American Protestantism.

[26] Bainton, *op. cit.*, pp. 105, 165 ff.
[27] Foster, *op. cit.*, pp. 453–470.
[28] *Dictionary of American Biography*, Vol. XXI, pp. 469, 470.
[29] See two of his more substantial books: *Reconstruction in Theology* (New York, The Mac-

In Henry Ward Beecher (1813–1887), a son of Lyman Beecher, Congregationalism produced a popularizer of some of the nineteenth-century trends.[30] The younger Beecher was even more a national figure than his father. After spending the earlier years of his ministry in the Middle West, in 1847 he came as the first pastor of the newly organized Plymouth Church (Congregational) on Brooklyn Heights, just across the East River from New York City. There he preached for forty years. He attracted huge audiences, mainly from the older American stock which was moving into the growing metropolis. Through his sermons and his contributions to such periodicals as *The Independent* and *The Christian Union,* both of them frankly Christian and the latter of his founding, and later *The Outlook,* he was the most widely influential American preacher of the third quarter of the century. He was not a theologian and reacted against much of the Calvinism in which he had been reared. Although he shared in the revival of 1857–1858 which began in New York, he sought to draw men to the Christian life by preaching the love of God in Christ rather than by the compulsive methods of Finney. He early accepted the theory of evolution and proclaimed that as an interpretation of the way God works in the world it was not only consistent with the Gospel but made possible a richer and deeper understanding of God's helpfulness. He stressed moral character, was an anti-slavery advocate, and championed free trade. He attempted to rise above denominationalism and theological controversy.

Henry Ward Beecher was succeeded in the pastorate of Plymouth Church by Lyman Abbott (1835–1922). Abbott was more famous as a writer than as a preacher. Of Congregational lineage, his father had been a clergyman of the liberal wing and was better known as an educator and as the author of the Rollo books, for the instruction of boys, than as a pastor. Lyman Abbott himself was first a lawyer, then, under the impulse of the revival of 1857–1858 and the influence of Beecher, entered the ministry. He always remained a loyal admirer of the older man and believed him innocent of the offense charged in a court case which clouded the latter's later years. At first fairly conservative theologically, through study and editorial writing he moved towards the liberal wing. But he did not become either a Unitarian or a Universalist and remained in the stream of "progressive orthodoxy." Never an original or creative thinker or a radical, he was near the vanguard of many causes, theological, political, moral, and social. As pastor of Plymouth Church from 1887 to 1899 he transformed it from a rostrum for great preaching to an institution whose members sought to serve the underprivileged about them. His main contribution was

millan Co., 2nd ed., 1903, pp. xiii, 257) and *Theology and the Social Consciousness. A Study of the Relation of Social Consciousness to Theology* (New York, The Macmillan Co., 1902, pp. xviii, 252).

[30] Lyman Abbott, *Henry Ward Beecher* (Boston, Houghton Mifflin Co., 1903, pp. xxxviii, 457), *passim;* Foster, *The Modern Movement in American Theology,* pp. 81 ff.; Lyman Beecher Stowe, *Saints, Sinners and Beechers* (Indianapolis, The Bobbs-Merrill Co., 1934, pp. 450), pp. 231–335.

through periodicals, chiefly *The Christian Union* and *The Outlook* but earlier other journals. For many thousands he aided the religious adjustment to the currents of thought of the age.[31]

Richard Salter Storrs (1821–1900), a younger contemporary of Beecher and an older contemporary of Abbott, was for over fifty years, beginning in 1846, pastor of the Church of the Pilgrims (Congregational) in Brooklyn. The third of his name, from a long line of New England ministers, son of a friend of Lyman Beecher, he was a graduate of Andover and a warm admirer of Park. A great pulpit orator, a popular lyceum lecturer, a great figure in the New York-Brooklyn area, he was regarded by many as impeccably orthodox. Yet, while believing in the miracles of Jesus, he did not teach that Jesus appealed to them as the chief proof of his divinity, nor did he hold to Old Testament prophecies of Christ as conclusive evidence. He valued the New Testament above any other book. In a series of lectures he saw in the history of Christianity additional confirmation of the faith. He also believed that Christianity ensured the progress of the human race.[32]

George Angier Gordon (1853–1929) was very different from any of the other Congregational preachers whom we have mentioned but also had the ear of thousands—although a more limited clientele—in the effort to formulate the accord of Christian faith to the intellectual climate of his day. Born in Scotland on a farm, he came to the United States in his late teens. In spite of an early struggle with poverty, he acquired a theological education in Bangor and then a college education in Harvard. In Harvard he won the respect of its great philosophers of the time—James and Palmer. He became pastor of Old South Congregational Church in Boston in 1884 and continued in its pulpit, already famous, until his death. Markedly influenced by Plato, Aristotle, Kant, and Hegel, he was described as a philosopher who knew how to preach. Despising sham and with a rugged character and intellect, in the capital of Unitarianism and Universalism he differed frankly from them both and upheld the doctrine of the Trinity.[33]

THE PRESBYTERIAN RESPONSE

In general, the main stream of the Presbyterianism of the United States was more resistant to the nineteenth-century currents of thought than was Con-

[31] Abbott, *Reminiscences, passim;* Brown, *Lyman Abbott, Christian Evolutionist, passim.*

[32] *Dictionary of American Biography,* Vol. XVIII, pp. 101, 102; Richard Salter Storrs, *The Divine Origin of Christianity Indicated by Its Historical Effects* (New York, Anson D. F. Randolph & Co., 1884, pp. xiv, 674), *passim.*

[33] *Dictionary of American Biography,* Vol. VII, pp. 419–421; Foster, *op. cit.,* pp. 81 ff.; George A. Gordon, *Humanism in New England Theology* (Boston, Houghton Mifflin Co., 1920, pp. viii, 105), pp. 86 ff.; *Book of the Fortieth Year, issued in grateful and affectionate recognition of the fortieth anniversary of the installation of George A. Gordon D.D., LL.D. as Minister of the Old South Church in Boston* (Boston, Old South Church of Boston, 1924, pp. x, 316), *passim;* George Angier Gordon, *My Education and Religion. An Autobiography* (Boston, Houghton Mifflin Co., 1926, pp. 352), *passim.*

gregationalism. It continued to hold to the Westminster Confession, to which much of pre-nineteenth- and early nineteenth-century Congregationalism had subscribed. It knew dissent. We have seen the separation of the New School from the Old School Presbyterians, the former the product of influences issuing from Congregationalism. But, as we have also noted, after about a generation the two were reconciled. In their reunion they continued to adhere to the Westminster formulation of faith. From time to time individuals were charged with heresy. With its structure of church courts from presbytery to General Assembly Presbyterianism could act on such cases in a way which Congregationalism, with its looser organization, could not. It was able, therefore, more nearly to close its ranks and present a united front against departures from its historic position than could Congregationalism. Yet even in such circumstances American Presbyterianism partly accommodated itself to the intellectual temper of the age. In this it resembled the Presbyterian and Reformed churches in the British Isles and the Continent of Europe.

The Presbyterian Church did not know the division brought by the Unitarians in Congregationalism, but early in the nineteenth century it began to be disturbed by the theological trends represented by Edwards, Hopkins, and Emmons which entered chiefly through the connexion with New England Congregationalism. In 1817 the Synod of Philadelphia lumped Hopkinsianism with the Arian, Socinian, and Arminian heresies.[34] The "New Haven theology" accentuated the conflict, which issued in the rupture between the Old School and the New School.

The chief centre for training the ministry of the largest body of Presbyterians, the Presbyterian Church in the U.S.A., was long Princeton Theological Seminary. As we have seen, it was begun in 1812 as an official organ of that church. At first its faculty was inclined to take a conciliatory position in the conflicting currents but in the late 1830's it lined up firmly with the Old School.[35] Even before that time Auburn Theological Seminary had been organized in New York State by those who regarded Princeton as too narrow.[36] In 1836, as we have noted, Union Theological Seminary was founded in New York City by men of New School and Plan of Union sympathies and completely independent of the General Assembly.[37]

The great figure at Princeton during the larger part of the century was Charles Hodge (1797-1878).[38] Of Scotch-Irish stock, he was reared in a devout home of the New Light Presbyterian tradition. Deeply religious from his happy

---

[34] Thompson, *A History of the Presbyterian Churches in the United States*, p. 86.
[35] *Ibid.*, pp. 113, 114.
[36] *Ibid.*, pp. 85, 86.
[37] *Ibid.*, p. 114.
[38] A. A. Hodge, *The Life of Charles Hodge* (New York, Charles Scribner's Sons, 1880, pp. viii, 620; an admiring biography by a son, with many of his father's letters and extracts from his journals), *passim; Dictionary of American Biography*, Vol. IX, pp. 98, 99.

childhood, growing up with a simple belief in the love of God and nurtured on the Westminster Catechism, while a student in the College of New Jersey during a revival he made a public profession of faith. He graduated from Princeton Theological Seminary in 1819 and there was profoundly influenced by Archibald Alexander, its first professor, noted as a preacher, for his devotion to Evangelical religion, and for his "singular attainments in holiness."[39] In 1820 he became a member of the faculty and with the exception of 1826–1828 when he studied in Europe he remained on it until his death at an advanced age. From 1822 to 1840 he was professor of Oriental and Biblical literature and thereafter had the chair of systematic theology. During his years in Europe he spent much time in Germany, formed a lifelong friendship with Tholuck, and made the acquaintance of some of the outstanding theological and Biblical scholars of the day, among them Neander and Hengstenberg. In his own theological thinking he especially felt the impress of François Turretin (1623–1687), a staunch Calvinist, vigorous defender of the Synod of Dort and of the Helvetic Consensus (1675), a statement of scholastic Calvinism, against the liberalizing trends in the French theological centre Saumur. Turretin's *Institutio Theologiae Elencticae* (1679–1685) had been the text in Alexander's classroom, and in his old age Hodge still regarded it as "one of the most perspicuous books ever written."[40] He was also influenced by Benedict Pictet (1655–1724), theologian and hymn-writer, who similarly held to the Calvinism of the Helvetic Consensus.

A man of deep emotional piety which was centred on the love of God in Christ, Hodge exerted a profound influence on his students both in the classroom and in his Sunday afternoon conferences. A scholar of solid learning and familiar with contemporary thought, he was the outstanding representative in America in his lifetime of Augustinianism in its stiff Calvinistic form. He wrote extensively, partly in books and partly in the journal which he founded in 1825 and edited for forty years and which eventually bore the title *Biblical Repertory and Princeton Review*. Of his books the one which made the greatest impact was his *Systematic Theology*.[41] It and some of the others were widely read on both sides of the Atlantic.

Hodge believed in the verbal inspiration and infallibility of the Scriptures. To his mind theology as he outlined it was unshakably founded on the Bible and was the faith once for all delivered to the saints. Any variation from it was error. At the semi-centennial of his election to a professorship he declared with satisfaction: "I am not afraid to say that a new idea never originated in this

[39] *Dictionary of American Biography*, Vol. I, pp. 162, 163.
[40] Hodge, *op. cit.*, p. 553. Yet he was partly shaped by the Scottish "common sense" philosophy. S. E. Ahlstrom in *Church History*, Vol. XXIV, pp. 266, 267.
[41] Charles Hodge, *Systematic Theology* (New York, Charles Scribner's Sons, 3 vols., 1872–1873).

seminary."[42] He was by nature optimistic and believed that infants dying in infancy would be saved, as would the great majority of the human race.[43]

Believing as he did, it was natural that Hodge should stand firmly for what came to be called Princeton theology against all variations from the kind of Calvinism which it represented. He was vigorous in his criticism of Taylor and especially of the trends at Andover. He opposed the theological currents that were entering the Presbyterian Church through New England Congregationalism and favoured the division which cut off the New School with what to him was its heretical taint.

Charles Hodge was followed in his Princeton chair by his son, Archibald Alexander Hodge (1823–1886). The younger Hodge had deep reverence for his father. He had been a missionary in India until ill health brought him home. Less learned than his sire, he was more widely read, had richer human sympathies, and in his fervent personal religion had flashes of mystical insight. Honest, frank, and generous, he had great influence with his students.[44] His *Outlines of Theology* went into many editions and was long used as a textbook.[45]

The younger Hodge was succeeded by Benjamin Breckinridge Warfield (1851–1921).[46] With a command of modern language, keeping abreast of theological scholarship, writing extensively, Warfield continued the Hodge tradition without concessions, held to the plenary inspiration of the Bible, was committed to Calvinism, and regarded the Westminster Confession as the final crystallization of the very essence of Evangelical religion.

James McCosh (1811–1894) was also in Princeton, but as president of the College of New Jersey, soon to be Princeton University, and not in the seminary. He also exerted a marked influence on Presbyterianism in the United States and on theological thought. A native of Scotland, a pupil of Thomas Chalmers, a pastor who went with the Free Church at the time of the Disruption, while he reacted against the "moderatism" which he knew in his youth, he was influenced by Reid and Stewart and was an intuitionalist and an outspoken critic of John Stuart Mill. He came to the United States in 1868 as president of the New Jersey institution and under his administration the college prospered. He was also a great teacher and his philosophy of religion was inspired by an uncompromising theism.[47]

[42] A. A. Hodge, *op. cit.*, p. 521.

[43] Loetscher, *The Broadening Church*, p. 41.

[44] *Dictionary of National Biography*, Vol. IX, pp. 97, 98.

[45] A. Alexander Hodge, *Outlines of Theology* (New York, R. Carter & Brothers, 1880, pp. 678).

[46] *Dictionary of American Biography*, Vol. XIX, pp. 453, 454. Among his books see Benjamin Breckenridge Warfield, *Calvin and Calvinism* (New York, Oxford University Press, 1931, pp. v, 428).

[47] William Milligan Sloane, editor, *The Life of James McCosh, Chiefly Autobiographical* (New York, Charles Scribner's Sons, 1897, pp. vi, 287), *passim; Dictionary of American Biography*, Vol. XI, pp. 615–617.

With its tendency to adhere to its doctrinal basis as expressed in the Westminster Confession, the Presbyterian Church in the United States of America knew heresy trials. Some were local and confined to presbyteries and synods, and others engaged the attention of the General Assembly.

The most famous of the Presbyterian heresy trials of the nineteenth century was that of Briggs.[48] Charles Augustus Briggs (1841–1913), after graduation from the University of Virginia and two years of theological study in the United States, had four further years of similar study in Berlin. In 1874 he became professor of Hebrew in Union Theological Seminary in New York City and in 1890 was moved into a new chair of Biblical theology in that institution. His address on his induction into that chair led to the veto by the General Assembly of his appointment. He had already alarmed the conservatives. In *Whither?* published the year before, he declared that many different interpretations had been given to the Westminster theology and that departures from its standards were numerous. While generously declaring that they ranked high in the roll of American theologians, he attacked both the older and the younger Hodge. But he pled for tolerance on the part of all parties, was eager for Christian unity, and advocated the reconstruction of theology, polity, worship, and Christian life and work on the basis of divine truth as the only orthodoxy. He earnestly desired organic unity, maintained that in its achievement the Church of England was entitled to lead, and welcomed the recently issued Chicago-Lambeth quadrilateral as a guide.[49] Union Theological Seminary, founded by men of New School and Congregational proclivities, had at first been independent of ecclesiastical control. Then, in 1870, in the burst of good will which accompanied the reunion of the Old and the New School, it had given to the General Assembly the right to review appointments to its faculty. In 1892 Briggs was tried for heresy by the New York Presbytery but was acquitted.[50] Such questions were raised as the inerrancy of the Scriptures, the authorship of Isaiah, and progressive sanctification after death. The prosecution appealed to the General Assembly and the latter body suspended Briggs from the ministry.[51] Union Theological Seminary contended that the authority which it had granted to the General Assembly did not extend to the right to veto the transfer of a member of its faculty from one chair to another, severed its connexion with the Presbyterian Church, and retained Briggs.

As might have been anticipated from *Whither?* Briggs eventually sought

[48] *Dictionary of American Biography,* Vol. III, pp. 40, 41; Loetscher, *op. cit.,* pp. 27–33, 48–62.
[49] Charles Augustus Briggs, *Whither? A Theological Question for the Times* (New York, Charles Scribner's Sons, 1889, pp. xv, 303), *passim.*
[50] *The Defense of Professor Briggs before the Presbytery of New York December 13, 14, 15, 19, and 22, 1892* (New York, Charles Scribner's Sons, 1893, pp. xx, 193), *passim.*
[51] John J. McCook, compiler, *The Appeal in the Briggs Case before the General Assembly of the Presbyterian Church in the United States of America* (New York, J. C. Rankin Co., 1893, pp. 378). In another form *The Case against Professor Briggs* (New York, Charles Scribner's Sons, five parts, 1893).

admission to the Protestant Episcopal Church and was given orders. Although he believed in the principles and methods of the higher criticism, he was essentially conservative and stood firmly for the virgin birth of Christ.[52] In 1904, in view of his zeal for Christian unity, a unity which he wished to see embrace all branches of the Church, he resigned the chair of Biblical theology and devoted his time to symbolics and irenics. A man of positive opinions, deeply affectionate, he won wide respect as a scholar, especially in his planning and editing the two series *International Critical Commentary* and *International Theological Library.*

Another heresy trial, although not attracting quite so much attention, was of a man who defended Briggs. Henry Preserved Smith (1847–1927) had twice studied in Germany and so was familiar with the Protestant scholarship of that country. He taught church history and then the Old Testament at Lane Theological Seminary. Conservative, yet convinced by Wellhausen of the validity of the critical method, he was convicted of heresy by his presbytery (1892) and then, on appeal, by the General Assembly, because he could not affirm the verbal inerrancy of the Scriptures. He spent most of his later years (1913–1925) as librarian in Union Theological Seminary in New York. He was the author of a number of books which became standard.[53]

Another case which did not come formally to trial was that of Arthur Cushman McGiffert (1861–1933). McGiffert had a degree from Marburg, was a friend and defender of Smith, and later was president of Union Theological Seminary in New York. Although the General Assembly of 1899 affirmed the inerrancy of the Scriptures, the infallibility of all statements made by Jesus Christ, the belief that the Lord's Supper was instituted by Christ Himself, and the doctrine of justification by faith alone as against views which he was alleged to have put forth, to avoid prolonged litigation McGiffert quietly withdrew from the jurisdiction of the Presbyterian Church and became a Congregationalist.[54]

In a quite different category in Presbyterianism, but also on occasion a storm centre, was Thomas DeWitt Talmadge (1832–1902).[55] Although he was reared and for a time was a minister in the Dutch Reformed Church, most of his fame came while he was pastor of the Central Presbyterian Church in Brooklyn (1869–1895). There he attracted huge congregations. Opposition was not to his theology, for to him "higher criticism meant lower religion,"[56] but to his methods of preaching. His enemies declared that he was a pulpit clown and

---

[52] Charles Augustus Briggs, *The Incarnation of the Lord* (New York, Charles Scribner's Sons, 1902, pp. x, 243), *passim;* Charles Augustus Briggs, "The Virgin Birth of Our Lord," in *American Journal of Theology*, Vol. XII, pp. 189–210.

[53] Loetscher, *op. cit.*, pp. 63 ff.; *Dictionary of American Biography*, Vol. XVII, pp. 278, 279.

[54] *Dictionary of American Biography*, Vol. XXI, pp. 527–529; Loetscher, *op. cit.*, pp. 71–74.

[55] Louis Albert Banks, editor, *T. DeWitt Talmadge, His Life and Work* (London, O. W. Binkerd, 1902, pp. xvi, 500); T. DeWitt Talmadge, *T. DeWitt Talmadge as I Knew Him* (New York, E. P. Dutton and Co., 1912, pp. 439); *Dictionary of American Biography*, Vol. XVIII, pp. 287, 288.

[56] Talmadge, *op. cit.*, p. 253.

mountebank. In 1879 he was tried by the Brooklyn Presbytery on the charge of "falsehood and deceit and . . . using improper methods of preaching, tending to bring religion into contempt." He was acquitted, but by a close vote. At the height of his popularity his sermons were published in about 3,500 newspapers. He lectured widely and was again and again in England. He knew some of the prominent public figures of his day both there and in the United States. From 1890 until his death he edited *The Christian Herald,* a religious journal that appealed to a popular clientele.

A contrasting kind of preacher was seen in Henry Sloane Coffin (1877-1954). He did not come into his full stride until after 1914. A graduate of Yale and of Union Theological Seminary in New York and after 1926 president of the latter institution, from 1905 to 1926 he was minister of the Madison Avenue Presbyterian Church in New York City. Familiar with modern scholarship, often known as a liberal but akin to the mediating theologians of Germany, he was a noted preacher, lecturer, and teacher and was a moderator of his church.[57]

An older colleague of Coffin on the faculty of Union Theological Seminary and a younger colleague of Briggs, William Adams Brown (1865-1943) was also of the mediating temperament. Remaining in the Presbyterian Church, even more than Briggs he laboured for Christian unity. His *Christian Theology in Outline* sympathetically took account of contemporary currents of thought, was strongly Christocentric, and was widely used as a textbook.[58]

By the year 1914 the forces making for modifications of inherited beliefs had become sufficiently potent to alter the confession of faith of the Presbyterian Church in the U.S.A. In the early 1890's an attempt at revision failed.[59] However, in 1903 changes were adopted which affirmed that God loves all mankind, said that "all dying in infancy are included in the election of grace" and that the good deeds of unregenerate men "come short of what God requires" instead of being "sinful," omitted the accusation that the Pope is "antichrist," and added articles on the Holy Spirit and on "the love of God and missions" which made it obligatory on all believers to contribute "to the extension of the Kingdom of Christ throughout the earth." Moreover, the revision declared that "the doctrine of God's eternal decree is held in harmony with the doctrine of His love for all mankind, His gift of His Son to be the propitiation for the sins of the whole world, and His readiness to bestow His saving grace on all who seek it."[60] As time passed most Presbyterian theological seminaries became less opposed to Biblical criticism.[61]

[57] *Who's Who in America,* Vol. XXVI, p. 518.

[58] William Adams Brown, *Christian Theology in Outline* (New York, Charles Scribner's Sons, 1906, pp. xiv, 468); William Adams Brown, *A Teacher and His Times* (New York, Charles Scribner's Sons, 1940, pp. xiv, 391, autobiographical).

[59] Loetscher, *op. cit.,* pp. 39–47.

[60] *Confession of Faith,* Chap. XVI, sec. 3, Chaps. XXV, XXXIV, XXXV. Declaratory Statement; Loetscher, *op. cit.,* pp. 83–89.

[61] Loetscher, *op. cit.,* pp. 74–82.

THE GERMAN REFORMED CHURCH: THE MERCERSBURG THEOLOGY

While the response of the Presbyterian Church in the United States of America to the currents of the age was being made in the manner which we have summarized, a quite different reaction was being seen in another member of the Reformed family, the German Reformed Church. It centred in Mercersburg, Pennsylvania, in the theological seminary of that church.

Founded at Carlisle, Pennsylvania, in 1825, the seminary, after being in New York for a few years, was moved to Mercersburg in 1837 and there was closely connected with Marshall College. In 1853 Marshall College was transferred to Lancaster, Pennsylvania, and combined with Franklin College under the joint name of Franklin and Marshall College. The seminary followed in 1871.[62] In the thirty-four years between 1837 and 1871 developments took place which made a profound impression on the German Reformed Church and through it on the Evangelical and Reformed Church, which came into being in the next century.

The pioneer was Frederick Augustus Rauch (1806–1841).[63] Born and educated in Germany, he arrived in the United States in 1831, the following year became a member of the seminary faculty and was ordained in the Reformed Church, in 1835 was made president of the school in Mercersburg which became Marshall College, and also taught in the seminary when it was transferred to Mercersburg. An Hegelian, he was the first to introduce Hegelianism to America in English. His career was cut short by early death, but his influence was perpetuated through his *Psychology* and by one of his students who long taught in the seminary and in Franklin and Marshall College.

The most potent figures in shaping the Mercersburg theology were Philip Schaff and John Williamson Nevin (1803–1886). We have already met Schaff. Nevin[64] was reared a Presbyterian. He was a student in* Union College in a period of revivals and in Princeton Theological Seminary when the tensions between those who favoured and those who opposed revivals were acute. During Charles Hodge's long absence in Europe he substituted for him in Princeton. From 1830 to 1840 he was on the faculty of the newly founded Western Theological Seminary in Pittsburgh. He made himself familiar not only with Hebrew and other ancient languages but also with French and German. He read extensively in the recent and current German theological and Biblical literature. He found German Idealism congenial and was impressed by Schleiermacher's emphasis on Jesus Christ and on the Christian faith as life.

---

[62] Binkley, *The Mercersburg Theology*, pp. 10–12.

[63] Howard J. B. Ziegler, *Frederick Augustus Rauch, American Hegelian* (Lancaster, Penn., Franklin and Marshall College, 1953, pp. xvii, 103), *passim*.

[64] Theodore Appel, *The Life and Work of John Williamson Nevin* (Philadelphia, Reformed Church Publication House, 1889, pp. 775), *passim;* S. F. Brenner, "Nevin and the Mercersburg Theology," in *Theology Today*, Vol. XII, pp. 43–56; J. H. Nichols in Slosser, *They Seek a Country*, pp. 238–250.

His discovery of Neander's pioneer efforts in church history was determinative. From Neander he caught a glimpse of development in Christian history. He plunged into a reading of the Church Fathers and was thrilled with the continuity and organic life of the Church. The Oxford Tracts also had an effect on him. In 1840 he accepted a quite unexpected invitation to head the struggling seminary at Mercersburg. Four years later he was joined by Schaff.

Schaff's inaugural address at Mercersburg on "The Principle of Protestantism," made in German and translated by Nevin, aroused controversy. In it Schaff stressed the continuity of Protestantism with the previous history of the Church and declared that the basic tenet of Protestantism is that Christ is all in all, that the Reformers had not said the last word, and that much still remained to be done in the theological realm. The preceding year Nevin, in a tract, *The Anxious Seat,* had also provoked criticism by attacking the revivalism then regnant in many of the churches for what he deemed its excessive emotionalism and subjectivism.

Together Nevin and Schaff were the chief creators of the Mercersburg theology. They were akin to the mediating theologians of Germany. Schaff had studied under outstanding representatives of that attitude and had been amanuensis to Tholuck. He and Nevin made Christ central. They stressed the incarnation rather than the atonement and laid emphasis on the Church as the body of Christ. Schaff dissented vigorously from Strauss and Renan and held that the existence of the Church for over eighteen centuries was conclusive proof of the dependability of the picture of Christ given in the Gospels. He sought the unity of the Church. Nevin especially had a high view of the Church and of the sacraments. In *The Mystical Presence, A Vindication of the Reformed or Calvinistic Doctrine of the Holy Eucharist*[65] he maintained that the Reformed creeds had taught that the Eucharist is participation in the body and blood of Christ for spiritual nourishment and growth in grace and that in later years the Presbyterians and Reformed had neglected much of the true significance of the Lord's Supper. Here he and his old teacher, Charles Hodge, differed openly. Nevin also stressed the catholic nature of the Church. He and Schaff, obviously, were exhibiting a trend which was represented in England by the Oxford movement and in Germany by Löhe.[66]

As one of the tangible fruits of the Mercersburg theology a liturgy was prepared by a committee which had first Nevin and then Schaff as chairman. It sought to unite the best in the ancient Catholic liturgies with the best in the Reformed liturgies and was published in 1857.[67]

The Mercersburg movement met active opposition in the German Reformed

[65] Philadelphia, J. B. Lippincott Co., 1846, p. 256.

[66] Binkley, *op. cit., passim;* Nichols in Slosser, *op. cit.,* pp. 238–250; Schaff, *The Life of Philip Schaff,* pp. 92–170, 197–220.

[67] Binkley, *op. cit.,* pp. 100, 101; Schaff, *op. cit.,* pp. 202, 203.

Church. The liturgy especially was criticized. It was a long time before harmony was restored, but in 1887 a revised liturgy, called the *Directory of Worship,* was officially adopted.[68]

RESPONSE IN THE PROTESTANT EPISCOPAL CHURCH

The intellectual currents of the day could not but be felt in the Protestant Episcopal Church. With its high standard of education for its clergy and with a laity largely from the middle and upper levels of income and education, it was as susceptible as the other denominations ministering to the older stock which had a background of establishment in Europe or America.

The Episcopal Church felt the impact of the new currents largely through the response that was being made in the Church of England. Thus *Essays and Reviews* and *Lux Mundi* were read and the Colenso controversy was followed with interest. In 1865 the House of Bishops approved the excommunication of Colenso and endorsed a letter which accused the authors of *Essays and Reviews* and Colenso of "infidelity."[69] In 1894 a "Pastoral Letter" was issued by a number of bishops, but not as an official pronouncement of the House of Bishops, which arraigned as "novelties . . . subversive to the fundamental verities of Christ's religion" the denial or passing over of the virgin birth of Christ and which affirmed that "fixedness of interpretation is of the essence of the creeds" and that this applied not only to the facts but also to the doctrines recorded in those documents.[70]

These attitudes did not win universal assent. After his suspension from the ministry by the Presbyterian General Assembly, as we have seen, Briggs was ordained in the Episcopal Church, and as early as the 1870's prominent clergy publicly held that "theologians must learn to look upon the naturalists as their allies rather than their antagonists" and that natural science "must be of service to the interpretation of the Bible, for it must tend to increase the knowledge of the truth."[71]

Yet a later scholar, writing of the history of his church, declared of this period that "in the production of religious literature of permanent value the Episcopal Church was weak" and that "in the field of scholarship the deficiency . . . was even more marked." Of only two of the Episcopal Church's scholars could it be said that their work was known and valued abroad. They were A. V. G. Allen of the Episcopal Theological School in Cambridge, Massachusetts, and William Porcher Du Bose of Sewanee, Tennessee. Sanday described the latter as "the wisest Anglican writer on both sides of the Atlantic."[72]

[68] Binkley, *op. cit.*, pp. 105–118.
[69] Addison, *The Episcopal Church in the United States 1789–1931*, pp. 246, 247.
[70] *Ibid.*, pp. 252, 253.
[71] *Ibid.*, pp. 249–251.
[72] *Ibid.*, pp. 224, 225.

Phillips Brooks (1835–1893), the greatest preacher to emerge from the Protestant Episcopal Church and one of the outstanding preachers of the century, was a "broad churchman" who was unafraid of the new knowledge and was sensitive to Coleridge, Tennyson, Maurice, Robertson, and Bushnell. From a long line of New England ancestors who on his mother's side were deeply religious and on his father's were marked by business ability and integrity, he was baptized in a Unitarian church. But when he was still a young child his parents, dissatisfied with what they regarded as the cold intellectualism of Unitarianism, became Episcopalians. Phillips Brooks graduated from Harvard and the Episcopal seminary in Alexandria, Virginia, was for several years a pastor in Philadelphia, and in 1869 came to Trinity Church, Boston. His preaching soon attracted throngs. Large of frame, strikingly handsome, radiating human sympathy and spiritual light, pouring out his sermons in a rapid torrent of words, he regarded preaching as "the communication of truth by man to men" and the "bringing of truth through personality." His approach was positive, stressing the eternal Christian verities. When, in 1891, he was elected Bishop of Massachusetts some of the conservatives and high-churchmen were critical, but the House of Bishops confirmed the choice. His early death was lamented as a public calamity.[73]

Response in Denominations Recruited Chiefly by Revivalism from the Lower Economic and Educational Levels of the Older Stock

What responses were seen in the denominations which owed their numerical strength chiefly to revivalism and which, drawing their membership mainly from the lower economic and educational levels of the older stock, by the end of the nineteenth century enrolled more than three-fifths of the Protestants of the United States? We have thus far devoted most of our attention to the Congregationalists, Presbyterians, Reformed, and Episcopalians. But they together included only about a fifth of the Protestant church members. The denominations mostly drawn from the nineteenth-century immigration, chiefly the Lutherans, constituted another fifth. It is upon the fifth embraced by the Congregationalists, Presbyterians, Reformed, and Episcopalians that studies of nineteenth-century American theological and Biblical scholarship have usually been concentrated, because from these denominations, with their superior educational level, more books and periodicals of a high intellectual character issued than from the other churches. Yet they reveal very little of what the four-fifths of the Protestants who were in the other denominations were thinking.

To give an accurate and well-rounded account of the responses of the three-

[73] Alexander Viets Griswold Allen, *Life and Letters of Phillips Brooks* (New York, E. P. Dutton and Co., 2 vols., 1900), *passim.*

fifths who were in denominations whose membership was largely through revivalism and from the older American stock, white and Negro, would require much more research than we have yet seen, and the ephemeral nature of most of the record would render the attempt at such a picture frustrating. Much of the record would be in sermons which either were never committed to writing or, if written, early disappeared. Some would be in periodicals of which complete files could not be found. A substantial amount of evidence would be in the hymns which were most popular in expressing the aspirations of those who sang them. Of them some survived, especially in such widely used collections as the *Gospel Hymns* of Moody and Sankey, but others were forgotten with the passing of the generations which treasured them. The literature issued in connexion with the Sunday Schools that helped to shape the thought of millions would afford useful clues, but it was not all from one source nor would an examination of what came from the publishing houses which provided a substantial proportion of it necessarily be representative of the whole. Widely used devotional literature would provide information, but most of that quickly perished.

Moreover, no hard and fast line of demarcation separated the constituencies of the main groups of denominations. The sermons of such men as Henry Ward Beecher, Thomas DeWitt Talmadge, and Phillips Brooks had an enormous circulation which crossed denominational lines. Although the Unitarians and Universalists were relatively few, their writings circulated widely. For example, the father of David Starr Jordan on a farm on the frontier in western New York read William E. Channing, Theodore Parker, and James Freeman Clarke and, leaving the Baptists because of his doubts about "eternal damnation," joined the Universalists.[74]

The attacks of Robert G. Ingersoll (1833–1899) on Christianity aroused irate rebuttals from the loyal, irrespective of denominational affiliation, or won gleeful assent from the unregenerate. Son of an itinerant evangelist whose preaching was patterned on that of Finney and who had been heard in the Broadway Tabernacle, Ingersoll in his strictures on the Bible and the Christian faith displayed no great intellectual depth but reflected some of the questioning of the day and appealed to many with little or no knowledge of Christianity. A great orator who was prominent in Republican politics, an excellent trial lawyer, gayly optimistic, full of *joie de vivre,* generous to the unfortunate, loyal to his friends, with a spotless family life, he had rebelled against his father's theology and was appalled by the Mosaic law and the cruelties to which the Old Testament seemed to give divine sanction. Yet he expressed a warm admiration for some of the teachings of Jesus. He was an enthusiastic Darwinian. In his assault on Christianity he brought to the lecture platform the fervour and the skill in

[74] David Starr Jordan, *The Days of a Man. Being Memories of a Naturalist, Teacher, and Minor Prophet of Democracy* (Yonkers-on-Hudson, World Book Co., 2 vols., 1922), Vol. I, pp. 46–50.

public appeal which characterized many of the evangelists in their advocacy of the faith.[75]

To a greater or less extent almost all the denominations which were recruited from the older American stock conformed to revivalism. In those with which this chapter has thus far been concerned revivalism met opposition, in some more than others. However, as we have repeatedly seen, the marked increase of church membership in the partially de-Christianized descendants of the pre-nineteenth-century immigration and among the Negroes was mainly in those denominations which were enthusiastically committed to it.

Of the churches which whole-heartedly endorsed revivalism, the largest denominational families were the Baptists and Methodists. In 1916 the two were about equal in size, each with approximately seven million members. Together they enrolled more than half the Protestants in the country. The Baptists were stronger in the South, among both the whites and the Negroes, and the Methodists were stronger in the North and had a smaller proportion of Negroes.[76] Because of limitations of space, it is to these that we must confine our attention, and to them only in a summary manner.

The Response of Baptists

In the South Baptists were late in concerning themselves seriously with the questions propounded by the intellectual movements of the revolutionary age. Before the Civil War, the issues were barely on the horizon of that vast majority, white and Negro, among whom the Baptists made their chief gains. After that struggle, the South was so long impoverished and higher education was so backward that not until late in the century did the challenge presented by the intellectual currents attract more than superficial attention.[77] Here and there a Baptist scholar was taking account of them, but the most prominent preachers concerned themselves with stressing the "old-time religion" which had been the theme of revivalism from frontier days.

John Albert Broadus (1827–1895) was outstanding. Born in western Virginia, converted in a revival in his teens, a graduate of the University of Virginia, he taught New Testament in the Southern Baptist Theological Seminary when it was founded (1859) in Greenville, South Carolina. The seminary was suspended because of the war. Renewed on the coming of peace, in 1873 it was moved to Louisville, Kentucky. Broadus went with it and in 1889 became its president. He was earnest in his Evangelicalism, a noted preacher, a member of the International Lesson Committee and of the International Sunday School Com-

[75] Cramer, *Royal Bob. The Life of Robert G. Ingersoll, passim.*

[76] Bureau of the Census, *Religious Bodies, 1916,* Vol. I, pp. 19–21.

[77] For an instance of the impoverishment and the struggle of one youth, later a leader in the Southern Baptist Convention, to gain an education, see Charles E. Maddry, *An Autobiography* (Nashville, Broadman Press, 1955, pp. xiii, 141), *passim.*

mittee, and a trusted leader in the Southern Baptist Convention. In him no hint was seen of the new intellectual challenges which were stirring the outer world.[78]

The "Whitsitt controversy" of 1896–1899 which nearly tore the Southern Baptist Convention apart raged over the application to Baptist history of the methods of scholarship that characterized the revolutionary age. William Heth Whitsitt (1841–1911), a graduate of the University of Virginia and of the Southern Baptist Theological Seminary, had spent two years of study in Leipzig and Berlin and had there become familiar with current procedures in historical research. As professor of church history in the Southern Baptist Theological Seminary and at the time of the controversy also its president, he came out in print with the statement that believers' baptism was restored in England by the Baptists in 1641. The assertion countered the teaching of the Landmark element in the Convention that from the days of the Apostles direct continuity of believers' baptism had existed and that the Baptists were its heirs. He was vigorously attacked and after two years deemed it wise to resign.[79]

Whitsitt was followed as president of the Southern Baptist Theological Seminary by Edgar Young Mullins (1860–1928).[80] Mullins added to that post the professorship of theology. As head of the leading institution for the training of Southern Baptist clergy, as president of the Southern Baptist Convention for three years (1921–1924), as president of the Baptist World Alliance, and through his books Mullins exerted a wide influence in Baptist circles. The son and grandson of Baptist ministers, he was born in Mississippi and reared in Texas. Following the Baptist pattern, in his youth he was converted in a revival (1880). He had hoped to be a foreign missionary, and since for reasons of health that seemed inadvisable he was long connected with the home administration of the Foreign Mission Board of the Southern Baptist Convention. He came to the Southern Baptist Theological Seminary from a pastorate in Newton Centre, on the outskirts of Boston. In theology he was a moderate Calvinist and little affected by the scientific thought of the century. Yet he was concerned with the impact of scientific thought on Christianity and was an able apologist. By his poise, firmness, and staunch adherence to Evangelicalism as held by the majority of his constituency he did much to restore the unity in the Convention that had been jeopardized by the controversy which had centred around his predecessor.[81]

The leading Biblical scholar of the Southern Baptists in the nineteenth

[78] Archibald Thomas Robertson, *Life and Letters of John Albert Broadus* (Philadelphia, American Baptist Publication Society, 1901, pp. xiv, 462), *passim.*

[79] *Encyclopedia of Southern Baptists*, p. 1496; Gill, *A. T. Robertson*, pp. 78 ff.; Barnes, *The Southern Baptist Convention, 1845–1953*, pp. 136–139.

[80] *Dictionary of American Biography*, Vol. XIII, pp. 322, 323; *Encyclopedia of Southern Baptists*, p. 930.

[81] As an example of his writing see Edgar Young Mullins, *The Christian Religion in Its Doctrinal Expression* (Philadelphia, The Judson Press, pp. xxiv, 514).

century was Archibald Thomas Robertson (1863–1934).[82] From a once wealthy Virginia plantation family impoverished by the Civil War, he struggled up for an education in North Carolina and the Southern Baptist Theological Seminary. He taught in that seminary from 1888 to his death. His special field was the New Testament. He made himself a master of the requisite languages, especially Greek, and wrote prodigiously. He was an expert on the text of the New Testament, was not afraid of textual criticism, was familiar with the work being done in it on both sides of the Atlantic, and presented it to his constituency together with his own independent conclusions.[83] Nor did he hesitate to set forth in popular form the varying theories of the authorship of the Gospels. But he also held to the dependability of the Gospels for a knowledge of Christ and came out flatly for the virgin birth and bodily resurrection of Christ and for the authenticity of the sayings attributed to the risen Lord.[84] He also stood firmly for John the beloved disciple as the author of the Fourth Gospel.[85] He was active in the work of his Convention and in the initiation of the Baptist World Alliance.

The most outstanding Southern Baptist pastor and preacher in the latter part of the nineteenth century was George Washington Truett (1867–1944).[86] He was born and reared on a farm in the mountains of North Carolina during the hard days of reconstruction that followed the Civil War. He was much influenced by his mother and his mother's uncle, the latter famous as a preacher in revivals and camp-meetings. Converted in his nineteenth year in a revival, he began and headed an academy in the North Carolina mountains to give an education to the youth of that region. Still in his early twenties, he went with his parents to Texas. There he was ordained, helped raise the debt which was crippling Baylor University, and was graduated from that institution. In 1897 he became the pastor of the First Baptist Church of Dallas, Texas, and continued in that post for the rest of his life. A great reader with a photographic memory, he found nothing in the many books he devoured to weaken his earnest Evangelical faith or his passion to see his hearers converted and grow in the faith. A man of complete integrity and natural eloquence supported by profound conviction, he built up a large church in the growing city which was his home and became a national and international figure. He was president of the Southern Baptist Convention and of the Baptist World Alliance. He conducted evangelistic meetings in many parts of the country and in Latin America.

[82] Gill, *A. T. Robertson, passim.*

[83] A. T. Robertson, *Studies in the Text of the New Testament* (New York, George H. Doran Co., pp. xi, 192), *passim.*

[84] As in A. T. Robertson, *Commentary on the Gospel According to Matthew* (New York, The Macmillan Co., 1911, pp. xi, 294), *passim.*

[85] A. T. Robertson, *Epochs in the Life of the Apostle John* (New York, Fleming H. Revell Co., 1935, pp. 253), *passim.*

[86] Powhatan W. James, *George W. Truett. A Biography* (New York, The Macmillan Co., 1939, pp. xv, 281), *passim.*

From this brief account of the men who did most to shape the thought of the Baptists of the South it must be clear that they held true to the Evangelical tradition which was associated with revivalism and through which the Southern Baptist Convention had grown. That Convention was predominantly rural or semi-rural. Only towards the end of the century as urbanization mounted in the South did large city churches multiply. On the eve of 1914 an awareness began to be seen of the intellectual currents associated with the revolutionary age. For the most part they were resisted, and such aspects of them as the evolutionary hypothesis and the higher criticism were rejected.

In the North the attitudes of Baptists were somewhat different from those in the South. For the majority revivalism continued. However, among a minority the intellectual currents began to have an effect. Some reacted against them. Others made a partial adjustment to them. Still others accepted the methods and many of the conclusions, at times whole-heartedly and even with enthusiasm. The adjustment first developed in New England, where the currents were running strong in Congregationalism, both orthodox and Unitarian. It spread to New York State and then, in more radical form, to the Middle West.

Alvah Hovey (1820–1903) represented a sturdy adherence to traditional convictions but had an irenic attitude towards the new trends.[87] A graduate of Newton Theological Institution, for the more than half-century from 1849 to his death he was a member of the faculty of that pioneer Baptist seminary and for thirty years (1868–1898) its president. Staunchly conservative, he was so quietly confident that the truth would prevail that he viewed the fresh approaches with equanimity though not with acceptance.

Augustus Hopkins Strong (1836–1921) stood for a Calvinism which in his later years was modified by what he called "ethical monism."[88] Strong was born in Rochester, New York, of New England stock. His father had been converted under Finney. He himself was converted while an undergraduate at Yale after hearing Finney and through weeks of spiritual struggle and was graduated from Rochester Theological Seminary in 1859. He had hoped to become a foreign missionary, and although he was prevented by ill health from fulfilling that purpose he never lost his deep and active interest in the missionary enterprise. He had a year of travel and study in Europe, acquired a knowledge of the German language, and through it continued to make himself familiar with German theological and Biblical scholarship. For four years he was pastor in Haverhill, Massachusetts, and then, from 1865 to 1872, had a church in Cleveland, Ohio, where John D. Rockefeller was a member. The two formed a lifelong friendship, one result of which was the marriage of a son to Rockefeller's daughter. For forty years, from 1872 to 1912, Strong was president and

---

[87] *Dictionary of American Biography*, Vol. IX, p. 270.

[88] *Dictionary of American Biography*, Vol. XVIII, pp. 142, 143; Carl F. H. Henry, *Personal Idealism and Strong's Theology* (Wheaton, Ill., The Kampen Press, 1951, pp. 233), *passim*.

professor of Biblical theology in Rochester Theological Seminary. There he had as a colleague Walter Rauschenbusch, of whom we are to hear more in the next chapter. He wrote many books, chief among which was his *Systematic Theology*. First published in 1886 it went through six revised editions[89] and was long and widely used as a text in theological seminaries. The earlier editions of the book were conservative and Calvinistic. In later editions Strong incorporated his personalistic idealism and ethical monism. He was influenced by Lotze, chiefly through the personalism of Borden Parker Bowne, of which we are soon to say more. He regarded evolution as the ordinary means of God's operation, but without excluding creation, the incarnation, the miracles, or the resurrection. He accepted the methods of higher criticism but not all of the conclusions put forward by their advocates. He held that they gave a larger view of Christ. He stressed the Trinity, the deity of Christ, substitutionary atonement, and supernatural regeneration.

William Newton Clarke (1861–1912), a younger contemporary of Strong, like him was of old New England stock and a native of New York State. He did most of his writing and teaching in that state.[90] However, he went much further in the attempt to readjust Christian theology to the changed conditions of his age. The son of a Baptist minister, he graduated from Madison University, later to be called Colgate University, and from the theological school associated with it, a school which in the next century was to be united with Rochester Theological Seminary. His pastorates included one in Newton Centre in a church at the foot of the hill which was crowned by Newton Theological Institution. There he was a warm friend of Hovey. He began as a moderate Calvinist. A transparently honest soul, through reading and reflexion he moved gradually towards a position quite different from that of Hovey but one which did not cost him the latter's friendship. After an interval as a pastor and teacher in Canada, in 1887 he became pastor of the Baptist church in Hamilton, New York, the seat of Colgate University, and from 1890 to his death was professor of theology in that institution. Frail of body and a slow worker, he did not write many books, but those that he wrote exerted a wide influence. The one which had the largest circulation was a textbook growing out of his class lectures. It passed through many editions and was noted for its clarity and its frank statement of a liberal position on historic Christian beliefs.[91] His most

[89] *Systematic Theology* (Rochester, E. R. Andrews, 1886, pp. xxix, 758); *Systematic Theology* (Philadelphia, Griffith and Rowland Press and American Baptist Publication Society, 3 vols., 1907–1909).

[90] *William Newton Clarke, A Biography* (by his widow) *with Additional Sketches by His Friends and Colleagues* (New York, Charles Scribner's Sons, 1916, pp. viii, 261), *passim;* Clarke, *Sixty Years with the Bible, passim.*

[91] William Newton Clarke, *An Outline of Christian Theology* (New York, Charles Scribner's Sons, 15th ed., 1906, pp. ix, 488).

mature book was centred on God.[92] Some of his views resembled those of the Ritschlians, but he had arrived at his conclusions independently and was not conscious of having been significantly indebted to German theological thought. Serene, with a deep religious experience, recoiling from theological brawls, never in any danger, so he said in his later years, of losing his faith in God and Jesus Christ,[93] hating hypocrisy or subterfuge, Clarke was content to set forth his convictions with all the clarity and candour that he could command. He accepted the theory of evolution and the methods of Biblical criticism. He moved too far for some and not far enough for others. While not regarding the virgin birth, the miracles, or the precise details of the resurrection as essential, he believed that the direct revelation of God was made once for all in Christ, that the critical study of the Gospels had enabled the living personality of Jesus to stand out more clearly than before in its uniqueness and grandeur, and that the character which Jesus opened to men is the real character of God. He was emphatic that God is both holy and love, that He could not be holy if He were not love, and that He could not be love if He were not holy. He taught that the glory of Christianity is salvation and that, rightly understood, salvation is Christianity. Salvation he regarded as a fact of personal experience and as ethical. He believed that the God Who is in Christ is the only God there is and that saviourhood belongs to the very essence of God. He endorsed the doctrine of the Trinity but held that it needed reformulation to accord with the peculiar needs of the current age.

Much more radical than Strong or Clarke in seeking to re-think Christian theology and beliefs about the Bible in terms of the revolutionary currents of the day was the group of scholars whom William Rainey Harper gathered about him in the early days of the University of Chicago. Strong had attempted to induce Rockefeller to finance the establishment of a great university in New York City which would be frankly Christian and have the highest standards of scholarship and research. To his disappointment Rockefeller was persuaded to undertake the adventure in the metropolis of the Middle West. This was done by bringing together an existing Baptist college in that city and a Baptist theological seminary in Morgan Park, on the outskirts of the city, to form the nucleus of the new University of Chicago.

William Rainey Harper (1856–1906) was an Old Testament scholar of distinction.[94] Of Scotch-Irish stock, he was precocious, graduating from Muskingum College at fourteen and taking his doctorate of philosophy at Yale when he was not yet nineteen. He loved languages and especially Hebrew and was a

[92] William Newton Clarke, *The Christian Doctrine of God* (New York, Charles Scribner's Sons, 1909, pp. xii, 477).

[93] Clarke, *Sixty Years with the Bible*, p. 4.

[94] Thomas Wakefield Goodspeed, *William Rainey Harper, First President of the University of Chicago* (University of Chicago Press, 1928, pp. ix, 240), *passim*.

superb teacher. For a time he was head of Granville Academy, the preparatory department of Denison University, and while there made his commitment to the Christian faith and became a Baptist. At twenty-two he began teaching Hebrew in the Baptist theological seminary in Morgan Park. Abounding in energy and a prodigious worker, he was active in the local church, organized summer schools and a correspondence course for the study of Hebrew, and, as we have seen, was early connected with Chautauqua. He wrote textbooks and began a journal for the study of Hebrew. In time he broadened the curriculums of the summer schools and correspondence courses to include not only Hebrew but also the cognate languages and Old and New Testament interpretation and theology. In 1886 he went to the Yale faculty. There he was enormously successful as a teacher of undergraduates and in the Divinity and Graduate Schools and maintained his summer schools and correspondence courses. In 1891 he was induced to become president of the University of Chicago and brought to the post his customary enthusiasm and administrative ability. He died early, but not before having begun the fulfilment of his dream of making the institution a real university and gathering about him a notable group of scholars. He himself was often attacked as unorthodox, but he had no taste for controversy, sought in his teaching to be constructive rather than destructive, and to the end remained firm in what he regarded as the essentials of the Christian faith. Genial, friendly, he seldom if ever seemed hurried. In addition to his burdens as president and author, for eight years he was superintendent of the Sunday School of the neighbouring Baptist church and helped work out for it a new and systematic course of study.

In the Divinity School of the University of Chicago Harper gathered about him a notable company of scholars. Although they varied among themselves, they had in common a fearlessness in facing the new knowledge brought by the age and an eagerness to re-think in its terms inherited beliefs. They had a sense of adventure in helping to initiate a university and a zest in helping it to push forward the frontiers of man's search for truth. They tended to rebel against what they deemed the conventions of the past and to seek to make a fresh start. Like others in the university, they were given complete freedom for research, teaching, and speech. Some were more radical than others, but collectively they aroused suspicion among conservatives and several of them were vigorously denounced.

The member of the faculty of the Divinity School who provoked the most controversy in the early years of the University of Chicago was George Burman Foster (1857–1918).[95] A graduate of Rochester Theological Seminary, a Baptist, for a time a pastor, he studied in Göttingen and Berlin, was associate professor and then professor of theology in the University of Chicago from 1895 to 1905,

[95] *Dictionary of American Biography,* Vol. VI, pp. 547, 548.

and was professor of the theology of religion from 1905 until his death. He was thoroughly familiar with European Biblical and theological scholarship, delighted in debate, and crossed swords on the one hand with an ultra-conservative Baptist minister in Chicago and on the other with the militantly sceptical lawyer Clarence Darrow. He moved far from the Evangelical orthodoxy of his early years. One of his former students, himself later eminent in theology, declared that for Foster "radical criticism was instrumental; the conservation of genuine religious values was the end," that "he knew what religion was, for it was his daily life," that "he could make more daring excursions into the realm of doubt than would have been spiritually safe for a less deeply religious man," and yet that "he was a remarkably sympathetic interpreter of points of view other than his own."[96] In a book which bore the challenging title *The Finality of the Christian Religion* and which he said reflected his own experience, Foster raised the question: "Is Christianity the ultimate religion?" In answering it he believed that what he called "authority-religion," whether Catholic or Protestant, was in process of dissolution, that it was impossible "to make primitive Christianity as such the criterion of our theory and practice in life for all time," yet the Gospel is that "God is like Jesus." He declared that "Jesus was what he taught, and taught what he was. But it must be that God is as good as Jesus is. Then we may have the faith which the Gospel requires—faith in God the Father, in His fatherly grace in forgiving sins, and in an eternal life."[97]

Another outstanding figure in the first generation of the University of Chicago was Gerald Birney Smith (1868–1929).[98] A Baptist clergyman, a graduate of Brown and of Union Theological Seminary, after two years in Berlin, Marburg, and Paris he spent his life in the thriving young institution. In his earlier years he was a Ritschlian and was influenced by the mystical piety of Hermann, under whom he had studied in Marburg. His emphasis on experience rather than on Biblical teaching as a basis of theology led him more and more to heed the claims of science and democracy. He sought to find a vital religion which would not rest on authoritarian dogma and took an empirical approach to theological reconstruction. Honest, with a deep sense of spiritual power, he never developed a system of theology of his own but sought to instill in his students a method of critical and constructive thinking.

Shailer Mathews (1863–1941), for years dean of the Divinity School of the University of Chicago, a New Testament scholar, a theologian, and a historian, made his chief contribution in the field of the social gospel.[99]

---

[96] George Burman Foster, *Christianity in Modern Expression*, edited by Douglas Clyde Macintosh (New York, The Macmillan Co., 1921, pp. xiii, 294), pp. v, vi. See also Mathews, *New Faith for Old*, pp. 67–69.

[97] George Burman Foster, *The Finality of Christian Religion* (University of Chicago Press, 1906, pp. xv, 518), *passim*, especially pp. xi, xii, 494, 515, 518.

[98] *Dictionary of American Biography*, Vol. XVII, pp. 269, 270.

[99] Mathews, *op. cit., passim*.

Ernest DeWitt Burton (1856–1925), the third president of the University of Chicago, was a New Testament specialist, fully acquainted with the results of historical criticism. He was committed to the methods, although not to all the conclusions. He had reached that position after painful struggle, for he was emotionally attached to the conservatism in which he had been reared. He sought to make the new views contribute to a more understanding use of the New Testament and to a deepened Christian faith. He had wished to become a foreign missionary, but physical frailty made that course inadvisable. Somewhat reluctantly, he was persuaded by Harper to come to the University of Chicago from a New Testament chair in the Newton Theological Institution. He made the move (1892) because he felt that "the battle for Christianity in this country for the next quarter century" was "to be waged somewhat more fiercely in the Mississippi Valley than on the New England coast." A man of unfailing courtesy and complete and fearless integrity of mind and action, he undertook a number of missions only indirectly associated with the field of his specialization and was highly successful in them. Some were for the world-wide extension of the Christian faith. Others were for the improvement of education under Christian auspices. Yet he was also an inspiring teacher of the New Testament and produced many books and articles on it. By some experts he was classed as "the most eminent New Testament scholar." As president he proved to have unusual gifts of promotion and administration and in the brief years before cancer terminated his work led the university into fresh avenues of achievement.[100]

Although their views on theology and the Bible brought them under severe attack in some conservative circles and in parts of the religious press, members of the faculty of the Divinity School of the University of Chicago, led by Harper, sought in a variety of ways to spread the methods and conclusions which they had developed. They did it through the summer schools and correspondence courses which Harper had initiated, through scholarly journals, and through more popular periodicals and literature.[101]

Members of the faculty of the University of Chicago also took the lead in the organization of the Northern Baptist Convention (1907). Both Henry Pratt Judson, Harper's successor as president, and Mathews were early presidents of the Convention. Burton was the creator of its Board of Education and chairman of the committee which was responsible for formulating an important further step in the organization of the Convention.[102]

THE RESPONSE OF THE METHODISTS

Like the Baptists, the Methodists of the United States were late in producing

[100] Goodspeed, *Ernest DeWitt Burton, passim,* especially pp. 27, 32, 43, 44.
[101] *Ibid.,* p. 39, 40.
[102] *Ibid.,* pp. 70–73; Matthews, *op. cit.,* pp. 109–113.

scholars who concerned themselves with the revolutionary currents of thought radiating from Western Europe and who did it in such fashion as to command respect among the highly educated. Like the Baptists, the Methodists were chiefly recruited from those in the older stock of limited educational background. They, too, were committed to revivalism and stressed the kind of experience which characterized Evangelical Protestantism—the conversion of the individual through repentance, faith, and the grace of God in Jesus Christ. As was true of the Baptists, the Methodists had their major early growth on the frontier. Unlike the Baptists, who had multiplied in the eighteenth century through the Great Awakening from secessions from the Congregational constituencies in New England, they were relatively weak in that region. Therefore, rather more than the Baptists, they were out of touch with the stimulus which was being given to Congregationalists, both Unitarian and orthodox, by contact with German scholarship. Significantly, as we have seen, the first among Baptists to make major efforts at the adjustment of theology to German and British thought were in New England and among those of New England ancestry in the adjacent New York. So, also, the leader of the Methodist effort to re-think its theology, Borden Parker Bowne, whom we are to meet in a moment, was of New England stock and did most of his teaching and writing in Boston.

Methodists early were concerned with the Calvinism which prevailed, at least in theory, among the majority of their fellow American Protestants. Being Arminian by heritage and conviction in the sense that they believed that the prevenient grace of God was operating on all men, and that all might accept the salvation freely offered through Christ, they often debated the issue with Calvinists, especially the Baptists, for the latter were appealing to much the same constituency and for the most part professed to hold to the Particular wing of their denomination with its Calvinistic theology. They also challenged the Congregationalists and Presbyterians. For many years a standard theological treatise among them was an English work, *Theological Institutes,* by Richard Watson (1781–1833) which set forth the Arminian position.

An able leader in the debate with the Calvinists was Nathan Bangs (1778–1862).[103] Born in Connecticut, it was as a young man in Canada that he became a Methodist. For a few years after 1800 he was an itinerant Methodist preacher in Upper and Lower Canada. Then he returned to the United States and made his major contributions as agent of the Methodist Book Concern, as the initiator and editor of Methodist journals, including the *Christian Advocate,* and as the chief founder of the Methodist Missionary Society. In these capacities he helped to shape Methodist thought. He challenged the Calvinist doctrines, for with their adherence to predestination, election, irresistible grace,

---

[103] Abel Stevens, *Life and Times of Nathan Bangs, D.D.* (New York, Carlton & Porter, 1863, pp. 426), *passim,* especially pp. 175–180, 208–210.

and the perseverance of the saints they hampered response to the call of the Methodist preachers to repentance and faith. He also attacked Hopkinsianism, for while he regarded it as having so modified Calvinism that some of the latter's features to which Methodists took exception were softened, it had not entirely removed them.

Wilbur Fisk (1792–1839), a younger contemporary of Bangs, was especially active in the debate. A native New Englander, a graduate of Brown, he was one of the earliest American Methodists to have a college education. He was principal of Wilbraham Academy and the first president of Wesleyan University, in Middletown, Connecticut. Living in that time and region, he was especially concerned both with the spread of Unitarianism and Universalism and with the Calvinism of the Congregational majority. He attacked Universalism and Unitarianism, but his sharpest controversy was over Calvinism. He declared that Calvinism prepared the way for Universalism, that the doctrine of predestination made God the author of sin, destroyed the free agency and the accountability of man, arrayed God's secret decrees against His revealed Word, and marred the moral attributes of God. He also asserted that the doctrine of election, while professing to vindicate free grace and the mercy of God, destroyed them altogether, and that it made God partial and a respecter of persons and limited the atonement. He differed from all the various strains of Calvinism, including Hopkinsianism and the New Haven theology of Taylor, and held to the articles of religion as set forth in the Methodist Book of Discipline which maintained that all men are corrupt as the offspring of Adam and that they cannot in their own strength turn and do what is acceptable to God without the grace of God assisting them. He stood for what was called "gracious ability"—the ability given by God's grace to repent and have saving faith.[104]

Daniel Denison Whedon (1808–1885) helped to reinforce and shape Methodist thought.[105] A graduate of Hamilton College, he was converted under Finney, became a Methodist, from 1833 to 1843 taught at Wesleyan where he was under the influence of Fisk, then was on the faculty of the University of Michigan and was dismissed because of his open anti-slavery stand. From 1856 to 1881 he was editor of the *Methodist Quarterly Review*. In that position he had an opportunity to express his convictions and have a wide hearing among his fellow Methodists. He was familiar with some of the movements across the Atlantic, reacted against Locke and Paley, and welcomed Reid, Stewart, and Cousin. His major contribution was in his advocacy of Wesleyan Arminianism as against Calvinism. He stressed the freedom of the will and in doing so rejected Edwards and the modifications of Calvinism by Taylor and others. In

[104] George Prentice, *Wilbur Fisk* (Boston, Houghton Mifflin Co., 1890, pp. iv, 289), pp. 111 ff.; Wilbur Fisk, *Calvinistic Controversy: Embracing a Sermon on Predestination and Election; and Several Numbers on the Same Subject. Originally Published in the Christian Advocate and Journal* (New York, T. Mason and G. Lane, 1837, pp. 273), *passim.*

[105] *Dictionary of American Biography*, Vol. XX, pp. 43, 44.

his emphasis on the freedom of the will he was in accord with a trend in American life as seen in such men as Emerson which made much of the ability of the individual to shape his own development and with the related movement in revivalism which assumed that the individual could by his own act accept the salvation offered by God in Christ.[106]

William Fairfield Warren (1833–1929) by virtue of his long life and his strategic position in Methodist education did much to mould Methodist attitudes towards the new currents of thought.[107] A native of Massachusetts, a graduate of Wesleyan, for a time a student in Andover Theological Seminary, in 1856–1857 he attended the Universities of Berlin and Halle. From 1861 to 1866 he was professor of systematic theology in the (Methodist) *Missionsanstalt* in Bremen. He thus was in a unique position to bring to American Methodism an acquaintance with theological, Biblical, and philosophical developments in Europe. Returning to the United States, he became a member of the faculty of the Methodist General Biblical Institute, then in Concord, New Hampshire, and accompanied it to Boston, where he became the first president of the Boston Theological Seminary into which it was transformed. He also was the first president of Boston University, in which that seminary was the initial department. Indeed, he was the chief creator of Boston University. He continued to teach in the seminary (1867–1920) and at two different periods was its dean. His most widely read utterance was an address, *A Quest for a Perfect Religion*. It went into a number of English editions and was translated into several foreign languages. Theologically Warren was conservative and held to inherited Methodist views. But he also believed in the essential soundness of the contemporary critical approach to the study of the Bible, was not afraid of Darwin and Spencer, and helped to guide Methodism to the kind of adjustment to these fresh approaches to knowledge which saved it from serious internal conflicts over the issues raised by them.

Miner Raymond (1811–1897) was highly influential in formulating the thought of American Methodism and his large Systematic Theology was long standard.[108] He had only a secondary school education, but for a number of years he was principal of Wilbraham Academy and from 1864 to 1895 taught in Garrett Biblical Institute in Evanston, Illinois. He largely followed Whedon on the controversial issue of the freedom of the will and in general represented the main stream of Methodist Arminianism.

Others who were influential in Methodist thought were Thomas Osmond Summers (1811–1897), English born, largely self-educated, who was dean and professor of theology in Southern Methodism's first theological school, that of

---

[106] Samples of some of these views are in D. D. Whedon, *Public Addresses, Collegiate and Popular* (Boston, John P. Jewett and Co., 1852, pp. 174).

[107] *Dictionary of American Biography*, Vol. XIX, pp. 490–492.

[108] *Dictionary of American Biography*, Vol. XV, pp. 413, 414; Miner Raymond, *Systematic Theology* (Cincinnati, Hitchcock and Walden, 3 vols., 1877–1879).

Vanderbilt University, author of a standard theology, long editor of books of the Methodist Episcopal Church, South, and secretary of many of its General Conferences;[109] and John Miley (1813–1895), professor of systematic theology in Drew Theological Seminary, whose book in that field was a comprehensive statement, beginning with theism and going on to the more specifically Methodist doctrines, including an emphasis on free will.[110] Wilbur F. Tillett (1854–1936), who taught at Vanderbilt beginning in 1882, was of great assistance in helping Southern Methodists to adjust to current intellectual trends.[111]

In general, the Methodism of the United States came to the end of the nineteenth century without a sharply defined theological position. Like many Protestant churches on both sides of the Atlantic, it was beginning to show the effects of the impact of the intellectual currents of the age. Yet no controversy arose over attempts at adaptation which were as intense as those in the Congregational, Presbyterian, or Baptist churches. Heresy trials there were, but not as shaking as those in Presbyterianism. As in most other Protestant churches in Europe and America, attitudes varied and much latitude developed in the interpretation of official statements of doctrine. In general, Methodism retained much of the warm revivalism and Evangelicalism which it had inherited. As the level of education in its growing membership rose through the multiplication of its schools and colleges and as its extensive publications mounted in volume, Methodism gave to its constituency an increasing amount of religious education. Much of the emphasis, however, was on morality rather than dogma.

In the closing years of the century a distinct slant was given to large segments of American Methodism by Borden Parker Bowne (1847–1910).[112] He was quite the most distinctive and influential theologian in American Methodism in the nineteenth century and his effect continued far into the twentieth century.

The factual record of Bowne's life is quickly summarized. He was born on a farm in New Jersey of Puritan ancestry. The family was staunchly Methodist. His father was a local preacher of sterling character, opposed to slavery and liquor. His mother had in her something of the mystic. In the family, in accordance with the Methodism of the day, an emphasis was placed on Christian per-

---

[109] *Dictionary of American Biography*, Vol. XVIII, pp. 207, 208; J. J. Tigert, editor, Thomas O. Summers, *Systematic Theology* (Nashville, Publishing House of the Methodist Episcopal Church, South, 2 vols., 1888).

[110] John Miley, *Systematic Theology* (New York, Eaton & Mains, 2 vols., 1892, 1894).

[111] *Who Was Who in America*, Vol. I, p. 1240.

[112] Francis John McConnell, *Borden Parker Bowne. His Life and His Philosophy* (Cincinnati, Abingdon Press, 1929, pp. 291), *passim;* José A. Fránquis Ventura, *Borden Parker Bowne's Treatment of the Problem of Change and Identity* (Rio Piedras, Puerto Rico, The University, 1930, pp. xvi, 260), *passim.* Some of Bowne's writings are *Theism* (Cincinnati, American Book Co., 1902, pp. 323); *The Christian Revelation* (Cincinnati, Curts & Jennings, 1898, pp. 107); *The Atonement* (Cincinnati, Jennings & Pye, 1900, pp. 152); *The Immanence of God* (Boston, Houghton Mifflin Co., 1905, pp. 153); and *Studies in Christianity* (Boston, Houghton Mifflin Co., 1909, pp. vii, 399).

fection. Bowne graduated from New York University, was ordained, and went to Europe. In Germany he studied with Lotze. He was caustic in his criticism of the pessimism of the later years of Strauss. Philosophically minded, he believed that atheism could never be held in good faith. He was also intensely critical of Spencer, at that time in high favour in many quarters. From 1876 to his death he was on the staff of Boston University, brought there by Warren, and refused invitations to the faculties of Yale and Chicago. His subjects were philosophy, theism, and ethics, with seminars on Spencer and Kant. For the latter he had warm admiration but pointed out what he believed to be serious mistakes in his thinking.

The philosophy which Bowne taught he first called objective idealism and in it showed the influence of Lotze. Later he termed it transcendental empiricism, meaning that man's experience is not limited to the senses. Living at a time when mechanistic determinism was popular, he rejected every argument which would limit the freedom of the self and the relation of the self to the Unseen behind the universe. He brought all philosophy and religion to the pragmatic test of life. His philosophy was usually known as personalism and it was this word which he preferred. He was a convinced theist, holding that the decisive argument for that position is the intelligibility of the universe.

Bowne helped Methodism to clear away antipathy to modern thought. He accepted the methods of the historical criticism of the Bible and stoutly defended, even though unsuccessfully, his colleague Hinckley J. Mitchell of the Old Testament department when the latter was attacked for his espousal of some of the conclusions of the higher criticism. Conservative in his Christology, he believed in the virgin birth but did not make it an article on which the faith of the Church would stand or fall. While he rejected its inerrancy and infallibility, he held that God had revealed Himself in the Bible. He maintained that Christianity was superior to all other religions and stood firmly for the great redemption wrought by Christ. He was tried for heresy by the New York East Conference but was completely vindicated.

The Revision of the Translation of the Bible

A project which occupied the attention of leading Biblical scholars of the older Protestantism of the United States in the second half of the century was the revision of the translation of the Bible into English. In 1870 the Convocation of Canterbury organized a committee of British scholars to undertake a revision to take advantage of recent scholarship and especially of the discovery of older and better texts of the originals than had been available to the translators of 1611 and to adapt the language of the King James Version to the existing state of the English language without altering the idiom or vocabulary. In 1871 a committee of American scholars was formed, with Philip Schaff as chairman, to be associated by correspondence with the British committee. The committee was made up of men from several denominations of the older American stock. The revision of the New Testament was published in 1881 and that of the Old Testament in 1885. On some readings the American committee differed from their English colleagues. In 1901 an American edition, called the American Standard Version, was published which incorporated their changes. It was evidence of the growing competence of American Biblical scholarship. Many conservatives viewed it with alarm and even with antagonism, believing that it had upset some of the proof texts on which they relied.[113]

NATIVE MOVEMENTS OF THOUGHT OUTSIDE THE CHURCHES AFFECT MANY WITHIN THE CHURCHES

As the century wore on, currents of thought of American origin affected intellectuals within the Protestant churches, especially those of the older stock. Some of their formulations were outside the standard churches and tended to be critical of them, but were profoundly religious. William James (1842–1910) and Josiah Royce (1855–1916), both of the Harvard faculty, were outstanding. James was noted both as a psychologist and as a philosopher—and for a vivid, readable literary style. Among others of his writings, his little essay *The Will to Believe* and his longer *Varieties of Religious Experience* assisted many thoughtful Christians in their faith. His *Pragmatism* reinforced an existing tendency. Royce represented a post-Kantian idealism, made much of the Absolute, and spoke of the "beloved community," a phrase which some of his readers transferred to the Church.[114]

To many Americans science and religion seemed to be chronically hostile—as in John William Draper's *History of the Conflict of Religion and Science,* published in 1873, and in Andrew Dickson White's (first president of Cornell and a devout Episcopalian) *A History of the Warfare of Science and Theology in Christendom,* issued in 1897. John Fiske sought to reconcile them, and his writings, popular in form, had a wide reading.[115] Edward Livingston Youmans (1821–1887) and his brother, William Jay Youmans (1838–1901), through extensive writing gave impetus to the vogue of Herbert Spencer and the advances of science.[116]

Popular literary figures of the period had an ambiguous impact. Although Mark Twain (Samuel L. Clemens, 1835–1910) bitterly rejected the Calvinism in which he had been reared, adopted naturalism, and became a deep pessimist,

---

113 Weigle, *American Idealism,* pp. 222, 223; Schaff, *The Life of Philip Schaff,* pp. 354, 389.
114 See a thoughtful treatment in Gabriel, *The Course of American Democratic Thought,* pp. 269–389.
115 Edward A. White, *Science and Religion in American Thought. The Impact of Naturalism* (Stanford University Press, 1952, pp. viii, 117), *passim.*
116 *Dictionary of American Biography,* Vol. XX, pp. 615–617.

the influence of his writings was not clearly anti-Christian.[117] Walt Whitman (1819–1892) in his voluminous prose writings and especially his poetry, notably his many-editioned *Leaves of Grass,* earlier flouted Christian morals but in later life came to have a deeper appreciation of religion. Yet his effect was to undermine orthodox Christianity.[118]

THE BEGINNINGS OF FUNDAMENTALISM

The adjustments to the new currents of thought which were being made in denominations of the older American stock could not but arouse alarm among conservatives. In the closing decades of the nineteenth century as the impact of the currents was intensified and the attempted adjustments mounted, the rank and file of church members were little affected. However, some men began to be deeply concerned. They were mainly in the denominations which had grown through revivalism based on the heritage of the Evangelical awakenings and in the conservative wings of Presbyterianism and Congregationalism. In the latter third of the century they began to come together to take common action for defense of what they believed to be the Evangelical faith. The movement was eventually called Fundamentalism because it sought to preserve what its adherents were convinced were the fundamental truths on which the Christian faith rested. It did not reach its crest until after 1914, but it had been foreshadowed a generation earlier.

Preliminaries to the movement were in the form of conferences. What was regarded as the first Bible conference met in Swampscott, Massachusetts, in 1876. The following year what was called a prophetic conference was held in the Church of the Holy Trinity in New York City. It was made up of those who held to the pre-millennial advent of Christ and sought to rebuke the theologians who advocated post-millennial interpretations of Scripture. The crucial difference between the two views was that the pre-millennialists maintained that evil was to be sovereign in the present age, while the post-millennialists looked for improvement in human civilization culminating in an ideal society and crowned by the second coming of Christ and His thousand-year reign. In 1885 a further conference was convened, this time in Chicago, with the purpose of solidifying conservative Protestantism. Some foreign scholars came to reinforce the Americans.[119]

A landmark in the development of Fundamentalism was the Niagara Bible Conference of 1895. On that occasion the Five Points of Fundamentalism were set forth—the inerrancy of the Scriptures, the deity and virgin birth of Christ, substitutionary atonement through Christ, the physical resurrection, and the

[117] Gabriel, *Religion and Learning at Yale,* pp. 192–194.
[118] Matthiessen, *American Renaissance,* pp. 517 ff.; *Dictionary of American Biography,* Vol. XX, pp. 143–152; Stewart, *American Literature and Christian Doctrine,* pp. 43 ff.
[119] Cole, *The History of Fundamentalism,* pp. 31–33.

coming bodily return of Christ to the earth. Several present at the gathering deplored the use by Moody in the Northfield conferences of such men as Henry Drummond and W. R. Harper, who, so they held, misrepresented Christianity.[120]

Other steps were taken to further what the Fundamentalists believed to be the true Gospel. Conference centres were established at Winona Lake, Indiana, and Denver for teaching the Bible according to their views. Literature was prepared for popular distribution. In 1908 Lyman and Milton Stewart founded the Los Angeles Bible Institute and the Stewart Evangelistic Fund.[121] Between 1909 and 1915 twelve small paper-covered books were issued which were said to have had a circulation of about three million and which dealt with such themes as the deity of Christ, the purpose of the incarnation, the personality and deity of the Holy Spirit, proof of the living God as illustrated in answers to prayer, personal salvation, evangelism, and world-wide missions. Negatively they were directed against the higher criticism of the Scriptures, Darwinianism, evolution, Mormonism, Christian Science, Spiritualism, and the Roman Catholic Church. Positively they emphasized salvation by grace, the efficacy of prayer, consecration, evangelism, and missions. In the years which immediately preceded 1914 several champions of Fundamentalist views appeared.[122]

A work which had a wide and continuing circulation was the *Scofield Reference Bible*.[123] By 1943 nearly two million copies had been sold. The author, Cyrus Ingerson Scofield (1843–1921), had served in the army of the Confederate States of America. After the Civil War, as a lawyer, he had been a member of the legislature of Kansas and United States attorney for Kansas. He was converted in 1879 and was ordained as a Congregational minister. Over twenty-five years, interrupted by seven years as pastor in Moody's home town, he was pastor of a church in Dallas, Texas, where a theological seminary perpetuated his influence. He devoted his later years to the Scofield Correspondence Bible School and to lecturing in America and Europe.[124] The forewords to the successive books and extensive explanatory notes of the Bible which bore his name displayed impressive erudition and in them he was aided by a number of outstanding conservative scholars. The *Scofield Reference Bible* saw the Bible as a unity, narrating by infallible inspiration the story of man from his creation through the long preparation for Christ recorded in the Old Testament, to the birth,

---

[120] *Ibid.*, p. 34.

[121] *Ibid.*, pp. 34, 35.

[122] Arthur Gabriel Hebert, *Fundamentalism and the Church* (Philadelphia, The Westminster Press, 1957, pp. 156), pp. 17–19; Norman F. Furniss, *The Fundamentalist Controversy, 1918–1931* (New Haven, Conn., Yale University Press, 1954, pp. viii, 199), pp. 11, 12.

[123] *The Scofield Reference Bible. The Holy Bible Containing the Old and New Testaments . . .*, edited by C. I. Scofield (New York, Oxford University Press, new and improved edition, 1909, 1917, pp. vi, 1362); Arno C. Gaebelein, *The History of the Scofield Reference Bible* (New York, Loizeaux Brothers and Our Hope Publications, 1943, pp. 71), *passim*.

[124] *Twentieth Century Encyclopedia of Religious Knowledge*, Vol. II, p. 1003.

teaching, atoning death, and resurrection of Christ, the coming of the Holy Spirit, the early spread of the faith, and the interpretive epistles, and culminating in the consummation of the divine-human drama as foretold in the Apocalypse. It held to the Mosaic authorship of the Pentateuch, to the Genesis account of the creation (although the seven "days" might be eras rather than of twenty-four hours each), and to Daniel as the author of the book which bears his name, offered explanations for the passages in which the Bible seems to contradict itself, and set forth the order of events to come as forecast in Daniel, the Apocalypse, and elsewhere.[125] It was the chief literary expression of "dispensationalism." By thousands, probably by millions, its notes were regarded as authoritative.

On the eve of 1914 the attitudes expressed by the Fundamentalists, although not always bearing that designation, were held by a large proportion of the Protestants of the older stock. They were akin to those of many conservative Protestants in Europe, but they were not identical with them and had a distinctive flavour which arose from the nature of American revivalism and of the accompanying intellectual environment.

RESPONSE IN THE PROTESTANT CHURCHES OF THE NINETEENTH-CENTURY IMMIGRATION

Before 1914 the Protestant churches which arose from the nineteenth-century immigration responded to the intellectual currents of the age chiefly by resistance. Those who sought accommodation to them were silenced by the conservative majority. As we have seen, the leaders who were chiefly responsible for founding the churches in their new environment were Pietists with a conservative theological outlook or, among the German and Scandinavian Lutherans, held staunchly to the Augsburg Confession and for the most part represented the Lutheran revival in Europe with its protest against the eighteenth-century Enlightenment. Moreover, the churches were so engrossed in the tasks of organization and of gathering into their folds their natural constituencies that their leaders paid little attention to the currents which were affecting the older American bodies.

We have seen how the attempt of Samuel S. Schmucker to modify Lutheranism to conform to the American scene was frustrated by the surge of conservative immigration. For the most part others who sought accommodation to the American milieu were passed by.[126]

The leader in the movement from Americanization to a conservative Lu-

---

[125] C. Norman Kraus, *Dispensationalism in America. Its Rise and Development* (Richmond, Va., John Knox Press, 1958, pp. 151), pp. 15 ff., 111–130.

[126] Carl Mauelshagen, *The Effect of German Immigration upon the Lutheran Church in America, 1820–1870* (Athens, University of Georgia Press, 1936, pp. 252), *passim;* S. E. Ahlstrom, "The Lutheran Church and American Culture. A Tercentenary Prospect," in *The Lutheran Quarterly,* Vol. IX, pp. 321–342.

theran position was Charles Porterfield Krauth (1823–1883). His father, Charles Philip Krauth (1797–1867), was the first president of Pennsylvania (later Gettysburg) College, helped found Gettysburg Theological Seminary, and, while he made use of revivals and was a friend of Schmucker, was more conservative than the latter. The younger Krauth was a pupil of Schmucker and at first tended to conform to his views. Later, under the influence of the German immigration and its adherence to the renewed European forms of confessionalism, he became a conspicuous champion of conservative views. He was a diligent student of German theology and especially of the older symbolical books and the literature associated with them, and his scholarship commanded respect. He was one of the chief architects of the General Council and the major figure in the new seminary in Philadelphia. Although in debate he stood stoutly for his convictions, he did not allow controversy to mar his personal friendships. His *magnum opus, The Conservative Reformation and Its Theology,* was widely used and had a pronounced influence in promoting Lutheran confessionalism and the resistance to conformity to the American environment.[127]

The outstanding figure in nineteenth-century Lutheran immigration was Walther, of the Missouri Synod. A great organizer and with a vigorous intellect, he had, as we have seen, reacted against the rationalism of his troubled youth and had become an unwavering supporter of a phase of the revived Lutheran orthodoxy.

With a few exceptions late in the century, not until after 1914 did the nineteenth-century immigrant churches begin to give evidence of adjusting themselves to the intellectual outlook and methods of the revolutionary age. Early trends towards eighteenth-century rationalism were countered by a surge of Lutheran confessionalism.[128]

Response in the Roman Catholic Church

In responding to the nineteenth-century currents the Roman Catholic Church had a record somewhat like that of the Protestant immigrant churches. Its energies were absorbed in holding its hereditary constituency to the faith, in erecting churches and institutions, and in recruiting and training its clergy. Except for the Irish, language was also a barrier. More than the Protestant immigration, the Roman Catholic newcomers were faced with the struggle for existence and were of a low educational level and had neither leisure nor preparation for

---

[127] *Dictionary of American Biography,* Vol. X, pp. 501–503; Wentz, *A Basic History of Lutheranism in America,* pp. 150, 243, 244; Charles Porterfield Krauth, *The Conservative Reformation and Its Theology as Represented by the Augsburg Confession and in the History and Literature of the Evangelical Lutheran Church* (Philadelphia, J. B. Lippincott Co., 1871, pp. xv, 840); Ferm, *The Crisis in American Lutheran Theology, passim.*

[128] Paul W. Spaude, *The Lutheran Church under American Influence* (Burlington, Iowa, The Lutheran Literary Board, 1943, pp. xvi, 435), pp. 244 ff., 362 ff.

concerning themselves with the intellectual currents which were moving in the world around them.

We have seen the storm aroused over the issue of Americanism. The American hierarchy declared that the charge of heresy was completely unfounded and insisted that they and their fellow American Catholics were entirely orthodox and repudiated the views of which they were accused. Dissensions arose from time to time between members of the hierarchy and between national groups, but they were over matters of policy and not of dogma. It seems significant that the Modernist movement had few adherents in the United States. No major personage in that country came under condemnation. The trustees of the Catholic University of America were prompt to adhere to the Papal encyclical *Pascendi dominici gregis* (1907), which outlawed Modernism, and took steps to see that no books containing Modernist teachings were in the library. *The New York Review,* a learned journal begun in 1905 and edited by professors of St. Joseph's Seminary in that city, was under suspicion but suspended publication in 1908. In 1909 William Laurence Sullivan, a priest, a graduate of the Catholic University of America, who had taught theology in Washington from 1900 to 1907, became a Unitarian. He was later prominent as a Unitarian pastor. He seems to have been the outstanding casualty. Modernism was chiefly confined to Europe.[129]

Conservatism prevailed in the education of the clergy. We have remarked the place which the Sulpicians had in some of the early theological seminaries. They continued to dominate a large proportion of the diocesan seminaries. Their Paris mother house was a firm centre of orthodoxy and stood sternly against the entrance of any possible taint of Modernism. It was to be expected that the record in the United States would be similar. Yet McQuaid, champion of conservatism, regarded the Sulpicians as the most dangerous liberals in America. The accentuation of the study of Aquinas by Rome led to emphasis upon the *Doctor angelicus* in the seminaries in the United States, but without the vigorous thought which it provoked in some quarters in Europe.[130]

SUMMARY

Any one looking back over this long chapter cannot but be impressed with what was suggested at the outset. The movements of thought in the nineteenth-century Christianity of the United States which grew out of the revolutionary age were partly indigenous and partly stimulated by what entered from the other side of the Atlantic. They began earlier and were more prominent among the Congregationalists, the Presbyterians, the Reformed, and the Episcopalians —denominations serving the older American stock which insisted on a high

[129] Ellis, *The Life of James Cardinal Gibbons,* Vol. II, pp. 169–171; *Who's Who in America,* Vol. XII, p. 2982.

[130] Cross, *The Emergence of Liberal Catholicism in America,* pp. 41, 42, 146 ff.

level of education for their clergy and which had a laity better educated, on the average, than that of the denominations drawing their constituencies from the rank and file of the older stock.

In Congregationalism the movements were chiefly departures from the inherited Calvinism and the debates which they occasioned. Unitarianism had a high view of the nature of man and stood for man's progress through his own efforts. Early centres of ministerial training of Trinitarian Congregationalism, notably Andover Theological Seminary and the Yale Divinity School, modified the inherited Calvinism and took cognizance of the methods of Biblical study which were being developed in Europe. Both Andover and Yale were distrusted by conservatives, but the controversy waxed more intense around the former than the latter. In the later decades of the century Oberlin also moved towards the new views. Critical methods in Biblical study and departures from Calvinism became dominant among the majority. Biological evolution was generally accepted. Horace Bushnell helped the transition to be achieved with a minimum of strain. Although not a scholar, Henry Ward Beecher, the most popular Congregational preacher in the third quarter of the century, gave impetus to the movement away from the traditional convictions but with a positive emphasis on much that was dear to Evangelicalism. The more scholarly Lyman Abbott continued the popularization of the new views. The still more scholarly George A. Gordon fully accepted the general approach to the Bible and theology associated with the intellectual climate of the day, but not all the radical conclusions. A substantial minority of Congregationalists held to conservative positions. However, by the end of the century they made their stand, not on Calvinism, but on such issues as the inerrancy of the Scriptures, the deity and virgin birth of Christ, the substitutionary atonement, and the premillennial second coming of Christ.

The chief centre of Presbyterian orthodoxy was Princeton Theological Seminary. There Charles Hodge stood firmly for unadulterated Calvinism and rejected the modifications developed in Andover and Yale. He was followed by his son, Archibald Alexander Hodge, and the latter in turn by Warfield. Union Theological Seminary in New York City, reflecting New School and Plan of Union views, and for some years closely related to the General Assembly of the Presbyterian Church in the U.S.A., was a focus of what in Germany would have been called a mediating theology. The most famous Presbyterian heresy trial of the latter part of the century had as its defendant Charles A. Briggs, a member of the Union faculty. The seminary stood by him and severed its official connexion with the Presbyterian Church. Henry Preserved Smith, suspended from the ministry by the General Assembly, was given haven on its faculty. Arthur Cushman McGiffert, also of its faculty, avoided a heresy trial in the General Assembly by becoming a Congregationalist. Yet soon after 1900 the

Presbyterian Church in the United States of America modified its version of the Westminster Confession.

The German Reformed Church experienced a unique development through the faculty of its seminary at Mercersburg. In it John Williamson Nevin and Philip Schaff were the chief figures. The Mercersburg movement was critical of revivalism, stressed the historical continuity of the Church, and gave birth to a liturgy which was deeply indebted to the early Christian centuries and the Catholic tradition.

The Protestant Episcopal Church tended to reflect the views and controversies which were developing in the Church of England. Its greatest preacher, Phillips Brooks, made his adjustment to the new currents of thought without any great struggle and in his sermons stressed the positive aspects of the faith as he understood them.

The denominations that owed their growth mainly to revivalism, for most of the century depended on a ministry which, with a few exceptions, had little formal education, and made their chief appeal to those of a similar background were late in experiencing the full impact of the new currents. The largest denominational families in this category were the Baptists and Methodists.

Not until the closing decades of the century did Baptists become really aware of the changing intellectual climate. Even then, in the South the general trend was towards a stalwart conservatism. In the North, Augustus H. Strong held to a mild Calvinism but began to show the effects of the thought that had long been stirring on the other side of the Atlantic. William Newton Clarke moved further towards acceptance. The initial theological faculty of the University of Chicago was still more radical.

Methodists had less difficulty than Baptists in making an adjustment to the new currents of thought. Most of the men who led in it, as was true of the Baptists, were in the North. Outstanding were Daniel Denison Whedon, who was familiar with the Scottish "common sense" philosophers and Cousin; William Fairfield Warren, who had had a long residence in Germany; and especially Borden Parker Bowne, who, like the latter, was for many years connected with Boston University. Yet some in the South, notably in Vanderbilt University, did much to soften the impact upon the Methodism of that region.

A reaction mounted against accommodation to the trends in Biblical scholarship and theological thought. In the latter part of the century it took a somewhat different form from the earlier conservatism. It did not attempt to defend Calvinism and rejoiced in an evangelism which assumed free will to accept or reject the Gospel. It stressed what it deemed the basic truths of the Gospel and therefore came to be known as Fundamentalism. It did not reach its peak until after 1914, but before that year it was being propagated by an extensive literature, including the *Scofield Reference Bible*. The explanatory notes of that edition of the Bible supported the inerrancy of the Scriptures and emphasized what its editor regarded as God's plan of salvation—a plan which began with the creation as described in Genesis, came to its climax in the virgin birth, atoning death, and resurrection of Jesus Christ, the incarnate Son of God, and was to culminate in the "last things" as set forth in Biblical prophecy.

The Protestant denominations which had the nineteenth-century immigration as their major constituency for the most part either were Pietistic or represented a revival of the historic Reformation symbols. Especially in Lutheranism was this the case.

The Roman Catholic Church in the United States was troubled but little if at all by the intellectual questions propounded by the revolutionary age. In the flurry over "Americanism" its leaders protested their orthodoxy. Many of its clergy were trained by Sulpicians, staunch conservatives. The seminaries faithfully conformed to the Papal commands to teach scholastic philosophy and Aquinas, and the church in America was only slightly tainted by Modernism.

Here, then, were reactions to the intellectual aspects of the revolutionary age which were akin to what we have seen in Western Europe and which were deeply indebted to it. Like the Christianity of Western Europe they were marked by a varying degree of acceptance on the one hand and by rejection on the other.

CHAPTER VIII

The Effect of Christianity on the
United States of America

To what extent and in what ways did Christianity affect the United States of America in the nineteenth century? How far and in what fashion did it modify the new nation which was emerging in the midst of the forces shaping the revolutionary age? To what extent did it mould the morals and the social, economic, and political life and institutions of the country?

A complete picture is impossible—partly because of the limitations of space, partly because for millions of individuals who professed allegiance to the Christian faith data are unobtainable. Even more of an obstacle is the difficulty of separating the influence of Christianity from other factors.

Although a complete picture cannot be given, we can indicate some aspects of life into which the Christian faith entered as at least one creative factor. At times we can say that it was the major factor.

What in some ways was the most important aspect was the impact individually on the millions who constituted the nation. As we have seen, a growing proportion, although in 1914 still a minority, were members of churches. Presumably those who did not have a formal church connexion had also felt the influence of Christianity to a greater or less extent. Many of them had once been members of a church or at least had been given instruction in Christianity but for one or another reason had allowed the connexion to lapse. The form of Christianity to which they were exposed was for some the Protestantism of the older stock, for others the Protestantism of the nineteenth-century immigration; for still others, mostly of the nineteenth-century immigration, it was Roman Catholicism, and for a small minority it was Eastern Orthodoxy. Upon all of them played the intellectual, social, political, and economic attitudes, institutions, and customs of the nation. Upon most of these Christianity had left an impress and through them had had a share in making the individual what he was.

Yet to determine precisely to what extent and exactly in what ways any individual showed the effects of Christianity would be impossible. At best only an approximation could be arrived at. To generalize for the entire nation would be absurd. For instance, we cannot know whether even for church members the degree of conformity to Christian standards of morality increased or declined as the proportion of church members in the population rose. The temptation is to say that, as the percentage of church members mounted, the degree of discipline exercised by the churches lessened and the trend was towards conformity to the general level. Yet this cannot be proved. We know that in the early part of the century many Protestant congregations took positive action against members who transgressed the ethical codes to which the majority subscribed. Thus Baptist churches on the frontier took cognizance of charges against their members of drunkenness, fighting, malicious gossip, lying, cheating, sexual irregularities, gambling, horse racing, and failure to pay just debts. If guilty, the offender might be excluded from membership.[1] As church membership burgeoned, such measures faded into desuetude. But whether this was accompanied by a general lowering of the moral life of the membership we do not know.

What we can attempt with some hope of dependable conclusions is to point out the manner in which Christianity entered into particular aspects of the life of the nation. We have already hinted at the fashion in which Christianity contributed to education and so to intellectual life. We will now speak of the ways in which it helped shape the ideals of the country and of the manner in which it stimulated efforts to attain those ideals through reform movements, through programmes for bringing the collective life to the nation to conformity to Christian standards, and through leaders in the government.

Throughout the nineteenth century Christianity exerted its influence on American society as a whole primarily through the Protestantism of the older stock. By the end of the century the Roman Catholic Church was beginning to make itself felt, mainly through such institutions as hospitals but also through its attitude towards organized labour. In the twentieth century its influence grew, as did that of the Protestantism of the nineteenth-century immigration.

THE AMERICAN DREAM

The ideals of the country were deeply indebted to the Protestantism of the older stock. Thus "America," the most widely sung of the patriotic songs, was written by a New England Baptist clergyman, Samuel Francis Smith (1808–1895), while a student in Andover Theological Seminary. With its zeal for liberty and its dependence on God it breathed the spirit which had been nourished

---

[1] William Warren Sweet, *Religion on the American Frontier. The Baptists 1783–1830, a Collection of Source Material* (New York, Henry Holt and Co., 1931, pp. ix, 652), pp. 48, 49. On the practice of Protestant churches about 1842 see Robert Baird, *Religion in the United States of America* (Glasgow, Blackie and Son, 1844, pp. xix, 725), pp. 426–428.

on the Evangelical revivals.[2] The great seal of the United States was obviously inspired by the Christian faith.[3] Here was what was called the American dream, namely, the effort to build a structure which would be something new in history and to do so in such fashion that God could bless it. Later in the century the dream again found expression in the lines of Katherine Lee Bates (1859–1929), daughter and granddaughter of New England Congregational ministers, in her widely sung hymn, written in 1893, "America the Beautiful," with the words "O beautiful for pilgrim feet whose stern impassioned stress a thoroughfare for freedom beat across the wilderness. America, America, God mend thy every flaw, confirm thy soul in self control, thy liberty in law. . . . O beautiful for patriot dream that sees beyond the years thine alabaster cities gleam undimmed by human tears. America, America, God shed His grace on thee, and crown thy good with brotherhood from sea to shining sea."[4]

The American dream was compounded of many strains. Some were clearly of Christian origin, among them the Great Awakening and other revivals which helped to make Christian liberty, Christian equality, and Christian fraternity the passion of the land. Some have seen revivalism and the search for Christian perfection as the fountain-head of the American hope.[5] Here, too, must be placed Unitarianism and, less obviously from Christian inspiration, Emerson, Transcendentalism, and the idealism of Walt Whitman. We must also remember those who reacted against the dream as a kind of myth—among them Melville, Hawthorne, and Henry James the elder, all of them out of a Christian background.[6]

Reform Movements

With such a dream arising, at least in part, from the Protestant heritage of the United States and built into the foundations of the nation, it is not surprising that many efforts were made to give it concrete expression. A number were in the nature of movements to relieve or remove social ills.

Significantly, the initiation and leadership of a major proportion of the reform movements, especially those in the first half of the nineteenth century, came from men and women of New England birth or parentage and from either Trinitarian or Unitarian Congregationalism. Several of the movements were given a marked impetus by revivalism. Quakers, some from New England, had a larger share than their proportionate numerical strength would have warranted. We do well to remind ourselves that from men and women of New

---

[2] *Dictionary of American Biography*, Vol. XVII, pp. 342, 343.

[3] Volume I, p. 123.

[4] *Dictionary of American Biography*, Vol. XXI, p. 59.

[5] Timothy L. Smith, *Revivalism and Social Reform in Mid-Nineteenth Century America* (New York, Abingdon Press, 1957, pp. 253), *passim*.

[6] R. W. B. Lewis, *The American Adam. Innocence, Tragedy, and Tradition in the Nineteenth Century* (University of Chicago Press, 1955, pp. lx, 205), *passim*.

England ancestry also issued the Church of Jesus Christ of Latter Day Saints, the Seventh Day Adventists, Christian Science, the American Board of Commissioners for Foreign Missions, the American Home Missionary Society, the American Bible Society, and New England theology. The atmosphere was one of optimism, of confidence in human progress, and of a determination to rid the world of its ills. The Hopkinsian universal disinterested benevolence, although holding to original sin and the doctrine of election, inspired its adherents to heroic endeavours for others, looked for the early coming of the Millennium, and was paralleled by the confidence in man's ability cherished by the Unitarians, Emerson, and the Transcendentalists.

We should recall the number of movements for the service of mankind which arose from the kindred Evangelicalism of the British Isles and the Pietism of the Continent of Europe—among them prison reform, anti-slavery measures, legislation for the alleviation of conditions of labour, the Inner Mission, and the Red Cross.

We cannot take the space to record all the efforts for the removal or alleviation of collective ills. A few of the more prominent must serve as examples of what a complete listing and description would disclose. Several were born in the early decades and persisted throughout the century. Others were ephemeral. Some disappeared with the attainment of their purpose. Still others sprang up late in the century to meet conditions which arose from fresh stages of the revolutionary age.

THE ANTI-SLAVERY MOVEMENT

The movement to end Negro slavery began before 1815 and mounted after that year until, as a result of the Civil War, emancipation was achieved.

Long before 1815 the Christian conscience was leading some to declare slavery wrong and to act accordingly. For example, in 1693 the Philadelphia Yearly Meeting of Friends declared that its members should emancipate their slaves and in 1776 it determined to exclude from membership all who did not comply.[7] In the latter year Samuel Hopkins, from whom the Hopkinsian strain of New England theology took its name, asked the Continental Congress to abolish slavery.[8] As we have seen, Methodism early took a stand against slavery. Beginning at least as far back as 1789 various Baptist bodies condemned slavery.[9]

After 1815 anti-slavery sentiment mounted, chiefly among Protestants and those of Protestant background of the older stock. The nineteenth-century immigration, whether Protestant or Roman Catholic, was not so much concerned, for very few if any among them held slaves: they were mostly in the Northern

[7] Weigle, *American Idealism*, p. 162.
[8] *The Works of Samuel Hopkins, D.D.* (Boston, Doctrinal Tract and Book Society, 3 vols., 1852), Vol. II, pp. 549 ff.
[9] Sweet, *op. cit.*, p. 79.

states where slavery had disappeared or was on the way out, or were too poverty-stricken to own slaves.

The anti-slavery movement took many forms. Benjamin Lundy (1789–1839), a Quaker, was a pioneer in preparing the way for anti-slavery societies.[10] It was he who turned the attention of William Lloyd Garrison (1805–1879) to the subject. Garrison, Massachusetts born of Nova Scotian parentage, was by temperament and conviction a reformer. Chiefly remembered because of his incessant advocacy of "immediate and unconditional abolition," he also espoused a great variety of other causes—among them women's rights, prohibition, and justice to the Indians. Incurably optimistic, dogmatic, and utterly fearless, in his youth a devout Baptist, in spite of his friendship for the Quaker poet John Greenleaf Whittier (1807–1892) he eventually attacked the orthodox churches for what he deemed their cowardly compromising on the slavery issue and in his invariably ardent manner was emphatically unorthodox and denied the plenary inspiration of the Bible.[11]

A marked impulse came to the anti-slavery movement through the Finney revivals. Finney himself, while opposed to slavery, placed his chief emphasis on evangelism, but from his converts issued much of the leadership of the anti-slavery campaign. Theodore Dwight Weld (1803–1895) was especially active.[12] Weld was the son and grandson of New England Congregational ministers. As a youth he became one of Finney's band of evangelists and gave himself to winning young men. A strong temperance advocate, through the influence of a favorite teacher, Charles Stewart,[13] another Finney convert, he devoted himself to the anti-slavery cause. A group of young men influenced by him enrolled in Lane Theological Seminary and had to leave because of their open anti-slavery position. The majority then went to the infant Oberlin. They and others employed some of Finney's techniques as they sought to win adherents to the cause. Weld contributed to the anti-slavery convictions of such men as Joshua R. Giddings and Edwin M. Stanton, enlisted John Quincy Adams, and helped provide ideas which underlay Harriet Beecher Stowe's *Uncle Tom's Cabin*. He shunned publicity for himself and sought to avoid fame.

Wendell Phillips (1811–1884), from a prominent Massachusetts family, in his teens was converted under the preaching of Lyman Beecher. Although he later broke with the churches because he believed that they were insufficiently outspoken against social evils, he remained a devout Christian. He was remembered

10 *Dictionary of American Biography*, Vol. XI, pp. 506, 507.

11 *Ibid.*, Vol. VII, pp. 168–171; Russel B. Nye, *William Lloyd Garrison and the Humanitarian Reformers* (Boston, Little, Brown and Co., 1955, pp. vii, 215), *passim*.

12 Gilbert Hobbs Barnes, *The Antislavery Impulse, 1830–1844* (New York, D. Appleton-Century Co., 1933, pp. ix, 298), *passim; Dictionary of American Biography*, Vol. XIX, pp. 625–627; Gilbert H. Barnes and Dwight L. Dumond, editors, *Letters of Theodore Dwight Weld, Angelina Grimké Weld and Sarah Grimké (1822–1844)* (New York, D. Appleton-Century Co., 2 vols., 1934), *passim*, especially Vol. I, pp. v–xxvii.

13 *Dictionary of American Biography*, Vol. XVIII, p. 162.

chiefly for his fearless advocacy of abolition, but he also stood for equal rights for women, for opportunity for the freedmen, and for prohibition.[14]

The anti-slavery movement and other contemporary reforms and philanthropies were given leadership and financial undergirding by Arthur Tappan (1786–1865)[15] and his younger brother, Lewis Tappan (1788–1873).[16] Reared in a devout New England home, for a time, to the grief of their parents, they swung towards Unitarianism. They returned to orthodoxy and were powerful supporters of Finney. Through Arthur's initiative, the two made a fortune in business in and near the growing New York City and devoted it to causes in which they believed. Arthur especially assisted the American Board of Commissioners for Foreign Missions, the American Bible Society, the American Education Society, and the American Home Missionary Society. He was a major financial supporter of Finney and the struggling Oberlin, fought tobacco and prostitution, championed temperance and Sunday observance, assisted theological students in Yale and Andover, and contributed to Auburn Theological Seminary, Kenyon College, and Lane Theological Seminary. He became the first president of the American Anti-Slavery Society (organized 1833) and then withdrew from it because under Garrison's influence it was also including women's rights in its programme. He was then elected president of the freshly founded American and Foreign Anti-Slavery Society. An older brother, Benjamin Tappan (1773–1857), was long a lawyer in Ohio, where he was a partner of the redoubtable Edwin M. Stanton and for a time was in the United States Senate. Religiously unorthodox, he opposed slavery but was not an abolitionist.[17]

An approach to the problem of slavery which for some years had a popular following was that of the American Colonization Society.[18] It sought a way other than general abolition for the solution of the problem and provided a programme on which moderates in both North and South could unite. It was organized in 1817 with the purpose of affording an opportunity for free Negroes to find homes in Africa. Thus it would remove the racial tensions resulting from the presence of Negroes in a predominantly white society and encourage slave-holders to voluntary emancipation. The hope was cherished that through the colony the conversion and progress of the people of Africa would be furthered. The Colonization Society was endorsed by a number of prominent

---

[14] Oscar Sherwin, *Prophet of Liberty. The Life and Times of Wendel Phillips* (New York, Bookman Associates, 1958, pp. 814), *passim.*

[15] *Dictionary of American Biography,* Vol. XVIII, pp. 298–300.

[16] *Ibid.,* pp. 303, 304.

[17] *Ibid.,* p. 300.

[18] Early Lee Fox, *The American Colonization Society 1817–1840* (Baltimore, The Johns Hopkins Press, 1919, pp. 231), *passim; Memorial of the Semi-Centennial Anniversary of the American Colonization Society Celebrated in Washington January 15, 1867, with Documents Concerning Liberia* (Washington, Colonization Society Building, 1867, pp. 191), *passim;* Bacon, *Leonard Bacon,* pp. 206, 209; Bodo, *The Protestant Clergy and Public Issues, 1812–1848,* pp. 112–138, 147–149.

public figures, by church bodies, and by leading Protestant clergymen. Through it a colony of free Negroes was established in the region on the west coast of Africa hopefully named Liberia. Samuel J. Mills, prominent in the initiation of the American Board of Commissioners for Foreign Missions and the American Bible Society, was active in the early stages of the Society and died on the return voyage as an agent in finding a location for the colony. During the first eighteen years of its existence the Society provided the means to settling about 3,300 Negroes in Africa and in suppressing the remnants of the trans-Atlantic slave trade, now illegal. In 1847 the independent Republic of Liberia came into being. After general emancipation as a result of the Civil War, the Society aided some of the freedmen to go to Liberia and in other ways sought to help that country.

We must not take the space to narrate even the main outlines of the long struggle which ended in emancipation. In it many moved by the Christian faith were notable, mostly of the Protestantism of the older stock. For example, in addition to those whom we have mentioned, Elijah Parish Lovejoy (1802–1837), whose death at the hands of a mob brought him into enduring prominence as one of the outstanding martyrs of the cause, was the son of a clergyman and was himself licensed by the Presbytery of Philadelphia.[19] Dissensions over the issue divided churches, not only on the national scale which we have noted, but also locally in some places in the North. In 1846 the American Missionary Association, later to have an important share in educating the freedmen, was founded in part as a protest against what some supporters of the American Board of Commissioners for Foreign Missions believed to be the lack of a forthright anti-slavery stand by that body.[20] Some of the more extreme abolitionists broke all connexion with the churches because of what they regarded as the compromising attitude of these bodies towards the issue.

The slavery issue was aggravated by several factors. At least two were the product of the revolutionary age. Under the impact of the Industrial Revolution, the sectional difference between the North and South was heightened. On the one hand the North, with its free labour, largely from Europe, was giving itself more and more to manufactures; on the other hand the South remained agricultural, producing food and cotton for the factories of the North and of England. By creating a demand for cotton and through the invention of the cotton gin, which made the cleaning of cotton relatively easy and inexpensive, the Industrial Revolution rendered profitable the raising of that staple by the plantation system through Negro slave labour. Earlier anti-slavery societies had flourished in Virginia, where slavery had become a burden. In the deep South, where cotton was raised in quantity, slavery was upheld and even the American

[19] *Dictionary of National Biography*, Vol. XI, p. 434. On others see Cole, *The Social Ideas of the Northern Evangelists 1826–1860*, pp. 192 ff.

[20] Beard, *A Crusade of Brotherhood*, pp. 29–31.

Colonization Society had few advocates. Under these circumstances, the abolition movement in the North, born of the Christian conscience, accentuated in the slave states the resistance to emancipation. Moderates in both North and South sought to ease tensions, but tempers mounted and the Civil War ensued. After the defeat of the South, radicals in the North wrote into the constitution of the United States not only emancipation but also articles designed to assure the Negro full equality with the white. In the mid-twentieth century they had not yet fully accomplished their purpose.

THE PEACE MOVEMENT

Another of the reform movements was that for international peace. It was given a major impetus by men whose consciences were roused by the spectacle of the wars of Napoleon and in one or another form continued throughout the nineteenth and into the twentieth century. After 1914 it was to unite with similar movements in Europe to bring into being the League of Nations and its successor, the United Nations.

In the United States some of the pioneer voices were those of Quakers and Christians of related convictions.[21] David Low Dodge (1774-1852), a native of Connecticut, at one time a teacher, later a successful business man in New York City, a devout Christian and progenitor of a long line of men and women of wealth centred in that city who were active in Christian causes and some of whom we have met, as early as 1809 wrote a pamphlet in which he said that it was wrong for a Christian to engage in war. His father-in-law, a Connecticut clergyman who had been much influenced by Whitefield, was won to and joined in the promotion of peace. Several other clergymen came out with declarations that a Christian profession was inconsistent with war.[22]

Soon after the end of the Napoleonic Wars and of the second war between the United States and Great Britain, peace societies came into being. In 1815 Dodge founded the New York Peace Society.[23] That same year Noah Worcester (1758-1837), a self-educated Congregational minister with Unitarian convictions and with an ancestry of New England clergymen, completely convinced that non-resistance was the proper attitude of a Christian, organized the Massachusetts Peace Society in William Ellery Channing's study.[24]

The chief American proponent of peace in the third and fourth decades of

[21] Allen, *The Fight for Peace*, pp. 5-7.
[22] *Ibid.*, pp. 8, 9.
[23] Curti, *The American Peace Crusade, 1815-1860*, pp. 6-8; *Dictionary of American Biography*, Vol. V, pp. 344, 345.
[24] *Dictionary of American Biography*, Vol. XX, pp. 528, 529; Galpin, *Pioneering for Peace*, pp. 21, 22; Curti, *op. cit.*, pp. 9-12; N. Worcester, *The Friend of Peace. To Which is Prefaced a Solemn Review of the Custom of War; Showing that War is the Effect of Popular Delusion and Proposing a Remedy* (Greenfield, Mass., Ansel Phelps, 1817, pp. 281), *passim;* Allen, *op. cit.*, pp. 365-369.

the nineteenth century was William Ladd (1778–1841).[25] Born in New Hampshire to wealth, a graduate of Harvard, for some years a sea captain, in 1819 Ladd became interested in the peace movement. A study of the Bible had convinced him that all war, defensive as well as offensive, was wrong. Joyously sanguine, clear-headed, not a fanatic, he devoted his abounding energies to the promotion of peace. The better to advance the cause, he was licensed as a Congregational minister. He proposed as a feasible ideal a congress of nations to formulate principles of international law and to provide for the general welfare of mankind. To that he would add a court for settling international disputes by judicial decision or diplomatic arbitration. He was chiefly responsible for the organization of the American Peace Society (1828), a project in which Dodge, along with others, joined. In 1837 he persuaded that body to condemn all war. He travelled widely in the United States and Europe to further the organization of peace societies and education for peace and in the end wore himself out.

Ladd's mantle fell on another New England Congregationalist, Elihu Burritt (1810–1879).[26] Self-educated, prodigiously learned, deeply religious and finding spiritual strength not only in the Congregational fellowship but also in Quaker meetings and Anglican services, after Ladd's death Burritt threw himself into the cause of peace. He spent much of his time in the British Isles. He initiated the League of Universal Brotherhood and induced about twenty thousand Britons and Americans to pledge themselves to complete abstinence from war. Almost single-handed he brought about the Brussels Peace Congress (1848) and he was active in furthering successor conferences. In the United States he organized eighteen state peace conventions. He promoted the programme formulated by Ladd—a congress of nations, a world court, and the codification of international law. As a means of furthering peace and international coöperation he also stood for free trade and cheap international postage rates.

The close inter-locking of the peace movement with other reform projects was seen in many individuals, and, among others, strikingly in the Grimké family. Sarah Moore Grimké (1792–1873), her sister Angelina Emily Grimké (1805–1879), and their brother Thomas Smith Grimké (1786–1834) were from a wealthy, socially prominent South Carolina family.[27] All were deeply religious, and the sisters eventually joined the Friends. The sisters were strong anti-slavery advocates and Angelina married Weld. They were also advocates of women's rights. Modest, cultured, naturally retiring, in a day when it was widely deemed improper for members of their sex they addressed meetings, mainly in behalf of emancipation. Their brother, a Yale graduate, a lawyer,

[25] Curti, *op. cit.*, pp. 34–37, 42–50, 68 ff.; Allen, *op. cit.*, pp. 370–375; *Dictionary of American Biography*, Vol. X, pp. 527, 528.

[26] *Dictionary of American Biography*, Vol. III, pp. 328–330; Curti, *op. cit.*, pp. 88, 143–188; Christina Phelps, *The Anglo-American Peace Movement in the Mid-Nineteenth Century* (New York, Columbia University Press, 1930, pp. 230), pp. 103–149; Allen, *op. cit.*, pp. 399 ff.

[27] *Dictionary of American Biography*, Vol. VII, pp. 634–636; Allen, *op. cit.*, pp. 375–380.

prominent in the politics of the state, was a warm temperance proponent, a thoroughgoing pacifist who stood staunchly against the use of force in South Carolina's nullification policy, and a worker for educational reform. In his view education should be based solidly on the Scriptures, should include higher education for women, and should have a wider range of subjects on the curriculum, including the ones emerging from the revolutionary age, than simply the traditional ancient languages, mathematics, and philosophy.

The Mexican War, the Crimean War, the Civil War, and then the Franco-Prussian War, all coming as they did within a little over two decades, seemed to set back the cause of peace.

The nearly four and a half decades between 1871 and 1914 gave a breathing space unpunctuated by serious wars in the Occident except the brief and comparatively bloodless Spanish-American conflict (1898). Advocates of peace utilized them in efforts to achieve a lasting peace in the face of the mounting armaments. Largely under the leadership of Protestant clergymen, the American Peace Society revived. In 1866 the Universal Peace Society was launched, with Alfred Henry Love (1830–1913) as its president from the beginning to his death. A Philadelphia merchant inspired by Burritt and the Friends, Love promoted popular peace education.[28] He took the full pacifist position and was unhappy because the American Peace Society sanctioned the Northern side in the Civil War. After the war he worked for the reconciliation of North and South. He agitated for international arbitration and sought arbitration in the disputes between employers and employed in the labour troubles which came in the latter part of the century with the mounting industrialization. The Woman's Christian Temperance Union had a peace department which in 1887 began a continuing campaign for peace.[29] Although a large proportion of the clergy were slow to come out for peace, several of their number who had more than local prominence, among them Henry Ward Beecher, Bishop Matthew Simpson of the Methodist Episcopal Church, Washington Gladden, Josiah Strong, and Edward Everett Hale, espoused measures for international organization.[30] A clergyman, Robert McMurdy, was at the heart of the National Arbitration League, which held a convention in 1882.[31] The indomitable Julia Ward Howe (1819–1910), outstanding champion of woman's rights, a Unitarian, organized (1871) an American branch of the Women's International Peace Association and characterized it as Christian.[32] At a hotel on Lake Mohonk of which he was part owner the Quaker Albert K. Smiley began in 1895 annual conferences on international arbitration and peace.[33] In 1909 over two hundred clergymen

---

[28] Curti, *Peace or War*, pp. 75–80; *Dictionary of American Biography*, Vol. XI, pp. 431, 432; Allen, *op. cit.*, pp. 466–477.

[29] Curti, *Peace or War*, p. 117; Allen, *op. cit.*, p. 281.

[30] Curti, *Peace or War*, pp. 109–111.

[31] *Ibid.*, p. 137.

[32] Allen, *op. cit.*, pp. 278, 279.

[33] *Ibid.*, p. 482; *Dictionary of American Biography*, Vol. XVII, p. 231.

of Massachusetts wrote to the Congress in opposition to an increase in the navy or any step towards preparation for war.[34] In 1914 the Church Peace Union was formed with a generous endowment from Andrew Carnegie. It organized the World Alliance for International Friendship through the churches.[35] The Intercollegiate Peace Association was begun in 1904 at Goshen College, a Mennonite institution, and ten years later units were in more than a hundred colleges.[36] The organizations with palpably Christian origin and motivation were paralleled by many others whose Christian rootage was not so obvious. But all arose in Christendom and mounted in the closing decades of the nineteenth century and on the eve of the holocaust of 1914–1918.

When wars came, the Christian forces sought to reduce the suffering and moral degeneracy which were their inevitable accompaniment. In the Confederate armies Lee and Jackson especially, deeply religious men that they were, sought to further the religious welfare of their men. Chaplains were active and in some camps religious revivals broke out. The Young Men's Christian Associations also concerned themselves with the troops. In the Northern armies the United States Christian Commission, organized in 1861 at the initiative of YMCA leaders, served the troops in a number of ways. Its president was a Presbyterian layman, George H. Stuart (1816–1890). It was paralleled by the Ladies Christian Union. Late in the war Ladies Christian Commissions were organized. The American Bible Society distributed Testaments and Bibles to both Confederate and Union soldiers. The United States Sanitary Commission worked independently and not on so frankly a Christian basis but had back of it much support by Christians.[37] During the Spanish-American War, much shorter in duration, the YMCA promptly moved to care for the men in the armed forces.[38]

THE CRUSADE FOR TEMPERANCE

At the beginning of the nineteenth century in the United States as in Europe the use of alcoholic beverages was general. Here, as in the British Isles and Northern Europe, it had reached alarming proportions. In the United States, as in much of Protestant Europe, movements for moderation in the use of alcoholic beverages or for total abstinence sprang up, initiated and supported by consciences made sensitive by the Christian faith. In the United States they led, as they did not in Europe, to the prohibition by law of the manufacture and sale

[34] Eleanor Tupper and George E. McReynolds, *Japan in American Public Opinion* (New York, The Macmillan Co., 1937, pp. xiii, 465), p. 90.

[35] Allen, *op. cit.*, p. 508; Curti, *Peace or War*, p. 205.

[36] Curti, *Peace or War*, p. 212.

[37] Hopkins, *History of the Y.M.C.A. in North America*, pp. 88–98; Sweet, *The Story of Religion in America*, pp. 317–319; J. William Jones, *Christ in the Camp or Religion in Lee's Army* (Richmond, Va., B. F. Johnson & Co., 1887, pp. 528), *passim*.

[38] Hopkins, *op. cit.*, pp. 455, 456.

of alcoholic beverages. The Roman Catholic Church had temperance societies quite independent of the Protestant movement.

As in so many other reform movements, we must content ourselves with the barest outlines of the crusade.

From time to time before the nineteenth century individual ministers had preached against the evils of drunkenness and here and there such religious bodies as the Quakers, Presbyterians, and Methodists had taken action condemning the distillation and sale of liquor.[39]

On the eve of 1815 the movement mounted, partly as an outgrowth of the revivals. In 1785 Benjamin Rush (1745-1813), the most eminent physician in the country in his day, came out with a treatise against the use of "ardent spirits."[40] In 1808 Rush's treatise came into the hands of Lyman Beecher. It inspired him to preach a series of sermons on the subject and to induce the Congregational Association of Connecticut to take action. Temperance societies sprang up in a number of places.[41]

After 1815 the temperance movement expanded and became one of the causes espoused by the growing constituencies recruited from the Evangelical forces and the revivals. In 1825 Lyman Beecher preached a series of six sermons on the subject which, printed, had a wide circulation. He demanded that the liquor traffic be made unlawful.[42] Temperance societies multiplied. In 1826 the American Temperance Society, later called the American Society for the Promotion of Temperance, was organized. It had as a special agent a clergyman who travelled extensively with the zeal of an evangelist. By 1835, it was said, over eight thousand local societies had been formed with a total membership of about a million and a half, four thousand distilleries had closed, about two hundred thousand individuals had ceased to use any kind of intoxicating beverage, and about two million had given up the use of distilled liquors. In 1836 the society was reorganized as the American Temperance Union and its pledge was stiffened from abstinence from ardent spirits to abstinence from all intoxicating liquors.

Several Protestant church bodies took action against the liquor traffic. Legislation was enacted by some of the states permitting local option to refuse to grant licenses for the sale of liquor.[43] For a number of years temperance societies were chiefly in New England and the sections of the West settled from New England.[44]

---

[39] Cherrington, *The Evolution of Prohibition in the United States of America*, pp. 15–69.

[40] Weigle, *American Idealism*, p. 175; Krout, *The Origins of Prohibition*, pp. 71 ff.

[41] Cherrington, *op. cit.*, pp. 73–87. See also Krout, *op. cit.*, pp. 83 ff.

[42] Cole, *op. cit.*, pp. 117–119; Stokes, *Church and State in the United States*, Vol. II, pp. 40, 41; Lyman Beecher, *Six Sermons on the Nature, Occasions, Signs, Evils, and Remedy of Intemperance* (Boston, T. R. Marvin, 8th ed., 1829, pp. 107); Krout, *op. cit.*, pp. 101 ff.

[43] Cherrington, *op. cit.*, pp. 97, 116–120; Bodo, *The Protestant Clergy and Public Issues, 1812–1848*, pp. 183 ff.

[44] Krout, *op. cit.*, pp. 129, 130.

The 1840's and 1850's witnessed the further increase of the temperance campaign. The Washingtonian Temperance Movement was begun in Baltimore by a club of drinking men who swore off the habit. However, it did not have a religious foundation. Out of it grew the Martha Washington temperance societies, for women. There were also the Order of the Templars of Honour and Temperance, the Sons of Temperance, and the Cadets of Temperance. A temperance society was formed of members of the Congress, and similar societies sprang up in several state legislatures. The Independent Order of Rechabites was introduced from England.[45] John Bartholomew Gough (1817–1886), a former alcoholic, who had not joined a church until after he had given up drink, became a notable and compelling lecturer on temperance.[46] Beginning in the 1830's Roman Catholic temperance societies spread rapidly. They were given a further impulse by the visit of Theobald Mathew, the Irish Capuchin temperance advocate, in 1849–1851.[47]

During the 1840's and 1850's prohibition laws were passed by a number of states. One of the most famous series of legislative measures was in Maine with Neal Dow (1804–1897) as the chief promoter. Reared a Quaker, Dow was in business in Portland, the chief city of the state. There, seeing the evils of intemperance, he organized the Maine Temperance Union, pledged to total abstinence. In 1846 the Maine legislature passed a prohibition measure. It proved too weak, and, owing to Dow's unflagging efforts, a more drastic law was enacted in 1851, reënacted with increased penalties in 1855, repealed in 1856, and again enacted in 1857.[48] In several other states the legislature prohibited the sale of liquor. In some instances the courts declared the act unconstitutional, in others it was vetoed by the governor, but in some it was put on the statute books or written into the constitution.[49] In Illinois Abraham Lincoln drafted a prohibitory law which passed the legislature but was rejected on a referendum to the electorate.[50]

The Civil War saw a recession in the temperance movement, partly because of the absorption of public opinion in the war and its associated issues, partly because of the lowering of morals brought by the conflict, including the heavy drinking in the armies. Most of the states returned to the license system and in 1875 only Maine, Vermont, and New Hampshire still had prohibitory laws. The brewers and others with financial interests in the liquor traffic organized to oppose prohibition. To obtain funds to fight the war, in 1862 Congress passed an internal revenue act which, among other features, placed a tax on liquor, thus

[45] Cherrington, *op. cit.*, pp. 123 ff.; Krout, *op. cit.*, pp. 138, 139, 182 ff.

[46] *Autobiography and Personal Recollections of John B. Gough* (Springfield, Mass., Bill, Nichols & Co., 1870, pp. 552), *passim;* Carlos Martyn, *John B. Gough, The Apostle of Cold Water* (New York, Funk and Wagnalls Co., 1893, pp. 336), *passim.*

[47] Ellis, *Documents of American Catholic History*, p. 279.

[48] Cherrington, *op. cit.*, pp. 135, 136; *Dictionary of American Biography*, Vol. V, pp. 411, 412.

[49] Cherrington, *op. cit.*, pp. 134–138; Krout, *op. cit.*, pp. 262 ff.

[50] Weigle, *op. cit.*, p. 179.

legalizing it. Saloons multiplied as a way of selling alcoholic beverages.[51]

After the Civil War the temperance movement revived, took additional forms, and again became a force with which to reckon. In 1865 a national convention brought together existing organizations into the National Temperance Society and Publication House. William E. Dodge (1805-1883), son of David Low Dodge and, like his father, prominent in business in New York and an ardent Christian, was its first president and held that post through the rest of his life.[52] In 1869 a state prohibition party was formed in Ohio, preceded in 1867 by similar tentative organizations in Illinois and Michigan. In 1869 the National Prohibition Party was created and during the rest of the century put a ticket in the field in each presidential election.[53] It was backed by many earnest Protestants.

In February, 1872, a national union of the Roman Catholic temperance societies was formed in a meeting at which delegates from over two hundred of them were present.[54] Some bishops were outspoken advocates of temperance. Archbishop Ireland was especially ardent, made war on the liquor traffic, and was called the "Father Mathew of the West." Largely through his influence the Third Plenary Council of Baltimore (1884) denounced the liquor traffic and advised Catholics engaged in it to seek more honourable means of livelihood. In 1887 Pope Leo XIII congratulated Ireland on his efforts, "through various excellent associations, and especially through the Catholic Total Abstinence Union" to "combat the destructive vice of intemperance."[55] In its pastoral letter the Third Plenary Council encouraged Catholic temperance societies. Yet Roman Catholic opinion and practice were sharply divided on the issue.[56]

A spectacular development in the 1870's was the Woman's Crusade. In 1873 in an Ohio town, led by Eliza J. Thompson, daughter of a governor and wife of a judge, seventy-five women gathered in a church, read a psalm, sang, and prayed, then went two by two to the saloons of the place and pled with the owner to give up his business. If he did not yield, they knelt, prayed, and returned day after day until he capitulated. The movement spread and hundreds of saloons closed their doors. But after six months the Crusade died down.[57]

More lasting was the Woman's Christian Temperance Union. Growing out of a meeting at Chautauqua, it was organized in Cleveland in 1874. Led by the brilliant Frances E. Willard (1839-1898), first as its corresponding secretary and then as its president, by 1883 through her incessant travels it had been organized

[51] *Ibid.*, pp. 181, 205.
[52] *Ibid.*, p. 206; Lowitt, *A Merchant Prince of the Nineteenth Century*, pp. 346, 347.
[53] Cherrington, *op. cit.*, pp. 165-167.
[54] Ellis, *op. cit.*, p. 279.
[55] Moynihan, *The Life of Archbishop John Ireland*, pp. 220, 221.
[56] Guilday, *The National Pastorals of the American Hierarchy* (1792-1919), p. 261; Cross, *The Emergence of Liberal Catholicism in America*, pp. 124-129.
[57] Weigle, *op. cit.*, pp. 206, 207.

in every state and territory in the country. In 1887 a world organization was formed with Miss Willard as president. She advocated political action and supported the Prohibition Party. A Methodist, of New England Puritan ancestry, she had earlier shown her ability by heading a college for women in Evanston, Illinois, in connexion with Northwestern University, a Methodist institution. Here was an expression of the growing independence and leadership of women, directed towards total abstinence, education on the evils of alcohol, and the prohibition of the liquor traffic.[58] Moreover, as the most powerful and widespread woman's organization of the latter half of the nineteenth century, the Woman's Christian Temperance Union was a potent force in the emancipation of women and their participation in public affairs.

Between 1880 and 1890 several states wrote prohibition into their constitutions. In 1880 Kansas led the way, followed by Maine in 1884. By 1890 North Dakota and South Dakota were also in the prohibition ranks. Vermont and New Hampshire remained there by earlier action. In several other states similar measures came near to adoption.[59]

A spectacular attempt by one individual to fight the saloon was that of Carry Amelia Moore Nation (1846–1911). From a family with a record of insanity, poorly educated, and with unhappy matrimonial experiences, she conceived a hatred of the saloons and deemed herself divinely commissioned to destroy them. Using a hatchet she smashed saloon fixtures in Kansas where liquor was sold in violation of the constitution, and carried her activities to other states.[60]

The most potent force in the fight against the manufacture and sale of alcoholic beverages was the Anti-Saloon League.[61] Organized in that centre of idealism and missionary zeal, Oberlin, in 1893, it had as its purpose enlisting support for prohibition from members of all parties. It had been preceded by similar movements in several parts of the country. Among them was the Oberlin Temperance Alliance, begun in 1874 with James H. Fairchild, president of Oberlin College, as its first head. A clergyman, H. H. Russell, a graduate of Oberlin, was the chief organizer and first superintendent of the Anti-Saloon League. The Anti-Saloon League made it appeal primarily to Protestants and Protestant churches and sought to bring together all the temperance advocates in a united attack on the liquor traffic.

The Anti-Saloon League did not win unanimous support from advocates of prohibition. Many believed the Prohibition Party to be the best means of obtain-

---

[58] Mary Earhart, *Frances Willard: From Prayers to Politics* (University of Chicago Press, 1944, pp. x, 418), *passim*.

[59] Cherrington, *op. cit.*, pp. 176–180.

[60] Herbert Asbury, *Carry Nation* (New York, Alfred A. Knopf, 1929, pp. xxii, 307, vii), *passim*; *Dictionary of American Biography*, Vol. XIII, pp. 394, 395.

[61] Peter H. Odegard, *Pressure Politics. The Story of the Anti-Saloon League* (New York, Columbia University Press, 1928, pp. x, 299), *passim*; Colvin, *Prohibition in the United States*, pp. 380 ff.; Cherrington, *op. cit.*, pp. 249 ff.

ing the objective and in 1913 adopted an enlarged programme for that method.[62] Some Roman Catholics in high position were critical. Yet the effort was made to keep the Anti-Saloon League from being exclusively Protestant and for many years a Roman Catholic priest was a vice-president. Several Roman Catholic bishops supported prohibition, even though not through the Anti-Saloon League, and a Catholic Clergy Prohibition League came into existence.[63]

Increasingly, prohibition spread, in great areas by states and in others by local option. On the eve of 1914 most of the country was "dry." Prohibition was written into the national constitution in 1919 as the eighteenth amendment.

REFORM OF CITY GOVERNMENTS

A quite different reform movement arose from the rapid growth of cities and the apathy of the public conscience in controlling the evil forces which took advantage of the situation. In 1892 Charles Henry Parkhurst (1842–1933) in stinging sermons pilloried the graft and corruption in the government of New York City, then under the control of a ring centring in Tammany Hall. He had come to New York in 1880 as pastor of the Madison Square Presbyterian Church. In 1891 he had been made president of the Society for the Prevention of Crime. As such he had access to information which proved the complicity of the city government, including the police, in prostitution, gambling-houses, and other evils in violation of the law. Denouncing them from his pulpit, he was challenged by the officials and the press and to reply to them, made a personal tour of the underworld, and disclosed what he found. The better elements organized, in New York a reform government was swept into power, and improvements were achieved in some other cities.[64]

WOMEN LEADERS IN REFORM AND PUBLIC SERVICE

The Woman's Christian Temperance Union was not the only or even the first instance in which, moved by their Christian faith, women of the older stock reared in the Protestant tradition braved the prejudice against their sex's embarking on such activities and fought collective ills.

An early outstanding figure was Dorothea Lynde Dix (1802–1887).[65] Born and reared in New England, she had an unhappy childhood due in part to a religiously fanatical father and suffered chronically from weak lungs. She was

---

[62] Colvin, *op. cit.*, pp. 406 ff.

[63] Odegard, *op. cit.*, pp. 24–29.

[64] C. H. Parkhurst, *My Forty Years in New York* (New York, The Macmillan Co., 1923, pp. xxiv, 256), pp. 106–145; Charles H. Parkhurst, *Our Fight with Tammany* (New York, Charles Scribner's Sons, 1895, pp. vii, 296), *passim;* Weigle, *op. cit.*, p. 215; *Dictionary of American Biography*, Vol. XIV, pp. 244–246.

[65] *Dictionary of American Biography*, Vol. V, pp. 323–325; Francis Tiffany, *Life of Dorothea Lynde Dix* (Boston, Houghton Mifflin Co., 1891, pp. xiii, 392), *passim.*

a member of Channing's congregation, taught his children, and was befriended by him. Intensely interested in the insane, she devoted her life to obtaining better care for them. When she was first aware of them, only eight asylums for the insane existed in the United States. For the most part the mentally ill were treated with appalling neglect and cruelty. She made personal investigations of their lot, by her findings aroused public opinion, and worked for a professionally trained personnel supported by taxation to care for the unfortunates. Between 1845 and 1852 she obtained legislation setting up hospitals for the insane in eleven states and in Canada and Nova Scotia. From 1854 to 1857 she travelled in the British Isles and the Continent of Europe investigating the provision—or lack of it—for the mentally unbalanced. During the Civil War she devoted herself to the men in the armed services as superintendent of the women nurses. But when peace was restored she returned to her labours for the insane.

Clara Barton (1821–1912), a younger contemporary of Dorothea Dix and like her of New England birth, was reared a Universalist but was never a church member. She first came to wide public notice by her service to the sick and wounded of the Civil War. After the war she spent some time searching for the missing of that conflict. During the Franco-Prussian War she assisted the Red Cross. She was chiefly remembered for her prolonged effort against many obstacles to introduce that movement to the United States. In 1881 the National Society of the Red Cross was organized and the following year the Senate ratified the Geneva Convention. She was president of the American Red Cross from its beginning to 1904.[66]

Lucretia Coffin Mott (1793–1880), of old New England Quaker stock, a preacher of the branch of the Society of Friends which arose from the teaching of Elias Hicks, had as her early major interest the abolition of Negro slavery. She and her husband, John Mott (1788–1868), were not only anti-slavery advocates but also pioneers in the struggle for equal rights for women.[67]

Julia Ward Howe (1819–1910) was the daughter of a deeply religious wealthy New York banker of Rhode Island birth and rearing who saw to it that she had an excellent education. Vivacious, one of the belles of the city, she married Samuel Gridley Howe, twenty years her senior. He was a man of chivalric zeal who fought with the Greeks for their independence, was a friend of Horace Mann, aided Dorothea Dix, was strongly anti-slavery, and gave much of his time to developing a school for the blind in Boston. Julia Ward Howe shared her husband's anti-slavery convictions. During the Civil War she rose to sudden fame as the author of "The Battle Hymn of the Republic," written in one night after visiting an encampment near Washington. She espoused many causes, in-

[66] *Dictionary of American Biography*, Vol. II, pp. 18–21; Ishbel Ross, *Angel of the Battlefield: The Life of Clara Barton* (New York, Harper & Brothers, 1947, pp. 305), *passim*.
[67] *Dictionary of American Biography*, Vol. XIII, pp. 288, 289.

:luding those for peace and for equal rights for women. In 1870 she issued an appeal to womanhood throughout the world to promote peace. She became president of the American Branch of the Woman's International Peace Association. She occasionally preached and, a Unitarian, championed liberal religion. She read widely in such authors as Comte, Hegel, Kant, Fichte, and Spinoza. Courageous, quick at repartee, with a sense of humour which contributed to a balanced judgement, to an advanced age she was widely influential.[68]

Elizabeth Cady Stanton (1815-1902), born in New York State and reared in a sternly religious home, was deeply indebted to a Presbyterian minister who introduced her to a better education than was usual for members of her sex and who did much to give her direction and purpose. But in later years she often attacked the churches for their slowness to promote woman's rights. She married a lawyer, Henry Brewster Stanton, an abolitionist, and gave herself to the causes of abolition, temperance, and equal rights for women. She had much to do with the Woman's Rights Convention which convened in Seneca Falls in 1848, was the first president of the National Woman's Suffrage Association (organized in 1869), and then was president of the National American Woman's Suffrage Association. She lectured widely, among other subjects on family life and the care of children.[69]

Susan B. Anthony (1820-1906) was of New England Quaker stock and was a member of the Hicksite branch of the Friends. A precocious child, she early developed a decided distaste for marriage. For some years she taught school. She organized the Woman's State Temperance Society of New York, was outspoken for abolition, and stood for equal rights for Negroes. When she was about thirty, Mrs. Stanton won her for the cause of woman's rights, a step for which she was prepared by the insistence of men that women should not speak in public. When the National Woman's Suffrage Association was organized, she became the chairman of its executive committee. From 1892 to 1900 she was president of the National American Woman's Suffrage Association. For some years she encountered ridicule and even mob violence in her public lectures, but she lived to be greatly revered as one of the leading women of her day—some said the greatest woman that the United States had produced.[70]

A friend and co-worker of Susan B. Anthony in the campaign for the equality of women with men was Lucy Stone (1818-1893). Born in Massachusetts, she was reared a Congregationalist, but in her student days at Oberlin she reacted against Finney's preaching and became a Unitarian. She was active as an antislavery lecturer. She also lectured indefatigably on the wrongs done to women.

---

[68] Louise Hall Tharp, *Three Saints and a Sinner. Julia Ward Howe, Louisa, Annie, and Sam Ward* (Boston, Little, Brown and Co., 1956, pp. x, 406), *passim; Dictionary of American Biography,* Vol. IX, pp. 291-293, 296, 297.

[69] *Dictionary of American Biography,* Vol. XVII, pp. 521-523.

[70] Katharine Anthony, *Susan B. Anthony. Her Personal History and Her Era* (Garden City, N.Y., Doubleday and Co., 1954, pp. x, 521).

She was president of the Woman's Rights Convention which met in 1850 in succession to the preliminary gathering of 1848. Her husband, Henry Brown Blackwell, was in full sympathy with her, permitted her to keep her maiden name, and helped in the campaign for woman's suffrage.[71]

Margaret Olivia Slocum Sage (1828–1918), widow of Russell Sage (1816–1906), was remembered as an outstanding philanthropist. She was left with a fortune gathered by her somewhat eccentric husband by methods made possible through the rapid growth of the country and by its laws. In accord with her deep religious convictions of the responsibilities of women of wealth and leisure, she distributed it to many enterprises and educational institutions, including the YWCA and the YMCA, and in 1907 gave ten million dollars to endow the Russell Sage Foundation for the improvement of social and living conditions in the United States. Across the years the Foundation contributed to a wide variety of projects, among them child welfare, recreation, the improvement of the peoples of the Southern highlands, and the training of social workers.[72]

A different story was that of Martha McChesny Berry (1866–1942). Born near Rome, Georgia, an Episcopalian, from a family of culture which had been impoverished by the Civil War and had by a brave fight in part recouped its fortunes, she became interested in the white mountaineers near her home. Most of them were illiterate and were struggling with extreme poverty. Some were making a hard living by distilling and selling whiskey contrary to the law. She began by giving them religious instruction and in 1902 initiated the Berry Schools for the boys and girls of the region. Under her leadership the schools grew and she was given national and international recognition.[73]

Again quite different, but also with a record of heroism and Christian faith, was the life of Helen Keller (1880–――). It was closely connected with the work of the husband of Julia Ward Howe. He headed, as we have suggested, the Perkins Institution for the blind in Boston. There he developed through Laura Bridgman, from infancy a deaf-mute, a method of reading. There, too, was educated through that method Anne Mansfield Sullivan, who had become almost totally blind early in life but had regained part of her sight. She was engaged to teach Helen Keller, who had been made a deaf and blind mute by early illness. In spite of what had been worked out at Perkins, Miss Sullivan had largely to devise her own methods. Her pupil proved intelligent and teachable. She learned to speak. She graduated from Radcliffe with honours. She grew into a religious faith in which she was helped by Phillips Brooks and which was centred on a simple, childlike trust in a Divine Friend. She became famous the

[71] *Dictionary of National Biography*, Vol. XVIII, pp. 80, 81.

[72] John M. Glenn, Lilian Brandt, and F. Emerson Andrews, *Russell Sage Foundation 1907–1946* (New York, Russell Sage Foundation, 2 vols., 1947); *Dictionary of American Biography*, Vol. XVI, pp. 291, 292.

[73] Harnett T. Kane with Inez Henry, *Miracle in the Mountains* (Garden City, N.Y., Doubleday and Co., 1956, pp. 320), *passim*.

world around and gave herself to aiding others, especially the blind.[74]

EMINENT PHILANTHROPISTS AMONG THE MEN

The nineteenth century saw a number of men, most of them moved by a Christian faith derived through the Protestantism of the older stock, become eminent as philanthropists. They had acquired wealth through the opportunities provided by a growing country and the machines developed in the revolutionary age. Regarding their wealth as a trust from God, they sought to use it for the welfare of their fellows. Others were not wealthy but obtained from men of wealth the means to make their dreams a reality.

One of the earliest philanthropic men of wealth was Elias Boudinot (1740–1821).[75] Of Huguenot ancestry, he was a devout Presbyterian, president of the General Assembly of his church, the first president of the American Bible Society, and was largely responsible for the choice of Princeton as the seat of the seminary of the Presbyterian Church. He was long a member of the Continental Congress, for a time was its president, and was a member of the first Congress under the constitution. He gave liberally of his wealth to religious and charitable causes.

Charles Loring Brace (1826–1890) had no wealth of his own but enlisted the support of those who possessed it.[76] Born in Connecticut of old New England stock, he graduated from Yale in 1846 and studied theology there for two years under Taylor. Religious doubts turned him from the ministry but did not prevent him from writing in after years *Gesta Christi, or a History of Human Progress under Christianity.*[77] He devoted his life to the underprivileged in New York City, then growing rapidly through the impulse of the revolutionary age. In 1853 he joined in organizing the Children's Aid Society. He spent his life mainly among the immigrants who were pouring into the city from Europe. Partly for them he established cheap lodging houses and industrial and night schools. He found employment for over 100,000 child waifs. Tolerant, convinced of the worth of every human soul, he insisted that those whom he served help themselves and thus be not pauperized or lose their self-respect.

Gerrit Smith (1797–1874) inherited wealth from his father, a partner of John

[74] *The Story of My Life by Helen Keller with Her Letters (1887–1901) and a Supplementary Account of Her Education, Including Passages from the Reports and Letters of Her Teacher, Anne Mansfield Sullivan* by John Albert Macy (Garden City, N.Y., Doubleday, Page and Co., 1926, pp. 441), *passim;* Helen Keller, *My Religion* (Garden City, N.Y., Doubleday, Page and Co., 1927, pp. viii, 208), *passim;* Van Wyck Brooks, *Helen Keller, Sketch for a Portrait* (New York, E. P. Dutton and Co., 1956, pp. 166), *passim.*

[75] George Adams Boyd, *Elias Boudinot, Patriot and Statesman 1740–1821* (Princeton University Press, 1952, pp. xiii, 321), *passim.*

[76] *Dictionary of American Biography,* Vol. II, pp. 539, 540; *The Life of Charles Brace Chiefly Told in His Own Letters, edited by His Daughter* (New York, Charles Scribner's Sons, 1894, pp. x, 503), *passim.*

[77] London, Hodder and Stoughton, 1889, pp. xxiii, 520. The first edition was in 1882.

Jacob Astor, and added to it through various investments, largely in land. He was a cousin of Elizabeth Cady Stanton.[78] Reared a Presbyterian, he espoused the cause of Church union. He advocated many of the reform movements of his day—abolition, the American Colonization Society, opposition to Freemasonry, temperance, vegetarianism, abstinence from tobacco, national dress reform, woman's suffrage, prison reform, the abolition of capital punishment, and Sunday observance. He was long a vice-president of the American Peace Society. He helped found the Liberty Party, was a member of Congress in 1853–1854, and later affiliated himself with the Republican Party. In the reconstruction years after the Civil War he favoured moderation to the former supporters of the Confederacy. He gave to the erection of churches, to theological seminaries and colleges, including Oberlin and his own *alma mater,* Hamilton College, to various missionary societies, and to needy individuals. He was a friend of the Tappans and often collaborated with them.

Anson Greene Phelps (1791–1853), born in Connecticut, first manufactured saddles in Hartford in that state and about 1812 moved to New York City. There he made a fortune, with investments in that and other cities. A devout Presbyterian, he gave liberally to such organizations as the American Board of Commissioners for Foreign Missions, the American Bible Society, the American Home Missionary Society, and the American Colonization Society.[79]

We have already met a son-in-law of Phelps, William Earl Dodge (1805–1883), son of David Low Dodge. In coöperation with Phelps in the family mercantile firm Phelps, Dodge and Company, he added to his inherited fortune by participating in a variety of enterprises in the burgeoning country, among them real estate, the Pennsylvania lumber industry, railroads, coal mining, and manufacturing. A friend of Finney, he contributed both time and money to a number of religious and philanthropic enterprises. Among them were the YMCA, the Evangelical Alliance, and, as we have seen, temperance and prohibition. By the time of his death he was said to be giving away an average of a thousand dollars a day to missionary societies, theological seminaries, the erection and support of churches, and individuals. He was one of the founders of Union Theological Seminary in New York City. He aided many colleges at home and abroad, supported education for the Negroes, and championed the cause of the Indians.[80] A son, William E. Dodge, Jr., carried on many of his interests.

Another son-in-law of Anson Greene Phelps, Daniel James, was of similar interests, and his son, Daniel Willis James (1832–1907), who became even more wealthy, chiefly through copper and railways, gave unobtrusively and generously to many charitable and religious causes. For example, it was he who pur-

[78] Ralph Volney Harlow, *Gerrit Smith, Philanthropist and Reformer* (New York, Henry Holt and Co., 1939, pp. vi, 501), *passim.*

[79] *Dictionary of American Biography,* Vol. XIV, pp. 525, 526; Cleland, *A History of Phelps Dodge 1834–1950,* pp. 3–20.

[80] Lowitt, *A Merchant Prince of the Nineteenth Century, passim;* Cleland, *op. cit.,* pp. 53–74.

chased the site and contributed largely to the erection of the new buildings of Union Theological Seminary in New York City.[81]

Andrew Carnegie (1835-1919), whose benefactions in his lifetime were said to exceed $350,000,000, seems to have owed his motive in giving only indirectly if at all to the Christian faith. His humble Scottish heritage through both his father and his mother had a strong strain of political and social radicalism. His father, a handloom weaver, was a Chartist. His mother's father was a friend and correspondent of William Cobbett. At least one of his relatives attacked the Established Church and advocated a republic. Through that background Carnegie, who was intensely loyal to his family, was nurtured in a commitment to human progress. The family came to the United States in 1848. By industry and ability Carnegie made a fortune in the rapid economic expansion of the country, at first through the Pennsylvania Railroad and later through his skill in developing the steel industry. Self-educated, with a strong literary bent, he was a friend of many of the great of his time in both the United States and Great Britain—notably, as an indication of his approach to human problems, of Herbert Spencer and John Morley. Yet he was not hostile to Christianity and, as we have seen, endowed the Church Peace Union. His was, rather, the humanism divorced from the Christian faith which arose in a culture deeply indebted to Christianity.[82]

In contrast, John Davison Rockefeller (1839-1937), whose gifts to philanthropic and religious enterprises by 1921 were said to have amounted to more than $500,000,000, seems to have been impelled in making them almost entirely by his Christian faith. Born in New York State, he attended a Baptist Sunday School and church as early as he could remember. When, in his teens, he came with his family to Cleveland, he affiliated himself at once with what was eventually the Euclid Avenue Baptist Church. There he was baptized at the age of fifteen, found his social life with its young people, attended their prayer and testimonial meetings, and taught a Sunday School class. His wife came from a deeply religious Congregational family. Her father, a business man and a member of the state legislature, had helped to organize Congregational churches, was ardently abolitionist and an operator of the Underground Railway which aided Negro slaves to escape to Canada, and, with his wife, worked and prayed for temperance. Rockefeller was never narrowly sectarian. Believing in tithing, in his early manhood he gave not only to Baptist causes but also to other denominations. After his marriage he was superintendent of the Sunday School of his church, and his wife supervised the infant department. He conducted daily family prayers and regularly attended the weekly prayer meeting of his

[81] *Dictionary of American Biography*, Vol. IX, p. 573.
[82] *Ibid.*, Vol. III, pp. 499–506.

church. The entire family were committed to the temperance movement.[83]

Disciplined, taciturn about his inmost feelings, deliberate, exact, Rockefeller declared again and again: "A man should make all he can and give all he can." His fortune was gathered chiefly through the petroleum industry, then in the early stages of its later prodigious development, and mainly through the Standard Oil Company. Like Carnegie, he had skill in choosing able associates and, taking advantage of the size and growth of the country, organized his business to promote efficiency and lower costs by large-scale operations. His methods brought on him much public criticism, but he did not allow himself to cherish rancour or to speak ill of any man. He appears always to have maintained in his business what he regarded as Christian ideals.

Rockefeller's benefactions mounted and in time were administered and reached their enormous proportions through a few institutions and organizations. Earlier, as his wealth multiplied and his generosity became known, he received countless appeals from individuals as well as institutions. He gave extensively through Baptist societies to education and to home and foreign missions. He turned for advice to men whom he had learned to trust. Among them were Baptist clergymen, chiefly Frederick T. Gates and Wallace Buttrick. In general the principles governing his contributions were to assist work already organized and of proven worth which was of a continuing character and would not disappear when his support was withdrawn, to give on the condition that the contributions of others would be stimulated, and, especially, to aid in such fashion that the beneficiary would be encouraged to be independent and self-reliant.

We have already seen the way in which Rockefeller made possible the University of Chicago: by 1910, the year of his final grant, he had put into that institution $35,000,000. He said that Harper, with whom he had a close friendship, had never asked him for money and had been successful in obtaining funds from others. Growing out of his interest in Negro education came (1903) the General Education Board, for education "without distinction of sex, race, or creed." Two years earlier, in 1901, the Rockefeller Institute for Medical Research had been launched. In 1909 the Rockefeller Sanitary Commission was begun for the purpose of eradicating hookworm in the South. In 1910 Rockefeller created his major philanthropy, the Rockefeller Foundation, "to promote the well-being and to advance the civilization of the peoples of the United States and its territories and possessions and of foreign lands in the acquisition and dissemination of knowledge, in the prevention and relief of suffering, and in the promotion of any and all of the elements of human progress." The attempt to obtain a charter from the Congress of the United States provoked

[83] Raymond B. Fosdick, *John D. Rockefeller, Jr., A Portrait* (New York, Harper & Brothers, 1956, pp. ix, 477), pp. 12–29.

intense and widespread criticism on the ground that the Foundation would perpetuate vast wealth without effective public control, and on the charge that it was being created by "tainted money" amassed by unrighteous means. Failing authorization by the Congress, in 1913 a charter was obtained from the New York State legislature. In that and the following year Rockefeller gave the Foundation $100,000,000 and through 1929 additional grants had increased the total to $241,608,359.74. The Rockefeller gifts through the Foundation and other agencies were made only after careful and often prolonged investigation. Increasingly the approach was non-sectarian.[84]

Daniel Drew (1792–1879) had a different record. A man of slight formal education, he combined unscrupulous business methods with a profession of Christian faith. In the lush period which immediately followed the Civil War he engaged in a number of financial undertakings which brought public scandal even in years which had grown all but callous to that kind of buccaneering. For a time he collaborated with the notorious Jay Gould and James Fisk. Bankrupt in his seventies, during his affluent decades he had built Methodist churches and had endowed a theological seminary and a school for girls which bore his name.[85]

THE SOCIAL GOSPEL

In the latter half of the nineteenth century the American dream and the churches were faced with the mounting urbanization and industrialization which were features of the revolutionary age in the United States as well as in Western Europe. The industrialization of the North had been accelerated by the Civil War and the demand for munitions and equipment for the armed forces. The war, too, was followed by marked moral deterioration in public and business life. The government, national, state, and urban, was honeycombed with corruption. Much of business was predatory, had no concern for honesty, and connived with officials of easy conscience to make fortunes at the expense of the general good. *Laissez faire* and the theory of "enlightened self-interest" with Adam Smith as an early expounder were dominant. As the first stages of the Industrial Revolution had brought conditions in Great Britain which the Christian conscience sought to correct, so in the United States, where that revolution was now coming to flood tide, evils appeared which challenged the Christian forces.

To meet the challenge, what was generally called the social gospel was formulated. An alternative designation was social Christianity. It was an attempt

---

[84] Raymond B. Fosdick, *The Story of the Rockefeller Foundation* (New York, Harper & Brothers, 1952, pp. xiii, 336), pp. 1–21; John D. Rockefeller, *Random Reminiscences of Men and Events* (New York, Doubleday, Page and Co., 1909, pp. vii, 188), *passim*; Allan Nevins, *Study in Power. John D. Rockefeller, Industrialist and Philanthropist* (New York, Charles Scribner's Sons, 2 vols., 1953), *passim*.

[85] *Dictionary of American Biography*, Vol. V, pp. 450, 451.

to bring the emerging society to conformity with Christian standards. Here was a movement—or, rather, movements—which continued dreams going back to the idealism of the radical Protestant groups that had been potent in the colonial period and had expressed itself in the reforms of the first half of the century. Yet some manifestations were new. They were in response to the changes in the American scene. They also reflected the optimism which was widespread in the latter part of the century in Western Europe as well as in the United States and which was associated with the older theory of progress reinforced by current interpretations of the theory of evolution. The social gospel had kinship with the Ritschlianism popular in some circles in Europe and was given early impetus by the writings of the English Christian Socialists. It was found chiefly in the Protestantism of the older stock. It had a variety of expressions. In our necessarily brief survey we can take the space for only a few of the more prominent figures and programmes.

Foreshadowings were seen in the first half of the century. Unitarianism and Transcendentalism, with their confidence in the essential goodness of man and the ability of man to shape his own future, were forerunners. Joseph Tuckerman (1778–1840), a clergyman, a graduate of Harvard, who had a city mission in Boston for the poor, was connected with the Benevolent Fraternity of the Churches, and wrote extensively, was one of the earliest pioneers.[86] A Unitarian clergyman, Edward Everett Hale (1822–1909), whose long life carried him to the eve of 1914, was a prominent representative of old New England stock, from 1856 to 1909 was pastor of the South Congregational (Unitarian) Church in Boston, and in his last years was chaplain of the Senate of the United States. He believed that it was the obligation of Christians to bring in the Kingdom of God and taught his congregation that a real Kingdom of God was to come in the world in which they lived. In 1870, at a time when the corruption in public life was near a peak, in a story, "Ten Times One Is Ten," he suggested how goodness could spread and coined the mottoes:

> Look up and not down
> Look forward and not back
> Look out and not in
> Lend a hand.

Lend a Hand Clubs and the Look-Up Legion were founded and spread far beyond the Unitarian fellowship. Hale's teaching contributed to the formation of the King's Daughters, the I.H.N. Clubs, the Order of Send Me, the Commercial Temperance League, and other organizations which sought to Christianize the world.[87]

[86] *A Memorial of Rev. Joseph Tuckerman* (Worcester, Mass., privately printed, 1888, pp. viii, 372), *passim*.

[87] Edward E. Hale, Jr., *The Life and Letters of Edward Everett Hale* (Boston, Little, Brown

In 1851 a book by Stephen Colwell, *New Themes for the Protestant Clergy,* showed the influence of Saint-Simon, Comte, and Sismondi. It accused the Church of being a bourgeois institution and held that in contrast it should give itself to bringing society more nearly in accord with the teachings of Jesus.[88]

The way for the social gospel was prepared by others in the churches of the older American stock, particularly but not exclusively in orthodox Congregationalism, through such forces as Hopkinsianism with its "universal disinterested benevolence" and the weakening of the inherited Calvinism. Horace Bushnell broke ground for the social gospel, especially by his *Christian Nurture* and his insistence that no partition exists between the natural and the supernatural. The Utopianism born of revivals and perfectionism also contributed to a post-millennarianism which would seek to improve society before the expected second coming and thousand-year reign of Christ.[89] Conservatives in the Protestant churches generally held that if individuals were really converted they would give themselves to fighting social ills. In 1864 some of them, from eleven denominations, organized the National Reform Association, which had among other objectives writing into the constitution of the United States the acknowledgement of God as the source of all authority and power in civil government, and His will, as revealed in the Bible, "as of supreme authority, in order to constitute a Christian government."[90] In 1870 Samuel Harris, later professor in the Yale Divinity School, while holding that the Kingdom of God would not come by any natural progress "but by the divine grace in Christ coming down upon humanity from above," viewed contemporary movements for social justice as of divine origin and believed that the Kingdom of God would progress towards a universal reign of justice and love.[91]

Washington Gladden (1836–1918), sometimes called the father of the social gospel, was of old New England stock. From 1882 to his death he was pastor and then pastor emeritus of the First Congregational Church in Columbus, Ohio. In his youth he had been profoundly influenced by Frederick W. Robertson and Horace Bushnell and through them had been helped to move from the extreme religious conservatism in which he had been reared. Before going to Columbus he had been on the staff of *The Independent* and had contributed to the chorus of denunciation of the Tweed ring which was battening off New York City. A prolific writer and lecturer as well as preacher, through his ma-

---

and Co., 2 vols., 1917), *passim,* especially Vol. II, pp. 40, 120–133, 214, 215; Jean Holloway, *Edward Everett Hale: A Biography* (Austin, University of Texas Press, 1956, pp. xi, 275), *passim.*

[88] Dombrowski, *The Early Days of Christian Socialism in America,* pp. 31–34.

[89] Hopkins, *The Rise of the Social Gospel in American Protestantism 1865–1915,* pp. 5, 6; Smith, *Revivalism and Social Reform,* pp. 225 ff.

[90] Hopkins, *op. cit.,* p. 17; Henry F. May, *Protestant Churches and Industrial America* (New York, Harper & Brothers, 1949, pp. x, 297), pp. 170 ff.

[91] Hopkins, *op. cit.,* p. 21.

ture years he helped to popularize the findings of Biblical criticism and the liberal theological views which were gaining in Congregational circles. His hymn "Oh Master let me walk with Thee" was sung for many years after his death. But he was chiefly remembered for his fearless speaking, writing, and acting on issues which were emerging from the mounting industrialization. He was critical of *laissez faire*. He did not believe that socialism had the answer, but he stood for the right of labour to organize, wished labour and capital to coöperate, and worked for government ownership of public utilities. He maintained that society could be Christianized by the application of the principle "Thou shalt love thy neighbour as thyself," and held this to be the chief business of the Church. The Church, he said, should concentrate its energies on realizing the Kingdom of God on the earth. He believed that the Church could accomplish this not by using force or espousing any one economic programme but by inspiring individuals with the love of justice and the spirit of service. He looked for a reformation in the attitude of the Church towards the working classes in which the Church would recognize that its welfare was bound up with theirs. The reformation would, he insisted, consist in the awakening of the Church to its social responsibilities. He called for "a new evangelism" which would have as its objective "the redemption of society." Gladden furthered municipal reform and for a brief time was a member of the city council of Columbus. He led in a bi-partisan committee to endorse the best candidates on the party tickets. He came to national prominence by his opposition to the solicitation by the American Board of Commissioners for Foreign Missions of a gift from Rockefeller, for he maintained that the latter's money was "tainted" by the methods through which it had been acquired. He stood up against an outburst of denunciation of the Roman Catholic Church by Protestants in the 1890's.[92]

In the 1870's several voices were raised on the problems presented by labour in the growing industries. The Episcopalians were concerned with the alienation of labour from the Church. Joseph Cook, a Congregational minister, a graduate of Andover Theological Seminary, called public attention to immoral conditions in the factories of Lynn, Massachusetts. Later by lectures in Boston and other cities which were given a wide circulation by newspapers in the United States and England, while rejecting socialism he excoriated the exploitation of women and children in industry and the inadequate wages paid and the slum conditions in which labourers were compelled to live. In 1872 the Christian Labour Union was organized with a Congregational clergyman,

[92] Washington Gladden, *Recollections* (Boston, Houghton Mifflin Co., 1909, pp. vi, 445), *passim;* Washington Gladden, *The Labor Question* (Boston, The Pilgrim Press, 1891, pp. 209), *passim;* Washington Gladden, *Working People and Their Employers* (New York, Funk and Wagnalls Co., 1888, pp. 241), *passim;* Washington Gladden, *The Church and Modern Life* (Boston, Houghton Mifflin Co., 1908, pp. vi, 221), *passim;* Washington Gladden, *Social Salvation* (Boston, Houghton Mifflin Co., 1902, pp. v, 240), *passim.*

Jesse Henry Jones, and a Methodist lay preacher, Edward H. Rogers, as prominent spokesmen.[93]

Henry George (1839–1897), through his advocacy of the single tax on the unearned increment in land values, influenced some men who became prominent in the social gospel movement. Reared in a deeply religious home in Philadelphia, he later became a Methodist but had little use for organized Christianity and most clergymen. He struggled with stark poverty in California, came to the conviction that in the growing prosperity of the country the rich were becoming wealthier and the poor poorer, and saw as a remedy not socialism, which he loathed, but what came to be known as the single tax. He set forth his thesis in *Progress and Poverty*, published in 1879 and 1880. This book, after having difficulty in finding a publisher, had an enormous circulation in the United States and England. George argued his theme with religious fervour and believed that in a true Christianity which attacks vested wrong a power resided that could make over the world. He became a national and international figure before burning himself out in his zeal.[94]

A younger contemporary of Henry George, Edward Bellamy (1850–1898), also contributed to the frame of mind which was receptive to the social gospel. Reared in a Baptist parsonage in a small town, he had his eyes opened to the extent of man's inhumanity to man by a trip to Europe, where the fruits of the Industrial Revolution were painfully apparent. He first attracted attention by a piece of fiction, *Looking Backward, 1887–2000*, which pictured an American Utopia of the year 2000. It sold over a million copies and was translated into several languages. Clubs arose with the purpose of transforming the United States from a capitalistic society to one in which industry would be nationalized. Many of the clergy and many social reformers were profoundly affected by it, with its high ethical and religious standards.[95]

Richard Theodore Ely (1854–1943) through his books had a wide influence especially upon Methodists, for whom some of his writings were required reading for ordination. Of an old New England family and reared in a strict Presbyterian home, while he later rejected some of the dogmas which he had been taught, he continued to be a convinced Christian. An economist and social scientist, he received some of his early formal training in Germany. He held that the Christian religion had all that was necessary for the solution of society's problems, especially in the command of love for one's neighbour. He was not a socialist, but he looked for the socialization of natural monopolies and the development by slow evolution of a Christian equalitarian society. The American Economic Association, which he had a large part in organizing, was

[93] Hopkins, *op. cit.*, pp. 38–49.
[94] Charles Albro Barker, *Henry George* (New York, Oxford University Press, 1955, pp. xvii, 696), *passim;* Hopkins, *op. cit.*, p. 60; Dombrowski, *op. cit.*, pp. 35–49.
[95] Dombrowski, *op. cit.*, pp. 84–95; *Dictionary of American Biography*, Vol. II, pp. 163, 164.

regarded by him as having its major work in the direction of practical Christianity. On its original membership roll were the names of twenty-three ministers, among them Washington Gladden and Lyman Abbott.[96]

John Bates Clark (1847–1938), regarded by some as America's greatest theoretical economist, came out of a deeply religious New England background, in his early student days had expected to enter the ministry, and in his undergraduate years was persuaded by Julius Seelye, president of Amherst, to become an economist. He was also profoundly impressed by Seelye's Christian faith. He held that society is morally based and that God was guiding it towards greater and greater moral well-being.[97]

Charles Monroe Sheldon (1857–1946) gave marked impetus to the social gospel. Of Scotch-Irish ancestry, he was a graduate of Brown and of Andover Theological Seminary. Beginning in 1889 he was pastor of the Central Congregational Church in Topeka, Kansas. There, with an interval from 1912 to 1915, he served until 1919. From 1920 to 1925 he was editor of the *Christian Herald*. Prominent in the movement for national prohibition, he was chiefly famous as the author of *In His Steps, or What Would Jesus Do?* Written in 1896 and 1897, it eventually went into thirty-six editions and sold over twenty-two million copies in more than twenty different languages. It set forth briefly in simple language and fictional form what the author believed following Jesus entailed in various aspects of life—social, economic, and political. It stirred up much debate. For one week in March, 1900, Sheldon had full editorial control of the *Daily Capital* of Topeka, as a widely publicized demonstration of what a newspaper should be if it attempted to do what Jesus would do.[98]

Organizations for the building of a Christian social order in the United States sprang up in the latter part of the century in an attempt to meet in a Christian fashion the problems brought by the mounting industrialization and the rise of labour unions. In 1872 a Christian Labour Union was organized in Boston. It was led by Jesse Henry Jones, a Congregational minister, and had as its object the reform of relations between capital and labour.[99] Although in the 1880's the leaders of the Protestant churches were almost unanimously against socialism, in the 1890's the attitude began to be modified. In 1889 the Society of Christian Socialists was organized.[100]

The chief creative figure in the Society of Christian Socialists was William Dwight Porter Bliss (1856–1926). The son of a New England Congregational missionary to Turkey, a graduate of Amherst and Hartford Theological Sem-

[96] Everett, *Religion in Economics*, pp. 75–98; Dombrowski, *op. cit.*, pp. 50–59; Richard T. Ely, *Social Aspects of Christianity and Other Essays* (New York, Thomas Y. Crowell Co., new ed., 1889, pp. x, 161).

[97] Everett, *op. cit.*, pp. 26–74.

[98] *Charles M. Sheldon, His Life Story* (New York, George H. Doran Co., 1925, pp. 309), *passim.*

[99] Dombrowski, *op. cit.*, p. 77; Hopkins, *op. cit.*, pp. 43 ff.

[100] Hopkins, *op. cit.*, pp. 174 ff.

inary, for a time he was a Congregational clergyman and then became a priest of the Protestant Episcopal Church. He had been influenced by Bellamy and by Maurice and Kingsley. In 1886 he had become a member of the Knights of Labour and in 1887 was a delegate to the convention of that movement. In 1891 he was appointed the organizing secretary of the Christian Social Union, inspired by the English Christian Social Union, and in that capacity lectured widely in the United States, Canada, and England and repeatedly preached in churches. In 1898 he founded the Union Reform League, which the next year merged into the Social Reform Union. He remained an ardent churchman. He organized the Church of the Carpenter in Boston and during his seven years' pastorate sought to make it serve social reform.[101]

Although most of the Protestant clergy rejected socialism, some believed that a similarity existed between it and the teachings of Jesus. In 1906 the Christian Socialist Fellowship came into being out of an exchange of letters in the columns of *The Christian Socialist,* a journal begun in 1903 by a minister in Iowa. It suffered from the anti-socialist reaction which followed World War I.[102]

A spectacular but relatively brief development in the social gospel movement centred in Iowa (later Grinnell) College in the 1890's. Its leading figures were the president, George A. Gates (1851–1912), and George D. Herron (1862–1925), both of them Congregational clergymen. Herron was reared in a devout Indiana home of Scottish parentage. He attracted attention by an address in 1890 on "the message of Jesus to men of wealth." In 1893 he was called to a professorship of applied Christianity which had been established in Iowa College at the instance of Gates. Gates, a graduate of Dartmouth and Andover Theological Seminary, had studied in Germany and had accepted the critical study of the Bible and the theory of evolution. Herron's classes were crowded. He lectured widely and wrote a number of books setting forth his convictions. He was sharply critical of the existing social and economic order and urged complete obedience to the teachings of Jesus that the Kingdom of God might come on earth. The Kingdom Movement spread and was reinforced by distinguished lecturers at Iowa College, by a periodical, and by the American Institute of Christian Sociology founded at Chautauqua in 1893 with Ely as president and Herron as organizer and chief instructor and with the endorsement of Gladden, Vincent, and other prominent figures. "Schools of the Kingdom" were held at Iowa College in the summers of 1894 and 1895 and were attended by hundreds of clergymen from several denominations. The Christian Commonwealth Colony arose in Georgia as an experiment in communal living and coined the term "social gospel." By 1898 Herron had become so radical and so pronounced a socialist that he lost the confidence of the churches. By 1901 he

[101] *Ibid.,* pp. 173–180; Dombrowski, *op. cit.,* pp. 95–106; *Dictionary of American Biography,* Vol. II, pp. 377, 378.
[102] Hopkins, *op. cit.,* pp. 235–237.

had faded out of the scene, branded as an advocate of "free love" and deposed from the ministry. The Kingdom Movement collapsed.[103]

More lasting were the efforts of Josiah Strong (1847–1916). Of old New England stock, Strong was a graduate of Western Reserve College and Lane Theological Seminary and was ordained into the Congregational ministry. In 1885 his maiden book, *Our Country,* appeared. It stressed the dangers of the over-accumulation and concentration of capital, had warm sympathy with labour, and expressed deep concern for social problems. Translated into foreign languages, it brought the author wide attention. In 1893 in *New Era* Strong had as his thesis that in the teachings of Jesus the Kingdom was set forth as an ideal society to be realized here and now. He wished the Church to achieve unity and to give itself to hastening the consummation of the Kingdom. Strong had first hoped to see his ideals promoted through the Evangelical Alliance. Under its auspices and through his organizing ability three conferences on social Christianity were held—in 1887, 1889, and 1893. However, the Evangelical Alliance proved too conservative to give the leadership which he believed the crisis called for, and in 1898 he initiated the League for Social Service. In 1901 the League was reconstituted as the American Institute for Social Service.[104]

The outstanding prophet of the social gospel, Walter Rauschenbusch (1861–1918), appeared late in the century.[105] As we have seen, he was from a Pietist ancestry.[106] He had back of him six generations of clergymen. His father, August, a Lutheran pastor, had come to the United States sent by the Langenberg Society, of Pietist origin, to hold the German immigrants to the faith. He arrived in 1846 and in 1850 became a Baptist out of deep conviction.[107] Walter Rauschenbusch was, then, born in a devout Baptist family, in Rochester, New York. He had part of his education in a *Gymnasium* in Pietist Gütersloh in Westphalia and was graduated from the University of Rochester and Rochester Theological Seminary. For several years, as a Baptist pastor, he served the German immigrants in New York City and acquired an intimacy with the common people. He read Tolstoy, Bellamy, Ruskin, and Marx. In 1891–1892 he studied history and theology in Berlin. While abroad he became acquainted with industrial conditions and through the Webbs was introduced to Fabian Socialism. While in New York City he joined with two other young Baptist

---

[103] *Ibid.,* pp. 184–200; Robert T. Handy in *Church History,* Vol. XIX, pp. 97–115; Dombrowski, *op. cit.,* pp. 132–193.

[104] Hopkins, *op. cit.,* pp. 113, 114, 259–262; Josiah Strong, *Our Country: Its Possible Future and Its Present Crisis* (New York, The Baker & Taylor Co., 1885, pp. x, 229), *passim; Dictionary of American Biography,* Vol. XVIII, pp. 150, 151; Strong, *The Challenge of the City, passim.*

[105] R. Sharpe, *Walter Rauschenbusch* (New York, The Macmillan Co., 1942, pp. xiii, 463), *passim;* Reinhart Müller, *Walter Rauschenbusch. Ein Beitrag zur Begegnung des deutschen und des amerikanischen Protestantismus* (Leiden, E. J. Brill, 1957, pp. x, 129), *passim.*

[106] Volume II, Chapter V.

[107] *Leben und Wirken von August Rauschenbusch,* an autobiography completed and edited by Walter Rauschenbusch (Cleveland, Peter Ritter, 1901, pp. xii, 274), *passim;* Carl E. Schneider in *Church History,* Vol. XXIV, pp. 3–14.

clergymen in forming the Brotherhood of the Kingdom. It expanded its roll to about a dozen and beginning in 1893 met annually to discuss issues connected with the Kingdom of God. Its members sought to exemplify the ethics of Jesus in their individual lives and to stress the social aims of Christianity. In 1897 Rauschenbusch went on the faculty of Rochester Theological Seminary in the chair of New Testament. Five years later he was transferred to the professorship of church history and held it until his death. His books became standard formulations of the social gospel. The ones which attracted most attention were *Christianity and the Social Crisis*,[108] *Christianizing the Social Order*,[109] and *A Theology for the Social Gospel*.[110]

Rauschenbusch was too good a historian to believe in the Utopian dream of the perfection of man in this life, but he held that in the present world progress was possible towards that ideal and that the moral forces inherent in Christian society could be mobilized for the regeneration of social life. In accordance with his Evangelical-Pietist heritage, he maintained that the fundamental contribution of the individual was the change in his own personality.[111] He was convinced that the Kingdom was the supreme end in the purpose of God, that it is always both present and future, that its origin, progress, and consummation were initiated by Christ, that it embraces the whole of human life and includes the transformation of the social order, that the Church must create the Kingdom, that for this the Church exists, and that God will in His own time bring the Kingdom to its completion.[112] Although suffering from deafness acquired while ministering to the poor during his New York pastorate, Rauschenbusch was active in the affairs of his denomination, and in personal intercourse his humour and graciousness disarmed many of his critics.

In the optimistic decades immediately preceding 1914, several denominations which served the older stock adopted programmes designed to put the social gospel into effect. In 1901 the Protestant Episcopal Church appointed a continuing commission to deal with the relations of capital and labour. That same year the National Council of Congregational Churches took steps towards establishing better relations with organized and unorganized labour and in 1910 appointed Henry A. Atkinson to the secretaryship of its Industrial Committee, a body which in 1913 was re-christened the Commission on Social Service. In 1907 the Methodist Episcopal Church (North) organized the Methodist Federation for Social Service. The following year the General Conference of that church adopted the Social Creed of Methodism. The document outlined standards for the employment of labour and stood for conciliation and arbitration in industrial dissensions and for "the recognition of the Golden Rule and

[108] New York, The Macmillan Co., 1907, pp. xv, 429.
[109] New York, The Macmillan Co., 1912, pp. xii, 493.
[110] New York, The Macmillan Co., 1917, pp. 279.
[111] *Christianity and the Social Crisis*, pp. 411, 412.
[112] *A Theology for the Social Gospel*, pp. 143–145.

the mind of Christ as the supreme law of society and the sure remedy for all social ills." At its initial meeting (1908) the Northern Baptist Convention urged its ministry and churches "to emphasize the social significance of the Gospel and to lend their aid to the united efforts of Christian men to arouse the civic conscience and to compel social righteousness in politics, commerce, and finance." By 1912 it was reported that twelve other denominations had pledged themselves to social service programmes. They were almost all those whose constituencies were of the older American stock and were mainly in the North, where industrialization was most pronounced. The Men and Religion Forward Movement, a lay evangelistic enterprise, in practice put its chief emphasis on social service and through its country-wide interdenominational meetings reached several hundred thousand with its messages. The desire for united social action was one of the major forces which brought into being (1908) the Federal Council of the Churches of Christ in America.[113]

Even a bare list of the men and women who championed the social gospel in its mounting tide on the eve of World War I would unduly prolong these pages. In addition to those we have mentioned a few can be picked out almost at random. Frank Mason North (1850-1935), a Methodist, was one of the founders of the Open and Institutional Church League (1894), a forerunner of the Federal Council of Churches, and was the chief author of the Social Creed adopted by the Methodists and in modified form by the Federal Council of Churches. His hymn "Where cross the crowded ways of life" was long sung as an expression of social concern.[114] The Unitarian Francis Greenwood Peabody (1847-1936), a member of the Harvard faculty, wrote a number of books which did much to spread and give content to the social gospel.[115] We have already met Shailer Mathews (1863-1941), a Baptist and dean of the Divinity School of the University of Chicago. Most of his numerous books dealt with social issues and Christianity.[116] Although not able to go as far as some of the advocates of the social gospel, Lyman Abbott through his editorial pen reached a wide clientele with his sturdy advocacy of social justice and his dissent from *laissez faire* and its outstanding defender, William Graham Sumner.[117] Henry Frederick Ward (1873——) was the chief inspirer and first editorial secretary of the Methodist Federation for Social Service and was later to be a prolific writer in that area.[118] Another Methodist, eventually (1912) a prominent bishop in his church, who

[113] Hopkins, *op. cit.*, pp. 284–317.

[114] *Dictionary of American Biography*, Vol. XXI, pp. 577, 578.

[115] As one example see Francis Greenwood Peabody, *The Christian Life in the Modern World* (New York, The Macmillan Co., 1914, pp. 234).

[116] Mathews, *New Faith for Old, passim.*

[117] Brown, *Lyman Abbott*, pp. 99–112.

[118] One of his early books was Harry F. Ward, *Social Ministry. An Introduction to the Study and Practice of Social Service* (New York, Eaton & Maine, 1910, pp. viii, 318).

was active in promoting the social gospel was Francis John McConnell (1871–1953).[119]

THE INSTITUTIONAL CHURCH

One expression of the social gospel was the institutional church. Serving the underprivileged in the great urban centres, it was an attempt to touch helpfully every aspect of the lives of its neighbourhood.[120] A few instances must stand as examples of what a full coverage would reveal. William S. Rainsford (1850–1933), born in Ireland, reared an Evangelical, from 1882 to 1906 was rector of St. George's, an Episcopal church in New York City which had once been in a fashionable community and, backed by the wealthy banker J. P. Morgan, remained as the neighbourhood changed to lower-income families. For a time under Rainsford's leadership it was said to be the largest and most active parish of the Protestant Episcopal Church. All pews were free. A modified form of Morning Prayer was worked out. Rainsford made the parish house a centre of social activities. Theologically he was a liberal and believed that he must be frank as well as constructive in his preaching.[121] Charles Stelzle (1869–1941) from a boyhood in New York's East Side knew poverty at first hand. After eight years as a machinist, he entered the ministry to bring the Gospel to the workingman. From pastorates in several working-class churches, in 1903 he became secretary of the Department of Church and Labour of the Board of Home Missions of the Presbyterian Church in the U.S.A. As such he sought to improve the relations between the churches and the labouring classes, spoke and wrote extensively, and through press releases in more than three hundred labour papers preached an ethical religion. When, in 1913, conservative opposition forced him out of his post, he gave himself to the Labour Temple which he had founded in 1910 on New York's East Side and made it into an institutional church with a variety of activities ministering to the whole life of the people with especial emphasis on their spiritual welfare.[122] Russell H. Conwell (1843–1925) was the creator of Grace Baptist Church, better known as the Temple, an institutional church in Philadelphia. Born in poverty on a New England farm in a deeply religious family, in college at Yale he was cynical and was known as an atheist. While serving in the Northern armies during the Civil War he was converted. For a time after the war he was a lawyer. Then he entered the

---

[119] Francis John McConnell, *By the Way. An Autobiography* (New York, Abingdon-Cokesbury Press, 1952, pp. 286), pp. 208 ff.

[120] Abell, *The Urban Impact on American Protestantism 1865–1900*, pp. 137–165. See a partial list in Strong, *The Challenge of the City*, pp. 281 ff.

[121] W. S. Rainsford, *The Story of a Varied Life. An Autobiography* (Garden City, N.Y., Doubleday, Page and Co., 1922, pp. 481), *passim; Dictionary of American Biography*, Vol. XXI, pp. 618, 619.

[122] Charles Stelzle, *A Son of the Bowery. The Life Story of an East Side American* (New York, George H. Doran Co., 1926, pp. 335), *passim;* Hopkins, *op. cit.*, pp. 280–283.

ministry. Coming to the Grace Baptist Church while it was still young, he saw it grow to large dimensions and become a beehive of social and religious activity. In connexion with it he founded Temple University for working men and women, many of whom had only their evenings for study. He also began and developed the Samaritan Hospital for the indigent sick. Much of the requisite money for it and the university he raised by lecturing, especially with the topic, "Acres of Diamonds."[123]

SOCIAL SETTLEMENTS

In addition to the institutional or "socialized" church, a number of social settlements came into being. They resembled the ones which we have found in England. Not all were of distinctively Christian origin, but most of them could be traced, at least indirectly, to a Christian motive.[124]

OPPOSITION TO THE SOCIAL GOSPEL

The social gospel aroused much criticism in conservative Protestant circles because most of its exponents were "liberals," accepting the historical criticism of the Bible and the theory of evolution, departing from features of the theology associated with Evangelicalism and revivalism, and believing in the indefinite progress of mankind rather than the growth of evil and the early second coming of Christ. To the Fundamentalists especially the social gospel seemed contrary to the Scriptures and hence was anathema.

Among many who shared in the opposition was a Baptist clergyman of Boston, named for the pioneer foreign missionary of his denomination, Adoniram Judson Gordon (1836–1895). Of New England strict Calvinistic rearing, a graduate of Brown and of Newton Theological Institution, he early rejected Frederick W. Robertson, current proposals for Christian unity, and the higher criticism. Positively he held to the pre-millennial second coming of Christ, was an ardent advocate of missions and prohibition, was the mainstay of the Industrial Temporary Home for immediate relief of those out of work, believed profoundly in answers to prayer, supported the New England Evangelization Society for preaching in the open air, while opposing Christian Science was committed to healing by faith and prayers for the sick, and established the Boston Missionary Training School akin to the ones in Germany which were created by Harms and Gossner.[125]

---

[123] Agnes Rush Burr, *Russell H. Conwell and His Work. One Man's Interpretation of Life* (Chicago, The United Publishers of America, 1926, pp. 438), *passim*.

[124] Strong, *The Challenge of the City*, pp. 288–308, contains a list with brief descriptions.

[125] Ernest B. Gordon, *Adoniram Judson Gordon, A Biography* (Chicago, Fleming H. Revell Co., 1896, pp. 386), *passim*.

MOUNTING INFLUENCE THROUGH PERIODICALS

Through its journalism the Protestantism of the older American stock exerted a marked and growing influence on the nation. Denominational periodicals, both Protestant and Roman Catholic, which were designed for circulation among the faithful, were legion. Their total circulation was enormous and they affected the opinions of their respective constituencies. However, some periodicals were intended to reach beyond the bounds of a particular church. Of them, two, *The Independent* and *The Outlook,* were especially widely read and were long lived. Their impact mounted in the third and especially the fourth quarter of the century.

The Independent was begun in 1848 with Leonard Bacon, pastor of First Church (Centre, Congregational) of New Haven, Connecticut, as senior editor. While initiated by Congregationalists and, as its name indicated, committed to the Congregational principle of independence, it was not the organ of any ecclesiastical body nor was it the mouthpiece of a political party. It dealt with political as well as religious issues. In pre-Civil War days it was opposed to the extension of slavery. It soon became the leading religious paper of the country and aroused much criticism.[126]

The Outlook, like *The Independent,* was begun by Congregationalists. For years Henry Ward Beecher wrote for *The Independent* and was its editor. After the Civil War he differed from its policy of support of the radical Republicans on reconstruction and in 1870 became the editor-in-chief of *The Christian Union,* a journal which sought to promote unity of feeling and coöperation of effort of all churches. Lyman Abbott contributed to both *The Independent* and *The Christian Union.* In 1876 he became joint editor with Beecher of the latter journal, assumed the major responsibility, and gradually transformed it to a weekly summary and interpretation of contemporary events. In 1881 Beecher retired from the editorship. In 1893 the name was changed to *The Outlook,* that, while still Christian in purpose and spirit, it might not be regarded as narrowly sectarian. Abbott was long its editor-in-chief. Theologically *The Outlook* was liberal. Eventually it had subscribers in every state in the Union and in every civilized country.[127] In the 1930's *The Independent* and *The Outlook* were combined but soon suspended publication.

THE GROWING ESPOUSAL OF CHRISTIANITY BY POLITICAL LEADERS

The rising proportion of church members in the population was paralleled by the growing commitment of the presidents to the Christian faith. All the presidents were from the older American stock and so far as they had a church connexion it was with the Protestantism of that constituency. Several in the

[126] Bacon, *Leonard Bacon,* pp. 304–313.
[127] Abbott, *Reminiscences,* pp. 326–350; Brown, *op. cit.,* pp. 66 ff.

first three-quarters of the century were not church members. Even Lincoln although after 1850 a regular attendant at a Presbyterian church, first in Spring field, Illinois, and then in Washington, never subscribed to a creed or was a member of a church. Yet under the burdens of his high office and the Civi War, his faith deepened and he became profoundly religious, believed in Goc as intimately concerned with the affairs of nations as well as individuals, and in the Bible as God's best gift to men. His second inaugural address was ample evidence of his earnest faith.[128]

Of the seven presidents of the three decades immediately preceding 1914 three, Arthur, Cleveland, and Wilson, were sons of clergymen, and Wilson espe cially was a man of staunch Christian faith which directed and sustained him Garfield had been converted in his teens in a "protracted meeting" and became a preacher of the Disciples of Christ. While in his later years he belonged to the progressive wing of his denomination and accepted much of the scientifi thought of his day, his faith determined his convictions on public issues and his optimistic confidence in democracy.[129] Reared in a deeply religious home Benjamin Harrison had thought seriously of entering the ministry, was fo forty years an elder in a Presbyterian church, was a teacher and superintenden in a Sunday School, and was prominent in the national councils of his denom ination.[130] McKinley was from youth a member of the Methodist Episcopa Church, regarded Christianity as the mightiest factor in civilization, and sough to guide his conduct by Christian principles.[131] Theodore Roosevelt was a life long member of the Dutch Reformed Church and believed in a virile Chris tianity. Taft's high sense of duty and his Unitarian affiliation seem to have been interrelated. To what extent their Christian faith determined the public policie of these presidents would be difficult to determine, but it may have contribute to the improvement in the moral tone of government after the nadir which followed the Civil War. That improvement was slow in coming, and unde some presidents of strong Christian faith corruption was still rampant.

The Contribution of the Protestantism of the Nineteenth-Century Immigration

The denominations which enrolled the majority of the nineteenth-centur immigration who had Protestant church affiliations made few contributions to the movements with which this chapter has been concerned. They were ab sorbed in establishing themselves, in winning the allegiance of their hereditar

[128] J. G. Randall, *Mr. Lincoln,* edited by Richard N. Current (New York, Dodd, Mead and Co 1957, pp. xiii, 392), pp. 385–389.

[129] W. W. Wasson, *James A. Garfield: His Religion and Education* (Nashville, Tennessee Boo Co., 1952, pp. xi, 155), *passim.*

[130] *Dictionary of American Biography,* Vol. VIII, pp. 332, 335; Harry J. Sivers, *Benjamin Har rison, Hoosier Warrior 1833–1865* (Chicago, Henry Regnery Co., 1952, pp. xxi, 344), pp. 58–62.

[131] *Dictionary of American Biography,* Vol. XII, p. 109.

constituencies, and in their internal theological and ecclesiastical issues. Here and there one of their members rose to prominence in his state or the nation. A child of that immigration, Walter Rauschenbusch, as we have seen, exerted a wide influence, but it was as a member of a denomination recruited mainly from the older American stock. The effects of the denominations of the new immigration were considerable but were chiefly in the moral and religious character of the individuals and families within their respective folds and not upon the nation as a whole. The latter impact was to come after 1914 and then was not to be as great as that of the denominations of the older stock.

The Contribution of the Roman Catholic Church

Since it also was made up mainly of the nineteenth-century immigration and had its energies largely engrossed in caring for those who by background were its children, the Roman Catholic Church exerted much less influence on the country as a whole than did the Protestant churches of the older American stock.

Yet by 1914 the Roman Catholic Church had a mounting effect on American life. Through its religious teachings and services and its extensive system of parochial schools it helped to shape the character of millions. Its many hospitals served not only its own members but also the communities in which they were located. We have noted the prominence of Roman Catholics in the movement for temperance.

The Roman Catholic Church was inescapably involved in the Civil War. Like the Protestant Episcopal Church, the Roman Catholic Church preserved its formal unity. However, within its episcopate profound differences existed. Bishop Lynch of Charleston openly defended secession and Archbishop John Hughes of New York as openly deplored it.[132] At the request of William H. Seward, Secretary of State, Hughes went to Europe to urge France to remain neutral and argued the Union case not only there but in other countries as well.[133] Abram J. Ryan (1838–1886), a priest, put the cause of Confederacy into verse and served as chaplain among the Southern troops.[134] Another priest, Edward Purcell (1808–1881), brother of John B. Purcell (1800–1883), the first Bishop of Cincinnati, came out in his paper, the *Catholic Telegraph,* for emancipation, first in August, 1862, and again after Lincoln's emancipation proclamation.[135] Nearly five hundred members of women's congregations nursed the sick and wounded in the military hospitals of the North and the South.[136] Sixty-seven priests were in the chaplaincy of either the Northern or the Southern armies.[137]

[132] Ellis, *Documents of American Catholic History,* pp. 356–365.
[133] *Ibid.,* pp. 379–382.
[134] *Ibid.,* p. 394.
[135] *Ibid.,* pp. 387–392.
[136] *Ibid.,* pp. 376–379.
[137] *Ibid.,* p. 385.

Since the Roman Catholic Church was largely urban and its members were
prevailingly workers in the factories and mines, it was deeply concerned in the
labour troubles which mounted in the latter part of the century as concomi
tants of the rapid industrialization of the country. Under the leadership of great
prelates such as Archbishops Gibbons and Ireland, Bishop John Lancaster Spald
ing of Peoria, and Keane, Bishop of Richmond, in spite of the opposition of
conservatives such as Archbishop Corrigan and Bishop McQuaid, the Roman
Catholic Church in the United States took a friendly attitude towards the
Knights of Labour, the first major American labour organization. The Knight
of Labour were founded in 1869 by a Freemason. The Archbishop of Quebec
regarded them as in the category of secret societies, membership in which had
been forbidden by Rome, and in 1884 obtained a decree supporting his position
At the outset the Knights of Labour had a ritual framed in part by a forme
student for the Baptist ministry and with some of the features which justified
the Archbishop of Quebec in placing it out of bounds for the faithful. The
archbishops of the United States, meeting in 1886, decided that the decree of
1884 was concerned with conditions in Canada and did not apply to their coun
try. At that time the Grand Master Workman of the Knights was Terence V
Powderly, a devout Roman Catholic, the organization had divested itself of an
oath of initiation, and it had no obligation to secrecy, no promise of blind
obedience, and no hostility to religion. To condemn it would alienate a large
element from the Roman Catholic Church. The Knights of Labour offered
to make any changes in their constitution which the ecclesiastical authorities
might require. Thanks to representations by Ireland and Keane in 1887 and by
Gibbons in 1888, supported by Manning of Westminster, Rome gave permission
to tolerate the Knights of Labour, provided changes were made in the consti
tution, especially to render it clear that Communism and socialism were not
approved. Powderly agreed but was not able to carry through the required
action. After 1893 the Knights of Labour declined. Powderly joined the Masons
and cooled towards the Roman Catholic Church. From the attitude of Gib
bons, Ireland, and Keane it was obvious that their church was not opposed to
organized labour. The friendliness of the Roman Catholic Church to labour
became crystal clear in the Papal encyclical *Rerum novarum* (1891).[138] In some
later labour unions, including the American Federation of Labour, numbers of
Roman Catholics had an active part and were not condemned for it by the
ecclesiastical authorities.

In general, in the 1880's and 1890's Roman Catholic spokesmen favoured com

[138] Ellis, *The Life of James Cardinal Gibbons*, Vol. I, pp. 486–546; Moynihan, *The Life of
Archbishop John Ireland*, pp. 211–214; Ellis, *Documents of American Catholic History*, pp. 460
472; Henry J. Browne, *The Catholic Church and the Knights of Labor* (Washington, The Catholic
University of America Press, 1949, pp. xix, 415), *passim;* Cross, *The Emergence of Liberal Ca
tholicism in America*, pp. 114 ff.

pulsory arbitration as the method for settling disputes between employers and employed. Their sympathies were with the workingmen, especially since many labour leaders were Roman Catholics.[139]

Henry George's single-tax movement brought embarrassment to the Roman Catholic Church and for a time seemed to threaten the favourable impression among workingmen created by the attitude towards the Knights of Labour. Edward McGlynn, through a pastorate in New York City, had been brought into intimate contact with the problems of unemployment and poverty. He was an outspoken advocate of George's programme and supported George in the latter's campaign for the office of mayor of that city. His ecclesiastical superior, Archbishop Corrigan, suspended him from his priestly functions (1886) and came out flatly for private property. In open defiance, McGlynn continued to speak for the single tax and did not obey a summons to Rome. After refusing to go within the specified time, McGlynn was excommunicated by Rome for disobedience. Later, through the action of the Papal legate, Satolli, McGlynn's teachings were adjudged by theologians to contain nothing contrary to faith and morals, the excommunication was removed, McGlynn was restored to his priestly functions (1892), and after some months Corrigan appointed him to a parish. The issue had caused dissension within the American clergy. Some of them, including at least one bishop, sympathized with McGlynn. Corrigan and McQuaid wished *Progress and Poverty* placed on the index of forbidden books. Gibbons objected on the ground that to place it there would give the book more publicity than it deserved, would further its sale, and would harm the reputation of the Roman Catholic Church. Rome compromised. The Congregation of the Inquisition decided (1889) that the teachings of George deserved condemnation but said that its judgement need not be made public. The whole affair had dragged out for years, had been aired in the press, and had added to the strain within the American hierarchy, with Corrigan and McQuaid leaders of one faction and Gibbons regarded as the spokesman for the other.[140]

Roman Catholics were concerning themselves with the problems of juvenile delinquency brought by the great cities. A pioneer was John Christopher Drumgoole (1816–1888). A native of Ireland, he was brought to the United States as a child, was reared in New York City, and became acquainted with the seamy side of the metropolis. Although deeply religious from boyhood, he was late in obtaining education for the priesthood. Ordained in 1869, in his midfifties, in 1871 he was given charge of a lodging house for waifs and newsboys in New York City. He soon made it a notable institution. By the time of his death it had cared for 1,600 or 2,000 children. In 1881 he built for that purpose

---

[139] Aaron I. Abell in *The Catholic Historical Review*, Vol. XLI, pp. 385–407.
[140] Ellis, *The Life of James Cardinal Gibbons*, Vol. I, pp. 547–594; Moynihan, *op. cit.*, pp. 231–233; Ellis, *Documents of American Catholic History*, pp. 473–475; Stephen Bell, *Rebel Priest and Prophet. A Biography of Dr. Edward McGlynn* (New York, The Devin-Adair Co., 1937, pp. xi, 303), *passim; Dictionary of American Biography*, Vol. VII, pp. 53, 54; Cross, *op. cit.*, pp. 119–124.

the Mission of the Immaculate Virgin. He believed that no youngster was in corrigible if he had placed before him the model of industry, hard work, and virtue.[141]

Although Pius IX had denounced the separation of Church and state, again and again the hierarchy in the United States expressed their approval of it as it existed in that country. In 1887, for example, in his sermon while taking possession of his titular church in Rome, Cardinal Gibbons called attention to Leo XIII's declaration that the Roman Catholic Church was not committed to any particular form of government and rejoiced that in his country the civil authorities protected that church without interfering in its internal affairs.[142]

Here and there before 1914 Roman Catholics were holding high office in the civil government of the United States. Thus two chief justices of the Supreme Court, Roger Brooke Taney (1777–1864), from an old Maryland family, and Edward Douglas White (1845–1921), educated in Roman Catholic schools and a veteran of the Confederate army, were of that faith.[143]

Summary

The American dream of creating in the New World a nation under the eye of God which would be free from the evils of the Old World was born mainly of the radical Protestantism which had sought refuge in the land of opportunity. The dream was fostered by the spiritual and often the physical descendants of these pioneers. From the Protestantism of that older stock were sprung most of the movements which sought to bring the dream to realization. In the fore part of the nineteenth century a great variety of such movements came into being. Some were out of Unitarianism. Numbers were closely connected with revivalism—the anti-slavery agitation, efforts to promote world peace, and the campaigns to promote temperance and to prohibit the manufacture and sale of alcoholic beverages. Many of the movements were of New England rootage, from Congregationalism, Unitarian or Trinitarian. Some were from the Friends. A number of the reformers were women committed to placing members of their sex on an equality with men in salaries, legal status, and the franchise. Most of the outstanding philanthropists among the men owed their motives to their Protestant heritage and faith.

In the latter part of the century, as industrialism mounted and cities multiplied in numbers and population, and in the atmosphere of optimistic belief in progress associated with the theory of evolution, what was known as the social gospel became potent. It was a logical development from the American

---

[141] Katherine Burton, *Children's Shepherd. The Story of John Christopher Drumgoole, Father of the Homeless* (New York, P. J. Kenedy & Sons, 1954, pp. viii, 236), *passim; Dictionary of American Biography*, Vol. V, pp. 462, 463.

[142] Ellis, *Documents of American Catholic History*, pp. 476–479.

[143] *Ibid.*, pp. 330, 581.

dream. It was associated with the liberalism which sought to adjust theology and the study of the Bible to the currents of thought of the revolutionary age. All who were committed to the social gospel were intent on better relations between capital and labour and on eliminating the evils that accompanied the Industrial Revolution and its attendant urbanization of the country. While many realized that the New Testament taught that the Kingdom of God is the gift of God and not man's creation, for the most part the proponents of the social gospel believed that Christians should do what they could to assist in the coming of the Kingdom. Some were Utopian, dreaming of a perfect society. The more thoughtful recognized that perfection as Christ envisioned it was not to be fully attained in this life, but were convinced that progress towards it could be made.

In these movements towards making the American dream actual, neither the Protestant churches of the nineteenth-century immigration nor the Roman Catholic Church had a large part. Both were too absorbed in caring for the vast tide from the Old World which was their hereditary constituency to address themselves to the challenge presented by the phases of the revolution with which the Protestantism of the older stock was concerned. Yet they were nourishing Christian character which could assist in meeting the challenge. Moreover, Roman Catholics dealt with some aspects of the challenge, notably alcoholism, the problem of a secularized education, and the issues presented by labour in the burgeoning industries. The latter especially involved them since a large proportion of the Roman Catholics were urban workmen and miners.

CHAPTER IX

The Christianity of the United States of America and the World-Wide Spread of the Faith

A STRIKING feature of the record of Christianity in the United States of America was a growing share in the world-wide spread of the faith. As we have hinted and as we are to see more in detail, the geographic expansion of Christianity was one of the most notable aspects of the revolutionary age. It mounted in the nineteenth century and was accelerated in the following century. In it the Christians of the United States had an increasing part, in spite of the fact that much of the energy of the churches was absorbed in winning the elements of the population which were threatened with de-Christianization, in caring for the immigrant tide, in reaching out to the Indians and the Negroes, and in meeting the multiform social, economic, and intellectual challenges brought by the revolutionary currents of the day. As was to be expected, most of the geographic outreach was by the Protestantism of the older stock. The churches which were composed of the nineteenth-century immigration, whether Protestant or Roman Catholic, were too much engrossed in the tasks immediately at hand to give much attention to what lay beyond the borders of the country. By 1914, however, they were beginning to participate in the global extension of the faith. Their participation was to increase in the decades which followed that year.

THE GROWING SHARE OF THE PROTESTANTISM OF THE OLDER STOCK

We have already recounted the beginnings of the foreign missions of the Protestantism of the older stock.[1] We have noted the inception of the American Board of Commissioners for Foreign Missions in 1810, at the outset interdenominational but mainly Congregational, and, in 1814, of the General Missionary Convention of the Baptist Denomination in the United States of America for Foreign Missions. We saw, too, the organization in 1816 of the American Bible Society, with a programme which included both the United States and other countries.

[1] Volume I, pp. 196, 197, 199.

Even to list all the societies which had missions beyond the borders of the United States as their objective would prolong these pages unduly. Some combined foreign and home missions. Several regarded missions to the Indians as part of the "foreign" assignment. In the course of time nearly every denomination had its missionary society or societies. Increasingly "missions," foreign and domestic, were considered to be the responsibility of the entire denomination. The societies were, therefore, official organs of the denominations. Here the United States was in contrast with the Continent of Europe, where the societies were independent of the ecclesiastical structure and each was dependent on a constituency which it cultivated. It was also in partial contrast with the British Isles, where some societies were agencies of the churches and others were not controlled by them. In addition to nationally organized denominational societies, scores of local or regional auxiliary societies came into being. A number of them were undenominational and were for special objects.[2]

THE RISING PARTICIPATION OF THE PROTESTANTISM OF THE NINETEENTH-CENTURY IMMIGRATION

In the latter part of the century the Protestant denominations which arose from the nineteenth-century immigration began to share in the extension of the faith in other lands. Some did it through existing agencies on the Continent of Europe. But as early as 1837 the Foreign Missionary Society of the Evangelical German Churches in the United States was organized with the hope that it would unite the efforts of all German Protestants, Lutherans and Reformed. The Reformed and Moravians would not coöperate, and "Lutheran" was substituted for "Evangelical" in the Society's name. The Society was closely associated with the General Synod. In 1841 a man was sent to India by the Ministerium of Pennsylvania, the first to be appointed for work abroad by American Lutherans. By 1869 the mission to India had grown and was amicably divided between the General Synod and the General Council. A Lutheran had begun a mission in Liberia in 1860 and in 1869 the General Synod assumed responsibility for it. The Evangelical Synod organized a foreign mission board in 1869. In the 1890's and the first decade after 1900 several Lutheran churches gave birth to foreign mission boards. By 1914 they had missions not only in India and Africa but also in China, Japan, Australia, and Latin America.[3]

MOUNTING COÖPERATION IN THE WORLD MISSION OF PROTESTANTISM

Late in the century the commitment to the world mission mounted rapidly among the Protestants of the United States, both in the denominations of the

---

[2] See a list in Beach and Fahs, *World Missionary Atlas*, pp. 18–31.
[3] Wentz, *A Basic History of Lutheranism in America*, pp. 110, 111, 191, 192; Beach and Fahs, *op. cit.*, pp. 21, 22. On the Missouri Synod, see Baepler, *A Century of Grace*, pp. 179, 180, 230–237.

older stock and in those of the newer immigration. It still actively enlisted only minorities, but the minorities were becoming larger and coöperation across denominational lines was increasing.

A major impetus was given by the Student Volunteer Movement for Foreign Missions. In the summer of 1886, as we have seen, a conference was convened by the Student Department of the Young Men's Christian Association and held under Dwight L. Moody's direction on the grounds of his school at Mt. Hermon, Massachusetts. Around a nucleus centring in Robert Parmelee Wilder (1863-1938), son of a Presbyterian missionary to India and then a student in Princeton, by the end of the conference an even hundred had gathered who declared that they "were willing and desirous, God permitting, to become foreign missionaries." Among the hundred was John R. Mott, then a student in Cornell. Out of that dedication came the Student Volunteer Movement for Foreign Missions. The next winter Wilder and one other travelled through the colleges, universities, and theological seminaries spreading the word that "all should go and go to all." Soon an executive committee was formed with Mott as chairman. A "watchword" was adopted—"The evangelization of the world in this generation." By it was meant, not the conversion of mankind in that brief time, but the giving of an opportunity to all men to hear the Christian message. The "declaration of purpose" was altered to read: "It is my purpose, if God permit, to become a foreign missionary." "Travelling secretaries," largely young missionaries and students planning to be missionaries, were sent each year through the institutions of higher learning to recruit "volunteers." Quadrennial conventions were held to bring the missionary appeal to each student generation. Mission study classes were organized and literature was prepared for them. As a result, thousands of students from most of the Protestant denominations were enlisted. Wilder and others carried the enthusiasm to Europe, and similar movements sprang up in the British Isles and on the Continent.[4]

The Student Volunteer Movement inspired the formation (1906) of the Laymen's Missionary Movement, which sought to provide the finances required to send the young men and women who were offering their lives. It gave rise to similar movements in a number of countries in Europe, Africa, and Australasia.[5]

Mott became an evangelist to students the world over. He was also the chief presiding officer of the World Missionary Conference held in Edinburgh in 1910, a gathering which was a landmark in the Ecumenical Movement and a precursor of the World Council of Churches. He was chairman of the Con-

---

[4] Robert P. Wilder, *The Great Commission. The Missionary Response of the Student Volunteer Movements in North America and Europe: Some Personal Reminiscences* (London, Oliphants, preface 1936, pp. 115), *passim;* Ruth Wilder Braisted, *In This Generation. The Story of Robert P. Wilder* (New York, The Friendship Press, 1941, pp. xvi, 205), *passim;* Mathews, *John R. Mott, World Citizen,* pp. 83, 84, 213-222.

[5] William T. Ellis, *Men and Missions* (Philadelphia, The Sunday School Times Co., 1909, pp. 313), pp. 71-80.

tinuation Committee of the Edinburgh Conference and as such was the chief organizer of the International Missionary Council, formed in 1921, and was its first chairman.[6]

The Foreign Missions Conference of North America, bringing together representatives of foreign missionary societies for the sharing of thoughts and later for coöperative action, dated from a meeting in New York in 1893. It met annually and in 1897 created a Committee of General Reference, which eventually, as the Committee of Reference and Counsel, became an increasingly important agency of joint effort.[7]

The Share of American Roman Catholics in the World Mission

The Roman Catholics of the United States were slow to assist in planting their church in other countries. This was to be expected. Until the flow of immigration was reduced to a trickle by World War I and subsequent legislation, the Roman Catholic Church, as its bishops said in their pastoral letter of 1884, had had to strain every nerve to carry on missions in the United States.[8] The United States itself was a mission field, until the eve of 1914 being under the Propaganda, and the Roman Catholic Church in that country received substantial assistance in personnel and funds from the faithful on the other side of the Atlantic.

However, the bishops were not deaf to the claims of other countries. In the pastoral letter in which they gave the reason for no larger participation in foreign missions, they urged that in every diocese an annual collection for the Society for the Propagation of the Faith be taken and that measures be initiated in each parish to give that society support.[9] The Archdiocese of Boston was particularly active. Thanks to successive archbishops and to diocesan directors of the Propagation of the Faith, for many years the see contributed more to that society than did any other diocese in North or South America and in 1904 gave more than any diocese in the world.[10] This was in spite of the fact that O'Connell, who was archbishop in the years that spanned 1914, was decidedly dissatisfied with the control of the Society for the Propagation of the Faith by a small group of French laymen.[11] At the request of the provincial council of 1833 the Roman Catholics of the United States concerned themselves with Liberia, but that enterprise was soon taken over by European missionaries.

From time to time Americans went as foreign missionaries in connexion with religious orders and congregations of which they were members, but the first

---

[6] Mathews, *op. cit.*, pp. 120–263.

[7] Hogg, *Ecumenical Foundations*, pp. 75, 76.

[8] Guilday, *The National Pastorals of the American Hierarchy (1792–1919)*, p. 263.

[9] *Ibid.*

[10] Lord, Sexton, and Harrington, *History of the Archdiocese of Boston*, Vol. III, pp. 337, 338.

[11] Theodore Roemer, *The Catholic Church in the United States* (St. Louis, B. Herder Book Co., 1950, pp. viii, 444), pp. 344, 345.

distinctively American Roman Catholic organization primarily for missions abroad was the Catholic Foreign Mission Society of America. It was begun in 1911 by two priests, James A. Walsh and Thomas F. Price. Its headquarters were at Maryknoll, overlooking the Hudson River, and for that reason its members were often called Maryknollers. Its initial field of operation was China, but in later years, as it grew, it sent its representatives to a number of other countries.[12]

BY WAY OF ANTICIPATION

In a later volume we shall see how in the next century the part of Americans in the world mission of Christianity greatly increased—through Protestantism, both of the older stock and of the nineteenth-century immigration, and also through Roman Catholics.

The mounting participation of Christians of the United States in the geographic expansion of Christianity more and more placed a distinctive stamp on the Christian communities which arose as a result of their labours, whether in Asia, Africa, or Latin America. As we trace the emergence of these communities we will note their debt to American Christianity and the emphases which they owed to it. None of the communities was an exact reproduction of an American pattern. They reflected their environment and conformed more or less closely to the traditions of their respective churches. But, whether Protestant or Roman Catholic, they bore something of the imprint of the American efforts.

---

[12] *Ibid.*, p. 347; George C. Powers, *The Maryknoll Movement* (Maryknoll, N.Y., The Catholic Foreign Mission Society of America, 1926, pp. xix, 167), *passim*.

CHAPTER X

British North America

NORTH of the United States lies a great expanse which by 1914 was comprised in two political units, Canada and Newfoundland. Combined with the latter was Labrador. Together they were British North America. Canada alone was slightly larger than the continental United States. However, since much of it was in the arctic and sub-arctic zones, it was more sparsely peopled than the United States. In 1911, although the total was mounting rapidly, the population was only 7,206,643. This was about 8 per cent. of that of the United States the preceding year and was less than that of the adjacent New York State. Newfoundland and Labrador were very thinly settled.

Canada was a relatively young nation, a member of the British Commonwealth. Its growth came in part through the forces of the revolutionary age—through immigration, the beginnings of industrialization and of the utilization of the vast natural resources of forests, minerals, and virgin soil by the machines of the day, and the development of railways and other means of transportation and communication. It will be remembered that the original settlements by Europeans, after the ephemeral Norse contacts, were by the French and that the English conquered the country in the eighteenth century—Acadia (Nova Scotia) in 1713, and the remainder during the Seven Years' War, with the confirmation of the cession by the Peace of Paris in 1763. British colonization followed, both in what were the later Maritime Provinces—Nova Scotia, New Brunswick, and Prince Edward Island—and in what was known as Upper Canada, the later province of Ontario. In the fourth quarter of the eighteenth century much of the colonization was by loyalists from the Thirteen Colonies who adhered to the mother country against their fellows revolting to create the United States. As early as 1839 a report by the Earl of Durham recommended the ultimate union of all British North America. As a first step, Upper and Lower Canada (the later Province of Quebec) were united by an act of Parliament passed in 1840. In 1867 the union was broadened to embrace Nova Scotia and New Brunswick in a federal state. In 1869 Rupert's Land, the territory stretching westward to the Rocky Mountains, was added. In 1871 British Columbia joined Canada. Prince Edward Island was included in 1873. In 1878 the British Government placed under Canada all the rest of North America which owed allegiance to it except Newfoundland and Labrador. The political bond was reinforced by the Canadian Pacific Railway, completed in 1886 and uniting East and West.

Another of the forces of the revolutionary age tended to counter the ties forged by the mechanical devices of the century. In Canada were rival nationalisms, chiefly French and British—the latter subdivided into English, Scottish, and especially Irish elements—with tensions heightened by the necessity of living together in a comprehensive political and economic structure. The rivalries were augmented by differences in the inherited forms of Christianity.

SIMILARITIES TO AND CONTRASTS WITH THE UNITED STATES

Canada had many similarities to the United States. Both nations were predominantly English-speaking and politically and culturally were deeply indebted to Great Britain. The population of both grew by immigration as well as by a high birth rate. Both had a westward-moving frontier. Both were endowed by nature with great natural resources. The growth of each was facilitated by the mechanical devices of the century.

Yet striking contrasts existed between the two countries. Canada had few Negroes and no history of Negro slavery and emancipation, no prolonged devastating civil war, and no record of Indian wars such as punctuated the course of its southern neighbour. But in the French it had a problem without exact parallel in the United States. The French, with a high birth rate and their own traditions and language perpetuating the Canada of pre-British days, were almost a distinct nation. The overwhelming majority in the province of Quebec, they spilled over into other provinces. In 1914 they were about a fourth of the population of Canada. Also unlike the United States, Canada received the bulk of her nineteenth-century immigration from the British Isles. In 1914 more than half the population of the country was of British ancestry. The elements from the Continent of Europe were relatively not as prominent as in the North and West of the United States.

The similarities and contrasts were marked in the religious scene. In both countries Protestants were in the majority, and the denominations which enrolled most of the Protestants were of British provenance. However, in Canada Roman Catholics constituted a larger proportion of the population than in the United States. The threat of de-Christianization seems not to have been as great, at least in the form of alienation from the Church, whether Roman Catholic or Protestant, as in the United States. Thus in 1911 more than 95 per cent. of the population of Canada were said to possess a church connexion[1] and in New-

[1] *The Canada Year Book 1912. Published by Authority of the Hon. George E. Foster, M.P., Minister of Trade and Commerce* (Ottawa, C. H. Parmelee, 1913, pp. xvi, 470), p. 34.

oundland in 1901 nearly 100 per cent. were in that category[2]—as against about 43.5 per cent. in the United States in 1910.[3]

The Roman Catholicism of Canada was distinct from that of the United States. Both were orthodox in creed and loyal to Rome. But in Canada the French elements were dominant. The internal tensions arising from differences of national origins were between the Irish and the French and were not as multiform as in the United States, nor were the Germans as prominent as in the latter country.

Canadian Protestantism was also different from the Protestantism on the southern side of the international boundary. In 1921 the largest Protestant bodies were the Presbyterians and Anglicans, the one Scottish and Irish, the other English in background. In that year they were about equal in size and together constituted about a third of the population of the country. The contrast with the United States was marked: there the Baptists were the largest Protestant denominational family and the Methodists next to them, with the Presbyterians and Episcopalians intellectually and socially prominent but decidedly in the minority. As might have been anticipated because of their strength in nineteenth-century England, the Methodists were more numerous in Canada than the Baptists. However, in 1921 they were outnumbered by both the Presbyterians and the Anglicans. Yet thirty years earlier they had enrolled more than either. Revivalism, the source of the growth of the Baptists and Methodists in the United States, was present but was less prevalent than in the latter country. Because of New England, where its predominance made it the strongest ecclesiastical body in the new republic at the outset of the nineteenth century, Congregationalism was much more prominent in the United States than in Canada. Since the German and Scandinavian immigration was smaller, both numerically and relatively, Lutheranism did not play as large a part in Canada as in its southern neighbour. Nor was Christianity as a whole as varied as in the United States, chiefly because the immigration was not as multiform but also because the Protestantism of Canada did not give birth to as many new movements as did that of the United States. The Disciples of Christ, the Church of Jesus Christ of Latter Day Saints, the Seventh Day Adventists, Christian Science, and Jehovah's Witnesses had repercussions in Canada, but they were not paralleled by impressive counterparts of Canadian origin. Canadian Protestantism was more colonial, more a reproduction of what was imported from other countries. Its vigour—for it had marked vigour—was displayed in other ways.

But if the Christianity of Canada differed from that of the United States, both were played upon by the currents of the revolutionary age. They were integral parts of Western Christianity and were subjected to the forces issuing

[2] *The Encyclopædia Britannica*, 11th ed., Vol. XIX, p. 480.
[3] Weber, *1933 Yearbook of the American Churches*, p. 299.

from Western Europe. Some of them threatened Christianity. Others made for enhanced vitality.

THE ROMAN CATHOLIC CHURCH

The Roman Catholic Church in Canada dated from the beginnings of French rule. Much of the settlement was in the heyday of the Catholic Reformation in France. Religious zeal, largely directed to the conversion of the Indians, competed with the fur trade as a major motive in the extension of French rule Three religious orders and congregations which were born of the Catholic Reformation—the Jesuits, the *Récollets* (from a reform of the Franciscans), and the Sulpicians—had leading roles. The Ursulines, also a fruit of that revival were outstanding as a channel for the participation of women. Both Montreal and Quebec had strong religious foundations.[4] As representatives of the extreme wing of the Protestant Reformation by their prominence in the inception of several of the Thirteen Colonies helped to shape the United States and the American dream, so in the making of Canada men and women who drew their inspiration from the Catholic Reformation placed an indelible stamp on the French elements of the nascent nation.

From these beginnings sprang some of the continuing characteristics of the Roman Catholic Church in Canada. In pre-British days the Gallicanism which prevailed in the contemporary church in France was eschewed, and direct dependence on Rome was stressed. Over the protest of some of the episcopate of France, Laval, the first Bishop of Quebec, refused to conform to Gallicanism and was a vicar apostolic, an appointee of the Pope. Thus he paralleled the bypassing of the Portuguese *padroado* in Asia by vicars apostolic who took their authority directly from Rome. Activism, austerity of life, and a zeal for martyrdom characterized the colony. A parish structure developed through which church wardens were elected by the parishioners and a representative element was introduced.[5]

The fore part of the eighteenth century witnessed a recession in the Roman Catholic Church in Canada which was a phase of the illness from which that church suffered in the mother country. Morals declined from the high standards which the church had sought to maintain in the early days of the colony. The presence of troops sent to combat the English contributed to the deterioration. Clergy were too few to supply all the parishes. The third Bishop of Quebec lived in France and refused to cross the ocean. His coadjutor and successor spent only a part of his time in his see.[6] Yet during these years the Grey Nuns, Sisters of Charity, a long-lived congregation, were begun.[7]

[4] Walsh, *The Christian Church in Canada*, pp. 23–43; Brasseur de Bourbourg, *Histoire du Canada*, Vol. I, pp. 63 ff.

[5] Walsh, *op. cit.*, pp. 43–48; Brasseur de Bourbourg, *op. cit.*, Vol. I, pp. 77 ff.

[6] Walsh, *op. cit.*, pp. 67–71.

[7] Keefe, *The Congregation of Grey Nuns*, pp. 99 ff.

The British conquest was followed by a strengthening of the Roman Catholic Church in the former New France. The English deemed it the part of wisdom to show favour to the Roman Catholic Church. The Thirteen Colonies were beginning to be restive, and a dissatisfied French Canada would add to the menace to British rule. In contrast with the disabilities under which Roman Catholics laboured in the British Isles, the English authorities granted concessions to their Canadian Roman Catholic subjects. Although they had as yet no Anglican bishop in their American possessions, they permitted the Pope to give bulls of institution to Jean Olivier Briand to the see of Quebec and recognized him as "Superintendent of the Romish Church."[8] In view of the fact that the English had suppressed the Sulpicians and *Récollets* and did not permit the recruiting of clergy from France and since the Society of Jesus was dissolved by the Pope (1773), Briand set himself to fill the depleted ranks of the clergy with native-born young men. During the eighteen years that he held office he ordained 90 to add to the 138 priests whom he found on his accession to care for the 60,000 French constituting his flock.[9] Through his coöperation with the English Briand helped to make possible the Quebec Act (1774). That act was prompted chiefly by the desire to hold the loyalty of the French in the face of the growing revolt in the Thirteen Colonies. The French civil law was established side by side with the English criminal law, and the Roman Catholic Church was given its old privileges, among them the right to collect tithes from its constituency. When, some years later, an assembly was convened, Roman Catholics were allowed to sit in it on taking an oath of loyalty to the king.

The coming of British settlers wrought changes, but ultimately not to the disadvantage of the Roman Catholics. The war which issued in the independence of the United States brought in many loyalists, determined as they were to maintain their British allegiance. British merchants established themselves, at the outset chiefly in Quebec and Montreal. The loyalists pressed for better educational facilities and wished to make English the sole language, superseding French. In 1787 an Anglican bishop was appointed for Nova Scotia and in 1793 the redoubtable Jacob Mountain was created Anglican Bishop of Quebec. In 1791 the situation was somewhat eased by the Constitutional Act, which divided Canada into two parts, Upper and Lower. In Upper Canada, where loyalists predominated, English law and customs were standard. In Lower Canada, where the French were in the overwhelming majority, pre-conquest customs and practices continued, with the addition of representative institutions. The arrival of Irish Roman Catholic settlers, English-speaking as they were, made for fresh complications. However, the Irish added to the Roman Catholic population. In 1812 the latter was estimated at 160,000 in contrast with 20,000 Protestants. The clergy were being augmented by *émigré* priests from revolutionary

8 Walsh, *op. cit.*, p. 73; Brasseur de Bourbourg, *op. cit.*, Vol. II, pp. 1 ff.
9 Walsh, *op. cit.*, p. 75.

France. The British regime, consistently with its policy at home, did not object to their finding haven in Canada.[10]

The second war between Great Britain and the United States (1812–1814), a phase of the Napoleonic Wars, further improved the status of the French Canadians and their church. The British Government was eager not to alienate them and thus throw them into the arms of its enemies. The able Roman Catholic bishop Joseph-Octave Plessis (1763–1825), a native of Montreal, who led the Canadian church from 1806 to his death, seized the opportunity. He was allowed to assume the title of "Catholic Bishop of Quebec," was given an annual stipend by the state, and was accorded a seat in the legislative council. Later, in 1819, he was permitted to have four auxiliary dioceses, a step which was confirmed by the Holy See. Rome raised him to the rank of archbishop. However, Plessis was foiled in his ambition to keep under the authority of his see all the dioceses in British North America. Edmund Burke (1753–1820), an Irish priest who had been a pioneer in Upper Canada and had then been sent to Nova Scotia, on the ground that the French hierarchy were not sufficiently concerned for the needs of his fellow countrymen, by direct appeal to the Pope obtained the creation of Nova Scotia as an independent vicariate apostolic with himself as its head.[11]

The progress of the Roman Catholic Church in Upper Canada was largely due to Alexander Macdonell (1760–1840).[12] A Highland Scot, he had had a remarkable record as a pastor in his native land and as chaplain in the British army, said to have been the first Roman Catholic to have been given such an appointment since the Reformation, when in 1803 he led a number of Highland Roman Catholics to Upper Canada. They settled in Glengarry, named for his birthplace and regarded as the cradle of his church in Upper Canada. In 1816 he was appointed vicar apostolic and in 1826 bishop and as such had a major part in organizing and enlarging the Roman Catholic Church in Upper Canada. He recruited and trained a body of clergy and so won the confidence of the British authorities that in 1831 he was appointed to the legislative council of the province.

The nineteenth-century immigration of Roman Catholics from Europe presented a problem to the Roman Catholic Church in British North America. Could it be held to the faith? If so, could it be successfully integrated in one ecclesiastical structure with the French Canadians? The Irish constituted the

[10] Ibid., pp. 77–80; Brasseur de Bourbourg, op. cit., Vol. II, pp. 25–73.

[11] Walsh, op. cit., pp. 80–82; Brasseur de Bourbourg, op. cit., Vol. II, pp. 101–180; Brother Alfred, Catholic Pioneers in Upper Canada (Toronto, The Macmillan Co. of Canada, 1947, pp. xiv, 251), pp. 93–116.

[12] The Catholic Encyclopedia, Vol. IX, pp. 489–491; Hugh Joseph Somers, The Life and Times of the Hon. and Rt. Rev. Alexander Macdonell, D.D., First Bishop of Upper Canada 1762–1840 (Washington, The Catholic University of America Press, 1931, pp. lx, 232), passim. See also Wm. Perkins Bull, From Macdonell to McGuigan. The History of the Growth of the Roman Catholic Church in Upper Canada (Toronto, The Perkins Bull Foundation, 1939, pp. 501), passim.

major non-French element. They came in large numbers in the 1820's and 1830's and especially after the famine which followed the potato blight of the 1840's. In 1911 slightly over one million, or about a seventh of the population of Canada, were of Irish origin.[13] As in the United States, most of them were Roman Catholics and because of their experience in the Emerald Isle were loyal to their church. However, their intense Irish nationalism was the source, not only in Nova Scotia but elsewhere as well, of friction with the French Canadians. For the latter as for the former the Roman Catholic Church was the symbol and chief bond of the nationalism to which they clung as against what became the British majority. They held to their language and institutions. The Irish were English-speaking and had their own traditions. They would not be assimilated to the French. Conflict ensued and the problem of welding the two together was more persistent and difficult than that presented by the rival nationalities in the United States, for in that country the second and third generations of immigrant stock became English-speaking and tended to conform to the surrounding culture. Scottish Highlanders who had conserved their Roman Catholic faith as against the dominant Presbyterianism were a part of the immigration, although not nearly as numerous as the Irish. In 1911 the population of German provenance, many of them Roman Catholics, totalled about 400,000; 129,103, most of them Ruthenian Uniates, were from the Austro-Hungarian Empire, 45,411 were Italians, predominantly Roman Catholic, 33,365 were Poles, and 9,593 were Belgians, also almost all by heredity of that faith.[14]

The province of Quebec and its overwhelming French majority continued to constitute the heart and the main strength of the Roman Catholic Church in Canada. The Act of Union of 1840 had been in part provoked by a rebellion in Lower Canada led by Louis Joseph Papineau that had as its goal the setting up of a French republic. However, the Roman Catholic bishops and clergy opposed the revolt, and an act of Parliament (1851) guaranteed to all Her Majesty's subjects in Canada "the free exercise and enjoyment of profession and religious worship":[15] the Roman Catholic Church was not disturbed in its control of its children. To counter the drift of French Canadians southward into the United States, a determined effort was made by the Roman Catholic authorities to keep them in Canada. This was furthered by the creation of new parishes in the province of Quebec, colonization congresses and societies, and annual agricultural congresses.[16] The Roman Catholic clergy were accorded distinctive privileges and functions which strengthened their position. Their right to tithes, in kind or in money, continued to be recognized by the civil

---

[13] Shortt and Doughty, *Canada and Its Provinces,* Vol. XI, pp. 26, 27; Brasseur de Bourbourg, *op. cit.,* Vol. II, p. 195.
[14] Shortt and Doughty, *op. cit.,* Vol. XI, pp. 26, 27.
[15] *The Catholic Encyclopedia,* Vol. III, p. 326; Wade, *The French Canadians,* p. 164.
[16] *The Catholic Encyclopedia,* Vol. III, p. 237; Wade, *op. cit.,* pp. 260, 261.

authorities. Whereas outside the province the civil officials kept the registers of births, marriages, and deaths, in Quebec the vital statistics as recorded by the parish priests were accepted by the civil courts. In Quebec the practice dating from colonial days of elected parish church councils persisted. The members, known as churchwardens, managed the property of the parish under the direction of the priest. Thus the church was closely integrated into the life of the parish.[17]

In 1911, Roman Catholics constituted five-sixths of the population of the province of Quebec. In Prince Edward Island and New Brunswick they were slightly less than half and in Nova Scotia between a quarter and a third of the whole.[18] The French element was augmented by the Acadians. Some had escaped the deportation of 1768. With their high birth rate, by 1815 they had increased to 25,000 and by 1864 to 80,000. In 1901 they numbered 139,000.[19]

Although they remained a minority in the rapidly growing regions west of Ontario, Roman Catholics multiplied in that vast area and were cared for by their church. In 1843 they constituted a little more than half of the Red River Settlement, near the later Winnipeg. In 1820 a French Canadian priest, Joseph Norbert Provencher, was appointed bishop in the area and in 1847 was created Bishop of St. Boniface (Manitoba). To help him he invited the Oblates of Mary Immaculate, a congregation of nineteenth-century French origin.[20] Alexander Antonin Taché (1823–1894), an Oblate, French Canadian by birth, followed Provencher as bishop and in 1871 was created archbishop of the new ecclesiastical province of St. Boniface. His earlier years in the West had been spent among several Indian tribes, and Indians remained his chief love, but he was esteemed the main organizer of his church in the region between Ontario and the west coast.[21] Additional Roman Catholics came to the vast West. Among them were Germans, Poles, English, Irish, and French. Especially numerous were the Ruthenians, Uniates of the Greek rite: some became Protestants, others Russian Orthodox, and some Seramphimites, members of the Independent Greek Church of Canada. However, French Canadian and English Redemptorists were appointed to care for them, and for that purpose adopted the Byzantine rite. In 1913 a bishop was consecrated for them.[22] Roman Catholics were also on the Pacific coast. In 1847 Modeste Demers was created the first Bishop of Vancouver.[23]

---

[17] *The Catholic Encyclopedia*, Vol. III, p. 238.
[18] *The Canada Year Book 1912*, pp. 32, 33.
[19] *The Catholic Encyclopedia*, Vol. III, p. 237.
[20] Morice, *History of the Catholic Church in Western Canada*, Vol. I, pp. 65 ff., 91 ff., 226, 227.
[21] *The Catholic Encyclopedia*, Vol. XIV, p. 427; Morice, *op. cit.*, Vol. II, pp. 121, 150, 151; Joseph-Étienne Champagne, *Les Missions Catholiques dans l'Ouest Canadien (1818–1875)* (Ottawa, Éditions des Études Oblates Scolasticat Saint-Joseph, 1949, pp. 208), pp. 69–204.
[22] Attwater, *The Catholic Eastern Churches*, pp. 87, 88; *The Catholic Encyclopedia*, Vol. VI, p. 750; Shortt and Doughty, *op. cit.*, Vol. XI, pp. 188 ff.; Dawson, *Group Settlement. Ethnic Communities in Western Canada*, pp. 275 ff.
[23] *The Catholic Encyclopedia*, Vol. III, p. 236.

Roman Catholics were zealous in missions to the Indians and Eskimos. Their efforts for them were extensive and far-flung. The Jesuits reëntered Canada in 1842 and eventually had missions along the northern shores of Lakes Huron and Superior.[24] Major responsibility for the Indians farther west was assumed by the Oblates of Mary Immaculate. This entailed extensive travel and often much hardship and danger, for the effort was made to reach the Indians and Eskimos where they were and to allow them to continue their accustomed way of life in such aspects as did not conflict with Christian faith and morals.[25]

As in many other countries, the relation of the Roman Catholic Church to education was often thorny. In 1841 an education act created separate primary and normal schools for Roman Catholics and Protestants. However, in 1871 denominational schools supported by public funds were abolished in New Brunswick and a similar act was passed in Manitoba in 1890. In both provinces vigorous objections were raised and a compromise was reached, in New Brunswick in 1874.[26] Upper Canada was the scene of a long and complicated struggle. Macdonnell had inaugurated Roman Catholic elementary schools. In the 1840's mixed schools for Roman Catholics and Protestants were assisted by government funds. In the 1850's Ryerson, a Protestant and chief superintendent of education in the province, wished free public elementary education for all children. The Roman Catholic bishops were convinced that Roman Catholic children should go to Roman Catholic schools and pressed for state aid for them. They were supported by the Protestant minority in Lower Canada who wished separate schools for their children.[27] The eventual solution in most of the provinces was free compulsory elementary and secondary non-sectarian education. In some provinces separate schools were maintained for minority groups, mostly Roman Catholics. In the province of Quebec two systems existed—one French and Roman Catholic and the other Protestant and English. There the *Société d'Éducation* promoted primary schools and was aided by the law of parish schools.[28]

The Roman Catholic Church in Canada was not content with schools on a primary and secondary level: it also supported higher education. In 1854 it inaugurated Laval University in Quebec and in 1876 erected a branch in Montreal.[29] What became St. Francis Xavier University was begun in Nova Scotia in 1853. In its growth it was deeply indebted to James J. Tompkins (1870–

---

[24] Brasseur de Bourbourg, *op. cit.*, Vol. II, pp. 274 ff.

[25] Morice, *op. cit.*, *passim*, especially p. 292; *Fifty Years in Western Canada. Being the Abridged Memoirs of Rev. A. G. Morice, O.M.I., by D. L. S.* (Toronto, The Ryerson Press, 1930, pp. x, 267), *passim;* Katherine Hughes, *Father Lacombe, The Black-Robe Voyageur* (New York, Moffat, Yard and Co., 1911, pp. xxi, 467), *passim.*

[26] Walsh, *op. cit.*, p. 232; *The Catholic Encyclopedia*, Vol. III, p. 237.

[27] Franklin A. Walker, *Catholic Education and Politics in Upper Canada* (Toronto, J. M. Dent and Sons, 1955, pp. xii, 331), *passim.*

[28] *The Catholic Encyclopedia*, Vol. III, p. 235.

[29] *Ibid.*, p. 236.

1953). A native of Nova Scotia who had his seminary training in Rome, in the years immediately after 1900 Tompkins did much in raising funds for it.[30] Before the end of the century New Brunswick had a college with power to grant the bachelor's degree and the Oblates maintained a university in Ottawa. In addition, twenty-three institutions bearing the name of college, some of them with the power to grant degrees, mainly through Laval University, were founded between 1800 and 1900. For the training of clergy in Quebec and Montreal Laval University had theological faculties, a seminary was maintained in Quebec, and in Montreal the Sulpicians created a seminary to which students came from more than forty dioceses in the United States and Canada and in which by 1914 more than a score of bishops of the two countries had studied. The Sulpicians were also responsible for the founding of the Canadian College in Rome.[31]

The growth of the Roman Catholic Church in British North America was vividly demonstrated by the rapid expansion of the hierarchical structure. By 1906 that church was served by eight ecclesiastical provinces, each headed by an archbishop. In addition, in these provinces were twenty-five dioceses and three vicariates apostolic. Of the provinces the two with the largest number of faithful were Quebec and Montreal. The latter had slightly more than the former. Together they contained about three-fourths of the Roman Catholics of British North America.[32] By 1900 Rome had recognized Canada by conferring the dignity of cardinal on one of its hierarchy. Elzéar Alexandre Taschereau (1820–1898), a native of Quebec who had studied in Rome, was appointed Archbishop of Quebec in 1871 and was raised to the purple in 1886.[33]

The vitality of the Roman Catholic Church in North America was further seen in the growth of orders and congregations of "religious." In 1907 more than twenty communities of priests, ten of brothers, and seventy of sisters were maintained. Of these the Sulpicians had the longest continuing existence in the country. Most of the orders and congregations were of European origin, but eventually they were recruited chiefly in Canada. Of the congregations of women thirteen had originated in Canada, eleven of them in the nineteenth century. The largest was the Grey Nuns and the next largest the Sisters of Providence.[34]

A nineteenth-century trend of the Roman Catholic Church in British North America was towards ultramontanism and opposition to Gallicanism, Protestantism, and all liberal trends. By French Canadian ultramontanism was meant

[30] George Boyle, *Father Tompkins of Nova Scotia* (New York, P. J. Kenedy & Sons, 1953, pp. 234), pp. 32 ff.
[31] *The Catholic Encyclopedia*, Vol. III, p. 240.
[32] *Ibid.*, p. 238.
[33] *Ibid.*, Vol. XIV, pp. 462, 463.
[34] *Ibid.*, Vol. III, pp. 238, 239. For a brief description of the orders and congregations engaged in domestic and foreign missions see Bourassa, *Le Canada Apostolique*, pp. 1–119.

French Canadian nationalism and resistance against assimilation by the English. It also supported Pius IX and his Syllabus of Errors and his insistence on the supremacy of the Church over the state. French Canadian liberalism was largely political and was indebted to Lamennais, Lacordaire, and English liberalism. Ultramontanism had a leader in Ignace Bourget (1799–1885), Bishop of Montreal and titular archbishop, who assumed the full administration of the diocese of Montreal in 1837. The Sulpicians, long powerful in the diocese, were at odds with him, for he denounced them as the last refuge of Gallicanism and favoured the Jesuits. He also entered into controversy with the liberal *Institut Canadien*. The Fifth Provincial Council (1873) supported him and the Sixth (1878) set forth emphatically the claims of the Roman Catholic Church as a perfect society, warned the faithful against books written by non-Catholics, and forbade them to attend Protestant religious services.[35] Bourget organized the *Programme Catholique* to work for legislation favouring the Roman Catholic Church. It urged Roman Catholics to vote only for men who pledged themselves to adhere to the doctrines of their church and to throw their weight to changes demanded by the church, especially in questions of marriage, education, and the erection of parishes. The Propaganda discouraged criticism of the *Programme*. In the election of 1875 Bourget blacklisted candidates who supported doctrines condemned by the Syllabus of Errors and who opposed intervention by the Pope in affairs of government. Bourget was reinforced by Louis-François Richer Laflèche (1818–1898). Formerly a missionary among the Indians, in 1870 Laflèche was appointed Bishop of Three Rivers in the province of Quebec. However, Taschereau eventually placed himself against the more extreme features of the *Programme Catholique* and of its successor, the *Castors,* which sought to weed out liberals from the schools of Quebec. Under Leo XIII, more conciliatory than Pius IX, Rome condemned clerical interference in political elections and by giving Taschereau the cardinal's hat set back the cause of the extreme ultramontanists.[36]

The activities of extremists among the Roman Catholics provoked organized Protestant opposition. Wilfred Laurier, himself a French Canadian, leader of the Liberal Party from 1887 to 1919, and a champion of coöperation between the British and French elements in Canada, insisted that Canadian liberalism was not identical with German, French, or Italian liberalism and as early as 1876 warned Roman Catholics that if they organized a Catholic party it would be countered by a Protestant party. Indeed, a Protestant Defense Association was formed in Montreal in opposition to the *Programme Catholique.* In Ontario an Equal Rights Association came into being to checkmate the Catholic

[35] Walsh, *op. cit.,* pp. 204, 205; *The Catholic Encyclopedia,* Vol. II, pp. 721, 722; Wade, *op. cit.,* pp. 341–349; Léon Pouliot, *La Réaction Catholique de Montréal 1840–1841* (Montreal, Imprimerie du Messager, 1942, pp. 119), *passim.*
[36] Walsh, *op. cit.,* pp. 233–235; Wade, *op. cit.,* pp. 356–382.

League in its efforts to obtain privileges for the Roman Catholic Church. It soon extended its efforts to other parts of Canada. The issue was often joined over the question of separate schools for Roman Catholics and the use in them of the French language.[37]

Like the Roman Catholic Church in the United States, that in Canada may be said to have been recognized by Rome as coming of age when in the same year, 1908, it was removed from the jurisdiction of the Congregation for the Propagation of the Faith and accorded a status corresponding to that in the historically Roman Catholic countries of Europe. In 1899 Canada was given an apostolic delegate, and in 1909 a plenary council was held.[38]

The vigour of the Roman Catholic Church in Canada showed itself in a number of other ways. The shrine of Ste. Anne de Beaupré a few miles from the city of Quebec became famous as a centre of pilgrimages and of miracles. The miracles of healing began in the seventeenth century. Eventually equipped with several alleged relics of St. Anne, the traditional mother of the Virgin Mary, with a new church erected in 1876 which Leo XIII raised to the rank of a minor basilica in 1887 and served by the Redemptorists, it attracted thousands.[39] The growing industrialization of the latter part of the nineteenth century was a challenge which, under the stimulus given by the encyclical *Rerum novarum,* was met by the organization of Catholic trade unions. Early in 1901 Archbishop Louis Nazaire Bégin of Quebec, appealed to by both trade unions and employers in a labour dispute, came out for arbitration and a continuing board of conciliation. His recommendation was accepted by both parties. In 1907, at clerical suggestion, a labour federation with Roman Catholic membership was inaugurated in the pulp and paper industry on the Saguenay River in Quebec. Further organizations emerged after 1914 and the movement assumed major dimensions.[40]

Earlier than those of the United States, the Roman Catholics of Canada began to participate in the wide-flung missions of their church. By the year 1914, in addition to their extensive share in the missions to the Indians and Eskimos of British North America, Canadian Roman Catholics had gone to Africa, Ceylon, China, Chile, India, Japan, New Guinea, Ecuador, Peru, Bolivia, Colombia, and Nicaragua, and at least one congregation had arisen primarily for foreign missions.[41]

In general, Roman Catholics, especially of French nationality, seem to have held to their ancestral church. In spite of Protestant missionary efforts and the movement headed by Charles Chiniquy, a former Quebec priest, in 1902 the

[37] Walsh, *op. cit.,* pp. 235–239.
[38] Shortt and Doughty, *op. cit.,* Vol. XI, p. 111.
[39] *The Catholic Encyclopedia,* Vol. I, p. 539.
[40] Allan Brockway Latham, *The Catholic and National Labour Unions of Canada* (Toronto, The Macmillan Co. of Canada, 1930, pp. v, 104), pp. 36 ff.
[41] Bourassa, *op. cit.,* pp. 120 ff.

number of converts to Protestantism in the province of Quebec was estimated as being only between 30,000 and 40,000.[42]

PROTESTANTS

Long before 1914 the majority of the population of British North America was not Roman Catholic but Protestant, chiefly by reason of immigration, at first to a large extent from New England to Nova Scotia, then by loyalists who sacrificed their homes in the Thirteen Colonies rather than renounce allegiance to the king, and in the nineteenth century mainly by overflow from the British Isles.

Most of the immigration was after 1815 and at a time when awakenings were revitalizing the Protestant churches of the British Isles. One of the repercussions was the success in holding to the faith the large majority of the immigration to British North America and the emergence of strong churches in that area. Much influence was exerted through societies in the British Isles and by individuals from the mother country.

To the founding and growth of the Church of England, among both the colonists and the Indians and Eskimos, major assistance was given by the Society for the Propagation of the Faith;[43] the Society for Promoting Christian Knowledge;[44] the Church Missionary Society;[45] the Upper Canada Clergy Society (eventually merged with the Society for the Propagation of the Gospel in Foreign Parts);[46] the Stewart Mission Fund;[47] the Colonial and Continental Church Society (earlier the Colonial Church and School Society);[48] the New England Company, which had been organized in the seventeenth century to support missions to Indians in New England but after the independence of the United States had transferred most of its efforts to the parts of North America which remained under the British crown;[49] the Church of England Society for Newfoundland, formed in London in 1823 by leading Evangelicals as the Society for Educating the Poor of Newfoundland;[50] and the Mission to the Free Coloured Population of Canada, begun in 1854 through Lord Shaftesbury and others.[51]

The planting and nourishing of Presbyterianism was assisted by the Glasgow Colonial Society, organized in 1825 "for promoting the moral and religious in-

[42] McNeill, *The Presbyterian Church in Canada, 1875–1925*, pp. 99, 100.
[43] Thompson, *Into All Lands*, pp. 118–125, 128–155, 242–273, 502, 507.
[44] Allen and McClure, *Two Hundred Years*, pp. 312–330, 368–372.
[45] Vernon, *The Old Church in the New Dominion*, pp. 123–125.
[46] *Ibid.*, p. 87.
[47] *Ibid.*, p. 87; Waddilove, The Stewart Missions, *passim*.
[48] L. Norman Tucker, *From Sea to Sea the Dominion* (Toronto, Prayer and Study Union of the M.S.C.C., 2d ed., 1911, pp. 181), p. 45.
[49] *History of the New England Company* (London, Taylor and Co., 1871, pp. xv, 353), *passim*.
[50] J. D. Mullins, *Our Beginnings; being a Short Sketch of the History of the Colonial and Continental Church Society* (no date or place, pp. 35), pp. 1–12.
[51] *Ibid.*, p. 21.

terests of the Scottish settlers in North America";[52] by missionaries sent by the Associate Synod of the Secession Church and by individual ministers of that church beginning as early as 1765;[53] by ministers sent from the Thirteen Colonies;[54] by personnel and funds from the Free Church of Scotland to colleges and for missions in the West;[55] by numbers of young men who came to the Presbyterian ministry in Western Canada; and by missionaries sent by the Colonial Committee of the Church of Scotland.[56]

Methodism seems to have been first introduced, as least in Upper Canada, from south of the border. With the itinerants came the camp-meeting, then in the first flush of its exuberance on the Western frontier. The War of 1812 aroused resentment against the United States and made difficult the work of Methodist preachers from that country. However, Methodist missionaries came from the British Isles.[57]

Congregationalism was brought in from New England before the independence of the United States. Later the London Missionary Society assisted it with money and personnel. In 1836 the Congregational Union of London, moved by the desire to aid clergy in Canada, appointed a committee from which sprang the Colonial Missionary Society. Numbers of Congregational ministers joined the immigrant tide from the British Isles.[58]

Baptist beginnings were deeply indebted to Henry Alline (1748–1784), a native of Rhode Island and a New Light Congregationalist, who as an itinerant evangelist from 1776 to 1783 was in what became the Maritime Provinces.[59] The ranks of British North American Baptists were reinforced by loyalists. Soon after the independence of the United States, ministers came from that country, especially to Upper Canada, several of them sent by the Baptist missionary societies of New York and Massachusetts. Some ministers were from the British Isles.[60] In 1837 the Baptist Canadian Missionary Society was organized in England to raise funds to assist Baptists in Canada.[61]

By the year 1820 Quakers were well established in British North America,

[52] Balfour, *Presbyterianism in the Colonies*, pp. 17–19.

[53] James Robertson, *History of the Mission of the Secession Church to Nova Scotia and Prince Edward Island from its Commencement to 1765* (Edinburgh, John Johnstone, 1847, pp. 285), p. 20; John M'Kerrow, *History of the Foreign Missions of the Secession and United Presbyterian Church* (Edinburgh, Andrew Elliott, 1867, pp. ix, 518), pp. 37 ff., 106 ff.

[54] McNeill, *op. cit.*, pp. 4, 5.

[55] Balfour, *op. cit.*, p. 42.

[56] McNeill, *op. cit.*, p. 103.

[57] Sanderson, *The First Century of Methodism in Canada*, Vol. I, pp. 27–32, 36–38, 44, 89, 97, 174.

[58] John Wood, *Memoir of Henry Wilkes, D.D., LL.D., His Life and Times* (Montreal, F. E. Grafton & Sons, 1887, pp. iv, 280), pp. 17, 20–23, 44, 84.

[59] Levy, *The Baptists of the Maritime Provinces 1753–1946*, pp. 22–36.

[60] Stuart Ivison and Fred Roser, *The Baptists in Upper and Lower Canada before 1820* (University of Toronto Press, 1956, pp. 193), *passim*.

[61] Fitch, *The Baptists of Canada*, pp. 114, 118–121.

although, as elsewhere, as a minority. They arose chiefly by immigration.[62]

The Disciples of Christ came by contact with the United States, partly by immigration and partly in other ways. Alexander Campbell himself preached in Upper Canada in 1855. Their first church seems to have been organized in 1830.[63]

Although much help in the planting of Protestantism in British North America was from the British Isles and the United States, increasingly the churches were self-supporting, recruited and trained their own ministry, and took steps to extend their faith both in their own country and outside their borders. As in so much of our narrative, a full account would lengthen our pages beyond all proper bounds. We must confine our attention to the larger denominations and deal with them only in highly condensed summaries.[64]

THE CHURCH OF ENGLAND IN CANADA

The Church of England entered the nineteenth century in British North America with both advantages and disadvantages. The advantages arose from the fact that at the outset it was the established church and by 1815 had an episcopate. In 1787 Charles Inglis (1734–1816) was consecrated bishop subject to the Archbishop of Canterbury and with royal letters patent which constituted him Bishop of Nova Scotia and its dependencies. The dependencies were interpreted as including New Brunswick, Prince Edward Island, Upper and Lower Canada, Newfoundland, and Bermuda.[65] In 1793 Jacob Mountain (1749–1825) was consecrated Bishop of Quebec, with a see which included Lower and Upper Canada and their dependencies.[66] However, what looked like a favoured position entailed handicaps. Because it was the official church, the Church of England was regarded as serving the upper classes and not the rank and file. In the Maritime Provinces and especially in Upper Canada rural frontier conditions prevailed, and the revivals and camp-meetings which characterized similar communities in the United States at the time spread to the traditionally Protestant elements in the population of British North America. As in the United States the Protestant Episcopal Church was ill adapted to the situation, so in the regions north of the international boundary the Church of England did not modify its methods to win those who, if they were religiously inclined, found the informal, emotional methods of the revivals congenial. Moreover, at the beginning of the century, in England the established church was still suffering from conditions which it inherited from the eighteenth century and was unable

---

[62] Dorland, *A History of the Society of Friends (Quakers) in Canada*, pp. 30–103.

[63] Reuben Butchart, *The Disciples of Christ in Canada since 1830* (Toronto, Canadian Headquarters Publications, Church of Christ [Disciples], 1949, pp. xv, 674), pp. 64 ff., 74, 81.

[64] For more extended treatments, both also only summaries, see Walsh, *The Christian Church in Canada, passim,* and Clark, *Church and Sect in Canada, passim*.

[65] Vernon, *The Old Church in the New Dominion*, pp. 72–80.

[66] *Ibid.,* p. 82.

to rise fully to the challenge presented by the new doors opened to it overseas. It had as yet too few clergy who were willing to share in the adventure of the burgeoning colonies, and some of those who crossed the Atlantic were of less than desirable character.[67]

Yet the Church of England overcame many of these handicaps, partly because of its leadership. It was fortunate in its early bishops. Inglis, born in Ireland, had been a missionary of the Society for the Propagation of the Gospel in Delaware and rector of Trinity Church in New York City. As bishop he travelled extensively through Nova Scotia, New Brunswick, Prince Edward Island, and Lower Canada, administering confirmation and arranging for regular Anglican worship. He was chiefly responsible for the founding of King's College, in Windsor, Nova Scotia, later federated with the University of Dalhousie.[68] Jacob Mountain brought with him a family which included a brother and a nephew, both clergymen, and a son, George Jehoshaphat Mountain (1789–1863), who became the third Bishop of Quebec. He stood for the dignity of his office and his church and at times this brought him criticism. When he arrived Lower and Upper Canada had seven active clergymen. When he died they had sixty-one, three of them archdeacons and forty-eight of them missionaries of the Society for the Propagation of the Gospel in Foreign Parts. Eight times he went over his huge diocese in official visitations. He attracted to Canada a number of able and devoted priests.[69] One, Charles James Stewart (1775–1837), a younger son of the Earl of Galloway, who early felt called to be a missionary and who chose Canada as against India, deliberately remained unmarried, devoted his fortune and his stipend to the advancement of the Church of England in his adopted country, repeatedly journeyed to England to obtain recruits and financial aid, and as the second Bishop of Quebec (1826–1837) travelled over his diocese again and again, baptizing, confirming, and providing for his widely dispersed flock.[70] John Strachan (1778–1867) was one of the greatest administrators and ecclesiastical statesmen that the Church of England in Canada knew. Born in Scotland of a layman devoted to the Scottish Episcopal Church and reared a staunch churchman, he came to Canada in 1799. He was first a schoolmaster and, while after a few years he was ordained, he never ceased to be active in education. He promoted the establishment of grammar schools, had a major part in the inauguration of King's College, later to become the University of Toronto, and when that institution was secularized he was the chief founder

[67] Clark, *op. cit.*, pp. 108 ff.

[68] Vernon, *op. cit.*, pp. 73–79; Heeney, *Leaders of the Canadian Church*, pp. 1–34.

[69] Thomas R. Millman, *Jacob Mountain, First Lord Bishop of Quebec. A Study in Church and State 1793–1825* (University of Toronto Press, 1947, pp. viii, 320), *passim;* Vernon, *op. cit.*, pp. 82–86; Armine W. Mountain, *A Memoir of George Jehoshaphat Mountain* (Montreal, John Lovell, 1866, pp. 477), *passim;* Heeney, *op. cit.*, pp. 35–74.

[70] Vernon, *op. cit.*, pp. 87, 88; Waddilove, *op. cit., passim;* J. Langtry, *History of the Church in Eastern Canada and Newfoundland* (London, Society for Promoting Christian Knowledge, 1892, pp. 256), pp. 43–50.

of Trinity College, Toronto. In 1827 he was made Archdeacon of York, in Upper Canada, and in 1839 was consecrated the first Bishop of Toronto. A man of marked initiative, prodigious energy, pronounced convictions, believing firmly in an aristocratic rather than a democratic society, and intent on the full establishment of the Church of England in Canada, he was often the centre of controversy. He built up his diocese, recruited and trained clergy, and in 1851 held a diocesan synod of clerical and lay delegates, said to have been the first of its kind in the British Empire.[71]

Disestablishment came to the Church of England in Canada. The Church of England was never fully established in British North America in the sense in which it was in the mother country, but it had a privileged position and was controlled and in part supported by the state. It lost this connexion, as was in accord with what was happening elsewhere in the colonies and with a trend in much of Christendom. In Canada disestablishment was not caused by anti-clericalism. It arose out of contention among the various denominations and was accomplished only after long and at times bitter debate. The Constitutional Act of 1791 made special provision for the support of the "Protestant" clergy, and to that end in place of endowments and tithes, the prevailing practice in England, set aside one-seventh of the lands in Upper Canada and one-seventh of such lands in Lower Canada as were not already occupied by the French inhabitants. Soon after the act was passed, the Presbyterian clergy, representing the established Church of Scotland, claimed a share in the "clergy reserves." Other Protestant bodies also insisted on participation. After three decades of strife, in 1854 the Canadian legislature transferred the lands to the municipalities within which they were situated, safeguarding the interests of the existing clergy. Later the proceeds were commuted in a capital fund to serve as a permanent endowment.[72]

Closely following the settlement of the complicated dispute over the clergy reserves and as a phase of the complete separation of Church and state, the independence of the Church of England in Canada was achieved. Successive steps were taken which resulted in a comprehensive autonomous structure. Beginning in the 1850's, with the one in Toronto as a path-breaker, diocesan synods became a regular procedure. In that decade, bishops began to be elected. In 1860, at the request of the synods of Quebec, Toronto, and Montreal, an ecclesiastical province was created with a metropolitan at its head and including not only the three dioceses but also Nova Scotia and Fredericton—but not Newfoundland or Rupert's Land. In 1868, on the death of the first archbishop, the

[71] A. N. Bethune, *Memoir of the Right Reverend John Strachan, D.D., LL.D., First Bishop of Toronto* (Toronto, Henry Rowsell, 1870, pp. viii, 385), *passim;* Vernon, *op. cit.,* pp. 91–106; Heeney, *op. cit.,* pp. 77–95; Walsh, *op. cit.,* pp. 169–177.
[72] Shortt and Doughty, *Canada and Its Provinces,* Vol. XI, pp. 235–236; Vernon, *op. cit.,* pp. 107–111; "Church Establishment and Endowment in Upper Canada," in *The Canadian Historical Review,* December, 1934, pp. 351–375.

bishops to the province of Canada chose his successor, thus symbolizing their independence of the crown. In 1861 a provincial synod had been held. In 1874 the ecclesiastical province and synod of Rupert's Land were created. In 1890 a conference was held in Winnipeg which framed a constitution for the entire Church of England in Canada and the first general synod convened in Toronto in 1893.[73] The Church of England in Canada, while attaining full autonomy, remained a part of the Anglican Communion.

As the century proceeded, the Church of England in Canada continued to prosper. The better to care for the mounting population, dioceses were increased in number and clergy were recruited and trained. More and more they were natives of Canada. The church was less and less dependent on the mother country for its priests. The growth was in the older parts of the country, but especially in the West and North: there it was among the Indians and Eskimos and the rapidly rising white population.[74] It was dramatized by the election as the first primate of all Canada of Archbishop Machray, who had been outstanding in the building of the church in the West. Robert Machray (1831–1904), a Highland Scot of Presbyterian parents, had become an Anglican while a student in Cambridge. He went to Rupert's Land as bishop in 1865. Making his headquarters at Winnipeg, never marrying, he gave himself to the vast area included in his diocese and was creative, not only in the life of his church, but also in educational and other public affairs of the region.[75] In 1883 the Domestic and Foreign Missionary Society was formed, modelled after the organization with the similar name of the Protestant Episcopal Church in the United States of America. In 1902 the Missionary Society of the Canadian Church was constituted. In 1904 the two were merged under the latter name. All baptized members of the church were regarded as members and it had a woman's auxiliary.[76]

The Anglo-Catholic movement was strongly represented, especially in the episcopate. The Evangelicals were also vigorous. They were responsible for the organization in 1869 of the Evangelical Association of the United Church of England and Ireland in the Diocese of Toronto and (1873) of the Church Association of the Diocese of Toronto. The Evangelicals founded Wycliffe College in Toronto, first incorporated as the Protestant Episcopal Divinity School and with its initial building in 1882. It became the largest theological college of the Church of England in Canada and was characterized by missionary zeal.[77]

[73] Shortt and Doughty, *op. cit.*, Vol. XI, pp. 235–239; Walsh, *op. cit.*, pp. 208, 209; Neill, *Anglicanism*, pp. 300–302.

[74] L. Norman Tucker, *Western Canada* (London, A. L. Mowbray & Co., 1908, pp. xii, 164); Arthur Lewis, *The Life and Work of the Rev. E. J. Peck among the Eskimos* (New York, A. C. Armstrong and Son, 1904, pp. xvi, 349), *passim;* S. Gould, *Inasmuch. Sketches of the Beginnings of the Church of England in Canada in Relation to the Indian and Eskimo Races* (Toronto, 1917, pp. xiv, 285), *passim.*

[75] Vernon, *op. cit.*, pp. 119–168; *Dictionary of National Biography,* Second Supplement, Vol. II, pp. 522, 523.

[76] Vernon, *op. cit.*, pp. 176–178, 186, 187.

[77] *Ibid.*, p. 179.

PRESBYTERIANISM

Presbyterianism entered British North America through a number of channels. Huguenots were present in the French period but never achieved an ecclesiastical organization. Not far from the middle of the eighteenth century German and Dutch Reformed settled in Nova Scotia. Before and after the independence of the United States Presbyterian bodies of that country with Irish and Scottish provenance conducted missions in Nova Scotia and Upper Canada. Among the loyalist settlers in Upper Canada were Presbyterians to whom the Reformed Church in America sent pastors. Continuing foundations of Presbyterianism in Nova Scotia were laid by missionaries from the Secession groups in Scotland—the Burghers and the Anti-Burghers. Before 1815 the Church of Scotland had entered the Maritime Provinces. Its representatives came into conflict with the Synod of Nova Scotia, organized in 1817 by the Burghers and Anti-Burghers. In 1833 they formed a presbytery in New Brunswick and a synod in Nova Scotia and Prince Edward Island. In 1818 Burgher ministers inaugurated a presbytery for Lower and Upper Canada. It was erected into a synod in 1820 but was reconstituted as the United Presbytery of Upper Canada. In 1831 it became the United Synod of Upper Canada. Lower Canada also had a presbytery. The year 1831 likewise saw the formation of the Synod of the Presbyterian Church of Canada in Connexion with the Church of Scotland. The Disruption of 1843 in Scotland brought division in the following year in Upper and Lower Canada and New Brunswick. In the decade 1850–1860 eight distinct self-governing Presbyterian bodies existed in what was to become the Dominion of Canada.[78]

Such diverse origins made for tensions between the several Presbyterian churches. Scottish and Irish elements predominated and the two were sometimes at loggerheads. The Church of Scotland congregations, perpetuating the tradition of the Establishment, tended to be recruited from the more substantial and socially prominent.[79] In general, too, at the outset the Scots and the Irish, like the several other ethnic groups in British North America and the United States, tended to be clannish and to regard their congregations as social as well as religious centres and did not reach out to the general population. They found distasteful the frontier revivalism which entered from south of the border.[80]

As we have suggested, the representatives of the Church of Scotland in Canada claimed a share in the clergy reserves. They did this on the ground that as the established church in Scotland their kirk had as much right to them as had the Church of England. Indeed, in the 1820's the members of the Church of

---

[78] McNeill, *The Presbyterian Church in Canada, 1875–1925*, pp. 1–16; Gregg, *History of the Presbyterian Church in the Dominion of Canada, passim;* Walsh, *op. cit.*, pp. 210, 211; Shortt and Doughty, *op. cit.*, Vol. XI, pp. 253–274.

[79] Clark, *op. cit.*, pp. 140, 141.

[80] *Ibid.*, pp. 135–138.

Scotland in Upper and Lower Canada asked the home government for the un-equivocal establishment of the Church of Scotland.[81]

Gradually the union of the various Presbyterian bodies was achieved. In 1860 the Synod of the Presbyterian Church of Nova Scotia (Secession) and the Synod of the Free Church of Nova Scotia merged. The idea of a general union of all Presbyterians in British North America began to be discussed. In 1861 the synod of the United Presbyterian Church in Canada (Secession) joined with the synod of the Presbyterian Church in Canada (Free Church) to form the Canada Presbyterian Church. In 1870 it gave birth to the General Assembly of the Canada Presbyterian Church with 4 synods, 17 presbyteries, and 292 ministers. In 1868 the Synod of the Maritime Provinces in Connexion with the Church of Scotland was formed. In that year the progress of union had reduced the eight Presbyterian bodies to four. The political union of 1867 encouraged further steps towards Presbyterian union. In 1875, after negotiations which had begun in 1870 and which had aroused opposition in some quarters, especially among those related to the Church of Scotland, the four bodies formally came together to form the Presbyterian Church in Canada.[82]

The Presbyterian Church in Canada expanded the missionary efforts of its constituting bodies. In 1875 there were 169 mission fields in the West and 53 in the East. About 40 per cent. of the funds then came from the British Isles and about 60 per cent. from the Canadian church. In the following decades a marked increase took place. The outstanding leader in the West was James Robertson (1839–1902). He had studied theology in Princeton and in Union Theological Seminary in New York City and at the time of his appointment as superintendent of missions in the West (1881) was pastor of a church in Winnipeg. An activist, organizer, and administrator, he travelled throughout the West to the Pacific coast and in the North to the gold fields on the Yukon. He launched the Church and Manse Building Fund to enable him to initiate Presbyterian operations wherever he saw the promise of a new town or city. He journeyed to Eastern Canada and to the British Isles to recruit personnel and in the vast area for which he was responsible organized presbyteries. By the time of his death he had started 642 missions and 121 augmented charges. In 1913, later regarded as the peak year, 1,150 centres received aid, including 287 augmented charges.[83] Not much was done among the Indians, but something was attempted for immigrants of non-Christian ancestry.[84] Foreign missions were undertaken in the New Hebrides in 1848, in India in 1857, in Trinidad in

[81] Gregg, *op. cit.*, pp. 406–439; Walsh, *op. cit.*, pp. 173–176; W. Stanford Reid, *The Church of Scotland in Lower Canada. Its Struggle for Establishment* (Toronto, Presbyterian Publications, 1936, pp. 192), *passim*.

[82] McNeill, *op. cit.*, pp. 16–32; Walsh, *op. cit.*, pp. 212–214.

[83] McNeill, *op. cit.*, pp. 104, 105, 107–109; Walsh, *op. cit.*, pp. 273–275; Shortt and Doughty, *op. cit.*, Vol. XI, pp. 284–290.

[84] McNeill, *op. cit.*, pp. 112, 113.

1868, in Formosa in 1871, in North China in 1888, in British Guiana in 1885, in Korea in the 1890's, and in South China in 1892.[85] In accord with the movement which had begun in Europe, in 1908 the General Assembly authorized the inauguration of an Order of Deaconesses, and in 1910 an earlier school in Toronto was renamed the Presbyterian Missionary and Deaconess Training Home.[86]

Provision was made for training an indigenous ministry. By the middle of the nineteenth century several institutions for theological education had been begun. In the second half of the century they were augmented and new ones were opened.[87]

Canadian Presbyterians could not ignore the currents of thought which were part of the revolutionary age. Not much was heard of them until the second half of the century. John Watson, on the faculty of Queen's University, and George Paxton Young, on the staff of Knox College, early called attention to the issues raised by Biblical criticism, and George Monro Grant, said to have been the most influential Presbyterian churchman in Canada in his day, defended Wellhausen. In 1866 Grant preached a sermon in which he assailed the extreme confessionalism of all the churches and held that it took the attitude: "Abandon thought, all ye who enter here."[88] Although at least some of the teachers in the theological schools were aware of the new currents, their attitude in general was conservative. One who was regarded as a progressive used in his classes Hodge's *Systematic Theology.* Modifications were made in the Westminster Confession, but they did not have to do with central doctrines.[89]

Heresy trials followed. In 1876 and 1877 Daniel James Macdonnell, a minister in Toronto, was arraigned because he doubted the doctrine of eternal punishment. Several sprang to his defense, among them the much loved John Bower Mowat (1825–1900), a well-known conservative of the faculty of Queen's College. Macdonnell was able to sign a statement which satisfied the Assembly, but as late as 1889 he still desired a revision of the Westminster Confession. In 1893 John Campbell, of Montreal, was brought before his presbytery and then his synod because he could not affirm the "entire inerrancy of the inspired revelation of the Old Testament" and held to "gradual revelation." Like Macdonnell, he eventually subscribed to a statement which the synod accepted with relief. No other men were brought to trial for heresy. The opinion prevailed that religious thought must cease to be sectarian and that, as Grant said (1894), the "churches must accept conclusions arrived at in accordance with the canons

85 *Ibid.,* pp. 120–125; Andrew Thomson, *The Life and Letters of Rev. R. P. Mackay* (Toronto, The Ryerson Press, 1932, pp. xiv, 192), pp. 62 ff.

86 McNeill, *op. cit.,* pp. 149, 150.

87 Shortt and Doughty, *op. cit.,* Vol. XI, pp. 275, 276; McNeill, *op. cit.,* pp. 70–84.

88 McNeill, *op. cit.,* pp. 203, 204; Walsh, *op. cit.,* pp. 212, 213; William Lawson Grant and Frederick Hamilton, *Principal Grant* (Toronto, Morang & Co., 1904, pp. 531), pp. 481 ff.

89 McNeill, *op. cit.,* pp. 59, 62, 63, 85–90.

of universal validity, or perish morally in a scientifically educated age."[90]

Some changes took place in church customs. Musical instruments, especiall[y] organs, were introduced. Hymns as well as Psalms were sung. The emphas[is] on the Communion, with careful preliminary preparation, fasting, preachin[g] self-examination, joint criticism, the use of metal tokens, and the "fencing" [of] the table, was gradually modified. By the close of 1906, in deference to the fea[r] of the transmission of disease through the use of the common chalice, in fort[y] five congregations individual cups had been adopted.[91]

On the eve of 1914 the Presbyterians shared with the Anglicans and Metho[d] ists the distinction of being the largest Protestant bodies in Canada. This wa[s] partly because of the many Canadians who were of Scottish and North of Ire[-] land ancestry. It was also because, in contrast with their earlier ethnic exclu[-] siveness, they were reaching out to unchurched elements in the populatio[n] particularly in the West, who were of other national backgrounds. Proportio[n] ately, like the Anglicans, they constituted a larger percentage of the populatio[n] than in the United States.

METHODISM

In 1914 the third in size of the Protestant denominations in Canada was Meth[-] odism. It had been the largest in 1891. Proportionately to the others, it wa[s] stronger than in the British Isles but not as prominent as in the United States.

As with the Anglicans and Presbyterians, so with the Methodists, the begin[-] nings in British North America were well before 1815. Like Presbyterianism[,] Methodism entered through several different channels. Some Methodist pioneer[s] were loyalists. After the independence of the United States, Methodist preach[-] ers came from that country, appointed by the Methodist Episcopal Church[.] With their emotionalism and their attack on frontier vices, they appealed t[o] the humbler elements of society. Frontier conditions akin to those south o[f] the border prevailed in much of Upper Canada, and the Methodist preacher[s] stressed camp-meetings and revivals. With its itinerant ministry and its form o[f] organization, Methodism flourished. It adopted the episcopal form of govern[-] ment and in Upper Canada remained in official connexion with the Methodis[t] Episcopal Church until 1828.[92] The war of 1812–1814 for the moment checke[d] the growth, for many of the preachers returned to the United States. But afte[r] the war revivals again broke out, more preachers entered from across the border[.]

[90] *Ibid.*, pp. 87–89, 204–210.

[91] *Ibid.*, pp. 210–215.

[92] Clark, *Church and Sect in Canada*, pp. 84–86, 93–96; *Cyclopædia of Methodism*, pp. 29–50[;] Shortt and Doughty, *Canada and Its Provinces*, Vol. XI, pp. 303–306. For the lives of some of th[e] pioneer preachers from the United States and the early history of Methodism in Canada, see Joh[n] Carroll, *Case and His Contemporaries; or the Canadian Itinerants' Memorial; Constituting a Bio[-] graphical History of Methodism in Canada from Its Introduction into the Province, till the deat[h] of the Rev. William Case in 1855* (Toronto, Samuel Rose, 4 vols., 1867–1874), *passim;* Lando[n] *Western Ontario and the American Frontier*, pp. 13 ff.

and some came from Ireland.[93] Before 1812 Methodist preachers from England had reached the Maritime Provinces.[94] As an outgrowth of the war, at the request of Methodists in Montreal Methodist missionaries were sent from England to Lower Canada. Tensions ensued, and in 1820 by agreement Lower Canada was assigned to the (English) Wesleyan Methodist Missionary Society.[95]

In 1824 the Methodists of Upper Canada formed a conference of their own within the Methodist Episcopal Church of the United States. In 1828 that conference became independent as the Methodist Episcopal Church of Canada. In 1833 it coalesced with the British Conference. The change entailed dropping the episcopate and other alterations in polity. Seven years later, in 1840, the Wesleyan Methodist Church in Canada became autonomous, but in 1847 it returned to the fold of British Methodism. In 1855, in conjunction with the Methodism in Lower Canada, it was constituted an affiliated self-governing branch of English Methodism.[96]

Other forms of Methodism were propagated, mainly from the British Isles. In 1837 the Methodist New Connexion determined to open a mission in Canada. In 1841, on recommendation of its pioneer representative, the Methodist New Connexion merged with the Canadian Wesleyan Methodist Church to form the Canadian Wesleyan Methodist New Connexion.[97] In 1829 the first preacher of the Primitive Methodist Church arrived in Upper Canada. More missionaries were sent from England; the church took root and in 1883 had 98 travelling preachers, 214 local preachers, and 8,090 members.[98] In 1831 the Bible Christian Church sent its first two missionaries to British North America. Others followed and the church was firmly planted in Prince Edward Island and Upper Canada and grew.[99]

A comprehensive union of Methodism in British North America was achieved by successive stages. In 1855 John Beecham, the senior missionary of the British Conference, brought into being the Eastern British American Conference, made up of the Wesleyan Methodist churches in Nova Scotia, New Brunswick, Prince Edward Island, and Newfoundland. In 1874 the Methodist Church of Canada was formed by the union of the Eastern British American Conference and the Conference of the Wesleyan Methodist Church in Canada. In it was included the New Connexion Church, a step made possible by the provision, distinc-

[93] Clark, *op. cit.*, pp. 96–100.
[94] Findlay and Holdsworth, *The History of the Wesleyan Methodist Missionary Society*, Vol. I, pp. 292–314.
[95] *Ibid.*, pp. 390 ff.; Shortt and Doughty, *op. cit.*, Vol. XI, p. 307; *Cyclopædia of Methodism*, pp. 51 ff.
[96] Findlay and Holdsworth, *op. cit.*, Vol. I, p. 407; Sanderson, *The First Century of Methodism in Canada*, Vol. I, pp. 105–109, 141–146; Walsh, *The Christian Church in Canada*, pp. 214, 215; Landon, *op. cit.*, pp. 75 ff.
[97] *Centennial of Canadian Methodism*, pp. 102–104.
[98] *Ibid.*, pp. 184 ff.
[99] *Ibid.*, pp. 205 ff.

tive of the New Connexion, for lay representation at conference meetings
For a time the Methodist Episcopal, Primitive Methodist, and Bible Christian
Churches remained aloof, but in 1883 they entered. Thus, by the census of 1891,
the Methodist Church of Canada was shown to have 17.8 per cent. of the population, ahead of the Presbyterians, who had 15.9 per cent., and of the Anglicans, who were credited with 13.7 per cent. of the population. It was not quite
half as large as the Roman Catholic Church.[100]

Methodists expanded into the West. At first this was by way of missions to
the Indians and through men sent from Britain. Later it was chiefly by men
from the East and from the tide of immigration which poured into the prairies
during the latter part of the century. In 1883 the Methodist Conference of
Manitoba and the North-West held its first meeting.[101]

Canadian Methodists also reached out beyond the borders of their country.
In 1873 they inaugurated a mission in Japan.[102] In 1891 the first party of Cana-
dian Methodists arrived in China, soon to begin an enterprise in Szechwan
Province.[103]

As were the other churches, Methodists were prominent in education. As
early as 1829 they took steps to undertake higher education for their young
people and in 1836 Upper Canada Academy opened its doors. In 1841 it became Victoria College, later to be Victoria University. Other institutions were
founded, among them Mount Allison University in the Maritime Provinces and
colleges for women in Hamilton and Whitby, Ontario. In 1872 the Wesleyan
Theological College of Montreal was established in connexion with McGill
University. In 1873 Wesley College was founded in Winnipeg, a unit of the
University of Manitoba. The Methodists also had a college in Newfoundland.[104]

Egerton Ryerson (1803–1882) was long the leading Methodist figure in education and as well was outstanding in other aspects of Canadian Methodism.[105]
He was born in Upper Canada, the son of a loyalist. In his late teens he was
converted and, to his father's intense disgust, became a Methodist. Later he was
a Methodist preacher, for a time an itinerant. He began the *Christian Guardian*.
He early and repeatedly tilted with Strachan on a number of issues, including
education and the clergy reserves: a vigorous advocate of the separation of
Church and state, he could not but be in opposition to the able and convinced
Anglican. For a few years he was secretary of the missionary society of his

[100] Shortt and Doughty, *op. cit.*, Vol. XI, pp. 310, 311; Walsh, *op. cit.*, pp. 215, 216.

[101] J. H. Riddell, *Methodism in the Middle West* (Toronto, The Ryerson Press, 1946, pp. xii,
371), pp. 1–318.

[102] *Centennial of Canadian Methodism*, pp. 257, 266–268.

[103] MacGillivray, *A Century of Protestant Missions in China (1807–1907)*, p. 113; George J.
Bond, *Our Share in China* (Toronto, The Missionary Society of the Methodist Church, 1911, pp.
268), *passim*.

[104] *Centennial of Canadian Methodism*, pp. 301–329.

[105] Ryerson, *The Story of My Life, passim*; Sissions, *Egerton Ryerson, His Life and Letters,
passim*; Landon, *op. cit.*, pp. 84 ff.

church. He became the first principal of Victoria College. From 1844 to 1876 he was superintendent of schools in Upper Canada. To study education he travelled extensively in the United States, England, and the Continent of Europe. In spite of opposition he gave to public education in Upper Canada the form which shaped it for many decades—thus paralleling the labours of Protestant clergymen which we have found in several of the states south of the border. He stood for universal, free, and compulsory primary and industrial education and for giving to religion and morality, but not to sectarianism, central place in the system. Active though he became in politics and education, religion never ceased to be his primary interest.

BAPTISTS

Baptists were not as prominent in British North America as in the United States. Yet, numerically a bad fourth, by 1914 they ranked after the Methodists, Presbyterians, and Anglicans as one of the largest Protestant denominations. As we have suggested, they had their origins as fruits of revivals in Nova Scotia in the second half of the eighteenth century. In 1800 an association was formed of nine Baptist churches, eight of them in Nova Scotia and one in New Brunswick. Free Baptists appeared, Arminian in theology and believing in open Communion. Loyalists accounted for the beginnings of Baptist churches in Upper Canada, also in the second half of the eighteenth century. In 1829 two Scottish ministers were induced to come to Canada and one of them organized (1830) the first Baptist Church in Montreal. In spite of ephemeral efforts, not until 1851 did the Baptists of Upper and Lower Canada achieve a continuing organization. Only in 1944 was the Baptist Federation of Canada formed, embracing the large majority of that denomination in the Dominion.[106]

Baptists spread into the West. In 1869 a deputation from the Baptists of Ontario went to the Northwest Territories, but not until 1873 was the first missionary sent to Manitoba. The enterprise grew, churches multiplied, and in 1907 the Baptist Convention of Western Canada was organized, which included the area from Manitoba to British Columbia.[107]

Baptists inaugurated missions in other countries. In 1845 a missionary was sent to Burma by the Baptists of the three Maritime Provinces. For some years contributions were made by the Baptists of Upper and Lower Canada through the American Baptist Missionary Union, but in 1866 a Canadian auxiliary was formed, followed in 1874 by a society independent of the United States. A mission was soon begun among the Telugus in India. In this the Baptists of the

[106] Short and Doughty, *op. cit.*, Vol. XI, pp. 347 ff.; Walsh, *op. cit.*, pp. 216–219; Levy, *The Baptists of the Maritime Provinces 1753–1946, passim;* Landon, *op. cit.*, pp. 100 ff.
[107] C. C. McLaurin, *Pioneering in Western Canada: A Story of the Baptists* (Calgary, C. C. McLaurin, 1939, pp. 401 ff.), pp. 32–107.

Maritimes joined in 1875, discontinuing their Burma effort. In 1897 a mission was opened in Bolivia.[108]

Baptists made provision for higher education and for the training of their ministry. The most prominent institutions were Acadia College, opened in 1839, and McMaster University, first in Toronto and later in Hamilton, Ontario, going back to 1860, but with a university charter granted in 1887. Brandon College, in Manitoba, opened in 1889, became affiliated with McMaster.[109]

SMALLER PROTESTANT AND EASTERN BODIES

Space does not permit more than the briefest mention of the smaller Protestant and Eastern bodies represented in British North America, and of these we must not extend our pages by a complete list. Congregationalism came to Nova Scotia from New England about 1760 but was greatly weakened by the exodus of pastors and people during the war in which the Thirteen Colonies achieved their independence. In Upper and Lower Canada Congregationalism was introduced both from England and from New England. Its great organizer was Henry Wilkes, from England, aided by the London Missionary Society. In Ontario it did not grow much after 1860. In 1906 the comprehensive Congregational Union of Canada was formed.[110] Lutherans remained a small minority but in 1901 numbered 94,100, over three times as many as Congregationalists. At the outset they were partly from the United States and partly from Europe. Some came to Nova Scotia from Pennsylvania in 1772. Those in the Maritimes were long allied with the Pittsburgh Synod, a connexion growing out of a mission begun in 1850. The Missouri Synod organized a district in Ontario in 1879. Other synods in the United States extended their operations to Canada.[111] The Quakers, a very small minority, arose first from immigration from New England, England, and the United States. In Upper Canada they found themselves in frontier conditions. In 1867 the Canada Yearly Meeting was formed and adopted as its discipline that of the mother Yearly Meeting of New York. Divisions developed, chiefly by contagion from the United States. An early one (1828) centred around the teaching of Elias Hicks. A second, in 1881, was partly over the adoption of revivalism.[112] When, in 1870, the Russian Government demanded military service of the Mennonites, pacifists, they refused it. Indeed, they had left Prussia for Russian territory in the previous century on the assurance that it would not be required of them. In the 1880's, encouraged by the grant of a large block of land in Manitoba by the Canadian Government together with a promise of exemption from military service and the guarantee of

[108] Shortt and Doughty, *op. cit.,* Vol. XI, pp. 358, 367.
[109] *Ibid.,* pp. 357, 368, 369, 374.
[110] *Ibid.,* pp. 379–384; Walsh, *op. cit.,* p. 220.
[111] Shortt and Doughty, *op. cit.,* Vol. XI, pp. 384–386; Walsh, *op. cit.,* p. 221.
[112] Dorland, *A History of the Society of Friends (Quakers) in Canada, passim.*

ther privileges, several thousand came from Russia and made continuing settlements.[113] In 1899 some thousands of Dukhobors reached Canada. Peter Verigin, who arrived late in 1902, became their leader. They settled on virgin land in Saskatchewan, lived their communal life, and, like the Mennonites, were granted exemption from military service. Later they divided. In 1909 Verigin led one company to new holdings in British Columbia. In their convictions and practices some of the Dukhobors ran afoul of Canadian law.[114] Other bodies and movements, most but not all of them entering from the United States, were the Church of Christ Scientist, the Seventh Day Adventists, the United Brethren, the Church of the Nazarene, the Disciples of Christ, the Churches of Christ, the Church of Jesus Christ of Latter Day Saints, the Reorganized Church of Jesus Christ of Latter Day Saints, the Evangelical Association, the Swedish Mission Covenant of America, the Church of the New Jerusalem, Jehovah's Witnesses, the Christadelphians, and various branches of the Plymouth Brethren.[115] Evangelists from the United States added Canada to their field: the most notable was Dwight L. Moody.[116]

Some movements were indigenous. Such was the one headed by Ralph Horner, who began within the Methodist Church but broke with it, largely on the issue of entire sanctification. The separation came in 1895.[117] In 1891 P. W. Philpott led a defection from the Salvation Army which carried with it many officers of that organiation and founded in several cities what were called Mission Churches.[118]

PROTESTANT MOVEMENTS MEET THE CHALLENGE OF THE REVOLUTIONARY AGE

Protestantism in British North America adopted or devised methods to meet the challenges brought by the rapidly changing conditions of the revolutionary age. Some were foreign in origin but had distinctive developments in Canada. Such were the Young Men's and Young Women's Christian Associations.[119] Such, too, were the Sunday Schools, the Young People's Society of Christian Endeavour, and the Epworth League. The Westminster Guild, later simply the

---

[113] S. K. Francis, *In Search of Utopia: the Mennonites in Manitoba* (Glencoe, Ill., The Free Press, 1955, pp. xv, 294), *passim;* Dawson, *Group Settlement. Ethnic Communities in Western Canada,* pp. 95–171.

[114] Harry B. Hawthorne, editor, *The Doukhobors of British Columbia* (Vancouver, The University of British Columbia, 1955, pp. xii, 288), *passim;* John P. Zubeck and Patricia Anne Solberg, *Doukhobors at War* (Toronto, The Ryerson Press, 1952, pp. ix, 250), pp. 1–98; Dawson, *op. cit.,* pp. 1–91.

[115] W. E. Mann, *Sect, Cult, and Church in Alberta* (University of Toronto Press, 1955, pp. xiii, 165), pp. 9–18; Shortt and Doughty, *op. cit.,* Vol. XI, pp. 394–400; Dawson, *op. cit.,* pp. 175–272.

[116] Clark, *op. cit.,* pp. 401, 402.

[117] *Ibid.,* pp. 416–418.

[118] *Ibid.,* pp. 427, 428.

[119] On the Young Men's Christian Association see Murray G. Ross, *The Y.M.C.A. in Canada, The Chronicle of a Century* (Toronto, The Ryerson Press, 1951).

Guild, was a Canadian variation of Christian Endeavour.[120] The temperance movement had the official support of more than one denomination.

A unique enterprise was that begun and long directed by Wilfred Grenfell Wilfred Thomason Grenfell '(1865–1940) was a physician who, during his student days in London, was deeply impressed by Moody and two Moody converts J. E. K. and C. T. Studd. For a time he devoted himself to the underprivileged boys of London and then shared in what the mission ships were doing for the fishermen on the North Sea. In 1891, learning of the needs of the fishermen on the north shores of Newfoundland and the bleak coast of Labrador, he began a mission to them. Practical, completely unselfish, athletic, courageous, he set himself to improve the lot of the hardy folk who made a precarious living in scattered, isolated settlements. His hospital ships and ultimately small hospitals on shore cared for the sick. He nurtured coöperative stores. He organized kindergartens, schools, and recreation, fought liquor dealers, and initiated fox farms, a sawmill, and orphanages. He sent scores of boys away for education. He obtained personnel and financial support from outside, and in 1912 the International Grenfell Association was incorporated to aid him.[121]

SUMMARY

The new nation which developed in the nineteenth century in British North America was largely the product of the revolutionary age. It was really two nations. The French element survived the British conquest of the preceding century, multiplied through a high birth rate, and clung to its inherited language and the Roman Catholic faith as symbols and bulwarks of its integrity. Beside it and beyond it an immigration poured in which was predominantly British, but with significant elements from the United States and the Continent of Europe. Especially in the last few decades before the events of July and August, 1914, brought the nineteenth century to a stormy end, large numbers from many nations peopled the prairie provinces of the West. By the latter half of the century a combination of political action and railroads and telegraphs—inventions of the revolutionary age—had welded into one all the vast area except Newfoundland and Labrador, and before the twentieth century had reached its halfway mark they were to be brought in. Here was a nation which on the eve of 1914 had a larger population than Scotland and Wales combined. In 1914 it had far more people than Denmark and Norway together and had more than Sweden. Because it began later, the frontier stage passed more quickly than in the United States. In the latter part of the century industrializa-

---

[120] McNeill, *The Presbyterian Church in Canada, 1875–1925*, pp. 172 ff.

[121] Of the extensive literature, see Wilfred Grenfell, *Forty Years for Labrador* (Boston, Houghton Mifflin Co., 1932, pp. 372); Wilfred Grenfell, *A Labrador Doctor. The Autobiography of Wilfred Thomason Grenfell* (Boston, Houghton Mifflin Co., 1919, pp. 441); Wilfred T. Grenfell, *Down North on the Labrador* (London, James Nisbet and Co., no date, pp. 229).

tion and urbanization proceeded apace, bringing with them some of the conditions and problems which marked them in other lands.

Christianity displayed great vitality in rising to the challenges posed by these developments. By the end of the century a much larger proportion of the population professed to have a religious affiliation than in the United States.

The Roman Catholic Church retained the allegiance of the overwhelming majority of the French Canadians and was vigorous in its internal life and its missionary outreach. It also held most of the nineteenth-century immigration who were by ancestry among its children. It faced difficulty in the rivalries between the French and the Irish, English-speaking as the latter were and intensely race-conscious as both groups were. It lost many of the Ruthenian Uniates.

Through immigration Protestants became the majority of the population, although not as large a majority as in the United States. In that Protestantism the Anglo-Saxon denominations were predominant. The most numerous were the Anglicans, the Presbyterians, and the Methodists, with the Baptists a less prominent fourth. In the course of the century the principle was established, after a long and at times bitter struggle, that no church was to be especially favoured by the state. Except in French Canada, primary education, supported by the government, was non-sectarian. More than in the huge neighbour to the south, the universities were secular state institutions. But associated with some of them were denominational colleges. Revivalism, introduced from the United States, was present, notably in frontier days, but was less characteristic of Protestantism than it was south of the border. Numbers of denominations and movements which originated in the United States entered but were not as prominent as in their native land. Somewhat paralleling the achievement of political unity, each major Protestant denominational family moved towards a nation-wide structure. The larger Canadian Protestant denominations were members of the Federal Council of the Churches of Christ in America, and some other organizations tied the Protestants of Canada and the United States together. The Protestants of Canada were experiencing less pain in adjusting themselves to the intellectual currents of the age than were those of the United States. Canadian Protestants, like Canadian Roman Catholics, were becoming active in spreading the faith to other lands.

The new nation was being profoundly moulded by Christianity. Its Christianity differed from that on the other side of the Atlantic. Like the Christianity of the United States, it was activistic and did not put forth as marked efforts to meet in fresh ways the intellectual currents of the day as did the Christianity of Western Europe. Nor did the Protestantism of Canada show as much intellectual ferment or spawn as many new denominations and movements as did that of the United States. Yet Canadian Christianity gave increasing evidence of approaching a maturity that would deal constructively with all phases of the revolution in the midst of which it was set. Almost every aspect of the life of Canada bore the imprint of the faith whether that Canada was French or Anglo-Saxon. This was true of moral standards, of the family, and of education. Politically Canada was largely the child of Anglo-Saxon democracy. That democracy, as we have repeatedly seen, was deeply indebted to Protestantism, and especially to what in the broad sense is described as Puritanism and Evangelicalism. The Canadian dream was not identical with what we have called the American dream, but both were what they were in no small degree because of Christianity and especially of Protestantism.

CHAPTER XI

Greenland; The British, Danish, and Dutch West Indies; The British and Dutch Enclaves on the Mainland of South and Central America

I N THE Western Hemisphere, mostly between North and South America, were islands and mainland possessions of powers which were traditionally Protestant. Greenland, in the extreme north, was also under Protestant rule. Most of the islands were in the Caribbean Sea and the others, the Bahamas and Bermuda, had similarities to them. Britain had the lion's share, but the Danes held Greenland and the Virgin Islands and the Dutch owned some of the Leeward Islands and of the Lesser Antilles. On the mainland were British Honduras and British and Dutch Guiana.

On most of the islands and on all of the mainland possessions Europeans were only minorities. In Greenland Eskimos were in the majority. On the West Indian islands Negroes were predominant, with Hindus a substantial minority on Trinidad. Negroes were also large elements in British and Dutch Guiana. In British Guiana Hindus were numerous, and Javanese were a sixth or a seventh of the population of Dutch Guiana. British Guiana had a few thousand Portuguese, mainly from Madeira. A few Chinese were found, chiefly in British Guiana. Aborigines were minorities in British and Dutch Guiana and, either as purebloods or as mixtures with Negro and some white blood, in British Honduras.

The presence of the Negroes, Hindus, Javanese, Portuguese, and Chinese was due to the demand for cheap labour. Only through that labour could the dominant white minority hope to make a living.

The labour problem was complicated by the abolition of slavery. Within the British possessions it came in 1834 as the result of legislation enacted the preceding year. That legislation had been put on the statute books largely because of pressure from the Christian conscience sensitized by Evangelical Protestantism. In response to the rising anti-slavery conviction in Western Christendom, a conviction arising partly from the Christian conscience and partly from humanitarian sentiment which was directly or indirectly the fruit of Christianity, emancipation in the Danish islands occurred in 1848 and in the Dutch islands and Surinam (Dutch Guiana) in 1863. With the removal of the compulsion of slavery, many of the Negroes proved undependable as labour. To meet the growing demand of the white plantation owners labourers were imported from several regions, often under contracts which were little better than slavery. From them arose the Indian, East Indian, Chinese, and Portuguese elements.

The challenge which the situation presented to Christianity was obvious. It was to make the inherited faith of the white minority more than nominal, to win to the faith the non-white majority, non-Christian by ancestry, to improve the moral character of the population, and to raise the educational and economic level of the underprivileged. Roman Catholics and Protestants shared in meeting the challenge. Since the governments were predominantly or entirely of their branch of the faith, Protestants were more active in most of the islands and on the mainland than were Roman Catholics.

In the brief space which is all that we can allot, we must content ourselves mainly with generalizations and a few concrete facts, and these only for some of the islands and mainland possessions.

Because of the arctic climate and the ice which covered most of the land, the population of the great island of Greenland was sparse. It was scattered along the south shores, in 1911 was between 13,000 and 14,000, and was made up mostly of Eskimos or of the offspring of unions between Danes and Eskimos. Missions begun in the preceding century by Egede and the Moravians were continued, and by the close of the nineteenth century almost all the scanty population were professed Christians. Thanks to the efforts of the missionaries and the teachers trained by them, the majority were literate. In 1900 the Moravians withdrew and the Danish state church was left the sole ecclesiastical body.[1]

The Virgin Islands, held by Denmark from their purchase in 1733 to their sale to the United States in 1916, had a predominantly Negro population which by the end of the nineteenth century totalled a little more than 30,000. Less than a fourth were Roman Catholics.[2] A number were Anglicans.[3] Somewhat fewer were Lutherans, the result of long-continued missions. The Moravians carried on the missions which they began in the eighteenth century. To prepare for emancipation the government inaugurated schools for the slaves and entrusted them to the Moravians, but with the provision that the instruction be non-sectarian. Although for a time the membership in the Moravian churches increased, by the end of the century it had declined on at least one of the

---

[1] Schulze, 200 Jahre Brüdermission, Vol. II, pp. 5, 7, 12, 15, 22–26, 35, 36, 38–43; Greenland (London, H. M. Stationery Office, 1920, pp. 37), pp. 5, 6, 13, 15; Knud Rasmussen, The People of the Polar North. A Record Compiled from the Danish Originals and Edited by G. Herring (London, Kegan Paul, Trench, Trubner & Co., 1908, pp. xix, 358), pp. 99 ff., 285, 289, 290.

[2] The Catholic Encyclopedia, Vol. XIII, p. 191.

[3] Thompson, Into All Lands, pp. 171, 525.

islands and moral conditions were said to have deteriorated, with a high percentage of illegitimate births.[4]

The Dutch West Indian Islands, some off the coast of Venezuela and some east of the Virgin Islands, at the end of the nineteenth century had a population of slightly less than 52,000. The largest island was Curaçao, near Venezuela. Protestantism was confined chiefly to those of Dutch blood. The Negroes, who constituted the large majority of the population, were overwhelmingly Roman Catholic. That form of the faith made substantial gains in the nineteenth century, in the latter half chiefly under the Dutch Dominicans.[5]

The largest of the British West Indies, both in area and population, was Jamaica. By the end of the nineteenth century its inhabitants numbered not far from 900,000. They were mostly Negroes. From the time of the English occupation (1655) until 1792 the Roman Catholic Church was proscribed. Even when toleration came, the numbers of Roman Catholics remained small. Jesuits arrived in 1837, first from the English province. Then, in 1894, responsibility was transferred to the Maryland-New York province of the Society of Jesus. Sisters of more than one congregation assisted.[6]

Until 1870 the Church of England in Jamaica was established. At the outset of the nineteenth century, as was to be expected from existing conditions in the mother country, the moral and religious quality of that church was low. Most of the whites were profligate and inattentive to religious observances, and the clergy did little to better the situation. But in the nineteenth century, partly as a reflexion of what was taking place in England, improvement was seen. In 1797 the Assembly made larger financial provision for the clergy and church buildings and required the former to devote a portion of each Sunday to the instruction of the slaves. In 1815 the Assembly set about increasing the number of the clergy and giving more instruction to the slaves. This was in part to counter the activities of the Methodists. In 1824 a bishopric was created which bore the name of Jamaica and included that island in its jurisdiction. To offset the Nonconformist missionaries, regarded as responsible for discontent among the slaves, on the eve of emancipation some white colonists formed the Colonial Church Union. In 1861 the Jamaica Home and Foreign Missionary Society was organized. Disestablishment at first seemed a handicap, but after the necessary though painful adjustment the church gained. A theological college was maintained to train an indigenous clergy. Mission stations multiplied and a mission

[4] Schulze, *op. cit.,* Vol. II, pp. 134–142; Jens Larsen, *Virgin Islands Story: A History of the Lutheran Church, Other Churches, Slavery, Education, and Culture in the Danish West Indies, now the Virgin Islands* (Philadelphia, Muhlenberg Press, 1950, pp. xii, 250), *passim.*

[5] *The Catholic Encyclopedia,* Vol. IV, pp. 569, 570; C. P. Amelunxen, *De Geschiedenis van Curaçao* (no place or publisher, preface 1929, pp. 227), pp. 169–174, 178.

[6] Francis X. Delany, *A History of the Catholic Church in Jamaica* (New York, Jesuit Mission Press, 1930, pp. xi, 292), *passim;* Descamps, *Histoire Générale Comparée des Missions,* p. 580.

was conducted in Africa.[7] Assistance came from the Church Missionary Society,[8] the Society for the Propagation of the Gospel in Foreign Parts,[9] and the Society for Promoting Christian Knowledge,[10] but before the latter part of the century the first two discontinued most of their aid and the church was dependent for support chiefly on its members in the island.

If all of their branches were included, Baptists were ultimately more numerous in Jamaica than any other denomination.[11] Their appeal was chiefly to the Negroes and in the fore part of the century that brought down on them the criticism of some who feared that Negro unrest and rebellion would result. On the coming of emancipation, Baptist missionaries fought the apprentice system as a continuation of slavery in disguise. In 1842 the Jamaica Baptist Missionary Society was organized with the West Indies as its objective. Beginning in 1843 a number went from Jamaica to West Africa under the (English) Baptist Missionary Society. With the aid of the latter a school was begun in the 1840's to train Jamaicans for the ministry.[12]

Methodists were also numerous in Jamaica. The indefatigable Thomas Coke, who did much to initiate the world-wide spread of Methodism, visited the island in 1789. Resident missionaries followed and directed their efforts primarily to the Negroes. Like the Baptists, they were accused of undermining the slavery on which the prosperity of the island was regarded as depending. The whites tended to leave the Methodist churches and the latter to be entirely Negro. In the 1880's the Methodism of Jamaica became independent of that in the British Isles and a conference was formed with George Sargeant as its president. Sargeant had been responsible for the opening, in 1875, of a high school and a theological college for the education of indigenous leadership. In 1904, at the request of the Annual Conference, the Wesleyan Methodist Missionary Society reluctantly resumed charge and reinforcements to the clergy were renewed from England.[13]

Although the Anglicans, Baptists, and Methodists were the largest of the denominations on Jamaica, a number of others were represented. Among them were the Moravians, who had been there longer than the latter two, Presby-

---

[7] J. B. Ellis, *The Diocese of Jamaica. A Short Account of Its History, Growth and Organization* (London, Society for Promoting Christian Knowledge, 1913, pp. 237), pp. 46, 53–57, 60–68, 96, 139 ff., 155.

[8] Stock, *The History of the Church Missionary Society*, Vol. I, pp. 346, 347.

[9] Thompson, *op. cit.*, pp. 274, 275.

[10] Allen and McClure, *Two Hundred Years*, pp. 373, 445, 521.

[11] Price, *Bananaland*, p. 12.

[12] Ernest A. Payne, *Freedom in Jamaica: Some Chapters in the Story of the Baptist Foreign Missionary Society* (London, The Carey Press, 1933, pp. 112), *passim*.

[13] Peter Duncan, *A Narrative of the Wesleyan Mission to Jamaica: with Occasional Remarks on the State of Society in that Colony* (London, Partridge and Oakey, 1849, pp. xii, 396), *passim*; Peter Samuel, *The Wesleyan-Methodist Missions in Jamaica and Honduras Delineated* (London, 1850, pp. ix, 320), *passim*; Findlay and Holdsworth, *The History of the Wesleyan Methodist Missionary Society*, Vol. II, pp. 63–132, 358, 394–398, 444–473.

terians of more than one Scottish branch, Congregationalists, both from the United States and from Great Britain, the Disciples of Christ, the Seventh Day Adventists, the African Methodist Episcopal Church, the Church of God, and several others, including some of Negro origin.[14]

What resulted from these multiform efforts to win the population and to mould the life of Jamaica? By the early years of the twentieth century nearly every home had some kind of connexion with a church or a Sunday School. Yet the permeation of the faith and conformity to its standards were uneven. A large proportion of the children were born out of wedlock. The African heritage of witchcraft and paganism persisted in distorted forms, some of them mixed with elements derived from Christianity. Much of this situation was an aftermath of slavery and the fruit of adverse economic conditions.[15] On the positive side were some lives of noble character, the aid given to the adjustment of freedmen to their new status, the raising of the level of education and leadership, and Negro missionaries to Africa.[16]

The second largest island in the British West Indies was Trinidad. Discovered by Columbus, it remained under Spanish rule for three centuries, until its capture by the British in 1797 during the wars of the French Revolution and Napoleon and its formal annexation in 1802. Since the possession of Jamaica by the English dated from the middle of the seventeenth century and Trinidad had been in their hands a much shorter time, the Roman Catholic Church was much stronger than on the other island. At the outset of the British occupation support was given by the government to the Roman Catholic Church. In 1820 the Port of Spain, the capital, was made the seat of a bishop and later the see was raised to an archiepiscopate. Most of the clergy were not native-born but were from England, Ireland, and France.[17] After the coming of British rule, Protestantism was introduced. The Church of England grew, assisted by the Society for the Propagation of the Gospel in Foreign Parts and the Church Missionary Society. After the disestablishment of the church (1870), the island was made a separate diocese. The Scottish Presbyterians sent their first missionary in 1836 and the Canadian Presbyterians in 1867. The Methodists were few and largely immigrants from other islands.[18]

The Church of England was represented in most of the British West Indies. In 1883 it was given the status of an ecclesiastical province with an archbishop

---

[14] Latourette, *A History of the Expansion of Christianity*, Vol. V, pp. 54–56; George McNeill, *The West Indies* (Edinburgh, The Foreign Missions Committee of the United Free Church of Scotland, 1911, pp. 92), *passim*.

[15] Price, *op. cit.*, pp. 12, 25, 154–166; Joseph J. Williams, *Voodoos and Obeahs. Phases of West India Witchcraft* (New York, Dial Press, 1933, pp. xvii, 257), pp. 142, 208, 215, 216.

[16] Price, *op. cit.*, pp. 134–138.

[17] *The Catholic Encyclopedia*, Vol. XII, p. 291; Marie-Joseph Guillet, *Les Dominicains Français a l'Ile de la Trinidad (1864–1895)* (Tours, Marcel Cattier, 1926, pp. vi, 458), *passim*.

[18] Latourette, *op. cit.*, Vol. V, pp. 58, 59.

as its head, but bound to Canterbury.[19] The Church of England was especially strong on the densely populated and predominantly Negro Barbados. Here was Codrington College, devoted to the training of clergy for the West Indies and associated with a plantation on which a significant experiment in Christian philanthropy was pursued.[20]

Methodism was also widely represented in the West Indies, mainly among the Negroes.[21]

In British Guiana, formerly Dutch, but taken by England during the wars of the French Revolution and Napoleon, the Church of England experienced a rapid growth in the nineteenth century. Not until 1899 was it disestablished. Other forms of the faith, including especially Presbyterianism, introduced as it was from Scotland, received financial aid from the state. British Methodism and Congregationalism were strongly represented and by 1914 some other denominations, among them the Seventh Day Adventists, had come. In that year the overwhelming majority of the Negroes and Chinese and, of course, the ruling white minority were ostensibly Christian, most of them Protestants, and the Portuguese labourers were also in the Christian ranks, as Roman Catholics. The labourers from India largely remained non-Christian.[22]

In Dutch Guiana, with a smaller population, the largest Christian bodies were the Moravians, by far the most numerous, the Roman Catholics, the Dutch Reformed, and the Lutherans, in the order named.[23]

In the sparsely populated British Honduras, in the nineteenth century Christianity was represented mainly by the Roman Catholic Church, which from 1888 had there a separate prefecture apostolic, and by Protestant minorities. The Roman Catholicism was badly mixed with superstition of pagan origin but was improving in quality.[24]

In the islands and the mainland enclaves with which this brief chapter has dealt we have an example of a pre-nineteenth-century period of the revolutionary age complicated by the nineteenth-century stage. Here was a situation and here were problems inherited from the period of the expansion of Western Christendom which began in the fifteenth century and in which the chief sufferers were non-Occidental peoples. In that period the indigenous peoples of the West Indian islands all but disappeared and their places were taken by slaves imported from Africa. Indigenous folk survived in Greenland, British

---

[19] Thompson, *op. cit.*, p. 286; Neill, *Anglicanism*, pp. 313–315.

[20] Benjamin C. O'Rorke, *Our Opportunity in the West Indies* (Westminster, Society for the Propagation of the Gospel in Foreign Parts, 1913, pp. 136), pp. 89 ff.; Frank J. Klingberg, editor, *Codrington Chronicle, an Experiment in Anglican Altruism on a Barbados Plantation, 1710–1834* (Berkeley, University of California Press, 1949, pp. vii, 157), *passim*.

[21] Findlay and Holdsworth, *op. cit.*, Vol. II, pp. 133 ff.

[22] Latourette, *op. cit.*, Vol. V, pp. 63–65.

[23] *Ibid.*, pp. 65, 66; H. Weiss, *"Ons Suriname"* (The Hague, Boekhandel van den Zendings-Studie-Rad, preface 1911, pp. 186), *passim*.

[24] Latourette, *op. cit.*, Vol. V, pp. 61, 62.

Honduras, and the Guianas, but in small numbers. In the nineteenth century Hindus, Javanese, and some Portuguese and Chinese were added. The Christian conscience, acting directly or indirectly, brought an end to slavery. The large majority of the former bondsmen were won to an acceptance of the Christian faith. However, that acceptance, while it raised the religious, moral, and educational level of the freedmen, did not eliminate all the ills which had accompanied servitude. Improvements were made as a phase of the general quickening and advance of Christianity in the nineteenth century, but the problems inherited from the fifteenth, sixteenth, seventeenth, and eighteenth centuries were only partially resolved.

CHAPTER XII

Latin America

A^s we pass to a vast area of which the Danish, Dutch, and British possessions in the West Indies and on the mainland of South and Central America constituted but minor fringes, we come to major challenges to Christianity.

Some of the challenges were inherited from the pre-nineteenth-century stages of the revolution which issued from Western Christendom. Here was the major portion of the globe which had been occupied by Spain and Portugal in the vast explosion of conquest from the Iberian Peninsula in the fifteenth, sixteenth, and seventeenth centuries. In the eighteenth century the borders of the territories affected continued to be pushed forward, although more slowly. Another Latin power, France, held a few islands in the West Indies, chiefly the western portion of the island of Haiti, and the inhospitable Cayenne, the eastern small third of Guiana.

In that huge portion of the land surface of the globe, in the nineteenth century new nations emerged from colonial empires and in the twentieth century, endowed by nature with great natural resources, they were burgeoning in wealth and population. The largest of these nations, Brazil, the creation of the Portuguese, embraced more square miles than the United States of America without Alaska. In the southern part of South America, mostly south of the Tropic of Capricorn, the population, swelled by nineteenth-century immigration from Western Europe, in the year 1914 was predominantly white. In most of the other nations the pre-Columbian peoples constituted a majority, dominated by white minorities, with mestizos a substantial element and sometimes sharing in the rule. Here and there, mostly in the tropics, were large Negro elements, descendants of slaves brought from Africa.

Nineteenth- and twentieth-century Latin America posed a challenging problem to Christianity and especially to the Roman Catholic Church. The region had been the scene of the largest-scale missionary effort of that church in the preceding three centuries. To it more of its missionaries had gone than to all the rest of the world in that period. Here was the field to which the Catholic Reformation had directed its major energies for the geographic expansion of the faith. As a result the majority of the population professed allegiance to the Roman Catholic Church. Non-Christian minorities remained. They were mostly of Indians and in general in jungles, upper reaches of rivers, mountain fastnesses, and on other frontiers of white occupation. In them late in the eighteenth century the borders of the faith were still being pushed forward. The expulsion of the Jesuits from the Spanish and Protuguese domains and the decline of missionary conviction brought by the Enlightenment slowed down the advance, but on the eve of the nineteenth century it was continuing. The elements of the population with white blood in their veins, whether pure or mixed, were ostensibly Christian and those of pre-Columbian ancestry had mostly conformed. The Roman Catholic Church, too, had begun and maintained the oldest universities in the Western Hemisphere and in other ways had furthered education. An indigenous body of clergy was emerging. Under the altered conditions brought by the nineteenth- and twentieth-century stage of the revolutionary era would the faith continue with mounting vitality? Would the enhanced vigour be seen which we have noted in the Roman Catholic Church in Europe, the United States of America, and British North America?

One of the most thought-provoking facts about the course of Christianity in the nineteenth century was the anemic condition of the Roman Catholic Church in Latin America. Although the large majority of the population were baptized and regarded themselves as Catholics, Latin America did not produce enough priests to care for them. The Church still depended on Europe to make good the deficit and to provide most of the missionaries to the remaining non-Christians. Nor did the Latin American Church produce more than a handful of missionaries to other countries. It was parasitic and a liability rather than an asset to the Roman Catholic Church as a whole. It proved less resistant to the corrosive scepticism and the militant anti-clericalism which issued from Western Europe than did that church in Europe. What caused this weakness?

Under these circumstances would Protestantism move in to repair the distress of Christianity? Protestantism was very weak in Spain and Portugal. The Inquisition had stamped out the beginnings of the sixteenth century and only scant footholds had been obtained in the nineteenth century. Similarly, in Latin America the Inquisition had nipped in the bud any incipient Protestantism before the nineteenth century. To the Spaniards and Portuguese Protestantism seemed culturally alien. Could it gain a foothold except through immigration? Would movements akin to it arise spontaneously? Could it be given productive rootage by missionaries from abroad?

The questions propounded by the situation would not be quickly answered. The nineteenth century only gave hints at the outcome. The twentieth century would shed more light, but, as is the way with history, the future would even then be hid. Only trends could be noted, and without assurance that they would continue.

As we venture on an attempt to summarize the course of Christianity in Latin America in the nineteenth century we must first remind ourselves of the conditions on the eve of that era—for it was an era. Then we must seek to draw a comprehensive even though brief picture of the political changes which marked the century. We must note the economic conditions, the shifts in population, and especially the intellectual currents which played on the region as a whole. Then we must say something of the over-all developments in the Roman Catholic Church. Next will come a brief comprehensive account of the entrance of Protestantism. That must be followed by a rapid country-by-country survey of the record of the Roman Catholic Church and of the early developments in Protestantism.

THE EVE OF THE NINETEENTH CENTURY

A striking feature of Latin America on the eve of the nineteenth century was the colonial policies of Spain and Portugal. They were autocratic, paternalistic, and directed from the mother countries by the appointees of the crown. This was especially true of the stronger country, Spain. Most of the officials in Spanish America were Spanish born and reared. Some creoles, American-born Spaniards, were appointed: one of the many viceroys had been from their ranks. A large proportion of the members of the *cabildos,* or city councils, were creoles. For the most part, however, the civil officials were from Spain and numbers had bought their offices from impecunious kings, hard pressed for money for their wars or luxuries. Portugal's regime was not as strict as that of Spain. It was more tenuous, for Portugal suffered from mounting poverty and weakness and its chief colonial ventures were in Asia and the East Indies.

In Spanish America society was sharply stratified, with Spanish born peninsulares at the top; next the creoles, holders of the less important offices, landowners, business and professional men, and artisans; then the mestizos, usually descendants of irregular unions; fourth the Indians, thousands of whom laboured in mines and plantations in conditions little better than slavery and that in spite of the Laws of the Indies placed on the statute books by the pressure of the Christian conscience; and lowest of all the Negroes, slaves of African provenance.

Brazil was much more thinly settled than Mexico and Peru, the centres of pre-Columbian civilizations and of Spanish power. Its population was chiefly on the coast. White, Indian, and Negro blood freely intermingled. The stratification was not racial but economic and was relatively fluid. The white stock tended to deteriorate through distaste for labour, improper diet, and sexual indulgence.

The economy of colonial Spanish America depended on gold and silver mines, farming, cattle, and industry. Foreign trade was strictly controlled and in principle was confined to closely regulated channels. In practice clandestine commerce flourished, partly through Spanish interlopers and partly by way of English, Dutch, French, and Portuguese ships.

Brazil made its living partly from agriculture, much of it devoted to producing sugar for export, and partly, although later than Spanish America, from gold-mining. Diamonds were also found. In theory foreign trade was controlled from Lisbon, but in fact the monopoly was more easily evaded than was that of the mother country in Spanish America.

In Spanish America a score or more of universities, the chief in Mexico City and Lima, capped the educational structure and encouraged culture. However, they were of varying quality and were largely for the training of the clergy. Literature, art, and architecture were distinctly behind those of Spain. Yet they were present, and printing presses multiplied. Before the end of the eighteenth century the Enlightenment was beginning to make itself felt.

The intellectual life of Brazil was much more meagre than that of Spanish America. In the colonial period Brazil did not have a university and its few schools were for the privileged. It possessed no printing press until 1808.[1]

The record of the Roman Catholic Church in colonial Spanish America was mixed. On the one hand were zeal and heroism in winning the Indians to the faith. The mission was the characteristic frontier enterprise, rather than the farm or the fur trade as in British and French America. The large majority of the Indians were brought into the Roman Catholic Church. In the thickly populated Mexico and Peru this was by mass conversion. On the more sparsely settled fringes and in the river valleys and plains, as on the Orinoco and in Paraguay, it was mainly through settled communities gathered by the patient labour of missionaries. The Indians had in the missionaries champions who fought against their exploitation by the owners of plantations and mines. Yet much of the conversion was superficial, and superstition and thinly veiled paganism survived. Many of the clergy were unworthy of their calling. Sometimes the home government used America as a dumping ground for priests who had caused trouble in Spain. Indeed, the Inquisition, formally introduced in 1569, devoted much of its attention to self-seeking and immoral priests. Moreover, by successive Papal bulls, Rome early granted to the crown the right of patronage (*real patronato de las Indias*), which conceded to the king more power over the Church in the colonies than that, already great, which he possessed in Spain. The crown was given the authority to appoint all the clergy, from bishops and archbishops to those in the humblest posts, and to determine such matters as the location and erection of churches and monasteries. In theory appointments were subject to the approval of Rome, but in practice that restriction was usually ignored. Without royal permission no missionary could come to the New World or, once there, could leave. Missions were largely supported financially by the crown. Only slowly were men born in America admitted to the clerical ranks. Indians and mestizos were long excluded. Yet by the end of the eighteenth century a majority of the bishops in Spanish America were from the colonies,

[1] Herring, *A History of Latin America*, pp. 155–168, 187–217, 225–227, 230–240.

most of them creoles.[2] The Church became very wealthy. It was said that near the end of the colonial era the Church owned one-half of all productive real estate in Mexico. One must add that it maintained many schools and charities.[3]

In Brazil the Roman Catholic record before the nineteenth century was also mixed. The Jesuits were relatively more active than in Spanish America, both in converting the Indians and in seeking to protect them against exploitation by the colonists. Other orders were also represented. Here, too, the crown had the right of patronage and through it exercised absolute control over appointments. The ranks of the seculars were often recruited from the dregs of the priesthood in Portugal. Until 1676 and 1677 Brazil had only one bishop, and while in those years the see of São Salvador (Bahia) was raised to metropolitan rank with three dioceses under it, the four were scarcely sufficient for adequate care of the vast area. In 1759 the suppression of the Society of Jesus in the Portuguese domains dealt a severe blow to the Church.[4] Because the Jesuits were more prominent—as contrasted with Franciscans and Dominicans—than in Spanish America, their departure was a more serious blow to Christianity in Brazil than in the Spanish domains.

Although progress was being made towards recruiting and educating an indigenous clergy, especially in Spanish America, Europe was still the chief source. The interruption of political independence came before either Spanish or Portuguese America was producing enough priests to care for the professedly Roman Catholic population.

THE COMING OF POLITICAL INDEPENDENCE

The French Revolution and the Napoleonic Wars initiated revolutionary changes in Latin America. They had as their aftermath the political independence of the region. Political independence, often closely associated with the influx of revolutionary political thought, was not achieved quickly for all the region. Steps toward it began a few years before 1815. Haiti, Mexico, Central America, Spanish South America, and Brazil early attained the goal, but Cuba did not become free of Spanish rule until 1898.

The independence of Spanish America was largely the work of creoles in revolt against the rule of the Spanish-born whites, but in places it was supported by Indians and mestizos and was stimulated by contagion with the ideas

---

[2] Huonder, *Der einheimische Klerus in den Heidenländern*, pp. 20–38; Ryan, *The Church in the South American Republics*, pp. 19–24; *Recopilación de Leyes de los Reinos de las Indias* (Madrid, Boix, 4 vols., 1841), Book I, Title 6; Mecham, *Church and State in Latin America*, pp. 2, 11–24, 29, 38–44; Latourette, *A History of the Expansion of Christianity*, Vol. III, pp. 87, 88–102; Herring, *op. cit.*, pp. 169–186.

[3] Mecham, *op. cit.* pp. 46–49.

[4] Latourette, *op. cit.*, Vol. III, pp. 160–167.

of the Enlightenment,[5] the French Revolution, and the successful revolt of the Thirteen Colonies which created the United States of America.

Preliminary uprisings gave indication of a basic unrest among the underprivileged. In 1780 a revolt broke out in Peru led by Tupac Amaru, legal heir of the Incas, who had been educated by the Jesuits and had been given a Spanish title. Tupac Amaru championed the grievously oppressed Indians. His movement was suppressed in a blood bath, but not until many Spaniards had also been killed by the outraged aborigines. The news of the outbreak of the French Revolution provoked riots among the mulattoes and Negroes on the island of Haiti. The scene was confused. Toussaint l'Ouverture, grandson of an African chief and formerly a slave but now wealthy, assumed the leadership and by 1801 was master of most of the island—the eastern portion, Spanish, as well as the western portion, French. An expedition sent by Napoleon forced Toussaint's surrender and he died in a French prison (1803), but in 1804 the French portion of the island won its independence. The Spanish eastern portion had a chequered history. For a time Spain reasserted her authority, but she was forced out in 1821. A republic was proclaimed which fell victim the following year to the president of Haiti. In 1844 the Dominican Republic was founded, to be annexed again by Spain in 1861. Spanish rule finally ended in 1865. In 1788 Tiradentes led the workers in Minas Geraes, in Southern Brazil, in demanding the emancipation of the slaves and national independence. The year 1792 saw the suppression of the rebellion and the execution of its leader.

In Mexico the initial steps towards independence were taken by a priest, Miguel Hidalgo y Costilla (1753–1811). Born and educated in America, he had read the French philosophers, especially Rousseau, and had joined the Masons. In a village pastorate to which he had been banished because of his radical views he learned several Indian dialects and helped his flock improve their vineyards, plant mulberry trees to feed silkworms, and establish simple industries. He fostered an orchestra. In 1810 he raised the standard of revolt. His followers were mostly Indians, but some were mestizos and a few were creoles. For a time he seemed to sweep all before him. He was especially intent on freeing the underprivileged from oppression by the Spaniards. Theoretically he was loyal to Ferdinand VII, whom Napoleon had ousted from the throne, and was zealous for religion. But he proved deficient as an organizer and military leader; he was captured by treachery and shot.[6]

One of Hidalgo's lieutenants, José María Morelos, carried on the struggle. A poorly educated mestizo, a priest, he proved to be an able soldier and administrator. In 1813, in control of much of the southern part of the country, he de-

---

[5] Arthur P. Whitaker, editor, *Latin America and the Enlightenment* (New York, D. Appleton-Century Co., 1942, pp. xiii, 130), *passim*.

[6] Herring, *op. cit.*, pp. 254, 255; Romanell, *Making of the Mexican Mind*, pp. 36, 37; Kelley and Byam, *Blood-Drenched Altars*, pp. 152–158.

clared Mexico independent and in 1814 published a constitution. He, too, was eventually taken by the Spaniards and shot (December 22, 1815). Yet guerrilla warfare continued.

Then came another kind of movement. The promulgation in Spain of the liberal constitution of 1820 alarmed the higher clergy and the wealthy creoles. The leadershsip was seized by the ambitious, unprincipled, and wealthy creole Augustin de Iturbide (1783–1824). His programme called for the establishment of the Roman Catholic Church, independence, and equal rights for those born in Europe and America. He took Mexico City in 1821 and independence was ostensibly won. The following year he had himself proclaimed emperor. But he proved incompetent, was deposed and exiled, and on his return was shot. Independence was preserved, but under shifting regimes.[7]

In Spanish South America the chief architects of independence were Simón Bolívar (1783–1830) and José de San Martín (1778–1850). To Bolívar was chiefly due the independence of Venezuela, Colombia, and Ecuador, and he shared in winning that of Bolivia and Peru. San Martín was the liberator of Argentina and Chile and in 1821 proclaimed in Lima the independence of Peru.

Bolívar, born in Caracas in a wealthy creole family, had as a tutor an admirer of Rousseau who took *Émile* as his guide for the education of his charge. Going to Europe in his late teens, he continued his admiration for Rousseau, read Hobbes, and was much influenced by Spinoza. Outwardly he conformed to the Roman Catholic Church, but he could scarcely be called religious. In 1809, when he was back in Venezuela, a junta was formed in Caracas by the creoles which professed to exercise authority in the name of Ferdinand VII. It proclaimed equal treatment of Spaniards and Americans, the abolishment of Indian tribute, the end of the importation of slaves, and other reforms in line with ideas derived from revolutionary sources in Europe. In 1811 a congress declared Venezuela independent, but it was not until 1823, after a number of reverses and considerable fighting, that the last royalist forces were dislodged. In 1819 Bolívar won a battle that ensured the independence of New Granada (the later Colombia), and was acclaimed there, as in Venezuela, as the Liberator. He dreamed of bringing together Venezuela, New Granada, Ecuador, and Peru into one state, Gran Colombia. He proved victorious in Ecuador, met San Martín, and was greeted with enthusiasm in Lima. The decisive blow was given to the royalist forces near Ayachucho in Peru in December, 1824. Factions, local particularisms, and corruption frustrated the dream of Gran Colombia, and Bolívar died, worn out, late in 1830, after receiving the last rites of the Church from a friendly bishop.[8]

[7] William Spencer Robertson, *Iturbide of Mexico* (Durham, N.C., Duke University Press, 1952, pp. ix, 361), *passim*.

[8] F. Loraine Petre, *Simon Bolivar, "El Liberator," A Life of the Chief Leader in the Revolt against Spain in Venezuela, New Granada, and Peru* (London, John Lane, 1910, pp. xv, 459),

San Martín was a striking contrast to Bolívar. Like the latter he was born in America of Spanish stock, like him he was responsible for freeing a large part of South America from Spanish rule, and like him he died a disappointed man. But there the resemblance stops. San Martín was a soldier by training and had served in the army in Spain. The creoles of Buenos Aires had long been restive under Spanish rule and had thrived on an illicit foreign trade, chiefly with the English. In 1810, because of the unseating of Ferdinand, a junta was set up in his name and dominated by creoles. In 1816 a constitution was adopted and independence declared. In 1812, a member of a branch of the Masons, convinced of the necessity of independence, San Martín returned to Argentina. There he offered his services to the government. In 1814 he was made commander of its forces. In 1817 he led his army across the Andes into Chile, routed the Spaniards, and was hailed in Santiago as deliverer. He moved on to Peru and in 1821 entered Lima and declared the independence of the country. After meeting Bolívar he withdrew, returned to Chile and Argentina, and, discouraged by the civil strife, took refuge on the other side of the Atlantic. There he died, unhonoured except by a few friends.[9]

Even to name the other figures and to outline the details of the struggles which issued in the independence of Spanish America would carry us far beyond the proper limits of this chapter. Before the nineteenth century had half spent its course Spain had lost all of her once magnificent American empire except Cuba and Puerto Rico. Her ties with these were severed as a result of war with the United States in 1898. All the fragments of her empire except Puerto Rico ultimately became republics. In all the struggles the revolutionary political ideas of the age that had been formulated in Europe had a part. But they were mingled with other elements—personal ambitions and rivalries, regional and local particularisms, and economic conditions. To few if any of them did antagonism to Christianity contribute. Much indifference existed, but the Roman Catholic Church and its faith were accepted. Bolívar advocated the separation of Church and state but he never repudiated the Roman Catholic faith. San Martín stood for Roman Catholicism as the state religion.[10] Anticlericalism developed and was chronic throughout most of the century. Many, yielding to intellectual currents issuing from Europe, became thorough sceptics, but except for Protestant, Orthodox, and Jewish immigrants and the pagan Indians on the frontiers of Western civilization the vast majority regarded themselves as Catholics and their culture as Catholic. The cultural tie with Spain continued and the influence of the Spanish church was strong.

The political record in Brazil was somewhat different but issued in much the

---

passim; Memoirs of Bolívar . . . with an introduction . . . , by H. L. V. Ducoudray Holstein (Boston, S. G. Goodrich & Co., 1829, pp. 383), *passim.*

[9] Margaret H. Harrison, *Captain of the Andes. The Life of Don José de San Martín, Liberator of Argentina, Chile and Peru* (New York, Richard R. Smith, 1943, pp. xiii, 216), *passim.*

[10] Mecham, *op. cit.,* p. 53.

same way—in independence and a republican form of government. The transition was accomplished with very little of the fighting that punctuated the process in Spanish America. To escape the armies of Napoleon, in 1808 the Portuguese court transferred its headquarters to Rio de Janeiro. In 1815 Brazil was given what corresponded to dominion status within the Portuguese Empire. In 1822, in protest against the effort of Lisbon to assert its authority, Pedro, son of King John, who had returned to Portugal, declared the independence of the country. He was crowned emperor and with the aid of the Scottish adventurer Lord Cochrane made good his status. In 1831 Pedro, long unpopular, abdicated and went to Portugal. His five-year-old son succeeded him as Pedro II. Well educated by a deeply religious tutor, on taking over the rule in his middle teens the second Pedro proved an honest, intelligent monarch, a loyal Roman Catholic, but too liberal for the stricter of that church. He governed through a constitution resembling that of England. Under him the country prospered. But sentiment for a republic grew and in 1889 he abdicated. He died in France in 1891.

THE GENERAL COURSE OF POLITICAL LIFE

Before the end of the nineteenth century all the Latin American countries were under republican forms of government, but this did not always mean order and stability. The republics had constitutions, most of them bearing evidence of the influence of similar documents in the United States of America and of European liberalism. In country after country, however, a strong man ruled with the aid of an army until unseated by another strong man, often by extra-constitutional procedures. The social stratification of colonial days persisted, and the masses, poverty-stricken and poorly educated or actually illiterate, could not make their voices heard effectively through the ballot. In several countries corruption was rife. Revolution followed revolution.

GROWTH IN WEALTH AND POPULATION

In spite of shifts in government and the extreme poverty of the masses, advances were made in national wealth and population mounted. The area was rich in natural resources of soil, minerals, and forests. Some had been exploited in the colonial period. In the nineteenth century they were further developed—largely for food, drink, and raw materials for the cities and industrial centres of Western Europe, the United States of America, and Canada, burgeoning as they were under the impulse of the Industrial Revolution. To mention only the more important exports: beef, wool, and wheat came from Argentina, beef and wool from Uruguay, coffee from Brazil, Colombia, and Central America, sugar from Argentina, Brazil, Cuba, Puerto Rico, and the island of Haiti, tobacco from Cuba and Puerto Rico, tropical fruits from Central America, nitrate and copper from Chile, tin from Bolivia, various metals from Peru, and silver, gold, lead, and copper from Mexico. Factories were only in their infancy and oil wells were still mostly in the future.

Immigration poured into the portions of South America which were in the Temperate Zone. The majority were from Italy, Spain, and Portugal, but a substantial proportion were from Germany, and before 1914 Japanese were beginning to find homes in Brazil. The English and Scotch controlled much of the commerce and built and ran the railways of Argentina. By the end of the nineteenth century most of the population in Southern Brazil, Uruguay, Argentina, and Chile were of pure European ancestry.

INTELLECTUAL AND PHILOSOPHICAL CURRENTS FROM WESTERN EUROPE

Intellectual currents of the revolutionary age entered from Europe. They were felt directly only by members of the educated minority. Although the masses were largely illiterate, among the ruling classes were men of high intelligence and culture. Through travel and reading they kept in touch with much that was being thought in Europe. With important exceptions their contacts were more with the Continent, and especially France, than with the British Isles. The commercial contacts with Great Britain did not necessarily entail the entrance of philosophical ideas from that island.

The Enlightenment had begun to penetrate to Spanish America before the nineteenth century. Some teachers in the universities had studied in Europe and had brought in ideas which were current there in the eighteenth century. Partly through them the Enlightenment played an important part in several of the movements for independence.

The nineteenth century saw a variety of philosophies enter Latin America. Nineteenth-century Latin America did not produce an original system of thought to equal the outstanding ones of Europe. However, the intellectuals (*pensadores*) had great prestige and were often very influential not only in thought and education but also in politics. Some inherited wealth. Others came up from poverty. With notable exceptions they were liberals and critical of the Church. Most of them, even when outspokenly anti-clerical, remained nominal Roman Catholics. Very few became Protestants. In this they were like their counterparts in contemporary Latin Europe. Victor Cousin was the exponent in France of a personalistic, pluralistic idealism akin to the system of Karl Chr. Fr. Krause (1781–1832), who developed what he called panentheism, a combination of pantheism and theism. Championed by H. Ahrens (1808–1872), that system penetrated Latin America as Krausism, philosophic spiritualism, or spiritual eclecticism. It came partly through contacts with the University of Oviedo in Spain, where Sanz del Rio had championed it. In the third quarter of the nineteenth century the curriculum of the University of Mexico was dominated by it. Earlier it had been influential there, in Uruguay, Brazil, Cuba, Colombia, Chile, and Buenos Aires.[11] French Comtian Positivism had a profound influence in the latter half of the nineteenth century. In Mexico it determined educational reforms. It was potent in Uruguay, affected Chile, Cuba, Bolivia, and Argentina, and dominated thought in Brazil during the early decades of the republic. Indeed, the revolution of 1889 which brought in the republic in Brazil had Comtian Positivists as its leaders. The words "order and progress" on the flag of Brazil were from Positivism. In the last thirty years before 1910 French Comtian Positivism was in the ascendency in much of Latin America but was already being challenged by other movements of thought. In time its political philosophy and dictatorial political practices provoked the consolidation of all other systems in opposition to it. In addition to Comte, Guyau, Fouillée, Renan, and Taine made an impact. In contrast, Kant, Hegel, and the German pessimistic thinkers had little or no effect.[12]

COMMON FACTORS AND TRENDS IN THE ROMAN CATHOLIC CHURCH

Although much variety existed and in each country distinctive developments occurred, several factors and trends in the Roman Catholic Church were common throughout Latin America. Some were prominent in Spanish America but not in Brazil, but similarities were seen in the course of the Roman Catholic faith in both areas.

A factor in both Spanish and Portuguese America was the formal adherence of the majority of the population to the Roman Catholic Church. Leaders of political movements were often indifferent or sceptical. Many were anti-clerical. Numbers of intellectuals tended to regard Christianity as untenable by enlightened minds. Among the masses the faith was held in ignorance and compounded with superstition, garbled survivals of pagan conceptions and practices, and, in some places, a crude animistic spiritualism. Yet, except among the Protestant minorities and the non-Christian Indians on the frontiers, Roman Catholic baptism was almost universal. As was true in a large part of Europe, it was regarded as belonging to the cultural heritage, much as Protestant baptism was in the rest of Western Europe and Orthodox baptism in Russia and among non-Moslem elements in Greece and the Balkans. If asked, even those who never darkened the doors of a church except for baptisms, weddings, and funer-

---

[11] Ardao, *Espiritualismo y Positivismo en el Uruguay*, pp. 19–62; *The Catholic Encyclopedia*, Vol. XI, p. 364; F. S. C. Northrop in *Civilisations*, Vol. V, No. 4, pp. 523 ff.; John Theodore Merz, *A History of European Thought in the Nineteenth Century* (Edinburgh, William Blackwood and Sons, 4 vols., 1914), Vol. III, p. 591, Vol. IV, p. 190; Crawford, *A Century of Latin-American Thought, passim.* On Krausism, from a Roman Catholic standpoint, see Marcelino Menéndez y Pelayo, *Historia de los Heterodoxos Españoles,* second edition by Miguel Artigas, Vol. VII (Madrid, Victoriano Suárez, 1932, pp. 519), pp. 345 ff.

[12] Ardao, *op. cit.,* pp. 286 ff.; Northrop, *op. cit.,* Vol. V, No. 4, pp. 523 ff.; Crawford, *op. cit.,* p. 8.

als would say that they were Catholic. Here was a feature of their tradition which gave a degree of unity and continuity.

Another and closely related factor was expressions of Roman Catholic piety. Gigantic statues of Christ were often prominent features of the landscape, such as the one which crowned a hill towering above the harbour of Rio de Janeiro and the Christ of the Andes, on the border between Argentina and Chile. Pilgrimage centres, often associated with what were believed to have been appearances of the Virgin Mary and akin to those in the Roman Catholic portions of Europe, had national significance. Among them were the ones hallowed by Our Lady of Guadalupe, in Mexico, and Our Lady of Apercida, in Brazil.

A factor all but universal in Spanish America but not so marked in Brazil was the shock brought to the Roman Catholic Church by independence and the inevitably painful adjustments. Crises arose from the disorders which were features of the wars of independence, from the Spanish birth of many of the clergy, from the historic patronage exercised by the crown, from the insistence of new governments on the transfer to them of that authority, from the unwillingness of Madrid to surrender its prerogatives, and from the political situation in Spain which made Rome hesitate to go counter to Spanish claims.

In the fighting which punctuated the struggle for independence the clergy were divided. In some places, as in Mexico, the higher clergy stood for a monarchical form of government, and leadership in the fight for independence was initially by village priests. In contrast, in Venezuela several of the higher clergy, the foreign-born, and the regular clergy sided with the cause of independence, while others, including some of the native-born, held to the king.[13] In Argentina, on the other hand, the creoles among the clergy worked for independence and aided it financially. In general the bishops and the Spanish clergy opposed the movements for independence.[14]

The prolonged disorder accompanying the struggle and the civil disturbances in Spain, both during and after the Napoleonic occupation, reduced the missionaries on the frontier and hampered the sending of reinforcements. For instance, in Venezuela in 1817 the Capuchins of Catalonia who the previous year had about 29 centres caring for approximately 21,000 Indians were arrested because they had sided with the mother country. The majority either died of exposure or hunger or were shot. Their flocks disintegrated.[15] During the struggles for independence in Bolivia all but one of the Franciscan missions among the Chiriguanos on the north-western edge of the Gran Chaco were destroyed.

[13] Watters, *A History of the Church in Venezuela 1810–1930*, p. 53.

[14] Mecham, *Church and State in Latin America*, pp. 62–73.

[15] Watters, *op. cit.*, p. 65; *Informe sobre el Estado Actual de los Distritos de Reduccion de Indijenas Alto Orinoco, Central y Bajo Orinoco, y Medidas que Reclaman, Presentado a su Excelencia el Podor Ejecutivo por el Visitador Nombrado al Efecto* (Caracas, Diego Campbell, 1850, pp. 98), *passim*, especially the first chart in the appendix; J. Fred Rippy and Jean Thomas Nelson, *Crusaders in the Jungle* (Chapel Hill, University of North Carolina Press, 1936, pp. x, 401), pp. 165, 166.

In 1814 some of the centres were plundered. Not for a quarter of a century could the enterprise be renewed.[16]

For several years the Popes supported the king. An encyclical of 1816 urged the bishops to bring their flocks to obedience to him.[17] The following year the Papal Secretary of State, the usually astute Consalvi, refused to receive any communication from the new governments. Obviously these governments would not acknowledge any bishops sent from Spain. Yet in the years 1814–1820 the Pope confirmed the appointment by the king of eight bishops in America, some of them to sees in regions where insurrection existed against the royal authority.[18] When the revolution of 1820 brought the anti-clericals to power in Spain the Pope refused the request of the liberal regime to urge the American clergy to support the Spanish cause. However, in 1824, after the absolutism of Ferdinand VII had been restored in Spain, a Papal encyclical urged that same clergy to rally to the king[19]—in spite of the progress of independence in the former colonies. Presumably Rome viewed the movements for independence as continuations of the French Revolution and hence odious, and felt bound to support "legitimacy." Much of the attitude of Rome was due to pressure from the Spanish embassy to the Holy See. From 1814 to 1820 and from 1824 to 1833 the ambassador was a staunch opponent of all agents of the revolutionary governments and in the interval 1820–1824 the *chargé* was equally intransigent.[20] Papal authority in Spain itself had long been so compromised by the crown that prudence seemed to advise against any step which might further breed resistance in the Spanish church to the administrative authority of the Pope.

Clearly the Spanish Government would not relinquish its long-standing claim to patronage, for in it was a means of reasserting, through the Roman Catholic Church, its rule in the New World. Equally obvious was the insistence of the new governments that appointments to ecclesiastical posts had devolved upon them as the inheritors of the powers of the crown.

The Holy See attempted to end the impasse by appointing vicars apostolic with episcopal status, a device which had long been employed in South and East Asia as a way of circumventing the Portuguese in their claims in that area under their *padroado*. In 1822, partly at the suggestion of a creole priest sent by the Chilean dictator O'Higgins, and against the opposition of Madrid and the Spanish embassy in Rome, Juan Muzi was consecrated Archbishop of Filipos, appointed vicar apostolic, and sent with jurisdiction over all America with the power to consecrate more titular bishops. In Buenos Aires, although San Martín welcomed him, the authorities ordered him to leave. In Chile he was at

[16] Lemmens, *Geschichte der Franziskannermissionen*, pp. 320, 321.

[17] Ayarragaray, *La Iglesia en América y la Dominación Española*, pp. 183, 184; Mecham, *op. cit.*, pp. 77, 78.

[18] Mecham, *op. cit.*, p. 78.

[19] *Ibid.*, pp. 79, 80; Ayarragaray, *op. cit.*, p. 184.

[20] Mecham, *op. cit.*, pp. 82, 83.

first received with enthusiasm, but when he refused to accept the nominees of the government for ecclesiastical posts criticism became so sharp that he left the country (1824). The future Pius IX was one of his staff and gained first-hand impressions which were later to stand him in good stead.[21]

The condition of the Spanish American church was becoming increasingly grave. It is said that in 1826 only ten of the thirty-eight episcopal sees had occupants, and of these two were incapacitated and two left within the year. Vast areas were without episcopal supervision.[22] By 1829 not one bishop was left in Mexico.[23]

Gradually conditions improved, owing partly to the recognition of the independence of the successor governments by Rome, partly to working arrangements between them and the Holy See, partly to a growing stability in the new states, and to no small extent to clergy from Europe. The achievement was in the face of the opposition of the Spanish Government. Madrid was long adamant against any concessions in ecclesiastical affairs to the successor regimes.

The attitude of the Papacy changed. Not long after the seeming failure of the Muzi mission, Ignacio de Tejada, a priest, came to Rome (December, 1824) representing Gran Colombia. By his ability, perseverance, and discretion he won his way and in time became the agent of other republics as well. Using him as a precedent, the Holy See, in spite of the protests of the Spanish embassy, received delegates from the new states, not as political dignitaries, but as concerned purely with ecclesiastical affairs and with the express stipulation that no political recognition of the rising governments was entailed.[24] In 1827 Leo XII preconized (formally approved) six candidates for bishoprics presented by Colombia. It was the first direct Papal action contrary to Spanish patronage. Ferdinan VII vigorously objected and insisted that in the future the Pope await his nominations for the episcopate. Negotiations followed in which Spain proved unyielding. Leo XII so far relented that in 1828 he preconized several, only one as a proprietory bishop, namely, as functioning in his own name, and the rest as vicars apostolic. But even that step met with wails from Spain.[25] Pius VIII, whose brief pontificate was from late March, 1829, to November 30, 1830, at first refused to consecrate bishops.[26] In 1830 the Mexican envoy threatened a further impasse by declaring that his government would receive only proprietory bishops and would refuse vicars apostolic.[27] Rome temporized by saying that in view of the turbulence still existing in America only vicars apostolic could wisely be appointed. But Pius VIII had already decided to consent to proprie-

[21] *Ibid.*, pp. 88–92; Ayarragaray, *op. cit.*, pp. 235 ff.; W. J. Coleman in *Worldmission*, Vol. VIII, p. 79; Coleman, *The First Apostolic Delegation in Rio de Janeiro*, pp. 2–6.

[22] Watters, *op. cit.*, pp. 89, 90.

[23] Mecham, *op. cit.*, p. 97.

[24] *Ibid.*, pp. 95–97.

[25] Coleman, *The First Apostolic Delegation in Rio de Janeiro*, p. 9.

[26] *Ibid.*, pp. 12, 13.

[27] *Ibid.*, p. 13.

tory bishops when death removed him. His successor, Gregory XVI, recognizing that the independence of the Spanish American countries was an established fact, unwilling longer to postpone action because of Spanish intransigence, and troubled by the threatened ruin of the churches, in 1831 preconized seven proprietory bishops for Mexico. The following year he appointed vicars apostolic for Argentina and Chile, and in 1833 he preconized four bishops for New Granada. Yet in hone of these acts did he grant to the new regimes the power of presenting names to him for his automatic approval. While willing to accept some names suggested to him, he expressly instructed the bishops of America to refuse to concede to the emerging governments the right of patronage such as his predecessors had given to the Spanish and Portuguese crowns.[28] That continued to be the policy of the Papacy. True to the ultramontane trend in the nineteenth century, here as elsewhere the Holy See insisted upon its control of the structure and administration of the Roman Catholic Church. In December, 1835, Gregory received Tejada as *chargé* for New Granada, thus formally recognizing the political autonomy of that government, and the following year named an inter-nuncio extraordinary to New Granada, the first of such appointments to a Spanish American republic.[29]

Slightly earlier, in 1830, a nunciature had been set up in Rio de Janeiro, ostensibly for Brazil, but with the secretly given authority of an apostolic delegate to all South America, Mexico, and the Caribbean.[30] From 1808 to 1821, when Brazil was the seat of the Portuguese Government, a nunciature to that court had been there. It was transferred to Lisbon when Brazil became independent. The creation of a nunciature in Brazil was preceded by several years of preliminary steps. The secrecy of designating the nuncio as apostolic delegate to Spanish America was to avoid an open affront to the Spanish Government. During its initial years the Rio nunciature made its influence felt in improving conditions in Argentina, but with the establishment of the inter-nunciature in Bogotá supervision of the Church in New Granada passed to that office. The Rio nunciature had an important part in helping to make provision for the Church in Uruguay, a country then in the early years of its independence and greatly unsettled. It also sought to assist in Chile, Bolivia, and Peru but seems to have had less effect than in Argentina and Uruguay. With the decision of the Holy See to recognize the independence of the Spanish American countries, increasingly the negotiations were with the individual governments.

One of the most urgent needs of the Roman Catholic Church in Latin America was indigenous clergy. In colonial days, although they were increasing, they had been insufficient in numbers and were largely under the direction of foreign-born ecclesiastical superiors. The disorders attendant on the achievement

28 Mecham, *op. cit.*, pp. 100–105.
29 *Ibid.*, pp. 105, 106.
30 Coleman, *The First Apostolic Delegation in Rio de Janeiro, passim.*

of political independence reduced the supply from Europe and militated against recruitment and training of American-born replacements. In 1858, partly at the instance of a priest from Chile, but with the initiative and financial assistance of Pius IX, a college was opened in Rome which was eventually called the Collegio Pio Latino Americano Pontifico. After various vicissitudes, it was given a substantial building, erected in 1887–1888. The college was placed permanently under the direction of the Jesuits. It was the source of professors for several seminaries and one ecclesiastical university in Latin America and thus multiplied its contribution towards the strengthening of a native priesthood. In its building was held, significantly, the first general council for Latin America, and one of its graduates was the first South American cardinal.[31]

The creation of theological seminaries and of the South American College in Rome could not quickly meet the needs of the professedly Roman Catholic population in Latin America. Into the twentieth century the recruits in Latin America were far from sufficient to give the pastoral care required for a healthy religious life,[32] and the quality of a large proportion of the indigenous parish priests and regulars was lamentably low.

To fill the void, both to care for the Roman Catholic population and to press forward the frontiers of the faith among the non-Christian Indians, priests, lay brothers, and sisters came from many lands. Before 1914 they were mostly from Europe. After that year and especially during and after World War II an increasing proportion were from the United States and Canada. Germany, Austria, Holland, and Italy shared. Portugal was the source of some for Brazil.[33] The Spanish church continued to feel a special responsibility. For example, in 1844 Spanish Lazarists arrived in Mexico and before long were in charge of two seminaries. By 1868 they had six houses in that country.[34] In 1899 St. Xavier's College, locally known as Colegio de Ultramar, was founded in Burgos for the preparation of clergy for Spanish America.[35]

In spite of some improvement, at the end of the nineteenth century the Roman Catholic Church was still dependent on assistance from other countries, mainly from Europe. Secularism had made great inroads, and among the educated sceptical intellectual currents from Europe and non-Christian systems of philosophy, notably Comtian Positivism, were undercutting the faith. Many of the upper classes held to the Church because they valued it as a bulwark of the established order against the radical social theories which marked the revolutionary age. But while willing that their sons should enter the Society of Jesus, they

[31] *The Catholic Encyclopedia*, Vol. I, pp. 425, 426.
[32] John J. Considine, *Call for Forty Thousand* (New York, Longmans, Green and Co., 1946, pp. 319), pp. 9–16.
[33] Latourette, *A History of the Expansion of Christianity*, Vol. V, pp. 73, 74.
[34] B. Paradela, *Resumen Histórico de la Congregación de la Misión en España, desde 1704 a 1868* (Madrid G. Hernández y Galo Sáez, 1923, pp. xv, 477), p. 435.
[35] *Fides News Service*, Dec. 30, 1939.

regarded with horror the suggestion that any of them should become secular priests.

In every country a struggle was seen in one form or another between clericals and anti-clericals. Although nominally Roman Catholic, the anti-clericals, largely moved by the kind of liberalism which gave rise to anti-clericalism in the Roman Catholic portions of Europe, strove to reduce the influence of the Church in politics and education and to loosen the tie between it and the state. In some countries they brought about disestablishment. The clericals sought to preserve the favoured status of the Church, partly to protect themselves and partly as an insurance against what they looked upon as forces of disorder.

THE BEGINNINGS OF PROTESTANTISM

The independence of the Latin American countries was accompanied and followed by a degree of religious liberty which varied from country to country and from time to time. At the outset, in all the countries the Roman Catholic Church was accorded a privileged position. In most of them it continued to enjoy preference throughout the century. In some it was fully established. In others separation of Church and state was accomplished, but usually with the Roman Catholic Church, as representing the faith of the majority and because of its historic position, able to exert a special influence and to obtain aid, direct or indirect, from the government.

Under these conditions Protestantism gained a continuing foothold but laboured under handicaps. It entered partly through immigration and partly through missions. Some of the latter were among the non-Christian Indians and some were to the Roman Catholics. As we have suggested, to those reared in the Portuguese or the Spanish tradition Protestantism seemed alien, not only religiously but also culturally. The missions were chiefly from Great Britain and the United States, eventually mainly from the latter. We will say something of Protestantism in our country-by-country survey. Here, however, it seems wise to speak of beginnings which extended to more than one country.

Early Protestant effort was through James Thomson, a Scot, who came first as an agent of the British and Foreign School Society to promote the Lancastrian method of education. He acted as a correspondent of the British and Foreign Bible Society and commencing in 1827 was for some time its official agent in Mexico and the Caribbean. He arrived in Buenos Aires and was there and elsewhere in the River Plate region until 1821. Aided by Roman Catholics, he organized a Lancastrian society which soon reported about a hundred schools with approximately five thousand children. He went on to Chile, Peru, and Colombia, obtained the support of San Martín, and in the heyday of the liberalism, in part a fruit of the Enlightenment, which pervaded circles, lay and clerical, friendly to independence, enlisted enthusiastic support. He also furthered the circulation of the Scriptures in Peru. In 1825 he brought into being the National Bible Society of Colombia. In Mexico he found a welcome in similar quarters. He returned to Mexico in 1842 and circulated an edition of the Bible, without notes, which had the endorsement of Roman Catholic authority. Through him and other agents the British and Foreign Bible Society furthered the translation of the Bible into some of the Indian languages in Peru and Mexico. Here was paralleled what we have found on the contemporary Continent of Europe. Although later conservative reactions seemed to put an end to what Thomson and the British and Foreign Bible Society had so hopefully begun, precedent was established for further efforts.[36] As early as the 1830's the American Bible Society was getting Bibles into South America and Mexico. Indeed, in 1833 it sent an agent, Wheelwright, to Chile.[37]

Many in the United States of America took a great interest in the emergence of independent republics, outwardly akin to their own, and this led to early attempts to begin Protestant missions in them. In 1823 the American Board of Commissioners for Foreign Missions sent two young men, Theophilus Parvin and John C. Brigham, to Buenos Aires, with a commission to explore South America. Parvin remained in Buenos Aires. In 1825 he returned to the United States; in 1826 he was ordained by the Presbytery of Philadelphia, was married, and went back to Buenos Aires at his own expense. The next year he was joined by another Presbyterian, also at his own charges. Brigham, after extensive travels, reported to the American Board that the time did not seem propitious for Protestant missions. However, he was later influential in having the American Seamen's Friend Society place chaplains in several South American ports.[38]

A pioneer Protestant enterprise, at the outset primarily to non-Christian Indians, was the Patagonian Missionary Society, later the South American Missionary Society, Anglican in affiliations. It arose from the efforts of Allen Francis Gardiner (1794-1851), an officer in the British navy, who wished to be a missionary to peoples otherwise untouched by the Gospel. In 1845 Gardiner made an unsuccessful attempt to found a mission in Patagonia. In 1851 in another effort, this time on inhospitable Tierra del Fuego, he and his party died of starvation and exposure. The report of their heroism stirred others to carry on what they had begun. Headquarters were established on the Falkland Islands, British territory since late in the eighteenth century. Missions to the aborigines were carried on in the Argentinian and Paraguayan Chaco, Southern Chile, and Patagonia. The scope of the Society was extended to Roman Catholics and to British sailors, merchants, and settlers. In 1869 Waite Hocking Stirling

[36] Webster E. Browning, *Joseph Lancaster, James Thomson, and the Lancastrian System of Mutual Instruction with special reference to Latin America* (privately printed, 1926, pp. 42), *passim;* Goslin, *Los Evangelicos en la América Latina*, pp. 16–27; Canton, *A History of the British and Foreign Bible Society*, Vol. II, pp. 77–84, 92–97.
[37] Dwight, *The Centennial History of the American Bible Society*, Vol. I, pp. 144, 221–223.
[38] J. O. Oliphant in *Church History*, Vol. XIV, pp. 85–103.

(1829–1923), secretary of the Society and then superintendent of its missions, was consecrated Bishop of the Falklands with jurisdiction for the Church of England over all South America except British Guiana.[39]

Bishop Stirling in his wide-flung diocese found much of his responsibility in English sailors and business men. They were found in most ports. To care for them chaplaincies were established by the British Government and for years were subsidized by it. However, they did not attempt to reach out to the non-British population. In 1910 the vast see was divided and a new one was added for Argentina and Eastern South America.[40]

Although some other British missions arose in Latin America, the most extensive Protestant efforts were from the United States of America, largely because, since that country and Latin America were in the Western Hemisphere, shared in republican forms of government, and were associated in inter-American and Pan-American conferences and later in the Pan American Union, Christians of the great northern neighbour felt a peculiar responsibility for the region. In seeking to meet it, the Roman Catholics of the United States were to take an active part, but mostly in the twentieth century. However, long before 1914 the Protestants of the United States were conducting missions in all the Latin American republics, in spite of marked cultural differences and the distrust, fear, and dislike of many Latin Americans for their fellow Americans of the United States.

We must not take the space so much as to name all the Protestant undertakings. Some we are to see in our country-by-country pilgrimage. Here we pause to note that among the most widespread efforts were those by the Methodists, the Baptists, especially the Southern Baptists, the Presbyterians, and the Seventh Day Adventists. More than in most parts of the world the "faith" missions, theoretically undenominational, were prominent. Movements such as those of the Pentecostals were present in several of the republics and had a phenomenal growth, especially in the twentieth century.

William Taylor (1821–1902) was largely responsible for introducing Methodism to the west coast of South America and to Brazil. A man of magnificent physique and great endurance, even more than John Wesley he made the world his parish. He had been an evangelist in California during the gold rush days and had also preached in Australia, South Africa, Canada, Great Britain, and India. In 1877 he began a tour of South America with the purpose of establishing self-supporting missions. The financial undergirding was to come through schools, staffed from the United States and sustained by fees and subscriptions from local residents. Most of the missionaries who came in answer to his call

---

[39] Latourette, op. cit., Vol. V, pp. 102–104. See especially the footnotes for extensive bibliographical references.

[40] For bibliographies see ibid., pp. 105, 106. For a comprehensive picture see E. F. Every, The Anglican Church in South America (London, Society for Promoting Christian Knowledge, 1915, pp. 155), passim.

were in Peru, but some were in Bolivia, Central America, and Brazil. In 1884 Taylor was made bishop for Africa, and his Latin American commitments were maintained by the Transit and Building Fund Society of Bishop Taylor's Self-Supporting Missions. In 1904 the responsibility was assumed by the Missionary Society of the Methodist Episcopal Church.[41]

In 1891 Myron A. Clark, a representative of the International Committee of the Young Men's Christian Association, functioning for the Associations of the United States and Canada, arrived in Brazil. By the year 1914 the International Committee had sent secretaries to help Associations in Buenos Aires, Montevideo, and Valparaiso. In that year the *Federación Sudamericana de Asociaciónes Cristianas de Jovenes* (South American Federation of Young Men's Christian Associations) was organized to coördinate what was being done on the continent and to assist in the training of secretaries. In 1902, after a transient preliminary effort early in the 1890's, continuing assistance began in Mexico. Although Protestant in origin, in Latin America the YMCA eventually was predominantly Roman Catholic in membership.[42]

It was in 1914 that the Committee on Coöperation in Latin America was formed with headquarters in New York City. It brought together for counsel and action a large proportion of the Protestant missionary organizations in the United States and Canada which were operating in Latin America and embraced ten regional groups in that area.[43]

We must remember that in 1914 Protestants in Latin America were minorities. They continued to grow after that year, but by mid-twentieth century they were still but a fraction of the population, in most countries a small fraction.

MEXICO

As we start our country-by-country survey of the course of Christianity in Latin America, it is natural to begin with Mexico. Here had been one of the chief centres of Spanish power. In population it was the largest of the countries of Spanish America and in area second only to Argentina. Mestizos were the most numerous, the Indians a substantial minority, and the whites (creoles) the smallest element but extremely important in the upper reaches of Church and state.

The course of Christianity could not but be affected by the shifts in the political scene. That scene was profoundly influenced by continuing and basic nonpolitical factors. One was the poverty of the country. In spite of vast mineral

[41] Taylor, *Story of My Life, passim;* William Taylor, *Our South American Cousins* (New York, Phillips & Hunt, 1882, pp. 366), *passim;* Goodsil F. Arms, *History of the William Taylor Self-Supporting Missions in South America* (New York, The Methodist Book Concern, 1921, pp. 263), *passim;* O. von Barchwitz-Krauser, *Six Years with William Taylor* (Boston, McDonald & Gill, 1885, pp. 332), *passim.*
[42] Latourette, *World Service,* pp. 204–207, 226, 233.
[43] Parker, *Directory of World Missions,* p. 67.

treasures—gold which had attracted the original *conquistadores*, silver, lead, copper, zinc, and the petroleum which lured foreign investment late in the nineteenth century and in the opening decades of the twentieth century—less than a tenth of the land was arable and for the majority of the population the struggle for mere existence was often desperate. As in much of the rest of the world of the revolutionary age, cities burgeoned, especially the historic capital, Mexico City. With notable exceptions, the creoles tended to be Castilian in out-look and to favour a conservative, centralized government. Some of them had a high degree of culture. They were inclined, often strongly, to support the Church, the landowners, and the army. The mestizos were divided among vari-ous shades of liberalism, were distrustful of a strong central regime, for to them it smacked of monarchy, and favoured a federal form of government with much authority in the states. The Indians, lowest in the economic scale, were usually pawns in the factional contests. Changes in administration were generally by *coup d'état*. A military leader would rally others of his kind and perhaps a few lawyers, would issue a *pronunciamento* containing a programme of reform, would attempt to seize power by force of arms, and, if successful, would rule, ostensibly through constitutional forms, until ousted by another general.

In the political seesaw the Roman Catholic Church now seemed to profit and then appeared to lose. At times anti-clericals were in power and at other times those favouring the Church were in control. For the most part the Centralists, chiefly creoles, were allied with the Church, and the Liberals, largely mestizos, and the intellectuals among the creoles took measures against it.

Following the death of Iturbide, Roman Catholicism was recognized as the state religion, and toleration of other forms of the faith was opposed. During the struggles for independence, although the number of clergy had declined by a third, the Church had nearly trebled the value of its properties and was said to have a fourth of the nation's wealth. Under creole governments its holdings continued to mount and it became the most powerful institution in the coun-try.[44]

Periodically the Liberals sought to curb the Church. The picture was compli-cated by rival forms of Masonry. The Scottish Rite Masons stood with the Con-servatives, and the York Rite, organized by two priests, sided with the Liberals. In 1828 and 1829, when the *Yorkinos* were in power, the properties of the mo-nastic orders and the Inquisition were taken over by the state.[45]

In 1830 a Conservative regime seized control. In 1831 it abandoned the previ-ously jealously guarded claim to be the inheritor of the patronage of the Spanish crown.[46] Something of the status of the Church can be seen from the fact that

[44] Mecham, *Church and State in Latin America*, p. 402.
[45] *Ibid.*, pp. 403, 404; Callcott, *Church and State in Mexico 1822–1857*, pp. 37 ff., 56 ff.; Kelley and Byam, *Blood-Drenched Altars*, pp. 181 ff.
[46] Mecham, *op. cit.*, p. 407.

in 1833 Mexico had 1,007 parishes and that 781 of them were regularly filled and 226 were served by temporary appointments.[47]

However, in 1833 the Liberals, emphatically anti-clerical, were once more in the saddle. The missions of Upper and Lower California were taken out of the hands of the regulars, their lands and buildings were confiscated and divided among the settlers and Indians, the parishes were assigned to the secular clergy, the Pious Fund of the missions was expropriated, and part of it was used to support the seculars. A few months later this step was followed by the nationalization of the properties of all the missions in the country. Parishes were ordered set up in mission areas and seculars assigned to them. The University of Mexico, with its faculty of priests, was suppressed and its property, together with that of another church college of higher education, was ordered assigned to public education. The collection of tithes by the state for the support of the Church was abolished. All laws compelling the fulfilment of monastic vows were repealed. The state assumed the authority to make all appointments to ecclesiastical posts. The bishops protested and some left the country to avoid compliance.[48]

The Liberals had moved too rapidly. The majority were scandalized by what they regarded as an attack on religion. Until 1855, with occasional minor ebbs, the tide turned in favour of the Church. Antonio López de Santa Anna (1795–1876), utterly unscrupulous, who fancied himself the Napoleon of the Western Hemisphere, periodically a national figure from the fall of Iturbide to 1855 and in the turmoil of Mexican politics five times president, led a Conservative reaction. Several of the Liberal ecclesiastical measures were revoked, including the one which gave the government the power of filling ecclesiastical offices, and the privileges of the Roman Catholic Church were partly restored. From 1834 to 1846, under shifting governments in some of which Santa Anna was prominent, no serious attack was made on the Church or its property. To meet the expense of the disastrous war with the United States (1845–1848) the clergy were required to make a substantial cash contribution. In the early 1850's, under Santa Anna's last presidency, the Jesuits were allowed to reënter the country to assist in the education of the masses and much of their property was restored to them.[49]

The revolution of 1855 which finally rid Mexican politics of Santa Anna was followed by fresh measures to reduce the wealth and power of the Roman

---

[47] Callcott, *op. cit.*, p. 95.

[48] Mecham, *op. cit.*, pp. 407–415; Callcott, *op. cit.*, pp. 85, 93; Kelley and Byam, *op. cit.*, pp. 101 ff. The decree of 1833 seems not to have seriously affected the Dominican Missions in Lower California. Because of epidemics and chronic syphilis the population was already declining. The final blows were given by the lawlessness of those passing through in 1849 on their way to the mines of Upper California. Peveril Meigs, *The Dominican Mission Frontier in Lower California* (Berkeley, University of California Press, 1935, pp. v, 192), p. 156.

[49] Mecham, *op. cit.*, pp. 416–425.

Catholic Church. By that time the Church had an income greater than that of the national government. Popular feeling rose against it. In 1855 a decree restricted the jurisdiction of ecclesiastical and military courts. The Church and the army united to oppose it, but it was confirmed by Congress. This step was followed by a decree forbidding any corporation, civil or ecclesiastical, to hold real estate which was not devoted directly to worship. Property not so used was to be sold and the proceeds, if of ecclesiastical holdings, were to be turned over to the Church. That decree was also approved by Congress. The clergy and the Pope condemned the measure. Feelings ran high and the Jesuits were once more expelled. In 1857 legislation was enacted which was designed to protect the poor against the exorbitant fees of the clergy for the performance of religious services. The constitution of 1857 contained provisions further restricting the clergy. It guaranteed freedom of the "expression of ideas" and of association, and prohibited religious vows. The clergy threatened excommunication to government officials who took the oath of allegiance to the document.[50]

In the pulsations between anti-clerical and pro-clerical regimes, late in 1857 the Conservatives came to power on a programme which included the inviolability of ecclesiastical property, the restoration of the former fees for clerical services, censorship of the press, the Roman Catholic faith as the sole religion of the country, immigration only from Roman Catholic countries, and the annulment of the constitution of 1857.

However, in December, 1860, after winning a battle with the Conservatives the Liberals established themselves in the capital under a full-blooded Indian, Benito Juárez (1806–1872), who was recognized by the United States as the legitimate president. Juárez had already adopted more drastic anti-clerical procedures than had any of the preceding Liberal governments. They included the nationalization of Church property, the suppression of all religious communities of men, the partial suppression of communities of nuns, civil marriage, the performance of religious services by priests without charge, the complete separation of Church and state, full religious liberty, the prohibition of participation by public officials in acts of religion, and the abolition of religious oaths—all in the name of "God, liberty, and reform."[51]

Then came foreign intervention, culminating in the setting up at the instance of Napoleon III and with the support of French bayonets of a regime with the hapless Maximilian (1832–1867), the generous-hearted younger brother of the Hapsburg ruler Francis Joseph, as emperor. Intervention was at first jointly by England, Spain, and France, ostensibly partly for the collection of foreign loans

[50] *Ibid.*, pp. 427–440. For documents by Melchor Ocampo, one of the Liberals, ranging in date from 1841 to 1861, see the volume bearing his name, *La Religion, la Iglesia y el Clero* (Mexico, D.F., Empresas Editoriales, S.A., 1948, pp. 236). It is one of a series, *El Liberalismo Mexicano en Pensamiento y en Accion*, edited by Martin Luis Guzmán.

[51] Mecham, *op. cit.*, pp. 440–445; Callcott, *Liberalism in Mexico 1857–1929*, pp. 1–13.

Inspiring it were Mexican Conservatives and clericals and the ambition of Napoleon III to build a French colonial empire. England and Spain soon withdrew, and Napoleon, pursuing the invasion, persuaded Maximilian to accept the proffered throne. Maximilian reached Mexico City in 1864. Liberal by conviction, he sought to win the support of both Liberals and Conservatives. Neither would have him. The Liberals, led by Juárez, kept up an insistent guerrilla resistance. The Conservatives were alienated by his refusal to restore the ecclesiastical property nationalized by the Juárez regime. Napoleon, troubled by developments in Europe and by the pointed warning of the United States, now freed of its weakening Civil War, began withdrawing his troops (1865). Refusing to abdicate, in 1867 Maximilian, defeated and captured by Juárez, was shot.[52]

With the defeat and death of Maximilian, the Liberals were again on top and the legislation separating Church and state and curtailing the privileged position of the Church was renewed. Juárez, returning to power, became more and more dictatorial. Unrest against him developed, but his sudden death (1872) removed him from the scene. He was followed by Sebastián Lerdo de Tejada. Under both Juárez and Lerdo the liquidation of ecclesiastical properties was resumed. Most of those alienated passed into private hands, but some were held for the Church by proxies and others of the new proprietors paid large sums to the clergy for the renunciation by the Church of its claims. In 1873 sections were written into the constitution which confirmed the separation of Church and state, civil marriage, the illegality of monastic vows, the prohibition of the acquisition of real estate by religious institutions, and the substitution of a simple affirmation for a religious oath. The following year fresh legislation forbade religious instruction in any public institution, the performance of religious acts outside the churches, and the use of church bells except as a summons to religious services.[53]

In 1876 Lerdo was overthrown by Díaz. With the exception of 1880–1884, when he was still a force in the government, Díaz was president continuously from 1877 to 1911. José de la Cruz Porfirio Díaz (1830–1915) was of lowly birth of a mother who was part Indian. He was educated for the Church but in his late teens, under the influence of Juárez, abandoned the clerical career for the law. A man of action, he led in the defeat of Maximilian. Later he broke with Juárez. During the long period of his power he gave the country internal peace, furthered the development of natural resources through foreign capital, built railways, developed industries, and won the respect of foreign powers for his government. Yet the condition of the masses deteriorated. Most of the land was in the hands of a few families and the majority of the population were little better than serfs. Díaz came to power as a Liberal, but he more and more brought the nation under a centralized rule with himself as master.

[52] Mecham, *op. cit.*, pp. 445–453.
[53] *Ibid.*, pp. 453–455; Callcott, *Liberalism in Mexico 1857–1929*, pp. 77–102.

Under Díaz the enforcement of the laws restricting the Church was relaxed. Although he was a thirty-third-degree Mason, only nominally a Roman Catholic, and fitfully enforced the restrictions on the Church, his second wife was warmly religious and the Church regained some of its lost ground. Religious processions and services appeared outside church buildings, monastic orders existed clandestinely, gifts and bequests to the Church increased, new churches were constructed, colleges and elementary schools in the hands of the clergy multiplied, at least two congregations of women were founded, one to serve in hospitals and one to care for orphans, the number of priests more than trebled, and five new archbishoprics and eight new bishoprics were created. Yet, while he suggested to Rome men to be named as bishops and had semi-official relations with resident apostolic delegates, Díaz refused the overtures of the Pope for the establishment of diplomatic relations with the Vatican and the renewal of the former tie between Church and state.[54]

In 1910 the aging Díaz was forced out of power by a popular revolt led by Madero. Clerical forces opposed Madero and under the patronage of the hierarchy the National Catholic Party was organized to resist impending social and economic changes. In spite of clerical opposition, Madero was overwhelmingly elected president. But he proved unequal to the office and was ousted (1913) by Francisco Huerta and murdered. In general the Church supported Huerta.

In the revolt against Huerta which, led by Carranza, broke out within a few weeks, much of the popular animus was directed against the Church. Many outrages were perpetrated on clergy and churches.[55] Since the renewed and intensified anti-clerical measures came chiefly after 1914, we must postpone more than this brief mention.

The position of the Roman Catholic Church in Mexico was complicated by intellectual currents from Europe. Through José María Luis Mora (1794-1850), a historian and author of the reform plan of 1833, British Utilitarianism, especially as expressed by Jeremy Bentham and Adam Smith, was potent. Krausism was influential in the latter part of the century. Comtian Positivism came, had a following among what corresponded to the bourgeoisie, largely wealthy landowners, and, opposed to Krausism, for a time was a force to be reckoned with in education. It was to Gabino Barreda, a convinced Positivist and the leader in introducing that philosophy, that Juárez entrusted his Ministry of Education. Yet the Positivists did not attack the Roman Catholic Church or found a church of their own. In the end Mexican Positivism became more Spencerian than

[54] Mecham, *op. cit.*, pp. 456–459; Herring, *A History of Latin America*, p. 343; Callcott, *Liberalism in Mexico 1857–1929*, pp. 120–154. For actions creating the new archdioceses and dioceses, see Jesus Garcia Gutierrez, *Bulario de la Iglesia Mexicana, Documentos relativos a erecciones, desmembraciones, etc. de diócesis mejicanas* (Mexico, D.F., "Buena Prensa," 1951, pp. 545), pp. 45–48, 55–64, 73–110, 153, 159, 203–208, 309–312, 338, 339, 361, 385–394, 411–415, 457, 465 ff.

[55] Mecham, *op. cit.*, pp. 459–463; Kelley and Byam, *op. cit.*, pp. 250 ff.; Callcott, *Liberalism in Mexico 1857–1929*, pp. 196 ff.

Comtian.[56] The revolution of 1910 brought changes in the philosophic outlook. The Positivists had supported Díaz, and the revolt against his rule was accompanied by a rejection of their philosophy.[57] Since the full force of the new philosophic movements did not come until after 1914 we must reserve their description for the twentieth-century stage of our story.

Mexico was not without efforts to fill the gap left by the deportation of Spanish priests. Thus in 1828 Papal approval was given for the College of Our Lady of Zapopan. In it a number of clergy received their education.[58]

In the latter part of the century a slight revival was seen in the missions to the Indians that had all but lapsed in the disorders and from the hostile measures of the state. For instance, in 1872 the Josephites undertook a mission to the Tarahumara, the largest tribe in the north of Mexico. In the seventeenth century the Jesuits had begun to introduce the faith and the majority had adopted it. The Society of Jesus resumed operations in 1900. In the twentieth century the religion of most of the Tarahumara was ostensibly Christian and gave many evidences of the influence of beliefs and customs of Christian origin, but it also had many non-Christian features.[59] In the 1890's the mission seminary bearing the name of Peter and Paul, a nineteenth-century foundation in Rome, was placed in charge of Lower California and sought to revive the faith in that inhospitable and sparsely settled region.[60]

In the nineteenth century Protestantism made its appearance in Mexico, as was to be expected. On the immediate north was the United States, and the Protestantism of that country was thriving and was sending missionaries to many parts of the world. Although in the shifting fortunes of Conservative and Liberal regimes the degree of freedom for Protestant missionary activity fluctuated from intolerance to tolerance and much of popular sentiment was hostile, Protestant representatives persevered and Protestants increased in number. In the 1820's an agent of the American Bible Society and James Thomson of the British and Foreign Bible Society were in the country. During the war with the United States some soldiers of the invading armies distributed New Testaments.[61] In 1852 Melinda Rankin began a school, mainly for Mexicans, at Brownsville, Texas, across the mouth of the Rio Grande from Mexico. In 1865

[56] Leopoldo Zea, *El Positivismo en Mexico* (Mexico City, El Colegio de Mexico, 1943, pp. 254), *passim;* Leopoldo Zea, *Apogeo y Decadencia del Positivismo en Mexico* (El Colegio de Mexico, 1944, pp. 303), *passim;* Romanell, *Making of the Mexican Mind,* pp. 42 ff.; Crawford, *A Century of Latin-American Thought,* pp. 247 ff.

[57] Leopoldo Zea, *La Filosofia en Mexico* (Biblioteca Minima Mexicana, 1955, pp. 261); Romanell, *op. cit.,* pp. 60 ff.

[58] *Historia Breve y Compendiosa del Colegio Apostolico de Propaganda Fide de N. Sra. de Zapopan* (Guadalajara, C. M. Sainz, 1925, pp. 112, 131B, 22C, vi), *passim.*

[59] Schmidlin-Braun, *Catholic Mission History,* pp. 515, 685; William C. Bennet and Robert M. Zingg, *The Tarahumara, an Indian Tribe of Northern Mexico* (University of Chicago Press, 1935, pp. xix, 412), pp. 236–325.

[60] Schmidlin-Braun, *op. cit.,* p. 685.

[61] Goslin, *Los Evangelicos en la América Latina,* p. 93.

she made her way to Monterey. There she purchased property and subsidized converts as missionaries.[62] From her enterprise eventually came the efforts of the American Board of Commissioners for Foreign Missions. In 1859 a Mexican celebrated what is said to have been the first Protestant Communion in the country.[63] In the Liberal portion of the 1850's some priests had left the Roman Catholic Church and it was one of their number who officiated. In the 1850's a priest of the Protestant Episcopal Church began services. That church was reinforced by former Roman Catholic clergy. In the years of Liberal government which followed the downfall of Maximilian, a number of societies from the United States undertook operations. Among them were the Northern and Southern Presbyterians, the Northern and Southern Methodists, and the Baptists.[64] Later other bodies from the United States arrived, including the Disciples of Christ. In 1888 a conference of most of the Protestant denominations convened in Mexico City and outlined plans for coöperation.[65] Not far from 1914 Protestants counted about 22,000 communicants.[66] Relatively few were from the pure-blooded Indians and almost none from the upper classes.[67]

CENTRAL AMERICA

In colonial days Central America included all the territory south of Mexico to the Isthmus of Panama. It was administered from Guatemala by captains-general under the viceroyalty of New Spain. At the beginning of the nineteenth century it had a population of about a million—mostly Indians, some a mixture of Spanish, Indian, and Negro blood, and a small ruling white minority.

Independence of Spain was declared in 1821 as an echo of similar action in Mexico. For a brief time Central America was included in Iturbide's ephemeral empire. In 1823, with the deposition of Iturbide, independence from Mexico was proclaimed by an assembly in Guatemala City under the name of "the United Provinces of Central America."

The union was torn by provincial jealousies and, as in Mexico, by struggles between those who advocated a strong central government allied with the Church and the Liberals, who were anti-clerical and stood for a federal state. In 1838, after fighting and mounting disorder, even federalism failed and the

[62] Melinda Rankin, *Twenty Years among the Mexicans. A Narrative of Missionary Labor* (Cincinnati, Chase & Hall, 1875, pp. 199), *passim*.

[63] Báez-Camargo and Grubb, *Religion in the Republic of Mexico*, pp. 87, 88.

[64] Goslin, *op. cit.*, pp. 94–104; Latourette, *A History of the Expansion of Christianity*, Vol. V, pp. 114, 115; James Garvin Chastain, *Thirty Years in Mexico* (El Paso, Tex., Baptist Publishing House, introduction 1927, pp. 191), *passim*; E. T. Westrup, *Beginnings. A Saga of Protestantism in Mexico* (Monterey, 1942, pp. 34), *passim*; G. B. Winton, *A New Era in Old Mexico* (Nashville, Tenn., Publishing House Methodist Episcopal Church, South, 1905, pp. viii, 203), *passim*; *Mexico* (New York, Department of Missions, National Council of the Protestant Episcopal Church, 1927, pp. 110), *passim*.

[65] Goslin, *op. cit.*, p. 105.

[66] Beach and St. John, *World Statistics of Christian Missions*, p. 74.

[67] Báez-Camargo and Grubb, *op. cit.*, p. 99.

union broke apart. The successor states were Guatemala, Honduras, El Salvador, Nicaragua, and Costa Rica. In 1903, through a move supported by the United States and to make possible the building of the Panama Canal, Panama separated from Colombia and became the sixth Central American republic. Although officially republics, most of the states continued to suffer from revolutions, dictatorships, and clashes with one another. In the nineteenth century the economy of Central America depended increasingly on coffee and bananas.

The nineteenth-century record in Guatemala was that of Liberal, anti-clerical regimes which alternated with ones having the support of the Roman Catholic Church. At the outset the government was under the influence of the Church. Then, in 1831, the Liberals took over. During their rule the archbishop, a Dominican, Spanish-born, and opposed to independence, was deported, together with the Franciscans, Dominicans, and *Récollets*. Members of all religious orders were forbidden entry, religious toleration was decreed, and the president was declared to have the right to appoint to ecclesiastical offices. Marriage was made a civil contract, divorce was legalized, the number of church holidays was reduced, and nuns were allowed to leave their convents.

The downfall of the Liberal regime, in 1838, with the attendant dissolution of the Central American union, was followed by a pro-clerical government which lasted from 1838 to 1871. During most of that time the country was under the domination of an illiterate Indian, Rafael Carrera. The regulars were permitted to return, the Jesuits, excluded since 1767, were allowed back, and in 1852 a concordat was concluded with Rome, one of the two first with any Spanish American country. The Roman Catholic faith was declared the sole religion, the clergy were given control of education and the censorship of books, tithes were continued, and the Church was assisted from the national treasury. Carrera, as president, was accorded by Rome the right of patronage. Carrera had the enthusiastic support of the Indians. The upper classes, the higher clergy, and the foreigners backed him because he controlled the masses, stood for the rights of property, and, with occasional deviations, supported the Church. He built roads, reduced the national debt, gave an honest financial administration, and improved agriculture.

Carrera died in 1865. In the absence of his strong hand, in 1871 the Liberals once more came to power. Anti-clerical measures followed. From 1871 to his death in battle in 1885 in a futile attempt to bring about the union of Central America, Justo Rufino Barrios was master of the country. Although he was professedly a Roman Catholic, under him the Jesuits, the archbishop, and a bishop were expelled, tithes were abolished, all ecclesiastical property, including that of the religious orders and congregations, was nationalized, civil marriage was made obligatory, priests were forbidden to wear clerical garb in the streets, monastic life whether of men or of women was proscribed, and the cemeteries were secularized. In 1884 a concordat partly eased the tensions between Church and state. Under it the state abandoned its claim to patronage and the Papacy disavowed the privileged position of the Church. But the anti-clerical legislation remained on the books into the twentieth century.[68]

Bible societies had been transiently represented, but the first resident Protestant mission established in Guatemala was under the Liberal regime of Barrios. In 1882 John C. Hill of the Presbyterian Church in the U.S.A. reached the country, his travelling expenses paid by Barrios. For years the only station was in the capital. In 1899 the Central American Mission, founded in 1890 by Cyrus I. Scofield, famous for his widely used reference Bible, began operations.[69] Early in the twentieth century the Southern Baptist Convention undertook a mission. The Plymouth Brethren came in 1900.[70]

In El Salvador, a smaller adjoining republic, the record was not unlike that in Guatemala. In 1841 an independent republic was set up under Conservatives. Its constitution recognized the Roman Catholic faith as the sole religion of the country. At the request of the government, in 1842 the Pope created an episcopal see for El Salvador. The first bishop made himself obnoxious by interfering in politics and placing one of his creatures in the presidency and was ordered out of the country. For a time a Liberal government forced his successor to take refuge in Guatemala, but the coming to power of Conservatives made possible his return. In 1862 a concordat was ratified with the Holy See with much the same terms as that with Guatemala. The Conservatives were in power from 1863 to 1871 and were led by a former Dominican who favoured the Church. Beginning in 1871 Liberals again were in the saddle, as in Guatemala. Much the same religious measures were taken as in the neighbouring country and were written into a constitution adopted in 1883 which remained in force into the twentieth century. Church and state were separated, monastic orders were forbidden, public education was divorced from religious instruction, no cleric could teach in a public school, and religious liberty was guaranteed. Yet the property of the Church was not nationalized, and in the main friendly relations were maintained between the civil and ecclesiastical authorities.[71]

Protestantism was introduced in 1896 by the Central American Mission and what seems to have been the first Protestant church in the country was organized in 1898.[72] In 1911 the Northern Baptists of the United States gained a foothold.[73]

---

[68] Mary P. Holleran, *Church and State in Guatemala* (New York, Columbia University Press, 1949, pp. 359), pp. 73 ff.; Mecham, *op. cit.*, pp. 373–379.

[69] Brown, *One Hundred Years*, pp. 825, 826; Grubb, *Religion in Central America*, pp. 32–36, 61–66; *The Central American Bulletin*, Vol. VIII, No. 4, Oct., 1902, pp. 4, 7; Goslin, *op. cit.*, pp. 84–86, 89.

[70] Beach and St. John, *op. cit.*, p. 74.

[71] Mecham, *op. cit.*, pp. 379–383.

[72] Goslin, *op. cit.*, p. 88; Grubb, *op. cit.*, pp. 76, 77.

[73] White, *A Century of Faith*, pp. 201–207.

Honduras, contiguous with both Guatemala and El Salvador, paralleled its two sister republics in its religious history. Its independent government was inaugurated by Conservatives (1840) with many masses. The next year the Pope appointed as bishop a nominee of the government. From then until 1880 the regimes were friendly to the Church, and three successive constitutions established the Roman Catholic faith and forbade the public exercise of any other. The concordat concluded with Rome in 1861 was almost identical with the earlier one with Guatemala. The constitution of 1880 was the work of Liberals. The concordat was revoked in that year and Church and state were separated. Subsequent steps in 1894 and 1906 further restricted the Church. Monastic houses were forbidden. Civil marriage was the only legal form and divorce was permitted by legal process. Religious teaching in the public schools was proscribed. In theory religious liberty was the rule, but the strong Catholic sentiment of the population made difficult the entrance of Protestantism. Yet priests were few, the church was poverty-stricken, and religion was at a low ebb.[74]

By the year 1914 Protestantism was represented in Honduras by the Central American Mission, the English Methodists, the Southern Baptists, the California Friends, the Seventh Day Adventists, the Plymouth Brethren, and the Church of England.[75]

The politics of Nicaragua were long troubled by the rivalry of the two cities León and Granada. It had begun in colonial times. In the nineteenth century León was the cultural centre and controlled by Liberals, mostly small landowners and professional men. Granada had an aristocratic tradition, upheld by large planters and merchants, and was a Conservative stronghold. Politics were troubled by the ambitions of foreigners.

Yet the Roman Catholic Church did not have quite as stormy a course as in the three republics to the west and north. A concordat was signed with the Vatican in 1862 by which the latter conceded to the civil government the right of presentation to ecclesiastical posts, and the government agreed to support the Church. In 1862 tithes were abolished. Asylum was given to the Jesuits expelled from Guatemala, but in 1881 the members of the Society were driven out for instigating riots.

A Liberal revolt in 1893 brought to power the unscrupulous José Santos Zelaya. In 1909 Zelaya was forced into exile, but in his sixteen-year rule anti-clerical measures were adopted. Adverse legislation had the effect of terminating the concordat and dissolving the union of Church and state. Because of his opposition Bishop Ulloa y Larrios was banished to Panama.

Following the fall of Zelaya the Conservatives were in control. Although Church and state were still separated, the constitution promulgated in 1911 declared that the majority of the population were Roman Catholics. Yet other

74 Mecham, *op. cit.,* pp. 383–386.
75 Beach and St. John, *op. cit.,* p. 74; Grubb, *op. cit.,* pp. 84–86.

cults were permitted if they did not oppose Christian morality and public order. Instruction in the Roman Catholic faith, paid for by the government, was required in the public schools.[76]

Protestantism was represented chiefly by the Moravians (who gained entrance in 1849 through the Mosquito Coast, then under British protection), the Central American Mission, and the American Bible Society.[77]

In contrast with the other Central American states, Costa Rica was predominantly white in population and had a high literacy rate. After its declaration of independence, in 1838, for a brief time a sharp swing from Conservatives to Liberals and then again to Conservatives was seen, but the population was predominantly on the side of the latter and from 1842 to 1883 they were in power. In 1850 Pope Pius IX gave the country a bishopric and in 1852 a concordat was signed on the same date as was that with Guatemala and with much the same terms. Although earlier constitutions declared that the Roman Catholic faith was the only religion to be tolerated, the ones of 1860 and 1871, while making Roman Catholicism the state religion, stipulated that other cults should be permitted. In 1878 a theological seminary was begun for the preparation of an indigenous clergy. Priests were few and declined in proportion to the population. Numbers of them were foreign.[78]

In 1883 a regime less friendly to the Church came into control. In that year the government forbade Jesuits entrance to the country and in the ensuing agitation the bishop was expelled for siding with them. The concordat of 1852 was then abrogated and diplomatic relations with the Vatican were severed. A decree prohibited the establishment of religious communities and another secularized the cemeteries. But with the death of the anti-clerical president peace between Church and state was reëstablished and from 1886 on it continued. In 1908 diplomatic representatives were exchanged with the Vatican.[79]

Under these conditions, with a population for the most party loyally Roman Catholic, Protestantism did not gain much of a foothold. In 1914 it was represented by the Central American Mission, the Jamaica Baptist Union, and the Seventh Day Adventists.[80]

When, in 1903, Panama broke away from Colombia and became an independent republic under the protection of the United States, Liberal sentiment, strong for many years in that area, brought about the separation of Church and state. Because of political disturbances in the preceding century the Church was

[76] Mecham, op. cit., pp. 386–388.

[77] Beach and St. John, op. cit., p. 74; Grubb, op. cit., pp. 90–92; H. G. Schneider, Moskito. Zur Erinnerung an die Feier des fünfzigjährigen Bestehens der Mission der Brüdergemeine in Mittel-Amerika (Herrnhut, Missionsbuchhandlung, preface 1899, pp. viii, 230), passim.

[78] John and Mavis Biesanz, Costa Rican Life (New York, Columbia University Press, 1944, pp. x, 272), pp. 203, 204.

[79] Mecham, op. cit., pp. 388–391.

[80] Beach and St. John, op. cit., p. 74.

weak. Very few native sons entered the priesthood.[81] Although the constitution adopted in 1904 recognized that the Roman Catholic faith was that of the majority of the nation, it granted no special privileges to the Church, guaranteed religious freedom, and had no religious tests for office in the state. Under the new government religious instruction was permitted in the public schools and representatives of the Church were allowed to teach in them. Government aid was given to Roman Catholic schools.[82]

Protestantism was introduced by Methodists from Britain and the United States, the Salvation Army, the Seventh Day Adventists, and the California Quakers.[83]

The Latin Caribbean

In the Caribbean there were, by 1914, three republics which must be classed with Latin America. In addition Puerto Rico, since 1898 belonging to the United States, was in that category.

Religiously Haiti entered upon its career as an independent country under severe handicaps. Its population was overwhelmingly Negro. During French rule, which had lasted from 1676 to 1804, the clergy, exclusively white and of poor quality, had paid relatively little attention to the blacks. The latter had acquired a superficial smattering of Christianity, but African animism persisted as voodooism and obeah.[84]

For several decades after independence the Church was very weak. The government regarded the church buildings as its property and maintained that services could be held in them only with its permission. Rome insisted on controlling the Church and to that the civil authorities, demanding the power of ecclesiastical appointment, would not agree. After 1830 episcopal supervision lapsed for thirty years. The clergy were few and Christian marriage almost died out. Attempts were made by the Papacy to establish working relations with the state, but failed.

At last, in 1860, a concordat was concluded under which the Church was put on a basis to which both it and the state agreed. The bishops were to be nominated by the president of the republic, paid by the state, and appointed by the Pope. Priests were to be appointed by the bishops but approved and supported by the state. Under the concordat a hierarchy was created. In 1864 French priests, nuns, and lay brothers were introduced and thereafter were in charge of the religious, educational, and charitable activities of the Church. Provision was made for training a native priesthood, but very few availed themselves of

[81] Guillerma Rojas y Arrieta, *History of the Bishops of Panama,* translated and edited by T. J. McDonald (Panama, La Academia, 1929, pp. xvi, 255), pp. 207 ff.

[82] Mecham, *op. cit.,* pp. 391, 392.

[83] Beach and St. John, *op. cit.,* p. 74; Grubb, *op. cit.,* pp. 111–113.

[84] Joseph J. Williams, *Voodoos and Obeahs. Phases of West India Witchcraft* (New York, Dial Press, 1933, pp. xvii, 257), pp. 56 ff.

it. The Roman Catholic Church provided most of the schools.[85]

Officially Haiti had religious liberty. Under it Protestantism entered. By 1914 six American societies, one British, and the Jamaica Baptist Union were represented in Haiti or the Dominican Republic. Significantly, two of the earliest of these were Baptist and Methodist Negro bodies.[86]

The Dominican Republic, occupying the eastern end of the island of Haiti, independent in 1844, under the rule of Spain from 1861 to 1865, and again independent in the latter year, had Roman Catholicism as its official religion. The Pope reëstablished the hierarchy in 1848, but the clergy were compelled by the president to be submissive to the state. Under the brief restoration of the rule of Spain a Spaniard was made archbishop. He displaced native priests from the more important posts and substituted his fellow countrymen. The Dominican clergy, therefore, were not unhappy when Spain relinquished its control. On the whole, the relations of Church and state remained friendly. Before 1914 two of the clergy, one of them the archbishop, had served as president of the republic. By an arrangement with the Holy See the archbishop was appointed by the Pope from a list of three candidates, natives or residents, submitted by the Congress of the republic. Most of the clergy were natives. Some were of high quality, but others were quite unworthy. They were too few: shortly before 1914 the priests numbered·only 88 for a population of about 600,000, the vast majority professedly Roman Catholics. In 1908 relations between Church and state were temporarily troubled by the question of the ownership of the buildings and lands occupied by the Church. Both Church and state claimed it and the former won in the instance over which the issue was raised. On the whole, as in many other Latin American countries, the women were more devout than the men. Yet although the latter might be free-thinkers the vast majority insisted that they were Catholics.[87]

Remaining under Spain until 1898, the Church in Cuba experienced some of the vicissitudes of the politics of that country. In an anti-clerical period in 1837–1841 the property of the religious orders was seized by the state and after long controversy the state agreed (1861) to pay the Church an annual rental for what had been put to secular uses. Some of the intellectual currents of the revolutionary age made themselves felt. For example, a priest, Felix Varela y Morales (1787–1853), in teaching philosophy attacked scholasticism.

Since in the Spanish period all the bishops and most of the clergy were appointed from Madrid, the rebellion which issued in the intervention of the United States and independence was directed in part against them. In conse-

[85] Mecham, *op. cit.*, pp. 340–349; *The Catholic Encyclopedia*, Vol. VII, p. 115.

[86] Beach and St. John, *op. cit.*, p. 75.

[87] Mecham, *op. cit.*, pp. 349–354; *The Catholic Encyclopedia*, Vol. XIII, p. 464; Otto Schoenrich, *Santo Domingo. A Country with a Future* (New York, The Macmillan Co., 1918, pp. xiv, 418), pp. 185 ff.

quence, one of the early acts of the republic was to sever the tie between Church and state and to guarantee religious liberty. Thanks to the firmness of the military governor from the United States who administered the country while the republic was being set up, the Church escaped the expropriation of its property by the state. The first native archbishop was consecrated in 1899. Positivism made itself felt, especially through Enrique José Verona y Pera (1849–1933).[88]

Protestantism had gained a slight foothold in Cuba before 1898—through the American Bible Society in 1882 and the Southern Baptist Convention in 1886. After independence other Protestant bodies entered from the United States and by 1914 eleven of them were represented.[89]

Puerto Rico had a record not unlike that of Cuba. During the long period of Spanish rule the crown had the right of patronage. In the anti-clerical period in Spain in the 1840's the Church was despoiled of much of its property and the only two religious communities, the Dominicans and Franciscans, were disbanded. With the return to power of the Conservatives in Spain a new concordat was entered into with Rome (1851). After the cession to the United States the Roman Catholic Church had complete freedom.[90] In the years which immediately followed about a dozen Protestant bodies began operations. Relatively they had more success than in Cuba. Most of the impact and growth of Protestantism, as elsewhere in Latin America, came after 1914.[91]

THE FRENCH POSSESSIONS

The French possessions in the Lesser Antilles and South America need not long detain us: their population was small and they did not play a large part in the total Christian scene. In the first half of the nineteenth century Jean Marie Robert de Lamennais, founder of the School Brothers of Ploermel, and Libermann, who revived the Society of the Holy Ghost, concerned themselves with Guadeloupe. Members of their congregations went to the island, and partly at their instance a bishopric was created for it (1850) as a suffragan see of the Archdiocese of Bordeaux. Two congregations of sisters also came to help.[92] Similarly, members of the Society of the Holy Ghost and of three congregations of sisters went to Martinique. The abolishment of slavery, one of the fruits of the Revolution of 1848, made their work even more imperative. Martinique was also placed (1850) under a diocese tied to the Archdiocese of Bordeaux.[93] French Guiana, sparsely settled and largely a penal colony, was ecclesiastically in the Prefecture Apostolic of Cayenne, erected in 1731.[94]

---

[88] Crawford, *A Century of Latin-American Thought*, pp. 218 ff.; Mecham, *op. cit.*, pp. 354, 359; *The Catholic Encyclopedia*, Vol. IV, pp. 560, 561.

[89] Beach and St. John, *op. cit.*, p. 76.

[90] *The Catholic Encyclopedia*, Vol. XII, p. 293.

[91] Beach and St. John, *op. cit.*, p. 75.

[92] *The Catholic Encyclopedia*, Vol. VII, p. 44.

[93] *Ibid.*, Vol. IX, p. 731.

[94] *Ibid.*, Vol. VII, p. 63.

VENEZUELA

Venezuela was possessed of great mineral wealth, especially in petroleum and iron, which was exploited in the twentieth century. But in the nineteenth century it was comparatively poor and suffered from much domestic fighting and from dictators. Its population was predominantly mestizo, with minorities of whites, Indians, and Negroes. The struggle for independence is said to have cost it a fourth of its people, a toll which was especially heavy on its young men. In the conflict the Church was dealt heavy blows from which it did not fully recover.

From its declared independence of Spain until 1830 Venezuela was in theory part of the Gran Colombia which Bolívar sought to construct from the former viceroyalty which comprised the later Venezuela, Colombia, and Ecuador. Ecclesiastical policy was determined by the programme for that inclusive state. In 1824 an elaborate law was enacted to govern the relations with the Church.[95] It affirmed the right of the state to continue the exercise of patronage which the kings of Spain had held. Among other functions it declared that the state had the power to erect new dioceses or reorganize old ones; to permit or call national or provincial councils and synods; to suppress existing monasteries or hospitals and to permit or prevent the founding of new ones; to regulate the administration of tithes; to fix parochial fees; to control missions to the Indians; to nominate those presented to the Pope for episcopal or archiepiscopal sees; to grant or refuse permission for the publication of Papal bulls or decrees; to name men to all the positions in the Church; and to erect new parishes. The law also contained minute regulations for filling ecclesiastical vacancies. Because of the lax discipline in the monasteries and the decline in membership, in 1821 houses were ordered suppressed which had less than eight members and their property was to be applied to education and charity. In 1826 the admission of novices under twenty-five years of age was forbidden. In 1828 Bolívar issued decrees which favoured the Church but aroused much anti-clerical criticism. In all the subsequent changes in government no action was taken abrogating the essential features of the Law of Patronage.[96]

Soon after the separation from Gran Colombia trouble developed between Church and state. Anti-clericalism had been more pronounced in Venezuela than in New Granada, the later Colombia. Bentham had been taught in the state universities and colleges in place of religious subjects. The Masons had criticized the clergy for opposing the distribution of Bibles. The clergy had been accused of impeding the establishment of friendly relations with foreigners

[95] Carlos Sanchez Espejo, *El Patronato en Venezuela* (Caracas, 1953, pp. xxi, 198), pp. 110 ff.; Watters, *A History of the Church in Venezuela 1810–1930*, pp. 100–103 (the text is translated on pp. 222–237); Mecham, *Church and State in Latin America*, pp. 112–115; W. W. Pierson in A. Curtis Wilgus, editor, *The Caribbean Area* (Washington, The George Washington Press, 1934, pp. vii, 604), pp. 438–439.

[96] Watters, *op. cit.*, pp. 118–121.

and foreign governments.[97] Although the breach with Gran Colombia was ascribed to a "conservative" oligarchy, that regime was as radical in its attitude towards the Church as any which followed. It was dominated by the powerful José Antonio Páez (1790–1873), who had come to maturity on the range as a cattle man and in guerrilla war. Páez determined to make the state supreme in all aspects of the national life. Because Archbishop Méndez, who owed his appointment to Bolívar, objected to the attitude of the government on religion and placed reservations on his oath of loyalty to the state, he was banished (1831). Two other prelates were exiled for the same reason. In 1832 they submitted unconditionally and were permitted to return. The tithe was abolished in 1833. In 1834, to encourage immigration, freedom of religion was decreed. In 1836 Méndez was again exiled for criticism of government measures and for refusing to give canonical institution to two men presented by the head of the state. He died in New Granada (1839).[98]

Méndez lamented the low state of the Church and said that the faith of the majority was limited to baptism and the last rites. Clergy were too few to give adequate pastoral care. The Church had lost prestige and could not offer sufficient financial compensation to induce men to enter the priesthood. In the fore part of the 1840's some attempts were made to restore the missions to the Indians and to attract missionaries from abroad, but with only occasional success.[99]

From 1846 to 1861 the Monagas brothers, José Tadeo and José Gregorio, were the chief figures. Their attitude towards the Church was ambiguous. Orders were issued not to admit any foreign priest without the permission of the government. The Jesuits were expelled and soon all foreign clergy, secular and regular, were commanded to leave the country. Yet chairs in ecclesiastical subjects were ordered established in all the national colleges and appropriations for the support of the Church were increased. But in 1855, of the 475 parishes only 154 were regularly filled.[100]

From 1861 to 1870 a near approach to chaos ensued from attempts at federalism as against centralism. However, for a brief time, 1861–1863, Páez was dictator and under him in 1862 a concordat was signed in Rome by Antonelli, the Papal Secretary of State, and was approved by the council of state in 1863. While it conceded to the president the right of patronage, it had clauses which were favourable to the Church.[101]

The principal figure from 1870 to 1888 was Antonio Guzmán Blanco (1829–1899). Professedly a Liberal and a federalist, well educated and cosmopolitan, spending much of his time in Paris, a Masonic grand master, noted for luxurious living, he was emphatically anti-clerical. His anti-clericalism seems to have

[97] *Ibid.*, pp. 108–115.
[98] *Ibid.*, pp. 125–140; Mecham, *op. cit.*, pp. 121–126.
[99] Watters, *op. cit.*, pp. 156–158.
[100] *Ibid.*, pp. 163–168; Mecham, *op. cit.*, pp. 126–128.
[101] Watters, *op. cit.*, pp. 168–172; Mecham, *op. cit.*, pp. 128, 129.

been due in large part to his personal vanity and the ambition to bring the Church fully under his control. His antagonism was stiffened by the attitude of the clergy: many of them sought to give to the political resistance to him a religious sanction.

The anti-clerical measures of Guzmán Blanco began early in the 1870's. Archbishop Guevara y Lira was exiled without judicial procedure and priests who supported him were either imprisoned or expelled from the country. The theological seminaries which Guevara had nurtured in an attempt to strengthen the Church with a Venezuelan clergy were destroyed. Priests were to receive their education in the national university and here Papal infallibility was repudiated. Communities of nuns which Guevara had fostered were broken up. Civil marriage and the civil registry of births, marriages, and deaths were decreed. Restrictions were placed on the inheritance of property by priests, and the prohibition of the marriage of the clergy was removed. Subventions to the Church were suspended. Public education was declared to be free, lay, and obligatory and parish schools were abolished. Guevara, in his refuge in Trinidad, proved obdurate and suspended from their ecclesiastical functions priests who yielded to Guzmán Blanco. But eventually under pressure, apparently from Pius IX, who wished to bring peace to the Venezuelan church, he resigned. Guzmán Blanco insisted on the full right of patronage and gave cavalier treatment to a Papal legate sent to restore peace. The Church was charged with being obscurantist and opposed to progress.[102]

In the later years of his dictatorship Guzmán Blanco had less unfriendly relations with the Church. The Church had been cowed and on his return from France in 1888 the occasion was celebrated by a *Te Deum* in the cathedral. He even sponsored the introduction from France of the Sisters of Charity of St. Joseph of Tarbes to serve in hospitals and to share in the education of girls.[103]

After Guzmán Blanco's death the Roman Catholic Church made a slow recovery. The dictators who succeeded him, ruling as president or through their creatures in that office, were masterful men. Cipriano Castro (1858–1924), who held power from 1899 to 1908, had never gone to school and had come up through the rough and tumble of civil war and with the support of a private army. Juan Vicente Gómez (1857–1935) had had little formal education, had been a lieutenant of Castro, and had taken the occasion of the latter's absence for medical care to supplant him. Under Castro and Gómez most of the anticlerical laws were kept on the statute books but were not strictly enforced. The constitution of 1904 declared Roman Catholicism to be the religion of the state, but by the constitution of 1914 it was deprived of that position. Various orders and congregations were allowed to enter, at least two by invitation of the government. Yet the prohibition against monasteries was not revoked. In 1900 ec-

---

[102] Watters, *op. cit.*, pp. 184–213; Mecham, *op. cit.*, pp. 131–134; Pierson, *op. cit.*, pp. 442–444.
[103] Mecham, *op. cit.*, pp. 134, 135.

clesiastical seminaries were again permitted. In that year the archbishop was authorized to bring in fifty Spanish regulars to serve in the missions to the Indians. Various attempts were made, at least partly with the financial support of the state, to renew the missions as a means of "civilizing" the Indians. Yet the missions did not attain the dimensions or the success that had been theirs in colonial days. Nor did the Roman Catholic faith regain the place in the country as a whole which it had held under Spanish rule.[104]

Protestantism had difficulty in gaining an entrance in Venezuela and down to 1914 made little headway. From the 1820's the American Bible Society was intermittently represented and its agents often faced popular hostility. In the 1880's Plymouth Brethren came. In the late 1880's and 1890 the Methodist Episcopal Church made a futile effort to gain a foothold. The year 1897 saw the establishment of continuing enterprises by the Christian and Missionary Alliance and the Presbyterian Church in the U.S.A. By 1914 beginnings had also been made by the Scandinavian Alliance of North America, the Scandinavian Free Church, the Hebron Home Institute and Missionary Association, and the Canadian Brethren. After that year they grew and others entered.[105]

COLOMBIA

By its geography Colombia was cut off from the quick influx of ideas from the outer world. Two-thirds of its area was mountain and jungle draining into the Orinoco. The large majority of its population were on the high plateaus and valleys of the Magdalena and Cauca rivers, which emptied jointly into the Caribbean. In the nineteenth century about a fifth of the people were white, nearly three-fourths mestizos, and the remainder divided about equally between Indians and Negroes.

As in Mexico and to a less extent in Venezuela, the chronic controversies and civil wars were between Conservatives, standing for a strong central government and the perpetuation of the privileges of the upper classes and the Church, and the Liberals, championing the sovereignty of the several departments (or states) into which the country was divided, universal suffrage, and the separation of Church and state.

The controversy over the relation of Church and state was more acute than in any other Latin American country except Mexico. The upholders of the Church were convinced that the nation must be committed to the Roman Catholic faith and were intensely hostile to any dissent. The Liberals, no less ardent, drew their inspiration largely from the men of the Enlightenment—Voltaire, Montesquieu, and Rousseau.

[104] Watters, *op. cit.*, pp. 214–221; Ryan, *The Church in the South American Republics,* pp. 78, 79; Mecham, *op. cit.*, pp. 135, 136.
[105] Grubb, *The Northern Republics of South America,* pp. 103–107; Goslin, *Los Evangelicos en la América Latina,* pp. 79–82.

From the failure of Bolívar's dream of Gran Colombia, made final by his death in 1830, until 1849 Colombia, now independent, was generally under the rule of Conservatives. The constitution framed in 1831 for New Granada, as the country was then called, declared the Roman Catholic faith to be the religion of the republic and no other was allowed. It maintained that the state had the duty to protect the citizens "in the exercise of the Roman Catholic Apostolic religion." Yet the government claimed more extensive rights of patronage than had ever been exercised by the Spanish crown. In addition, in 1836 a law made the civil courts supreme in several realms which heretofore had been regarded as belonging exclusively to the Church. But in 1835, thanks in no small degree to the skilful diplomacy of Tajeda, Pope Gregory XVI recognized the independence of New Granada, the first Spanish American republic to be accorded that honour, and by preconizing four bishops and an archbishop fully restored the hierarchy.[106]

In the late 1830's and the 1840's, when they were in power, although they supported the Roman Catholic Church and permitted the Jesuits to return, the Conservatives took measures which ran counter to what the more ardent churchmen wished. They permitted the use of the works of Jeremy Bentham as texts in the schools. They sought to enforce a law which forbade admission to the novitiates in monasteries before the age of twenty-five. They abolished the tithe and reduced the state subsidy to the Church.

In 1849 the Liberals won control of the government and with slight interruptions held it until 1880. Pressure on the Church was occasionally eased, but measures were taken which were distinctly anti-clerical. The Jesuits were expelled (1850)[107] and although in a few years they were allowed to return (1853) and a college was put under their direction, they were later (1861) again ordered out of the country. In place of the tithe a fixed income was set for the clergy. Separate ecclesiastical courts were abolished and the supreme court was accorded jurisdiction over ecclesiastical cases. The theological seminary of the archdiocese was incorporated in the national college, thus giving the state control of education for the priesthood. In 1853 the separation of Church and state was effected, said to have been the first act of that kind in all Latin America. Civil marriage was made obligatory and cemeteries were secularized. In the constitution of 1858 religious liberty was guaranteed. In 1861 all religious houses were ordered suppressed and the property of religious corporations was confiscated. For their opposition to the Liberal programme one archbishop was exiled, another was imprisoned, and several other prelates and clergy were imprisoned or exiled. Because of the resistance of the clergy, some churches were closed. Indian missions suffered.[108]

106 Mecham, *op. cit.*, pp. 141–145.
107 Pérez, *La Compañía de Jesus en Colombia y Centro-América despues de su Restauración,* Part I, *passim.*
108 Mecham, *op. cit.*, pp. 148–155; Ryan, *op. cit.*, pp. 60, 61.

A Conservative turn in the tide came in 1880 and continued beyond 1914. That year marked the coming to the presidency of Rafael Núñez (1825–1894). An intellectual and civilian who had spent a number of years in Europe observing and studying, he was at first a Liberal. However, partly under the influence of Herbert Spencer, he came to believe in the slow evolution of institutions. He ended by becoming a convinced Conservative, holding that progress for Colombia depended on Catholic morality, centralization in government, and vigorous economic controls by the state. Yet he favoured religious tolerance. From 1880 to 1894 he was the leading man in the country. Weary of strife and resentful of attacks on the Church, the majority welcomed his strong and pro-clerical administration. Out of a civil war in 1884 and 1885 Núñez emerged as victor and the head of a coalition of Conservatives and moderate Liberals in the National Party. In 1886 a constitution was adopted and, amended in 1904 and 1905, continued in force into the twentieth century. The constitution was declared to be that of "the Republic of Colombia," as against the designation "the Republic of New Granada" adopted in 1831 and altered in 1861 to "the United States of Colombia"—the change of 1886 being evidence of the triumph of centralization. It said that "the Catholic Apostolic Roman Religion is that of the nation; the public authorities will protect it and cause it to be respected as an essential element to social order." Yet it also went on to affirm: "It is understood that the Catholic Church is not and shall not be official, and shall preserve its independence."[109]

A concordat followed (signed December 31, 1887, and approved by the Congress in 1888) which governed relations with the Holy See well beyond 1914. It provided that the Roman Catholic Church was to enjoy complete liberty and independence of the civil power; that canonical legislation, independent of the civil law, would be respected by the authorities of the republic; that the Church should have the right to acquire property, but that the property was to be taxed in the same manner and to the same extent as private property; that members of the clergy were to be exempt from military service; that, with the authorization of ecclesiastical authority, religious orders and associations of both sexes could be constituted; that in all schools, universities, and colleges education and public instruction would be in conformity with the dogmas and morals of the Catholic religion, that religious instruction would be obligatory in them, the pious practices of the Catholic religion would be observed, and the texts used, both in religious and other subjects, would be selected by the ecclesiastical authorities; that the president of the republic could recommend to the Pope men to fill archiepiscopal and episcopal sees, that the Pope would treat the nominations with respect and would give opportunity to the president to say whether a candidate was objectionable for civil or political reasons; that, after consultation with the civil government, the Holy See could establish new dioceses and

109 Herring, *A History of Latin America,* pp. 480–482; Ryan, *op. cit.,* pp. 60, 61.

alter the boundaries of existing ones; that in the marriages of Roman Catholics the provisions of the Council of Trent would be observed and the ceremony would be witnessed by a functionary determined by law simply to verify it for record in the civil register; that in the churches a prayer would be said regularly for the president; and that the Holy See granted to the government the property of convents and religious associations which had already been extinguished and in return the government would make an annual financial contribution to the Church. Subsequent conventions (1892 and 1898) adjusted other issues, including the special privileges of the Church (*fuero eclesiástico*), the control of cemeteries, and the amount of the state's subvention to the Church. In 1902 a further convention had to do with missions to the Indians. It provided for their state support with the aid of the Church as "instruments of civilization and culture" and making effective national control. They were thus continuations of the frontier policy of colonial days.[110]

Although the close association of Church and state formalized in these documents was maintained into the twentieth century, the Liberals were restive and staged unsuccessful insurrections. They demanded the complete separation of Church and state and full freedom of speech and institutions.[111]

Under these conditions Protestantism had difficulty in gaining entrance. Although the constitution of 1886 declared that "no one shall be molested because of his religious opinions nor compelled by the authorities to profess beliefs nor to observe practices contrary to his conscience" and permitted "the exercise of all forms of worship which are not contrary to Christian morals nor to the laws,"[112] the sentiment of the majority and the control exercised by the Roman Catholic Church all but nullified the religious liberty thus guaranteed.

Yet during the years of Liberal government a slight Protestant foothold was obtained. On invitation of an officer of a British legion which had served under Bolívar and who, with his descendants, remained in the country and held to his ancestral Presbyterianism, in 1856 a representative of the Presbyterian Church in the U.S.A. reached Bogotá. In 1861 a congregation, all foreigners, was organized in that city, and in 1869 a building was dedicated for it and a school for girls was opened. A school for boys followed in 1885 and in that year the first Colombians were received into the Church. Before 1914 the Presbyterians established centres in a few other cities.[113] In the 1880's the American Bible Society had an agent in the country and in 1912–1913 the Gospel Missionary Union, with headquarters in Kansas City, sent two men.[114]

[110] Mecham, *op. cit.*, pp. 156–164. On the Franciscans, see Arcila Robledo, *La Orden Franciscana en el América Meridional*, pp. 67–69.

[111] Mecham, *op. cit.*, p. 167.

[112] W. Reginald Wheeler and Webster E. Browning, *Modern Missions on the Spanish Main. Impressions of Protestant Work in Colombia and Venezuela* (Philadelphia, The Westminster Press, 1925, pp. xii, 334), pp. 223, 224.

[113] *Ibid.*, pp. 230–236.

[114] Grubb, *op. cit.*, pp. 70, 71.

ECUADOR

Ecuador, lying athwart the equator and named for it, was one of the fragments of Bolívar's Gran Colombia. It had a higher proportion of Indians and a somewhat smaller proportion of whites than its northern neighbour. The victim of the ambitions of adjoining republics, it lost to Colombia and Peru much of the territory to which it laid claim.

During the first years of independence from Gran Colombia, a step taken in 1830, the country was ruled alternately by two rivals, Juan José Flores, a soldier who had served under Bolívar, and Vicente Rocafuerte, a Liberal intellectual, scion of a wealthy aristocratic family, who had spent much time in the United States, France, England, and Mexico. Although Flores had little interest in religion, he backed the Roman Catholic Church as the sole religious body. Rocafuerte professed the Roman Catholic faith but gave his support to anti-clerical measures. He sought to take education out of the hands of the Church, attempted to introduce Protestantism, and advocated the reform of the clergy and a better education for the priesthood. In 1843 Rocafuerte left the country, followed in 1845 by Flores.[115]

From a fifteen-year-long period of near anarchy (1845–1860) with ephemeral regimes, usually Liberal, Ecuador was rescued by García Moreno. Gabriel García Moreno (1821–1875) was one of the most remarkable men in the history of Latin America. Born in Guayaquil, the son of a Spanish merchant, he was educated in law at the Central University in Quito. He was in Europe not far from 1848 and what he saw there of the effects of the revolutions of that year, reinforced by what he observed later in a period of exile to that continent, confirmed him in his conviction that the Roman Catholic faith and the Conservative ideal held the only hope of escape from chaos, whether for his own little country or the Western world. In this he reminds us of an older contemporary, Juan Donoso Cortés of Spain.[116] He engaged actively in Ecuadorian politics, partly as an editor and partly in the civil strife of the tumultuous decades. He seized power in 1860 and was president from 1861 to 1865 and from 1869 to his assassination.

Deeply religious, feeding his soul on *The Imitation of Christ,* García Moreno sought to improve the character of the Church and to give it a dominant and exclusive position in the life of the nation. He was responsible for a concordat (1862) which among other features made Roman Catholicism the only religion of the republic; agreed that no cult or society condemned by the Church would be permitted; provided for a seminary in every diocese; declared that instruction in all the universities, colleges, and public and private schools must conform to Roman Catholic doctrine and that the bishops should have the exclusive right to designate texts for religious and moral instruction and could prohibit books

[115] Herring, *op. cit.*, pp. 502–504; Mecham, *op. cit.*, pp. 170–174.
[116] Volume I, pp. 422, 423.

"contrary to religion and good custom"; made necessary the authorization of the diocesan prelate for all teachers in private or public institutions; permitted free communication of clergy and people with the Holy See without interference of the civil government; made the ecclesiastical courts fully independent of the civil courts; accorded the right to the president to propose to the Pope nominations for the episcopacy and to appoint prebends and canons and to select the parish priests from lists sent him by the ordinaries; granted to the Holy See the power to erect new dioceses and specified that because the existing ones were too large additional ones should be created; recognized the right of the Church to acquire property; allowed the diocesan authorities to admit and establish new orders and promised the aid of the government in such steps; and assured the assistance of the state in missions among the non-Christians in the republic. To make the concordat effective a Papal legate was sent to supervise the much-needed reform of the clergy and four new dioceses were created. Provincial councils were called which dealt with the curriculums and discipline of the seminaries and the Church was purged of many unworthy priests. To cap his loyalty to the Roman Catholic faith, García Moreno had the Congress dedicate Ecuador to the Sacred Heart of Jesus. He undertook other measures to improve the religious, moral, and educational life of the country. He was responsible for the coming of the Jesuits. Teaching orders and congregations were introduced, especially from France. The Jesuits were authorized to establish institutions of learning.

The energies of García Moreno were not confined to religion and education. He put the country on a better financial basis, attracted foreign capital, sought to improve agriculture, and, the soul of honesty, gave his own salary to charity and strove to eliminate corruption.[117]

García Moreno met opposition, both from intellectuals and from political rivals. For example, Juan Montalvo (1832–1889), who had spent time in Europe, was an advocate of justice and liberty, attacked tyranny and obscurantism, and was a vigorous critic.[118]

After García Moreno succumbed to the assassins' machetes and bullets, for some years the country oscillated between short-lived Conservative and Liberal regimes. Something of the sad condition of the Church can be seen in the fact that a German Jesuit sent in 1886 to take charge of the ecclesiastical situation suspended nearly all the indigenous clergy and installed an almost entirely new hierarchy.[119]

[117] Ryan, *op. cit.*, pp. 64–67; Herring, *op. cit.*, pp. 504, 505; Mecham, *op. cit.*, pp. 174–185; *The Catholic Encyclopedia*, Vol. VI, pp. 379–381; Williams, *The People and Politics of Latin America*, pp. 561–565. On the Franciscans, reinstituted in Ecuador in 1895 and sharing in education and missions to the Indians, see Arcila Robledo, *op. cit.*, pp. 79, 80. On the Jesuits see Pérez, *op. cit.*, Part I, pp. 369 ff., 441 ff.

[118] Crawford, *A Century of Latin-American Thought*, pp. 170–173.

[119] Ryan, *op. cit.*, p. 68.

Then, in 1895 the Liberal anti-clerical Eloy Alfaro seized power and with a four-year interval (1901–1905), a few months of it marked by a brief Conservative reaction, held it until after 1914. Various anti-clerical measures were taken. In 1899 legislation was enacted which was contrary to the concordat and that document was in effect terminated. Civil marriage and divorce were permitted. Religious toleration was enjoined by law. The founding of new monasteries was prohibited. Tithes were abolished. Public education was made essentially secular. A constitution proclaimed in 1906 separated Church and state. Yet a department of worship was maintained to administer ecclesiastical patronage.[120]

Missions to non-Christian Indians were revived, not only under García Moreno but under later, anti-clerical regimes. They were chiefly staffed from Europe—by Franciscans, Salesians of Don Bosco, Jesuits, and Dominicans.[121]

Protestantism was slow in establishing a continuing foothold in Ecuador. James Thomson was briefly in the country. In 1877 William Taylor touched there. In 1828 an agent of the British and Foreign Bible Society and in 1886 a representative of the American Bible Society visited Guayaquil. In 1896, under the Liberal government, agents of the Gospel Missionary Union settled in that city and the following year gained entrance to Quito. Within a few years they were at work in other centres. In 1900 Methodists from the United States obtained the consent of Alfaro to open normal schools: these institutions lasted only three or four years, but in that short span of time a church of about 350 members was gathered in Quito. In 1904 the Seventh Day Adventists began operations.[122]

PERU

Peru had been the centre of Spanish rule in South America. In its capital, Lima, "the City of Kings," the desiccated body of Pizarro, displayed in the cathedral for all to see, was a continuing symbol of the conquest. Church and state were closely allied.

Under independence the relations between Church and state continued, with modifications. Anti-clericalism was not as rampant as in most of the other Spanish American countries. Political independence came as a result of external pressure, first from San Martín and then from Bolívar. The bishops supported the cause of the king and either were exiled or voluntarily left the country. Many of the lower clergy, native Peruvians and numbers of them mestizos, actively endorsed independence. On some of them the Enlightenment had impinged and had led them to espouse the liberalism associated with the French Revolu-

[120] Mecham, *op. cit.*, pp. 186–190.

[121] Lemmens, *Geschichte der Franziskanermissionen*, p. 288; *Revista de la Exposición Missional Española*, Nov., 1928, pp. 75–78; Berg, *Die katholische Heidenmission als Kulturträger*, Vol. I, p. 224; Freitag in *Zeitschrift für Missionswissenschaft*, Vol. XI, pp. 175, 176.

[122] Grubb, *op. cit.*, pp. 31–34; Goslin, *op. cit.*, pp. 72–75.

tion. In 1826 only one bishop remained between Ecuador and the Straits of Magellan. He was opposed to independence and Bolívar took most of his authority from him. In 1835 the Pope preconized the first republican archbishop, thus establishing relations with independent Peru, but without formal recognition of that status or of the right of presenting him with a candidate. In the constitution of 1828 the Roman Catholic faith was called the religion of the state and the exercise of any other religion was forbidden. In later constitutions —1839, 1856, and 1860—the prohibition was relaxed to the extent of confining it to the public exercise of any other cult. In the 1850's, under Liberals, the exemption of clergy from the jurisdiction of the civil courts was terminated and tithes were abolished, but the state paid the hierarchy and financially assisted the seminaries, colleges, and hospitals of the Church. The constitution of 1860, a document which remained in force until after 1914, was the work of a Conservative government. It defined the exercise of the patronage by the state and the relations with the Holy See. Although no formal concordat existed, in 1875 Pope Pius IX conceded the right of patronage as it had been enjoyed by the kings of Spain. Yet the bull did not prove entirely satisfactory to the Peruvian Government and not until 1880 did the latter assent to it. By a law enacted in 1901 the Church and religious orders were allowed to acquire property, but could not receive it by bequest. Religious instruction by the Church was obligatory in public primary and intermediate schools. Marriages were required by law to be celebrated according to the rules of the Council of Trent, but after 1897 weddings of persons not of the Roman Catholic faith were exempted. Not until 1915 was religious toleration explicitly the subject of legislation.[123]

Strong though the Roman Catholic Church was politically, it did not succeed in making its faith more than a social convention among the majority or in preventing religious indifference. It more and more failed to attract to its priesthood scions of the aristocracy or even of the middle classes. Most of the clergy came from the less desirable elements.[124] Many were of inferior moral character and were deficient in education. Recurrent civil strife handicapped efforts to remedy conditions. Vacillating policies of the government were further obstacles. For example, in 1887 the Jesuits were expelled but later were permitted to return. In 1899 an attempt to abolish all religious communities was made but failed.[125] The Church had its critics among the intellectuals. Thus Manuel González Prada (1848-1918), the most distinguished Peruvian writer of the century, an admirer of Rousseau, was anti-clerical and said that the Catholicism of the country was idolatry.[126] The trend towards the secularization of the intellectual life was further seen when San Marcos, the oldest university

[123] Mecham, *op. cit.*, pp. 197–219.
[124] *Ibid.*, 216, 217. On the Franciscans see Arcila Robledo, *op. cit.*, pp. 111 ff.
[125] Ryan, *op. cit.*, pp. 71–73.
[126] Crawford, *op. cit.*, pp. 173–182.

in the country and one of the two oldest in the Americas, founded and long maintained by the Dominicans, was taken out of the hands of the Church and placed under the state. The act was a symbol of what the revolutionary age did to the realm of thought not only in Peru but elsewhere in Latin America.

Efforts to convert the non-Christian Indians were renewed, but they were carried on by missionaries from Europe—Franciscans, Augustinians, and Dominicans.[127]

Not until the 1880's did Protestantism become a continuing feature of the Peruvian scene. James Thomson arrived in 1822 at the invitation of San Martín to organize an educational system for the country on the Lancastrian plan and was there a little over two years. He was aided by a friendly priest. He introduced the New Testament in his schools but did not seek directly to win the students to Protestantism. He also distributed Bibles and New Testaments for the British and Foreign Bible Society and in this was assisted by some of the clergy, including the archbishop. In the decades which followed, the British and Foreign Bible Society and the American Bible Society from time to time succeeded in circulating copies of the Scriptures. In 1849 a church was organized to serve the English colony. In the 1860's the South American Missionary Society sent a clergyman to minister to the English residents, especially in Callao, the port of Lima, and some Peruvian children were pupils in the school which was conducted. Additional representatives of the Society came, but in the 1870's the efforts were discontinued. The redoubtable William Taylor was in Peru in 1877–1878 and inaugurated a mission programme designed to be self-supporting through schools. In 1887, however, the last of his schools closed. In 1884 the Presbyterian Church in the U.S.A. made an effort to care for sojourners from that country but abandoned it in 1896.

The beginning of continuing Protestantism among the Peruvians was through Francisco G. Penzotti. Penzotti, a carpenter by trade, was Italian-born and came to Montevideo at the age of thirteen. There through hearing Methodist preaching he became a Protestant. He went to Peru in the 1880's as a colporteur of the American Bible Society. He gathered a small church in Callao, the first in the country for Spanish-speaking people. On the ground that he was thus violating the constitution of Peru, although he was careful to have its meetings private, some of the Roman Catholic clergy had him imprisoned (1889). The case was prolonged and eventually attracted wide interest in the United States. In 1891 on a decision of the supreme court he was set free. His release was a major step towards religious liberty. Methodist missionaries from the United States carried on the congregation that he had gathered in Callao.

---

[127] Lemmens, *op. cit.*, pp. 303–306; Bernardino Izaquirre, *Historia de las Misiónes Franciscanas y Narración de los Progresos de la Geografía en el Oriente del Perú* (Lima, Talleres Tipográficos de la Penitenciaria, Vols. X, XI, XII, 1925, 1926), *passim;* Schmidlin-Braun, *Catholic Mission History*, p. 679.

By 1914 several other Protestant agencies had established themselves and, sometimes in face of bitter opposition by the clergy, reached additional centres. Among the societies were the Regions Beyond Missionary Union, followed by the Evangelical Union of South America, the Holiness Church of California, the Salvation Army, the Seventh Day Adventists, the Independent Baptist Missionary Movement, and the Church of the Nazarene. Yet in 1914 Peruvian Protestants were still few.[128]

BOLIVIA

Bolivia, named for Bolívar, had an unfortunate geography and history. Alto Peru in colonial days, at the close of the nineteenth century four-fifths of its population, nine-tenths of them Indians and mestizos, largely illiterate, eked out a scanty subsistence on the high tablelands which constituted two-fifths of the country's area. The other fifth of the population, mostly in a condition little better than serfdom, worked the great landed estates which covered much of the eastward-stretching valleys and plains comprising three-fifths of the area. During the nineteenth century all the seaboard and much of the inland territory of the hapless republic was grabbed by its neighbours—Brazil, Peru, Paraguay, Chile, and Argentina.

Internally, Bolivia was the victim of shifting governments. In the early days of its independence two men, both honest and patriotic, successively attempted to save it from its internal and external enemies—Antonio José de Sucre and Andrés Santa Cruz, the latter the son of a Spanish father and an Indian mother who was said to have imperial Inca blood in her veins. For a time Santa Cruz seemed to have achieved his ambition of uniting Bolivia and Peru, but in 1839 an army from Chile shattered the dream and the dreamer was exiled. A spate of revolutions combined with a disastrous war with Chile (1879–1893) brought a low ebb to the country's fortunes. In the 1880's and 1890's recovery was accomplished, although slowly. Progress and internal and foreign peace continued under Liberal rule until after 1914.

Religiously the Bolivian record was chequered. In the struggle for independence the hierarchy stood staunchly by Spain and the archbishop sought to reform the Church. But several of the lower clergy, some of them irked by the disciplinary measures, supported the effort to throw off the Spanish yoke. The constitution of 1826 declared the Roman Catholic religion to be that of the country "to the exclusion of all other public cults." The tie between Church and state continued and not until 1905 was the constitution amended to permit the public exercise of all cults. In 1851 an agreement was signed with the Holy

128 Wenceslao Oscar Bahamonde, *The Establishment of Evangelical Christianity in Peru (1822–1900)* (Hartford, Conn., mimeographed, 1952, pp. vi, 183), *passim*; Goslin, *op. cit.*, pp. 59–71; Browning, Ritchie, and Grubb, *The West Coast Republics of South America*, pp. 77–85; Barclay, *History of Methodist Missions*, Vol. III, pp. 792–818.

See in which the latter conceded the right to the president to present the men for ecclesiastical dignities and the competence of the state's courts in civil cases involving ecclesiastics. The state permitted the Church to own property and subsidized it. Yet in 1880 tithes were abolished. The state did not give the Church any authority over the public schools but permitted religious instruction outside the regular hours. On the elementary level public schools far outnumbered church schools. However, in secondary and higher education institutions conducted by Jesuits, Franciscans, and teaching congregations of men and women were regarded as superior to the ones maintained by the state. Up to 1908 cemeteries were under the control of the Church and until 1911 the only legal marriage was according to the regulations of the Council of Trent. The overwhelming majority of the population outwardly conformed to the Roman Catholic faith, but for the masses of the Indians that religion was mixed with elements of pagan provenance, and the Church's fiestas were often an excuse for drunkenness and license. The rural clergy were usually but little if any better than their parishioners. Efforts were not wanting to improve the education and moral character of the clergy. For instance, in 1859 a presidential decree ordered the establishment of seminaries. Some bishops also worked for reform. But the level of the parish priests seems to have deteriorated. Franciscans from Europe had missions to the Indians.[129]

Protestantism was late in gaining continuing access to Bolivia. In 1827 an agent of the British and Foreign Bible Society visited several centres. Gardiner, whose sacrificial vision and death inspired the formation of the Patagonian, later the South American Missionary Society, was in the country in 1846 and two men were sent to reach the Indians. But severe opposition led to their withdrawal. In 1883 and 1884 a representative of the American Bible Society was twice in Bolivia. In the 1890's the Canadian Baptists established residence, mainly through a school, and in 1901 the Methodist Episcopal Church obtained a foothold. The Seventh Day Adventists came in 1907. Two years later the Bolivian Indian Mission, interdenominational, was organized.[130]

CHILE

Chile was constituted of the narrow ribbon of land between the South Pacific and the crest of the towering Andes. It stretched from the rainless desert of the North, rich in nitrates, through the fertile central valley and the forest region to the semi-antarctic South of the continent. Its people were largely a mixture of Araucanian Indian and Spanish blood. In the nineteenth century small but

---

[129] Mecham, *op. cit.*, pp. 220–235; Ryan, *op. cit.*, pp. 53, 54. On the Franciscans see Arcángel Barrado Manzano, *Las Misiones Franciscanas en Bolivia* (Seville, Imprenta San Antonio, 1946, pp. 82), *passim;* Lemmens, *op. cit.*, pp. 320–325; Berg, *op. cit.*, Vol. II, pp. 301, 302; Schmidlin-Braun, *op. cit.*, p. 680.

[130] Browning, Ritchie, and Grubb, *op. cit.*, pp. 125–128; Goslin, *op. cit.*, pp. 56–58.

important minorities were added by immigration from England, Ireland, Germany, France, Italy, and Serbia. The extremes were marked between the wealthy minority, predominantly white, and the poverty-stricken minorities who festered in the cities, tilled the soil, and worked in the mines.

In Chile, as in other Spanish American countries, the course of nineteenth-century history was punctuated by struggles between Conservatives and Liberals. The Conservatives, supported by the majority of the propertied classes and the clergy, stood for a strong central government and the privileges of the Roman Catholic Church. The Liberals favoured decentralizing the government and, although nominally Catholic, wished to curtail the Church. In the latter part of the century parties proliferated and the distinction between Conservatives and Liberals was not as sharply drawn as earlier. All parties insisted upon having the state continue the patronage which had been exercised by the Spanish crown in colonial days. Nor was the separation of Church and state achieved until 1925.

The scene was complicated by the contributions of intellectuals. Andres Bello (1781–1865), a Venezuelan who did most of his creative work in Chile, called "the greatest Spanish humanist since the Renaissance," had spent many years in England and there had been strongly influenced by James Mill and Jeremy Bentham. He was also much interested in Scottish philosophy. He wrote prodigiously, was a great teacher, and was the first rector of the University of Chile.[131] A pupil of Bello, José Victorino Lasterría (1817–1888), read Comte Rousseau, Montesquieu, and Bentham, and admired the United States. He advocated the separation of Church and state and while rejecting Spanish civilization wished to retain Christianity.[132] Francisco Bilbao (1823–1865), a disciple of Lasterría living in exile, believed Christianity to have been the greatest forward step in history but held that the Roman Catholic Church had deformed it.[133]

The relations of Church and state varied according to circumstances and the attitude of the head of the civil government. Bernardo O'Higgins, natural son of the last royal governor and the leader in achieving Chilean independence, maintained comparatively friendly relations with the clergy. However, the Bishop of Santiago, although a creole, so obdurately opposed the revolution and the work of "impenitent Voltaireans" that O'Higgins exiled him to another province. He expelled three other ecclesiastics from the country.[134] Under the successor of O'Higgins tithes were abolished, the clergy were paid directly by the state, some of the religious houses were suppressed, and the properties of several of them were assigned to the schools which James Thomson was organ-

[131] Crawford, *A Century of Latin-American Thought*, pp. 52–57; Galdames, *A History of Chile* p. 351.

[132] Crawford, *op. cit.*, pp. 69–74; Galdames, *op. cit.*, p. 352.

[133] Crawford, *op. cit.*, pp. 69–74; Galdames, *op. cit.*, p. 352.

[134] Mecham, *op. cit.*, p. 248; Silva Cotapos, *Historia Eclesiástica de Chile*, p. 202.

izing. It was also under him that the ill-starred Papal mission of Juan Muzi came to Chile. The suppression of the diocesan seminaries was a blow to the secular clergy. However, citizenship was confined to Roman Catholics and the public or private worship of any other than the Roman Catholic Church was forbidden.[135] In 1833 under Conservatives a constitution was framed which remained in force until 1925. Although it recognized the Roman Catholic faith as that of the republic, it expressly provided that patronage belonged to the state and that the civil government could grant or refuse permission to admit decrees of councils or Papal bulls, briefs, and rescripts. Consistently with this position, the Conservative government required bishops to take an oath to respect the patronage of the state and refused to recognize a bishop who had not been presented to Rome by the government. The Conservative government included a faculty of theology when it founded (1842) the University of Chile. It forbade, under heavy penalties, attacks on the Roman Catholic religion. The Jesuits were permitted to return. In the 1850's foreign congregations of men and women entered the country.[136] In the course of the nineteenth century several branches of the Franciscans were represented, including the Capuchins and the Third Order and coming from Italy, Germany, and Spain. They served parishes, staffed missions, schools, and hospitals, and had some recruits from the Chileans.[137] In the 1870's a Liberal regime abolished the ecclesiastical privilege (*fuero eclesiástico*) in civil and criminal cases and allowed Protestants to be buried in designated portions of Roman Catholic cemeteries. It broke off diplomatic relations with the Vatican over the latter's refusal to confirm the nomination by the government of a Liberal for the archbishopric made against the wishes of the clergy. In 1884 the civil ceremony in marriage was rendered compulsory. Some of the anti-clerical measures were put through by a minister of the interior, José Manuel Balmaceda, who had studied for the priesthood but had had his faith shaken by reading philosophical and scientific works.[138] On the eve of 1914 a large proportion of the population, although professedly Catholic, were increasingly tolerant of other faiths, but not so much from conviction as from religious indifference.[139]

Protestantism gained continuing entrance earlier than in any other of the republics on the west coast of South America. After the notable but ephemeral labours of James Thomson, from 1841 onward Chile always had Anglican chap-

[135] Mecham, *op. cit.*, pp. 249–251; Silva Cotapos, *op. cit.*, pp. 207–214, 224, 225; Galdames, *op. cit.*, pp. 226, 227.

[136] Mecham, *op. cit.*, pp. 252–257; Frances Kellam Hendricks, *Church and State in Chile before 1891* (Urbana, Ill., 1931. Abstract of a doctoral dissertation. Pp. 6); Silva Cotapos, *op. cit.*, pp. 232–246, 290.

[137] Arcila Robledo, *op. cit.*, pp. 237 ff.; Silva Cotapos, *op. cit.*, pp. 234, 235; Lemmens, *op. cit.*, pp. 314–316; Schmidlin-Braun, *op. cit.*, pp. 678, 679.

[138] Mecham, *op. cit.*, pp. 257–264; Galdames, *op. cit.*, pp. 316, 317. On a survey of the relations between Church and state, with useful excerpts from documents, see Miguel Cruchaga, *De las Relaciones entre la Iglesia i el Estado en Chile* (Santiago, Chile, "El Independiente," 1883, pp. 186).

[139] Mecham, *op. cit.*, p. 267; Galdames, *op. cit.*, p. 429.

lains who served the English communities. In 1845 David Trumbull arrived from the United States. He first served the English-speaking community and in 1847 organized for it the Union Church of Valparaiso. He became a Chilean citizen and was largely responsible for the setting aside of some of the legal disabilities under which Protestants had laboured. Churches using Spanish were organized in Santiago in 1868 and in Valparaiso the following year. In 1865 the constitution was officially interpreted as permitting Protestant religious services indoors. Protestants were also allowed to conduct schools in which their doctrines were taught. In 1873 the Presbyterian Church in the U.S.A. took over, by invitation, what had been begun by the American and Foreign Christian Union. In 1877 William Taylor came and in 1904 the Methodist Episcopal Church assumed responsibility for what he had started. Among its earliest preachers was a former Roman Catholic priest. The Christian and Missionary Alliance was also represented. Not far from 1914 the Pentecostal movement sprang from the conviction of a Methodist missionary. After that year it grew to large proportions, and entirely with Chilean leadership.[140]

PARAGUAY

With the smallest population of the South American countries, Paraguay had a troubled history. The famous Jesuit missions with their paternalistically governed communities (reductions) of Indians included all the Paraguay of the nineteenth century and extended beyond it. The forced withdrawal of the Jesuits (1769) only a little more than a half-century before independence from Spain and preceded (1750) by the transfer, in spite of Jesuit resistance, of part of the territory to the merciless exploiting Portuguese brought the first major disaster. The Franciscans who followed the Jesuits were unable to keep their charges to the level attained under their predecessors. Whether the inability of the Indian Christian communities to resist the destructive currents which then assailed them was due to the weakness of the methods employed by the Jesuits, as the latters' critics averred, or whether it arose from defects inherent in the Indian character, as the apologists of the Jesuits maintained, the unhappy aftermath was undebatable.

When independence was declared, in 1811, both of the rule of Spain and of the regime in Buenos Aires which vainly attempted to assert its authority over Paraguay, the majority of the population were nominally Roman Catholics, mostly Indians. But the course of the Church for the next two-thirds of a century was one of unrelieved tragedy. The three dictators who dominated the country from 1811 to 1870 insisted on making the Church a tool of their despotism.

---

[140] Mecham, *op. cit.*, p. 254; Goslin, *op. cit.*, pp. 45–53; Browning, Ritchie, and Grubb, *op. cit.*, pp. 27–32; Wheeler and others, *Modern Missions in Chile and Brazil*, pp. 112 ff.; Barclay, *op. cit.*, Vol. III, pp. 792–818.

The first of the dictators, José Caspar Rodríguez de Francia (1757–1840), who ruled from 1814 to his death, had a doctorate of theology but, although ostensibly a Catholic, was in reality a sceptic. He reduced the Church and its clergy to complete subservience, took control of all ecclesiastical property, and when the bishop, pressed by his exactions, went insane, he appointed as vicar-general a man who would do his will. Relations with Rome were broken off, and Francia became in fact if not in theory the head of a schismatic church. He abolished the religious orders and forbade religious processions. He commanded the priests to marry. The clergy, many of them ignorant, lazy, and dissolute, were cowed and were compelled to report to him what they heard in the confessional. Francia promoted the economic welfare of the country, but kept it almost completely isolated from the outer world.

The successor of Francia, Carlos Antonio Lopéz (1795–1862), a mestizo, president from 1841 to 1862, had also been educated in theology but, while outwardly conforming to the Roman Catholic faith, was a scoffer. He found it convenient to restore relations with the Holy See and obtained the approval of the Pope for his nominee to the bishopric, his own brother, Basilio, who was complacently compliant. He opened the country to trade and sought to encourage immigration. He introduced the telegraph, built roads, aided the construction of a railway, and so effectively promoted education that at the time of his death most of the men could read. He restored many parishes and gave the priests civil as well as ecclesiastical authority. Yet he required the clergy to report to him what had come to them in the confessional. When, in 1859, Basilio Lopéz died, the Pope demanded that the next bishop be a non-Paraguayan appointed from Rome, responsible to the Holy See and not to the dictator, and that the Church have its property returned to it. Carlos Antonio Lopéz demurred. Pius IX then threatened to put the land under an interdict but eventually accepted the president's nominee.

On his death Carlos Antonio Lopéz was followed by a son, Francisco Solano Lopéz (1827–1870), whom he had trained for the post, partly by sending him to Europe for education. The younger Lopéz, dissolute, overweeningly proud, reduced the bishop, a weak man, to servile compliance and made him and the clergy agents for espionage. He also had them instruct the populace to regard him as the Lord's anointed and to support him in an aggressive foreign policy. That policy led to war with Argentina, Uruguay, and Brazil which ended in complete defeat (1870), the cession of much of the country's territory, the death of most of the able-bodied males, the halving of the population by famine and disease, the occupation of Paraguay by the conquerors, and the breeding of a fresh population by unions between the troops of the victors and the remaining women. Only the reciprocal jealousies of Brazil and Argentina prevented the extinction of the country by partition.

For a generation after 1870 the unhappy land was racked by revolts and not until 1912 was some degree of order and stability achieved. The Church did not make a full recovery, even to its low state at the beginning of independence. The constitution adopted in 1870 declared the Roman Catholic religion to be that of the state but, partly to encourage immigration, permitted the free exercise of other religions. The state gave a modest subsidy to the Church. The president had the power of ecclesiastical patronage, a claim which the Vatican did not formally acknowledge but in which it tacitly acquiesced. The bishop was required to be a Paraguayan. No religious instruction was allowed as part of the curriculum of the public schools. In number and quality the clergy were inadequate. For example, between 1881 and 1911 only sixty were graduated from the country's sole theological school. Even in the twentieth century only about a third of the population were on the parish registers. This meant that two-thirds were without a formal connexion with the Church.[141]

Even with the freedom of worship granted by the constitution of 1870, Protestant missionaries were slow in coming to Paraguay. Representatives of the South American Missionary Society began arriving in 1889, of the Inland South America Missionary Union in 1902, and of the Christian Missions in Many Lands (Plymouth Brethren) in 1909.[142]

ARGENTINA

Argentina, in area the second largest of the Latin American countries, had most of its history in the nineteenth and twentieth centuries. Lying almost entirely in the South Temperate Zones, with the fertile Pampa at its heart, easily accessible from the sea, and sparsely populated at the time it achieved its independence, from the mid-nineteenth century onward it attracted a mounting immigration from Europe. The immigration was mostly from Italy and Spain, with a substantial minority from France and with other European countries and Turkey represented. By the end of the nineteenth century the population was overwhelmingly white, with here and there a dash of Negro and Indian blood. Wealth was chiefly from cattle, sheep, and grain, mainly exported to Europe and stimulated by the demand in that region of the industrial populations which were a feature of the revolutionary age. Economic development was furthered by foreign capital, predominantly from Great Britain. Indeed, from the economic standpoint, in much of the nineteenth century Argentina was a part of the British colonial empire. For example, its railways were built by British capital and managed by British citizens. In the country's rapid growth the

---

[141] Mecham, *Church and State in Latin America*, pp. 235 ff.; Ryan, *The Church in the South American Republics*, pp. 69–71; Arthur Elwood Elliott, *Paraguay. Its Cultural Heritage, Social Conditions and Educational Problems* (New York, Bureau of Publications, Teachers College, Columbia University, 1931, pp. xiv, 210), pp. 65 ff.

[142] Beach and Fahs, *World Missionary Atlas*, p. 94.

apital, Buenos Aires, from being a small, sprawling city at the outset of the ineteenth century, by mid-twentieth century was the largest metropolitan cenre in the entire Southern Hemisphere.

Argentina's course as an autonomous nation dated from 1810 and 1816. In he former year a group of citizens in Buenos Aires assembled to create a govrnment in the name of Ferdinand VII. In the latter year delegates assembled n Tucumán declared "the United Provinces of South America" independent f Spain.

As in much of the rest of Latin America the record was one of a series of trong men, usually ruling under constitutional forms but not bound by them. Iere, too, a chronic struggle went on between proponents of a federal structure vith much power retained by the provinces and those favouring a strong cenral government. In Argentina the latter were chiefly in Buenos Aires. The picure was made distinctive by the Gauchos, hardy horsemen who were the roduct of the wide Pampa with its cattle-raising. Generally having a mixture f Spanish and Indian blood, for the most part they were illiterate, hard fighting, and hard drinking. Nominally Roman Catholic, their religion was compounded of a thin veneer of Christianity with superstitions of varied origin. They were usually allied with *caudillos,* provincial or local leaders who emerged n the rough and tumble of the times.

Intellectual currents from Europe and the United States entered through various men. Sarmiento, of whom we are to hear more in a moment, was much mpressed by Horace Mann. Agustín Enrique Alvarez Suárez (1857–1914), ounder of the University of La Plata, a secular idealist, an admirer of Carlyle, Iorace Mann, and Emerson, wished to substitute schools for the Church. The irst president and real creator of the University of La Plata was Joaquín V. Gonzáles (1863–1923). He continued the educational work of Sarmiento, wrote oluminously, was patriotic, a democrat, and a lover of Spain. Carlos Octavio Bunge (1875–1918), a novelist and sociologist, was critical of the Spanish character and maintained that Hispanic America was the victim of laziness, sadess, and arrogance. José Ingenieros (1877–1925), born in poverty, psychologist nd sociologist, as a scientist won respect in Europe and was one of the favorite uthors of Latin American youth. Emerson was among his heroes. He advocated morality without dogma. Alejandro Korn (1860–1936), an Argentinian f German parents, rejected Positivism.[143]

In the first decades of independence the Roman Catholic Church was the ictim of adverse circumstances from which it only slowly recovered. Already veak, from 1812 to 1834 it did not have a bishop. Without episcopal discipline, he clergy deteriorated and, with no one to ordain, were in danger of becoming xtinct.[144] Bernadino Rivadavia, the strongest figure in the government from

---

[143] Crawford, *A Century of Latin-American Thought,* pp. 95–142.
[144] Ryan, *op. cit.,* p. 50.

1821 to 1827, had been in Europe and was a warm admirer of Jeremy Bentham and the French Utopians. He sought to reform the Church. To that end tithes and ecclesiastical privilege were abolished, some religious orders were suppressed, no one under twenty-five years of age was allowed to enter those that were left, membership of any one monastery was not to number less than sixteen or over thirty, an annual accounting of the administration of each monastery was to be made to the state, properties of the Church not actually used for worship were put under the control of the government, and the Church was aided from the public treasury. When Muzi arrived as a representative of the Pope, he was refused permission to perform any official function unless the Holy See would recognize the independence of the country. Although many of the clergy supported Rivadavia's reforms, others were loud in their criticism.[145]

Juan Manuel de Rosas was the next strong man and the dominant figure from 1829 to 1852. In theory he was for a federal form of government but in fact he exercised all but absolute power. Although having little or no religious conviction, he favoured the Church, but with the condition that it submit to his control. He was insistent on the right of patronage by the state and that meant himself. He also was inexorable on non-recognition of any Papal bull, brief, or rescript which had not been given the exequatur of the minister of foreign affairs. Under these restrictions the religious orders and congregations were permitted and the Jesuits were allowed to return: consent was given to filling the see of Buenos Aires, by a man first named vicar apostolic and then proprietory bishop, but Rosas kept him strictly in hand. Rosas had disciplinary measures adopted to suspend, remove, or imprison immoral priests and reformed the ecclesiastical courts. Pictures of Rosas were required to be placed close to the altars of the churches. In 1847 the Jesuits were expelled for refusing to conform to the commands of Rosas. During these years several intellectuals were committed to the liberalism then abroad in Europe, some of them influenced by Lamennais and one of them under the spell of Saint-Simon.[146]

After the elimination of Rosas a constitution was framed (1853) which continued to be the basic law of the country until well along in the next century. Under it the federal government was to support the Roman Catholic religion, but all inhabitants were accorded the right freely to practice their religion and aliens were given a similar right. The president was required to be a Roman Catholic and was accorded ecclesiastical patronage, selecting a bishop from names proposed by the Senate. He was also entrusted with granting or refusing, on advice of the supreme court, the publication of documents from the Holy

---

[145] Mecham, *op. cit.*, pp. 276–279; Zuretti, *Historia Eclesiastica Argentina*, pp. 219–230; Kennedy, *Catholicism, Nationalism, and Democracy in Argentina*, p. 19.

[146] Mecham, *op. cit.*, pp. 279–286; Herring, *A History of Latin America*, pp. 604, 605; Zuretti, *op. cit.*, pp. 235–246; Kennedy, *op. cit.*, p. 10.

See and from councils and with concluding agreements with the Pope. Congress had the power to promote the conversion of the Indians, to make rules governing ecclesiastical patronage, and to confirm or reject concordats with Rome.[147]

Gradually the conditions of the Roman Catholic Church improved. In 1885 the state created a new diocese north of Buenos Aires. Under the presidency of Bartolomé Mitre (1862–1868) Buenos Aires was made the seat of an archbishop (1865). Argentina had previously been in the Archdiocese of Charcas, the later Sucre, in Bolivia. Now it was created an ecclesiastical province.[148]

Domingo Faustino Sarmiento (1811–1888) seemed to some to have brought a secularist and even an atheist reaction. Born in the western part of the country, he was intended by his mother for the priesthood. He had relatives in the clergy, one of them later a bishop. He knew the Bible well and as a boy had helped in church services. He seems not to have violently rejected the faith and could speak of it sympathetically. For years he was an exile in Chile because of his vigorous opposition to Rosas. There he read extensively in current European literature, edited a journal, and wrote books, including the widely circulated novel *El Facundo,* which won him recognition in Europe as well as in South America. He travelled in Europe and the United States and conceived a great admiration for the latter. Later he was President of Argentina (1868–1874) and then and in subsequent official positions did much to promote education. He sought to increase the number of schools, raise the quality of the teachers, and bring in better teaching methods. He fought compulsory religious instruction in the schools and wished to de-Hispanize South American culture.[149]

Further improvement in the religious life was effected. Various orders and congregations staffed from Europe assisted. For example, Franciscan missions were reinforced from Spain; Lazarists from France had missions in Patagonia; in 1875 the first Salesians of Don Bosco arrived from Italy; Brothers of Christian Schools from France opened a college in 1891; Italian Redemptorists and Italian Capuchins shared in promoting the religious life; and Irish Passionists came to care for immigrants from the Emerald Isle. Various other congregations of men and women from France, Italy, and Spain were represented and some recruited members in Argentina.[150] To meet the challenge of the growing population new dioceses were created—three of them in 1897, one in 1907, and two in 1910. Yet in spite of government financial aid to diocesan seminaries the number of clergy was inadequate.[151] Soon after 1900 congresses of Argentinian Catholics were held for social action and in 1910 a Catholic university was

---

[147] Mecham, *op. cit.,* pp. 287, 288; Zuretti, *op. cit.,* pp. 247–249; Kennedy, *op. cit.,* pp. 12–15.

[148] Mecham, *op. cit.,* pp. 290, 292; Zuretti, *op. cit.,* p. 259; Kennedy, *op. cit.,* pp. 10, 11.

[149] Allison Williams Bunkley, *The Life of Sarmiento* (Princeton University Press, 1952, pp. xv, 566), *passim.*

[150] Zuretti, *op. cit.,* pp. 273, 274, 276, 288–292.

[151] *Ibid.,* pp. 294–296, 308, 309; Mecham, *op. cit.,* p. 302.

founded.[152] Occasionally relations with the Vatican were strained and at one time an open break occurred. But in 1892 it was healed. However, no concordat was entered into.[153] Although religious instruction was not permitted in the public schools during the regular hours, it could be given by authorized ministers of the several faiths before and after those hours to children whose parents requested it. In addition, Roman Catholics maintained schools, especially beyond the elementary grades.[154]

Protestantism was represented partly by immigrants and foreign residents and partly by missions to non-Christian Indians and to Roman Catholics. As early as 1831 the Anglicans had a church building in Buenos Aires. The Scottish Presbyterians were not long in following their example. German Protestants were cared for. Welsh and South African Protestants had a settlement in Chubut Valley in the South. Baptists from the United States and Waldensians constituted small minorities. The Danish Lutherans had a congregation.

For non-Protestants the British and Foreign Bible Society and the American Bible Society were long active. As we have seen, James Thomson was early in Buenos Aires but was ordered to leave the country. The South American Missionary Society was loyal to the vision of Allen Gardiner. The Presbyterian Church in the U.S.A. sent a representative in 1829, made another attempt in 1854, but finally withdrew in 1859. The Methodist Episcopal Church sent two men in 1836 and after an interruption resumed operations in 1843 and continued them without another lapse. Southern Baptists came in 1903, the Disciples of Christ in 1906, and by 1914 other groups were represented. An especially notable enterprise was by William Case Morris, an Englishman, who devoted himself to the children of Buenos Aires, particularly through schools for the underprivileged.[155]

URUGUAY

Uruguay, the smallest of the South American republics, was long a subject of contest between Spaniards and Portuguese. In the colonial period Jesuit missions tended to hold the region for Spain. Spanish control was made effective in 1776, but in the years of revolt against Spain, in 1817 Brazilian forces captured Montevideo and in 1825 Argentina and Brazil fought for the area until, in 1828, through British diplomacy, both agreed to recognize and defend the independence of Úruguay. The country then had a population of about sixty thousand. Population mounted, partly by immigration from Spain and Italy, and was predominantly white. The wealth of Uruguay was chiefly in cattle and sheep raised on the fertile soil.

[152] Zuretti, *op. cit.,* pp. 314, 315.
[153] Mecham, *op. cit.,* pp. 293–296.
[154] *Ibid.,* pp. 301, 302.
[155] Browning, *The River Plate Republics,* pp. 49–59; Beach and Fahs, *op. cit.,* p. 94; Goslin, *Los Evangelicos en la América Latina,* pp. 29 ff.

Until 1903 Uruguay, although with a growing population, suffered from political instability. The contending parties were the *Colorados* ("Reds"), who professed to stand for the common man, liberalism, and national independence, and the *Blancos* ("Whites"), made up of merchants, the higher clergy, and the owners of landed estates, who asserted that they were the defenders of order and of the faith. During his rule in Argentina the *Blancos* had the support of Rosas. From 1843 to 1851, backed by Rosas, they besieged Montevideo, held by the *Colorados* with Brazilian aid. In the 1860's Uruguay was caught in the war of Brazil and Argentina against Paraguay. In spite of the disorder railways were built, cities grew, lands were fenced, and immigrants created an urban middle class. *Colorado* strong men ruled from 1875 to 1896, some of them under the guise of constitutionality, but in 1896 a civil war broke out, as a result of which the *Blancos* were given control of a third of the provinces.

In 1903 José Batlle y Ordóñez (1856–1929) came to power and in one way or another remained dominant until his death. He remade the country into what it became in the twentieth century. The son of a former president and a *Colorado*, he himself was elected to the presidency in 1903. But his first term was troubled by civil war and he was then absorbed in the reconstruction which followed it. After his first term he spent four years in Europe (1907–1911) in studious observation and became especially impressed by the Swiss Government and its programme. In 1911 he began his second term as president and commenced putting into force the changes of which he had dreamed. He sought to educate the country through the editorials in his newspaper, *El Dia,* and under his insistent guidance Uruguay traversed the pathway towards a welfare state. Among his measures were freedom of speech and of the press, compulsory free primary and secondary schools, the right of labour to organize and strike, the eight-hour day, minimum wages, workingmen's compensation, old age pensions, state monopoly of insurance and electric light and power, state ownership of railways, university education for women, and state control of banking.[156]

In the meantime, in spite of the political unrest which characterized the country during much of the nineteenth century, intellectual currents were entering from Europe. They chiefly affected the educated but spread beyond them. The rationalism of the Enlightenment and Deism had their day. Krausism and a philosophic form of Spiritualism enjoyed a vogue. Positivism was very influential in the 1880's and made an impact on education, literature, politics, and religion. About 1890 the Jesuits led in a criticism of Positivism. Darwin and Spencer had repercussions. Carlos Vaz Ferreira, a philosopher and teacher who began writing in the 1890's, was critical of the mechanistic approach of Taine and Spencer and was attracted by William James. José Enriqué Rodó (1872–1917) rejected Positivism and attempted to harmonize Hellenic paganism with

[156] Simon G. Hanson, *Utopia in Uruguay. Chapters in the Economic History of Uruguay* (New York, Oxford University Press, 1938, pp. viii, 262), *passim.*

Judaism and Christianity. Batlle, earlier a Roman Catholic, went through a Positivist stage, but his favourite work on philosophy was by the Krausist Ahrens.[157]

The attitude of the government towards religion varied. The constitution of 1830 which theoretically remained in force until 1919 declared the Roman Catholic faith to be that of the state but did not prohibit other religions. As in other Latin American countries, the government claimed ecclesiastical patronage. Although the government contributed financially to the support of the Church the amount was insufficient and the difference was made up by fees, contributions from individuals, bequests, and income from real estate. In theory the *Blancos* stood for the Church and the *Colorados* were anti-clerical, but in their times in power the former did not rescind the ecclesiastical measures enacted by the latter when they were in control. In 1838 the Franciscan houses were suppressed. In 1859 the Jesuits, admitted a few years before, were expelled, but in 1865 they were permitted to return under a presidential ruling that congregations devoted to education should be allowed. In 1880 the Church's control of marriage, cemeteries, and the legitimatization of births was cancelled and the registration of vital statistics, heretofore a function of the clergy, was made the exclusive charge of justices of the peace. Although the Church was not disestablished until 1919, the connexion had been so loosened that before that date the tie had been all but severed.[158]

The Roman Catholic Church in Uruguay long suffered from inadequate episcopal supervision. In spite of a request by the Congress in 1830, only in 1878 was the Diocese of Montevideo created and the country given a bishop. Until then it was part of the see of Buenos Aires. For some years a vicar apostolic was in charge. Especially outside Montevideo, the clergy were too few for the population.[159]

Protestantism was represented in part by immigrants. Waldensians began arriving from Italy in 1856, continued to grow by immigration and natural increase, and spilled over into Argentina. Until after 1914 their pastors were from Italy.[160] Both the British and Foreign and the American Bible Society were active for a number of decades before 1914. The Methodist Episcopal Church dated the inception of its mission from 1839. But it was not until after 1900 and almost on the eve of 1914 that other bodies entered—the Plymouth Brethren in 1904, the Seventh Day Adventists in 1906, the Southern Baptists in 1908, and in that same year the International Committee of the Young Men's Christian Association. Obviously only slight headway was made before 1914.[161]

---

[157] Crawford, *op..cit.*, pp. 79–94; Ardao, *Espiritualismo y Positivismo en el Uruguay. Filosofías Universitarias de la Segunda Mitad del Siglo XIX* (Mexico, Fondo de Cultura Económica, 1950, pp. 287), *passim*, especially pp. 108, 109, 157–207, 262–272.

[158] Mecham, *Church and State in Latin America*, pp. 332–336.

[159] *Ibid.*, pp. 331, 332; Ryan, *The Church in the South American Republics*, pp. 73–75.

[160] Browning, *op. cit.*, pp. 62, 63.

[161] *Ibid.*, p. 66; Beach and Fahs, *op. cit.*, p. 94.

BRAZIL[162]

In the second half of the nineteenth century huge Brazil, occupying almost half of South America, had a striking growth. The country displayed great variety. Nearly half was in the thinly peopled valley of the Amazon. Another large region was the semi-arid North-east. The most populous and economically highly developed section was in the South, from the southern edge of the tropics in Minas Geraes into the Temperate Zone to Rio Grande du Sul and the northern border of Uruguay. Production of food and raw materials for industrialized Europe increased in the vicinity of tropical Bahia and Pernambuco—sugar, tobacco, and cotton. São Paulo became an important centre for coffee consumed in Europe and North America. In the South herds of cattle were multiplying. Thousands of miles of railways were constructed. After 1874 immigration, in the 1850's and 1860's a swelling stream, became a torrent. Its chief sources were Italy, Germany, Spain, and Portugal.

Yet in spite of the zeal of Pedro II for schools and his initiative in sending talented youths to Europe for education, at the time of his abdication and the inauguration of the republic (1889) out of a population of fourteen million only about a quarter-million were in primary grades.[163]

In Brazil the relations between Church and state were usually less strained than in other Latin American countries. A large proportion of the clergy favoured severing the tie with Portugal, a step made easier because independent Brazil was still ruled by a member of the historic House of Braganza. The constitution promulgated in 1824 made the Roman Catholic faith the religion of the country but permitted the private exercise of other cults. In accord with colonial precedent the state paid the clergy. A nearer approach to religious liberty and tolerance of dissenting bodies existed than in most other parts of Latin America. The historic control of the Church by the Portuguese crown continued with the right of patronage. In this the crown was supported by the clergy, for the latter were Gallican in their attitude towards the Papacy. The Pope acquiesced, although not without an effort (1827) at asserting himself.[164] We have seen that in 1830 the Holy See set up a nunciature for Brazil with authority over the rest of Latin America.

In the 1820's the government took measures to reform the regulars. They were not numerous but in comparison with the secular clergy were wealthy. In 1828 foreign regulars were forbidden to enter or reside in the country, the creation of new orders or congregations of either sex was interdicted, and orders

---

[162] No adequate history has been written of the Roman Catholic Church in Brazil, but a bibliography which would prove useful is in *Revista (Trimestrial) do Instituto Historico e Geographico Brasileiro Fundado no Rio de Janeiro em 1838*, Vol. 220, July–September, 1953 (Rio de Janeiro, Departamento de Imprensa Nacional, pp. 338).

[163] Herring, *op. cit.*, pp. 697–701.

[164] Mecham, *op. cit.*, pp. 307–311; Kennedy, *Catholicism, Nationalism, and Democracy in Argentina*, p. 5.

and congregations which obeyed superiors outside Brazil were expelled. Three years later, with the concurrence of the Papal nuncio, reform of the orders continued and some of their houses were closed.[165]

The highminded Pedro II, described as a "liberal Catholic," wished the further reform of the orders and insisted upon his full control of the Church. Supported by the Papal nuncio and the bishops, he forbade the entrance of novices into the orders and congregations. He also declared that his was the right to name to all positions in the Church without consultation with the prelates.[166]

In the 1870's a controversy troubled the Church which had as its focal point the membership of the clergy in the lodges of the Freemasons. Masonry seems to have entered Brazil in the closing years of the eighteenth century. It flourished and made for independence. Although he was Grand Master, Pedro I prohibited further Masonic meetings, and Masonic agitation is said to have contributed to his abdication (1831). As early as the eighteenth century more than one Pope had condemned Masonry and forbidden the faithful to become members, but the decrees had not received the *placet* of the state and so had not been officially published in Brazil. As a phase of the Enlightenment which gained currency in Portugal under Pombal and penetrated to the Brazilian clergy, numbers of the latter, including bishops, became Masons, and Masons were admitted to predominantly lay Catholic benevolent and religious associations. Pedro II and his prime minister were Masons and did not permit the publication of Pius IX's denunciation of the fraternity. While the clergy must have been aware of the Papal proscription, they had not been compelled to take formal cognizance of it. Their attitude towards Masonry was part of a pattern of liberalism and Gallicanism which included a movement to abolish the requirement of clerical celibacy and wished to make the Brazilian church administratively independent of Rome.

The issue came to a head in 1872. In that year the Bishop of Rio de Janeiro rebuked a priest for delivering a discourse at a Masonic reception and ordered him to abjure Masonry. The priest refused, the bishop, invoking the anti-Masonic Papal bulls, suspended his right to preach and hear confessions, and the priest threatened to appeal to the council of state. That year the newly consecrated Bishop of Olinda, a Capuchin, an ardent ultramontane, forbade the proposed mass at a Masonic celebration in Recife (Pernambuco). When his command was heeded, the Masons published a list of clergy and lay members of Catholic confraternities who held membership with them. Thereupon the bishop commanded all the priests to sever their connexion with the order and the confraternities to exclude members who were Masons. The bishop brought the controversy to the attention of Pius IX. The Pope praised him, empowered him to continue his campaign, and ordered him to convey the instructions to all the

---

[165] *Ibid.*, pp. 312, 313; Badaro, *l'Église au Brésil*, pp. 52–56.
[166] Mecham, *op. cit.*, p. 314; Badaro, *op. cit.*, p. 61.

Brazilian episcopate. Since the Papal command had not received the *placet* of the state, in complying with it the bishop had violated the law of Brazil. Of the twelve prelates only one other, the Bishop of Pará, obeyed the Pope and told the Masonic members of the confraternities to withdraw from one or the other affiliation. Pedro II now urged the Pope to take a conciliatory attitude and through his Secretary of State Pius IX instructed the bishops to restore the confraternities to their former status. Not content with this victory, Pedro commanded the Bishops of Olindo and Pará to withdraw within fifteen days the interdicts which, as part of their anti-Masonic campaign, they had placed on Pernambuco and Pará. Since they did not obey, they were arrested, tried, and condemned to prison (1874). The following year they were released. Many regarded the bishops as martyrs and the state suffered a loss of prestige. In a test of strength between the Church and the state, as in the *Kulturkampf*, the state had lost—and in a land where the Church was much weaker than in Germany.[167]

The liberalism of Pedro II facilitated the spread in Brazil of many intellectual currents from contemporary Europe. They continued to enter under the republic. Positivism was especially influential. Those committed to it championed the abolition of Negro slavery, the separation of Church and state, and civil marriage as essential to liberty.[168] Ruy Barbosa (1849-1923), said to have been the greatest orator, linguist, and writer of the Brazil of his day, greatly admired England. He passed through an anti-Catholic stage but, although fighting the Jesuits and abominating dictatorships, came back to Christianity. The religion of a younger contemporary, Euclydes da Cunha (1868-1909), a noted writer, was a mixture of Indian anthropomorphism and African animism.[169]

When, in 1889, Brazil became a republic, the Positivist influence made for the separation of Church and state, a step taken in January, 1890. The state relinquished its long-standing practice of patronage and its *placet* to Papal documents, freedom of worship was guaranteed, and both federal and state governments were forbidden to subsidize any religion. Religious corporations were granted the right to acquire and hold property. All religious holidays except Sunday were abolished, civil marriage was made compulsory, and cemeteries were secularized. An effort to exclude the Jesuits was defeated, but the formation of new houses and congregations of "religious" was prohibited. Brazil continued to have an ambassador to the Vatican.[170]

Disestablishment seemed to work to the advantage of the Roman Catholic

---

[167] Mary Crescentia Thornton, *The Church and Freemasonry in Brazil, 1872-1875. A Study in Regalism* (Washington, The Catholic University of America Press, 1948, pp. viii, 287), *passim;* Mecham, *op. cit.,* pp. 317-321; Ryan, *op. cit.,* pp. 89-92; Flavio Guerra, *A Questão Religiosa do Segundo Imperio Brasileiro. Fundamentos Históricos* (Rio de Janeiro, Irmaos Pongetti, 1952, pp. xix, 265), *passim.*

[168] Mecham, *op. cit.,* pp. 322, 323.

[169] Crawford, *op. cit.,* pp. 190-198.

[170] Mecham, *op. cit.,* pp. 323-326; Badaro, *op. cit.,* pp. 77 ff.

Church. Although religious instruction in the public schools could be given only after school hours, the Church maintained a large number of elementary and secondary schools. Various orders, including the Jesuits and Benedictines, and teaching congregations of women conducted many of the latter. Hospitals and other charitable institutions were supported. The quality of the clergy was improved. Most of the immigration was at least nominally Roman Catholic and to care for it more dioceses and archdioceses were created. The *União Catolica Brasileira,* organized in 1907, a lay movement, concerned itself with political issues which affected the faith. It fought secret societies condemned by the Church, divorce, and immoral literature, and stood for the teaching of religion in the public schools and the continuation of the embassy to the Vatican.[171]

As we have hinted, immigration, like that in Argentina and Uruguay, constituted a challenge. The total was slightly larger than in Argentina, well over three million in the nineteenth century. As in the latter country, the largest number were from Italy, the next largest from Portugal (in contrast with Argentina, where the Spaniards were second). Spaniards were third and Germans were fourth. From 1820 to 1915, 122,830 Germans were said to have reached the country and by the latter year those of German blood in Brazil were reported to number about 250,000.[172] Of them some were Protestants and others Roman Catholics.

We have no comprehensive record of how successful the Roman Catholic Church was in holding to the faith those who historically were its children. One foreign observer shortly after 1914 wrote that he did not find as much rationalism and antagonism to religion as in Argentina, but that teachers told him that in the state schools at least nine-tenths were non-religious and the other tenth were nominally Roman Catholic.[173] Such efforts as were made to reach the immigrants seem to have been mostly by foreign clergy. Thus the Pious Society for Missions, usually known as the Pallottines, founded in Italy in 1835 to serve immigrants in America, by 1914 had fourteen missions in Brazil.[174] For years the Italians in Rio Grande do Sul, the southernmost state, were without clerical ministrations. In 1896, at the invitation of a local bishop, Capuchins from Savoy began to come and served not only Italians but also native Brazilians.[175] In 1888 Missionaries of St. Charles Borromeo, a congregation founded in Italy to minister to Italian immigrants to the New World, arrived in Brazil.[176] German

[171] Mecham, *op. cit.,* pp. 327, 328; Julio Cesar de Morais Carneiro, *O Catolicismo no Brasil (Memória historíca)* (Rio de Janeiro, Agir, 1950), pp. 213 ff.

[172] L. E. Elliott, *Brazil Today and Tomorrow* (New York, The Macmillan Co., 1917, pp. x, 338), pp. 56–72.

[173] Clayton Sedgwick Cooper, *The Brazilians and Their Country* (New York, Frederick A. Stokes Co., 1917, pp. xvi, 403), p. 115.

[174] *The Catholic Encyclopedia,* Vol. XII, p. 107.

[175] *Capuchins Missionnaires. Missions Françaises. Notes Historiques et Statistiques* (Paris, Société et Librairie Coopératives St. François, 1926, pp. iv, 86), pp. 36–42.

[176] *The Catholic Encyclopedia,* Vol. X, p. 368.

Franciscans cared for Italian immigrants.[177] In 1924 in Rio Grande do Sul, of the Germans 157,000 were said to be Roman Catholics and of these slightly more than four-fifths were said to be affiliated with the Church.[178]

Much of the population of Brazil, widely scattered as it was, had no resident priests. From time to time missionaries, largely foreign, made itinerant missions, preaching penance, confession, and proper relations between the sexes. In the absence of priests lay leaders conducted prayers in chapels, some of them rude, and conducted funerals. In the rural districts most of the religious life was in the hands of these laymen. Some of them started movements which stressed a Messianic hope.[179] Thus in 1837 in the state of Pernambuco an *illuminado,* as he was called, preached the imminent coming again of Don Sebastian, who had been killed three hundred years before in battle with the Moors, and declared that he would reign in Portugal and Brazil and reward those faithful to him.[180] In 1890 a woman while taking Communion swooned and from her mouth drops of blood fell which were popularly believed to be the blood of Christ from the consecrated wafer. The news spread and the site became a pilgrimage centre and contributed to a movement led by a priest, Father Cicero, which had political manifestations.[181]

As with efforts to reach the immigrants, so the missions to the non-Christian Indians were mostly by orders and congregations staffed from Europe. Brazil had more Indians than any other South American country. It is said that in spite of the great immigration from Europe, between 1872 and 1912 the proportion of Indians in the population rose from 7 to 13 per cent.[182] The missions ranged over most of the country—from Rio Grande do Sul in the extreme South to Pará in the North, from the coast to Mato Grosso in the centre, to the western tributaries of the Amazon, and to the territory between Venezuela and British Guiana. In the missions a number of orders and congregations shared, among them the Pallottines, the Society of the Divine Word (Germans), Italian Capuchins, French Dominicans, Belgian Benedictines, Italian Silesians, Dutch, Italian, and German Franciscans, Jesuits, and Holy Ghost Fathers.[183]

In the second half of the twentieth century Protestantism was declared to be growing proportionately in Brazil more rapidly than in any other country. By 1914 it had only made a beginning, partly through immigrants and foreign resi-

---

[177] P. Cletus Espey, *Festschrift zum Silberjubiläum der Wiedererrichtung der Provinz von der Unbefleckten Empfängnis im Süden Brasiliens 1901–1926* (Werl i. Westf., Franziskus-Druckerei, 1929, pp. 175), *passim.*

[178] Braga and Grubb, *The Republic of Brazil*, p. 52.

[179] *Ibid.,* p. 37.

[180] R. B. Cunninghame Graham, *A Brazilian Mystic. Being the Life and Miracles of Antonio Conselheiro* (London, William Heinemann, 1920, pp. xii, 238), pp. 42, 43.

[181] Braga and Grubb, *op. cit.,* p. 38.

[182] Cooper, *op. cit.,* p. 334.

[183] Freitag in *Zeitschrift für Missionswissenschaft,* Vol. XI, pp. 183–186; Lemmens, *Geschichte der Franziskanermissionen,* pp. 275, 276; Elsner, *Die deutschen Franziskaner in Brasilien* (Trier, Paulinus-Druckerei, 1912, pp. 136), pp. 81–87.

dents and partly by conversions from nominal Roman Catholics. Of the large German population, in 1924 over nine-tenths of the 183,289 of Protestant ancestry in Rio Grande do Sul were said to have a church affiliation. The pastors came from Germany. In the early days of the immigration some were paid by the Brazilian Government. Later pastors were sent from Basel and Barmen. Most of the German Protestants were members of the German Evangelical Church of Brazil, representing the union of Lutherans and Reformed which characterized much of the Fatherland in the nineteenth century. Some were in congregations of the Missouri Synod, and smaller minorities were in other churches, among them Baptists and Seventh Day Adventists.[184]

Protestant missions primarily for Roman Catholics were chiefly but not entirely from the United States. The Methodist Episcopal Church was represented from 1834 to 1842. Continuing Methodist operations were by the Methodist Episcopal Church, South, and began in 1867. A strong fellowship of Congregational churches, conservative theologically, arose out of the initiative of Robert Reid Kalley, a Scottish physician, who arrived in 1855. The first church was organized in 1858 and its first pastor, a Brazilian, was trained in Spurgeon's college in London. In 1892 Kalley inaugurated the Help for Brazil Mission, later merged in the Evangelical Union of South America. In 1913 the Congregational Union was brought into being by delegates from fourteen churches. The next year a theological seminary was opened. Presbyterianism was the outgrowth of missions by the Presbyterian Church in the U.S.A., begun in 1859, and the Southern Presbyterian Church, started in 1868 and assisted by colonists who came from the Southern states after the Civil War.[185] Baptists, who soon after 1914 constituted the largest of the Protestant denominations gathered from Roman Catholics, arose from white refugees after the Civil War and from missions of the Southern Baptist Convention. Beginnings which proved ephemeral were made in 1859. Two Baptist churches of settlers from the Southern states were organized near Campinas in 1873, and in 1881 the first missionary came for the Portuguese-speaking population.[186] The British and Foreign Bible Society and the American Bible Society were long represented, the former beginning in 1819 and the latter in 1876. In the 1870's the National Bible Society of Scotland also sent Testaments. The Protestant Episcopal Church, the Seventh Day Adventists, the Young Men's Christian Associations of the United States and Canada, the Plymouth Brethren, the Inland South America Missionary Union, and the Swedish Free Mission were in the country before 1914. The

[184] Braga and Grubb, *op. cit.,* pp. 50–52; Schlatter, *Geschichte der Basler Mission 1815-1915,* Vol. I, pp. 89, 90; Ferdinand Schröder, *Brasilien und Wittenberg, Ursprung und Gestaltung deutschen evangelischen Kirchentums in Brasilien* (Berlin, Walter de Gruyter & Co., 1936, pp. 413), *passim.*

[185] Braga and Grubb, *op. cit.,* pp. 53–80; Wheeler and others, *Modern Missions in Chile and Brazil,* pp. 335–352.

[186] A. R. Crabtree, *Baptists in Brazil* (Rio de Janeiro, The Baptist Publishing House of Brazil, 1953, pp. 236), *passim.*

Pentecostals had only barely begun the remarkable growth which they were to have after 1914.[187]

SUMMARY

A backward look reveals a striking contrast between the record of Christianity in Latin America and that in the United States and British North America. Both areas had been peopled chiefly from Europe and in both the nineteenth-century increase by immigration from that continent had been notable. Both had been played upon by the forces of the revolutionary age. Yet in the United States and British North America Christianity, whether Roman Catholic or Protestant, was much more vigorous than in Latin America. Down to 1914 the Eastern Churches, although represented, were small minorities, somewhat more so in Latin America than in the United States. In Latin America neither the Roman Catholic Church nor the Protestant churches produced enough indigenous clergy to care for their adherents, to reach out to the non-Christian Indians, or to share in the world-wide spread of the faith. That was to be expected of Protestantism, for it had not been present before the nineteenth century, was culturally alien, and except through immigrants of Protestant ancestry was late in gaining footholds and had gathered only a few converts. Yet the largest body of Protestant immigrants, the Germans, until after 1914 were receiving their clergy from the Fatherland. This was in marked contrast with the United States, where clergy early began to arise from the nineteenth-century German immigration. For the Roman Catholic Church the difference between Latin America and the United States and British North America was especially thought-provoking. In the United States the Roman Catholic Church was predominantly of the nineteenth-century immigration. But while it drew some of its clergy and members of orders and congregations from Europe, especially at the outset, long before 1914 the increasing majority were native-born and it was beginning to participate in the global extension of the faith. In British North America from the dawn of the century the French were producing their own clergy and the nineteenth-century immigration, mainly Irish, was more and more doing likewise. In the United States Protestantism was rapidly reaching out to the unchurched, white and Negro, had widespread missions to the Indians, was operating them through indigenous initiative, and by 1914 was carrying more than half of the burden of Protestant missions in other lands. The Protestantism of British North America, although younger than that of the United States, was fully as vigorous. The Protestantism of the United States was responding positively to the stimulus of the intellectual currents of the age and from it were issuing movements which were helping to shape the national life. From Latin America no significant contributions were coming to Roman

---

[187] Braga and Grubb, *op. cit.*, pp. 65–82; Beach and Fahs, *World Missionary Atlas*, p. 94.

Catholic thought and in general the Church was a bulwark of social and political conservatism. Constructive efforts to meet the social problems of the revolutionary age were mainly from the Church's critics.

What accounted for the differences in the nineteenth-century course of Christianity in Latin America and in the United States and British North America? The causes seem to have been multiple. Perhaps not all are discernible. Certainly no dependable appraisal can be made of the proportionate share of each in the total picture.

One factor in the contrast in the Roman Catholic scene was nationality. In the United States the leadership and vigour were chiefly among the Irish and Germans—for reasons which we have discussed elsewhere. Little came from the Italians, and the Spaniards and Portuguese were small minorities—except the Mexicans in the South-west. In Canada the Roman Catholic Church was the symbol and tie of French nationalism against the British majority and the Irish were also numerous. In Latin America Irish were either non-existent or very few and German Roman Catholics were minorities. The nineteenth-century immigration was predominantly from Spain, Italy, and Portugal, and in Spain and Portugal the Roman Catholic Church was given a peculiarly stormy time by the revolutionary currents and did not respond with as much creative vitality as in France, Germany, and Italy. The anemic conditions of Latin American Christianity might be thought to be due to the fact that so much of the population was Indian, mestizo, and, in places, Negro. But the Roman Catholic Church was fully as weak in the sections where the population was predominantly white—for example, in parts of Argentina, Uruguay, and Rio Grande do Sol in Brazil—as in areas where mestizos, Indians, and Negroes constituted the majority.

Also basic was the inheritance from the colonial era. The domination of the crown in Portuguese and especially in Spanish America made for a passive Christianity. In both the United States and Canada the prevailing tradition in colonial days was self-government with a minimum of control from the mother country. That was true in both Church and state. In Latin America, on the other hand, the ranking civil and ecclesiastical officials were appointed by the crown and most of them were from across the water. From Europe came the majority of the missionaries and the higher clergy.

In Spanish America in the struggle for independence the inherited handicap was a source of weakness. The movements away from Spain were largely led by creoles, who were antagonistic to the Spanish-born, including those among the clergy. For years the Spanish crown clung to its right of patronage as a way of maintaining its authority in the revolting colonies. Each of the successor governments insisted on a similar right. Rome long hesitated to take sides. To acknowledge the claim of Spain would offend the new regimes. To refuse to do so would jeopardize the already shaky administrative control of Rome in Spain. As a result, for some of the most crucial years the episcopate in Spanish America was almost extinct.

The colonial inheritance of lack of experience in self-government contributed to the stormy political record of most of the Spanish American republics. Civil strife and revolutions were endemic, and orderly government was only slowly and painfully achieved in some and was tragically absent in others. We need not be surprised that this inheritance made for weakness in the Roman Catholic Church.

In every one of the Latin American countries, although more in some than in others, the Roman Catholic Church was weakened by the struggle between conservatives, who usually supported the Church, and liberals, who sought to curtail it and to bring in a secular state. Here was a parallel to what was taking place in contemporary Latin Europe in the conflicts between clericals and anticlericals and in Germany in the *Kulturkampf*. But in Latin America the Roman Catholic Church entered the revolutionary age much weaker and more poorly equipped to cope with that struggle than in Europe.

Another factor was the low quality of the Latin American clergy, both seculars and regulars. This seems to have dated from the colonial period, when an indigenous clergy was only slowly developing and when much of what emerged was from the mestizos, who, originally mostly from irregular unions of whites and Indians, tended to be socially and morally inferior.

Some of the weakness of Latin American Christianity must be attributed to the fashion in which the faith had spread among the peoples of pre-Columbian ancestry. It was largely by mass conversions and in the frontier missions was by paternalistic methods. The expulsion of the Jesuits from the Spanish and Portuguese possessions badly crippled some of the more important missions, and that only a few decades before the storm of revolution broke. As a result, the Christianity of most of the Indians was superficial and often mixed with distorted remnants of pre-Christian cults and attitudes.

Brazil was not subject to some of these factors. There no prolonged struggle for independence took place. Nor was the conflict between clericals and anticlericals as pronounced as in most of Spanish America. Yet here the colonial Church was weaker than in much of Spanish America and entered the nineteenth century severely handicapped by both the paucity and the poor quality of the clergy.

Whatever the causes, in Latin America Christianity rose much more weakly to the revolutionary age than in the United States and the British North America. Indeed, in no other major region predominantly Christian by profession at the outset of the nineteenth century did the faith suffer as severely from the forces of the era.

Yet it would be false to the facts to say that in Latin America Christianity was moribund, kept alive only by transfusions from the Church in other countries. Here and there revivals were seen in the Roman Catholic Church, even though affecting only minorities. In more than one centre the traveller found new church buildings. In the churches and shrines the characteristic figure of Christ was of a powerless and pathetic corpse. But the huge statues of Christ towering over cities and nations were evidence of another kind of piety. That was especially notable in the Christ of the Andes, which commemorated peace between Chile and Argentina and symbolized hope for the continuation of amity. Popular shrines of nineteenth-century origin springing from appearances of the Virgin Mary were indications of the sort of faith which we have noted in Roman Catholic circles in Europe. In the twentieth century Roman Catholic missionaries from the United States remarked what they interpreted as a widespread even if shallow and ill-informed Catholicity. Protestantism, though in most places in 1914 recently arrived and dependent on foreign leadership, after that year in several countries was to display marked vitality. In the contrast between the de-Christianizing forces issuing from the revolution and the revivals in Christian faith which we have noted in Christendom in Europe, the United States, and British North America, Latin American Christianity displayed much less vigour than in these other regions. But it was not dead.

CHAPTER XIII

Australia

A s we pass from the Americas and move eastward and southward we come
to two outposts of Western Christendom, Australia and New Zealand.
Although at the beginning of the nineteenth century each was the home of
non-European peoples, Australia of aborigines of Stone Age culture and New
Zealand of more recently arrived Polynesians, in each, and especially in Australia, the population was scanty, as was that of the Indians in most of the
Americas, and before the century had ended both countries, like the Americas,
were overwhelmingly European in blood and culture. As were the Americas,
they were an extension of Western Europe and, like the United States, British
North America, Argentina, Uruguay, and Southern Brazil, were the products
of that explosion of the population of Western Europe which was one of the
features of the nineteenth-century stage of the revolutionary age. Yet, unlike
the Americas, even British North America and the United States, they were
peopled almost entirely from the British Isles. How far did Christianity accompany that explosion? What, if any, vitality did it display? We will address ourselves first to Australia and then to New Zealand.

We naturally compare Australia with British North America. Both grew to
maturity as parts of the British Empire and then as nations in the Commonwealth. Both were huge: in spite of the fact that Australia was often counted
as the sixth continent rather than an island it was smaller than British North
America, about 3,000,000 square miles as against the latter's approximately 3,750,-
000 square miles. In both regions the spread of population was limited by
climate. In each the white population was predominantly in the South and
South-east—in Australia because this was in the Temperate Zone and reason-
ably well watered, whereas the North was in the tropics and most of the centre
was arid or semi-arid; in British North America because this area was also in
the Temperate Zone and the North was arctic or sub-arctic. But in British
North America the West became more thickly settled than in Australia. In
both Australia and British North America political unity of contiguous or nearly
contiguous states or provinces was achieved. In British North America before
1914 all were drawn in except Newfoundland and its dependency, Labrador,
and after 1914 they were included. In Australia New South Wales, Victoria,

South Australia, Western Australia, and Queensland, together with Tasmania (formerly known as Van Diemen's Land), were granted responsible government by an act of Parliament in 1850 and at various times in the 1850's it was inaugurated in each of them. On January 1, 1901, they came together in the Commonwealth of Australia. The fact that this was more than three decades after the formation of the Dominion of Canada was indicative of a later maturity which was also reflected in the religious life. Canada, too, was more populous than Australia. In 1911 the total stood at 7,206,643[1] as contrasted with 4,425,083 in Australia in 1910.[2] A larger proportion of the population of Australia than of Canada was in cities. Eventually two, Sydney and Melbourne, contained more than a third of the population of Australia, whereas the two largest in Canada, Montreal and Toronto, had only about an eighth of the country as a whole. One reason was that the rural population of Australia was largely absorbed in raising sheep and cattle, although by the latter part of the century wheat-growing increased and dairying was important. Pastoral and agricultural development was stimulated by the presence of markets in industrialized Western Europe, mainly Britain. In Australia industrialization mounted, but it was chiefly in the large urban areas and was mostly for local markets rather than export.

OBSTACLES

The initial peopling of Australia from the British Isles was unfavourable to Christianity. Here were no settlements established from deeply religious motives, as in several of the future United States, with a strong missionary purpose, as in French Canada, or from sturdy political loyalties, as by refugees in the Maritime Provinces and Upper Canada from the Revolution in the Thirteen Colonies. For more than a generation Australia and Tasmania were penal colonies, the compulsory dumping ground of undesirable elements of the British Isles. The main convict settlements were in or near Sydney, soon to become and to remain the leading city of Australia. The contrast was striking with the founding of Boston and Philadelphia. To be sure, not all who were deported to Australia were hardened criminals. Many had been guilty of what were later esteemed minor offenses. Some from Ireland had been involved in movements against English rule. Yet in the main, for several decades the majority were from the dregs of British society. In 1840 transportation to New South Wales was ordered stopped. The last convicts shipped to Tasmania were landed in 1852. But for another sixteen years some were being sent to Western Australia. It is said that from first to last 137,161 came to Australia and Tasmania as convicts.[3] Eventually the majority of the immigration was voluntary and in 1914

---

[1] *The Encyclopædia Britannica*, 14th ed., Vol. IV, p. 694.
[2] Wilson, *Official Year Book of the Commonwealth of Australia*, 1939, p. 352.
[3] Giles, *The Constitutional History of the Australian Church*, pp. 23–25.

only a minority of the population were of convict descent.

Some later conditions also presented obstacles to Christianity. The discovery of gold in the 1850's in several places led to the growth of mining camps where, as contemporaneously in California, moral conditions were adverse. In the extensive immigration which ensued were many Chartists and other radicals. In 1848 the Constitutional Association was formed with a Chartist programme. Militant agitation followed among the miners with a revolt, quickly suppressed, which Marx hailed as a phase of the class struggle. Labour unions became prominent as early as the 1870's and 1880's, and as elsewhere organized labor was usually indifferent or hostile to religion and some of its leaders were intensely critical of the Church.

If under these circumstances Christianity was less vigorous in Australia than in British North America we need not be surprised. Yet it displayed much more vitality than in Latin America. In the early part of the century it was chiefly dependent on the British Isles for its clergy. But long before 1914 it was beginning to produce them and by that year an increasing proportion were born and educated in Australia. Moreover, the Christians of Australia were sharing in the spread of the faith beyond their own country. They felt a special responsibility for the islands to the east and north, but they also reached out to Africa and to East and South Asia.

Protestantism was more nearly predominant in Australia than in Canada. In the early years of the twentieth century those classified under it constituted about four-fifths of the total population as against about three-fifths in Canada. The difference was accounted for by the absence of the French element in Australia. As was to be expected, the largest Protestant denominations were the ones which led in the British Isles. In 1921 those claiming affiliation with the Church of England were about 40 per cent. of the population and Presbyterians and Methodists each were about 12 per cent. Baptists and Congregationalists were relatively less numerous—Baptists about 2 per cent. and Congregationalists not quite one and a half per cent. The Churches of Christ enrolled about one per cent. The Plymouth Brethren, the Seventh Day Adventists, and the Salvation Army claimed still smaller percentages. The absence of a substantial immigration from North-western Europe accounted for the smallness of the Lutheran bodies—only slightly more than one per cent. of the population, in striking contrast with the United States and even with Canada.[4]

We will begin with a sketch of the development of the chief Protestant bodies and go on to a brief account of the Roman Catholic Church.

The Planting and Growth of Protestantism

The Church of England came with the first contingent of convicts and even-

4 Wilson, *op. cit.*, p. 381.

tually was represented in all the country. Richard Johnson sailed as chaplain with the initial ship in 1787, held the first service in Australia, and, at his own expense, built the first church. He was in the country until 1800.[5] The outstanding figure in the Church of England in the pioneer years was Samuel Marsden (1765–1838).[6] A sturdy Yorkshire man, an Evangelical, he owed his appointment to William Wilberforce. He sailed for New South Wales in 1793 and with one visit to England served for over forty years. He was not only in Australia but also concerned himself with introducing the faith to New Zealand and Tahiti. Practical, indefatigable, in Australia in addition to doing much to plant the Church he conducted schools, partly at his own expense, served as civil magistrate, helped to develop agriculture, and laboured for the social and moral improvement of women, convicts, and aborigines.

The first Bishop of Australia was William Grant Broughton (1788–1853). He came to Australia in 1829 as archdeacon, for the country at that time was under the Bishop of Calcutta. He was consecrated bishop in 1836 and when, in 1847, his huge diocese was divided, he became metropolitan. A high-churchman, he enlisted the aid of the Society for the Propagation of the Gospel in Foreign Parts and the Society for Promoting Christian Knowledge, travelled extensively, saw to the erection of churches and schools, and stimulated the sending of many clergy from England.[7]

As the population grew and the Church of England spread, additional dioceses were created. Tasmania was given one in 1842. The year 1847 saw three others—Melbourne, Newcastle, and Adelaide. Perth was made the centre of one in 1857, and in 1860 one was erected for Queensland with Brisbane as its seat. Later still other dioceses were added. Near the end of the century the title of metropolitan was changed to Archbishop of Sydney and in 1905 Victoria became a province under the Archbishop of Melbourne.[8]

Extensive assistance from the British Isles came to the Church of England in Australia. This was in part financial from the Society for the Propagation of the Gospel in Foreign Parts, the Society for Promoting Christian Knowledge, the Australian Church Missionary Society, the Western Australia Church Missionary Society, the Colonial and Continental Church Society, and substantial sums from Miss (later Baroness) Burdette-Coutts.[9] Much of the aid was in person-

[5] Giles, *op. cit.*, pp. 39–41; King, *Australia*, pp. 12–14.

[6] John Rawson Elder, editor, *The Letters and Journals of Samuel Marsden 1765–1838* (Dunedin, Coulls Somerville Wilkie and A. H. Reed, 1932, pp. 580), *passim;* S. H. Johnstone, *Samuel Marsden. A Pioneer of Civilization in the South Seas* (Sydney, Angus & Robertson, 1932, pp. xiii, 256), *passim;* J. B. Marsden, editor, *Memoirs of the Life and Labours of the Rev. Samuel Marsden of Paramatta, Senior Chaplain of New South Wales, and of His Early Connexion with the Missions to New Zealand and Tahiti* (London, The Religious Tract Society, c. 1858, pp. viii, 326), *passim.*

[7] *Dictionary of National Biography*, Vol. II, pp. 1373, 1374; Giles, *op. cit.*, pp. 43–47; Thompson, *Into All Lands*, pp. 207 ff.

[8] King, *op. cit.*, p. 19; Thompson, *op. cit.*, pp. 213–217; K. R. von Stieglitz, *The Story of the Church in Van Diemen's Land* (no place or publisher, preface 1954, pp. 72), p. 39.

[9] Giles, *op. cit.*, pp. 53, 54, 144, 145; Allen and McClure, *Two Hundred Years: The History of*

nel.[10] A unique project, in its beginnings staffed by young men from England, was the Bush Brotherhoods. They had their inception in 1897 when the Bishop of Rockhampton in Queensland asked Bishop Westcott of Durham for clergy. Realizing the strain of isolation, Westcott suggested that two or more live in a community and seek from that centre to cover a district. The plan was admirably adapted to the thinly settled districts in Queensland and New South Wales.[11]

The Anglicans eventually took steps to raise up and train an indigenous clergy and in this were increasingly successful. For example, the first Bishop of Bathurst was Samuel Edward Marsden, grandson of Samuel Marsden and born in Australia but educated in England. Although All Saints' College which he had a share in founding in Bathurst was not specifically for theological education, from its graduates several became clergymen.[12] In 1904 a diocesan theological college for Tasmania was opened.[13] In 1913 three Anglican theological colleges existed in Victoria, with a total of about one hundred students.[14] Yet, whether from England or native-born, the clergy were quite insufficient in number for the vast area of a growing country, and much use was made of lay readers.[15]

Gradually the Church of England in Australia developed an organization which enabled it to act comprehensively, at first for individual colonies and then for the country as a whole. At the outset the bishops were appointed from England with letters patent from the home government. In 1850, soon after the creation of several dioceses and the designation of Broughton as metropolitan, at the latter's instance a conference of the bishops met in Sydney for consultation on common action.[16] Subsequently diocesan conferences and synods were held in which the bishop, clergy, and laity were normally represented. Gradually the necessary authorizations were obtained from the colonial legislatures and ratified by the home government to enable the dioceses to have an increasing degree of autonomy.[17] Separate provinces were created, each with a metropolitan. In 1873, arising from a recommendation made by an informal gathering of seven of the bishops in 1868, a general synod convened. It was composed of ten bishops and about three clergy and three laymen from each diocese. It adopted a con-

---

the Society for Promoting Christian Knowledge, 1698–1898, pp. 330–346; J. D. Mullins, *Our Beginnings: being a Short Sketch of the History of the Colonial and Continental Church Society* (no place, publisher, or date, pp. 35), *passim;* Thompson, *op. cit.*, pp. 206–219.

[10] See some of it in G. H. Jose, *The Church of England in South Australia 1836–1856* (Adelaide, Church Office, 1937, pp. 70), pp. 17–21; Thompson, *op. cit.*, p. 215.

[11] King, *op. cit.*, pp. 37, 38.

[12] Watson A. Steel, *The History of All Saints' College, Bathurst 1873–1934* (Sydney, Angus & Robertson, 1936, pp. 217), pp. 16, 126, 127, 161 ff.

[13] W. R. Barrett, *History of the Church of England in Tasmania* (Hobart, The Mercury Press, pp. 92), p. 56.

[14] *Official Report of Congress on Union of Churches. Melbourne, August 31st to September 4th, 1913* (no place, publisher, or date, pp. 124), p. 8.

[15] King, *op. cit.*, pp. 45, 46.

[16] Giles, *op. cit.*, pp. 75 ff.

[17] *Ibid.*, pp. 63–134.

stitution under which synods continued to meet regularly. It had a primate, elected by the bishops from among the metropolitans. However, until after 1914 the Church of England in Australia, unlike its sisters in Canada and South Africa, was not fully autonomous and remained a part of the Church of England.[18]

The Presbyterianism of Australia was, obviously, of Scottish origin and its early growth was chiefly dependent on immigrants and aid from Scotland. Presbyterian services in Australia were begun in 1794 in Botany Bay by a Scottish convict. But he escaped in less than two years. Continuing Presbyterianism dated from 1803 from a group of free immigrants near Sydney.

The chief figure in early Australian Presbyterianism was the sturdy, able, and controversial John Dunmore Lang (1799–1878). A graduate of the University of Glasgow, he was attracted to Australia by the report of a brother on the needs of the Presbyterians in New South Wales. He was ordained in 1822 for the express purpose of inaugurating a Presbyterian church in Sydney and arrived there in 1823. He at once began the erection of a church building and was said to have been the first to administer the Communion in Australia after the Presbyterian fashion. He was six times in Britain, partly to obtain a grant towards the erection of a college in Sydney for the education of young men and of candidates for the ministry, partly to encourage free emigration to offset the influence of the convict element, and partly to foster the emigration of Protestants to keep New South Wales from becoming Roman Catholic. He served repeatedly on the legislative council and then the parliament of New South Wales. He advocated a United States of Australia. He travelled extensively in Australia as well as abroad. More than once he was in difficulty with the ecclesiastical authorities of his church. In 1832 the Presbytery of New South Wales was created embracing all Australia. In 1837 Lang led in the organization of the Synod of New South Wales independent of that Presbytery and claiming full autonomy as against any church. In 1840 it united with the Presbytery to form the Synod of Australia. Lang became convinced that the Church should completely separate itself from the state and should depend for support entirely on voluntary contributions. For a time the Synod deposed him from the ministry, largely for alleged contumacy. The case was carried to Scotland, both to the General Assembly and to the Court of Session, the supreme court of the country, and then to the Privy Council. Lang won and was reinstated.[19]

In the meantime the Disruption in Scotland led to a Free Church movement which resulted in the formation of the Synod of Eastern Australia (1846). However, in 1865 a union was effected which brought together the Synod of Eastern Australia and three other bodies in New South Wales.[20]

---

[18] *Ibid.*, pp. 146 ff.; Neill, *Anglicanism*, pp. 309–311.
[19] White, *The Challenge of the Years*, pp. 7–13; *Dictionary of National Biography*, Vol. XI, pp. 530–532; Latourette, *A History of the Expansion of Christianity*, Vol. V, pp. 139, 140.
[20] White, *op. cit.*, pp. 22, 23.

Presbyterianism continued to grow, not only in New South Wales but also in the other Australian colonies and in Tasmania. Clergy came from Scotland and Ireland. They were recruited in Australia as well and provision was made in more than one centre for their preparation. The congregations did not rely entirely on financial assistance from the mother countries. They became financially independent, except for government grants, of which we are to hear more in a moment, and also raised funds to assist in the founding of other congregations in the growing country.[21] Presbyterian congregations were organized in Victoria in the 1830's. The Church of Scotland, the United Presbyterian Church, and the Free Church were all represented in the next decade. The Disruption and the financial burdens which it threw upon both the Church of Scotland and the Free Church of Scotland for a time prevented much financial assistance to Australian Presbyterianism, but that did not stop the latter's growth, whether in Victoria or elsewhere. Clergy continued to come from Scotland. In 1854 the Presbytery of Melbourne ceased to be a part of the Church of New South Wales and constituted itself the Synod of Victoria. In 1867 the majority of the Presbyterians of Victoria came together, and in 1870, with the termination of state aid and by it the removal of an obstacle to their adherence, the dissenting minorities joined the Presbyterian Church of Victoria.[22] What seems to have been the first Presbyterian service in Tasmania was held in Hobart in 1823. A presbytery was organized in 1835 with Lang as moderator. The Disruption of Scotland brought disunion, but in 1896 reunion was accomplished.[23] The year 1837 saw the arrival of the first Presbyterian clergyman in South Australia—from the United Secession Church. As elsewhere, various branches of Presbyterianism were soon represented, but in 1865, slightly earlier than in Victoria, the United Presbyterian Church, the Church of Scotland, and the Free Church came together as the Presbyterian Church of South Australia.[24] As late as 1878 only one Presbyterian congregation was to be found in all Western Australia. The following year the Church of Scotland and the Free Church coöperated in sending a clergyman. But in 1892, when the first presbytery was formed, it comprised only three congregations. By 1901 two other presbyteries had been organized and in that year a general assembly met.[25] The indefatigable Lang held the first Presbyterian service (1845) in what later became Queensland. It was he who induced some immigrants to come to the region. The first church was organized in 1849 and in 1863 the Presbyterian Church of Queensland was formed. In 1876 an institution opened for the preparation of clergy.[26]

[21] *Ibid.*, pp. 14–83.
[22] Æneas Macdonald, *One Hundred Years of Presbyterianism in Victoria* (Melbourne, Robertson & Mullins, 1937, pp. 190), pp. 13–56.
[23] Latourette, *op. cit.*, Vol. V, pp. 150, 151.
[24] Harvey, "Notes on Australian Church History" (Ms.).
[25] *Ibid.*
[26] Alexander Hay, *Jubilee Memorial of the Presbyterian Church of Queensland, 1849–1899* (Brisbane, Alex. Muir & Co., 1900, pp. viii, 220), pp. 2, 5.

The several state Presbyterian churches formed in 1901 the Union of Presbyterian Churches embracing all Australia. A high degree of autonomy was left to the member churches, but a common doctrinal standard was adopted and the General Assembly of Australia had functions which it performed for them all, including supervision of missions to the aborigines.[27]

Methodism first entered Australia through laymen. With assistance from the British Isles it grew rapidly. In 1812 the first class meeting was held in Sydney and others soon followed. Aid was asked from the Methodist Conference of Great Britain. In response Samuel Leigh was sent. He arrived in 1815 under government license as a schoolmaster and Marsden welcomed him. He travelled widely, organizing Sunday Schools and Methodist classes, helping to found a branch of the British and Foreign Bible Society, and starting a tract society and an asylum for the poor. After a few years his health failed and at Marsden's suggestion he turned his attention to New Zealand. In 1820 after a nine months' stay there he went to England to prepare for that new mission.[28] Other ministers came from Britain, members increased, and in 1855, with the encouragement of the British Conference, the first Australasian Conference convened in Sydney. Following a plan suggested by the parent church, it formed the Australasian Wesleyan Methodist Connexion, partly independent of that body.[29]

Much of the increase of Methodism in New South Wales and elsewhere in Australia was due to Joseph Orton, appointed in 1831 as the second general superintendent.[30] In 1836 he held what was said to have been the first public religious service in Melbourne. A Methodist Society was soon organized and in 1841 a resident minister arrived for it.[31] In 1849 the Primitive Methodists sent a minister to Melbourne and two years later the Wesleyan Methodist Association, later the United Methodist Free Church, was represented in Victoria.[32] With the growth of population through the development of gold-mining and the coming from Great Britain of more ministers to meet the challenge, by the year 1855 Victoria was served by twenty Methodist circuits and seventeen clergy.[33]

Methodism was introduced and made progress in all the other Australian colonies. In 1820 three Methodist soldiers started a class meeting in Hobart. The

[27] White, *op. cit.*, p. 55.

[28] Colwell, *A Century in the Pacific*, pp. 223–227, 231, 235, 236; Alexander Strachan, *The Life of the Reverend Samuel Leigh . . . with a History of the Origin and Progress of the Missions in those Colonies* (London, The Wesleyan Mission House, 1870, pp. vi, 418), pp. 13–83.

[29] Findlay and Holdsworth, *The History of the Wesleyan Methodist Missionary Society*, Vol. III, pp. 134–140.

[30] *Ibid.*, pp. 49 ff.

[31] *Ibid.*, pp. 82–87; Colwell, *op. cit.*, pp. 279–282.

[32] Colwell, *op. cit.*, p. 283; *Autobiography of the Reverend Joseph Townend with Reminiscences of His Missionary Labours in Australia* (London, W. Reed, United Methodist Free Churches Bookroom, 1869, pp. iii, 252), pp. 84 ff.

[33] Findlay and Holdsworth, *op. cit.*, Vol. III, pp. 92–100; Colwell, *op. cit.*, pp. 283–287; Symons, *Life of the Rev. Daniel James Draper*, pp. 130 ff.

next year a minister from England was assigned to Tasmania. In the 1840's and 1850's the Tasmanian churches attained self-support. In 1854, so rapid was the progress, Tasmania had twenty-three chapels, eleven other preaching places, and eight ministers. Twenty years later these totals had increased to ninety-seven chapels and other preaching places and fifteen ministers.[34] In proportion to the other denominations, Methodists were more numerous in South Australia than in New South Wales or Victoria. In 1876 in that colony they enrolled more than either the Anglicans or the Presbyterians.[35] Although it arrived in 1830 through immigrants, in Western Australia Methodism developed more slowly than in the other colonies and not until 1900 was a separate conference formed.[36] In 1863 a Methodist district was created for Queensland, but still attached to New South Wales. Thirty years later it was given a distinct conference and in 1894 the Primitive Methodists, the Bible Christians, and some of the United Free Methodists joined in it with the Wesleyan Methodists.[37]

Australian Methodism felt the repercussions of awakenings and fresh methods elsewhere in its global fellowship and especially in the British Isles. For example, in the 1860's William Taylor, from the United States, whom we have met in Latin America, made two long visits to Australia as an itinerant preacher and helped to raise money for chapels and schools.[38] In the 1880's a native of Yorkshire, William George Taylor, was appointed to a downtown church in Sydney from which the constituency was moving to the suburbs and transformed it into the successful Central Methodist Mission, after the pattern which was being developed in England to meet similar situations.[39]

In spite of unions in individual states, up to 1892 four separate Methodist churches existed. The Methodist Ecumenical Conference of 1881 gave an impetus towards comprehensive union and on January 1, 1902, Methodism became one throughout Australia.[40]

Baptists appeared early but, as we have suggested, were much less prominent than the Anglicans, Presbyterians, and Methodists. Percentage-wise they did not loom as large as in Canada. Why this was so is not clear. One conjecture has it that, since a number of Baptist ministers were trained by Spurgeon and tended to depend on vast "tabernacles" of the kind which that great preacher erected in London, they did not effectively reach the urban population of Australia with its distinct problems and habits. Clearly the kind of frontier and rural conditions did not exist in which Baptists and Methodists flourished in

[34] Findlay and Holdsworth, *op. cit.,* Vol. III, pp. 66–68, 79.
[35] Harvey, *op. cit.;* Symons, *op. cit.,* pp. 47 ff.
[36] Findlay and Holdsworth, *op. cit.,* Vol. III, pp. 120–126; Colwell, *op. cit.,* pp. 336–358.
[37] Findlay and Holdsworth, *op. cit.,* Vol. III, pp. 143, 144; Colwell, *op. cit.,* pp. 363–373.
[38] Taylor, *Story of My Life,* pp. 255–326.
[39] Colwell, *op. cit.,* p. 561; William George Taylor, *The Life-Story of an Australian Evangelist with an Account of the Origin and Growth of the Sydney Central Methodist Mission* (London, The Epworth Press, 1920, pp. 347), *passim.*
[40] Rouse and Neill, *A History of the Ecumenical Movement 1517–1948,* p. 301.

the United States. The absence of a system of circuits such as that adopted by the Methodists worked to the relative disadvantage of the Baptists. From 1831 to 1834 a Highland minister served a congregation which he gathered in Sydney.[41] In 1834 a minister arrived in Sydney, sent in response to a request to the Baptist Missionary Society, in 1836 a church was incorporated in that city, the first in the country, and in the course of the next three decades several Baptist churches sprang up in New South Wales.[42] In 1838 laymen began Baptist services in Melbourne. A clergyman came from England in 1842 and the next year a church was organized. By 1862 enough churches existed in Victoria to constitute an association. Both General and Particular Baptists were represented in the colony. In 1871 a home missionary society was formed to help found new churches and to further theological education. For several years Baptists and Congregationalists coöperated in the latter, but in 1889 a separate Baptist theological college was opened. In 1835 Baptist churches were organized in two centres in Tasmania.[43] In South Australia Baptist beginnings in the 1830's and 1840's were troubled by divisions and dissensions. The coming to Adelaide of a minister, Silas Mead, from England in 1861, on invitation from local leaders, marked the dawn of a better day. Under his initiative a church was organized, a building erected, and mission work in the city undertaken. Other ministers arrived, additional churches were formed, and in 1863 they came together in the South Australian Baptist Union. Lay preachers were active. Missionaries were sent to India.[44] Apparently the first Baptist services in Western Australia were held, in Perth in 1894, by a layman. In the 1890's several churches were organized and the Baptist Union of Western Australia was formed.[45] In Queensland the Baptists organized their own church in 1855 after having joined for six years with Presbyterians and Congregationalists in a United Evangelical Church.[46] Until well after 1914 the Baptists of Australia continued to draw many of their ministers from England, partly through the Baptist Missionary Society of that country.[47]

Congregationalism early appeared in Australia through the enterprise of the London Missionary Society in the South Seas in the 1790's. It increased in the succeeding decades, partly by immigration and partly by aid from Britain. Some of the original contingent in Tahiti eventually made their homes in New South Wales. Through them a congregation assembled (1829) and a chapel was erected (1833). The Colonial Missionary Society, organized in London in 1836

---

[41] A. Crowther Smith in *The Christian Century*, Vol. XLVIII, p. 885.

[42] Harvey, *op. cit.;* Torbet, *A History of the Baptists,* p. 181.

[43] Harvey, *op. cit.;* Torbet, *op. cit.,* pp. 182, 183.

[44] H. Estcourt Hughes, *Our First Hundred Years. The Baptist Church in South Australia* (Adelaide, South Australia Baptist Union, 1937, pp. 349), *passim.*

[45] Leslie J. Gomm, *Blazing New Trails. The Story of the Life and Work of William Kennedy, Pathfinder, Preacher, and Pioneer* (Glebe, J. H. Packer, 1935, pp. 208), pp. 35–39 and *passim.*

[46] Harvey, *op. cit.*

[47] Torbet, *op. cit.,* p. 186.

to assist Congregationalism in the colonies, sent a man to New South Wales (1840). In 1864 Camden College was begun both as a school for boys and to train young men for the ministry.[48] In 1872 New South Wales had twenty-five Congregational chapels.[49] A Congregational church was formed in Melbourne in 1839. It was reinforced by men sent by the Colonial Missionary Society, in 1860 a Congregational Union was organized in that city, and the following year a college was opened for the training of clergy.[50] In Tasmania the first Congregational church dated from 1832, led by a minister who arrived in 1830 at the instance of a layman. In 1834 the Congregationalists hopefully formed the Van Diemen's Land Colonial Missionary and Christian Instruction Society, which, assisted by the Colonial Missionary Society, brought out clergy and aided weak churches.[51] An agent of the Colonial Missionary Society who arrived in 1837 introduced Congregationalism to South Australia. In 1850 the Congregational Union was started and not many years later it had at least fifteen centres and a chapel-building society.[52] Congregational beginnings in Western Australia were usually due to laymen, but the Colonial Missionary Society assisted with funds and clergy.[53] That society also sent a missionary to Queensland who served the first Congregational church in that colony (gathered in 1853). The Congregational Union of Queensland was organized in 1861.[54]

The Churches of Christ arose from colonists and from preachers from Great Britain, especially Scotland, and the United States. They sprang up in the 1840's and 1850's in South Australia and Victoria, in the 1860's in New South Wales and Tasmania, in the 1870's in Queensland, and in the 1890's, from South Australia, in Western Australia. In 1875 the South Australia Evangelist Committee was organized to further the movement. The Australian College of the Bible was founded, also in South Australia, to prepare leadership.[55]

Lutheranism was not as prominent in Australia as in the United States, Canada, or Brazil, but it was present and was well organized. It arose partly from immigrants who opposed the Union of Lutherans and Reformed in the Fatherland.[56]

[48] Harvey, *op. cit.;* Colwell, *op. cit.,* p. 226.
[49] John Dunmore Lang, *An Historical and Statistical Account of New South Wales from the Founding of the Colony in 1788 to the Present Day* (London, Sampson Low, 2 vols., 4th ed., 1875), Vol. II, p. 449.
[50] Harvey, *op. cit.*
[51] *The Twenty-Third Report of the Tasmanian Colonial Missionary and Christian Instruction Society in Connection with the Tasmanian Congregational Union* (Hobart Town, Burnet, 1859), *passim.*
[52] James Bickford, *Christian Work in Australasia* (London, Wesleyan Conference Office, 1878, p. vii, 344), pp. 160, 161; *Report of the Tenth Annual Meeting of the Congregational Union of South Australia, held April 19th, 20th, and 21st, 1859* (Adelaide, J. T. Shawyer, 1859, pp. 8), *passim;* Edward S. Kiek, *Our First Hundred Years. The Centenary Record of the South Australian Congregational Union* (no place, publisher, or date, pp. 123), *passim.*
[53] Harvey, *op. cit.*
[54] *Ibid.*
[55] Mason, *Jubilee Pictorial History of the Churches of Christ in Australasia, passim.*
[56] Theodor J. M. G. Hebart, *The United Evangelical Lutheran Church in Australia. Its History,*

Although by no means as many Protestant denominations were represented in Australia as in the United States, or even as in British North America, on the eve of 1914 an effort was made to bring about more coöperation and to discuss the possibility of union. In 1913 what was called a congress on the union of churches was held in Melbourne but was only for the state of Victoria. Its chief topics were theological education, coördination of home missions, and organic union. As an indication of the extent to which Australia was producing its own clergy, it found that in Victoria the Anglicans, Presbyterians, Methodists, Baptists, and Congregationalists had then about 250 theological students, a number of whom were not in residence. Some were from other states. The suggestion was made that joint effort in theological education be made something after the pattern of what was already being done in Montreal. Serious overlapping of efforts in home missions was reported, and the commission which studied the problem recommended that a united control of home missions be adopted. Statements were presented by the various bodies of what each deemed essential if organic union was to be achieved.[57]

The intellectual currents of the revolutionary age could not but have repercussions on Australian Protestantism. For example, in 1881 Charles Strong, pastor of the Scot's Church in Melbourne, was declared by the Presbyterian General Assembly of that province no longer to be a minister. The issue was the divinity of Christ, on which he was questioned but refused to reply.[58] Joseph Coles Kirby, a prominent Congregational minister, repudiated both Bushnell, to whom he had been earlier attracted, and the "new theology" of R. J. Campbell of City Temple, London, and affirmed his belief in the preëxistence and deity of Christ and especially in the substitutionary atonement.[59]

The Australian churches had far less influence on public affairs and in shaping the collective life of the country than their counterparts in Britain. Here and there a churchman stood out as an exception. We will see them in the Roman Catholic hierarchy. We also hear of them among Protestants, fighting vice, and advocating woman's suffrage, temperance, prison reform, and eugenics.[60]

THE ROMAN CATHOLIC CHURCH

The Roman Catholic Church in Australia was overwhelmingly Irish. At the outset the Irish element was largely of convicts. Later thousands came to escape the famine which sent other thousands to Great Britain, the United States, and British North America. After the famine had become only a hideous mem-

---

Activities, and Characteristics 1838–1948 (North Adelaide, Lutheran Book Room, 1938, pp. 336) passim.
[57] Official Report of Congress on Union of Churches, Melbourne, August 31st to September 4th 1913 (no place, publisher, or date, pp. 124), passim.
[58] The Australian Encyclopedia, Vol. II, p. 329.
[59] Kiek, An Apostle in Australia, pp. 67, 76, 183.
[60] Ibid., pp. 193 ff.

ory the influx from Ireland continued. For instance, not far from 1860 James O'Quinn, Bishop of Brisbane, brought in about six thousand on ships chartered for the purpose and under subsidy from the Queensland Government.[61] On the eve of 1914, official statistics of the church placed the number of Roman Catholics as 19.4 per cent. of the population.[62]

Before 1815 intermittent clerical care was given to the Roman Catholic convicts by some priests in their number. In 1817 Jeremiah Francis O'Flynn was appointed by Rome as Prefect Apostolic for Botany Bay, but the Vicar Apostolic of London held that this was a violation of his jurisdiction, O'Flynn came without permission from the British Government, and the governor deported him.[63]

When consecrated Vicar Apostolic of the Cape of Good Hope Edward Bede Slater was assigned Australia as part of his field. He obtained the appointment of two priests as chaplains. One of them, John Joseph Therry, went first to Sydney and then after some years to Tasmania. He struggled to alleviate the hard lot of the convicts, but his relations with the government were thorny.[64]

Better times for the Roman Catholic Church began with the arrival in 1833 of William Bernard Ullathorne as the first Vicar General for New South Wales. A remarkable man who was later to have an outstanding role in the English hierarchy, after three years in Australia he returned to the British Isles to recruit personnel for that country. He spent two years in the effort, and with success. He brought much unpopularity on himself in Australia among those who profited by it in seeking to end the convict system.[65]

The Roman Catholic Church was further strengthened by the consecration, in 1834, of a Benedictine, John Bede Polding (1794-1877), as the first resident Vicar Apostolic for Australia. In his early years he spent much of his time on horseback, traversing the rough outposts of settlement, ministering to his flock. He encouraged his priests to do likewise and developed a system resembling that of the early Methodist circuit riders in the United States. Like Ullathorne, he was openly critical of the transportation system, especially in its worst centres, Norfolk Island and Van Diemen's Land (Tasmania). He declared it to be horribly destructive of human values and said that transportation was often inflicted on individuals who were obnoxious to landlords as political agitators and was used to relieve the ruling classes of the annoyance or threat of their presence. In 1840 he and Ullathorne left for Europe to appeal for missionaries. In the five years since his arrival he had seen a single church and a few in process of erection increase to twenty-five churches and chapels, thirty-one primary

[61] *The Australian Encyclopedia*, Vol. II, pp. 68, 69.
[62] *The Australian Catholic Directory for 1910*, table after p. 193.
[63] O'Brien, *The Dawn of Catholicism in Australia, passim.*
[64] *Ibid.*, Vol. II, pp. 180, 206 ff.
[65] *From Cabin-Boy to Archbishop. The Autobiography of Archbishop Ullathorne* (London, Burns Oates and Washbourne, 1941, pp. xxiii, 310), pp. 60 ff.; Birt, *Benedictine Pioneers in Australia*, Vol. I, pp. 204 ff.; Murtagh, *Australia: The Catholic Chapter*, pp. 44-53.

schools, and a well-organized Roman Catholic population of 23,130.[66]

During their time in Europe Ullathorne and Polding developed a plan for the creation of a hierarchy for Australia. In 1842 it was approved by Rome. Polding was appointed Archbishop of Sydney and was given two suffragans, one for Hobart Town, in Van Diemen's Land (Tasmania), and one for Adelaide, in South Australia. This, it will be noted, was eight years before the restoration of the hierarchy in England. Broughton, as Anglican Bishop of Australia, formally protested the designation of Polding as Archbishop of Sydney.[67]

The newly appointed bishops set themselves to building up their church; one also continued the efforts of Ullathorne and Polding to remedy the evils of the transportation system and solve the problems arising from voluntary immigration. Robert William Willson, the first bishop of Hobart Town, not only brought Sisters of Charity, built colleges for higher education, promoted work with youth, and was a pioneer in the scientific treatment of the insane but also was chiefly responsible for the end of the penal settlement on Norfolk Island and reclaimed some of the individuals who were its victims.

A convert through contact with a French *émigré* priest in her English childhood, Caroline Jones Chisholm, who came to Sydney in the 1830's because of the ill health of her husband, gave herself to immigrant women and girls, attacked the abuses on the ships on which they came, established centres in which girls could be protected, helped them to find employment, and urged that immigration should be by family groups rather than by unattached individuals. To assist her the Family Colonization Loan Society was organized in England. She also advocated small land-holdings as a way of providing for the families.[68]

As the years passed, the Roman Catholic Church continued to grow, not only in members, but also in the numbers of clergy and dioceses and in its institutions. Religious orders and congregations increased. In 1910 it had in Australia 1,443 churches, 738 secular and 230 regular clergy, 466 brothers, 5,081 sisters, seminaries, and 85 charitable institutions. In its parochial and higher schools 112,315 pupils were enrolled.[69] Plenary councils of the bishops were held. In 1900 the first National Australian Catholic Congress convened and was followed by others in 1904 and 1909. A Catholic Young Men's Society was founded. The Australian Catholic Truth Society was begun (1900) to present the Roman Catholic faith to non-Roman Catholics.[70]

The Roman Catholic Church in Australia was fortunate in its leadership. In addition to Ullathorne and Polding, the latter was followed as Archbishop of Sydney by another Benedictine, Roger William Vaughan (1834–1883),

[66] Birt, *op. cit.*, Vol. I, pp. 265 ff.; Murtagh, *op. cit.*, pp. 41–48, 65, 66.

[67] Birt, *op. cit.*, Vol. II, pp. 1–56.

[68] Murtagh, *op. cit.*, pp. 53–79.

[69] *Australian Catholic Directory for 1910*, after p. 193.

[70] Murtagh, *op. cit.*, pp. 162, 175.

younger brother of the Cardinal Archbishop of Westminster. His decade in the post (1873–1883), first as coadjutor and then as successor, was cut short by his early death.[71] Vaughan was followed by Patrick Francis Moran (1830–1911). Appointed Archbishop of Sydney in 1884 and created cardinal in 1885, he had long made a special study of Australia. In his see he championed the right of labour to organize unions, then in the early and stormy stages of their bid for power, sought to mediate in a prolonged maritime strike which began in 1890, and was in the forefront of the movement for the federation of the Australian colonies which was achieved in 1900–1901.[72]

The Issue of Financial Support by the State

As in British North America, the question of financial support of the churches by the state was an early cause of controversy. The trend, as in most of Western Christendom, was away from subsidy by the government and eventually, at dates which differed from colony to colony, all assistance was terminated. The reason was not hostility to Christianity. It lay partly in the multiplicity of denominations and the conviction that to subsidize one to the exclusion of the others would be unjust. Here and there were churchmen, of whom Lang was notable, who on principle opposed a subsidy.

We need not go into the full story but will simply record a few highlights as typical. In 1836 an act was passed in New South Wales which provided for the annual distribution of a sum among the Church of England, the Roman Catholic Church, the Presbyterians, and the Wesleyans. It was to be applied towards the erection of churches, chapels, residences for clergy, and stipends for the clergy. All grants from the colonial governments ceased in New South Wales in 1862, in Tasmania in 1869, and in Victoria in 1871. In Tasmania the cutting off of financial aid was eased by a terminal grant for endowment and for stipends for clergy who had been aided by the state. It was divided among the Church of England, the Roman Catholic Church, the Church of Scotland, the Wesleyans, the Free Church of Scotland, and the Jews.[73]

The Vexed Question of Education

Australia was no exception to the struggle over education which we have found in country after country in the nineteenth-century Occident. Should it be by the churches with state aid? Should it be entirely in the hands of the state, and, if so, should religious instruction be given in the state schools? At first, the general policy was to have all schools conducted by the various denominations and with subsidies by the state. Such was the situation in New South

---

[71] Birt, *op. cit.*, Vol. II, pp. 405 ff.
[72] Murtagh, *op. cit.*, pp. 133 ff.
[73] Giles, *The Constitutional History of the Australian Church*, pp. 140–143.

Wales until 1841.[74] In that year legislation provided for state aid to existing schools, regardless of creed, on the basis of the number of students enrolled, and for setting up public schools where no other schools existed. In 1848 two boards were formed, one for the denominational and the other for the public schools, and the state aid was divided between them. However, eventually in all the Australian states legislation was passed which established free, compulsory, secular elementary education and which cancelled assistance to denominational schools. This was done against the vigorous protest of church leaders, especially Anglicans and Roman Catholics. Yet it was a Protestant clergyman who was the leading spirit in the New South Wales Public School League begun in 1874 which sought to make elementary education national, secular, compulsory, and free.[75] In some states non-sectarian religious education was given in the public schools in the form of Biblical history and morals. Moreover, parents were permitted to send their children to denominational elementary schools, and numbers of the latter were maintained, especially by the Roman Catholics.[76]

Throughout the country secondary education was mainly in denominational schools.[77] Higher and technical education was provided prevailingly by the state, but in connexion with the University of Sydney were four denominational colleges supported by government funds—Church of England, Roman Catholic, Presbyterian, and Wesleyan.[78]

Missions Among the Aborigines

The vigour of Christianity in Australia was evidenced not only in the efforts, largely successful, to hold the vast influx of population from Europe to at least a nominal adherence to the faith. It was also seen in attempts to make the coming of the white man a blessing and not a curse to the aboriginal population. Some undertakings were directly from Europe. Numbers were from Australia. They were through several denominations.

The aboriginal population dwindled rapidly in the contacts with the white man, partly because of appalling cruelties at the hands of the immigrants, partly from the diseases which came with the Europeans—the latter had developed partial resistance to them but they swept in epidemics through a people who had never before been exposed to them—and partly through the difficulty of adjusting to a different culture. The aborigines are said to have numbered about

---

[74] For a survey of the situation see William Westbrooke Burton, *The State of Religion and Education in New South Wales* (London, J. Cross and Simpkin and Marshall, 1840, pp. vii, 321, cxxxvi), *passim*.

[75] Kiek, *An Apostle in Australia*, p. 108.

[76] Murtagh, *op. cit.*, pp. 116 ff.; *The Australian Encyclopedia*, Vol. I, pp. 397–403.

[77] *The Australian Encyclopedia*, Vol. II, pp. 423–428.

[78] *Ibid.*, p. 604.

250,000 to 300,000 in 1788.[79] They all but died out in Tasmania.[80] By 1936 they had dwindled in Australia to 51,379 full-bloods and 24,718 half-castes. The large majority were in the areas with the smallest white population—Queensland, Western Australia, and the Northern Territory.[81]

Early in the nineteenth century Christians of various denominations were expressing concern for the aborigines. Even to enumerate the missions that were undertaken among them would unduly prolong this paragraph. Anglicans, Presbyterians, Methodists, Moravians, Lutherans, the undenominational United Aborigines Mission, the Aborigines Inland Mission, also undenominational, the Seventh Day Adventists, and the Roman Catholics had a share. The government gave financial assistance. The enterprises mounted in the latter part of the century.[82]

AUSTRALIAN CHRISTIANS UNDERTAKE MISSIONS OUTSIDE THEIR COUNTRY

While even down to 1914 some help, although diminishing and chiefly in personnel, continued to be given to Australian Christianity from the British Isles and the rapidly mounting population and the changing social conditions constituted a major challenge, the churches of the country increasingly reached out beyond its borders in the effort to spread the faith among other peoples. Before 1914 Anglicans, Presbyterians, Methodists, Baptists, Congregationalists, Disciples of Christ (Christians), Lutherans, and several undenominational bodies were active. They operated through more than twenty-five societies and had representatives in India, China, Africa, Japan, Korea, Melanesia, and Papua.[83] Here was vitality such as was not seen in Latin America but resembled that in Europe, the United States, and British North America.

SUMMARY

In Australia Christianity faced greater obstacles than in that other region which so closely resembled it: British North America. The initial peopling by convicts, the early growth of large cities with the difficulties which here as elsewhere they presented to the churches, the rapid rise of organized labour, and, by contrast, the thin dispersal of the population on the vast ranges devoted to raising sheep and cattle with the near impossibility of developing a normal

[79] J. S. Needham, *White and Black in Australia* (London, Society for Promoting Christian Knowledge, 1935, pp. 174), p. 22.

[80] James Bonwick, *The Lost Tasmanian Race* (London, Sampson Low, Marston, Searle, and Rivington, 1884, pp. 224), *passim*, especially pp. 172–175.

[81] Wilson, *Official Year Book of the Commonwealth of Australia*, 1939, p. 408.

[82] Needham, *op. cit.*, pp. 63 ff. For the record of an Anglican missionary see E. R. Gribble, *Forty Years with the Aborigines* (Sydney, Angus & Robertson, 1930, pp. 235), *passim*.

[83] Beach and Fahs, *World Missionary Atlas*, pp. 31–33.

parish life, and the semi-tropical climate which invited to outdoor sports and discouraged church attendance presented challenges peculiar to the country. In addition, the various intellectual currents of the revolutionary age which made for secularization poured into Australia as into other sections of the larger Occident.

In the face of these adverse conditions the achievement of Christianity was remarkable. As in British North America, the major part of the settlement came when the pulses of life were running strong in the Christianity of the British Isles. Even more than in British North America the immigration was from the British Isles and thus profited by the rising tide in that Christianity. Much assistance came from the mother country in funds and personnel in planting the faith in the new nation. The Australians themselves rapidly took the initiative, supported the clergy, erected church structures, and reached out into newly settled districts. Lay participation was prominent. As in British North America and unlike the United States, no new major denominations came out of Australian Christianity. For the most part the denominations were those of the British Isles, although in somewhat different proportion than there. As was to be expected in a people engrossed in building a new country, the temper of Christianity was activistic. Little was done in creative thought to meet the intellectual challenge of the age. The churches served the country through schools, institutions for the relief of suffering, and care for the underprivileged. From them, as elsewhere, came temperance movements, contributions to prison reform, and, especially, the shaping of individual lives and the collective character of the emerging nation. Increasingly efforts were made to protect the aborigines, to bring them the Christian faith, and to draw them into Christian communities. The churches reached out, too, to the vast population in Asia, to the peoples of the islands of the Pacific, and to Africa. Although the government adopted an adamant policy of a "white Australia" which set impassable barriers to the entrance of these teeming millions to the relatively underpopulated continent, the Christians of Australia felt an obligation to these their neighbours.

CHAPTER XIV

New Zealand

N EW ZEALAND, only slightly more than a thirtieth the size of Australia but lying entirely in the Temperate Zone, although settled, both by aborigines and Europeans, later than that country, in proportion to its area had a larger population. In 1916 its total was 1,149,225, a little over a fourth of that of Australia. Of this nearly 50,000, or a larger percentage of the whole than in the latter, were aborigines.

Christianity first came to the aborigines—the Maoris, a Polynesian people —nearly a generation before white settlement began. It was brought chiefly through Protestants and the pioneer was the redoubtable Marsden. While on a visit in England in 1807–1808 Marsden induced the Church Missionary Society, then only a little more than a decade old, to send missionaries. The first contingent arrived in 1814, led by Marsden, and on Christmas Day of that year he officiated at what seems to have been the first Christian service in the islands. Other missionaries followed. The language was reduced to writing, and hymns, catechisms, the liturgy, and parts of the Bible were translated. The first baptism was in 1825. By 1841 some of the old religious practices were waning, slavery, cannibalism, infanticide, and suicide were passing, and polygamy was dying. In its first bishop, George Augustus Selwyn (1809–1878), who arrived in 1842, the Church of England had a leader of outstanding ability, vision, and devotion.

Other denominations undertook missions to the Maoris. At the instance of Marsden the Methodists came (1822), led by Samuel Leigh. Late in the 1830's the Roman Catholics arrived, staffed by the recently founded Marists and with Jean Baptiste François Pompallier as vicar apostolic. Eventually Mormons, Seventh Day Adventists, two German societies, and Presbyterians were represented. In the number of converts gathered the Anglicans were first, the Roman Catholics second, the Methodists third, and the Mormons fourth.

Christianity did not have a smooth course among the Maoris. The white man's firearms accentuated the deadlines of the tribal wars, his firewater proved demoralizing, and for years population declined. Although most of the Maoris became Christian by religion, some of them developed cults which were a compound of that faith with remnants of pre-Christian days and novel contributions from the leaders. Yet eventually adjustment was made to European civilization, population recouped some of its losses, and the Maoris, most of them in the North Island, became an integral part of the new nation. Much of this achievement must be attributed to Christianity.[1]

Here on a small scale was what we have found in the Americas and Australia and what we shall later see more at length and on much larger dimensions. A striking contradiction was evident in what issued from Western Christendom in the revolutionary age. On the one hand were forces which brought disintegration, moral and social, to the peoples on whom they impinged. They came through traders whose only interest it was to exploit the aborigines for their own fancied profit. On the other hand, missionaries laboured to help the aborigines to a richer life, both spiritual and physical. At times they made what others appraised as mistakes, but in the main the results were positive and constructive, both in individuals and in the group as a whole.

Systematic European settlement began in 1840. Before that year immigrants had been filtering in, some transient, some continuing. Planned immigration was promoted by the New Zealand Company, primarily the creation of Edward Gibbon Wakefield (1796–1862). Although Wakefield had a Quaker ancestry, some of it related to Elizabeth Fry, his dominant motive seems not to have been religious. He devoted himself to colonization and had a large share in the founding of South Australia and in furthering self-government in Canada. He was convinced that the colonists should be of high moral character and was opposed to the continuation of the peopling of the new domains by convicts. His study of history impressed him with the role of those ruled by Christian purpose in the creation of the Thirteen Colonies. He wished to see colonization by similar groups, each centred around a particular denomination. At first the Church Missionary Society opposed the programme of the New Zealand Company as a threat to the Maoris. However, undeterred by initial lack of government support, colonization was pushed. British sovereignty over New Zealand was declared in the nick of time to forestall similar action by the French and with the reluctant consent of the missionaries. As a result, New Zealand did not have the convict element which loomed large in the early years of the settlement of Australia, and conditions favoured the emergence of a nation in whose life Christianity would have an integral part.[2]

Although the major growth of the churches in New Zealand was not through the special denominational colonies envisioned by Wakefield, two of the latter came into being and were important. Because of the growing religious tolerance in the British Isles, they did not spring from refugees from religious persecution

---

[1] Latourette, *A History of the Expansion of Christianity,* Vol. V, pp. 177–185, contains a longer summary and an extensive bibliography.

[2] A. J. Harrop, *The Amazing Career of Edward Gibbon Wakefield* (London, George Allen and Unwin, 1928, pp. 253), *passim;* Edward Gibbon Wakefield, *A View of the Art of Colonization, with Present Reference to the British Empire* (London, John W. Parker, 1849, pp. xxiv, 513), pp. 155–165; *Dictionary of National Biography,* Vol. XX, pp. 449–455.

as did some of the most important of the Thirteen Colonies nor did they have as large a part in shaping the ideals of the new nation.

One of the two was of Anglicans, sponsored by the Canterbury Association. Wakefield gave it support, but the leading spirit was a graduate of Christ Church, Oxford. The New Zealand Company promised it a block of a million acres and assured it of control until 1858 of all purchases of land within it. The initial contingents arrived in 1850 and 1851 and founded Christchurch. Difficulties inevitable in a pioneer undertaking arose, but when, in 1856, the first bishop of the new see arrived, he found a population of about five thousand, of whom approximately 70 per cent. were Anglicans, with five churches and nine clergymen. In time Christchurch became the second city in size in the country, dependent largely on stock-raising and the growth of cereals, but in the 1880's it still had the appearance of a university town with a distinctly ecclesiastical atmosphere.[3]

The other religious colony was founded by Scottish Presbyterians with its centre in Otago, like Christchurch on the South, sometimes called the Middle Island, and was begun slightly earlier. In the initial stages of its preparation it was assisted by the New Zealand Company. It was largely the work of laymen of the Free Church of Scotland and was endorsed by the General Assembly of that body. The name given it was first New Edinburgh but later changed to Dunedin, an old Celtic designation of Edinburgh. Two shiploads arrived in 1848, with Thomas Burns, a nephew of the poet Robert Burns, as minister and an outstanding leader. More settlers came and additional ministers. In 1854 the Presbytery of Otago was constituted. The discovery of gold in 1861 brought an influx of miners, which altered the character of the neighborhood, but progress continued, with the creation of a synod in 1866 with Burns as moderator and the founding of a theological hall and the University of Otago in 1869 with the preparation of ministers as an objective.[4]

The Church of England became the largest of the ecclesiastical bodies of New Zealand and in the 1920's was registered in the census as having almost exactly the same proportion of the population as in Australia—approximately 44 per cent. It owed much of its early vitality and organization to Selwyn. To Wakefield's intense irritation Selwyn sided with the missionaries in their opposi-

---

[3] Purchas, A History of the English Church in New Zealand, pp. 147–150; A. J. Harrop, England and New Zealand from Tasman to the Taranaki War (London, Methuen and Co., 1926, pp. xxiv, 326), pp. 247, 248; Samuel Butler, A First Year in Canterbury Settlement (London, Longmans, Green, Longmans, Roberts and Quen, 1863, pp. x, 162), passim; G. E. Mason, Round the World on a Church Mission (London, Society for Promoting Christian Knowledge, 1892, pp. x, 379), pp. 263–305.

[4] C. Stuart Ross, The Story of the Otago Church and Its Settlement (Dunedin, Wise, Caffin & Co., 1887, pp. x, 449), passim; Elder, The History of the Presbyterian Church of New Zealand, 1840–1940, pp. 42–52; William Gillies, The Presbyterian Church Trust: the Documents Relating to the Title and Administration of the Trust Property of the Presbyterian Church of Otago and Southland: with Historical Narrative (Dunedin, Reith & Wilkie, 1876, pp. 108), passim; John Hislop, History of the Knox Church, Dunedin (Dunedin, J. Wilkie & Co., 1892, pp. xviii, 160, 21), pp. 1–12.

tion to colonization by Europeans, but he won the friendship and respect of many of the latter. Although at first he met with opposition from the Church Missionary Society, which feared that separation from the Church of England was intended, he pushed through the formation of the Church of England in New Zealand. By the close of 1859 five bishoprics had been created, he had been made metropolitan, a constitution had been adopted, and in that year a general synod had convened. Selwyn wished to restrict the church to those in full communion, but some of the laity insisted that it should embrace as many as possible, even though their Christian faith was purely nominal. The latter view won. Resistance came from Christchurch to the authority of the general synod. A war between whites and Maoris from 1861 to 1871, waged chiefly in the North Island and because of the Maoris' resentment against what they deemed the encroachments of the whites on their lands and marked by strong reaction against Christianity as the white man's religion, set back the Church of England. However, recovery was achieved and advances were made.[5]

Presbyterians had begun coming to New Zealand before the first shiploads landed at Otago. They continued to arrive and eventually constituted about a fourth of the population, or more than twice the proportion that was theirs in Australia. Ministers were from the Church of Scotland, the Free Church of Scotland, the Irish Presbyterian Church, and the English Presbyterian Church. Within a few years, in spite of efforts to bring about an inclusive union, two Presbyterian churches arose, one in the North Island and the northern provinces of the South Island, and one in Otago and the southern part of the South Island. Not until 1901 was a comprehensive union achieved.[6]

The fourth largest denomination and the third largest Protestant body in New Zealand was Methodism. Yet proportionately it was not as strong as in Canada and Australia. Since Methodists early began missions among the Maoris it was natural that they should pay attention to colonists when they arrived and should be especially strong in Auckland, in the North Island where most of the Maoris had their home. They sprang up elsewhere, including Anglican Christchurch and Presbyterian Dunedin. Various branches of British Methodism were represented. While a New Zealand Methodist Conference was held in 1874, a country-wide union did not come into being until 1913.[7]

The first Baptist church in New Zealand was organized at Nelson in 1851. In 1881, as other churches appeared, the Baptist Union of New Zealand was

[5] Purchas, *op. cit.*, pp. 150 ff.; Jacobs, *New Zealand*, pp. 165–167, 186, 187, 224, 243; William Garden Cowle, *Our Last Year in New Zealand, 1887* (London, Kegan Paul, Trench & Co., 1888, pp. 403), *passim;* G. H. Curteis, *Bishop Selwyn of New Zealand and of Litchfield. A Sketch of His Life and Work* (London, Kegan Paul, Trench & Co., 1889, pp. xiv, 498), pp. 94–192; Neill, *Anglicanism*, pp. 288–292.

[6] Elder, *op. cit.*, pp. 158 ff.; Dickson, *History of the Presbyterian Church in New Zealand*, p. 277; Ross, *op. cit.*, p. 387; W. J. Comrie, *The Presbytery of Auckland: Early Days and Progress* (Dunedin, A. H. and A. W. Reed, 1939, pp. 261), *passim.*

[7] Colwell, *A Century in the Pacific*, pp. 381–407.

formed. In 1912 Baptists numbered 5,494.[8] Congregationalists, Churches of Christ, Quakers, and Seventh Day Adventists were present but were much smaller minorities.

The Roman Catholic Church was the second largest denomination and as in Australia among the white population was overwhelmingly Irish. Pompallier, the first vicar apostolic, arrived in 1836 with assignment primarily to the Maoris. Although trouble developed between him and his congregation, the Marists, over the issue of his authority as bishop, in 1842 he was appointed the first Vicar Apostolic of New Zealand. Six years later two dioceses, Auckland and Wellington, were created. In 1869 Dunedin was made the seat of a bishop. In 1885 a hierarchy was set up for New Zealand with Wellington as the metropolitan see. In 1906 the Roman Catholic population was said to be 126,995 and was served by an archbishop and three suffragans. In 1910 two ecclesiastical seminaries were conducted, one by the Marists and one provincial. The vitality of New Zealand Roman Catholicism was seen, among other ways, in the emergence, in 1884, of the Sisters of Our Lady of Compassion. The Society of St. Vincent de Paul was active, and in nearly every parish young men's clubs were to be found, bound together in the Federated Catholic Clubs of New Zealand.[9]

As in country after country in the nineteenth century, the question of the control of education became acute. For the first few years of the colony, the legislatures of the provinces into which New Zealand was divided subsidized denominational schools. However, when in 1875–1876 these legislatures gave way to a central government, that aid was terminated (1877) and a national system of free, compulsory, and secular elementary education was planned. In 1875 the northern Presbyterian General Assembly declared itself in favour of a national interdenominational system of education, but it condemned in the plan of 1877 the omission of the Lord's Prayer and Scripture reading at the opening of a school session—an omission due to Roman Catholic, Jewish, and secular opposition. Presbyterians continued to press for the inclusion of religious worship and instruction in the public schools. They also founded several colleges where worship and religious instruction constituted part of the programme. Since school buildings could be used for religious instruction after school hours, some denominations availed themselves of that privilege. The Anglicans had a few parochial and secondary schools. Sunday Schools were widely employed by Protestants for the religious education of their children. The Roman Catholics persisted in asking for state aid for their schools and in its absence built up a system of parochial schools which were supervised by the government and which in 1910 enrolled about thirteen thousand pupils.[10]

The New Zealand Christians were concerned in spreading the faith outside

[8] John Laird in *The Chronicle*, Vol. I, pp. 115–121, 124.
[9] *The Catholic Encyclopedia*, Vol. XI, pp. 40–43.
[10] *Ibid.*, p. 42; Elder, *op. cit.*, pp. 358 ff.; Purchas, *op. cit.*, pp. 217, 218, 239, 240.

their country. Through the Melanesian Mission, begun in 1849, the Anglicans coöperated with their fellow churchmen of England and Australia in missions in the Solomon, Santa Cruz, and Northern New Hebrides Islands. Through the New Zealand Church Missionary Society, organized in 1892, they shared with the mother society in Japan, China, India, and Africa. In 1866 the Presbyterians sent a missionary to the New Hebrides. The Foreign Missions Committee of the Presbyterian Church of New Zealand, dating from 1869 and with several auxiliary bodies, supported missionaries in China, India, the New Hebrides, and among the Chinese in New Zealand. Until 1913 the Methodist Church of New Zealand was a part of the General Conference of Australasia and participated in the missions of that body. Beginning in that year it became independent and took over full responsibility for an enterprise in the Solomon Islands. In 1885 the Baptists formed a society which concerned itself with India. The Congregationalists organized auxiliaries of the London Missionary Society. The Churches of Christ began a mission in Southern Rhodesia in 1906. By the year 1914 branches of the China Inland Mission and the Sudan Interior Mission had been formed in New Zealand.[11]

Coöperation among New Zealand Protestants progressed rapidly after 1914 and had its beginnings chiefly among youth and well before that year. Christian Endeavour was introduced in the 1890's. In 1896 John R. Mott brought about the organization of the Student Christian Movement as a branch of the World's Student Christian Federation. Bible classes sprang up for youth in various churches and in 1902 the Presbyterians initiated the Bible Class Union. Young Men's Bible Camps were held, some of them by Methodists, some by Baptists, and in 1907 they and the Presbyterians had conventions in Christchurch which found inspiration in a joint Good Friday service. When, in 1921, the Council of Religious Education was formed in which six denominations joined, followed in 1941 by the National Council of Churches, the Bible Class movement was regarded as having prepared the way for them.[12]

In New Zealand, the creation of nineteenth-century British colonization, the Christianity of the white majority was clearly a child of the Christianity of the British Isles of that period. All the major and some of the numerically minor denominations characteristic of those islands gained firm rootage—although not in the precise proportions as in the mother country. No new ones of substantial size appeared. Union on a national scale was achieved by each of the larger denominations. Some of the unions embraced divisions which had not yet fully come together in the British Isles and thus reflected the effect of the pioneer

[11] Beach and Fahs, *World Missionary Atlas*, pp. 33, 34; Alan A. Brash, *How Did the Church Get There?* (Christchurch, Presbyterian Book Room, preface 1948, pp. 72), *passim*.

[12] E. P. Blamires, *Youth Movement. The Story of the Rise and Development of the Christian Youth Movement in the Churches of New Zealand—as Seen by a Methodist* (Auckland, Forward Books, 1952, pp. 116), pp. 1–20; Rouse and Neill, *A History of the Ecumenical Movement 1517–1948*, p. 626.

environment. Most of the Maoris became professedly Christian, but only after a decade or more of agonizing strife. Although neither the white nor the Maori churches produced all their clergy but even in 1914 continued to draw some from the British Isles, increasingly clergy were emerging from the New Zealanders. The churches were also having a mounting share in the world-wide spread of the faith. How far if at all the advanced social legislation which characterized New Zealand could be attributed to Christianity would be difficult if not impossible to determine. Presumably it came at least in part from the humanitarianism that was deeply even though not obviously indebted to Christianity and which we have met in Europe, the United States, and Canada. Except for a period among the Maoris no strongly anti-Christian sentiment developed. Public education became secular, but as in the United States, Canada, and Australia that was more because of the inability of the churches to agree on the kind of religious instruction to be given than from antagonism to the faith. Here was clearly a vigorous Christianity.

CHAPTER XV

Introductory to the World Outside "Christendom"

THUS far we have given our chief attention to what was long called "Christendom." We have devoted most of our pages to what might be described as "Western Christendom." That has included Western Europe and has been made to embrace as well the regions in which, through immigration, peoples of Western European blood became the overwhelming majority. As we have again and again reminded ourselves, the multiform revolution which mounted in the nineteenth and twentieth centuries and which forms the context of our story had its rise in "Western Christendom" and from there had most of its initial spread. We have summarized the record in Eastern Europe, namely, Russia, the Balkans, and Greece, because Christians were in the large majority there. We have noted the fashion in which the revolutionary forces from "Western Christendom" impinged on Eastern Europe, on the indigenous peoples of the Americas, Australia, and New Zealand, and upon those of African descent whose progenitors Europeans imported to the Western Hemisphere. In much of Latin America mixtures of Indian and European blood were a majority, and in some places in the Americas African and European blood had mingled. But on the whole, Western Europeans and their descendants constituted the overwhelming proportion of the population in the Americas, Australia, and New Zealand.

We have repeatedly noted the striking contrast in the nineteenth-century course of Christianity in "Christendom." We have seen that at the outset of the century the prospect for the faith seemed grim. The revolution which had its rise in "Western Christendom" had begun and through it Christianity had been dealt such severe blows and the churches which were its vehicles had displayed so much lassititude and had so compromised themselves with the existing order that some observers predicted its early demise. As the century progressed the revolution increased, both in potency and in the variety of its expressions. The West appeared to be threatened with complete secularization, and the designation "Christendom," which in view of the actual character of Europe never had been fully descriptive of the real situation, seemed to be less and less justified.

On the other hand, the nineteenth century witnessed an amazing quickening of Christianity. It was marked in all the major branches, most notably in Protestantism, but also strikingly in the Roman Catholic Church and to a less extent in the Eastern Churches. The quickening was least noticeable in Latin America. Indeed, at the close of the century Christianity was weaker in that vast region than it had been at the outset: it displayed less inward resilience to the impact of the revolutionary forces than anywhere else in "Christendom." In Europe, the United States, British North America, Australia, and New Zealand the churches were much stronger in 1914 than at any time in the preceding hundred years.

When the explosion of the summer of 1914 set off the stage of the revolution which became more intense and widespread in the succeeding decades, Christianity was in a better position to meet it than it was to deal with the stage which came upon it in the closing years of the eighteenth century.

Here was a vivid example of what had characterized Christianity from its beginning. As the Christian historian views it, the incarnation, God's supreme gift to man, provoked man to his greatest crime, the crucifixion of the Son of God. Beginning with that first Good Friday what issued from the Gospel, perverted by man, threatened to nullify the Gospel. Examples, by no means exhaustive, were many of the forms of Gnosticism of the second and third centuries; the capture of the Church by *Romanitas* and the kind of prestige which came with the adoption of the Church by the Roman Empire and which was entirely contrary to the genius of the Gospel; the seizure by ambitious and self-seeking men of power in the Church and even in some of the institutions, such as the monasteries, which at their inception sought to embody afresh the ideals set forth in the Gospel; the corruption of the structure devised by the great medieval reformers in their effort to bring into being a Christian society; the use of the science which in part was the fruit of the Christian faith to challenge the faith; the employment of the machines which arose from that science to exploit the underprivileged; and the emergence in "Christendom" of political and social philosophies, notably Marxist Communism, which endeavoured to supplant Christianity. Yet always men and movements were seen which bore out the assertion that in the crucifixion and what followed "the prince of this world" was being "cast out," and that the "light shines in the darkness and the darkness has not overcome it."

Much of this again becomes vivid as we move into what constituted the home of the majority of mankind, the portion of the world outside "Christendom." When the nineteenth century dawned, for more than seven hundred years "Western Christendom" had been increasingly impinging on the rest of mankind and with the same contrasts which we have remarked in its inner history.

Earlier the features contrary to the Gospel had predominated. The Crusades, waged in the name of the cross, left a legacy of hate which into the twentieth century embittered relations between Moslems and Christians and between Western and Orthodox Christians. The thirteenth- and fourteenth-century enterprises of Western Europeans in Asia were commercial and missionary and were too slight and ephemeral to produce extensive or lasting results. But the stage of the expansion of "Christendom" which began in the fifteenth century was far more extensive than its predecessors. It was accompanied by the ruthless exploitation of non-European peoples, especially in the subjugation of the Indians of the Americas and the beginnings of the vast importation to the Americas of enslaved Africans. Yet it was also marked by a more vigorous and more nearly effective protest of the Christian conscience against that exploitation than had been seen in earlier centuries and by the formal conversion of millions with constructive efforts at making the coming of Europeans a blessing rather than a curse. In some areas, notably China, missionary penetration was more extensive geographically than were commercial and political contacts. Although in the expansion of "Christendom" of the fifteenth, sixteenth, seventeenth, and eighteenth centuries Protestantism and the Russian Orthodox Church participated, the major share was that of the Roman Catholic Church, chiefly through Spain and Portugal.

In the nineteenth century the expansion of "Christendom" and especially of Western Europe attained unprecedented proportions and through it the revolution issuing from "Western Christendom" began to have the global impact which was to be greatly augmented in the twentieth century. In it, what from the Christian standpoint were the contrasts in the effects were striking, but with the ameliorating and constructive features arising from Christianity more marked than in any of the previous stages of the expansion of "Christian" peoples.

To the nineteenth-century phase of the impact of "Christendom" upon the non-European majority of mankind we are to give most of the remainder of this volume. In view of the importance of that majority and of the later consequences of the impact we may seem to be dismissing this portion of our story with the minimal attention which smacks of the traditional self-centredness and attitude of superiority of the "white man." The choice of a relatively brief summary is for three reasons. (1) The author has already given to the subject the major part of the three volumes of his seven-volume *A History of the Expansion of Christianity* which have the sub-title *The Great Century*. To repeat them here would be a duplication which would be both unnecessary and, to both author and reader, fatiguing. (2) The story which we have thus far attempted is of primary importance to an understanding of the impact of the revolutionary age upon mankind as a whole. The nearly three volumes which we have assigned to the nineteenth-century stage of the revolution among the peoples from which it sprang are barely sufficient to portray the complexity of the contributions and response of Christianity if we are to appraise with any approach to adequacy the share of Christianity in the global development of the revolution. (3) Even more important: down to 1914 the revolution had only begun to be felt by that majority of mankind which was outside of "Christendom," and in most countries the churches which sprang up were almost infinitesimal minorities that were still dependent on the churches of "Christendom" for leadership, financial support, and vitality. Although the effects of Christianity were not limited to what were later called "younger" churches and were much more extensive than the numerical strength of these churches would indicate, as yet in most of the larger centres of population they were only beginning to modify the impact of "Christendom" and the revolution.

As we embark on our pilgrimage through the world outside "Christendom" we do well to remind ourselves of generalizations which apply to the whole. (1) Never before in the history of the human race had peoples of one portion of the globe penetrated to all the rest of the planet or dominated so large a proportion of mankind. That penetration was more widely economic than political or cultural. But by the end of the century most of the land surface of the globe was politically controlled by "Christian" peoples, and cultural change was proceeding at varying paces. (2) The leading motive in the expansion was economic. Possessing the mechanical appliances which were one of the aspects of the revolution, equipped with the facilities which these devices provided for more extensive transportation and communication than mankind had ever before known, and desiring raw materials and markets for the factories emerging from the Industrial Revolution and food for their rapidly growing populations, European and especially Western European peoples were ransacking the planet. (3) A closely associated motive was political. To ensure access to raw materials and markets and opportunity for the investment of the capital which was mounting as a feature of the revolution, "Christian" nations were bringing under their administration more and more territory. (4) Another motive was national prestige, accentuated by the nationalism which was another aspect of the revolution. (5) Among every people upon whom European peoples impinged, cultural changes began which were an extension of the revolution that had its inception within "Western Christendom." In the nineteenth century the cultures of some peoples, usually "primitive," suffered drastic disintegration. That was true in the Americas and many of the islands of the Pacific. In Africa and Asia by 1914 the disintegration had only barely begun. At the time it seemed spectacular, but after 1914 it was accelerated, and except in a few corners not readily touched by the currents of the day, by the mid-twentieth century every aspect of life was being profoundly altered. Never before had all the human race experienced such rapid cultural change or been beset by so many common problems. The planet was fast becoming a neighbourhood, but an extraordinarily quarrelsome neighbourhood which had the possibility of using the fruits of the revolution to destroy itself.

Under these circumstances, what role did the nominal faith of "Christendom" play? To an undetermined but significant extent it shared in the responsibility for various aspects of the revolution. But how far if at all did it modify the effects of that revolution outside "Christendom"?

1. Missionaries bore witness to the Christian faith more widely than it or any other religion had ever been proclaimed. Even though the resulting Christian communities were small and millions had yet not even heard so much as the name of Christ, at no earlier time had any religion been planted among so many tribes and nations.

2. Proportionately, in the nineteenth century the spread of the Christian faith was greater by Protestants than by either Roman Catholics or the Eastern Churches. Roman Catholics had led in the preceding centuries. With the revival in their church, they continued to have a large share and in 1914 in some sections of Asia and Africa their communities outnumbered Protestants. But, having had few missions to non-Christians before 1815, in the nineteenth century Protestantism relatively had a much larger growth outside "Christendom." From being a North-western European phenomenon, it became world-wide.

3. Less than in any earlier period since the first three centuries was the propagation of the faith the objective, either avowed or unavowed, of the policies of "Christian" governments and peoples. To be sure, David Livingstone, the leading European explorer of Africa and in his later years with a British consular commission, had as his controlling motive the opening of gateways for the Gospel; from time to time Western governments made attacks on missionaries an occasion for armed invasion, notably in China; missionaries obtained in treaties between China and Western powers the guarantee of permission to propagate their faith; and Western diplomatic authorities sought to curb the persecution of Christians in areas as distant from each other as the Ottoman Empire and Japan. Yet at no time was conversion as prominent in the programmes of Western imperialism as it was in the Portuguese and especially the Spanish conquests and colonial administration from the fifteenth into the eighteenth century. In the nineteenth century the French Government, even when in the hands of anti-clericals, made the protection of French missionaries the occasion for imperialistic ventures. Similarly the German Government found in attacks on German missionaries the excuse for demands on non-Western governments. But neither the French nor the German Government had as its object the spread of the faith. The chief empire-builder of the nineteenth century, Great Britain, never made the extension of its official faith an object of its annexations. In its possessions it accorded protection to missionaries, whether British or non-British, but simply as part of its policy of maintaining law and order. It subsidized schools maintained by missionaries, but because they were

schools and not because they were Christian. The passing of the propagation of the faith as a motive for imperialism was part of the trend towards the separation of Church and state which was a feature of nineteenth-century "Christendom." The separation arose from the increasing contrast in the former "Christendom" between Christians and their neighbours who were departing more or less openly from the traditional faith. It was evidence of the "secularization of the West" and it sprang from the awakenings in the churches.

4. Christian missionaries brought with them various aspects of Western civilization. Both Protestant and Roman Catholic missionaries were pioneers in creating schools which introduced Western forms of education. In vast areas these schools were long the only channels of the kind of education which was imperative if non-European peoples were to make a successful adjustment to the revolution issuing from "Christendom." Missionaries gave to hundreds of languages their first written form. Here, too, was assistance in meeting the revolutionary age. Protestants led in bringing Western medicine and surgery to China and much of Africa and shared in its introduction to a number of other countries. Both Roman Catholic and Protestant missionaries, and particularly the former, founded and maintained orphanages and other charitable institutions. Among many peoples missionaries led in according to women the status which was becoming theirs in nineteenth-century "Christendom."

5. The Christian conscience reduced the exploitation which accompanied the impact of "Christendom" on the world outside "Christendom." The abolition of Negro slavery was a striking example. In the British Empire and the United States it was a fruit of the Evangelical wing of Anglo-Saxon Protestantism. In Latin America it came chiefly through a humanitarianism which was less directly but still clearly of Christian rootage. As the awakenings in Protestantism mounted, they sensitized consciences and brought greater consideration by the rulers to the welfare of subject peoples in both the British and the Dutch colonial empires.

6. The influence of Christianity was beginning to be seen in non-Western persons and movements outside the churches and through them was entering into the cultural changes which were a phase of the revolution brought by the impact of "Christendom." It was not dominant and was often difficult to detect or, if recognized, to appraise. But it was mounting. Such were the Brahmo Samaj in India, the formation of the ideals and methods of Gandhi, after 1914 to be of major importance in India, and the contribution to the education and the dreams of Sun Yat-sen which on the eve of 1914 were entering into the revolution in China that overthrew the Confucian empire and began the hazardous experiment with a republic.

From these generalizations we turn to a region-by-region and at times a country-by-country pilgrimage through the world outside "Christendom."

CHAPTER XVI

Western Asia and North Africa

I N OUR survey of the world outside "Christendom" we naturally turn first to
Western Asia and North Africa, partly because of geographic propinquity
but also because much of the area once constituted a part of "Christendom" and
was torn away by the Moslem conquests which began with the Arab advance
in the seventh century and culminated in the invasions by the Ottoman Turks
in the fourteenth and fifteenth centuries. Here in the nineteenth century were
the dwindling but still resistant remnants of most of the oldest churches,
churches which in the first centuries of the Christian era enrolled the majority
of the Christians. With the exception of Rome they still perpetuated in name
all the original patriarchates. By the beginning of the nineteenth century they
had vanished in North Africa west of Egypt: in that vast region Christianity
was represented only by captives of the corsairs who preyed on the Mediterranean commerce of Europe. In Egypt, Ethiopia, and Western Asia the ancient
churches seemed to be ossified. They could make no converts from the dominant Islam, for Moslem law and practice visited death upon apostasy from that
faith. In their attempt to conserve their faith against the encircling Islam they
opposed any attempt at departure from their inherited structures and customs.
Their adherents constituted communities which were as much social and political as religious. Indeed, their Turkish masters treated them as "nations" and
governed them through their clergy. In their efforts to preserve what had come
to them from the past, the churches held to their ancient liturgies, which,
though often beautiful and expressions of deep religious feeling, were in the
languages of earlier days and unintelligible to the average worshipper. The
monastic life persisted but was usually stereotyped and remote from the currents
of the changing day. The bishops and the patriarchs were from the monks. The
parish clergy were generally married.

In the nineteenth century the chief effects of the revolutionary age were essays at reform, usually stimulated by contact with Roman Catholic or Protestant
missions, and the loss of members to one or the other of these branches of Christianity. Russian ambitions also played a part.

The effects upon the churches were only one aspect of the impact of the revolutionary age on North Africa and Western Asia. Politically major European

powers were seeking to extend their control in that area, or at least to keep their rivals from doing so. Chief among them were France, which under Napoleon invaded Egypt and later annexed Algeria and established protectorates over Tunisia and part of Morocco; Great Britain, which in 1878 took over the administration of Cyprus, annexing the island in 1914, and in the 1880's occupied Egypt with the purpose of bringing order in the country; Russia, moving into the Balkans and south of the Caucasus; Italy, adventuring mainly in Abyssinia; and Spain, with a sphere in Morocco. In contrast with the Crusades, these movements were purely secular, although at times seeking to use the churches as tools. Similarly the rising secularism in Europe found expression in the "Young Turks," who, many of them educated in Western Europe, through their Committee on Union and Progress seized power in Turkey in 1909 and began the transformation of their country into a secular state. The mechanical devices of the revolutionary age appeared—steamships, railways, the telegraph, and the Suez Canal, dug in the 1850's and 1860's largely by European capital and machinery. A beginning was made towards exploiting the vast petroleum resources of the region.

The full impact of the revolutionary age did not come until after 1914. It was only foreshadowed in the nineteenth century. During the greater part of the nineteenth century the power of the Ottoman Turks, once dominant in most of Western Asia and North Africa, was waning and section after section was breaking away. Yet until World War I the Turks were the legal rulers of much of the territory with which we are here concerned.

It was in the midst of these secularizing phases of the incursion of Europe that the reviving currents in Christianity made themselves felt. We will first say something of the course of the several ancient churches and then summarize the impact upon the region of the missions issuing from the churches of Europe and the United States.

THE OLDER EASTERN CHURCHES

Of the older Eastern Churches the one with originally the widest spread was that which is usually termed Orthodox. By the nineteenth century its main numerical strength was in Europe. Traditionally the Patriarchate of Constantinople was known as the Great Church and had a degree of priority over the other patriarchates. Its headquarters were in the Phanar district of Constantinople. In the course of the nineteenth century its administrative authority was progressively limited by the emergence of autocephalous churches in Greece and the Balkans but at the end of the century it still exercised a degree of control over the Orthodox, mostly Greeks, in Constantinople and Asia Minor. As the civil head in the Turkish Empire of what was called the "Roman nation," namely, the Orthodox, the Patriarch of Constantinople, often described as Ecumenical, had a kind of authority over the other patriarchs in that realm, namely, of Alexandria, Antioch, and Jerusalem, and over the bishops of Cyprus.[1]

The Orthodox Patriarchate of Alexandria claimed, as did its Coptic rival, to trace its succession from Mark. It had only a few thousand adherents, mostly Greeks and Syrians. Its incumbent was long appointed by the Patriarch of Constantinople and resided in Cairo. During the first half of the century Egypt, although still technically part of the Turkish Empire, was actually ruled by Mohammed Ali. He insisted that the patriarch live in Alexandria and in 1846 chose the holder of the title. Later in the century the Ecumenical Patriarchate successfully reasserted its authority. But in 1899 against the opposition of Constantinople Photios was translated to Alexandria from the Jerusalem Patriarchate and the Metropolitanate of Nazareth. This was said to be at the request of the Alexandrian clergy and people and also at the instance of Russia. Photios was a determined opponent of the Russian effort to use the Orthodox in the Levant as a tool and Moscow contrived his removal to Egypt where at that time it had no ambitions. In Egypt Photios met opposition from the Arabs, for they wished a patriarch of their own race, but his flock was augmented by the immigration of Greeks and Syrians. Before his death (1925) he had established a synod and had begun schools, hospitals, and other charitable enterprises.[2]

The ancient and at one time highly influential Patriarchate of Antioch was for centuries a bone of contention between the Orthodox and the Roman Catholics. Some of the incumbents were in communion with Rome and others sided with the Greeks. From the fore part of the eighteenth century two lines of patriarchs existed, one loyal to Rome and the other Orthodox. For many years the Orthodox patriarchs were Greeks, named by the Phanar. Since most of them could not speak Arabic and the large majority of their flock were Arabic-using, nationalistic restlessness developed against their rule. In 1898 when a Greek retired from the post, the bishops named a Syrian, Meletios. At first the Phanar would not recognize him and, supported by the French, delayed his confirmation by the Turkish sultan. The Russian Palestine Society supported him and the sultan yielded, giving him what was known as his *barat* (1900). The Phanar and the Patriarchs of Alexandria and Jerusalem refused to recognize him, but the Russian and the Rumanian churches stood by him. He succeeded in getting rid of three Greeks who were among his bishops. On the death of Meletios (1906) another Syrian succeeded him but was also deemed schismatic by the Greeks. With the decline of Antioch, since the fourteenth century the seat of the patriarch had been in Damascus. In the fore part of the twentieth century the faithful subject to him numbered about a quarter of a million. For the most part the lower clergy were poorly trained and many in the rural sections supported themselves and their families by other occupations. In 1904 a seminary

[1] Fortescue, *The Orthodox Eastern Church*, pp. 283, 284.
[2] *Ibid.*, pp. 285, 286; Attwater, *The Christian Churches of the East*, Vol. II, pp. 30, 31.

for their preparation was opened, but it was closed in 1912.[3]

The Orthodox Patriarchate of Jerusalem was officially recognized as such by the Council of Chalcedon in 451. In the nineteenth century, although most of its few thousand faithful were Syrian Arabs, all its occupants were Greeks. So, too, were the large majority of the Brotherhood of the Holy Sepulchre. That body, made up of a few score monks, who since at least the sixteenth century had looked after the holy places, was highly influential in the church. From its number were drawn the members of the synod which in theory governed the church. The latter part of the nineteenth century was punctuated by struggles between the partisans of Russia and the Phanar. Much of the financial support came from Russia and Russian pilgrims. Since Russia supported the Bulgars in their struggle for independence from the Phanar,[4] in 1872 Cyril II, the Patriarch of Jerusalem, refused to join with the other patriarchs in condemning them for their alleged heresy of philetism. His synod declared him deposed and chose a successor. In the ensuing struggle the Phanar and the Turkish and Russian governments were involved. The Russians forced the rival of Cyril to resign. On Cyril's death a patriarch was elected who sided with the Phanar against the Bulgars. On his demise (1882) Photios, always an enemy of Russia, was elected and after nearly two decades of complicated controversy, in 1899, as we have seen, became Patriarch of Alexandria. Not far from that time a Greek candidate was elected to the Jerusalem see. In 1908 the Arabs, who constituted the large majority of the faithful, moved by the mounting tides of nationalism, demanded that the church be administered by a mixed council in which they would be represented. After further controversy in which the patriarch favoured the Arabs, their request was granted (1911). Most of the parochial clergy were Palestinian Arabs and generally were ignorant.[5]

Since the fifth century, except for nearly four centuries (1191–1571) when the island was under the rule of Western Europeans and attempts were made, often by crude force, to compel subordination to Rome, the Orthodox in Cyprus were ecclesiastically independent of control by any of the patriarchates. After the Turkish conquest (1571) the Greek Cypriotes were included in the "Roman nation" and as such were under the civil authority of the Ecumenical Patriarch. But ecclesiastically they were autocephalous with their archbishop as the head of the hierarchy. During the Greek war of independence the Turks killed the archbishop, all three bishops, and many of the clergy and lay people for siding with Greece. The British occupation (1878) brought a degree of peace and the hierarchy was renewed through the consecration of four Cypriotes by bishops sent by the Patriarch of Antioch at the instance of the Ecumenical Patriarch. In 1900 controversy arose over the choice of an archbishop between two candidates,

[3] Fortescue, *op. cit.*, pp. 286–288; Attwater, *op. cit.*, Vol. II, pp. 34–39.

[4] Volume II, Chapter XXXIV.

[5] Fortescue, *op. cit.*, pp. 288–290; Attwater, *op. cit.*, Vol. II, pp. 40–48.

one favouring the British and the other standing for political union with Greece. After some years the latter was appointed. Monastic life was low and the parish clergy were of inferior quality.[6]

St. Catherine of Sinai, in the nineteenth century one of the oldest monasteries in the world, followed the rule of Anthony rather than Basil and at one time had been very rich. Although its abbot as archbishop was consecrated by the Patriarch of Jerusalem, its autonomy was recognized by Constantinople in 1575 and by the several patriarchs in 1782. In the nineteenth century its supporting properties in various countries with their administering monks, its resident monks, and the few lay folk who lived around or near it had shrunk, but in theory it was still an autocephalous Orthodox church. The abbot lived in a branch, or metachion, in Cairo. In the second half of the century a dispute between the abbot and his monks led the former to appeal to the Ecumenical Patriarch. But the Patriarch of Jerusalem objected to this infringement of what he claimed as his jurisdiction and in the ensuing struggle the Ecumenical Patriarch resigned and the abbot was deposed.[7]

The Coptic Church of the nineteenth century was the attenuated survivor of the dominant church of Egypt of pre-Moslem times. Professing to have been founded by Mark, it had been the church of the majority and a symbol and tie of Egyptian nationalism against the Orthodox Greek rulers of the Byzantine Empire. It had suffered from the Arab conquest and the long Moslem Arab rule. From time to time it had been severely persecuted. The animosity of the Moslem majority had been heightened by the Crusades, especially the one led by Louis IX of France directed against Egypt. The French invasion under Napoleon (1798–1801), the rule of Mohammed Ali and his successors, and the British occupation (which began in 1882) brought developments, some favourable and others unfavourable to the Copts. At the close of the century, in spite of conversions to Islam and losses to other Christian churches, the Copts numbered about 600,000, approximately one in fifteen of the population. Most of them were very poor, but some were in comfortable circumstances and a few were wealthy merchants and landowners.

Cyril IV, patriarch from 1854 to 1861, partly because of contact with Protestant missionaries sought to work reforms. They were chiefly in the improvement of education, the encouragement of Bible reading, the production and distribution of literature, and opposition to what seemed to him superstitious veneration of holy pictures.

Cyril V, patriarch from 1874 or 1875 to 1927, was conservative. Although personally frugal and devoting the large revenues of his see to the relief of the poor and other traditional forms of philanthropy, he vigorously opposed the efforts

---

[6] Fortescue, *op. cit.*, pp. 290–292; Attwater, *op. cit.*, Vol. II, pp. 110–113.
[7] Fortescue, *op. cit.*, pp. 310–312; Attwater, *op. cit.*, Vol. II, pp. 115–118.

of some of the younger laity to further education and lay participation in the management of the affairs of the church. The struggle went on for a number of years. In 1892 the khedive supported the laity and had Cyril confined to a monastery. In protest, most of the bishops retired to their monasteries. An interdict deprived a large proportion of the faithful of the services of the church and many of them went to the Orthodox churches. So great was the outcry which followed that in a few months Cyril was released and resumed his functions.

The reformers wished better education for the parish clergy. The latter were drawn largely from humble families; many of them could not read the liturgical language or even Arabic but memorized the service and said it by rote. Some were ordained deacons in adolescence before the canonical age of twenty-five. As a result and because of the extreme poverty of the masses, a large proportion of the Copts were grossly ignorant of the faith. But although the service was in Coptic, which few understood, the reading of the Epistles and the Gospels, while first in Coptic, was later in Arabic, the language of the people, and so made the faith intelligible. Moreover, preaching was not uncommon. Much of it consisted of the reading of uninspiring homilies, but some, especially in later years, was vigorous and had a marked appeal. As a part of the service the lives of the saints were often read, also in Arabic. But even the more devout took the Communion only once a year. In 1897 the number of bishops was increased to eighteen, but this did not necessarily entail improvement in diocesan administration, for most of the episcopate lived with or near the patriarch and constituted his curia.[8]

Since many of the laity gave a better education to their children than was common among their Moslem neighbours, the Copts were more prominent in business and had a larger share in positions under the state than their numbers would have given reason to expect.

In the nineteenth century the Ethiopian (Abyssinian) Church had four or five times as many adherents as the Coptic Church. Some of its clergy rejected as inaccurate the designation of monophysite which was often given them by outsiders and declared that they held to the two natures in Christ, although not as defined at Chalcedon. The head of the Ethiopian Church, the Abuna, was a Coptic monk appointed and consecrated by the Coptic Patriarch. Next in rank was the Echage, who was always an Abyssinian and appointed by civil authority. He was the head of the monasteries of his order and acted as a check on the Abuna and the Coptic Church. Bishops were from Coptic monasteries in Egypt and were chosen and appointed by the Coptic Patriarch. Their powers were not as great as in some other churches. Church buildings abounded and

---

[8] Attwater, *op. cit.*, Vol. II, pp. 201–211; Strothmann, *Die Koptische Kirke in der Neuzeit, passim*; S. H. Leeder, *Modern Sons of the Pharaohs, A Study of the Manners and Customs of the Copts of Egypt* (London, Hodder and Stoughton, 1918, pp. xvi, 355), *passim*; Fortescue, *The Lesser Eastern Churches*, pp. 252–290.

were erected as acts of piety. The language of the church was Ge'ez, which had ceased to be that of the people and was understood only by the more educated among the clergy. Most of the priests had slight education but were supposed to devote all their time to their clerical duties and not to have a gainful occupation. Monasteries were numerous and monks were honoured. The majority of the monks were in one or the other of two orders, but all claimed to follow the rule of Anthony. Again and again through its history the Ethiopian Church had been troubled by theological controversy. During much of the nineteenth century the chief debate was between those who held that Christ had three births (of the Father, from all eternity; of the Virgin Mary, in time; and of the Holy Ghost) and those who maintained that He had two births (combining that of the Virgin with that of the Holy Ghost). Cut off as they were in mountain fastnesses and encircled by Islam, the Ethiopian Christians were not much affected by the currents abroad in the other churches. However, both Roman Catholic and Protestant missionaries sought to win converts from them, and ambitious European imperialism strove to extend its control over the country—the Italians by an invasion in the 1890's with, for them, disastrous consequences and the Russians soon after 1900 by the conversion of the Ethiopians to Orthodoxy, also unsuccessful.[9]

Another church usually regarded by foreigners as in the monophysite tradition, but also disliking that term and holding to the two natures in Christ but in a non-Chalcedonian sense, was often known as Jacobite from its early history. It preferred, however, to call itself Syrian or sometimes Syrian Orthodox. It entered the nineteenth century with numbers greatly reduced from the time of its prosperity on the eve of the Arab conquest. Many of its former members had become Moslems and across the centuries numbers of others had adhered to Rome. Early in the twentieth century the Syrians totalled only about 100,000, in Syria, Mesopotamia, Palestine, and Egypt. They were organized under a Patriarch of Antioch and diocesan bishops. Monasteries were decayed and the lower clergy for the most part had little education and were poverty-stricken.[10]

Like the Jacobites, in the nineteenth century the Nestorians were a small remnant of a church which had once been widely extended in Asia. Preferring to call themselves merely Christians or the Church of the East, or alternatively Syrians or the Assyrian Church, in 1914 they numbered between 70,000 and 150,000. Most of them were in the mountains north of Mesopotamia, in the North-west, in the vicinity of Lake Van and Mosul, and a minority were in Persia, mainly in the neighbourhood of Lake Urmia. The successive patriarchs, unmarried, were from one family, the office usually passing from uncle to

[9] Attwater, *op. cit.*, Vol. II, pp. 212–224; Harry Middleton Murray, *The Church of Abyssinia* (London, Luzac & Co., 1928, pp. 302), *passim*; Augustus B. Wylde, *Modern Abyssinia* (London, Methuen and Co., 1901, pp. 497), pp. 157 ff.; Fortescue, *The Lesser Eastern Churches*, pp. 307–322.

[10] Attwater, *op. cit.*, Vol. II, pp. 225–233.

nephew, and the bishops, also unmarried, were generally recruited from families which had long had a monopoly of the office. By the nineteenth century monasticism, once prominent, had all but disappeared. The ecclesiastical language was Syriac. The parish priests were married and the post usually descended from father to son.[11]

The Armenians were said to be the first nation to accept Christianity, late in the third and early in the fourth century as the result of the labours of Gregory the Illuminator. Because of him the Armenian Church was often known as Gregorian.

In spite of persecutions by their enemies, often accompanied by massacres, the Armenians held to the faith. As we shall see, many became Roman Catholics and in the nineteenth century a few thousand became Protestants. But in 1914 about 3,500,000 held to the church of their fathers. In its theology that church did not conform to Chalcedon, but, like the Copts, the Ethiopians, and the Syrians, who also officially held to one form or another of the anti-Chalcedonian position, the real bond was not creedal but national or racial. Although geographically centred in or near their ancient home in the mountains north of Mesopotamia, many Armenians were found in other parts of the world. Yet for most of them their church remained a tie which, like Judaism to the Jews, helped to keep them in distinct communities. Indeed, like the Jews, the Armenians were disliked or even hated by their neighbours because so many of them were clever in financial dealings.

At the beginning of the nineteenth century the structure of the Armenian Church was not unified. The ranking ecclesiastic was a patriarch, also known as the catholicos, with his headquarters in Echmiadzin. But in Constantinople was an Armenian patriarch to whom the Turkish Government had given the oversight of all the non-Orthodox—namely, the Armenians, Syrians, Copts, Chaldeans, Georgians, and Ethiopians. Two other patriarchal sees existed with jurisdiction in particular areas.

The nineteenth century brought mixed vicissitudes to the Armenian Church and its people. Thanks partly to the Armenians themselves and partly to Protestant missionaries from the United States, the educational level of both clergy and laity was raised. Here and there, owing to intellectual currents from the West, scepticism appeared which was directed against the church. In the Turkish realms, through a structure promulgated in 1860 and sanctioned by the Ottoman Government in 1863, the direction of Armenian affairs was entrusted to a national assembly of whom six-sevenths were laymen elected by vote. A council composed of laymen chosen by the assembly supervised the civil interests of the Armenians, and another council, also chosen by the assembly and made up of ecclesiastics, supervised religious matters. The Patriarchs of Con-

---

[11] *Ibid.*, pp. 187–197; Fortescue, *The Lesser Eastern Churches*, pp. 114–159; Aubrey R. Vine, *The Nestorian Churches* (London, Independent Press, 1937, pp. 227), pp. 170 ff.

stantinople and Jerusalem were chosen by the assembly.

The Armenians were caught in the ambitions and machinations of the European powers, chiefly Russia and Great Britain. The two sought to checkmate each other in the decadent Ottoman realms. The Russians advanced their frontiers southward. In 1828, following a war with Persia, they annexed a section which included Echmiadzin and the year after acquired from Turkey additional Armenian land to the westward. In 1878 in her war with Turkey Russia occupied another slice of Armenia. The Russian Government eventually exercised control over the Armenian Church. To reduce Armenian nationalism, the use of the Armenian language was forbidden in Armenian schools, and in 1903 the revenue-producing properties of the church were confiscated.

In the 1880's, with the approval of the Turkish sultan, the Kurds preyed on the Armenians. In 1894–1896 tens of thousands of Armenians were massacred by the Turks and many more were rendered homeless and impoverished. In 1896, of the sixty-five dioceses in the Turkish realms only seven had bishops and twenty temporary vicars, with thirty-eight entirely unshepherded. The massacres were provoked partly by the chronic dislike of the Armenians and partly by the revolutionary movements among them which sought to throw off the alien yoke. They were the precursors to even more tragic massacres and deportations during World War I.[12]

THE ROMAN CATHOLIC CHURCH EXPANDS ITS EFFORTS

The nineteenth century witnessed the substantial expansion of the Roman Catholic Church in Western Asia and North Africa. This was partly by immigration and partly by the increasing missions which were a fruit of the reviving and mounting life in that church.[13]

The Roman Catholic Church was not a new-comer in Western Asia and North Africa. In the early centuries the Bishop of Rome had been potent in the area. Then came the break of the Monophysites and Nestorians from the majority church of the Roman Empire, followed by the conquests of the Moslem Arabs and the drifting apart of the Western wing of that church, acknowledging the authority of the Pope, and the Eastern wing, with the Ecumenical Patriarch as the ranking ecclesiastic. The Crusades were accompanied and followed by efforts of the Roman Catholic Church to win its "separated brethren." Some of them succeeded. Thus the Maronites, a people chiefly in the

[12] Attwater, *op. cit.*, Vol. II, pp. 244 ff.; Fortescue, *The Lesser Eastern Churches*, pp. 391 ff.; Leon Arpee, *A History of Armenian Christianity* (New York, The Armenian Missionary Association, 1946, pp. xii, 386), pp. 293–299; Malachia Ormanian, *The Church of Armenia, Her History, Doctrine, Rule, Discipline, Liturgy, Literature, and Existing Condition,* translated from the French by G. Sarcar Gregory and edited by Terenig Poladian (London, A. R. Mowbray & Co., 2nd ed., 1955, pp. xxvi, 219), pp. 71–75, 116–118, 133–137, 176–178.

[13] For a general survey see Konrad Lübeck, *Die katholische Orientmission in ihrer Entwicklung dargestellt* (Cologne, J. P. Bachem, 1917, pp. 152), *passim.*

Lebanon, monothelete in belief, conformed to Rome in the twelfth century and from the early part of the sixteenth century were continuously in communion with the Pope. In the revival of missions which issued from the Catholic Reformation fresh efforts were made, spectacularly but not exclusively in Abyssinia in the sixteenth and seventeenth centuries.[14]

The expansion by immigration was chiefly in North Africa. The French conquest of Algeria was begun in 1830 and was not completed until late in the 1850's. A French protectorate over Tunisia was established in the 1880's. Between 1800 and 1914 France and Spain acquired zones in Morocco. Immigration followed, chiefly to Algeria, where the European population numbered about 750,000 in 1914 and was mainly from France but also from Italy, Spain, and Malta. Most of it was at least nominally Roman Catholic. In 1838 a bishop was appointed for Algiers. In the next twenty years, with financial assistance from the French Government and the Society for the Propagation of the Faith, a well-organized diocese was brought into being. In time other dioceses were created. The most famous ecclesiastic was Charles Martial Allemand Lavigerie (1825–1892), who was appointed archbishop in 1866. In 1882 he was created cardinal and in 1884 was given the title of Archbishop of Carthage and Primate of Africa. His authority extended over Algeria, Tunisia, and the Sahara.[15]

Although almost all his flock were Europeans, the redoubtable Lavigerie did not confine his vision or his plans to them. He sought to make his see one from which Christianity would be spread throughout Africa, among both Moslems and pagans. To this end he brought into being (1868) the *Société des Missionnaires de Notre Dame d'Afrique*. Its members were known, from their garb, an adaptation of the Arab dress, as the White Fathers. Through them and their associated sisters Lavigerie's dream astonishingly approached realization. They laboured not only in North Africa among Moslems but also in large areas south of the Sahara, chiefly for pagans.[16]

Roman Catholic missionaries through most of North Africa and Western Asia directed their efforts mainly to bringing non-Roman Catholic Christians to allegiance to Rome. They sought to reach Moslems as well as Christians, but they could not hope to have many converts among the followers of the Prophet: custom and Moslem law were all but insuperable obstacles.

Some of the non-Roman Catholic converts were incorporated into the Latin rite. In the latter part of the nineteenth century, however, as their number mounted, the emphasis was on encouraging the Uniate bodies. That was the Papal policy. The term "Uniate" was not quite a happy one. It seemed to have

[14] Attwater, *The Christian Churches of the East*, Vol. I, pp. 142 ff., 165 ff.; Latourette, *A History of the Expansion of Christianity*, Vol. III, pp. 79, 80.

[15] A. Pons, *La Nouvelle Église d'Afrique ou le Catholicisme en Algérie, en Tunisie et au Maroc depuis 1830* (Tunis, Librairie Louis Namura, no date, pp. xv, 343), *passim*.

[16] Kittler, *The White Fathers, passim;* S. Bouniol, editor, *The White Fathers and Their Mission* (London, Sands and Co., 1929, pp. 334), *passim*.

the inference that a distinction existed within the portion of the Church which recognized the Pope as its head between those of the Roman rite and those who did not hold to it, as though the latter, in contrast with the former, were not really Catholics. Rome held that all were Catholics and officially designated Uniates as Catholics of the Eastern Rites. In 1862 Pius IX erected the Congregation of the Propagation of the Faith for Eastern Rites (*S. Congregatio de Propaganda Fide pro Ritibus Orientalibus*) as a department of the Congregation for the Propagation of the Faith. In 1917 it became independent of the latter as the Sacred Congregation for the Eastern Church, later the Sacred Eastern Congregation.[17] Leo XIII was especially eager to honour the Eastern Churches in communion with Rome and vigorously supported their rites and customs against those who would bring them into conformity with the Roman rite. He also founded colleges for them.[18] The Uniates kept their ecclesiastical language, their liturgies, and many of their customs, so far as these did not clash with the authority of the Pope and the basic principles of the Church of Rome. The variety was cherished as evidence of the inclusive, Catholic character of the Roman Communion. Uniates (if we may continue to use that awkward designation) attracted only a minority from the Eastern Churches—about fifty-six out of a thousand in the first half of the twentieth century.[19]

The churches of the Eastern rites in Western Asia and Egypt in communion with Rome were the Melkites, the Uniate Copts, the Syrian Uniates, the Chaldeans, the Armenian Uniates, and the Maronites.

The Melkites were Uniates of the Byzantine rite who were found in Syria, Palestine, and Egypt. Although they spoke Arabic, they insisted that they were Greeks, descended from the Greeks of Hellas. They were under one whom Rome recognized as the Patriarch of Antioch. Early in the nineteenth century they were severely persecuted by the Orthodox. Their outstanding leader in the nineteenth century was Maximos III, who was patriarch from 1833 to 1855. Through his efforts the Turkish Government was persuaded (1846) to recognize the Melkites as a separate nation under the civil jurisdiction of himself and his successors. He also made his authority effective in Egypt and Palestine and erected churches in those countries. Yet his years in office were marked, as was characteristic of the Melkites, by many dissensions, both within his flock and with their neighbours. He and his successors assumed, some without authorization from Rome, the title of Patriarch of Antioch, Alexandria, Jerusalem, and all the East.[20]

The Uniate Copts were the result of missions, at first by the Franciscans, to whom were later added Jesuits and the African Missionaries of Lyons. They

[17] Attwater, *op. cit.*, Vol. I, pp. 21, 22; Fortescue, *The Uniate Eastern Churches*, p. 38.
[18] Fortescue, *The Uniate Eastern Churches*, pp. 39–42.
[19] Attwater, *op. cit.*, Vol. I, p. 23.
[20] Fortescue, *The Uniate Eastern Churches*, pp. 210–220; Strothmann, *op. cit.*, p. 75.

dated from the eighteenth century, but it was not until 1893 that they had churches for their sole use, turned over to them by the Brothers Minor, and it was only in 1899 that Rome advanced the first of their number to the rank of Patriarch of Alexandria and the Copts. That same year Leo XIII initiated a seminary in Egypt to educate priests for the Coptic rite. The Uniates were mainly from the poorest of the Copts and in 1894 numbered 5,000. But in 1946 they had increased to 63,000.[21]

The Syrian Uniates, from the Jacobites, had a broken history which dated from the Crusades, but chiefly from the sixteenth century. Michael Jarweh, accounted the first Patriarch of Antioch of their rite, died in 1801. Between 1820 and 1850 their numbers were increased by the submission of five Jacobite bishops to Rome.[22]

The Chaldeans were Uniates recruited from the Nestorians. They dated from the sixteenth century when a dispute over the succession in the office of patriarch (or catholicos) led to one of the claimants' submitting to Rome and being recognized by the Pope as patriarch of such of his rite as would follow him. From time to time the succession of Chaldean patriarchs lapsed, but in 1834 an appointment by Rome to that office was followed by an unbroken continuity. In the course of the nineteenth century the Chaldeans increased by accessions from the Nestorians. For example, soon after 1902 about twenty thousand followed two bishops in moving over to them.[23]

From the end of the twelfth century for nearly two hundred years, through contact with the Crusaders, a substantial proportion of the Armenians were in communion with Rome, and after that time individuals and groups maintained the connexion. By 1742 their number had so increased that Benedict XIV established a patriarchal see for them. In 1830 French influence obtained their recognition by the Turkish Government as a separate nation, or civil entity. Internal dissensions, seemingly chronic, troubled the Armenian Uniates. One of them was provoked by a Papal bull of 1867 which reduced the participation of laity in ecclesiastical affairs. But the Uniates continued and in the twentieth century produced Agagianian, patriarch and cardinal.[24]

The Maronites continued the connexion with Rome begun late in the twelfth century. Their head had the title of Patriarch of Antioch. In 1860 massacres by their neighbours, the Druzes, and by others eliminated several thousand Maronites and rendered even more thousands homeless.[25]

Roman Catholic missionaries of various orders and congregations conducted numerous schools. Some were only for Christians. Others also enrolled Moslems. Outstanding was the University of St. Joseph in Beirut, a Jesuit institu-

---

[21] Attwater, *op. cit.*, Vol. I, pp. 133–135.
[22] *Ibid.*, pp. 153–155.
[23] *Ibid.*, pp. 198–202; Strothmann, *op. cit.*, p. 74.
[24] Attwater, *op. cit.*, Vol. I, pp. 181–185.
[25] *Ibid.*, pp. 166–169.

tion.[26] With it was associated a seminary for the preparation of clergy, the largest of its kind of the Oriental rites.

The French Government sought to further its political interest in North Africa and Western Asia by championing the cause in that region of Roman Catholics and Roman Catholic missionaries.

PROTESTANT MISSIONS ENTER AND MULTIPLY

The nineteenth century witnessed the rapid growth of Protestant missions in North Africa and Western Asia.[27] They were a phase of the remarkable burst of Protestant missionary activity which was one of the fruits of the awakenings in Protestantism in that century. Protestant missions in Western Asia and Northern Africa were chiefly but not entirely from the British Isles and the United States and were mainly from constituencies which had been deeply affected by the Evangelical movements. In general Protestant missions were directed towards revitalizing the ancient churches in the hope that they would become more active in reaching the Moslems. With some exceptions, they did not seek to win converts to Protestantism but hoped that those whom they touched would remain within their ancestral communions, would re-invigorate them, and would make them missionary-minded. To this end they prepared and circulated translations of the Bible in the vernaculars, conducted schools, and sought friendly contacts with both clergy and laity. The result was that minorities were attracted to them, but the majority in the several Eastern Churches, conservative, rejected the innovators, and the latter were forced out or withdrew and formed congregations which were usually called Evangelical and were Protestant in character. The largest was that in Egypt gathered chiefly from the Copts by the United Presbyterians of North America. In 1895 it had 4,554 members.[28] In the next half-century it had a very substantial growth. Some Protestant missionary effort was directed towards the conversion of the Jews, numerous and widely scattered in that area. Much attention was given to schools, for both Christians and Moslems, and to hospitals.

The major British efforts were through the British and Foreign Bible Society and the Church Missionary Society. The former operated from Constantinople and in Tunis, Algeria, Syria, Palestine, Egypt, and Ethiopia.[29] The Church Mis-

[26] H. Charles, *Jésuites Missionnaires, Syrie proche Orient* (Paris, Gabriel Beauchesne, 1929, pp. 114), pp. 20 ff.

[27] For a general survey see Julius Richter, *Mission und Evangelisation im Orient* (Gütersloh, C. Bertelsmann, 2nd ed., 1930, pp. vi, 294), pp. 59 ff.; Latourette, *op. cit.,* Vol. VI, pp. 18 ff.

[28] Charles R. Watson, *Egypt and the Christian Crusade* (Philadelphia, Board of Foreign Missions of the United Presbyterian Church of North America, 1913, pp. xi, 288), *passim.*

[29] Canton, *A History of the British and Foreign Bible Society,* Vol. II, pp. 1 ff., Vol. III, pp. 212 ff., Vol. IV, pp. 404-438.

sionary Society was in Constantinople, Palestine, Egypt, the Sudan, Mesopotamia, and Persia.[30]

Of the societies from the United States, the American Board of Commissioners for Foreign Missions began what were the most extensive missions from that country. They had their inception during the years when the New School Presbyterians coöperated with the Congregationalists in that organization. They were originally in Asia Minor, Armenia, Constantinople, Persia, and Syria. When the New School and the Old School Presbyterians reunited, a friendly division of fields was effected (1870). The Presbyterians assumed responsibility for Persia and Syria, and the American Board, now an organ only of the Congregationalists, continued in Asia Minor, Armenia, and Constantinople, with chief attention to the Armenians.[31] Out of the efforts of the American Board came Evangelical congregations, the first in 1846. In 1847 and, by a new imperial charter, in 1850 the Protestants were accorded legal status as a civil community. Eventually antagonism between the old church and the Evangelicals declined. Evangelical pastors were often asked to preach in Gregorian churches and numbers of students preparing for the Gregorian ministry were in schools of the American Board.[32]

Many schools and several colleges were maintained by Protestant missions. Of them the most famous were Robert College, in Constantinople, which opened its doors in 1863 and in its early decades was frequented chiefly by Bulgarians and Armenians, the American College for Girls, which was begun in 1871 in Constantinople and in a few years was removed to the Asiatic side of the Bosporus, and the Syrian Protestant College, later (1920) called the American University of Beirut.[33]

Scores of physicians gave their lives under Protestant auspices in several parts of North Africa and Western Asia.[34]

Some Protestant missionaries, especially as the century wore on, believed that their function, rather than to make formal conversions, was to influence individuals who would remain in their respective faiths but with characters essentially Christian and through them to modify the surrounding collective life.[35]

---

[30] Stock, *The History of the Church Missionary Society*, Vol. I, pp. 221–235, Vol. II, pp. 140–155, Vol. III, pp. 113–125, 512–536, 751–754, Vol. IV, pp. 105–136.

[31] Rufus Anderson, *History of the Missions of the American Board of Commissioners for Foreign Missions to the Oriental Churches* (Boston, Congregational Publishing Society, 2 vols., 1892), *passim;* Peter Kawerau, *Amerika und die Orientalischen Kirchen. Ursprung und Anfang der Amerikanishem Mission unter Der Nationalkirchen Westasiens* (Berlin, Walter de Gruyter & Co., 1958, pp. xi, 772), *passim.*

[32] James L. Barton, *Daybreak in Turkey* (Boston, The Pilgrim Press, 2nd ed., 1908, pp. 306), pp. 168, 174, 175.

[33] Stephen Beasley Linnard Penrose, *That They Might Have Life. The Story of the American University of Beirut* (New York, The Trustees of the American University of Beirut, 1941, pp. xviii, 347), *passim.*

[34] For some of them see Latourette, *op. cit.,* Vol. VI, pp. 45, 52 (n. 300).

[35] As a striking example by a son of the founder of the Syrian Protestant College and himself a

An interesting incident in the Protestantism in Western Asia was the Anglo-Prussian bishopric in Jerusalem. The project arose at the suggestion of Frederick William IV of Prussia. He looked with kindly eye upon the Church of England and would have been glad to introduce some of its features, including its episcopate, in the Prussian church. He also dreamed of promoting, through the Jerusalem episcopate as a pioneer enterprise, union among Protestants. His agent in England was Bunsen. The incumbent was to be in the Anglican episcopal succession, was to be named alternately by England and Prussia, and was to ordain German clergy on their subscription to the Augsburg Confession and Anglicans on their adherence to the Thirty-nine Articles. In 1841 an act of Parliament cleared the way for the participation of the Church of England. The plan had the endorsement of the Archbishop of Canterbury and of the Bishop of Oxford, Wilberforce, but was vigorously opposed by the Tractarians. Three men in succession held the post, but in 1886 the Prussian Government withdrew and the Jerusalem bishopric continued as purely Anglican.[36]

THE RUSSIAN PHASE

Russian interest was primarily political, not religious. Thus through assistance to the Eastern Churches, not all of them Orthodox, the Russian rulers sought to further their long-standing ambition to profit by the increasing weakness of a chronic enemy, the Ottoman Empire. We have already seen the efforts in Ethiopia and Jerusalem and the consequences for the Gregorian (Armenian) Church. In 1882 the Imperial Orthodox Palestine Association was constituted. It collaborated with the Orthodox Missionary Society. In 1898 the Russians had 64 schools with 6,739 pupils in Syria and Palestine and in the ensuing six years the number of students doubled. Medical clinics and at least one hospital were opened. In the 1890's over twenty thousand Nestorians entered into the Russian Orthodox Church to obtain protection against the Kurds and the Persian Government. In Russia the Brotherhood of St. Cyril and St. Sergius was formed (1903) to assist the mission. The defeat of Russia by Japan in 1905 reduced enthusiasm for the Russian connexion.[37]

SUMMARY

In spite of a rising tide of missionary effort from Europe and the United States, chiefly Roman Catholic and Protestant and in lesser dimensions Russian Orthodox, except by immigration Christianity made little numerical gain in the nineteenth century in North Africa and Western Asia. The immigration

---

president of that institution, see Howard S. Bliss, "The Modern Missionary," in *The Atlantic Monthly*, May, 1920.

[36] Rouse and Neill, *A History of the Ecumenical Movement 1517–1948*, pp. 288–290; Latourette, *op. cit.*, Vol. VI, pp. 39, 40; Stock, *op. cit.*, Vol. III, pp. 276–278.

[37] Lübeck, *Die russischen Missionen*, pp. 24–45.

was substantial, mainly from France but also from Italy, Spain, and Malta, was chiefly to North Africa, especially Algeria, and was predominantly Roman Catholic. It resulted in the renewal of the Roman Catholic hierarchy in North Africa. If the ancient non-Roman Catholic churches of North Africa and Western Asia grew in that century it was by the excess of births over deaths, not by conversions. As a result of the labours of missionaries, minorities left these churches to become either Roman Catholics of the Latin or Uniate rites or Evangelicals (Protestants). Very few converts were made from the Moslem majority and not large numbers from the Jews. Missionary schools, literature, and medical service extended the influence of Christianity among some Moslems and members of the ancient churches. Yet on the whole the latter went on, resistant to change. The situation was complicated by the imperialistic ambitions of European powers, mainly Britain, France, and Russia. France and Russia especially sought to further their interests, the former by championing the Roman Catholics and the latter the Orthodox. Difficult of measurement yet clearly important was the influence of missionaries, especially Protestant missionaries, in stimulating Arab nationalism. The Arab nationalism which was to have striking expressions in the twentieth century had its inception in part in the stimulus given by the vernacular literature produced by the missionaries, in the men trained by them in the production of that literature, and among those educated in mission schools.

CHAPTER XVII

India

As we move eastward from Western Asia we come next to India. Like Western Europe a peninsular extension of the Eurasian continent, India was even more diverse in cultural complexion. It had a greater multiplicity of languages. Religiously it was also more diverse. Hinduism in one form or another was the faith of the majority, but Moslems constituted a substantial proportion of the population, animists were numerous, Sikhs were an important minority, Buddhists, although sadly dwindled from their earlier prominence, were still to be found, Jains continued, Parsees constituted small but wealthy enclaves, and Christians had for centuries been part of the scene. The caste structure, associated with Hinduism, was pervasive. Politically, India had never been fully united. From time to time one or another ruling house had brought a large part of the country under its sway, but none had succeeded in conquering the whole.

In the nineteenth century the revolution which issued from Western Christendom was beginning to be felt. Its impact mounted as the century proceeded, but the changes which followed were only preliminary to the more sweeping ones of the twentieth century.

The coming to India of the revolutionary age was intimately associated with British rule. That rule had begun under the East India Company. At the outset a purely commercial enterprise, to protect its trade the Company began to control territory. Then to safeguard its holdings against Indian and European rivals it felt itself constrained to embark on the conquest of the entire country. By about the middle of the nineteenth century the conquest had been practically completed. All but a few enclaves held by the Portuguese and French were acquired. In 1858 control was shifted from the East India Company to the British crown. The major part of the country was included in what was known as British India, governed directly. About a third of the area and a fifth of the population were embraced in the native states. Some of them had been allies of the British; others had resisted British arms but, defeated, had been permitted to continue. The largest were of the size of European kingdoms; others were only a few square miles in extent. The native states were under British supervision and their foreign affairs were completely in British hands. At British initiative and with British capital railways were constructed, telegraph lines spanned the country, and a comprehensive postal service was created. An educational system was established on the British model, and English became the medium of instruction. Indians went to Britain for their education. As a result, not only were mechanical appliances of the revolutionary age introduced, but the intelligentsia were increasingly familiar with the ideas of that age as transmitted to them through the medium of the English language and British education.

CHRISTIANITY AT THE OUTSET OF THE NINETEENTH CENTURY

At the outset of the nineteenth century Christianity was represented in India by the Syrian Christians, the Roman Catholic Church, and Protestantism. All were minorities, but in the ensuing hundred years the latter two—and especially Protestantism—were to have a marked growth. As we have repeatedly remarked, in the nineteenth century Protestantism displayed a greater proportionate numerical increase as well as more adjustment to the revolutionary age than did the other branches of the faith. In India the numerical growth was particularly striking.

Tradition had it that the Syrian Christianity dated from the Apostle Thomas. Commercial relations between India and the Mediterranean world in the first Christian centuries made possible churches in centres of that trade on the south coast, but we do not know that they existed. Christians were certainly in Northwest India as early as the fourth century, we hear of them in South India at least as far back as the sixth century, and inscriptions variously estimated as dating from the seventh to the tenth century attest to their presence in later days. Whether that presence had been continuous is not clear. In the thirteenth and fourteenth centuries travellers from Western Europe found Christians in the South.[1] In the sixteenth century Jesuits, supported by the Portuguese, brought them into communion with Rome. In the seventeenth century a substantial proportion of the Syrian Christians broke the Roman connexion and became affiliated with the Jacobite Church. At the beginning of the nineteenth century the Syrian Christians, most of them in the South-west on the Malabar Coast, were divided into three groups—those conforming to Rome and with Latin as their ecclesiastical language, those adhering to Rome but holding to their old customs and with Syriac as their ecclesiastical language, and the Jacobites, also using Syriac in their services.[2] The Jacobites tended to be a separate caste, not seeking to win converts, in their mores conforming in a number of

[1] Latourette, *A History of the Expansion of Christianity*, Vol. II, pp. 280–282; Brown, *The Indian Christians of St. Thomas*, pp. 43–91.
[2] Latourette, *op. cit.*, Vol. III, pp. 263–265; Brown, *op. cit.*, pp. 92–131.

ways to the culture about them, but maintaining inherited Christian forms of worship.[3]

The Roman Catholic Church was represented in the main in four kinds of constituencies. One was its adherents in the Portuguese possessions and those who, issuing from those possessions but residing elewhere, regarded themselves as Portuguese. A second was the Syrian Christians who adhered to Rome, both those of the Latin and of the Syrian rite. A third was made up of converts outside the Portuguese or Syrian elements and found in several parts of the country. The fourth was in the small French enclaves. Through the *padroado,* or right of patronage, granted it centuries earlier, the Portuguese crown insisted that it had authority to appoint the bishops, not only in the Portuguese possessions, but also throughout all India. Because of the decline of Portuguese power, the waning of religious zeal in Europe, the expulsion of the Jesuits from Portuguese territories, the dissolution of the Society of Jesus by the Pope, and the French Revolution, at the beginning of the nineteenth century the Roman Catholic Church was losing ground.[4]

As we have seen,[5] active missions by Protestants began in 1706 with the arrival of German missionaries under Danish auspices. For years the German missionaries were aided by funds from English sources. The East India Company forbade missionaries in its territories, but in 1793 in the renewal of its charter Evangelicals obtained better provision for chaplains for its troops and a few of the chaplains began efforts for Hindus as well as for professed Christians. William Carey, of the (English) Baptist Missionary Society, arrived in 1793 and eventually made his headquarters at Serampore, a Danish possession near Calcutta. There he and his colleagues, notably William Ward and Joshua Marshman, before and after 1815 translated the Bible in whole or in part into more than a score of languages, set up a printing press for its publication and distribution, and founded a college to prepare Indian Christians to reach non-Christians. From there they also furthered the founding of missions elsewhere in India and in Burma and the East Indies. In 1813, when the charter of the East India Company again came up for renewal, Evangelicals, among whom Wilberforce was prominent, obtained provision for an Anglican ecclesiastical establishment with a bishop and three archdeacons and what amounted to permission for missionaries to live and work in territories controlled by the Company. A few years before 1815 the London Missionary Society and the American Board of Commissioners for Foreign Missions had sent representatives to India.[6] But by 1815 Indian Protestant Christians were still very few.

[3] Brown, *op. cit.,* pp. 167 ff. For a survey, largely of the Roman Catholic connexion, see Tisserant, *Eastern Christianity in India,* pp. 1–97, 163.

[4] Latourette, *op. cit.,* Vol. VI, pp. 71–73.

[5] Volume I, pp. 88, 180–182.

[6] Latourette, *op. cit.,* Vol. VI, pp. 106–109.

THE ROMAN CATHOLIC CHURCH HAS A STRIKING GROWTH

In 1911 official figures gathered by the church showed 2,223,546 Roman Catholics in India. Of them, 296,148 were in Portuguese territory and 25,918 were in the French enclaves. The statistics were admittedly inexact and were slightly higher than those gathered by the government.[7] In the preceding half-century the total had risen from 1,017,969 in 1861 to 1,131,672 in 1871, 1,389,306 in 1881, 1,625,943 in 1891, and 1,860,876 in 1901.[8]

The growth had come about partly through the excess of births over deaths in the Roman Catholic population but also through the widespread efforts of an augmented force of missionaries and of Indian priests. How many the personnel numbered at the beginning of the century we do not know, but in 1912 India was served by 966 European and 1,142 Indian priests, 440 lay brothers, and 2,778 sisters.[9] It seemed clear that all categories showed a marked growth in the preceding hundred years.

The foreign staff was from a number of countries and from several orders and congregations. Here was evidence of the revival in the Roman Catholic Church in Europe which had among its expressions the re-invigoration of existing orders and congregations, the emergence of new congregations,[10] and the mounting urge to carry the faith to the uttermost parts of the earth. Of the older orders we hear of the Benedictines, the Augustinians, the Carmelites, the Capuchins, and the Jesuits. The newer congregations were represented, among others, by the Oblates of Mary Immaculate, the Salesians, the Sisters of St. Joseph of Annecy, the Society of the Divine Word, and the Holy Ghost Fathers. The *Missions Étrangères* of Paris, the Mill Hill fathers, the Salvatorians, and the Milan Society shared in the Roman Catholic expansion. Seculars also came. The countries from which missionaries were derived included France, Italy, Belgium, Germany, Switzerland, England, Holland, and Ireland.[11]

Not all of the foreigners or the indigenous staff could devote their energies to the winning of non-Christians. Even at the beginning of the twentieth century, with the much augmented personnel of European and Indians, the European priests were said to have been so occupied in pastoral care of Christians and in schools that a large proportion had little time to give to seeking converts.[12]

The rapid increase of European missionaries from countries other than Portugal and their spread over so large a proportion of the area of India brought repeated and painful clashes between the Holy See and Portugal. Enfeebled by prolonged civil strife, in the 1830's Portugal was unable to care adequately even

---

[7] *Catholic Directory of India, 1913* (Madras, The Catholic Supply Society, pp. 532, xxxv), p. 435.
[8] *Catholic Directory of India, 1912* (Madras, The Catholic Supply Society, pp. 544), pp. 466–497.
[9] Streit, *Atlas Hierarchicus,* p. 187.
[10] Volume I, pp. 324 ff.
[11] Latourette, *op. cit.,* Vol. VI, pp. 79–92.
[12] Schmidlin-Braun, *Catholic Mission History,* pp. 596, 597.

for the dioceses which under the *padroado* were clearly hers. Anti-clericalism was in the saddle, and orders and congregations, the traditional source of reinforcements, were being suppressed.[13] In 1831 all four *padroado* sees were vacant. In 1832 the Propaganda requested the king either to fill the dioceses or to renounce his privileges. When he made no reply, Rome created vicariates apostolic, but for areas remote from the Portuguese possessions, and abolished three of the four sees which were subject to the *padroado*. The Portuguese were unreconciled, and what was known as the Goan schism resulted. The Goan ecclesiastical authorities expelled the missionaries of the Propaganda, and the Archbishop of Goa excommunicated the vicars apostolic and ordained six hundred priests, some of them palpably unworthy. Various efforts were made to achieve a settlement and in 1857, 1860, and 1861 agreements were entered into between Pius IX and Portugal which for a time looked promising. But friction continued. In 1886 a fresh adjustment was negotiated which granted the Portuguese crown the right of presentation not only to the traditional bishoprics but also to some others on the west coast not in Portuguese territory, and more Christians were transferred to the districts under the *padroado* than were lost to it: the church in Portugal was under such heavy attack that Rome felt constrained to be as considerate as possible to national pride. Yet even then many Portuguese remained unsatisfied and in 1928 a further compromise was attempted.[14]

The Holy See would not permit the palsied hand of Portugal to cripple the advance of the Roman Catholic Church in India. In 1884 Leo XIII appointed an apostolic delegate to the country. In 1886, the year in which a further stage in the settlement of the issue was reached, he set up a hierarchy for India. For comprehensive administration seven ecclesiastical provinces were created with an archbishop at the head of each, and various vicariates and prefectures apostolic were transformed into bishoprics.[15]

The Uniates of the Syrian rite constituted a recurring problem. In the fore part of the century they were at times restive under their bishops. At the request of some of them, in 1861 the head of the Chaldean Uniates sent a bishop to whom most of the Malabar Uniates submitted. The missionaries persuaded him that he was giving rise to a schism and he left. In 1874 another bishop was sent by the Chaldean Patriarch and under him a schism occurred which eventually dwindled. In 1887 Leo XIII, following his policy of strengthening the churches of the Oriental rites, separated the churches of the Syrian rite on the Malabar Coast from those of the Latin rite. He put them into two vicariates apostolic, but under Latin incumbents. In 1896 the Uniates were divided into three vicariates and at the head of each was a bishop of the Syrian rite. In 1911 a fourth

---

[13] Volume I, p. 424.

[14] Latourette, *op. cit.*, Vol. VI, pp. 73–77, Vol. VII, pp. 281, 282; Schmidlin-Braun, *op. cit.*, pp. 595, 596.

[15] Latourette, *op. cit.*, Vol. VI, p. 76; Schmidlin-Braun, *op. cit.*, p. 596.

vicariate was created. In that year the Uniates were said to number 665,084. Carmelites conducted seminaries for the preparation of indigenous priests.[16]

Although many of the missionaries were absorbed in education and in caring for the Christians, the Roman Catholic Church grew from conversions among non-Christians. Some were from the higher castes, but the majority were from the depressed classes and the animistic tribes of primitive culture. Thus the semi-nomadic Khonds, in the hills of Central India, were the source of several thousand converts. In Chota Nagpur, a plateau south of the Ganges and west of Bengal, in 1921, 175,000 Roman Catholics were counted, largely from the aborigines. The major pioneer was a Flemish Jesuit, Constant Lievens, who arrived in 1885. Largely through championing the cause of the illiterate masses against their landlords and the moneylenders and helping them win their cases in court, in the seven years before ill health forced his return to Belgium Lievens saw thousands in Chota Nagpur come into the Roman Catholic Church from Protestantism and paganism. Converts from the lower rungs of the social ladder tended to move *en masse*, by their natural groupings. The percentages of Indian Christians in the various social levels varied from section to section. In one diocese 95 per cent. were from the middle classes and only 4 per cent. from the lowest groups. In some other dioceses from 65 to 85 per cent. were from the depressed classes.[17]

Roman Catholics had no uniform practice in their treatment of caste. In some places Christians were regarded as forming a distinct caste. In others caste differences were observed. Rome endeavoured to ensure the admission of all castes to church services without distinction. In one archdiocese, where most of the Christians were from the lower castes, only youths from higher castes were prepared for the priesthood. In general Roman Catholics tended to regard caste as a social and civil affair without religious significance and to tolerate it.[18]

Much of the work of conversion and of instruction of the neophytes and their children was by Indian catechists. Some were resident, others itinerant, and still others travelling companions and secretaries to missionaries. The first approaches to non-Christians were made chiefly through them. They gave the initial instruction to catechumens, visited the sick, cared for the poor, the aged, and the crippled, and introduced Christian farmers to improved agricultural methods.[19]

Among other methods employed by Roman Catholics were plays presenting Biblical themes,[20] the production and distribution of literature,[21] and such phil-

---

[16] Konrad Lübeck, *Die katholische Orientmission in ihrer Entwicklung dargestellt* (Cologne, J. P. Bachem, 1917, pp. 152), pp. 149, 150; Tisserant, *op. cit.*, pp. 97–139.

[17] Latourette, *op. cit.*, Vol. VI, pp. 83–91.

[18] C. Becker, *Indisches Kastenwesen und Christliche Mission* (Aachen, Xaverius-Verlag, 1921, pp. 164), *passim*.

[19] The Capuchin Mission Unit (C.S.M.C.), Cumberland, Maryland, *India and Its Missions* (New York, The Macmillan Co., 1923, pp. xxi, 315), pp. 224–233.

[20] *Ibid.*, pp. 219–221.

[21] *Ibid.*, pp. 241–243.

anthropic institutions as hospitals, orphanages, refuges for widows, and leper asylums.[22] Measures were taken to improve the economic lot of Christians, drawn as a large proportion of them were from the lower social levels and at the time of their conversion in abject poverty. For example, in Chota Nagpur coöperative credit societies were formed for Roman Catholics, coöperative stores, rice banks, produce banks, and industrial schools were created, and cottage industries and improved methods of agriculture were encouraged.[23] In the Punjab the Capuchins obtained lands and on them gathered colonies of the underprivileged.[24]

Education was stressed, in part because of subsidies given by the government to schools regardless of their religious affiliation if they conformed to its educational standards. The use made of schools varied from diocese to diocese. In some, nearly all the mission centres had primary schools and secondary schools were maintained. Others did not have even primary schools. Sisterhoods conducted numbers of schools for girls. The Jesuits established several colleges of a grade beyond the secondary level which appealed to many by their high academic standards and enrolled non-Christians as well as Christians.[25] Much attention was paid to the preparation of Indian clergy. In the latter half of the century, partly on the insistence of Rome, increasing emphasis was placed on theological seminaries and several were opened.[26]

Evidences of vitality within the Roman Catholic communities were seen in the many organizations which enlisted laymen and women. Among the Syrian Christians in Malabar were various confraternities of the Virgin Mary, some of them with endowments in the form of land. The Men's Sodality of the Immaculate Conception of St. Peter's, Bandra, made annual pilgrimages and initiated a retreat for laymen. A sodality begun at Mangalore in 1879 sought to strengthen the religious life of its members by retreats, weekly meetings, monthly corporate Communions, and the celebration of annual festivals. Bombay had a unit of the Society of St. Vincent de Paul whose members administered poor relief by personal visitation. Temperance societies existed. A Catholic Indian Association formed in 1899 and seeking to promote solidarity among Roman Catholics embraced much of South India. A congregation of the third order of Discalced Carmelites drawn from the Uniates and founded in 1831 had among its purposes the holding of retreats for the laity, the publication of books, and the education of youths for the priesthood. Several congregations of Indian women arose, one of which ministered to Hindu widows, served catechumenates for women, founded orphanages for girls, and aided hospitals.[27]

[22] *Ibid.*, pp. 246–253.
[23] T. Van der Schuerin, *The Belgian Mission in Bengal* (Calcutta, Thacker, Spink & Co., 1922, 2 parts, pp. 100, 108), part 2, pp. 22–28.
[24] *Catholic Directory of India, 1916*, pp. 423–435.
[25] Latourette, *op. cit.*, Vol. VI, pp. 93, 94.
[26] *Ibid.*, pp. 94, 95.
[27] *Ibid.*, pp. 97, 98.

THE RAPID GROWTH OF PROTESTANTISM

In 1914 the number of baptized Protestants was about one million.[28] That was less than half the total of baptized Roman Catholics. However, since a century earlier Indian Protestants had numbered only a few hundred in contrast with at least a half-million and perhaps more than a million Roman Catholics,[29] the proportionate increase was much greater. In 1914 Protestant missionaries far outnumbered Roman Catholic missionaries—5,465[30] as against no more than 4,000 of the latter.

The rapid growth of the Protestant missionary body was due to a number of factors. The alteration of its charter in 1813 which in effect permitted the entrance of missionaries to the East India Company's territories was followed by even more favorable terms in the renewal of the charter in 1833, including the creation of two more Anglican bishoprics. The continued extension of the Company's territories with the bringing of more and more of the country under the *pax Britannica* facilitated missions, whether Roman Catholic or Protestant. Although the British *raj* was religiously neutral, the fact that Great Britain was predominantly Protestant and the active sympathy of some British residents, including outstanding officials, for Protestant missionary activity tended to further that branch of the faith. The coincidence of the expansion of the British domains with the awakenings in Protestantism and the increase of interest of Protestants in the geographic spread of the faith had much to do with the multiplication of Protestant missionaries. Protestants of the British Isles especially felt an obligation to the peoples made accessible by the British conquest.[31]

Protestant missionaries to India were from several countries and a number of denominations. In contrast with the Roman Catholics, the vast majority of whose missionaries were from the mainland of Europe, only about one in ten of the Protestant staff were from that continent. Nearly nine in ten were from the British Isles and the United States. In 1914 those from the United States were about five-sixths of those from the British Isles. Some also were from other members of the British Commonwealth—New Zealand, Australia, and Canada, with more from Canada than the other two.

Anglicans covered more of India than did any other non-Roman Catholic communion. In the course of the century dioceses increased in number and by 1914 the ecclesiastical structure embraced most of the country. The bishops included a number of able and devoted men who did much to promote the faith. It seems almost invidious to select any of them for mention. But certainly note

[28] Beach and Fahs, *World Statistics of Christian Missions*, p. 59.
[29] Latourette, *op. cit.*, Vol. VI, p. 73.
[30] Beach and Fahs, *op. cit.*, p. 59.
[31] Surveys of Protestant missions in India in the nineteenth century are to be found in Latourette, *op. cit.*, Vol. VI, pp. 99–193, with extensive footnote references to the authorities, and in Julius Richter, *Indische Missionsgeschichte* (Gütersloh, C. Bertelsmann, 2nd ed., 1924, pp. 570), pp. 138 ff., without bibliography or footnote references to the sources.

should be taken of Reginald Heber (1783–1826), the saintly hymn-writer, who died as the second Bishop of Calcutta after less than three months in India; of the doughty Evangelical, Daniel Wilson (1778–1858), Bishop of Calcutta from 1832 to his death; of Thomas Valpy French (1825–1911), another Evangelical, who first arrived in India in 1851, in 1878 became the first Bishop of Lahore, and in his later years inaugurated a mission in Muscat; and of Frederick Gell, Bishop of Madras from 1861 to 1899. A number of Anglican organizations sent representatives to India. The historic bodies, the Society for the Propagation of the Gospel in Foreign Parts and the Church Missionary Society, were the most prominent, the latter, with its Evangelical tradition, more so than the former, with its Anglo-Catholic constituency. The Society for Promoting Christian Knowledge, which in the eighteenth century had assisted the German Lutheran missionaries, early in the nineteenth century turned over its interests to its sister body, the Society for the Propagation of the Gospel in Foreign Parts. Among other Anglican organizations were the Church of England Zenana Missionary Society and the Zenana Bible and Medical Mission, both by women and for women, the Oxford Mission (Anglo-Catholic), the Fathers of St. John the Evangelist (popularly known as the Cowley Fathers), the Wantage Sisters, the (Women's) Community of St. Stephen, and the Cambridge Mission to Delhi. Missionaries also came from the Scottish Episcopal Church and the Church of England in Canada. Towards the end of the century increasing steps were taken to give the Anglican Communion a firm rooting in Indian leadership, and in 1912 Vedenayagam Samuel Azariah (1874–1945) was consecrated as bishop of a new diocese, Dornakal, the first Indian to be elevated to the Anglican episcopate. Not until after 1914, however, did the Anglican Communion in India become autonomous. In 1930 what was known as the Church of the Province of India, Burma, and Ceylon was formally set free from its connexion with the state.

One of the striking effects of the Anglican missions was on the Syrian Church. An Englishman, a devout Evangelical, who represented the East India Company in Travancore, became deeply interested in that church and wished to see it invigorated by the better training of its clergy, the translation of the Bible into the vernacular, and the enforcement of its discipline. Through him a representative of the Church Missionary Society arrived in 1816 and was followed by others. Like most Protestant missionaries in their contacts with the Eastern Churches in Western Asia, those sent to the Indian Syrians by the Church Missionary Society had no intention of making proselytes but sought by their counsel to instill fresh life and to help the Syrian Church to become active in winning its non-Christian neighbours. But, as in Western Asia, conflict arose between those influenced by the missionaries and the conservatives. A few of the clergy became Anglicans, but a larger group remained within the church of their fathers, hoping to effect improvements. After prolonged controversies which at times were taken to the civil courts, the reformers were forced out and constituted themselves and those who sided with them as the Mar Thoma Syrian Church. The separation occurred in the 1880's. The Mar Thoma Christians claimed to be the true successors of the church founded by the Apostle Thomas and to have preserved the faith uncorrupted by the superstitious practices which they asserted had crept into the majority body. They retained much of the liturgy and practices of the Syrian Church but were more evangelistic than the latter. Deprived of their old church buildings, they erected new ones. In 1889 they initiated the Mar Thoma Evangelistic Association, which from small beginnings eventually grew to large proportions and permeated the entire church with missionary zeal. They were in communion with the Anglicans and by the middle of the twentieth century numbered about 200,000.[32]

All of the major and some of the numerically minor Nonconforming churches of England were represented in India. The Baptist Missionary Society expanded from the beginnings made by William Carey. The London Missionary Society, represented before 1815, continued. The Wesleyan Methodists, moving in from Ceylon, first gave their attention mainly to British soldiers and European residents. Later they expanded chiefly among the Indians. The English Presbyterians had a small mission. The Plymouth Brethren were active. In 1914 the Salvation Army had one of the largest missionary staffs of any organization in the country. A number of undenominational missions for special projects were in action.

Scottish Presbyterianism, earlier disinclined to have an official share in foreign missions, moved by the Evangelical awakening took an active part in India. The first representative of the Church of Scotland to arrive was Alexander Duff (1806–1878).[33] Reared in a home which was profoundly committed to the Evangelical awakening and which had felt the touch of Simeon, and in his student years influenced by Thomas Chalmers, Duff went to India in 1829. There his chief contribution was in education. In a school in Calcutta he sought to show that Christianity and the learning which was entering from Europe were not incompatible with each other and thus to counter the agnosticism or atheism which might be bred by the science of the West which many of the Indians were eager to acquire. He taught in English and sought to expose his pupils to the Christian ideas by which, so he held, that language was permeated. His school was attended by sons of the upper castes. Several were converted. He made a deep impression on a number of Brahmins who did not become Christians and also left his impress on the form of education which was being devel-

---

[32] Brown, *The Indian Christians of St. Thomas*, pp. 132 ff.; Latourette, *op. cit.*, Vol. VI, pp. 113, 114; Neill, *Anglicanism*, pp. 324–329.

[33] For a bibliography on Duff see Latourette, *op. cit.*, Vol. VI, p. 115, n. 265. Also on Duff, chiefly on his accomplishments in promoting missions after his return to Scotland, see Olav Guttorm Myklebust, *The Study of Missions in Theological Education* (Oslo, Egede Institutet, 2 vols., 1955–1957), Vol. I, pp. 158–230, with the accompanying footnote references to bibliography.

oped by the British rulers. Following the precedent set by Duff, an outstanding contribution of the Scottish Presbyterians was in the field of education, not only in Calcutta, the main radiating centre of British trade and culture, but also in the other major centres, Bombay and Madras. Duff's example had a marked effect on the methods of other Protestant denominations. At the Disruption Duff and his colleagues chose to go with the Free Church, thus sacrificing the physical properties which they had built up. But the Free Church rose to the emergency and the Church of Scotland continued what he and the other dissidents had begun. The United Presbyterian Church, which was to join with the Free Church in forming the United Free Church of Scotland, also assumed a share in the missionary enterprise in India.

The denomination which had the most widely extended missions in India of any from the United States was the Methodist Episcopal Church.[34] Its pioneer, William Butler, arrived in 1856. But the rapid expansion was deeply indebted to William Taylor, whom we have already met, and to James Mills Thoburn (1836–1922). Thoburn went to India in 1859. Partly at Thoburn's invitation, Taylor came in 1870 and preached in cities in several parts of the country—to Europeans, Anglo-Indians, Parsees, and Indians, in English where that was understood and when necessary through interpreters. Taylor was four and a half years in India, where he encouraged self-maintaining congregations and called for locally supported missionaries, much as he was to do in South America. He and Thoburn urged that their church broaden its field. Thoburn especially insisted that it take all India into its purview. In response to the appeal, a structure was developed by the Methodist Episcopal Church which in principle covered the entire country. Thoburn also had a share in the extension of the missions of his church to Burma, Singapore, the Malay Peninsula, and the Philippines. In 1888 he was chosen as the first missionary bishop for India and Malaya. In 1914 the greatest numerical strength of the Methodist Episcopal Church was in the North. Here were more than four-fifths of its members and nearly two-thirds of its probationers.

In 1914 the churches served by the American Baptist Foreign Mission Society, the organ of the Northern Baptists, had more baptized members than any other branch of Protestantism except the Anglicans and the congregations connected with the Methodist Episcopal Church. Most of them were in the South and came through mass movements from the depressed classes.[35]

Presbyterians from the United States, of the Northern, the Southern, and the United Presbyterian Church, were prominent. So, too, was the American Board of Commissioners for Foreign Missions and, although in a more limited area and in the South, the (Dutch) Reformed Church in America.[36]

[34] Barclay, *History of Methodist Missions,* Vol. III, pp. 451–666; Latourette, *op. cit.,* Vol. VI, pp. 169–175, especially the bibliography in the footnotes.
[35] Latourette, *op. cit.,* Vol. VI, pp. 165–168; Torbet, *Venture of Faith,* pp. 253–287.
[36] Latourette, *op. cit.,* Vol. VI, pp. 161–165.

Lutheranism, indebted to missionaries from Germany, Sweden, Denmark, and the United States and divided into several synods and churches, was strongest in a wide area in the South-east but was also vigorously represented by the Gossner Mission in Assam and Chota Nagpur, which laboured chiefly among animistic peoples of primitive cultures.[37]

In 1914 the Basel Mission had the largest Protestant foreign staff from the Continent of Europe. In numbers of communicants, of the Continental Protestant societies it was second only to the Gossner Mission. The area which it served was on the south-west coast and included several social and linguistic groups. It made much of industrial and commercial enterprises to assist its constituency in an economic way and to help meet its own expenses. Its system of education had its apex in a theological seminary.[38]

The Young Men's Christian Association stressed Indian leadership and was aided by fellow movements from several countries, notably from the United States and Canada. On the eve of 1914 its outstanding Indian was Kanakarayan Tiruselvam Paul (1876–1931), who wished to make the YMCA help meet the needs of rural India.[39] Of the numbers of able North Americans who served with the YMCA, Sherwood Eddy (1871——) was one of the most colourful. In his student years he had been deeply impressed by Dwight L. Moody and, following the Moody tradition, he was primarily an evangelist. Although not confining his attention to them, he made students his major concern. He came to India in 1896 and, while addressing students in many parts of the country, for a number of years devoted himself chiefly to Tamil-speaking sections in the South. He was a warm friend of V. S. Azariah and with him and other Indians brought into being the National Missionary Society of India (1905). Another whom he influenced profoundly was Abraham, later a bishop of the Mar Thoma Church.[40]

As did the Roman Catholics in the nineteenth century, the Protestants drew the majority of their converts from the depressed classes and the hill tribes of primitive culture. Many of them came through mass movements which brought with them problems of adequate instruction, nurture, and discipline.[41]

Fully as much as the Roman Catholics, Protestant missionaries stressed education. Like the Roman Catholics, they were assisted by grants from a government which, religiously neutral, was prepared to aid schools, regardless of their connexions, if they maintained the educational standards which it set up. Many of the schools, particularly of an elementary grade, had their enrolments chiefly

[37] *Ibid.*, pp. 175, 176, 180–185.

[38] Schlatter, *Geschichte der Basler Mission 1815–1915*, Vol. II, pp. 54 ff.

[39] Latourette, *World Service*, pp. 105 ff.

[40] Sherwood Eddy, *Eighty Adventurous Years* (New York, Harper & Brothers, 1955, pp. 255), pp. 31–59.

[41] J. Waskom Pickett, *Christian Mass Movements in India. A Study with Recommendations* (Cincinnati, Abingdon Press, 1933, pp. 382), *passim*.

from Christian families. That was of major importance, particularly in view of the fact that the large majority of the Christians were from the lowest economic and social rungs of the population. In contrast with the dominant tradition in India, Protestant education was for girls as well as boys. Much attention was given to higher education and in most of the colleges a majority of the students and teachers were non-Christians. Not many converts came from them, but through them a leavening of the national life with Christian ideals was effected.[42]

Much emphasis was placed by Protestants, as by Roman Catholics, on the preparation and circulation of literature. More than the representatives of the other great wing of the faith, Protestants translated the Bible. They put it in whole or in part into all the languages which were spoken by the major segments of the population and into many of the languages of minority groups. Such organizations as the British and Foreign Bible Society with its numerous auxiliaries, the American Bible Society, the National Bible Society of Scotland, the Bible Translation Society, the Society for Promoting Christian Knowledge, and the Tranquebar Tamil Bible Society shared in this characteristically Protestant enterprise.[43] Protestants produced great quantities of other literature. In 1912 more than two score mission presses published Christian literature and in that year over a hundred magazines, newspapers, and periodicals were issued, most of them by missions rather than Indian Christians, either in English or in one of the vernaculars.[44] Among the agencies producing Protestant literature were the Christian Literature Society for India and Africa, organized in 1858 and by 1914 with four regional branches in India, the Calcutta Tract and Book Society and similar ones in five other major centres in India, all assisted by the Religious Tract Society of London, and the Board for Tamil Christian Literature formed in 1905 by twelve missions and societies in the Tamil area.[45]

A large number of societies sprang up, largely or entirely Indian in personnel and support, evidence that Protestant Christianity was taking sufficient hold to impel its adherents to spread the faith among their fellow countrymen. In 1914 at least fifteen existed, most of them begun in the 1890's or in the decade from 1900 to 1910.[46]

[42] *The Christian College in India. The Report of the Commission on Christian Higher Education in India* (London, Humphrey Milford, 1931, pp. xiii, 388), pp. 12–233.

[43] Gustav Warneck, *Abriss einer Geschichte der protestantischen Missionen von der Reformation bis auf die Gegenwart* (Berlin, Martin Warneck, 10th ed., 1913, pp. x, 624), p. 415; Richter, *op. cit.*, pp. 395–405.

[44] J. P. Jones, editor, *The Year Book of Missions in India, Burma and Ceylon, 1912* (The Christian Literature Society for India, 1912, pp. xvi, 780), pp. 341–343, 356–363, 638–648. An impressive set of lists of Christian literature compiled in 1917, 1918, and 1919 was bound under the back title *Surveys and Reports of Christian Literature in India, 1918.*

[45] Strong and Warnshuis, *Directory of Foreign Missions*, pp. 204, 205, 208.

[46] Latourette, *A History of the Expansion of Christianity*, Vol. VI, p. 188; P. O. Philip, *Report on a Survey of Indigenous Christian Efforts in India, Burma and Ceylon* (Poona, Scottish Missions Industries Co., 1928, pp. 14), *passim.*

Among other forms of Protestant missionary effort were hospitals, dispensaries, care for lepers, famine relief, agricultural colonies, missions to railway workers, and homes for boys.[47]

The great diversity of Protestantism in India with the multiplicity of denominations and societies was paralleled by many forms of coöperation and by a notable union of churches, the precursor of an even more significant union after 1914. Beginning in 1862 decennial all-India missionary conferences were held, each with a larger attendance than its predecessor. In its procedure the one in Madras in 1902 provided a precedent for the epoch-making World Missionary Conference which assembled in Edinburgh in 1910. Regional missionary conferences also met, in both North and South India. The one in Madras in 1900 set the pattern for the all-India one of 1902. The various conferences were composed mostly of missionaries, although some Indians were present in the later ones, evidence of the increasing rootage of Protestantism.[48] In 1905 the First General Assembly of the United Churches of South India convened, representing the Congregational churches which had sprung out of the labours of the London Missionary Society and the American Board of Commissioners for Foreign Missions. In 1908 the South India United Church came into being, composed of the Presbyterians, the Reformed, and the Congregationalists in that region, with the Congregationalists in the majority. The initiative was primarily from missionaries, not Indians.[49] The South India United Church constituted the nucleus around which gathered, in 1947, the Church of South India, which embraced Congregationalists, Presbyterians, Wesleyans, and Anglicans. Coöperation across denominational lines also existed in education—as in the Madras Christian College, formed in 1910 with the support of the Free Church of Scotland, the Church of Scotland, the Wesleyans, and the Church Missionary Society, and in the United Theological College of Bangalore, also begun in 1910. That year the theological department of Serampore College became interdenominational. It had been founded by English Baptists and through a charter from the Danish Government was the only institution in India which could confer degrees in divinity. By 1914 a number of other bodies and institutions made possible coöperation across denominational lines. The most inclusive was the National Missionary Council of India, Burma, and Ceylon, which came into being in 1912 from a conference initiated and presided over by John R. Mott as chairman of the Continuation Committee of the (Edinburgh) World Missionary Conference. It was the precursor of the National Christian Council of India, Burma, and Ceylon, formed in 1923. Mott stressed Indian participation, an em-

[47] Latourette, *A History of the Expansion of Christianity,* Vol. VI, pp. 191, 192.

[48] Hogg, *Ecumenical Foundations,* pp. 17–25.

[49] Bengt Sundkler, *Church of South India; The Movement Towards Union 1900–1947* (London, Lutterworth Press, 1954, pp. 457), pp. 36–49.

phasis arising from his vision of a world-embracing Christian movement rooted in each country in indigenous leadership.[50]

SUMMARY

To what extent did Christianity modify the revolution which, entering from Western Christendom under British auspices, was beginning to impinge on India?

Some of the effects are easy to discern. The numbers of Christians grew rapidly. As had been true for many centuries, Christianity continued to be strongest south of a line which could be drawn roughly from Bombay to Madras. But by 1914 its constituencies were increasing, not only in the South, but throughout much of the country. The growth was not through the ancient Syrian Church, for it remained encysted, a kind of caste. Thousands of the Syrian Christians were in communion with Rome, some with the Latin rite, and others as Uniates with their ancestral rites. Others, although fewer, through the influence of Anglican missionaries had hived off to form the Mar Thoma Church, more missionary-minded than its parent. The numerical increase was mainly through Roman Catholics and Protestants. By 1914 the former still outnumbered the latter, but proportionately the latter had displayed a more marked expansion. Roman Catholic missionaries were predominantly from the Continent of Europe. Protestant missionaries were mostly from the British Isles, the British Dominions, and the United States. The fact that the ruling power, although officially religiously neutral, was also officially Protestant tended to make for the growth of that branch of the faith. The large majority of the conversions of non-Christians, through both the Roman Catholic Church and Protestantism, were from the depressed classes and the animistic hill tribes. For these elements, underprivileged as they were, Christianity afforded a door of hope to larger opportunities. Here was a contribution to the drastic change in the status of these elements that was a feature of the revolution and that mounted after 1914. Both Roman Catholic and Protestant missions stressed education. That education embodied ideas of Western origin and in its higher ranges was through the medium of English. It therefore furthered the revolution. The fact that both Roman Catholics and Protestants fought some of the disabilities under which women had laboured and provided education for girls promoted a phase of the social revolution. Various aspects of culture were introduced or reinforced, such as Western medicine and methods of agriculture. Their results were mixed, for on the one hand they relieved suffering and reduced poverty and on the other hand by that very fact contributed to the growth of population which in the next century approached the explosive stage.

Less capable of accurate appraisal were other contributions of Christianity to

[50] Hogg, *op. cit.*, pp. 152, 153, 213.

the impact of the revolutionary age. One was the ideas which entered through the form of education furthered by the British rulers. The use of the English language as the medium of instruction opened the entire range of English literature, some of it non-Christian, but much of it shot through and through with Christian standards and conceptions. Many a British official sought to embody his Christian faith in the performance of his duties. Numbers of Indians who as non-Christians attended schools conducted by missionaries, while holding to their inherited religions, were influenced, some much, some little, by what they learned of Christianity. The Brahmo Samaj, a movement largely among Brahmin intellectuals, although not Christian, was theistic and deeply indebted to contacts with Christianity. One of its scions, Rabindranath Tagore, poet, philosopher, and educator, was famous both in India and abroad. The Servants of India Society, founded in 1905 for the purpose of furthering the progress of the country by the devotion of its members, seems to have been inspired by contact with the Cowley Fathers. Mohandas Karamchand Gandhi, whose contributions were to be mainly after 1914, in his formative years was profoundly influenced by the New Testament and the example of Christ, continued to embody what came to him from that source, and was to do more to shape the post-1914 India than any other man. Through him Christ helped to mould the India which issued from the revolution.[51] Most of the effects of Christianity outside the churches, including those by way of Gandhi, were through Protestantism.

In India Christianity had a greater and more positive share in the pre-1914 coming of the revolutionary age than in Western Asia. India was different, and in the next century was even more so because of the place of Christianity and especially of avowed and convinced Christians in the expanding impact of Western Christendom. On the eve of 1914 Indian leadership in the churches, whether Roman Catholic or Protestant, was rapidly mounting, partly because of the initiative of far-seeing missionaries, who recognized that to be securely planted Christianity must be in Indian hands and that the rising tide of nationalism was making imperative the early transfer of authority from foreigners to Indians.

---

[51] Latourette, *A History of the Expansion of Christianity*, Vol. VI, pp. 200–204.

CHAPTER XVIII

South-East Asia and the
Fringing Islands

SOUTH and east of India stretches a region which is a fringe of the continent of Asia, partly mainland and partly islands on the continental shelf. Most of it received much of its earlier civilization from India—Ceylon partly Buddhist and partly Hindu, Burma and Thailand (Siam) Buddhist, Cambodia Hindu and Buddhist, Annam, periodically part of China, more Confuciain than Indian, but still with a smattering of Indian culture, and the East Indies with potent enclaves of Buddhism and Hinduism. On the eve of the coming of the Europeans Islam also made its way into the region and became the dominant faith in the Malay Peninsula, in Java, and in southern portions of that northern extension of the East Indies which was conquered by Spain.

Western Christendom had had contacts with part of the area in the thirteenth and fourteenth centuries, but it was not until late in the fifteenth and in the sixteenth century that the impact began to have much effect. It came first through the Portuguese and Spaniards—the latter limited to the Philippines— and then through the Dutch and the English. The nineteenth century brought further inroads, with the extension of political conquest and of commerce. Contacts with Christianity through missionaries marked all these centuries, at first through Roman Catholics and then through Roman Catholics and Protestants. In the nineteenth century the contacts rapidly mounted. Christian communities arose, in most places small minorities, but in a few growing into substantial minorities and even majorities. Passing rapidly from land to land we will summarize the main features of these contacts.

CEYLON

On the sea highway, Ceylon was early touched by commerce from the Mediterranean world and then from Western Europe. In the sixteenth century the Portuguese conquered much of the island, to be supplanted by the Dutch in the seventeenth century. The Dutch, in turn, were expelled by the English during the wars of the French Revolution.

Ceylon may have had Christian communities in connexion with commerce with the Mediterranean and Mesopotamia before the sixteenth century, but if so, unlike the Syrian Christians in the adjacent South India, they disappeared. The majority of the population were Buddhists, and Moslems and Hindus constituted minorities.

It was through the Portuguese that Christianity was first firmly planted in Ceylon. The Portuguese began their conquest early in the sixteenth century. Roman Catholic missionaries accompanied or followed them, and thousands of the islanders conformed to the conquerors' faith. Little if any compulsion was used. The motives seem to have been a desire for release through Portuguese protection from social and economic disabilities suffered under the old order and for a share in the privileges which accrued to the ruling invaders. Here and there a prince and his nobles were baptized. By the beginning of the seventeenth century some portions of the island under the Portuguese were said to be predominantly Christian. Since Moslems were resistant to the Portuguese, in 1626 they were expelled from such parts of Ceylon as were in Portuguese hands.[1]

In the seventeenth century the Dutch, Protestants and commercial rivals, displaced the Portuguese. They regarded the Roman Catholic Church as allied with the Portuguese, and, indeed, not without cause, for the clergy of that church actively supported the Portuguese. The Dutch sought to substitute their form of Protestantism for Roman Catholicism. They expelled the priests, converted many of the church buildings to Protestant worship, and forbade both public and private meetings of Roman Catholics. They placed non-Christians and Roman Catholics under political disabilities, prohibited at least some non-Christian ceremonies, and are said to have imposed financial penalties for refusal to accept baptism and non-attendance at Protestant church services. The number of Protestants in 1722 was reported to be 424,392. Another estimate places the total in 1801 at 342,000. But the clergy were too few and most of such as were present were too little familiar with the language to give adequate care to the Christians. Roman Catholicism persisted and in 1801 may have had more adherents than Protestantism. Some Roman Catholics sought refuge in regions outside the Dutch domains, clergy from Goa ministered to the faithful, usually surreptitiously, and in the latter part of the eighteenth century the Dutch relaxed their restrictions.[2]

In 1795-1796 the British, taking advantage of the occupation of Holland by the French, drove the Dutch out of Ceylon and within a few years extended their rule to the portions of the island which had not submitted to the Dutch. The new regime was tolerant religiously, and with the disappearance of the pressures brought by the Dutch, the Protestant communities rapidly declined.

---

[1] Latourette, *A History of the Expansion of Christianity*, Vol. III, pp. 285–289.

[2] James Emerson Tennent, *Christianity in Ceylon: Its Introduction and Progress under the Portuguese, the Dutch, the British, and American Missions* (London, John Murray, 1850, pp. xv, 345), pp. 41–68.

Thousands openly renewed their connexion with the Roman Catholic Church and other thousands resumed the Buddhist and Hindu affiliations of their fore-fathers.[3]

As in much of the rest of the world, Roman Catholic missions in Ceylon mounted in the nineteenth century. In 1806 the British rulers granted full liberty of worship to Roman Catholics and in 1829 confirmed it by extending to the island the provisions of the Catholic Emancipation Act which was passed in that year. Under the adverse conditions during the Dutch period and in common with what was happening in India and elsewhere in the eighteenth century, the quality of religious life of the Roman Catholics had suffered a sad decline. But, partly in response to pleas from the Roman Catholics, by the middle of the nineteenth century, to the Goanese clergy European clergy had begun to be added. In spite of the opposition of the Portuguese on the basis of the *padroado,* Rome created vicariates apostolic and, later, bishoprics. In the course of time Roman Catholics increased in number and in quality. In 1873 the total was said to have been 184,399 as against 66,830 in 1806. In 1901 the total was reported to be 285,018, and in 1911, 339,300. Of the latter figure, nearly two-thirds were Sinhalese on the lowlands, slightly less than a third Tamils, and a few thousands Burghers (of mixed European and native blood) and Sinhalese in the high interior. Schools and clerical care accounted for an improvement in the religious life of the faithful.[4]

Soon after the establishment of British rule, and with the friendly assent of the British authorities, Protestant missionaries began arriving. They were mainly from the British Isles, but some were from the United States. The English Baptists were the first to begin a continuing mission (1812). They were followed, in 1814, by the Wesleyan Methodists. The Methodists came at the suggestion of the British chief justice of the island made through Wilberforce. Their pioneer party was led by the devoted Thomas Coke, and although he died on the outward voyage, his colleagues, undaunted, persevered. Anglican chaplains and the Anglican bishop were subsidized by the government until the 1880's. In 1817 the Church Missionary Society, partly through the urging of the chief justice, sent its first contingent. The Society for the Propagation of the Gospel in Foreign Parts had its initial representative on the ground in 1840. Other British organizations were also attracted. The American Board of Commissioners for Foreign Missions made its headquarters at Jaffna, in the extreme north, and concentrated its efforts on the Tamils. Protestants were not as numerous as in the Dutch era, but the growth was healthier.

The census of 1911 showed Roman Catholics and Protestants together to num-

---

[3] *Ibid.*, pp. 83, 84.
[4] Latourette, *op. cit.*, Vol. VI, pp. 216–221, with the accompanying footnotes.

ber about one out of ten of the population, a much higher percentage than in any other country on the mainland of South and East Asia.[5]

Burma presented a picture both like and unlike that of Ceylon. It was like Ceylon in that the religion of the majority was Buddhism, and of the same general kind as that of the southern island. Here, too, were non-Buddhist minorities. Here also in 1914 the rulers were British. However, in contrast with Ceylon, peoples of animistic religions and primitive cultures constituted substantial minorities. The Burmans proper, almost solidly Buddhist, were concentrated in the valleys. The animistic folk were in the hills and mountains which flanked the valleys. Some, notably the Shans, were being penetrated by Buddhism. The most numerous, the Karens, had no written form of their language. The British conquest was more slowly effected than in Ceylon. It was achieved in three stages. The first annexation was in the coastal provinces and followed a war in 1824–1826; the second, after a war in 1852, took a province in Lower Burma; and the third, comprising the rest of the country, was the outcome of a war in 1885–1886.

The record of Christianity in Burma differed strikingly from that in Ceylon. At the outset of the nineteenth century Burma had very few Christians. Roman Catholicism had been introduced in the seventeenth century largely under Portuguese auspices. In the eighteenth century the Barnabites made a few converts, but before 1815 their mission had come to an end.[6] In the nineteenth century Roman Catholic missions were slow in being revived. By 1914 they were represented by the *Société des Missions Étrangères* of Paris and the Seminary of Milan. Conversions were largely but not entirely among the Karens. Among immigrants from India and Anglo-Indians there were several thousand Roman Catholics.[7]

Also in contrast with Ceylon, in Burma Protestants were more numerous than Roman Catholics and their strength was due more to missionaries from the United States than to British societies. The introduction of Protestantism to Burma was at the initiative of the English Baptists. The Serampore group early translated part of the New Testament into Burmese and at Carey's suggestion two men, one of them his son Felix, went to the country. But Felix proved unfortunate and the other soon left for Ceylon.[8] The outstanding pioneer of Protestantism in Burma was Adoniram Judson (1788–1850).[9] One of the group

[5] *Ibid.*, pp. 221–224.

[6] *Ibid.*, Vol. III, pp. 293, 294.

[7] *Ibid.*, Vol. VI, pp. 226, 227.

[8] S. Pearce Carey, *William Carey* (New York, George H. Doran Co., 1923, pp. xiv, 428), pp. 257–269, 272–274, 319–322.

[9] Francis Wayland, *Memoir of the Life and Labors of the Rev. Adoniram Judson, D.D.* (Boston, Phillips Samson and Co., 2 vols., 1853); Stacy R. Warburton, *Eastward. The Story of Adoniram*

responsible for stirring the Congregationalists to inaugurate the American Board of Commissioners for Foreign Missions, Judson was a member of the original contingent sent by that body. They headed for India. In the long outward voyage Judson became convinced of the truth of the distinctive Baptist position on baptism and soon after arriving in Calcutta was immersed by one of the Serampore Trio. Since the East India Company, then hostile to missionaries, would not permit him to remain in its territories, he and his wife went to Rangoon. The Baptists of the United States rallied to his support. After incredible hardships he obtained a firm foothold in the country and reinforcements were sent him. Gifted as a linguist, he translated the entire Bible into Burmese, prepared other literature in that tongue, and did extensive work on an English-Burmese and a Burmese-English dictionary.

Stirred by Judson, the Baptists of the United States regarded Burma as their responsibility. By 1914 all the principal peoples of the country had been touched by them. Not many converts were won from the Burmans, staunch Buddhists as they were. The major numerical gains were among the animistic folk, mainly the Karens. The Karen language was reduced to writing, the Bible was translated and other literature was prepared, schools were begun and maintained, and clergy and teachers were recruited and trained for what in 1914 were the nearly 50,000 church members among that people.[10]

Anglicans also came, chiefly through the Society for the Propagation of the Gospel in Foreign Parts, and with numerical success chiefly among the Karens.[11] Methodists arrived—Americans in 1879 following up some of their Indian converts[12] and Wesleyan Methodists from Britain in 1887 feeling the compulsion of the peoples made accessible by the British conquest of Upper Burma (1885–1886).[13] A few other Protestant bodies began enterprises in Burma, but none were of large dimensions.

The chief tangible results of nineteenth-century Christianity in Burma were among the non-Burmese peoples, mainly the Karens. Despised by the Burmans as inferior, the Karens, educated in schools which combined Western subjects and attitudes with adaptations to local conditions and stimulated to a growing share in the churches, in which an increasing proportion were enrolled, aspired to political autonomy. That ambition was to bring serious complications in the next century which by Christian standards were ambiguous.

Judson (New York, Round Table Press, 1937, pp. xi, 240); Courtney Anderson, *To the Golden Shore. The Life of Adoniram Judson* (Boston, Little, Brown and Co., 1956, pp. xiii, 530).

[10] Torbet, *Venture of Faith*, pp. 31–51, 56–75, 206–252.

[11] Thompson, *Into All Lands*, pp. 384–393, 638–640.

[12] Barclay, *History of Methodist Missions*, Vol. III, pp. 583 ff.

[13] Findlay and Holdsworth, *The History of the Wesleyan Methodist Missionary Society*, Vol. V, pp. 381–391.

MALAYA

In the nineteenth century the lower part of the Malay Peninsula and Singapore, the island close to its extreme southern tip, became part of the British Empire. Singapore, Malacca, and the island of Penang, a few other islands, and a strip on the mainland constituted the Straits Settlements, a crown colony. The bulk of such of Malaya as was under British control was made up of the Federated Malay States and the Unfederated Malay States. The Malays were overwhelmingly Moslem. Attracted by the opportunities brought by the growing commerce of the revolutionary age, Chinese and Indians increasingly formed important elements of the population. In time Singapore became predominantly Chinese and Chinese were present elsewhere.

So far as is known, Christianity first came to Malaya through the Portuguese in the sixteenth century. Its main strength was in Malacca—until the founding of Singapore the chief mart on the straits which bore that name. The Portuguese took it in 1611 and under their regime Roman Catholicism became strong. In 1641 the Dutch dispossessed the Portuguese and the church buildings were either made over to Protestants or appropriated for secular purposes. The British took possession in 1795 but did not come into continuing occupancy until 1824.

In the nineteenth century Roman Catholicism, which had been eclipsed by the Dutch, was revived. The see of Malacca, long vacant because of the Dutch, was erased in 1838 by a Papal brief, and in 1840 the region was assigned to the *Société des Missions Étrangères* of Paris. At the outset Roman Catholics numbered only a few hundred and professedly were of Portuguese blood. In the course of the century converts were made, mostly from the Chinese, and the Bishopric of Malacca was revived, but with its seat in Singapore. In 1912 Roman Catholics were said to total 17,511.[14]

In the nineteenth century Protestantism, earlier represented by the Dutch, was chiefly indebted to the British and the Americans. Anglican chaplains came with the English and in 1869 were removed from the supervision of the Bishop of Calcutta and placed under the Bishop of Labuan. It was in the 1850's that the Anglicans seem first to have reached out to non-Europeans—with a mission of an Anglican congregation in Singapore to the Chinese in that city. In the next decade the Society for the Propagation of the Gospel in Foreign Parts began sending representatives. In time their activities were among the Chinese, Tamils, Sinhalese, and Malays. Singapore was made a separate diocese, with Siam added to it.[15] In 1856 the English Presbyterians began a mission among the Chinese, at the beginning among immigrants from the region of Swatow and Amoy, among whom were Christians who were the fruits of English Pres-

14 Launay, *Histoire Générale de la Société des Missions-Étrangères*, Vol. III, pp. 108, 109, 446, 534, 551; Streit, *Atlas Hierarchicus*, p. 99.
15 Thompson, *op. cit.*, pp. 395, 396, 403–406, 649.

byterian efforts in that region.[16] The Methodist Episcopal Church shared the honour with the Anglicans of having the strongest non-Roman Catholic mission in Malaya. Its inception was due to the wide-ranging vision of Thoburn. William F. Oldham, an English convert of the meetings in India associated with Taylor, and later a bishop, reached Singapore in 1885. The mission rapidly expanded, at first chiefly among the Chinese and Tamils, and had centres in Singapore, Penang, Malacca, and several places on the mainland. It made much use of schools and through them reached some of the Moslem Malays.[17] A few other Protestant bodies were active, but on a smaller scale.[18]

SIAM (THAILAND)

Siam, or Thailand as was the preferred name in the next century, was the one area in South-east Asia and the fringing islands which did not come under the political control of Europeans. More nearly solidly Buddhist than Burma and Ceylon, it offered greater resistance to the spread of Christianity than did either of those countries. Linguistically and racially the land was a mixture, with the Thai dominant.

Christianity entered first through the Roman Catholics and in the sixteenth century. Beginning in the seventeenth century that branch of the faith had been represented chiefly by the *Société des Missions Étrangères* of Paris. As was true in several other countries, a low ebb was reached in the latter part of the eighteenth century. At the dawn of the nineteenth century Christians were said to number only a thousand or twelve hundred. In 1841 Siam was made a separate vicariate apostolic. The first vicar apostolic, Pallegoix, was a man of outstanding ability. Although in 1849 missionaries were ordered out of the country, the coming to the throne in 1851 of a friend of Pallegoix brought a reversal of that decree. In 1856 a treaty between France and Siam guaranteed French missionaries the privilege of preaching, teaching, travelling anywhere in the realm, and building churches, schools, and hospitals. Roman Catholics tended to form distinct enclaves under the supervision of their church. In 1912 they were said to total about 36,000. In 1880 one of their number was raised to the priesthood and by 1900 about a score had that status.[19]

Protestantism did not arrive in Siam until the fore part of the nineteenth century. Then several efforts were made to introduce it, and by societies from at

[16] William Dale, *Our Missions in the Far East. A Historical Sketch of the Foreign Missions of the Presbyterian Church of England 1847–1907* (London, The Publications Committee, 1907, pp. 88), pp. 59–62.

[17] Barclay, *op. cit.*, Vol. III, pp. 650–663; W. F. Oldham, *India, Malaysia, and the Philippines. A Practical Study in Missions* (New York, Eaton & Mains, 1914, pp. viii, 299), pp. 224–248.

[18] Beach and St. John, *World Statistics of Christian Missions*, p. 64.

[19] Latourette, *op. cit.*, Vol. VI, pp. 241–243; Launay, *op. cit.*, Vol. II, p. 495, Vol. III, pp. 108, 115–122, 244–247, 338, 339; Streit, *op. cit.*, p. 99.

least three countries. The largest of the Protestant enterprises was that of the American Presbyterians. It was begun in 1840 and was continuous from 1847. Eventually the Presbyterians established centres in several parts of the country with churches, schools, a theological seminary, and hospitals. Their main numerical gains were in the North, where Buddhism was less firmly entrenched than in the South. A few other non-Roman Catholic bodies were represented, but the Protestant total did not equal that of the Roman Caholics.[20]

FRENCH INDO-CHINA

As a descriptive term "French Indo-China" was accurate only in the latter part of the nineteenth and the fore part of the twentieth century. Then it was a convenient summary of forces which played upon the diverse peoples of the area. East of the mountainous backbone were Tongking and Annam. At intervals they had been part of the Chinese Empire and had been permeated by Chinese culture. To the west of the mountains, and especially in the lower part of the valley of the Mekong—in Cambodia and Cochin-China—Indian cultural influence had been potent, with Hinduism and Buddhism as contributions to religion. French interest came in the wake of Roman Catholic missions and in the second half of the nineteenth century the French conquest, at the outset ostensibly in protection of French missionaries, brought all of the region under French control, part by direct annexation and part through the form of a protectorate over existing regimes. In the latter part of the century French administrative mastery was tightened. In French Indo-China Christians were more numerous than in any other country on the mainland from Ceylon to China.

Before the nineteenth century the Roman Catholic faith had gained a firm foothold in several parts of the region. Early in the seventeenth century Jesuits came. At the instance of one of them a movement was begun in France which issued in the *Société des Missions Étrangères* of Paris. In time that society became the most prominent of the missionary bodies. Several orders were also active in the region—Augustinians, Franciscans, and especially Spanish Dominicans from the Philippines. The Jesuits continued until the second half of the eighteenth century.[21] In the year 1800 the area later included in French Indo-China is said to have had 310,000 Roman Catholics.[22]

It was through missionaries that France gained her first territorial foothold. In the latter part of the eighteenth century, at the initiative of a Paris Society missionary who was vicar apostolic in Cochin-China, the French gave naval and military support to an aspirant to the throne. With French aid he founded a dynasty which survived in Annam into the twentieth century. In return France

[20] George Bradley McFarland, editor, *Historical Sketch of Protestant Missions in Siam 1828–1928* (Bangkok Times Press, 1928, pp. xvii, 386), *passim*.
[21] Latourette, *op. cit.*, Vol. III, pp. 296–298.
[22] Descamps, *Histoire Comparée Générale des Missions*, p. 547.

was promised an island off the mouth of the Mekong and a port on the coast of Annam.[23]

In what became French Indo-China the nineteenth century was marked by intermittent persecutions which were the occasion for French intervention and conquest, and by a striking growth in numbers of the faithful and in indigenous clergy. The chief storms of persecution were in the years 1833–1840 and 1857–1863. They seem to have sprung from the belief that Christianity was undermining the inherited culture of the country and from the fear of the use of the foreign faith as an instrument for European aggression. That fear was seen to be justified when in 1858, in response to an appeal by a French vicar apostolic, Napoleon III sent a naval expedition in which Spain joined. France played the leading part, annexed three provinces of Cochin-China, and extracted a treaty (1862) by which the King of Annam agreed to permit his subjects to embrace Christianity. Persecutions again broke out, and in 1874, under French pressure, a treaty was negotiated with the promise of greater freedom for missionaries and indigenous Christians. In 1883 and 1884 another war with France was marked by the massacres of missionaries and tens of thousands of Christians. French victory brought the firm establishment of French rule. In spite of the growing anti-clericalism of the French Government and its colonial administration, the numbers of Christians rapidly mounted. A combination of the devotion of the missionaries, economic advantages, such as lighter taxes, and instruction in crafts and methods of agriculture proved attractive.[24] On the eve of 1914 Christians numbered slightly less than a million in twelve vicariates apostolic, ten of which were in charge of the Paris Society and two under the Spanish Dominicans of the Province of the Holy Rosary, with headquarters in Manila.[25]

Protestantism was late in arriving. Although in the 1890's the Christian and Missionary Alliance, an American organization, sought to gain a foothold, not until 1911 did it succeed in establishing its first station.[26] The only other Protestants represented in 1914 seem to have been the Plymouth Brethren.[27]

THE EAST INDIES

The vast congeries of islands which Europeans of the nineteenth century called the East Indies or the Malay Archipelago was never all under one political structure. Nor was it racially, linguistically, or religiously a unit. It had been successively penetrated by Indian, Arab, and Western European culture. From India had come Buddhism and Hinduism. Through Arab contacts Islam had

---

[23] Latourette, *op. cit.*, Vol. III, p. 299.

[24] *Ibid.*, Vol. VI, pp. 247–251.

[25] Streit, *op. cit.*, p. 99.

[26] E. F. Irwin, *With Christ in Indo-China. The Story of Alliance Missions in French Indo-China and Eastern Siam* (Harrisburg, Christian Publications, 1937, pp. 164), pp. 25 ff.

[27] Beach and Fahs, *World Missionary Atlas*, p. 83.

supplanted the Indian faiths in much of the region. Western Christendom had been successively represented by the Portuguese, the Dutch, the English (briefly, during the wars of the French Revolution and Napoleon), and then again the Dutch. At the dawn of the nineteenth century the Portuguese retained the eastern end of Timor and some smaller islands, and the Dutch had widely extended holdings which had been returned to them by the English after their occupancy (1811–1818). Religiously Islam was the faith of the majority and had its chief strength on the island of Java, animism in one or another of its forms was held by a variety of tribes, Hinduism survived on the island of Bali and, as we are to see, Christianity was professed by minorities. In the course of the nineteenth century the Dutch extended their rule over most of the archipelago, the Portuguese remained in control of part of Timor, and the British made themselves masters of north-western sections of Borneo.

Christianity was first introduced to the East Indies by the Portuguese early in the sixteenth century. One of its pioneers was the indefatigable and far-ranging Francis Xavier. Spanish missionaries also came by way of the Philippines. The displacing of the Portuguese in most of the islands by the Dutch proved an obstacle to the spread of Roman Catholicism. The East India Company, through which the Dutch carried on their enterprise, made the Reformed Church one of its responsibilities and supported clergy whose function it was to care for its European employees and to win the East Indians to the faith. Accordingly a church arose which, after the East India Company was dissolved (1798), had the support of the state and continued to do so into the twentieth century. In the main centres of Dutch rule, notably in Amboyna, a large proportion of the population became members of that church.[28]

In the nineteenth century Christianity continued its growth, chiefly by natural increase and by conversions from animistic folk, but partly through the winning of Moslems, notably in Java, where Islam sat rather more lightly on its adherents than in most of the Moslem world. During much of the nineteenth century, and especially in the first half, the colonial administration viewed with jaundiced eye attempts to win non-Christians and especially Moslems to the faith. It feared that they would stir up unrest and cut down the profits of the Dutch. But the policy was softened in the latter part of the century. Indeed, through the rising tide in the religious life of Holland, and notably through the movement spear-headed by Kuyper,[29] the "ethical policy" was adopted which declared that as a "Christian power" the Netherlands had an obligation to further the welfare of the peoples under its colonial administration, to better the position of the native Christians, and to encourage Christian missions. One result of the

---

[28] Carel Wessel Theodorus van Boetzelaer van Dubbeldam, *De Gereformeerde Kerken in Nederland en de Zending in Oost-Indië in de dagen der Oost-Indische Compagnie* (Utrecht, P. Den Boer, 1906, pp. viii, 358), *passim*.

[29] Volume II, Chapter XXV.

change of policy was the subsidizing by the state of mission schools.[30]

In the nineteenth century the Roman Catholic Church did not have a very large part in the spread of Christianity in the East Indies. Even in the eastern portion of Timor, under Portuguese rule, the majority of the population continued to be non-Christian. By an agreement of 1847 the Dutch colonial government subsidized Roman Catholic personnel and public worship as it did that of the Protestant Church in the Netherlands Indies, but it attempted to keep Roman Catholic missionaries out of territories where Protestant missionaries were at work—as it also excluded Protestant missionaries from areas assigned to Roman Catholics. Jesuits came in 1859, and shortly after 1900 missionaries of other organizations began to arrive. But not until after 1914 was Roman Catholic growth pronounced.[31]

The major increase of Christians in the Netherlands East Indies in the nineteenth century was through Protestants. The state-supported Protestant Church in the Netherlands Indies had more members than any other ecclesiastical body. However, with the awakenings that marked the course of Protestantism in the Netherlands, the missionary societies which were a part of its fruitage saw in the East Indies an opportunity and obligation. Of them the largest was the Netherlands Missionary Society, which had been formed in 1797 under the inspiration of the London Missionary Society. Other societies sprang up representing special interests and theological viewpoints or for particular objects. A German organization, the Rhenish Missionary Society, in which Reformed and Lutherans combined, had extensive enterprises. The chief gains were among peoples of primitive non-Moslem cultures. They were especially numerous in the Moluccas and Celebes and, through the Rhenish Missionary Society, among the Bataks in Sumatra and among the peoples on Nias.[32] By the year 1914 the Netherlands East Indies had more baptized Protestants than were to be found elsewhere in all East Asia. The Rhenish Missionary Society was particularly fortunate in its pioneer leadership. Ludwig Ingwer Nommensen (1834–1918), who arrived in 1862, was a man of indomitable will, wise, far-seeing, a friend and father of his people, and placed on the enterprise which he led for more than a generation and on the church which arose from it the stamp of his vision and character.[33]

The British portion of Borneo included Sarawak, a British protectorate ruled

---

[30] Amry Vandenbosch, *The Dutch East Indies: Its Government, Problems, and Policies* (Berkeley, University of California Press, 3rd ed., 1942, pp. xiv, 458), pp. 208, 209; Pietertje Magdalena Frankel-VanDriel, *Regeering en Zending in Nederlandsch-Indië* (Amsterdam, A. H. Kruyt, 1923, pp. 128), pp. 46 ff.

[31] Latourette, *op. cit.*, Vol. V, pp. 294, 295; Schmidlin-Braun, *Catholic Mission History*, pp. 639–642.

[32] Latourette, *op. cit.*, Vol. V, pp. 277–293; Joh. Rauws *et al.*, *The Netherlands Indies* (London, World Dominion Press, 1935, pp. 186), *passim*.

[33] Joh. Warneck, *D. Ludwig I. Nommensen. Ein Lebensbild* (Barmen, Missionshaus, 3rd ed., 1928, pp. 142), *passim*.

by James Brooke and his descendants, Brunei, a British protectorate, British North Borneo, governed by the British North Borneo Company, and Labuan, latterly administered as part of the Straits Settlements. British control dated from the 1840's. Christianity entered soon after the British occupation. James Brooke, who had become Rajah of Sarawak with the purpose of suppressing piracy and head-hunting, increasing trade, and spreading Christianity, took the initiative in introducing Anglican missionaries (1848).[34] American Methodists began in 1901 through Chinese immigrants who were followed by a missionary (1903).[35] Roman Catholic missionaries came in the seventeenth century and the 1850's, but it was not until 1881 that a continuing enterprise was begun, by the Mill Hill fathers.[36]

THE PHILIPPINES

The Philippines were the northern portion of the East Indies and were distinguished from the southern portion by having been brought under Spanish rule in the sixteenth century. That rule was accompanied by extensive Roman Catholic missions, and at the dawn of the nineteenth century the majority of the population were Roman Catholics. Animistic tribes persisted in the remote mountain fastnesses, and in the South were Moslems whom the Spaniards called Moros, the name they had applied to the adherents of Islam in Spain. The Spanish missionaries, members of orders, were powerful, owned much of the land, and controlled the Church. Through them the Philippines contained more Christians than all the rest of South and East Asia. In the nineteenth century the number of Christians was said to have mounted from about four million to about seven million, an increase of two million by the excess of births over deaths, the other million by conversions.[37] Spanish rule, although paternalistic, had on the whole been mild and benevolent. Out of a motley congeries of tribes of animistic religion and primitive culture it had begun the creation of a nation with a common faith and with infusions of Western civilization which were more than a veneer.

In the closing years of the nineteenth century momentous changes were brought by the impact of the revolutionary age. Partly through contact with the ferment in Western Europe, a nationalistic movement sought independence from Spain and a rationalistic questioning of the Roman Catholic faith began to be heard. In 1898 the islands were annexed by the United States.

A combination of nationalism and rationalism brought about a major secession from the Roman Catholic Church. All the bishops were Spaniards and

---

[34] Thompson, *Into All Lands*, pp. 204, 205, 394–403, 656, 657.
[35] Frank T. Cartwright, *Tuan Hoover of Borneo* (Cincinnati, Abingdon Press, 1938, pp. 186), *passim*.
[36] *Zeitschrift für Missionswissenschaft*, Vol. III, pp. 326–328; Schmidlin-Braun, *op. cit.*, p. 642.
[37] Schmidlin-Braun, *op. cit.*, p. 634.

the regular clergy, Spaniards, tended to look down on the seculars, mostly Filipinos or mestizos. Aguinaldo, who in the 1890's led a revolt against Spain, accused the religious orders of appropriating the lands of the laity and usurping the prerogatives of the Filipino seculars. He demanded that Filipino bishops be appointed. He chose a Filipino priest, Aglipay y Labayan, to head the Filipino church. Aglipay called an ecclesiastical assembly, which approved his appointment. The original purpose was not separation from Rome but a hierarchy of Filipinos. Rome would not assent, and Aglipay, somewhat reluctantly, was elected (1902) archbishop of what was called the Independent Catholic Church of the Philippines (alternatively the *Iglesia Filipina Independiente,* or the Filipino Independent Church) and several other Filipino priests were made bishops. Through the influence of one of its prominent members who had been in touch with radical thought in Europe the new body adopted a theologically liberal position and sought fellowship with the Unitarians. It was therefore regarded by Rome as both schismatic and heretical. It sought to hold possession of the church buildings, but for the most part the American courts decided against it. One of the chief problems of the *Iglesia Filipina Independiente* was the quality of both its clergy and its laity. Few were highly educated. Yet it numbered hundreds of thousands of members and retained control of about a seventh of the church edifices.[38]

Annexation by the United States was followed by far-reaching changes. For the most part the people of the United States, when they thought about them at all, regarded the Philippines as a trust to be prepared for self-government and with the kind of democracy which the Americans had developed. One of the early steps towards the attainment of that goal was the beginning of a system of public education on the pattern with which Americans were familiar. It was secular, but many of the teachers who came to put it into effect had motives of Christian origin.

Also as an early sequel to annexation, if less extensive in its immediate effects, was the introduction of Protestantism. Because of the close alliance of the Roman Catholic Church with the civil government, under the Spanish regime Protestantism had been unable to gain a foothold. The British and Foreign Bible Society had attempted to distribute the Scriptures, in part in translation into one of the local languages, but with only transient success. Protestant missionary leaders in the United States saw in annexation a challenge and, spurred by the rapidly rising interest in foreign missions that characterized the nineteenth century, several denominations sent representatives who began continuing enterprises. Before many months the Northern Presbyterians and the Northern Methodists, the latter stirred by the kindling vision of Thoburn, had included the islands in their programmes. They were followed shortly by the Northern Baptists, the Disciples of Christ, the United Brethren, the Protestant

[38] Latourette, *op. cit.,* Vol. V, pp. 267, 268.

Episcopalians, the American Board of Commissioners for Foreign Missions, and the Christian and Missionary Alliance, and a little later by the Seventh Day Adventists and the Young Men's Christian Association. Except for the British and Foreign Bible Society, all the Protestant efforts were from the United States, and that organization soon divided responsibility with the American Bible Society. All but the Episcopalians directed their major attention to the Roman Catholic majority. Wishing not to be seeming to win proselytes from another Christian communion, the Episcopalians concentrated on Americans and the animistic Igorots. Faced with the monolithic structure of the Roman Catholic Church, Protestants early developed various forms of coöperation, among them a division of territory to avoid overlapping and the Union Theological Seminary in Manila. Protestantism grew rapidly in adherents and Filipino leadership and initiative quickly emerged.[39]

The Roman Catholic Church rose to the crisis presented by annexation, the protest led by Aglipay, and Protestantism. The Vatican sought to replace some of the Spanish bishops with Americans and to keep from returning to the islands those of the Spanish friars who were unacceptable to their flocks. Since in 1903 the number of regulars was only 246 as against more than 1,000 in 1898, the Roman Catholic Church had the opportunity of injecting fresh blood into its clergy. A number of American priests came, although some found adjustment to the situation so difficult that they returned home. To supply the islands with nationals familiar with American ways, Filipinos were sent to seminaries in the United States for education. Some Filipinos were raised to the episcopate. Several societies and congregations sent missionaries from European countries other than Spain. Recruits from Spain again began to arrive. Changes were effected in the Roman Catholic schools to meet the new conditions. Additional bishoprics were created.[40]

SUMMARY

From this rapid survey of South-east Asia and its fringing islands it must be apparent that in that region, as in India, Christianity was more to be reckoned with at the close than at the beginning of the nineteenth century. In each country not only were missionaries from the West far more numerous, but Christians of indigenous stocks had multiplied several fold and Christian communities were present among several peoples where they had not been known in 1815. The increase was chiefly but by no means entirely among folk of animistic religions and primitive cultures. It was through both Roman Catholics and Protestants. In all the countries the Roman Catholic Church had been present before the nineteenth century but had languished in the eighteenth century. In every

[39] *Ibid.*, pp. 270–272.
[40] W. Cameron Forbes, *The Philippine Islands* (Boston, Houghton Mifflin Co., 2 vols., 1928), Vol. II, pp. 60, 64; Schwager in *Zeitschrift für Missionswissenschaft*, Vol. IV, pp. 212–215.

country in the nineteenth century it was reinvigorated and expanded. Before 1815 Protestantism had been represented in Ceylon, in the East Indies, and, briefly, in Burma. In the nineteenth century it was strengthened where it had previously existed and in other countries was introduced for the first time. Although in 1914 in the area taken as a whole Roman Catholics far outnumbered Protestants, the proportionate growth of the latter was more impressive. As elsewhere, leadership in the nascent churches was still predominantly Western —paralleling the political and economic Western imperialism of the period. But indigenous leadership was beginning to emerge.

Christianity was having an increasing impact outside as well as within the circles of avowed adherents. It came partly through schools and medical service. Much, too, was felt in the policies of two colonial powers, Great Britain and the Netherlands. Each had among its officials men who endeavoured to put their Christian faith into practice both in their official duties and in their informal contacts. The coming to power of a frankly Christian government in the Netherlands, especially under Kuyper, brought a policy in the East Indies which had the welfare of the governed more at heart than had its predecessors. In Sarawak James Brooke sought to make his rule express his Christian faith. The programme of the United States in the Philippines was shaped to no small extent by consciences sensitized by Christianity. As elsewhere in the non-Occidental world, selfish exploitation still characterized much of the impact on that region of the allegedly Christian West. But in 1914 more than at the dawn of the nineteenth century it was being modified and in part countered by what issued from the Christian faith.

CHAPTER XIX

China

I N THE nineteenth century the Chinese Empire was the largest realm under one government outside Christendom. In population it contained in the Chinese themselves—who constituted the overwhelming majority—the most numerous fairly homogeneous body of mankind on the entire planet. In addition were several racial minorities. The Chinese had created one of the greatest civilizations thus far developed by man, and one which had profoundly influenced their neighbours. They regarded their country as the Middle Kingdom and looked upon other peoples with disdain as barbarians.

The civilization of China was based upon Confucianism. The Confucian tradition was perpetuated by a political structure built on the Confucian theory, by an educational system culminating in civil service examinations through which the bureaucracy was recruited and which indoctrinated the scholar and official class with Confucian principles, and by a family system permeated by Confucian ideals. Buddhism, Taoism, and an indigenous polytheism governed much of the religious life, but the pattern of life was largely determined by Confucianism.

At the outset of the nineteenth century the Chinese were proudly endeavouring to keep aloof from the Occident. They refused diplomatic relations on equal terms and permitted foreign trade only through one port, Canton, and on conditions which proved galling to the Westerners. Throughout most of the century they resisted the growing pressure of the Western world and attempted to preserve their historic way of life. They were handicapped by the progressive decay of the ruling dynasty, the Ch'ing, composed of the descendants of the Manchus who had conquered the country in the seventeenth century. In the seventeenth and eighteenth centuries the Manchus had given the empire some able rulers, but in the nineteenth century the quality progressively deteriorated and the dynasty proved quite incapable of providing the leadership which would enable the Chinese to adjust themselves successfully to the revolutionary currents impinging upon them from the expanding Occident.

Successive blows left the Chinese prostrate. The first was a war with Great Britain in 1839-1842, with resistance to the importation of opium as the ostensible cause, but fundamentally because of the unwillingness of the English to conform to the conditions imposed by China on their commerce. China was defeated, and treaties followed which gave the British possession of Hong Kong, opened five ports for foreign residence and commerce, and accorded foreigners extraterritorial status. These treaties satisfied neither the foreigners nor the Chinese and out of the ensuing friction came a second war, in 1856–1860, in which the British and the French joined in again defeating China. The treaties which were imposed on China in 1858 and 1860 opened more ports to foreign residence and commerce, allowed foreigners to travel anywhere in the empire, provided for diplomatic intercourse on the basis of equality, conceded to missionaries the privilege of teaching the Christian faith, and guaranteed to Chinese permission to become Christians. Then for a generation conservative and able Chinese and Manchus supported the dynasty in the effort to maintain the inherited Confucian culture. In 1894–1895 defeat by Japan, followed by steps which threatened the partition of the empire by European powers, stimulated efforts at radical adjustments to the mounting revolutionary forces. A violent and unintelligent conservative reaction in 1900 led by the Boxers provoked an invasion by the Western powers and Japan which made of China an occupied country. In 1904–1905 the Chinese were further humiliated by a war between Japan and Russia fought on their soil while they had to stand helplessly by.

In attempts to regain full independence, the Chinese took measures which resulted in drastic changes. In 1905 the historic civil service examinations were abolished and beginnings were made of an educational system modeled on those of Western origin. Thus one of the bulwarks of the Confucian civilization collapsed. A second bulwark disappeared in 1911–1912 when the Manchu rulers and with them the Confucian monarchy were swept into the discard. The Chinese entered upon a perilous experiment with a republic, adapted from what they saw in the West. Although they had demonstrated their ability in the development of a political structure which for centuries, with some interruptions, had held together in "China Proper" a land area nearly as large as that of Western Europe, and, in its widest extent, reached in the eighteenth century, an empire larger than all Europe, they had no experience with a republic and floundered about in their struggles to make it work. The near anarchy which followed did not reach its nadir until after 1914 and then, in mid-century, was followed by a Communist regime which destroyed most of such remnants of the Confucian civilization as had persisted.

Would Christianity become an integral and potent element in the new China which was emerging out of the impact of the revolutionary West?

Pre-Nineteenth-Century Christianity

Christianity had been introduced three times to China and twice had completely disappeared.

The first introduction was in the seventh century. It came when China was being ruled by the T'ang Dynasty, which at its height shared with the Arab Empire the distinction of having under it the most widely extended and most powerful realm on the contemporary planet. Many foreigners were attracted. Among them were Nestorian Christians from Central and Western Asia. Christians were found in a number of places. Most of them seem to have been foreigners, but some converts were made. In the middle of the ninth century, after Christianity had been present for slightly over two centuries, a proscription of Buddhism by the emperor was made to include Christianity. By some time in the tenth century no Christians remained.[1]

Christianity was introduced the second time in the thirteenth century, in connexion with the rule of the Mongols. The Mongols had brought under their sway China, Korea, much of Central and Western Asia, and part of Russia— the largest empire thus far seen. They were tolerant religiously and under that tolerance Christianity was represented by more than one of its branches. Nestorianism, which had survived among peoples on the borders of China, once more had centres in that country. Alans, Christians from the Caucasus, provided the Mongols with a military contingent. Western Europeans, Roman Catholics, made their way to China in various capacities. Many were merchants. Some were Franciscan missionaries. The Nestorians seem to have been largely and perhaps entirely non-Chinese. The Franciscans won a few thousand converts, some from Nestorianism, others from non-Christian faiths. But the revival of Christianity under the Mongols was short-lived. The expulsion of the Mongols and the end of their dynasty (1368) combined with other factors made for the disappearance of Christianity both within and on the borders of China. Traces may have survived into the sixteenth century, but early in the seventeenth century, after careful search, the Jesuits could discover no existing Christians.[2]

It was the Jesuits who once more introduced Christianity to China. Their pioneer in East Asia, Francis Xavier, died off the coast of China in 1552 in a vain attempt to enter the mainland. Later in that century other Jesuits arrived and one of them, Matteo Ricci, obtained a foothold in Peking. They were aided by the Portuguese colony in Macao, near Canton. Franciscans, Dominicans, and members of the *Société des Missions Étrangères* of Paris followed. Some came by way of the Philippines after the Spanish conquest of those islands. Towards the end of the seventeenth century, under the friendly eye of the Manchu emperor who is usually best known by his reign name, K'ang Hsi, Christianity prospered, and by the beginning of the eighteenth century Christians may have

[1] Latourette, *A History of Christian Missions in China*, pp. 51–55; A. C. Moule, *Christians in China before the Year 1550* (London, Society for Promoting Christian Knowledge, 1930, pp. xvi, 293), pp. 27–93; P. Y. Saeki, *The Nestorian Documents and Relics in China* (Tokyo, The Maruzen Co., 1937, pp. 515, 30, 96), *passim*.

[2] Latourette, *op. cit.*, pp. 61–77; Moule, *op. cit.*, pp. 78 ff.

numbered between 200,000 and 300,000, scattered in all the eighteen provinces except Kansu.

Then followed more than a century of adversity. A prolonged dispute, the "rites controversy," over the attitudes to be adopted towards Chinese culture and especially the ceremonies in honour of Confucius and the family ancestors, rent and reduced the missionary body and lost the friendship of the K'ang Hsi emperor. Persecutions in China, the decline of missionary zeal in Europe, the expulsion of the Jesuits from French, Portuguese, and Spanish territories, the dissolution of the Society of Jesus by the Pope, and the French Revolution seemed to presage a third disappearance of the faith from China. At the dawn of the nineteenth century Christians may have numbered 200,000 or even close to 300,000. They were served by Chinese as well as foreign priests. But imperial edicts proscribing the faith were still unrepealed and martyrdoms were not unusual.[3]

RENEWED ROMAN CATHOLIC GROWTH

As in many other parts of the world, the nineteenth century witnessed a revival in Roman Catholic missions and the growth of Roman Catholic communities. The renewal had begun before the first treaties but was furthered by them and by the mounting missionary interest in Roman Catholic circles in Europe. After 1815 reinforcements came to the missionary staff. The treaties of 1842–1844 with their opening of five ports to foreign residence, their cession of Hong Kong, and their provision of extraterritoriality brought enlarged opportunity. Imperial edicts of 1844 and 1846 permitted the erection of churches in the open ports and granted to Roman Catholics the liberty of exercising their faith. Although missionaries were forbidden to travel outside the five ports, if they did not do so too conspicuously they were not molested. The Society of Jesus, now restored, sent representatives to China. Bodies already present increased their staffs. In 1858 a new organization, the Seminary of Foreign Missions of Milan, sent men. For the better administration of the church, additional vicariates apostolic were created.[4]

The treaties of 1858 and 1860 greatly expanded the opportunities for missionaries, both Roman Catholic and Protestant. The one of 1860 with France promised to restore to the Roman Catholics their religious and benevolent institutions which had been confiscated in the persecutions. The Chinese text differed from the French text in providing that the toleration of the Roman Catholic faith would be published throughout the country and that French missionaries would be permitted to rent and purchase land in all the provinces and to erect on it

[3] Latourette, *op. cit.,* pp. 78–198; Arnold H. Rowbotham, *Missionary and Mandarin. The Jesuits at the Court of China* (Berkeley, University of California Press, 1942, pp. xi, 374), *passim;* Columba Cary-Elwes, *China and the Cross: A Survey of Missionary History* (New York, P. J. Kenedy & Sons, 1957, pp. xii, 323), pp. 73–180.
[4] Latourette, *op. cit.,* pp. 228–244.

such buildings as they wished. The French Government maintained a protectorate over Roman Catholic missions from whatever country they came. Although the Chinese protested that the French rather than the Chinese version of the convention of 1860 was authoritative, France, in an additional convention of 1865, virtually obtained the confirmation of the concession which the latter version incorporated.[5]

In the forty years after the treaties of 1858 and 1860 the Roman Catholic missionaries greatly expanded their activities. Orders, congregations, and societies at work before those years enlarged their staffs and additional ones sent representatives. Although most of the new arrivals were from France, Italian, Spanish, Belgian, and German missionaries also came. Official figures of 1896 and 1897 gave the total foreign missionary force as 759 and the number of the faithful as 532,448.[6]

Persecutions and riots punctuated the course of Christian missions, whether Roman Catholic or Protestant. They arose chiefly from popular resentment, often reinforced by the scholar class, who had been reared on Confucianism, against the threat of Christianity to the historic Chinese culture. The most serious one directed primarily against the Roman Catholics was in 1870 in Tientsin. It was as much anti-French as anti-Catholic. A mob destroyed an orphanage, the French consulate, and the adjoining church and killed several foreigners, especially Frenchmen, and a number of Chinese. Anti-Christian demonstrations followed in other parts of China. Foreign warships were dispatched to Tientsin, Chinese officials held responsible were punished, and an indemnity was exacted.[7] Roman Catholics suffered severely in the Boxer uprising. The precise number of those killed could not be determined, but one list reported five bishops, thirty-one other European clergy, nine European sisters, and two Marist lay brothers as having perished.[8] The total of Chinese Catholics who lost their lives seems to have been more than thirty thousand.

With the lowering of resistance and the beginning of rapid change which followed the disastrous war with Japan and especially the suppression of the Boxer outbreak, the number of Roman Catholics, both missionaries and Chinese, quickly mounted. The totals of foreign priests rose from 1,075 in 1901 to 1,469 in 1912.[9] At the close of 1912 Roman Catholics were said to number 1,431,258.[10]

The Roman Catholics placed their chief emphasis upon winning converts and

---

[5] *Ibid.*, pp. 276, 277, 309.

[6] *Missiones Catholicae Cura S. Congregationis de Propaganda Fide,* Rome, 1897. The 1895 edition gave the number of Catholics as 581,575, but the reason for the discrepancy is not clear.

[7] Latourette, *op. cit.*, pp. 346–356.

[8] L'Œuvre de la Propagation de la Foi, *Dix Années d'Apostolat Catholiques dans les Missions* (*1898–1907*), pp. 52, 53.

[9] Latourette, *op. cit.*, pp. 538, 539.

[10] *Zeitschrift für Missionswissenschaft,* Vol. IV, p. 42.

building the Church. Various methods were employed to attract catechumens. For a few decades after the treaties of 1858 with their toleration clauses some missionaries used their influence with consular authorities to intimidate Chinese officials and to interfere in lawsuits on the claim that those whom they favoured were Christians and were being brought into court because of their faith. As the news got abroad, litigants professed to be Christians to obtain the help of the powerful foreigner. However, since at least 1880 the official attitude of the church was unfriendly to that method and in 1908 the prohibition was reiterated and amplified. Famine relief was often given on condition that the recipients submit to instruction in the faith. Catechumens among the farmers were sometimes supported during the winter months when they were otherwise idle and with the provision that they learn the catechism. As an act of mercy, abandoned infants in danger of death were baptized, and they and others born to the poor were brought into orphanages and reared as Christians. Where possible, entire families rather than individuals were instructed, so that conversion would be by the natural groupings. Here and there Christians were gathered into villages. Much emphasis was placed on education. Elementary schools were provided for the children of Christians and in them the instruction was in the rudiments of reading and writing and in the tenets and practices of the faith. Until 1900 most of the secondary and higher education was for the preparation of teachers for these schools, catechists, and priests. With the rising demand after that year for education of a Western kind, more schools of secondary and higher grade were begun.

Missionaries were quite aware that a large proportion of the catechumens sought instruction from unworthy motives but hoped that after two or three generations of Christian nurture the character of their flocks would improve. They sought to raise up a Chinese clergy, but to ensure its loyalty to the faith insisted that candidates for the priesthood come from old Christian families.

In keeping with the general attitude of Westerners towards the Chinese, Roman Catholic missionaries treated the indigenous clergy as inferiors. Not until after 1914, with the rise of Chinese nationalism, did they begin to deal with them as equals. As the twentieth century advanced Rome insisted that more responsibility be placed on the Chinese priests and raised some to the episcopate.[11]

<h2>PROTESTANTISM</h2>

Protestantism was much later in being introduced than was the Roman Catholic form of the faith. But proportionately it made more rapid progress and touched the life of the country through a greater variety of channels.

The first Protestant missionary, Robert Morrison (1782–1834), an appointee of the London Missionary Society, reached China in 1807. Unlike the Roman

[11] Latourette, *op. cit.*, pp. 331–343, 547–562.

Catholic missionaries of the period, he had no Christian groups to which he could go clandestinely. He could remain in China only as an interpreter of the East India Company and in the strictly limited foreign mercantile community in Canton. Not until 1814 did he baptize his first convert. Yet in his little over a quarter-century in China he translated the Bible, prepared a Chinese-English dictionary, translated other Christian literature, wrote pamphlets on the faith, and was chiefly responsible for the founding of a Christian school, the Anglo-Chinese College, at Malacca.[12]

In the pre-treaty years other Protestant missionaries came, most of them from the British Isles and the United States. One German was outstanding—Karl Friedrich August Gützlaff, under the Netherlands Missionary Society. A few were able to remain in Canton and the neighbouring Macao, but others sought to reach the Chinese diaspora in the East Indies, Malaya, and Bangkok.[13]

The first treaties, with the opening of the five ports to foreign residence and the cession of Hong Kong to Great Britain, were followed by the arrival of additions to the Protestant missionary staffs of societies already represented and by the coming of new societies. Gützlaff, for example, with his enthusiasm and vision, was responsible for several German groups, including Basel missionaries to South China (among them a Swede) and Moravians who sought to penetrate Tibet by way of the Indian frontier.[14]

A movement of large dimensions which arose in the 1840's, in part through contact with Protestantism, was that which bore the name of T'ai P'ing. It impinged upon much of China with profound effects and in the next century was regarded by many as the initial stage of the revolution which issued from the impact of the West upon the empire. The leader of the movement, Hung Hsiu-ch'üan, had come in touch with Christianity through a Protestant missionary and through literature prepared by a Chinese Protestant convert. The movement arose in the South from a variety of causes. It sought to displace the Manchus by a new dynasty which it called T'ai P'ing, "Great Peace," with Hung as the first emperor. It had a marked religious character which derived some of its features from what Hung had learned of Christianity. It was in the tradition of other movements in China's history with political ambitions and religious features, but the earlier ones had not borrowed from Christianity. The T'ai P'ing forces moved north into the Yangtze Valley and established their headquarters at Nanking. Chinese and Manchus with Confucian training who saw in the movement a threat to law and order and the historic way of life rose to

[12] *Memoirs of the Life and Labours of Robert Morrison . . . Compiled by His Widow, with critical notices of his Chinese works by Samuel Kidd* (London, Longman, Orme, Brown, Green and Longmans, 2 vols., 1839), *passim;* Marshall Broomhall, *Robert Morrison, Master Builder* (London, Church Missionary Society, 1924, pp. xvi, 238), *passim.*

[13] Latourette, *op. cit.,* pp. 213–227; Herman Schlyter, *Karl Gützlaff als Missionar in China* (Lund, C. W. K. Gleerup, 1946, pp. viii, 318), *passim.*

[14] Latourette, *op. cit.,* pp. 244–270; Herman Schlyter, *Theodor Hamberg, den förste svenske Kinamissionären* (Lund, C. W. K. Gleerup, 1952, pp. 266), *passim.*

the support of the decrepit dynasty and put down the T'ai P'ing revolt, but no until 1864 and after the rebellion had been responsible for the death of hundred of thousands and had laid waste much of the lower valley of the Yangtze. Here was another of the perversions of Christianity which were features of the revolutionary age and which issued in colossal suffering.[15]

The treaties of 1858 and 1860 were followed by the reinforcement of the staff of societies already in China, by the coming of additional societies, and by the extension of Protestant missions throughout the country. The number of Protestant missionaries in China in 1858 was said to have been 81, representing 20 societies. In 1889, or in a little over thirty years, it was reported to be 1,296 (including 391 wives), from 41 societies. Of the 1889 total 56.5 per cent. were British, 39.5 per cent. were from the United States, and 4 per cent. were from the Continent of Europe.[16]

Of the Protestant societies the one which ultimately had the largest staff was the China Inland Mission. Its founder and leader was James Hudson Taylor (1832–1905),[17] usually more briefly known as Hudson Taylor. Reared in a devout Methodist home, in his teens he had the characteristic Evangelical experience of conversion through faith in the atoning work of Christ after a period of restless unhappiness. He dedicated himself to missions in China. He prepared by studying medicine and by living a life of complete dependence on God for all his needs, material as well as spiritual. He went to China in 1853 under the short-lived China Evangelization Society, which owed its origin in part to Gützlaff. After four years he severed his connexion with it because, contrary to what he believed to be a Scriptural injunction and indicating a lack of faith, it went into debt. For a time he lived without the undergirding of a missionary society, in trust in God. In 1860 his health gave way and with his wife he returned to England. There he completed his medical course. But he was burdened by the tragedy of China's millions, who, he believed, without the Gospel were going out into eternal darkness. He was convinced that God did not want them to perish but was simply waiting for some one to have the faith to claim His inexhaustible resources to give them a knowledge of Christ. In an act of

[15] The literature on the T'ai P'ing Rebellion is enormous and continues to appear. For a summary with extensive references to the sources see Latourette, *op. cit.,* pp. 282, 302. Major sources are Theodore Hamberg, *The Visions of Hung-Siu-Tshuen* (Hong Kong, 1854), and Thomas Taylor Meadows, *The Chinese and Their Rebellions* (London, Smith, Elder and Co., 1856, pp. ix, 656), pp. 137 ff. Excellent accounts are Wilhelm Oehler, *Die Taiping Bewegung* (Gütersloh, C. Bertelsmann, 1923, pp. 174), William James Hail, *Tseng Kuo-fan and the Taiping Rebellion* (New Haven, Conn., Yale University Press, 1927, pp. xvii, 422), and Eugene Powers Boardman, *Christian Influence upon the Ideology of the Taiping Rebellion* (Madison, University of Wisconsin Press, 1952, pp. xi, 188).

[16] Latourette, *op. cit.,* pp. 405, 406.

[17] James Hudson Taylor, *A Retrospect* (Philadelphia, The China Inland Mission, 3rd ed., no date, pp. 136), *passim;* Dr. and Mrs. Howard Taylor, *Hudson Taylor in Early Years. The Growth of a Soul* (Philadelphia, The China Inland Mission, 1912, pp. xxi, 511), *passim;* Marshall Broomhall, *Hudson Taylor, the Man Who Believed God* (London, The China Inland Mission, 1929, pp. xii, 244), *passim.*

surrender he decided that he would be that man. In 1865 he asked God for "twenty-four willing skilful workers"—two for each of the eleven provinces then without a Protestant missionary and two for Mongolia. To support them he organized the China Inland Mission. It was to be undenominational, accepting members of any Protestant body if they gave promise of being good missionaries. Its missionaries were to have no guaranteed salary but were to trust God for their subsistence. The Mission was never to go into debt. To avoid competition with other missions, no direct solicitation of funds was to be undertaken: China's spiritual needs were to be set forth with the faith that God would move His servants to supply what was required. The missionaries were to go to areas which were without other representatives of Protestantism. They were not to concern themselves with organizing congregations but were, rather, to present the Gospel to as many as possible and leave to others the gathering of converts into churches. The first appointees left for China in 1865 and the initial large party, of twenty-two, in 1866. Affiliated bodies sprang up in several countries in the Occident. In 1895 the China Inland Mission had 641 missionaries, 462 Chinese helpers, and 260 stations and out-stations. This, it will be seen, was approximately half the Protestant missionary force in China at that time. Never robust physically and often ill, Taylor retained the leadership until 1903 and, fittingly, died in Changsha, capital of Hunan, the province which had been most resistant to the entrance of foreigners. After his death the Mission continued its growth. It drew its strength from the kind of Evangelicalism represented by Taylor and was evidence of the extent of those convictions.[18]

The Boxer outbreak of 1900 brought death to even more Protestant than Roman Catholic missionaries, and, in the enlarged opportunity attending the progressive collapse of the old civilization which preceded and followed that fateful year, Protestants multiplied their efforts to aid the Chinese as they moved into the revolutionary age. Most of the societies previously in China enlarged their operations and others were represented for the first time. In 1914 Protestant missionaries were said to number 5,462.[19] This, it will be seen, was over four times the total of 1889 and also far more than the Roman Catholic missionary force.

The Protestant approach to China was multiform. In addition to what might be called the "broadcast" methods of the China Inland Mission the emphasis continued on the printed page in which Morrison had been a pioneer. Much attention was paid to translating the Bible. Some versions were in the classical language. Others were produced in the various vernaculars. For the benefit of the thousands who could not read the Chinese characters, more than one of the latter were in romanized forms. The British, American, and Scottish Bible so-

---

[18] Marshall Broomhall, *The Jubilee Story of the China Inland Mission* (London, Morgan & Scott, 1915, pp. xvi, 386), *passim*.
[19] *China Mission Year Book, 1915*, p. xiv.

cieties shared with less well-known agencies in the distribution of the Scriptures and greatly expanded their operations. Several societies and publishing houses. The chief of them, what became known as the Christian Literature Society, produced and distributed hundreds of thousands of copies of books, tracts, and periodicals. They also joined in spreading the Christian message as well as nourishing Christians in the faith. In a land which by tradition held the printed page in great respect, the use of the printing press was highly significant.[20]

Protestant missions also stressed education. From their beginning they had done so. During most of the nineteenth century theirs were the chief institutions through which a knowledge of Western learning could be acquired. So long as the historic civil service examinations survived they could not be popular, for they did not give the required preparation for those tests as well as did the traditional type of school and their graduates found employment chiefly in the missions and in foreign business firms. But when in 1905 the ancient examinations were swept aside and Western learning was in high demand, as one of the few easily available sources of that learning they flourished. In contrast with the Roman Catholics, the Protestants paid relatively slight attention to elementary schools and placed more emphasis upon secondary and higher education. Increasingly Protestants, and especially those from the United States, pooled the resources of two or more denominations in supporting their colleges and universities. The colleges and universities were strategically located, so that few major sections of the country were without one.[21]

Protestants were active in bringing Western medicine and surgery to China and were pioneers in the creation of medical and nursing professions utilizing the medical science of the Occident. The latter half of the nineteenth century witnessed striking advances in Western medicine. Antiseptics, anesthetics, vaccines, and the development of better treatment of such diseases as tuberculosis and of public health measures made rapid strides. The hospital and the dispensary with their physician or physicians and nurses utilizing these achievements became a characteristic feature of the Protestant mission station. The China Medical Missionary Association held its first meeting in 1890 and was the pioneer national organization of physicians practising Western medicine. The training of Chinese in that style of medicine was begun in connexion with mission hospitals, and before 1914 medical schools under Protestant auspices were appearing.[22] In 1913 William Wesley Peter, supported by the YMCA, inaugurated a programme of lectures on public health which reached most of the main centres of the country.[23]

In a wide variety of other ways Protestant missionaries sought to meet what

[20] Latourette, *op. cit.*, pp. 429–441, 646–652.
[21] *Ibid.*, pp. 441–451, 622–646.
[22] *Ibid.*, pp. 452–460, 638–640, 652–656.
[23] *Ibid.*, p. 590.

they deemed the clamant needs of the Chinese and in doing so introduced procedures adapted from what had been devised in the Occident. They initiated public playgrounds, units of the Red Cross, social service clubs, labour-saving machinery in the spinning of cotton, and methods for improving the quality of silk-worm eggs. They fought the age-long custom of binding the feet of women, combatted the production, sale, and use of opium (then a major curse which had been stimulated by Western merchants), sought to ameliorate the lot of the blind, the deaf, and the dumb, gave much attention to the relief of the periodic famines, founded orphan asylums (although not as many as those conducted by the Roman Catholics), stimulated interest in sports and physical education, and did much to acquaint Chinese with the principles and achievements of Western science.[24]

Protestant missionaries also sought through translations and through books of their own writing to familiarize the Chinese with Western history, international law, and other aspects of Occidental civilization which they believed would be of assistance to the Chinese in making their adjustment to the revolutionary age. One of the outstanding missionaries in the production of that literature was the Welsh Baptist Timothy Richard (1845–1919). The real founder of the English Baptist mission in China, he helped in famine relief and endeavoured to introduce Chinese scholars to Western science in the hope that it would contribute to the prevention of famines. As secretary of the Christian Literature Society in the 1890's and the years immediately after 1900 when to preserve their country from subjugation by the West the Chinese were groping towards an appropriation of such elements of Occidental culture as would save it from that fate, Richard produced books and articles on things Western which were eagerly read by leaders in the transition.[25]

Although they approached the Chinese from a number of angles, many Protestant missionaries were eager to help bring into being Chinese churches rooted in the soil which would become an integral part of the empire's life. The numbers of Chinese Christians of the Protestant wing of the faith increased rapidly —proportionately more so than did the Roman Catholics—although having entered China much later, in 1914 Protestantism had not enrolled as many as had the Roman Catholics. In 1898 Protestant communicants were said to have totalled 80,682 and in 1915, 268,652. In the latter year, with 268,652 communicants, 62,274 baptized non-communicants, and 190,958 others under Christian instruction, the total Protestant community was reported to be 526,108.[26] Protestants were also beginning the recruiting and education of a Chinese clergy and were more and more seeking to bring the Chinese churches to the point where

[24] *Ibid.*, pp. 460–465, 588, 599, 656–662.
[25] William E. Soothill, *Timothy Richard of China* (London, Seeley, Service & Co., 1924, pp. 330), *passim;* Timothy Richard, *Forty-Five Years in China. Reminiscences* (New York, Frederick A. Stokes Co., 1916, pp. 384), *passim.*
[26] Latourette, *op. cit.,* p. 680.

they would be self-governing, self-supporting, and self-propagating.

As in India, the multiplicity of societies and denominations stimulated efforts some of them strikingly successful, at coöperation across denominational lines Numbers were for special phases of the missionary programme, such as the translation of the Bible, medical care, Sunday Schools, and education on the provincial and national level. Still others were enterprises which enlisted the support of individuals of various denominations, such as the Christian Endeav our movement and the Young Men's and Young Women's Christian Associa tions. Unions of branches of the same communion but from different countrie were achieved. Thus in 1862 the missions of the Reformed Church in America and the English Presbyterian Church in and near Amoy joined in a single pres bytery: a Chinese church arose which was neither English nor American.[27] In 1912 the first general synod convened of the *Chung Hua Shêng Kung Hue* ("The Holy Catholic Church of China"), which sprang from the missions o the various societies of the Anglican Communion.[28] As in a number of other parts of the world, in several sections what were called comity agreements were entered into by two or more missions to prevent duplication of effort.

Comprehensive national missionary conferences embracing all China were held in 1877,[29] 1890,[30] and 1907.[31] Significantly, they met in Shanghai, the city which had grown to major proportions out of the commerce between China and the West. Thus, although not by design, they symbolized the close connex ion between Protestant missions and other phases of the impact upon China o the expanding and revolutionary Occident. It was also significant that they were frankly "missionary" conferences, composed mainly or entirely of men and women from the Occident, with few or no Chinese members. Hence they gave evidence of the dominance of the foreign element in the emerging Protestant enterprise. That was partly because Protestantism in China was too young to have produced many able Chinese leaders. It was also because Protestant mis sions, like their Roman Catholic counterpart, were as yet the ecclesiastical face of Western imperialism. Each national conference was larger than its predeces sor. Each gave rise to a more tangible organization for advancing and coördi nating the approach of Protestants to China. The 1907 conference, held on the centennial of the arrival of Robert Morrison, recommended a federal union under the title of the Christian Federation of China and projected provincia or regional councils made up of Chinese and foreigners and a national council

[27] *Ibid.*, p. 412.

[28] *China Mission Year Book, 1914*, pp. 218, 219.

[29] *Records of the General Conference of the Protestant Missionaries of China, held at Shanghai May 10–24, 1877* (Shanghai, Presbyterian Mission Press, 1878, pp. iii, 492), *passim.*

[30] *Records of the General Conference of the Protestant Missionaries of China, held in Shanghai May 7–20, 1890* (Shanghai, Presbyterian Mission Press, 1890, pp. lxviii, 744), *passim.*

[31] *China Centenary Missionary Conference Records* (New York, American Tract Society, no date, pp. xxxvii, 823), *passim.*

composed of delegates from the provincial councils to convene at least once in every five years.

In 1913 Mott came to China as chairman of the Continuation Committee of the (Edinburgh) World Missionary Conference of 1910; he held six regional conferences and (in Shanghai) a national conference. In them Chinese were more numerous than in the earlier conferences. In the national gathering comprehensive plans were made for furthering Protestantism in China, among them emphasis upon the training of Chinese leaders. The China Continuation Committee was organized to carry on the work of the conference, and not less than a third of its members were to be Chinese.[32] From the 1913 gathering, but not until after World War I, came the National Christian Council of China. Clearly Protestantism was becoming better rooted in China, with mounting Chinese leadership and with the designation "Christian" rather than "missionary."

The varied approach of Protestantism to China with its efforts to help the Chinese make a wholesome adjustment to the impact of the Occident had many results. Some were in the growth of churches and a wider acquaintance, even though superficial, with the Christian faith. Others were quite outside professedly Christian circles. Here they were more extensive than those of Roman Catholic missions. Perhaps because of their pre-nineteenth-century experience of chronic persecution, Roman Catholic missionaries made little attempt to influence the empire as a whole, but concentrated on building their church, and that as inconspicuously as possible. To trace all the ramifications of the influences of Protestantism on China and its changing culture would be impossible, for many were too intangible or too mixed with other factors to be measured. To describe even those which were fairly obvious would prolong this chapter out of all proper proportions. One spectacular and tragic contribution we have already noted—to the T'ai P'ing movement. Another, more ambiguous, was the share in the overthrow of the Ch'ing (Manchu) Dynasty and the inception of the republic. The major figure in that confused picture and the first provisional president of the republic was Sun Yat-sen. Sun Yat-sen owed his conversion and most of his formal education to Protestant missionaries. Precisely to what degree he was indebted to Protestantism for his idealism and the drive which made him outstanding in the revolutionary movement would be impossible to determine. Yet it is clear that Protestantism was in part responsible for him and thus for his place in the multiform revolution which convulsed China in the twentieth century.[33] A striking parallel was the contribution of Protestantism to India through Sun's contemporary, Gandhi.

[32] *The Continuation Committee Conferences in Asia 1912–1913*, pp. 321–367.
[33] On the education and baptism of Sun Yat-sen see Lyon Sharman, *Sun Yat-sen. His Life and Its Meaning. A Critical Biography* (New York, The John Day Company, 1934, pp. xvii, 418), pp. 9–27.

THE RUSSIAN ORTHODOX CHURCH IN CHINA

The Russian Orthodox Church participated, but in a numerically minor way, in the spread of Christianity in China. In 1685 a few Russian Orthodox, taken prisoners at Albazin on the Amur River, were brought to Peking, were given residence in the north-east corner of the city, and began a community which endured into the twentieth century. They were served by Russian clergy. In the eighteenth century a Russian mission, partly diplomatic and partly ecclesiastical, was maintained in Peking but did not attempt to convert the Chinese.[34] After the Russian treaty of 1858 some effort was made to win Chinese to the Orthodox faith. However, only a few conversions followed. In 1916 twenty missionaries and about five thousand baptized Chinese were reported.[35]

SUMMARY

As to most of the world outside the Occident, Christianity came to China in connexion with other aspects of the impact of the West. That impact was commercial and in the nineteenth century it was accompanied and followed by wars which issued in treaties that compromised the independence of the empire. Late in the century the partition of the country among European powers was threatened. After the Boxer outbreak China was virtually an occupied country, with the Westerners dominant.

Christianity was brought to China twice only to disappear, leaving few traces. The first introduction was in the seventh century, and not from Western Christendom but through the Nestorians from Central Asia. The second was in the thirteenth century, partly by Nestorians on the western fringe of China, partly by soldiers from the Caucasus, and partly by Franciscans from Western Europe who came in close association with merchants from that area.

The third introduction of Christianity was in the sixteenth century and was made possible by the Portuguese commercial power with its foothold in Macao and by the Spanish conquest of the Philippines. Until early in the nineteenth century that third advent of the faith was entirely through Roman Catholics. After what looked like a promising growth in the latter part of the seventeenth century, the eighteenth century brought adverse conditions which for a time seemed to presage a third extinction of the faith.

The commercial pressures of European powers, mainly Great Britain, in the mid-nineteenth century issued in wars against the resistant Chinese and treaties which gave Westerners access to China. Later in the century territorial ambitions were added to commercial pressures. Then began the collapse of the traditional civilization and the vast revolution affecting all aspects of the life of the Chinese which after 1914 swelled to ever greater proportions.

[34] Latourette, *op. cit.*, pp. 199, 200.
[35] *Ibid.*, pp. 486, 487.

The rising tide of life in both the Roman Catholic Church and Protestantism, which brought a striking growth in the missions of those two wings of Christianity, issued in rapidly mounting efforts to plant the faith in China. Roman Catholics expanded their staffs and for most of the century were under the protectorate of France. The first Protestant missionary arrived in 1807 and others followed. Missionaries helped in the negotiation of several of the treaties—Roman Catholics with French and British and Americans with British and American documents. Protestant missionaries multiplied even more rapidly than Roman Catholic personnel. In contrast with the Roman Catholics, who were prevailingly from the Continent of Europe, they were mostly from the British Isles and Dominions and the United States, at first more from the former but by 1914 more from the latter.

The Roman Catholics bent their efforts chiefly to creating the Church. By 1914 they could count nearly a million and a half in their fold.

In contrast, Protestants endeavoured in a variety of ways to broadcast the Gospel and to aid the Chinese in an adjustment to the Occidental invasion which would be of benefit to them. Proportionately adherents to their branch of the faith grew more rapidly than did the Roman Catholics, but in 1914 they still numbered only about a half-million. However, in education, medicine, and other aspects of the empire's life they were more influential than were the Roman Catholics. From them came unanticipated political effects—partly in helping to shape the T'ai P'ing movement in the mid-nineteenth century and partly in contributing through Sun Yat-sen to the fall of the Confucian form of government and the first experiments with a republic.

Although in 1914 its adherents numbered only about one in two hundred of the population—a much smaller percentage than in India—Christianity was having a pronounced effect upon the revolution which, arising from the impact of the Occident, in that year was still in its early stages.

CHAPTER XX

Korea

CHRISTIANITY was planted in Korea late and only after grievous persecutions. Its course was stormy and continued to be so as far into the twentieth century as the date of these volumes will permit us to recount it.

Korea's geographic position was unfortunate. The country was a peninsula which was located strategically between rival empires. For centuries the rivals were China and Japan. Later Russia and, after 1914, the United States loomed on the horizon. At the outset of the nineteenth century Korea was tributary to China, and its culture was partly that of its huge neighbour. It insisted on remaining aloof from the West. Only in 1876 was a treaty signed which partly opened the country to the outer world and that was with Japan. In the 1880's treaties followed with Western powers. Japan and China struggled for control and in 1894–1895 fought a war, part of which was waged on Korean soil. Japan won and her influence in the country mounted. In the 1890's Russia sought to extend her authority. Russia and Japan clashed, and in 1904–1905 a war between them left the latter incontestably the victor. In 1910 Japan formally annexed the country.

So far as we know, Christianity was first brought to Korea in the 1590's, and then only briefly. In that decade Hideyoshi, the master of Japan, sought to invade China by way of Korea. In his armies were a few Christians, the fruits of Roman Catholic missions. With them for a time was a Jesuit, but so far as is known such converts as he made were Japanese. The same decade saw the baptism of a few Korean slaves in Nagasaki, the chief centre of Christianity in Japan. When, also in the 1590's, the Japanese armies were withdrawn from Korea, presumably no Christians remained.[1]

The continuous presence of Christianity in Korea began in the 1770's. Through the periodic tribute embassies which went from Korea to Peking, books prepared by Roman Catholic missionaries in China were carried to Korea and were read in a scholarly circle. In 1783 a member of the embassy was baptized by missionaries in Peking. Returning to Korea he carried with him books and religious objects. A number of conversions followed, mainly from the official and scholar class. The converts made contact with the bishop in Peking and a Chinese priest whom he sent them arrived in 1793 but in 1801 was caught

---

[1] Dallet, *Histoire de l'Église de Corée*, Vol. I, pp. 2–10.

and executed. Indeed, from almost the beginning chronic and stubborn persecution was visited on the Christians. Anti-Christian edicts declared that Christianity threatened the loyalties inculcated by Confucianism and would be an opening wedge for European invasion. Yet a few Christians survived and in 1827 a letter from them reached Rome requesting aid.[2] In response Rome asked the *Société des Missions Étrangères* of Paris to assume the dangerous mission. Not until 1836 did one of its representatives succeed in making his way into the country. The next year a vicar apostolic arrived to whom the country had been assigned.[3] Heightened persecution promptly followed. In 1839 the vicar apostolic and his two foreign colleagues were tortured and executed. Several scores of Korean Christians suffered martyrdom.[4] In 1845 another vicar apostolic succeeded in making his way into the country and later was joined by other missionaries, all of the Paris Society. In 1857 he reported the number of Christians as being slightly over fifteen thousand.[5] In 1866 the storm of persecution again broke out and by September, 1868, two thousand Christians are said to have perished and two bishops and seven other missionaries to have been killed. The futile attempt of a French naval commander to come to their rescue both confirmed the Koreans in their fear that Christians were a threat to the independence of their country and gave them confidence in their ability to keep the foreigner at bay.[6] Yet, undiscouraged, Roman Catholic missionaries persisted in coming, and with the entrance of Korea into treaty relations with Western powers in the 1880's persecution lapsed. The numbers of Roman Catholics rapidly mounted. In 1900 they totalled 42,000 and in 1911 77,000.[7]

Protestants had a more extensive growth in Korea than did Roman Catholics. In the 1860's and 1870's their efforts included the translation of the New Testament into Korean and resulted in a few conversions. But not until 1884 did Protestant missionaries succeed in establishing residence in the country. In that year (Northern) American Presbyterians, (Northern) American Methodists, and Chinese Anglicans arrived. Eventually the numerically major missions were those of the American Presbyterians, both of the North and of the South. Presbyterianism was also strengthened by missionaries of that communion from Australia and Canada. Next were those of the American Methodists, also both Northern and Southern.[8] The Anglicans were represented by the Society for

---

[2] *Ibid.*, pp. 14–380, Vol. II, pp. 3–5.

[3] Launay, *Historie Générale de la Société des Missions-Étrangères*, Vol. II, pp. 575–583, Vol. III, pp. 62–71.

[4] *Ibid.*, Vol. III, pp. 67–77; Adrien Launay, *Société des Missions-Étrangères. Martyrs Français et Coréens 1838–1846 Béatifiés en 1925* (Paris, P. Tequi, 1925, pp. xv, 271), *passim*.

[5] Dallet, *op. cit.*, Vol. II, pp. 302 ff., 434.

[6] *Ibid.*, pp. 521 ff.

[7] *The Catholic Church in Korea* (Hongkong, Nazareth Printing Press, Paris Foreign Mission Society, 1924, pp. 106), p. 68.

[8] Paik, *The History of Protestant Missions in Korea, 1832–1910*, pp. 71–109, 185–187; Horace G. Underwood, *The Call of Korea* (Chicago, Fleming H. Revell Co., 3rd ed., 1908, pp. 204), pp.

the Propagation of the Gospel in Foreign Parts.[9] Some other organizations sent missionaries.[10]

The methods employed by Protestant missions resembled those in several other countries. The Bible was translated and circulated, partly with the aid of the Bible societies—British, Scottish, and American. Other Christian literature was produced. Protestant missionaries were pioneers in the introduction of Western medicine and in 1893 opened a medical school in Seoul in which several denominations coöperated. Protestant mission schools became major sources of Western learning, which in the decades immediately preceding 1914 was in great demand. Three Christian colleges arose—in Seoul and Pyeng Yang, major centres in the North and South, each supported by more than one American society. One of the three, Ewha, in Seoul, was for girls. Provision was made for theological education.[11]

Distinctive of Protestantism in Korea was the active part of the Korean Christians in the spread of the faith. One reason for this was a policy adopted early at the suggestion of John L. Nevius, a Presbyterian missionary in China during a visit in Seoul. It emphasized the winning of their neighbours by Christians, the support by their fellow Christians of Koreans giving their time to the Church and evangelism, the erection of church buildings by Korean gifts and in the local style of architecture, and the self-government of the Korean churches. But Nevius only gave impetus to what the Korean Christians were doing and continued to do on their own initiative.[12]

As in several other regions and countries, coöperation among Protestant missionary bodies increased with the years. The Presbyterians and Methodists agreed on allocation of responsibility for particular areas. In 1905 they joined in the General Evangelical Council and in 1912 formed the Federal Council of Missions.[13] This was in addition to the educational institutions which were supported by two or more missionary societies.

In its early years Protestantism in Korea grew very slowly. After 1895, however, the numbers rose rapidly—partly because of the emotional shock given by the Chino-Japanese War of 1894–1895 and the Russo-Japanese War of 1904–1905, followed as the latter was by the Japanese annexation. Numbers of Kore-

---

133–150; Barclay, *History of Methodist Missions*, Vol. III, pp. 741–757; Brown, *One Hundred Years*, pp. 409–414; J. S. Ryang, editor, *Southern Methodism in Korea. Thirtieth Anniversary* (Seoul, Board of Missions, Korea Annual Conference, Methodist Episcopal Church, South, no date, pp. 186, lxviii, 299), *passim*.

[9] Thompson, *Into All Lands*, pp. 460–466, 702, 703.

[10] Paik, *op. cit.*, pp. 179–184; Latourette, *A History of the Expansion of Christianity*, Vol. VI, p. 424.

[11] Paik, *op. cit.*, pp. 109, 118–120, 133–142, 217–242, 291, 296–325, 388–398; Latourette, *op. cit.*, pp. 424, 425.

[12] Paik, *op. cit.*, pp. 278–284; Latourette, *op. cit.*, p. 425; Wasson, *Church Growth in Korea*, pp. 23–29; Brown, *op. cit.*, p. 425.

[13] T. Stanley Soltau, *Korea, The Hermit Nation and Its Response to Christianity* (London, World Dominion Press, 1932, pp. 123), pp. 58 ff.

ans hoped that in Christianity they would find the answer to national weakness and their personal insecurity. Moreover, a partial religious vacuum existed. The native faith was a kind of animism. Buddhism, once popular, had long been declining and was weaker even than in China. Confucianism had been the philosophy of the educated, but the blows which were being dealt it in China had repercussions in Korea. For some, Christianity filled the gap. The high ethical demands of Christianity appealed to those who had been under the influence of Confucian standards.[14] In 1914 the number of Protestant communicants was not far from 85,000 and of baptized, including communicants, was approximately 96,000.[15]

With the eastward drive of Russia, the Russian Orthodox Church won converts among the Koreans. In 1899 or 1900 a Russian Orthodox mission was begun in Seoul.[16] By 1904 missions supported by the Russian Government among Korean immigrants in Russian territory near the border are said to have won between 8,000 and 9,000 converts.[17] Ten years later within Korea itself the Russian Orthodox Church was reported to have about 3,500 members.[18]

In 1914 Christians of all branches of the faith numbered about one out of a hundred of the population, or approximately the percentage in India and higher than in Japan or China, and that in spite of the fact that Christianity was a much more recent arrival than in any of these countries.

As in many other lands, by 1914 Christianity was making itself felt outside the churches as well as within them. Within them it was working characteristic changes in morals, religious practices, physical well-being, education, and the status of women. Outside them it was helping to introduce Western medicine and methods of education, features of the impinging revolutionary age. Among Protestants it was strengthening nationalistic aspirations for independence from Japanese rule. It was a stimulating factor in the emergence of a syncretic religious movement, Chuntokyo or Tonghak, which had political aspects. Its founder had had contact with Roman Catholicism and in its later stages it bore the impress of Protestantism. It combined elements from Buddhism, Confucianism, animism, and Christianity. In the 1890's it gave rise to a rebellion.[19]

[14] Brown, *op. cit.*, pp. 421–423; Wasson, *op. cit.*, pp. 15–23.
[15] Beach and St. John, *World Statistics of Christian Missions*, p. 62.
[16] Lübeck, *Die russischen Missionen*, p. 14.
[17] Raeder in *Allgemeine Missions-Zeitschrift*, Vol. XXXII, p. 522.
[18] Lübeck, *op. cit.*, p. 14.
[19] Paik, *op. cit.*, pp. 161–163; Charles Allen Clark, *Religions of Old Korea* (New York, Fleming H. Revell Co., 1932, pp. 295), pp. 144–172.

CHAPTER XXI

Japan

THE Japanese entered the new age with a strong prejudice against Christianity and with anti-Christian edicts which were not rescinded until the nineteenth century was more than half over. About the middle of the century the faith was re-introduced, or, better, re-inforced by a fresh wave of missionary enterprise—Roman Catholic, Russian Orthodox, and Protestant. Its career was chequered with alternating unpopularity, popularity, unpopularity, and popularity, but by 1914 it was a potent even though a minority force in the life of the country. As elsewhere outside the Occident, the course of Christianity in Japan was intimately associated with the impact of the West.

Christianity first appeared in Japan in connexion with Western merchants, Portuguese. The Portuguese reached Japan about the year 1542. In 1549 the pioneer Jesuit in South and East Asia, the heroic Francis Xavier, took advantage of their contacts to introduce Christianity. He was there until November, 1551. He won a number of converts and prepared the way for a continuing mission. The growth of the Church was rapid, especially in the South in ports frequented by the Portuguese. In 1587 Hideyoshi, the dominant political figure, came out with an edict against the faith which ordered missionaries to leave the country within twenty days and forbade the Portuguese merchants to bring more. It was not vigorously enforced and some even of Hideyoshi's entourage became Christians. The Jesuits persisted and Dominicans and Franciscans came by way of the Philippines. For a time the strong man who followed Hideyoshi, Iyeyasu of the Tokugawa family, looked with favour on the missionaries because of their association with the profitable commerce with the Westerners. Christians multiplied and at the beginning of the seventeenth century seem to have numbered between 200,000 and 750,000. Even the smaller figure would mean that a larger proportion of the population were Christians than in the nineteenth or the first half of the twentieth century. Iyeyasu and those of his family who succeeded him became convinced that Christianity threatened the internal order which they had established after long and debilitating civil strife and might jeopardize the independence of the land—much as in the Spanish conquest of the Philippines. Accordingly, stern measures were taken against it with severe and bloody persecutions. Since missionaries persisted in coming, to keep them out the Tokugawa stopped the commerce with the Portuguese and Spaniards and eventually closed the country tightly against all intercourse with the Occident except a strictly regulated trade with the Dutch through one port, Nagasaki. The anti-Christian edicts were posted throughout the country, and in places in which Christians were suspected of existing, particularly Nagasaki, where they had been especially numerous, the populace were required periodically to tread on emblems of the faith. Yet Christianity survived in the hills back of Nagasaki and in neighbouring islands. Christian objects were concealed behind Buddhist symbols, baptism was maintained, Christian prayers were said, and the Ten Commandments and some Christian doctrines were transmitted from generation to generation.[1]

With the renewal of the expansion of Europe in the nineteenth century the pressure became so marked that the rulers deemed it wise to re-open Japan to foreign intercourse. They took a leaf out of the lesson taught China by the wars of 1839–1842 and 1856–1860 and yielded without the bitter experience of their large neighbour. The first crack in the door appeared in 1853 as the result of an American naval expedition led by Perry. In 1858, at the instance of the United States of America, the first of a series of commercial treaties was signed which, somewhat on the pattern of existing agreements imposed on China, opened specified ports to foreign residence, provided for diplomatic intercourse, granted extraterritorial privileges to the foreigners, and fixed the custom duties. The foreigners might practise their religion, but toleration of missions among the Japanese and permission to the Japanese to accept Christianity were not included.

The Japanese proceeded to adjust themselves to the Western world. They reorganized their government, but in such fashion as to stress the inherited loyalty to the imperial institution and the military tradition. They feverishly adopted the mechanical devices of the Occident—railways, factories, steamships, the telegraph, the telephone, printing presses—and the education which undergirded these appliances. They built an army and navy on Western patterns. They adopted, with modifications in accord with their traditions, some of the Western forms of government. They engaged in foreign commerce and in time became formidable competitors with the West in the markets of East Asia. A proud people, they struggled, and with success, to free themselves from the limitations on their national sovereignty entailed in extraterritoriality and the fixing of their tariffs by treaty. Like the Western powers, they engaged in im-

[1] Cary, *A History of Christianity in Japan*, Vol. I, pp. 13–257; Léon Pagés, *Histoire de la Religion Chrétienne au Japon depuis 1598 jusqu'à 1651* (Paris, Charles Dounoil, 2 vols., 1869, 1870), *passim*; Schmidlin-Braun, *Catholic Mission History*, pp. 338–351; Latourette, *A History of the Expansion of Christianity*, Vol. III, pp. 322–335.

perialistic adventures in East Asia—adventures which at first were successful but which in the 1930's and 1940's brought them disaster.

Missionaries of the three major branches of Christianity—Roman Catholic, Orthodox, and Protestant—made their way to Japan soon after the first commercial treaties.

Roman Catholic missionary forces, with the fresh vigour born of the revival in their church in the new century, had been looking longingly towards Japan and had made various attempts at reëntering the country. Even before Perry Rome had created a vicariate apostolic for Japan and had appointed an incumbent (1846) from the *Société des Missions Étrangères* of Paris. Men were sent to the Ryu Kyus, for while not under the control of Japan the islands had connexions with that country. The treaty of 1858 between France and Japan permitted the French the free exercise of their religion in the three open ports and declared that the Japanese Government had abolished all practices in its domains injurious to Christianity. In 1859 missionaries of the Paris Society established themselves in Japan.[2]

In 1865, not long after the opening of a Roman Catholic church in Nagasaki, Japanese came to it who declared themselves to be Christians, descendants of the converts of the sixteenth and seventeenth centuries. The French missionaries soon discovered others. About ten thousand, persuaded that the missionaries were valid representatives of the faith of their fathers, affiliated themselves with them. Several times that number, while retaining some Christian practices which they had inherited, remained aloof. Since the anti-Christian edicts were still in force, Japanese officialdom, startled by the discovery of the crypto-Christians, imprisoned a number of them and deported several hundred to other parts of the country. The Western powers protested, but not until 1873, and then presumably only because it wished a revision of the treaties, did the Japanese Government order that the persecutions cease.[3]

In the succeeding decades additional missionaries came, some from the Paris Society and others from several orders—Dominicans, Franciscans, Trappists, and the Jesuits—and from the Society of the Divine Word. In 1891 Rome created a hierarchy for Japan, with Tokyo as the seat of an archbishop and with three suffragan sees.[4] In 1912 foreign priests numbered 152, Japanese priests 33, lay brothers 133, sisters 232, and catechists at least 165. The total of Roman Catholics in the country in that year was said to be 66,134.[5]

The methods employed by Roman Catholic missionaries were chiefly the winning of converts and the nourishing of them and their children in the faith. They included schools, partly because the Japanese were eager for education of a Western kind. Marists from France were especially prominent in the conduct

[2] Marnas, *La "Religion de Jésus" (Iaso Ja-kyō) Resuscitée au Japon*, Vol. I, pp. 78–384.
[3] *Ibid.*, pp. 475 ff., Vol. II, pp. 128 ff.; Cary, *op. cit.*, Vol. I, pp. 275–335.
[4] Marnas, *op. cit.*, Vol. II, pp. 365 ff.; Cary, *op. cit.*, Vol. I, pp. 336–372.
[5] Streit, *Atlas Hierarchicus*, p. 100.

of the schools. Sisterhoods also had schools for girls. In 1912 the Jesuits acquired land near the centre of Tokyo for a university, eventually to be given the name of Sophia, and in 1913 they obtained government authorization for the institution.[6] Orphanages were conducted and care was given to lepers.[7]

The lack of funds, due partly to the anti-clericalism which abounded in late nineteenth-century France, was a serious handicap to a more rapid extension of the Roman Catholic faith. So, too, was the obligation to give spiritual care to the descendants of the pre-nineteenth-century Christians, which absorbed much of the energies of the missionaries. Japanese, moreover, were inclined to accuse Roman Catholicism of inculcating a lack of patriotism and as evidence pointed to the attacks of the French Government on the Roman Catholic Church.[8] Yet, as if to counter that charge, in 1890 a Roman Catholic council meeting in Nagasaki permitted the faithful to participate in the rites at the shrines of the state-sponsored Shinto on the ground that they were purely civil and not religious and were ways of expressing loyalty to the nation.[9]

The Russian Orthodox Church had in Japan its most extensive mission anywhere outside the Russian Empire. For this the founder, Ivan Kasatkin, better known as Nicolai, his name in religion, was chiefly responsible. Nicolai came to Japan in 1861 as chaplain to the Russian consulate in Hakodate and with the purpose of being a missionary. One of his earliest converts was from the warrior gentry class, the *samurai*, who had sought his acquaintance with the purpose of killing him as one intent on enslaving the Japanese. The *samurai* was eventually ordained a priest of the religion which he had once hated. In 1872 Nicolai removed the headquarters of the mission from the North to Tokyo and acquired a site for it on a prominent hill. Funds came from Russia, but Nicolai wished the mission to be as Japanese in leadership as possible. Converts were gathered rapidly in the 1880's, when things Western were enjoying an undiscriminating popularity. With the nationalistic reaction against that popularity in the 1890's growth slowed. The Russo-Japanese War brought embarrassment, but Nicolai, remaining with his flock, urged them to be loyal to their country and growth continued during and after the conflict.[10] Nicolai died in 1912 and in the meantime had been made bishop and then archbishop. In that year the Orthodox totalled about 32,000. By 1914 the Russian staff consisted of one man, the bishop. The rest were Japanese. The Christians, at first numbering many from the *samurai*, eventually were largely from the humbler ranks of society.[11]

In 1914 Protestants were said to number 103,119 exclusive of Formosa, which was more than the combined Roman Catholic and Orthodox bodies. They were

---

[6] Berg, *Die katholische Heidenmission als Kulturträger*, Vol. I, pp. 37–372.

[7] Cary, *op. cit.*, Vol. I, pp. 365, 369.

[8] *Ibid.*, pp. 364–370.

[9] *Fides News Service*, July 4, 1936.

[10] Cary, *op. cit.*, Vol. I, pp. 375–423; Lübeck, *Die russischen Missionen*, pp. 16–23.

[11] *The Christian Movement in Japan, 1911*, pp. 289–292; *1913*, pp. 417, 418; *1914*, p. 22 and the statistical table.

the result of the efforts of missionaries who were predominantly from the United States and who in 1914 totalled 986.[12] As in a number of other countries, the approach of Protestant missionaries to Japan was multiform and addressed itself to several aspects of the life of the nation. Accordingly it had a wider and more varied effect than was achieved by the other branches of Christianity. In the planting of Protestantism Japanese early had a prominent part.

Before the first commercial treaties, Protestants had made a number of efforts to establish contact with the Japanese. An interpreter on the Perry expedition, S. Wells Williams, was a missionary to China. He had acquired a knowledge of the language through Japanese refugees whom he had befriended. In the expedition was a marine who had enlisted with the hope of gaining a knowledge of the country which would serve him as a missionary. He later accomplished his purpose.[13]

The first Protestant missionaries to become residents of Japan reached that country in 1859. They were all from the United States and were from three denominations—the Protestant Episcopal Church, the Presbyterian Church, and the (Dutch) Reformed Church of America.[14] One of them was Guido Herman Fridolin Verbeck (1830–1898). Born in the Netherlands and reared under Moravian influence, Verbeck came to the United States in his young manhood. In Japan he engaged in education and in Yedo, soon to be renamed Tokyo, headed a school which grew into the Imperial University. He became the adviser of officials who were eager for counsel from foreigners they could trust as they sought to guide their nation in the uncharted course of adjustment to that Western world which was thrusting itself on them. Through him or under his direction, translations were made of a number of Occidental legal documents to enable the Japanese to bring their laws and courts into such conformity to Western standards that the treaty powers would be willing to relinquish extraterritoriality. It was partly at his instance that the Japanese sent their first diplomatic mission of the century to Western governments. He also preached and taught the Bible.[15]

The American Board of Commissioners for Foreign Missions sent its first representative in 1869. It was moved to take the step in part through the prodding of a remarkable Japanese, Joseph Hardy Neesima (1843–1890).[16] Of *samurai* stock, as a lad Neesima conceived a consuming desire to go to the Occident, which was then looming large on the Japanese horizon, and there to acquire a knowledge of things Western. In 1864, in face of the laws which still

[12] *The Christian Movement in the Japanese Empire, 1915,* statistical table.

[13] Latourette, *op. cit.,* Vol. VI, pp. 381, 382.

[14] Cary, *op. cit.,* Vol. II, pp. 45 ff.

[15] William Elliot Griffis, *Verbeck of Japan* (New York, Fleming H. Revell Co., 1900, pp. 376), *passim.*

[16] J. D. Davis, *A Sketch of the Life of Rev. Joseph Hardy Neesima* (Chicago, Fleming H. Revell Co., 2nd ed., 1894, pp. 156), *passim;* Arthur Sherburne Hardy, *Life and Letters of Joseph Hardy Neesima* (Boston, Houghton Mifflin Co., 1892, pp. vi, 350), *passim.*

made such a step dangerous, he managed secretly to leave his country. Through the kindness of captains of American vessels he reached the United States and there was befriended by Thomas Hardy, the owner of one of the ships, whose name in gratitude he assumed. Through that generous assistance he obtained a college and theological education, the latter at Andover Theological Seminary. In 1874 he returned to Japan in connexion with the American Board. There he brought into being several churches and founded a school in the ancient capital, Kyoto, a centre of resistance to the invading civilization. The school, frankly Christian and known as the Doshisha, eventually grew into a university.

The rate of growth of Protestantism fluctuated. It was very slow in the 1860's. Then, with the removal of the anti-Christian edicts in 1873 and the coming of representatives of additional bodies, mostly American, among them the American Baptist Missionary Union (1872) and the Methodist Episcopal Church (1873), the numbers of Protestant Christians slowly increased. In the 1880's the totals rapidly shot upward. As we have suggested, this spurt was an accompaniment of a somewhat uncritical popularity of Occidental civilization and an eagerness by adopting it to be accepted as equals by the Western powers. Indeed, some Japanese urged that to obtain admission to the then dominant Christendom Japan should officially adopt Christianity. Thousands thronged public meetings in which the Christian faith was presented. Between 1882 and 1888 the numbers of Protestant church members leaped from 4,987[17] to 25,514.[18] Then came a reaction. The delay in the revision of the treaties and a resurgence of a nationalistic admiration for Japanese culture led to a cooling of enthusiasm for Western civilization, and so for Christianity. Many Japanese Protestants were restive under the foreign control of their churches and wished to interpret the faith in Japanese forms. Much of Western radical thought and some of the trends in the theology and Biblical studies in the Occident which were counter to the views introduced by the missionaries gained currency in Christian circles. Yet additional societies were represented, more missionaries came, and the number of Protestant church members in 1900 was 43,273, a marked increase over the preceding decade, although not as great as that in the 1880's.[19] The years between 1900 and 1914 witnessed more rapid proportionate growth than in the 1890's, although not as startling as in the 1880's. As we have seen, in 1914 the membership of Protestant churches was 103,119. In that year the Protestant denominations with the largest membership were first the Presbyterians, next the Congregationalists (under the Japanese name of *Kumiai*), then the Anglicans, followed by the Methodists, the Baptists, and the Disciples of Christ and Churches of Christ.[20]

[17] *Proceedings of the General Conference of Protestant Missionaries of Japan . . . 1883* (Yokohama, R. Meiklejohn & Co., 1883, pp. xviii, 468), statistical table opposite p. 184.
[18] Cary, *op. cit.*, Vol. II, pp. 164–209.
[19] *Ibid.*, pp. 212–296.
[20] *The Christian Movement in the Japanese Empire, 1915*, statistical sheet.

The methods employed by Protestant missionaries included the translation and distribution of the Scriptures; the preparation of literature for a people who became predominantly literate; the utilization of secular newspapers to spread a knowledge of the Gospel; a temperance movement; orphanages; leper asylums; famine relief; service to soldiers in the Russo-Japanese War; care for discharged prisoners; Sunday Schools; a rescue home for prostitutes and wayward girls; Young Men's and Young Women's Christian Associations; large public meetings for the presentation of the Christian message; hostels for students in government and private universities; prison reform; and schools for the deaf and blind. In a nation as avid for education as was Japan on its emergence into the Revolutionary age, much attention was given to founding and maintaining schools from kindergartens to universities. Since the government, with its larger resources, early set about the creation of an educational system which was an adaptation of what was seen in the West, its best schools and universities became better equipped and were more desired by students than those begun by the missions. Yet so great was the pressure for learning that the schools under Christian auspices were full, even though regarded as second or third choice. Moreover, Protestant colleges continued to lead in higher education for women.[21]

Coöperation among Protestants took a number of forms. National conferences of Protestant missionaries were held in 1872, 1883, and 1900.[22] In 1902 the Conference of Federated Missions came into being, and the Federation of Churches formed in 1911 collaborated with it.[23] A Continuation Committee of the Edinburgh Conference was created in 1913 as a result of a visit by Mott and in 1923 was succeeded by the National Christian Council.[24] Other conferences, gatherings, and projects for special objectives which crossed denominational lines were familiar features of Protestantism.

Protestantism in Japan had distinctive characteristics. Like Roman Catholicism and Orthodoxy, it was chiefly urban. More than the other two branches of Christianity, much of its leadership came from the *samurai* and from members of the middle classes, who had been profoundly affected by Western culture. Partly for this reason, it early tended to develop ecclesiastical structures which were independent of foreign control and to produce an educated clergy. We hear of Japanese Christians, with little or no suggestion from missionaries, undertaking social welfare projects and seeking to conduct business enterprises on Christian principles.[25] The *Mukyokai* ("no church church") movement had its origin in the teaching of Uchimura Kanzo (1861–1930).[26] Uchimura, of *sa-*

---

[21] *Ibid.*, pp. 149 ff.; Latourette, *op. cit.*, Vol. VI, pp. 400, 401.

[22] Cary, *op. cit.*, pp. 164, 294.

[23] Rouse and Neill, *A History of the Ecumenical Movement 1517–1948*, p. 388.

[24] Hogg, *Ecumenical Foundations*, pp. 212, 213.

[25] *The Christian Movement in the Japanese Empire, 1915*, pp. 289–312; Latourette, *op. cit.*, Vol. VI, pp. 404, 405.

[26] Uchimura Kanzo, *The Diary of a Japanese Convert* (Chicago, Fleming H. Revell Co., 1895,

murai stock, was converted in his student days in the Sapporo Agricultural School, for a time studied in the United States, returning to Japan taught in a government school but resigned because of his opposition to an ultra-nationalism which seemed to him to entail worship in which he as a Christian could not share, and then for more than thirty years gave himself to writing, teaching, and lecturing on Biblical themes. An intellectual, a pacifist, honest, and fearless, he attracted many among the intellectuals and business men. After his death his writings were circulated in hundreds of thousands of copies and his work was carried on by his disciples. *Mukyokai* stressed the study of the Bible, but it had no local or national organization, no sacraments, and no official connexion with the churches. It was a distinctly Japanese movement and continued its growth after Uchimura's death.

Although in 1914 its adherents were only about one in two hundred of the population of Japan, Christianity had an influence all out of proportion to its numerical strength. The vast majority of the Japanese regarded it as alien, not so much because it came to them from the West, for they were eager to take from the Occident whatever seemed to them of value—its science, machines, forms of education, and military and naval skills—but because to them Christianity appeared to be destructive of many of the values which they prized in their family life and in their mores. Moreover, it demanded much of the individual and made him stand against the pressures of the group in a manner which appeared to many to be un-Japanese. Yet more and more Japan bore the impress of Christianity. In the field of religion, for example, some forms of Buddhism, following Christian precedent, encouraged the singing of hymns and founded hospitals.[27] Some of the influence of Christianity was through missionaries and Japanese Christians. Much was through contact with literature, ideas, and institutions from a segment of mankind which had long been under Christian influence even though it was far from conforming fully to Christian principles and contained many who were rejecting the Christian faith.

---

pp. 212), *passim;* W. H. H. Norman in *The International Review of Missions,* Vol. XLVI, pp. 380–393; Otis Cary, "Uchimura Kanzo—Prophet, Patriot, Christian," in *The Japan Christian Quarterly,* Vol. III, No. 4.

[27] Henry Van Straelen, *The Religion of Divine Wisdom* (Kyoto, Veritas Shoin, 1957, pp. 236), p. 64.

CHAPTER XXII

The Islands of the Pacific

I N THE Pacific Ocean, stretching in a great arc from Midway and Hawaii on the North-east to New Zealand on the South-west, were hundreds of islands. On the western fringe were some, the largest of them New Guinea (Papua), which were continuations of the East Indies. At the advent of the nineteenth century the easternmost, from Hawaii to New Zealand, were peopled chiefly by Polynesians. North of the equator and west of Hawaii were islands, mostly small, inhabited by Micronesians. What were called Melanesians constituted the population of many of the islands in the Western Pacific. The Papuans were dominant in New Guinea. The lines between the various ethnic strains were not always sharply drawn. For example, Papuans constituted elements in much of Melanesia, and Melanesians and Polynesians were sometimes mixed.

At the outset of the nineteenth century all the peoples had in common one form or another of "primitive" culture including religions which were prevailingly animistic. All, too, had the experience in the nineteenth century of contacts with Occidental peoples, contacts which mounted in the twentieth century.

The contacts with the revolutionary West were, in general, of three kinds. The two earliest were for the most part contradictory—expressions of that ambiguous character of Christendom which we have repeatedly noted.

On the one hand were white traders and adventurers who exploited the inhabitants. They brought firearms which they sold to the islanders. Since those on the coast acquired them first they were able to use them in the chronic wars waged with rivals in the interior and thus intensified the deadliness of the conflicts heretofore fought with stone weapons. The traders brought in alcoholic beverages of a kind unfamiliar to the islanders, often with disastrous results. The white man kidnapped many—"black-birding" as it was sometimes called—for forced labour on his plantations. He also, usually unintentionally, introduced diseases to which through long contact he and his ancestors had developed a partial resistance but which among the islanders, without that experience, assumed epidemic and deadly proportions. The traditional cultures disintegrated and a reduction in population followed, on some islands to the point of near extinction.

On the other hand were missionaries. At the outset they were predominantly

Protestant, for, with most of Asia closed to them in the fore part of the nineteenth century, here was a region to which access, though difficult and often dangerous, was possible. Most of them were from the British Isles, Australia, and New Zealand. Congregationalists and Methodists bore the chief burden, but Anglicans and Presbyterians participated. Later came Roman Catholic missionaries. But throughout the nineteenth century Protestants, either foreign or indigenous, were in the majority. In some of the island groups, after initial resistance, wholesale conversions were seen. The missionaries then had the task of protecting the neophytes against the demoralizing contacts with white traders and of helping them construct a wholesome social order to take the place of the old, sometimes disintegrating as that was before their arrival. Missionaries reduced languages to writing, put the Bible into them, produced other literature, and conducted schools. They encouraged native rulers to enact laws conforming to Christian standards. They sought to promote peace and to prevent inter-tribal wars. They brought cannibalism to an end and stood for monogamous marriage. They fought drink, head-hunting, and sexual irregularities. In Protestant areas the churches became largely self-governing and from some of them Christians went as missionaries to non-Christian islands and to peoples of other languages, often at no small peril. In general advance was most striking among the Polynesians and Micronesians. In places it was marked among the Melanesians or peoples of mixed Polynesian and Melanesian blood. It was slowest among the Papuans and especially in New Guinea, large as was that island and physically difficult to penetrate.

In general Occidental governments lagged behind traders and missionaries, but by 1914 they had extended their authority over all the islands. The British had acquired the lion's share. The French obtained several islands and island groups. In accord with their policy in other quarters of the globe, they protected Roman Catholic missionaries, for the latter were for the most part of their nationality, and in that protection they found the excuse for annexation. As elsewhere outside Europe, Germany was late in entering the scramble for territory. However, it eventually appropriated several islands and a portion of New Guinea. The United States had an interest in Samoa and late in the century annexed Hawaii. Through his governments the white man brought internal order and promoted the adoption of Occidental culture and the development of economic life on patterns which he found profitable.[1]

An account of the spread of Christianity in the islands of the Pacific group

---

[1] For a comprehensive account of the spread of Christianity in this region, with footnote references to the appropriate authorities, see Latourette, *A History of the Expansion of Christianity,* Vol. V, pp. 198–263. See also Aarne A. Koskinan, *Missionary Influence as a Political Factor in the Pacific Islands* (Helsinki, Annals of the Academy of Science and Letters, 1953, pp. 163), *passim.* On Anglican missions, a comprehensive account is in C. F. Fox, *Lord of the Southern Isles. Being the Story of the Anglican Mission in Melanesia, 1849–1949* (London, A. R. Mowbray & Co., 1958, pp. XV, 272).

by group would prolong these pages far beyond all proper proportions. In spite of the vast area over which they were scattered, the islands had a total popula tion of only a few hundred thousand—perhaps as many as two million in 191. —and, although entire groups conformed to the faith, in 1914 only a minority of the Pacific islanders called themselves Christian. The full story would con tain the record of some of the most devoted lives, heroic deeds, and signal achievements in the history not only of Christianity but also of all mankind Here, however, we must confine ourselves to a few of the many island group involved and then only in brief summary.

We begin with the Society Islands, of which Tahiti was the largest, for it was to them that the initial contingent of Protestant missionaries to the Pacific islands came. The voyages of Captain Cook in the last third of the eighteenth century had disclosed the Pacific islands to the English-speaking world. The awakening missionary interest saw in them a challenge. In 1796 the newly or ganized London Missionary Society sent a contingent to the South Pacific. Most of them were placed on Tahiti. The first few years were discouraging. Several of the party soon left for New South Wales and two of those who remained "went native" with Tahitian wives. But about 1815 the tide turned. The dom inant chief espoused the faith and the population followed. The Bible was trans lated, schools were opened, and a code of laws was formed, with missionary advice, which embodied Christian ideals. Others of the Society Islands followed the example of the Tahitians. The extension of French authority over the islands at first, in 1842, in the form of a protectorate and in 1880 by full annexation began in the successful effort to defend French Roman Catholic missionaries who sought to establish themselves there. In 1886 the London Missionary So ciety withdrew and left the islands to French Protestants who had already entered. By the end of the century about three-fifths of the population were Protestants, about a fourth were Roman Catholics, and a few were won by the Mormons.[2]

The Picpus Fathers, a congregation which had come into being in Paris shortly after 1800,[3] introduced the Roman Catholic faith to the Society Islands In 1834 they landed on the Gambier Islands south-east of Tahiti and within four years won the population to a profession of Christianity.[4]

On the Tonga, or Friendly Islands, with a population in the third quarter of the century of perhaps 50,000, the dominant form of Christianity was Meth odism. Methodism arrived about the time of its entrance among the Maoris A mass conversion occurred in the 1830's, with weeping for sins, public confes

---

[2] Lovett, *The History of the London Missionary Society 1795–1895,* Vol. I, pp. 146 ff., 169 ff. 192–197, 208–215, 224 ff., 306 ff.; Latourette, *op. cit.,* Vol. V, pp. 205, 206; Schmidlin-Braun *Catholic Mission History,* pp. 666, 667.

[3] Volume I, p. 158.

[4] Louis-Eugène Louvet, *Les Missions Catholiques au XIXme Siècle* (Lyon, Œuvre de la Propa gation de la Foi, 1895, pp. xvi, 543), p. 514.

sion, and the joy of forgiveness. In 1839 a code of laws embodying Christian principles was enacted. In the 1880's the majority moved into a church, Methodist in polity and tied to the state. It severed the bond with the Methodist Church in New South Wales with which Tongan Methodists had been connected.[5]

The Fiji Islands, which had a Melanesian population declining in the nineteenth century and to which Indians were imported as indentured labourers on the white man's plantations, were annexed by Great Britain in 1874. Before the annexation Christianity had been firmly planted by Methodists from Tonga and Great Britain. For a time Christianity accentuated the inter-tribal conflicts, and that in spite of the efforts of missionaries to keep the Christians from engaging in war. Eventually the large majority of the Fijians became Methodists. The language was reduced to writing, the Bible was translated, a system of schools was introduced, and an indigenous ministry was recruited and trained. Little success was had in winning the Indians.[6]

New Caledonia was annexed by France in 1853 and the step assured the prosperity of the Roman Catholic mission, which had been begun before that date. Missionaries came from the Society of Mary, as they did to many other islands in the Pacific, and were assisted by at least four congregations of women. By the dawn of the twentieth century Roman Catholics numbered about 11,000.[7]

Hawaii had a unique record. Its original population was Polynesian. Described as being at the cross-roads of the Pacific, a generation before the arrival of the first missionary it had been frequented by Western sailors and traders, its population had begun to decline, and its traditional culture was disintegrating. One of the chiefs had utilized the firearms obtained from the traders to subdue his rivals and unite the islands under his rule, a rule which continued through his family until the white settlers deposed the last of its monarchs and set up a republic (1894). Annexation by the United States came in 1898.

Christianity made its chief gains among the indigenous population of Hawaii through representatives of the American Board of Commissioners for Foreign Missions. For many years American vessels had been touching at the islands and had brought Hawaiian youths to the United States. In the first flush of that foreign missionary interest which centred in New England and when most of Asia and Africa was inaccessible to its representatives, these young men seemed to offer possibilities. In a school established in Cornwall, Connecticut, several were prepared to return to their people as missionaries. In 1819 a party recruited by the American Board sailed from Boston. It included three Hawaiians but was predominantly white. It landed in 1820 and within a decade

---

[5] Colwell, *A Century in the Pacific*, pp. 420–437.

[6] Latourette, *op. cit.*, Vol. VI, pp. 219–226.

[7] J. B. Piolet, editor, *Les Missions Catholiques Françaises au XIXe Siècle* (Paris, Libraire Armand Colin, 5 vols., no date, last vol. in 1902), Vol. IV, pp. 276–332.

reinforcements had arrived, several of the chiefs and a member of the royal family had been converted, thousands were in mission schools, part of the Bible had been translated, and a code of laws had been adopted which, to the indignation of foreign residents and sailors, sought to restrain prostitution, drunkenness, and gambling and to ensure the observance of Sunday. In 1836 a mass movement into the Church began which was furthered by the revival methods then characteristic of much of the Protestantism of the United States. In the years 1839, 1840, and 1841 over twenty thousand, or about a sixth of the population, were received into membership. Although the annual number of accessions then fell off, the Hawaiians were rapidly becoming professedly Christian. The translation of the Bible was completed, the children of the chiefs, together with those of the royal family, were educated by the missionaries in a special school, and, with missionary counsel, a written constitution was adopted which included religious liberty and the declaration that no law should be enacted which was contrary to the Scriptures. Several missionaries, usually after severing their formal connexion with the Board, served the government in various capacities: one was in effect premier and another was in charge of education. In 1863, deeming its task accomplished, the American Board of Commissioners for Foreign Missions, while continuing some financial aid, turned over its responsibilities to the Hawaiian Evangelical Association, a body composed of clergy and laity, both indigenous and foreign.

The situation in Hawaii became progressively complicated by the continued decline of the indigenous stock and the arrival of other peoples, at the outset mostly as labourers on plantations. In 1920 42.7 per cent. of the population were Japanese, 9.2 per cent. were Chinese, 9.3 per cent. were pure-blooded Hawaiians, and 7 per cent. were a mixture of Hawaiians with other stocks. Koreans and Filipinos also came. A white minority existed drawn from various nationalities. On their arrival almost all the Japanese and Chinese were non-Christians. Many of the others were Roman Catholics. The Hawaiian Evangelical Association sought to meet the challenge. Other denominations came. By 1896 the influx of Portuguese and Filipinos together with accessions from the Hawaiians brought Roman Catholics almost to a numerical equality with Protestants.[8]

The conversion of the Pacific islanders continued after 1914, but in most of the smaller islands and island groups it had been completed by that date.

---

[8] On Hawaii see Latourette, *op. cit.,* Vol. V, pp. 247–256, and especially the footnote references to the authorities.

CHAPTER XXIII

Africa South of the Sahara: Madagascar

I N THE nineteenth century the largest body of peoples of primitive cultures
was in Africa south of the Sahara. Here, fully as sharply as in any other part
of the world, the contrasts were seen in the impact of the Western European
peoples who had long been professedly Christian. From the close of the fifteenth
until well into the nineteenth century the most obvious and extensive feature
of that impact was the slave trade. Millions of Africans were torn from their
homes and forcibly transported across the Atlantic to compulsory labour on the
white man's plantations. The inter-tribal wars and raids by which the victims
were obtained for the slave ships left several dead for each one delivered to the
white man and entailed a legacy of fear and hate. The trans-Atlantic voyages
were living hells. But as we have seen, in the nineteenth century the Christian
conscience brought to an end the importation of slaves to the Americas and the
abolition of slavery in the Western Hemisphere. In the British West Indies and
the United States that was chiefly through earnest Protestants. In Latin America
it was largely through a humanitarianism which was not avowedly Christian
but which came out of the Christian heritage. In Africa the traffic in slaves continued, mainly to supply the demand of Moslem Arabs and with the connivance
of some of the colonial administrations, mainly Portuguese, and, under the
thinly disguised form of contract labour, on the cocoa plantations on the Portuguese islands of San Thomé and Principe. Here and there, also in regions controlled by Europeans, forced labour which was tantamount to slavery persisted
into the twentieth century but was challenged, with increasing success, by the
conscience of the Western Christendom.

EXPLORATION AND PARTITION

In the nineteenth century began the penetration of Africa south of the Sahara
by European culture which after 1914 was to bring about the disintegration of
the traditional patterns of life. Indeed, it would issue in a vast revolution which
by the mid-century was rapidly mounting but even then seemed to be only in
its beginnings.

That penetration was partly by exploration, which opened the interior of the continent to the astonished eyes of Europe and America. It was also to a large extent by missionaries, both Protestant and Roman Catholic. It was accompanied and furthered by the partition of the region among Western European powers, chiefly in the 1880's.

Outstanding among the explorers were David Livingstone (1813–1873) and Henry Morton Stanley (1841–1904). Livingstone went to Africa as a missionary and to the end regarded himself as such and under divine compulsion and support in his efforts to open the continent and end the remnants of the Arab slave trade.[1] Born and reared in Scotland in a devout and humble home, from childhood through his teens he was employed in the cotton mill in which the family worked. He joined the Independent church in which his father was a deacon. Attracted by an appeal from Gützlaff for medical missionaries for China, he acquired an education in medicine and theology. He was appointed by the London Missionary Society but was sent, not to China, for the first Anglo-Chinese War then in progress closed that door, but to South Africa, where the picture painted by his future father-in-law, on furlough, Robert Moffat, of areas untouched by the Gospel appealed to his pioneering convictions. Of his arduous journeys, first in South Africa, later in Central Africa, disclosing the vast interior to the white man, and of his lonely death on his last expedition, we need not do more than speak. Since the directors of the London Missionary Society believed that his explorations lay outside the proper scope of their programme, his connexion with that body was severed (1857) and his later journeys were as a British consul. Some financial aid was then given by the British Government, but most of his expenses were met by private contributions and from his own funds, the proceeds of his books. Partly as a result of his appeals and partly because of the challenge of his heroism and of the areas he had disclosed to the outer world, a number of missionary enterprises were initiated in the regions which he had traversed.

Stanley became involved in Africa through his commission from the *New York Herald* to find Livingstone, who had been lost to sight from the European world in his final journeys in Africa's interior. Born out of wedlock, he had had a difficult childhood, part of it in a workhouse where sermons

---

[1] Of the enormous literature on Livingstone, the best and in many ways the definitive biography is George Seaver, *David Livingstone: His Life and Letters* (New York, Harper & Brothers, 1957, pp. 650). Older, but still valuable, is W. Garden Blaikie, *The Personal Life of David Livingstone* (Chicago, Fleming H. Revell Co., preface 1880, pp. 508). Among original sources are James I. Macnair, editor, *Livingstone's Travels* (New York, The Macmillan Co., 1954, pp. xvi, 429); David Livingstone, *Missionary Travels and Researches in South Africa* (London, John Murray, 1857, pp. ix, 687); David Chamberlin, editor, *Some Letters from Livingstone 1840–1872* (New York, Oxford University Press, 1940, pp. xxvii, 280); David and Charles Livingstone, *Narrative of an Expedition to the Zambesi and Its Tributaries and the Discovery of Lakes Shirwa and Nyassa, 1858–1864* (London, John Murray, 1865, pp. xiv, 608); *The Zambesi Expedition of David Livingstone 1858–1863*, edited by J. P. R. Wallis (London, Chatto & Windus, 2 vols., 1956); and *The Last Journals of David Livingstone in Central Africa from Eighteen Hundred and Sixty-Five to His Death* (New York, Harper & Brothers, 1875, pp. 541).

and religious teaching were combined with the floggings of a cruel, half-mad schoolmaster. Years of adventure followed which took him to the United States, brought him adoption and the name by which he was known to history, led to his active participation in the Civil War, and were marked by wide journeyings and incipient skill as a journalist. His finding of Livingstone (1872) after an arduous expedition brought Stanley fame. His days with Livingstone made a profound impression on him, and after his great predecessor's death he felt impelled to continue what it had left uncompleted. Like Livingstone, he had an iron constitution, resourcefulness, courage, and an indomitable will. Several journeys into the interior of Africa followed. One of them, in the valley of the Congo, was under the auspices of an organization (*Comité d'Études du Haut Congo,* later *Association Internationale du Congo*) of which the chief promoter and supporter was King Leopold II of the Belgians. The ostensible purpose was the free navigation of the river and the bringing of civilization to the peoples on its banks and tributaries. Five years, 1879–1884, were spent in exploration, in establishing centres for European trade, the chief of them Leopoldville, and in obtaining treaties from the local chiefs. Stanley thus laid the foundations of what was at first the Congo Free State and then the Belgian Congo.[2]

The exploration of the interior of Africa by Livingstone, Stanley, and other white men, mounting as it did as the century progressed, was followed by the partition of the area by the earth-hungry governments of Western Europe. In the latter part of the nineteenth century, that heyday of Western imperialism fed by the prosperity brought by the Industrial Revolution and the rising nationalism and by the optimism associated with the relative peace of the later decades, European statesmen entered into a scramble for the territory thus disclosed. The motives were mixed. Among them was the welfare of the Africans. But the primary impulse was national prestige, and the chief lure was trade and the exploitation of the fabulous natural resources as yet only dimly discerned. Much jockeying for advantage followed. An international conference held in Berlin in 1884–1885 at the instance of Bismarck reached agreement on general principles. By the year 1900 all Africa south of the Sahara except Liberia had been occupied by one or another of the European powers. Although, if all Africa be included, France had the largest share, most of it was in the Sahara and adjacent regions. Of the part of the continent south of the Sahara Great

[2] Of the prodigious literature by Stanley and on him, see *The Autobiography of Sir Henry Morton Stanley,* edited by his wife, Dorothy Stanley (Boston, Houghton Mifflin Co., 1909, pp. xvii, 551); Frank Hird, *H. M. Stanley, the Authorized Life* (London, Stanley Paul & Co., 1935, pp. 320); Ian Anstruther, *I Presume. Stanley's Triumph and Disaster* (London, Geoffrey Bles, 1956, pp. xiii, 207); Henry Morton Stanley, *How I Found Livingstone* (New York, Scribner, Armstrong & Co., 1872, pp. xxiii, 736); Henry Morton Stanley, *Through the Dark Continent* (New York, Harper & Brothers, 2 vols., 1878); Henry Morton Stanley, *The Congo and the Founding of Its Free State. A Story of Work and Exploration* (New York, Harper & Brothers, 2 vols., 1885); Henry Morton Stanley, *In Darkest Africa, or the Quest, Rescue and Retreat of Emin Governor of Equatoria* (New York, Charles Scribner's Sons, 2 vols., 1890).

Britain possessed by far the largest number of square miles, and Germany and Belgium (which took over the Congo Free State in 1908) were next. Portugal had slightly less, Spain very much less, and Italy had sections bordering on Ethiopia.

Through the several channels of trade, exploration, the establishment of European regimes, and Christian missions, by 1914 the disintegration of African cultures was in its initial stages.

THE PLANTING OF CHRISTIANITY: GENERALIZATIONS

Christian missionary effort had begun centuries earlier and mounted rapidly in the later decades of the nineteenth century. It was closely associated with the other phases of European advance—trade, exploration, and the establishment of colonial rule—but often frankly stood against features of these activities which were counter to Christian standards and always sought to make the contacts with the white man a blessing and not a curse and to assist the Africans to a wholesome adjustment to the invading culture.

By the mid-twentieth century a mass conversion of the Africans to Christianity was in progress. By 1914 that conversion was well under way in South Africa, but elsewhere only beginnings had been made and they irregularly.

Significantly, not only were the two chief explorers, Livingstone and Stanley, Protestants, the former with his faith as his driving and sustaining impulse and the latter also a convinced Christian, but the major colonial power, Great Britain, was officially Protestant, the chief movements to end the African slave trade were by Protestants, and in the nineteenth century Protestants had a larger share than Roman Catholics in the planting of Christianity. Here were additional reasons for calling those ten decades the Protestant century. But, as in so much of the history of Christianity, the record, from the standpoint of the Gospel, was ambiguous.

We cannot take the space for even a well-rounded summary account of the spread of Christianity in Africa south of the Sahara. That, fortunately, has already been made.[3] Here we must confine ourselves to a brief enumeration of the main stages of the spread of the faith and to a description, also telescoped, of the course of Christianity in a few of the more important political divisions.

---

[3] For a comprehensive account of both the Protestant and Roman Catholic wings of Christianity, see Latourette, *A History of the Expansion of Christianity*, Vol. III, pp. 240–246, Vol. V, pp. 319–464. Longer accounts, primarily of Protestant missions, are in Julius Richter, *Geschichte der evangelischen Mission in Africa* (Gütersloh, C. Bertelsmann, 1922, pp. viii, 813); in J. Du Plessis, *The Evangelization of Pagan Africa. A History of Christian Missions to the Pagan Tribes of Central Africa* (Cape Town, J. C. Juta & Co., 1930, pp. xii, 408); and especially in Groves, *The Planting of Christianity in Africa*, which, while giving most of its space to Protestant missions, includes Roman Catholic missions.

Pre-Nineteenth-Century Christianity

Christianity was first introduced to Africa south of the Sahara by the Portuguese in the course of their successful search for a sea route to the Indies. Christian missions continued in connexion with some of their trading centres. Numerically the most important pre-nineteenth-century Roman Catholic missions were in the southern part of the valley of the Congo, in Angola on the coast just south of the latter, and on or near the east coast in the Mozambique region. Although under Portuguese auspices, not all the missionaries were of that nationality. By the beginning of the nineteenth century most of the Christian communities had vanished, leaving few tangible traces.[4]

Before the nineteenth century Protestantism was represented on the southern tip of the continent by a settlement which came into being as a station between the Netherlands and the Dutch possessions in India, Ceylon, Malaya, and the East Indies. In 1795, when it was seized by the English, the colony consisted of about 21,000 whites, most of them Dutch and a minority who were descendants of French Huguenot refugees, and all of them at least nominally of the Reformed faith and served by ministers who were paid by the Dutch East India Company. A few slaves of non-European blood had been baptized.[5]

Late in the eighteenth century Protestant missions were begun on the Guinea coast. Here was Sierra Leone, founded by English Evangelicals as a refuge for freed slaves, including Negroes taken by British cruisers from slave ships. The Church Missionary Society sent its first missionaries to Sierra Leone—in 1806. The climate and its associated diseases took a heavy toll in missionary lives, but a continuing Protestant community arose.[6]

South Africa

The region south of the Sahara which by the end of the nineteenth century had the largest number of Christians was South Africa. Here out of the Dutch and Huguenot settlements, the British conquest, the later expansion of the Dutch—or, better, Afrikander—population, and the further extension of British territory and of immigration from the British Isles, a new nation arose. It was multi-racial, with Africans in the large majority (Bushmen, Hottentots, but chiefly Bantus of various tribes), whites a large minority (divided into the Afrikanders, with their own language, Afrikaans, and those of British birth or descent), and with smaller minorities of Coloured, Indians, and Chinese. The European elements were much less numerous, both proportionately and in totals, than in two commonwealths within the empire—Canada and Australia. They were, however, larger than in New Zealand—1,519,488 in 1921 as against

[4] Latourette, *op. cit.*, Vol. III, pp. 241–245; Groves, *op. cit.*, Vol. I, pp. 118–138.
[5] Latourette, *op. cit.*, Vol. III, pp. 245, 246; Groves, *op. cit.*, Vol. I, pp. 153–160, 164–166.
[6] Latourette, *op. cit.*, Vol. V, pp. 453, 454; Groves, *op. cit.*, Vol. I, pp. 184–189.

the latter's 1,218,913 in that year.[7] In the 1830's and 1840's, to escape British rule, many of the Afrikanders, then called Boers, trekked northward and founded republics—the Orange Free State, the Transvaal, and Natal. Natal was soon (1845) annexed by the British, but it was not until the South African War (1899–1902) that the two other republics were reduced to submission. A few years later (1910) the Union of South Africa was formally established. It was a self-governing dominion akin to Canada, Australia, and New Zealand in its position in the British Empire but had more of a unitary government than Australia. In it the Boers were given the same rights as those of British birth and descent, but between the two white elements tensions continued to exist. Immediately north of the Union were two other British territories, Bechuanaland and Rhodesia. Within the borders of the Union but not included in its structure was Basutoland, a protectorate, and between Natal, Transvaal, and Portuguese East Africa was another protectorate, Swaziland, also not in the Union.

Religiously the Boers or Afrikanders were almost solidly members of the Dutch Reformed Church (*Nederduits Gereformeerde Kerk*) or its offshoots. To them the Dutch Reformed Church was a symbol and tie of nationalism, as was the Roman Catholic Church for the French Canadians. During the nineteenth century it grew in both numbers and inner life. In the early decades of the century, the colonial government continued the salaries of its clergy in accord with British policy at that time in other colonies. In 1843 the church achieved a large degree of autonomy.[8] For many years the church suffered from a shortage of clergy. To meet the need ministers came from Scotland, where the Presbyterianism was akin to the Dutch Reformed Church, and from the Netherlands. Outstanding was Andrew Murray. He had wished to be a missionary, and in the call to South Africa he saw the channel for fulfilling that purpose.[9] He spent his mature life in the service of his adopted church. His greatest contribution was through two of his sons, John and Andrew. Both were sent to Scotland for their education and there came in touch with the awakenings which entered into the formation of the Free Church of Scotland. In their student days in Utrecht, where they went for their university education, they became members of a circle that had arisen from the *réveil,* which did much to renew the vigour of the Reformed Church in the Netherlands.[10] On their return to South Africa, both brothers developed into outstanding leaders. John Murray (1826–1882), quiet and scholarly, became one of the first faculty of the theological seminary at Stellenbosch (opened in 1859) and thus had a

[7] *The Encyclopædia Britannica,* 14th ed., Vol. XVI, p. 395, Vol. XXI, p. 47.

[8] John McCarter, *The Dutch Reformed Church in South Africa with Notices of other Denominations* (Edinburgh, W. and C. Inglis, 1869, pp. vi, 147), pp. 34, 43; Du Plessis, *The Life of Andrew Murray,* p. 80.

[9] Du Plessis, *The Life of Andrew Murray,* pp. 12–16.

[10] *Ibid.,* pp. 34–77.

large share in the training of an indigenous ministry. Andrew Murray (1828–1917) had an even wider influence. When only twenty-one he followed the trekkers to the new frontier in the Orange Free State and became the first pastor of the congregation in Bloemfontein. He also itinerated widely among the lonely ranches of the Boer farmers and pushed his journeys as far as what became the Transvaal. A spiritual child of the revivalism of Scotland and the *réveil* of the Netherlands, he was an ardent evangelist, fed his soul on the *Theologia Germanica* and other writings of the Christian mystics, was warmly in sympathy with the Keswick movement in England, gave his support to the South Africa General Mission, which had as its object deepening the spiritual life of the nominal Christians and carrying the Gospel to the Africans, and was the author of many books, one of which in its English translation, *With Christ in the School of Prayer,* had a wide circulation in other countries. He believed in the faith healing of disease and stood for full commitment to the will of God and holiness of life. He also fought the influx of rationalistic, theologically liberal currents into the Dutch Reformed Church. He made a marked contribution to characteristics of that church—emphasis upon individual piety, adherence to theological conservatism of a Reformed kind with rejection of the intellectual currents abroad in much of European Protestantism, and active concern to spread the faith among the Africans.[11]

The Dutch Reformed Church accompanied and followed its children as they migrated northward and eastward to the new frontiers and, reinforced by clergy recruited from its sons or imported from Europe, became identified with the Afrikanders. Its clergy were ardent supporters of the Boer cause in the South African War. Boer nationalism, intensified by that conflict, rallied to it even more strongly.[12] Yet some spoke for conciliation with the English. In protest against the views of a number, Andrew Murray urged that the church as such keep out of politics and not commit itself to any one party or programme.[13]

In a body as large as the Dutch Reformed Church divisions almost inevitably developed. Thus in the 1840's and 1850's an autonomous *Nederduits Hervormde Kerk* appeared in the Transvaal. The chief reason for separation from the similar church in the Cape was that the latter received financial aid from the British colonial government and was accused of being subservient to a regime which the settlers had left the Cape Colony to escape.[14] Dutch Reformed churches administratively independent of one another, of which the Transvaal body was one, arose as well in the Orange Free State and Natal. Eventually they coöperated through a federation which embraced the large majority of the Reformed. Secessions from the majority bodies also occcurred, on the one hand of theologi-

---

[11] *Ibid.,* pp. 78 ff.
[12] *Ibid.,* pp. 423–432.
[13] *Ibid.,* pp. 423, 431, 432.
[14] S. P. Engelbrecht, *Geshiedenis van die Nederduits Herformde Kerk van Afrika* (Pretoria, J. H. de Bussy, 1936, pp. x, 434), *passim.*

cal liberals[15] and on the other hand of ultra-conservatives.[16] The ultra-conservative *Enkel Gereformeerde Kerk* was akin to a similar body in the Netherlands and created its own university, resembling the Free University in Amsterdam.

Among the non-Afrikander whites the Anglican Communion had the largest number of professed adherents. Early in the nineteenth century the Society for the Propagation of the Gospel in Foreign Parts and the Society for Promoting Christian Knowledge gave financial assistance to efforts to care for the English settlers. The colonial government also aided with lands and funds. The vigorous life of the Anglican Communion in South Africa dated from the arrival (1848) of the first bishop, Robert Gray (1809–1872). Committed to the Anglo-Catholic view of the Church, then newly reinforced by the Tractarian movement, he brought to his vast diocese vision and energy. He travelled prodigiously and stimulated the formation of congregations, the erection of churches, and the enlistment of clergy, both from England and in South Africa. He also concerned himself with missions among the non-whites. In 1853 he became Metropolitan of the new (Anglican) Province of South Africa. Additional dioceses were created and missions among the non-whites were greatly expanded.[17]

Methodism was next to Anglicanism in its numerical strength among the white population of South Africa for three reasons: the immigration from the British Isles, the sending of ministers from England, and the financial subventions from the Wesleyan Methodist Missionary Society. The much-travelled American William Taylor was there in 1866 and with especially marked effects among the blacks. In 1883 the comprehensive South African Conference first convened, but although financial aid from the mother body ceased in 1902 it was not until 1927 that the Conference became fully independent.[18]

Presbyterianism—if the Afrikander churches be not included—was relatively weaker among the whites than in Canada, Australia, and New Zealand. Only in 1893 was a presbytery formed with a church in Cape Town as a nucleus. Four years later a General Assembly was constituted.[19]

Lutherans, Baptists, and Congregationalists had fairly substantial numbers among the whites but were much fewer than Anglicans, Methodists, or Presbyterians.[20]

The percentage of Roman Catholics among the population of European blood ranked after that of Anglicans, Methodists, and Presbyterians. It was much less

---

[15] Du Plessis, *The Life of Andrew Murray*, pp. 208 ff., 247 ff.; D. P. Faure, *My Life and Times* (Cape Town, J. C. Juta and Co., 1907, pp. 232, iii), *passim.*

[16] Du Plessis, *The Life of Andrew Murray*, pp. 81, 175–179.

[17] Thompson, *Into All Lands*, pp. 197–203, 287–334; Groves, *op. cit.*, Vol. II, pp. 139–142.

[18] J. Whiteside, *History of the Wesleyan Methodist Church in South Africa* (London, Elliott Stock, 1906, pp. viii, 479), *passim;* Union of South Africa, *Official Year Book . . . , No. 9, 1926–1927*, pp. 292, 293.

[19] Balfour, *Presbyterianism in the Colonies*, pp. 282–291; Union of South Africa, *Official Year Book . . . , 1926–1927*, pp. 294, 295.

[20] *The Encyclopædia Britannica*, 14th ed., Vol. XXI, p. 50.

than in Canada, Australia, and New Zealand. Not until 1820 did the British colonial government permit a congregation to be organized. A priest was then placed in Cape Town. In 1837 a vicariate apostolic was created for the Cape and by 1892 four others had been added in South Africa. Clergy were in part recruited from native-born whites.[21]

For Christianity the challenge presented by the revolutionary age was partly that of race relations which arose from bringing together in an effort to take advantage of the natural resources of the land peoples of many traditions— Afrikanders, folk from the British Isles, Bushmen, Hottentots, Coloureds, Bantus, Indians, and Chinese. That phase of the challenge became acute before 1914, especially in the Afrikander-British clash, in the contacts between Africans and whites, and between whites and Indians.

Much of the challenge was winning the non-whites to the faith. By 1914 very considerable progress had been made. Statistics varied. One set had it that in 1921 less than half remained pagan and included in the standard denominations slightly more than a third of the non-Europeans.[22] Another survey showed about two-thirds of a million baptized Christians in 1914, which was only about one-sixth of the non-Europeans.[23] Both agree that the overwhelming majority of the Christians were Protestants. Protestants were from ten times to more than twenty times as numerous as the Roman Catholics. Yet in 1914 the latter had a larger foreign staff than did the former,[24] and after that year were to make very considerable gains. As in other countries, Roman Catholic missionaries to non-Christians were predominantly from the Continent of Europe. Among the Protestants missionaries from the Continent of Europe slightly outnumbered those from the British Isles, with the Berlin Missionary Society having the largest contingent and with other German societies, Scandinavians, French, and Swiss represented. Missionaries from the United States were less than half those from the British Isles and only about a third of those from the European Continent. South African societies had more missionaries than the Americans, and of them the Dutch Reformed Church had more than half and also more than the Americans.[25]

Since the societies were so numerous and the non-European population was divided into many groups and tribes, even a well-rounded summary of the missions would outstrip the proper limits of this chapter. Only a few features can be included.[26]

---

[21] *The Catholic Directory of British South Africa*, 1910, p. 1; *Missiones Catholicae . . . MDCCCXCII* (Rome, S. C. de Propaganda Fide, 1892, pp. xxxvi, 682), pp. 346–355.

[22] *The Encyclopædia Britannica*, 14th ed., Vol. XXI, p. 50.

[23] Beach and St. John, *World Statistics of Christian Missions*, pp. 59, 104.

[24] *Ibid.*, pp. 70, 104.

[25] *Ibid.*, p. 70.

[26] For a useful collection illustrating various aspects see Horton Davies and R. H. W. Shepherd, compilers, *South African Missions 1800–1850* (London, Thomas Nelson and Sons, 1954, pp. xxiv, 232).

Before the British occupation quite a little effort was put forth by the Dutch to win the non-Christians in the vicinity of their settlements. True to their wide-ranging vision, the Moravians had also been represented.[27] But several factors kept the Afrikanders from maintaining the leadership that the Dutch had begun. With their rapidly mounting numbers due to a high birth rate, they themselves long suffered from a dearth of pastors and had few to spare for the Africans. As they moved to the frontier, mostly farmers, they came into conflict with the Africans, especially the Bushmen and the Hottentots, and sought to exterminate them or reduce them to slavery rather than convert them.[28]

Soon after the British took possession, the London Missionary Society, organized as it was in that very same year (1795), saw in the coincidence a challenge. In 1799 an initial contingent, led by a Dutchman, John Theodore Vanderkemp, arrived at Cape Town. With them began a continuing mission. One of the doughty pioneers, Robert Moffat (1795–1883), we have already met as the one who turned Livingstone's eyes to Africa. He was a notable missionary in his own right and one of his daughters married Livingstone.[29] The outstanding leader of the London Missionary Society's enterprise in South Africa was John Philip (1775–1851). Philip came to South Africa in 1819 and the following year was made superintendent of the London Missionary Society's undertakings in that area. A man of amazing physical energy and of pronounced convictions, he travelled indefatigably over the vast area which was his assignment, brought improvement in stations which under Vanderkemp's sincere but unwise supervision left much to be desired, and championed the cause of the natives. His accusations of cruelty to the latter were given wide publicity in Great Britain, where the anti-slavery agitation was at its height, and brought him much criticism in the Cape Colony, especially from the Afrikanders. It was at his suggestion that the French Protestants began their highly successful mission in Basutoland and it was largely through him that the Rhenish Missionary Society began operations in South Africa.[30]

As a result of the efforts of the London Missionary Society, Congregationalism enrolled a much larger proportion of the non-European than of the European Christians of South Africa. The Society pushed its frontiers northward to enter the doors opened by its great emissary, Livingstone.[31] It encouraged

[27] Du Plessis, *A History of Christian Missions in South Africa*, pp. 19–69.

[28] *Ibid.*, pp. 261–271.

[29] *Ibid.*, pp. 99–136; John S. Moffat, *The Lives of Robert and Mary Moffat* (London, T. Fisher Unwin, 1886, pp. xxii, 468), *passim;* Robert Moffat, *Missionary Labours and Scenes in Southern Africa* (London, John Snow, 1842, pp. xv, 624), *passim;* Edwin W. Smith, *Robert Moffat, One of God's Gardeners* (London, Student Christian Movement, 1925, pp. 251), *passim.*

[30] Du Plessis, *A History of Christian Missions in South Africa*, pp. 141–153.

[31] For the biography of one of the pioneers who married a sister of Livingstone's wife, see Edwin W. Smith, *Great Lion of Bechuanaland. The Life and Times of Roger Price, Missionary* (London, Independent Press, 1957, pp. xvi, 444). For Price's wife see Una Long, editor, *The Journals of Elizabeth Lees Price written in Bechuanaland, Southern Africa 1854–1883 with an Epilogue: 1889 and 1900* (London, Edward Arnold, 1956, pp. x, 564), *passim.*

the churches founded by it in the Cape Colony to become independent, financially and in other ways. In the twentieth century only one station remained with missionaries supported from Great Britain: it centred on a school most of whose graduates became teachers.[32]

In the nineteenth century the Wesleyan Methodists ultimately won more of the non-whites of South Africa than any other Protestant denomination or than the Roman Catholics. Their first missionary came in 1814 but was soon transferred to Ceylon and was succeeded by Barnabas Shaw, who arrived in 1816 and laid the foundations for the missions of his denomination. The Methodists combined white and non-white in their circuits and pushed their frontiers eastward and north-eastward. In 1886 they inaugurated the South African Missionary Society. By 1914 that society was responsible for more than 86,000 baptized Christians.[33]

Anglicans were next to the Methodists in the number of non-whites enrolled. Like the Methodists they did not draw a sharp colour line in their congregations. Although some of the latter were entirely of one race or the other, in many of them whites and non-whites were included and both were represented in their synods. Since the Anglican missionaries were predominantly Anglo-Catholic—a tradition going back to Robert Gray and maintained through the Society for the Propagation of the Gospel in Foreign Parts—various orders and congregations of men and women were represented and had a large part in the varied methods by which the mission of their church was pursued.[34]

Presbyterians did not have as large a proportion of the non-Europeans in their churches as did the Methodists, Anglicans, Dutch Reformed, Lutherans, or Congregationalists. But through several Scottish societies, most of them eventually merged in the United Presbyterian and the Free Church efforts and then in those of the United Free Church, they had centres scattered through much of the country. They stressed education, and their major educational institution was at Lovedale. There the programme was deeply indebted to a visit of Alexander Duff. In the adjacent Fort Hare, on land donated by the United Free Church, a college arose in 1916 in which several societies, churches, and governments and protectorates of South Africa joined to give higher education to non-Europeans. The outstanding creator of Lovedale was its second principal, James Stewart (1831–1905).[35]

---

[32] Lovett, *The History of the London Missionary Society 1795–1895*, Vol. I, pp. 572 ff.; *The One Hundred and Seventh Report of the London Missionary Society* (1902), p. 239; *The One Hundred and Fourteenth Report of the London Missionary Society* (1909), p. 210.

[33] Du Plessis, *A History of Christian Missions in South Africa*, pp. 165–181, 294–302; Whiteside, *op. cit.*, *passim;* W. Holden, *A Brief History of Methodism and of Methodist Missions in South Africa* (London, Wesleyan Conference Office, 1877, pp. viii, 519), *passim.*

[34] Du Plessis, *A History of Christian Missions in South Africa*, pp. 233–242, 353–359; Thompson, *op. cit.*, pp. 287 ff.; Osmund Victor, *The Salient of South Africa* (Westminster, Society for the Propagation of the Gospel in Foreign Parts, 1931, pp. vii, 190), *passim.*

[35] Du Plessis, *A History of Christian Missions in South Africa*, pp. 360–365; John Lennox, *The Story of Our Missions, South Africa* (Edinburgh, Offices of the United Free Church of Scotland,

In spite of the shortage of clergy to meet the needs of the rapidly multiplying congregations on the frontier, the Dutch Reformed Churches increasingly undertook missions for the non-Europeans. Not a few were at the instance of men, including Andrew Murray, who were deeply touched by the Pietist movements. Many were through what was called the Inland Mission of the Cape Colony and through the churches of the Orange Free State, Transvaal, and Natal. Some missionaries were obtained from the Netherlands, but increasingly the staff was Afrikander. The missions were in several parts of the country.[36] In addition the Dutch Reformed had a notable mission in Nyasaland.[37] Moreover, among the Afrikanders, largely farmers and with African servants, were those who sought through personal and domestic contacts to win the latter to the Christian faith.

Of the Protestant societies from the Continent of Europe the ones with the largest foreign staffs in 1914 were the Berlin Missionary Society, the Hermannsburg Mission, the *Société des Missions Évangéliques* (of Paris) and its associated Swiss socicety, the *Mission Romande,* and the Norwegian Missionary Society. Of these the one with the largest number of baptized adherents was Hermannsburg, and it did not have as many as the leading British societies.[38] The Hermannsburg Mission, begun by the Lutheran pastor Ludwig Harms,[39] specialized in sending out farmers and others without much formal education but with a warm, contagious Christian faith and with skills which would enable them to assist folk of primitive or near-primitive culture in their economic and collective life. It came to the Transvaal at the invitation of that republic's president. The Berlin Missionary Society also found its major field in the Transvaal. The Afrikanders were disposed to welcome the Germans as a counterpoise to the distrusted British missionaries. The outstanding French Protestant missionary was François Coillard (1834-1904). His great achievement was among the Barotse, whom he and his associates helped to make the difficult adjustment to the problems brought by the white man.[40]

The society from the United States with the major staff and numbers of converts—and it not as large in these respects as the leading British, Afrikander, and Continental European societies—was the American Board of Commissioners for Foreign Missions. Its main enterprises were among the Zulus in Natal and then among the Zulu young men who went to Johannesburg to labour in

---

1911, pp. 87), *passim;* Robert H. W. Shepherd, *Lovedale South Africa. The Story of a Century 1841-1941* (Lovedale, The Lovedale Press, 1941, pp. xiv, 531), *passim;* James Wells, *The Life of James Stewart* (London, Hodder and Stoughton, 1909, pp. xi, 419), *passim.*

[36] Du Plessis, *A History of Christian Missions in South Africa,* pp. 284–293.

[37] H. W. Retief, *Verowerings vir Christus: die Lewe van Dr. W. H. Murray van Nyasaland* (Stellenbosch, Die C. S. V. Boekhandel, foreword 1947, pp. 308), *passim.*

[38] Beach and St. John, *op. cit.,* p. 70.

[39] Volume II, Chapter IX.

[40] For the Continental European missions, especially the footnote references to the extensive literature on them, see Latourette, *op. cit.,* Vol. V, pp. 362–372.

the gold mines. Partly through the help of Zulu Christians in the 1890's the American Board reached out into Southern Rhodesia.[41]

Before 1914 only the foundations of the Roman Catholic Church among the non-European population in South Africa had been laid. The rapid numerical growth which was seen in the four decades after that year had only barely begun. But in the nineteenth century several centres were opened in various parts of the country. In this enterprise a variety of orders and congregations shared. The most notable establishment was Mariannhill, begun by German Trappists in 1882 on a site in Natal commanding a view of Durban and the sea. Here Africans were induced to settle and for them industrial, normal, and other schools were developed and a printing press and a hospital were created. In the course of the years more than a score of other centres were founded by the Trappists.[42]

As Christianity, and especially Protestant Christianity, made headway among the Africans, various movements arose which repudiated the white man's leadership. Some of them stemmed from an incipient African nationalism, as in the "Ethiopian" church founded in 1892. Others had fellowship with the African Methodist Episcopal Church of the United States. Many sprang from ambitious Africans who in this fashion found leadership. The movements had begun before 1914. After that year they rapidly proliferated.[43]

Marked though the progress was in holding the whites to at least a nominal adherence to the faith, in winning an increasing proportion of the non-whites, and in helping the latter to make an adjustment to the invading culture, the challenge of South Africa was by no means fully met. Race tensions remained and became even more acute in the next century. Here Gandhi, in an effort to gain justice for his fellow Indians, worked out, partly under the inspiration of Christ and friendship with a Protestant pastor's family, the methods of non-violent resistance which he was soon to practise on a larger scale in his homeland. But the problem of the contacts between the other elements was still unresolved and was rendered more acute by the misuse of the soil and by urbanization.

BECHUANALAND, RHODESIA, NYASALAND

In 1914 the vast territory north of the Union of South Africa was under

[41] *Ibid.*, pp. 360, 361; Du Plessis, *A History of Christian Missions in South Africa*, pp. 219–232, 303–309. For the life of an American Board missionary who was for a time pastor of early Dutch Reformed settlers see Edwin W. Smith, *The Life and Times of Daniel Lindley (1801–80), Missionary to the Zulus, Pastor of the Voortrekkers, Ubebe Omhlope* (London, The Epworth Press, 1949, pp. xxx, 456).

[42] Du Plessis, *A History of Christian Missions in South Africa*, pp. 366–372; Schwager, *Die katholische Heidenmission der Gegenwart im Zusammenhang mit ihrer grossen Vergangenheit*, pp. 132–145.

[43] Bengt G. M. Sundkler, *Bantu Prophets in South Africa* (London, Lutterworth Press, 1948, pp. 344), pp. 38–64.

British rule as the Bechuanaland Protectorate (in which Boer and British interests had been in conflict until the establishment of the British Protectorate in 1885), Rhodesia (South and North), and Nyasaland. Here the contrasts between the various ways in which Western Europe impinged on Africa were striking. The extension of British authority was deeply indebted to Cecil John Rhodes (1853–1902). The son of a clergyman of the Church of England and in his boyhood designed for his father's profession, Rhodes went to South Africa in search of health, there became wealthy, dreamed of the British occupation of vast areas in that and adjoining regions, and did much to fulfil his dream. Here came sportsmen in search of game and adventurers in quest of gold. Here, too, were missionaries, labouring for the temporal and eternal welfare of the Africans.[44] Livingstone had explored part of the area, especially that later embraced in Nyasaland, with the object of opening it to missions and of curbing the slave trade.

We have time simply to mention the main missions in Nyasaland and to call attention to the fact that they came in response to the challenge of Livingstone and his discoveries. The Universities' Mission to Central Africa, Anglican and the result of a direct appeal by Livingstone, had a tragic beginning in an involvement in native wars and the early death of its first bishop and several of his party. But it persevered and eventually gained access to the region from a base on Zanzibar and established continuing centres. Stirred by the death of Livingstone, both the Free Church of Scotland and the Church of Scotland assumed responsibilities in the region. The former had as its initiator James Stewart, already prominent in South Africa, and as its outstanding leader Robert Laws. Partly at the instance of Andrew Murray and of a brother-in-law of James Stewart and with a relative of the former as the first missionary, the Dutch Reformed Church of South Africa began a mission (1888) which ultimately had a larger white staff than either of the Scottish societies.[45]

UGANDA

Uganda, below the equator, in its highlands had a climate which because of the altitude was not unsalubrious. The ruling people were the Baganda, and among them Christianity, both Protestant and Roman Catholic, made striking advances before 1914.[46] His journeys brought Stanley to Uganda. There he in-

---

[44] As illustrating the contrast, see Constance E. Fripp and V. W. Hiller, editors, *Gold and the Gospel in Mashonaland 1888: being the journals of 1. The Mashonaland Mission of Bishop Knight-Bruce; 2. The Concession Journey of Charles Dunell Rudd* (London, Chatto & Windus, 1949, pp. ix, 246).

[45] Latourette, *op. cit.*, Vol. V, pp. 388–397, which contains bibliographical references. More recent than that volume are J. P. R. Wallis, editor, *The Zambesi Journals of James Stewart, with a Selection from His Correspondence* (London, Chatto & Windus, 1952, pp. xxvi, 276), and H. W. Retief, *William Murray of Nyasaland,* translated from the Afrikaans and abridged by Mary H. Le Roux and M. M. Oberholster-le Roux (The Lovedale Press, 1958, pp. viii, 196), *passim.*

[46] For summary accounts, with footnote references to the authorities, see Latourette, *op. cit.,*

structed the half-pagan, half-Moslem Mtesa, King of the Baganda, in the Christian faith and translated part of the Bible for him. Mtesa professed himself to be Christian and Stanley appealed to Europeans and Americans to send missionaries. Both the Church Missionary Society and the White Fathers responded. The representatives of the former were the first to arrive (1877) but the latter followed shortly (1879). For both Anglicans and Roman Catholics the initial years were marked by great difficulties, with many deaths, few conversions, and intermittent persecutions. The persecutions were due in part to the rivalries of the English, French, Germans, and Arabs for political control. In 1890 an Anglo-German treaty assigned the region to the British and in 1894 the British protectorate was formally declared. The coming of British rule brought internal peace. A mass movement, principally of the Baganda, into the Anglican and Roman Catholic forms of Christianity quickly followed. By 1914 the number of baptized Anglicans was only slightly less than 100,000, and that of Roman Catholics was about 134,000. In 1894 part of the territory was assigned by Rome to an English society, that of Mill Hill. In spite of their policy to require a catechumenate of four years, in 1914 the White Fathers had more Roman Catholics under their guidance than were to be found in any other vicariate south of the Sahara. Both Anglicans and Roman Catholics had schools, the former more than the latter, and were training an African staff and encouraging self-support.

THE BELGIAN CONGO

The large portion of Africa included in the Congo Free State, by 1914 to become the Belgian Congo, was the scene of extensive missions, both Roman Catholic and Protestant. The explorations of Stanley attracted the attention of the missionary forces.

The fact that the region was under the rule of the King of the Belgians and then passed to Belgium gave Belgian Roman Catholics a special interest in it. Leopold obtained from the Pope the reservation of most of the area to Belgian missions. Numbers of orders and congregations established themselves there and in 1914 more of them were represented than in any other political entity in Africa south of the equator. Most of the personnel was Belgian. In 1912 the Congregation of the Immaculate Heart of Mary with headquarters at Scheutveld, who had their initial field in Inner Mongolia, had upwards of half the Roman Catholic missionaries in Congo Belge. In that year the number of Roman Catholics was more than 100,000. After 1914 it was to multiply several fold.

The provision of freedom endorsed by Leopold for missionary activity by any branch of the faith and from any country encouraged Protestants to carry on extensive enterprises. Indeed, they were earlier active than were Roman Cath-

---

Vol. V, pp. 412–419, and Groves, *op. cit.,* Vol. III, pp. 88–97. See also Kittler, *The White Fathers,* pp. 112–213.

olics, and eventually more Protestant than Roman Catholic organizations were represented. They were mostly from the British Isles and the United States and were supported by several denominations and undenominational societies.

Both Roman Catholic and Protestant missionaries called the attention of the world to the exploitation of the Africans, not far removed from slavery, under the administration of Leopold.[47]

A Brief Look at Other Sections

Space permits only the barest mention of other portions of Africa south of the Sahara. There the complexion of the missionary body was in part determined by the European government which had control. In the British territories the missionaries were largely Protestant and British. In the German possessions German missions were numerous. French territories tended to be served by the French. But to these generalizations there were many exceptions. For example, in Nigeria, under British administration, the Southern Baptists of the United States began what became a large enterprise. Since in Portugal the Roman Catholic Church was distraught because of domestic difficulties,[48] few missionaries came from that country to Portuguese East Africa and West Africa. Moreover, Roman Catholic missionaries were found in lands governed by the officially Protestant Great Britain, and Protestant missionaries gained entrance to Portuguese territories. The Roman Catholic congregations with the largest number of missionaries and with more Christians under their care than any other of the orders and congregations were the White Fathers and the Holy Ghost Fathers (indebted to Francis Maria Paul Libermann, the convert from Judaism who became the first superior general).[49] Of the British Protestant agencies the Church Missionary Society was the most widely represented.[50]

Madagascar

Because of its geographic proximity to that continent, Madagascar can properly be noted in connexion with Africa. One of the largest islands in the world, more than twice the size of Great Britain or the main island of Japan, with a population of about 2,750,000 akin to the Malays, Polynesians, and Melanesians, it was the scene in the nineteenth century of a most dramatic chapter in the history of Christianity. The dominant tribe was the Hòva, whose home was on the central high plateau. At the outset of the nineteenth century not highly civilized, the Hòva, while still animists as were their fellow islanders, could not be called primitive. Moreover, one of their monarchs, Radàma I, had taken

---

[47] For summary accounts, with footnote references to the authorities, see Latourette, *op. cit.,* Vol. V, pp. 419–427, and Groves, *op. cit.,* Vol. III, pp. 108–125.

[48] Volume I, pp. 424–426.

[49] Volume I, pp. 338, 339.

[50] For statistics on the eve of 1914 see Beach and St. John, *op. cit.,* pp. 59, 103.

advantage of firearms acquired from the white man to extend his rule over much of the island. He was also eager to introduce European crafts and education. At that juncture, in 1818, the London Missionary Society, which almost since its formation had been contemplating the initiation of an enterprise on the island, sent its first representatives. Schools were opened, the Bible was translated, and boys were sent to England for training under the auspices of the Society but at the expense of the Hòva Government. At first not many converts were made and the years 1836–1861 were marked by persecution. Yet the faith continued to spread, in the late 1860's a new queen and her prime minister were baptized, and a mass movement into the faith followed, not only among the Hòva, but also among other tribes.

Conforming to what they had learned through the representatives of the London Missionary Society, most of the Hòva Christians were Congregationalists, but other denominations entered—Anglican, Lutheran (from Norway and the United States), and Friends. Roman Catholics also came, at first through a French secular priest who, appointed prefect apostolic of the Isle of Bourbon in 1829, died on his first trip to Madagascar. Other Roman Catholic missionaries followed and after much difficulty obtained a continuing foothold.

Annexation by France (1895) brought great changes. For a time Roman Catholic missionaries, being French, were favoured by the colonial authorities, and, because of the intense rivalry between the French and English in Africa in the 1890's, British missions were regarded with suspicion. To strengthen their branch of the faith the French Protestants sent representatives through the *Société des Missions Évangéliques* (of Paris) and worked in close coöperation with the London Missionary Society and the Friends. In 1905, about the time of the separation of Church and state in France, an anti-clerical governor was appointed and both Roman Catholics and Protestants faced restrictions.

Yet Christianity continued to spread. Protestant church·membership is said to have risen from 41,134 in 1898 to 74,817 in 1918; Protestant adherents to have mounted from 86,416 in 1898 to 449,126 in 1918, and Roman Catholics, approximately 170,000 in 1905, to have been 210,000 in 1911. Presumably, therefore, by 1914 about a fourth of the population of Madagascar considered themselves to be Christians.[51]

SUMMARY

In 1914 the impact of the revolutionary age on Africa was only beginning to be felt. Late in the eighteenth century white men had first penetrated the interior. But not until the second half of the nineteenth century did intrepid explorers disclose the heart of the continent to Europeans and Americans. It was only in the last quarter of the century that Western European powers parcelled

---

[51] Latourette, *op. cit.*, Vol. V, pp. 301–313 contains a summary account with footnote references to the literature and sources.

out among themselves Africa south of the Sahara. The great changes brought by the age were to come in the twentieth century.

On the whole, the effects of Western Christendom on Africa south of the Sahara were not as demoralizing in the nineteenth century as they had been earlier. From the fifteenth into the fore part of the nineteenth century the slave trade, for which nominal Christians were chiefly responsible, had piled up a record of almost unrelieved cruelty, suffering, and callous greed. In the course of that century the Christian conscience and the humanitarianism born of that conscience had eliminated the slavery in the Americas on which the trade had battened. That conscience continued to prod Europeans, especially the British, to end such remnants of the trade as were carried on by Moslem Arabs.

The record of Western Christendom was still ambiguous. The passion for riches and the zeal for national prestige were potent in African policies. The explorations of such men as Livingstone and Stanley in whom a Christian motive was strong opened the way for a civilization in which Christianity, while influential, was not dominant. Missionaries, both Protestant and Roman Catholic, endeavoured to make the coming of that civilization a blessing and not a curse. They sought to proclaim the Gospel and to win the Africans to its acceptance. They reduced languages to writing, translated the Bible, and bore the main load of the kind of schools which the Africans must have if they were to adjust themselves successfully to the invading culture. They pioneered in substituting Western medicine for the witch doctor. Their efforts multiplied in the later decades of the century. They sought to inculcate Christian ideals of family and sex. They contributed to the disintegration of the traditional patterns of life, but that disintegration would have come had never a missionary set foot in Africa. The missionary effort was not as destructive as it was constructive. Here and there the mass conversions had commenced which were to mount in the next century.

At the end of the century Protestant and Roman Catholic missionary staffs were about equal. At that time African Protestants outnumbered African Roman Catholics, but if South Africa be left out of the reckoning the two branches of Christianity had approximately the same numbers of adherents.

In Madagascar the record of Christianity was less compromised by the greed of Western Europeans than in Africa. The slave trade had never been as prominent, the English sought to erase such of it as existed, and missionaries were less hampered by the dark side of Western Christendom than on the neighbouring continent.

CHAPTER XXIV

The World Outside "Christendom":
A Summary Retrospect

As we pause to look back over the course of Christianity in that vast segment of the world which lay outside the historic "Christendom" and its extension in the Americas, Australia, and New Zealand, we require only a brief summary. Much that might go into it was given in the pages (Chapter XV) which served as an introduction to this portion of our story. However, it may prove helpful to remind ourselves of some of the recurring features of what we have rehearsed with some detail in the preceding eight chapters.

First, everywhere we have noted the mounting impact of "Christendom," mostly Western "Christendom," and of the revolutionary forces which issued from it upon the rest of mankind. That impact was predominantly economic and political, but with these aspects went other phases of that Western civilization which was undergoing revolution. By the year 1914 the majority of mankind were partially or entirely politically subject to "Christian" peoples, and the commerce and capitalism of Western "Christendom" were penetrating most of the globe.

Second, under the impact of the revolutionary forces the cultures of all mankind were undergoing changes. As was to be expected, the changes were most marked in Europe and in peoples of European ancestry. But they were also seen in varying degrees in all other peoples and cultures. They had already gone far among folk of "primitive" cultures on many of the islands of the Pacific. They had begun to be spectacular among the Chinese, that largest fairly homogeneous portion of mankind. The outer but as yet not the inner structure of life of the Japanese was transformed. In the twentieth century the changes were to become so breath-taking that in retrospect even those of the latter part of the nineteenth century would appear to have been hesitant and slow. But at the time they were startling.

Third, in connexion with the impact, Christianity had a geographic spread which was more extensive than it or any other religion had thus far known. Much of it came about through the adoption by non-European peoples of phases of a civilization which had long been under Christian influence. More obvious

was the formal adherence to the faith achieved through the labours of missionaries. A very few of the missionaries were Russian Orthodox. The large majority
were Roman Catholics and Protestants. Roman Catholic missions were renewed
after the pause in the eighteenth century and covered a wider portion of the
globe than even in the previous heyday of the sixteenth and seventeenth centuries. They stemmed almost entirely from the Continent of Europe and more
from France than from all other countries combined—and that in spite of the
corroding scepticism and the rampant anti-clericalism in that country. They
were the fruits of the revival of the Roman Catholic Church in Western Europe in the nineteenth century and were carried on either by the orders and
congregations which had been given fresh life by that revival or by congregations and societies newly sprung from it in the nineteenth century. Protestant
missionaries were chiefly the children of the awakenings of the nineteenth century and either represented the Pietist and Evangelical strains of Protestantism
or, in lesser numbers, were from the revival of the Catholic tradition in the
Anglican Communion and the stiffened confessionalism in some of the Lutheran bodies. They were predominantly from the British Isles, the United
States, and the British dominions. Proportionately Protestant missions grew
more rapidly both in numbers of their representatives, in territory covered, in
converts, and in effects upon the cultures among which they operated than Roman Catholic missions. Through missions among non-Christians as well as
through migrations of peoples by heredity of its branch of the faith, Protestantism for the first time was ceasing to be a North-western European phenomenon
and was becoming world-wide.

Fourth, as a result of the efforts of missionaries, with the exception of the
old churches in Western Asia and North-east Africa, existing Christian communities outside Western "Christendom" were growing and new Christian
communities were coming into being. For the most part the latter were small
minorities and chiefly of peoples of "primitive" or near-"primitive" cultures.
Relatively few included members from the higher castes of India, from the educated among the Chinese, and from the Japanese, and still fewer from the
Moslems.

Fifth, as yet most of the Christian communities which arose from the labours
of the missionaries were dependent for leadership and financial undergirding
upon missionaries and the supporters of missions. Superficially they seemed to
be the religious and ecclesiastical phase of Western imperialism. Yet the dream
of many of the missionaries was to make them self-supporting, self-governing,
and self-propagating and by the end of the century here and there the dream
was beginning to be realized. In the twentieth century rapid strides were witnessed towards the attainment of the goal.

Sixth, missionaries, and especially Protestant missionaries, were pioneers in introducing phases of Western civilization, chiefly in education, medicine, and surgery, which would assist the peoples among whom they lived to adjust to the age into which they were being hurried and to profit from the civilization which was being thrust upon them.

CHAPTER XXV

The Foreshadowing of Global Coöperation Among Protestants

A FEATURE of nineteenth-century Protestantism was growing coöperation across denominational lines. With some temporary reverses it mounted as the century went on and in the last two decades assumed global proportions. In the twentieth century the pace quickened. Here and there denominational lines were erased and unions of ecclesiastical bodies were achieved. In other instances federation was accomplished which preserved a degree of autonomy to the churches entering into it. But more inclusive was coöperation which did not entail either union or federation.

The impulse responsible for union, federation, or coöperation was of varied origin. In part it was an uneasy conscience. If the basic Christian command is love, the divisions among Christians, of whatever nature, are a sin against that love. In part the impulse was the conviction that certain objectives could be better attained by working together than by working separately.

Our narrative has disclosed much of the movement on national and international scales. We have seen, for example, the unions of Reformed and Lutheran in Germany; the Young Men's and Young Women's Christian Associations which enlisted individuals from many denominations and which, while Protestant in origin, attracted many Roman Catholics without severing their connexion with their church; the Federal Council of the Churches of Christ in America; and the several conferences of missionaries of India, China, and Japan. Somewhat similarly, beginning in 1858 the Conference of Swiss Churches brought together representatives of the cantonal Protestant bodies, and the Protestant Federation of France was inaugurated in 1905 from the stimulus given by the separation of Church and state in that year.[1] It remains to point out the first steps towards global coöperation. At some of them we have already hinted, but we must attempt to put them in the comprehensive pattern to which, in retrospect, they are seen to belong.

The movement was both similar and dissimilar to what was taking place in the Roman Catholic Church. As we have seen, that church was being knit to-

---

[1] Rouse and Neill, *A History of the Ecumenical Movement 1517–1948*, pp. 621, 629.

gether more closely than ever before under the Pope. The process was aided by the improved means of travel and communication which were features of the revolutionary age. The same means facilitated closer global ties among Protestants. Yet the unity being achieved among Roman Catholics had basic differences from that which was appearing within Protestantism. The Vatican Council of 1869–1870 made explicit a conviction long cherished in the Roman Catholic Church that the Pope had supreme authority both in administration and in defining what must be believed by all Christians. In contrast, because of its principles of justification by faith alone and the right and duty of each Christian to think for himself and be responsible only to God—the latter a principle with such palpable dangers that most of the great Reformers and their successors did not fully abide by it—Protestants could not consistently and would not in practice conform to any institution of the nature of the Papacy. For the most part the Protestant advances towards unity tacitly or explicitly held that no institution, whether church or bishop, was infallible or embodied the Gospel in its entirety. Yet they had at their heart the fulfilment of the prayer "that they [the followers of Christ] all may be one . . . that the world may believe." The dominant motive was effective witness to the Gospel and common action in bringing all men to accept the faith and to embody it in every aspect of their lives—namely, obedience to the commission to make disciples of all nations, baptizing them, and teaching them to observe all that Christ had commanded the intimate group of His followers.

It was significant and a foreshadowing of what eventually developed that William Carey, usually regarded as the outstanding pioneer of the nineteenth- and twentieth-century Protestant missionary movement, proposed in 1805 decennial conferences "of Christians of all denominations" to consider common problems.[2] However, at that time nothing came of Carey's idea and it was almost forgotten until later movements quite independently of it embodied it.

A nineteenth-century movement which persisted into the twentieth century, chiefly in its later years for calling for a week of prayer, was the Evangelical Alliance. It arose from the Evangelical awakenings of the nineteenth century and was critical of the Roman Catholic Church and the Anglo-Catholic movement in the Church of England. It tended to champion groups on the Continent of Europe which dissented from the state churches. Its members were individuals, not ecclesiastical bodies. In the 1830's and 1840's suggestions for some such organization were made in several countries. A preparatory meeting was held in London in 1843 in that well-known centre of Evangelical movements, Exeter Hall. The gathering which founded the Alliance took place in 1846, also in London. The attendance was predominantly British, but of the eight hundred present about 10 per cent. were from America and 6 per cent. from the

---

[2] *Ibid.*, pp. 311, 312.

Continent. Every few years the Evangelical Alliance held international meetings. In connexion with them careful surveys were made of contemporary religious conditions in the world. Some of its national branches published journals. It placed much emphasis upon religious liberty and also sought to promote missions. The American Evangelical Alliance was not organized until 1867, but thereafter for several years it flourished and had many state and city alliances as auxiliaries.[3]

Various world-embracing organizations were formed of movements with specialized functions. Like the Evangelical Alliance, they were fruits of the Evangelical-Pietist awakening. In 1855 representatives of the YMCA's in several countries convened in Paris in connexion with an international gathering of the Evangelical Alliance and brought into being the World's Alliance of Young Men's Christian Associations. An important but not the only prominent figure in the meeting was Henri Dunant, the chief inspirer of the Red Cross.[4] In 1894 the sister organization, the World's Young Women's Christian Association, was formed, with its doors open to the members of all churches.[5] The expanding Sunday School movement held the first of a series of world's conventions in London in 1889 and at the seventh, in Rome in 1907, the World's Sunday School Association was constituted.[6]

Several denominational families devised comprehensive structures, largely for fellowship and to form a common mind on specific issues. The bishops of the Anglican Communion were called together in 1867 to deal with the controversy arising from the views of Colenso. Beginning in 1888 what were known as the Lambeth Conferences met decennially. They disavowed any intention of becoming a synod with legislative powers over the multiplying national bodies which made up the Anglican Communion.[7] The Alliance of Reformed Churches throughout the World holding the Presbyterian System was organized in 1875; the Ecumenical Methodist Council, after 1951 called the Methodist Council, was founded in 1881; the International Congregational Council was formed in London in 1891; and the Baptist World Alliance was begun in 1905.[8]

A body from which came much of the leadership of what in the next century was known as the Ecumenical Movement was the World's Student Christian Federation. Arising out of the Evangelical-Pietist strains of Protestantism and deeply indebted in its inception to the Young Men's Christian Association, it was formed in 1895 by a small group meeting in Vadstena in Sweden. Its first general secretary and the one who was chiefly responsible for its inception and

[3] *Ibid.*, pp. 254, 255, 318–324.
[4] Clarence P. Shedd, *History of the World's Alliance of Young Men's Christian Associations* (London, S.P.C.K., 1955, pp. xvii, 746), pp. 102–137.
[5] Rouse and Neill, *op. cit.*, p. 607.
[6] *Ibid.*, p. 612.
[7] *Ibid.*, p. 264.
[8] *Ibid.*, pp. 613–615.

its growth was John R. Mott. The World's Student Christian Federation had as its purpose coöperation among the student Christian movements which were springing up in several countries out of the Evangelical-Pietist revivals of the latter part of the century. Its expressed objectives were to lead students to become disciples of Jesus Christ as only Saviour and Lord, to deepen the spiritual life of students, and to enlist students in extending the Kingdom of Christ throughout the world.[9] It was no accident that Mott became the first honorary president and that another of the former officers of the Federation was the first general secretary of the World Council of Churches, formed in 1948. Nor was it strange that Mott should be the most creative figure who emerged from the World Missionary Conference and that the meeting was looked back on in the next century as a milestone in the Ecumenical Movement.

The World Missionary Conference of 1910 had back of it more than a generation of experience of coöperation among Protestants in seeking to spread the Gospel throughout the world. Much had been in regional conferences and organizations. We must remind ourselves of the ones in India, China, and Japan; of the plans to divide the responsibility in the Philippines among denominations by regions; of other similar measures in various countries of what was called comity; of the Foreign Missions Conference of North America constituted in 1893 and its Committee of Reference and Counsel authorized in 1907; of the Association of German Mission Conferences formed in 1906 to coördinate various provincial conferences which overpassed confessional lines and which dated from 1879; and of *Der Ausschuss der deutschen evangelischen Missionsgesellschaften,* dating from 1885 and given a constitution in 1897.[10] From time to time Continental Missions Conferences had convened, the first in Bremen in 1866.[11] In 1819 secretaries of foreign mission societies with headquarters in London formed an association for consultation which met almost monthly.[12] Out of a sense of a common Scandinavian Lutheranism, beginning in 1863 northern Lutheran missions conferences convened which eventually were attended by missionary leaders from Sweden, Norway, Denmark, and Finland.[13] After a missionary convention held in New York in 1854 at the instance of Alexander Duff and another in that year in London growing out of the British unit of the Evangelical Alliance, more comprehensive conferences with increasing attendance were held in Liverpool in 1860, in London in 1878, again in London in 1888, and in New York in 1900. They were predominantly Anglo-American, reflecting the majority position which the British Isles and the United States had in the world-wide missions of Protestants, but in the later ones Continental

---

[9] Ruth Rouse, *The World's Student Christian Federation. A History of the First Thirty Years* (London, S.C.M. Press, 1948, pp. 332), pp. 52–64.
[10] Hogg, *Ecumenical Foundations,* pp. 68–71, 74–79.
[11] *Ibid.,* pp. 60–67.
[12] *Ibid.,* pp. 51, 52.
[13] *Ibid.,* pp. 53–60.

Protestantism was also represented. That in New York in 1900, called the Ecumenical Missionary Conference, attracted a huge attendance and helped to make widely known the dimensions which the Protestant foreign missionary enterprise had attained.[14]

The World Missionary Conference of 1910 arose directly from the Ecumenical Missionary Conference of 1900. Unlike it, however, it was made up of official representatives of organizations engaged in missions and was preceded by careful and comprehensive studies extending over a number of years and engaging the labours of hundreds of individuals. It was intended to formulate policies for future action. The two who had most to do with the success of the gathering were John R. Mott and Joseph H. Oldham. Mott had an important part in the preparations and presided at most of the sessions in Edinburgh. Oldham, slightly younger than Mott, was a Scot and came from a warmly Evangelical home. Scholarly, like Mott from the Student Christian movement, and profoundly religious (his *Devotional Diary* had wide use over many years), beginning in 1908, when he became secretary for the preparation for the conference, for twenty-eight years he gave himself to the gathering and to the programme to which it gave rise.

The Edinburgh Conference was more inclusive than any of its predecessors. For the first time the Continent of Europe was strongly represented. The German contribution to the science and theory of missions was notable. Only seventeen of the delegates came from the churches in Asia and Africa which were the outgrowth of nineteenth-century missions, but they had a part on the programme quite out of proportion to their numerical strength. One address, that of V. S. Azariah, soon to be the first Indian to be raised to the Anglican episcopate, was especially remembered. Here was evidence that these churches were coming of age, a foreshadowing of the important part which they were to have in subsequent stages of the Ecumenical Movement. Anglo-Catholics were also in attendance. They came on condition that the questions of faith and order which divided the churches and on which they had convictions differing from those of the Evangelical majority would not be discussed and with the understanding, on which the Germans also insisted, that the scope of the gathering be restricted to missions among non-Christian peoples: efforts to win converts from other Christian bodies were excluded. Several younger men from the British Student Christian Movement served as stewards. Among them were John Baillie, later to be a president of the World Council of Churches, and William Temple, son of an Archbishop of Canterbury, eventually himself to be appointed to that see and outstanding in the Ecumenical Movement.[15]

---

[14] *Ibid.*, pp. 37–50.

[15] *Ibid.*, pp. 123–144; Rouse and Neill, *op. cit.*, pp. 357–362. The preparatory papers and the discussions and findings of the conference are in *World Missionary Conference, 1910* (Edinburgh, Oliphant, Anderson & Ferrier, 9 vols., 1910); J. H. Oldham in *Religion in Life*, Vol. XXIX, pp. 329–338.

"Edinburgh 1910" had consequences which amply justified later generations in looking back to it as a milestone. The careful planning with the comprehensive studies helped in the formulation of policies on a world-wide scale. The inclusion of young men from the churches of Asia was recognition that missions from the Occident would not long remain what they then seemed to be, the ecclesiastical aspect of Western imperialism, but that if the Gospel was for all mankind the Christians of Asia and Africa must have a full share in the counsels of the Church. Although on the insistence of Anglo-Catholics questions of faith and order were expressly left off the official programme, one of the Anglo-Catholics, Charles R. Brent, while cordially assenting to that provision, in a moving statement from the floor declared that steps must be taken towards other devices through which they could be frankly faced. He gave a major impulse to a movement which was already under way and from which after World War I came the World Conference on Faith and Order. The Edinburgh Conference also contributed to the formation, in 1912, of the Conference of Missionary Societies of Great Britain and Ireland, paralleling the older but similar body in North America, and to the British Board of Study for the Preparation of Missionaries, in 1911. In 1912 the Swedish Committee of Coöperation of Missionary Societies came into being. Since by confining its attention to non-Christian peoples the Edinburgh Conference did not include Latin America in its scope, in 1913, to make good the omission, a conference on Protestant missions in that portion of the world was held in New York under the auspices of the Foreign Missions Conference of North America. From it came the Committee on Coöperation in Latin America.[16] Most important of all was the Continuation Committee of the Edinburgh Conference, with Mott as its chairman and Oldham as its secretary. Under it, from November, 1912, to April, 1913, Mott convened twenty-one conferences from Colombo to Tokyo. From them, after World War I, came national Christian councils. In 1913 Oldham began, as an organ of the Continuation Committee, *The International Review of Missions,* a quarterly journal which at once took front rank among the periodicals dealing with the Christian world mission in a comprehensive, scholarly fashion. After World War I also came, in 1921, the International Missionary Council, with Mott as its chairman and Oldham and A. L. Warnshuis as its secretaries. Through it the larger proportion of the Protestant missionary forces of the world were brought into coöperation.[17]

Here was a more inclusive unity than Protestantism had yet known. Some regretted that it could not have been even more comprehensive, bringing in the Roman Catholics and the Orthodox. An Italian Roman Catholic bishop wrote a letter applauding the Edinburgh Conference,[18] but the cordial participation of

---

[16] Rouse and Neill, *op. cit.,* pp. 360, 361, 375, 396.
[17] *Ibid.,* pp. 363–366; Hogg, *op. cit.,* pp. 144 ff.
[18] Hogg, *op. cit.,* pp. 132, 133.

Anglo-Catholics in a gathering which was primarily one of the Evangelical forces was as much of a step as could be taken at that time.

The fact that the World Missionary Conference was held only four years before the then quite unanticipated outbreak of World War I makes vivid a contrast which was to become even more striking in the decades ahead. Here was an effort at common planning and action by one of the major branches of Christianity—by its genius the most divided branch of the faith—inspired by the vision and purpose of bringing all mankind to obedience to Christ. On the other hand was the most wide-spread war thus far waged by man, breaking out in Christendom, having its most devastating destruction in the geographic heart of Christendom, and waged by devices which had been developed in Christendom.

CHAPTER XXVI

Retrospect and Prospect

B EFORE we pass to the stage of the revolutionary age which was introduced by the contrast between the World Missionary Conference of 1910 and World War I we would do well to cast our eyes back over the ten decades between 1815 and 1914 and to remind ourselves of the fashion in which during that century the contrast had again and again been seen.

We have noted at some length the vividness of the contrast between its *milieu* and the Roman Catholic Church. On the one hand, in the regions where it had been the dominant form of religion the Roman Catholic Church was being challenged—not by a fresh surge of life in Christianity as in the sixteenth century by the rise of Protestantism, but rather by a secular departure from all that men had called religion. Many dismissed the faith of the Church as untenable in light of the new knowledge presented by the intellectual aspects of the revolution. For others Christianity was tacitly or explicitly regarded as irrelevant to the real interests of men. Thousands scornfully rejected the Church as obscurantist and an enemy of the progress in which they confidently believed and sought to free the state, the family, and the education of youth from what they regarded as bondage to the Church. In the lands where conformity to the Roman Catholic branch of the faith had been traditional, the vast majority were still baptized into its fold: in Latin Europe and in areas which bordered on it, such as Southern Germany, Austria, Hungary, part of Switzerland, and Belgium, and in most of Latin America. Yet for an undetermined percentage the connexion was only nominal. Culturally nearly all might call themselves Catholic and in their mores and ideals give evidence of having been nurtured in a civilization which had long been under the influence of Christianity. But that did not prevent a rabid and rampant anti-clericalism.

On the other hand, the Roman Catholic Church experienced a striking revival. Officially it set itself against some of the outstanding features of the revolution which was sweeping across Christendom and rejected compromises with them, whether in theology, in education, in attitudes towards religion, or in the family. At the same time it became more closely knit under the central direction of the Papacy than ever before, and came out for the infallibility of the Pope in matters of faith and morals and for his supreme authority in administration.

A great forward surge was seen in the full dedication to the religious life. Old orders and congregations were infused with fresh vigour, the Society of Jesus was revived, and more new congregations were organized than in any previous century. The life of prayer was strengthened. Frequent reception of the Communion was encouraged, in the latter part of the century Eucharistic congresses appeared with emphasis upon the central rite of the Church, and the Liturgical Movement began with its stress on intelligent lay participation in the mass. The spiritual counsel of the Curé of Ars was sought by thousands. Devotion to the Virgin Mary was heightened. It was reinforced by the proclamation of the dogma of the immaculate conception and by what were devoutly believed to be appearances of the Virgin, notably in La Salette and Lourdes. In an effort to meet the intellectual challenge of the age theological activity and Biblical studies were revived. Some attempts to present the faith in such fashion as to be congruous with the current climate of opinion were officially condemned, notably what was called Modernism, and a solution was sought in reëmphasis on Thomas Aquinas. Numbers in the Roman Catholic Church, both clergy and laymen, were awake to the problems brought by the Industrial Revolution and in one way or another sought to solve them. Outstanding in such efforts was Leo XIII's encyclical *Rerum novarum*. Attempts to accommodate the Church to the liberal democratic movements met with a varied reception. Some were frowned on by the ecclesiastical authorities, but Leo XIII urged the faithful to work with the Third Republic in France. A new burst of missionary energy was seen which planted the Roman Catholic Church more widely than ever before. The vast emigration of the Church's children to the Americas and Australasia, especially to the United States, Canada, Australia, and New Zealand, was paralleled by herculean efforts, in a large degree successful, to hold them to the faith and to stimulate them to produce their own clergy and erect their own churches and schools. The area in which the least success was registered was Latin America. Missions multiplied among the non-Christian peoples of Asia, Africa, and the islands of the Pacific who were made accessible by secular phases of the revolutionary age. Not only were they more extensive than ever before: they were also more heartily supported by the rank and file of the faithful and were less dependent on governments than at any time since the conversion of the Roman Empire. Roman Catholic missions were to mount still further in the twentieth century, and that in spite of the heightened threats to the faith in those decades.

The contrast between the de-Christianizing features of the revolutionary age and the renewal of life in the Roman Catholic Church was most striking in France. In that country many of the challenges to Christianity had their most acute and spectacular manifestations. De-Christianization was regarded as having proceeded further in France than in any other country in Western Europe. Yet more of the fresh vigour in the Roman Catholic Church was seen in that land than in any other. More new congregations and societies were organized there than elsewhere, the most notable appearances of the Virgin Mary were in France, and from France more missionaries went to non-Christian peoples than from all the rest of the Roman Catholic Church.

Something of the same contrast was seen in the family of Orthodox Churches. In Russia, where was the largest of those churches, intellectual currents from Western Europe, the radiating centre of the revolutionary age, were leading many to question or discard the hereditary faith. Yet a revival was seen in the devotional life of thousands, missions were being carried on among non-Christian peoples in the vast reaches of the empire, and a few missionary enterprises among non-Christian peoples outside the empire were seen, notably in Japan. In the Balkans and Greece, owing to the decay of the Ottoman Empire and the rise of nationalism fed by contact with revolutionary Western Christendom, the Orthodox Churches were emerging from the long domination by the Moslems and were becoming independent of the Ecumenical Patriarch. Through emigration, Orthodox Churches were beginning to develop in the Americas, chiefly in the United States, and the growth was to be augmented in the twentieth century.

The contrast was still greater between the de-Christianizing features of the revolutionary age and Protestantism. The lands where Protestants were in the majority were even more the sources of the revolutionary movements which challenged Christianity than were those in which the Roman Catholic Church had been the dominant form of the faith. The tensions were not as explosive in Protestant as in Roman Catholic countries—perhaps in part because Protestantism found accommodation easier than did Roman Catholicism. But the Industrial Revolution first appeared in Protestant Britain. Political liberalism and parliamentary institutions which in Roman Catholic countries often became anti-clerical and which the Papacy long opposed first developed in Great Britain, where the established religion was Protestant. Much of the science which seemed to make Christianity untenable had its most prominent early formulations in Britain. That was true of geology as it was popularized by Charles Lyell, of evolution, closely associated with the name of Charles Darwin, and of the application of evolution to the theory of society and the development of civilization as propounded by Herbert Spencer. The form of socialism which eventually most shook the world and which was frankly anti-Christian had as its creator the ex-Protestant Karl Marx. The application to the Bible of the methods of historical criticism with results which tried the faith of many was most extensive in Protestant circles in Germany.

On the other hand, no branch of Christianity displayed such vigour in the nineteenth century as did Protestantism. The major currents of abounding life were through Pietism and the kindred Evangelicalism. A revival of confessional orthodoxy was also seen, sometimes inextricably mingled with Pietism—

as in the movement which with Walther as a leader in the United States gave rise to the Missouri Synod—and the Catholic tradition in the Church of England was reëmphasized. From Protestantism came the most daring attempts to re-think Christian theology in such fashion as to take account of the intellectual currents of the day and to apply to the Scriptures and to the history of Christianity the scholarly procedures of the revolutionary age. From Protestantism, mainly from its Pietist and Evangelical expressions, issued most of the novel attempts to deal with the social and moral problems accompanying the revolutionary age. They were seen, for example, in the Inner Mission in Germany, the Sunday Schools, the Young Men's and Young Women's Christian Associations, the Salvation Army, the Red Cross, the most widely successful of the anti-slavery movements, and the chief leadership in the movements for international peace. Protestantism had the widest proportionate geographic extension of any of the branches of Christianity in the nineteenth century. In 1815 it had been confined chiefly to North-western Europe, to the eastern fringe of North America in the United States and Canada, and to a few scattered minorities in the West Indies, on the coasts of Africa, and in India and the East Indies. By 1914 it had become world-wide. The spread was due partly to great migrations, but had it not been for the vigour which successfully held to the faith an increasing percentage of the migrant populations the change of habitat would have been followed by the abandonment of the hereditary religion. That percentage-wise the Pietist and Evangelical strains were more prominent in Protestantism in the new nations created by European peoples in the Americas and Australasia than in Europe was evidence of the debt which that branch of the faith owed to these movements. Protestantism was also extended by missions among the traditionally non-Christian peoples. By 1914 Protestant communities were to be found in nearly every country and island. In most places they were small minorities and were dependent financially and for leadership upon the Protestants of Europe and of the larger Europe in North America and Australasia. But by 1914 that dependence was beginning to wane and the Christian communities were becoming rooted among the peoples to whom the faith had been so recently introduced. The missions among non-Christians were mostly by bodies sprung from Pietist and Evangelical awakenings. Vitality was also seen in the fashion in which Protestants were increasingly finding ways of overpassing their differences and coöperating in their efforts to win mankind to the Christian faith.

The contrast between the forces working against Christianity and the vitality inherent in the faith had not appeared for the first time in the nineteenth century nor was it to end with that century. It had been present from the beginning and was most vividly seen in the seeming triumph of the opposition in the crucifixion, followed as that was by the resurrection of Christ and the birth of the Church. In a variety of ways it had characterized the succeeding centuries. It was to be accentuated after 1914, so much so that many, with their eyes only on one side of the contrast, declared that mankind was entering the post-Christian era. Yet the other facet of the contrast gave ample cause for the assertion that the twentieth century was one of the greatest days in the history of Christianity and that, if the world was viewed as a whole, never before had Christ been as influential in the affairs of the human race.

BIBLIOGRAPHY

As in the preceding volumes, the bibliography includes only those books and periodicals which have been cited more than once in the footnotes. For the others, fully and perhaps twice or three times as numerous, to which only one reference was made, the appropriate bibliographic data are given in the footnote where the citation occurs.

Abbot, Lyman, *Reminiscences* (Boston, Houghton Mifflin Co., 1915, pp. 509).

Abell, Aaron Ignatius, *The Urban Impact on American Protestantism 1865–1900* (Cambridge, Mass., Harvard University Press, 1943, pp. x, 275). Based on a doctoral dissertation.

Addison, James Thayer, *The Episcopal Church in the United States 1789–1931* (New York, Charles Scribner's Sons, 1951, pp. xii, 400). A sympathetic account by a competent scholar.

Adeney, Walter F., *The Greek and Eastern Churches* (New York, Charles Scribner's Sons, 1908, pp. xiv, 634). A standard work by a Protestant.

Allen, Devere, *The Fight for Peace* (New York, The Macmillan Co., 1930, pp. xi, 740). By a prominent pacifist.

Allen, Joseph Henry, *Historical Sketch of the Unitarian Movement since the Reformation* (New York, The Christian Literature Co., 1894, pp. xi, 254). By a Unitarian historian.

Allen, W. O. B., and McClure, Edmund, *Two Hundred Years: The History of The Society for Promoting Christian Knowledge, 1698–1898* (London, Society for Promoting Christian Knowledge, 1898, pp. vi, 551). A standard history based upon original sources.

Allgemeine Missions-Zeitschrift (Gütersloh, C. Bertelsmann, 1874–1895; Berlin, M. Warneck, 1896–1923).

The American Journal of Theology (Chicago, 1897–1920).

Anstadt, P., *Life and Times of Rev. S. S. Schmucker, D.D.* (York, Pa., P. Anstadt & Sons, 1896, pp. 392). Sympathetic. Important not only for Schmucker but also for the early history of the General Synod.

Arcila Robledo, Gregorio, *La Orden Franciscana en la América Meridional* (Rome, Pontificio Ateneo Antoniano, 1948, pp. xviii, 416). An official compilation.

Ardao, Arturo, *Espiritualismo y Positivismo en el Uruguay. Filosofías Universitarias de la Segunda Mitad del Siglo XIX* (Mexico, Fondo de Cultura Economica, 1950, pp. 287). Based on careful research.

Attwater, Donald, *The Catholic Eastern Churches* (Milwaukee, The Bruce Publishing Co., 1935, pp. xx, 309). By a Roman Catholic. Contains excellent bibliographies.

Attwater, Donald, *The Christian Churches of the East* (Milwaukee, The Bruce Publishing Co., 2 vols., 1947, 1948). A revised edition of earlier works by a Roman Catholic expert. Semi-popular.

The Australian Encyclopedia (Sydney, Angus & Robertson, 2 vols., 1925, 1926).

Ayarragaray, Lucas, *La Iglesia en América y la Dominación Española. Estudio de la Epoca Colonial* (Buenos Aires, J. Lajouane & Cia, 1920, pp. 321). Valuable for both its narrative and its documents.

[Babo, Bede] A Benedictine Monk, *Our Catholic Heritage* (New York, Benziger Brothers, 1950, pp. 344). A brief history arranged by states.

Bacon, Theodore Davenport, edited by Benjamin W. Bacon, *Leonard Bacon. A Statesman in the Church* (New Haven, Conn., Yale University Press, 1931, pp. xv, 563). Well done, by grandsons.

Badaro, F., *l'Église au Brésil pendant l'Empire et pendant la République* (Rome, Stabilimento Bontempelli, 1895, pp. xiii, 138). Critical of the government.

Baepler, Walter A., *A Century of Grace. A History of the Missouri Synod 1847-1947* (St. Louis, Concordia Publishing House, 1947, pp. vii, 408). Sympathetic.

Báez-Camargo, G., and Grubb, Kenneth G., *Religion in the Republic of Mexico* (London, World Dominion Press, 1935, pp. 166). A competent survey by Protestants.

Bainton, Roland H., *Yale and the Ministry. A History of Education for the Christian Ministry at Yale from the Founding in 1701* (New York, Harper & Brothers, 1957, pp. xiii, 297). By a member of the faculty of the Yale University Divinity School.

Balfour, R. Gordon, *Presbyterianism in the Colonies with Special Reference to the Principles and Influence of the Free Church of Scotland* (Edinburgh, Macniven & Wallace, 1899, pp. xi, 341). Based upon printed sources and secondary accounts, by the convener of the Free Church Colonial Committee from 1874 to 1881.

Barclay, Wade Crawford, *History of Methodist Missions* (New York, The Board of Missions of the Methodist Church. To be in 6 volumes. Vols. 1-3, 1949-1957). The standard survey.

Barnes, William Wright, *The Southern Baptist Convention 1845-1953* (Nashville, Broadman Press, 1954, pp. x, 330). A standard work, based on extensive research.

Barry, Colman J., *The Catholic Church and German Americans* (Milwaukee, The Bruce Publishing Co., 1953, pp. xii, 348). By a Benedictine, chiefly on the Cahensly movement.

Beach, Harlan P., and Fahs, Charles H., *World Missionary Atlas* (New York, Institute of Social and Religious Research, 1925, pp. 219). Standard.

Beach, Harlan P., and St. John, Burton, editors, *World Statistics of Christian Missions* (New York, The Committee of Reference and Counsel of the Foreign Missions Conference of North America, 1916, pp. 148). Authoritative.

Beard, Augustus Field, *A Crusade of Brotherhood. A History of the American Missionary Association* (Boston, The Pilgrim Press, 1909, pp. xii, 334). By a secretary of the Association.

Beecher, Lyman, *Autobiography, Correspondence, etc.,* edited by Charles Beecher (New York, Harper & Brothers, 2 vols., 1864-1865).

Benedict, David, *A General History of the Baptist Denomination in America and Other Parts of the World* (New York, Lewis Colby and Co., 1848, pp. 970). Contains a mine of information gathered from many sources.

Benson, Clarence H., *A Popular History of Christian Education* (Chicago, Moody Press, 1943, pp. 355).

Berg, Ludwig, *Die katholische Heidenmission als Kulturträger* (Aachen, Aachen Missionsdruckerei, 2nd ed., 3 vols., 1927). Based on careful research, warmly Roman Catholic and critical of Protestants.

Binkley, Luther J., *The Mercersburg Theology* (Lancaster, Pa., Franklin and Marshall College, 1953, pp. 156). A doctoral dissertation.

Birt, Henry Norbert, *Benedictine Pioneers in Australia* (London, Herbert & Daniel, 2 vols., 1911). By a Benedictine.

Bodo, John R., *The Protestant Clergy and Public Issues, 1812–1848* (Princeton University Press, 1954, pp. xiv, 291). Begun as a doctoral dissertation.

Bourassa, Henri, *Le Canada Apostolique. Revue des Œuvres de Missions des Communautés Franco-Canadiennes* (Montreal, Bibliothèque de l'Action Française, 1919, pp. 173).

Bracq, Jean Charlemagne, *The Evolution of French Canada* (New York, The Macmillan Co., 1924, pp. viii, 467). Sympathetic, containing much factual information.

Braga, Erasmo, and Grubb, Kenneth G., *The Republic of Brazil. A Survey of the Religious Situation* (London, World Dominion Press, 1932, pp. 184). By experts, Protestants, one of them a Brazilian.

Brasseur de Bourbourg, *Histoire du Canada de son Église et de ses Missions* (Paris, 2 vols., 1852). From the beginning to the mid-nineteenth century, by a French Canadian priest and based on both original sources and secondary materials.

Brown, Arlo Ayres, *A History of Religious Education in Recent Times* (New York, Abingdon Press, 1923, pp. 282). A semi-popular account by an expert.

Brown, Arthur Judson, *One Hundred Years. A History of the Foreign Missionary Work of the Presbyterian Church in the U.S.A. With Some Account of Countries, Peoples and Problems of Modern Missions* (New York, Fleming H. Revell Co., 1937, pp. 1140). An official history by a secretary emeritus of the Board of Foreign Missions.

Brown, Ira V., *Lyman Abbott, Christian Evolutionist. A Study of Religious Liberalism* (Cambridge, Mass., Harvard University Press, 1953, pp. ix, 303). Competent.

Brown, L. W., *The Indian Christians of St. Thomas. An Account of the Ancient Syrian Church of Malabar* (Cambridge University Press, 1956, pp. xii, 315). A comprehensive scholarly work.

Brown, Marianna C., *Sunday-School Movements in America* (Chicago, Fleming H. Revell Co., 1901, pp. 269). A competent survey.

Browning, Webster E., *The River Plate Republics. A Survey of the Religious, Economic and Social Conditions in Argentina, Paraguay and Uruguay* (London, World Dominion Press, 1928, pp. 139). By an expert, a Protestant.

Browning, Webster E., Ritchie, John, and Grubb, Kenneth G., *The West Coast Republics of South America, Chile, Peru and Bolivia* (London, World Dominion Press, 1930, pp. 183). A competent survey, stressing Protestantism.

Buckley, J. M., *A History of Methodists in the United States* (New York, The Christian Literature Co., 1896, pp. xix, 714). Sympathetic, by a Methodist.

Bureau of the Census. See [U.S.] Bureau of the Census.

Burns, J. A., *The Principles, Origin and Establishment of the Catholic School System in the United States* (Cincinnati, Benziger Brothers, 1912, pp. 415). A competent survey by a Roman Catholic.

Burton, Katherine, *In No Strange Land. Some American Catholic Converts* (New York, Longmans, Green and Co., 1942, pp. xix, 254). Sympathetic, in popular style.

Callahan, Adalbert, *Medieval Francis in Modern America. The Story of Eighty Years 1855-1935* (New York, The Macmillan Co., 1936, pp. xiv, 494). Laudatory.

Callcott, Wilfrid Hardy, *Church and State in Mexico. 1822-1857* (Durham, N.C., Duke University Press, 1926, pp. 357). Based on careful research.

Callcott, Wilfrid Hardy, *Liberalism in Mexico 1857-1929* (Stanford University Press, 1931, pp. xiii, 410). Carefully done.

The Canadian Historical Review (Toronto, 1920 ff.).

Canton, William, *A History of the British and Foreign Bible Society* (London, John Murray, 5 vols., 1904-1910). An official history.

Cartwright, Peter, *Autobiography of Peter Cartwright, with an Introduction, Bibliography, and Index* by Charles L. Wallis (New York, Abingdon Press, 1956, pp. 349).

Cartwright, Peter, *Autobiography of Peter Cartwright, the Backwoods Preacher*, edited by W. B. Strickland (New York, Hunt & Eaton, 1856, pp. 525).

Cary, Otis, *A History of Christianity in Japan* (Chicago, Fleming H. Revell Co., 2 vols., 1909). A standard work.

The Official Catholic Directory, 1940 (New York, P. J. Kenedy & Sons, 1940, pp. vi, 1107). Has in addition 157 pp. on Canada and 105 pp. on Ireland, England, Scotland, Wales, Cuba, and Mexico.

The Catholic Historical Review (Washington, The Catholic University of America Press, 1914 ff.). The official organ of the Catholic Historical Association.

Centennial of Canadian Methodism Published by Direction of the General Conference (Toronto, William Briggs, 1891, pp. 339).

Central American Bulletin (Dallas, Texas, 1895 ff.).

Cherrington, Ernest H., *The Evolution of Prohibition in the United States of America. A Chronological History of the Liquor Problem and the Temperance Reform in the United States from the Earliest Settlements to the Consummation of National Prohibition* (Westerville, Ohio, The American Issue Press, 1920, pp. 384). Sympathetic, based on extensive research.

The China Mission Year Book (Shanghai, Christian Literature Society, 1910-1919).

The Christian Century (Chicago, 1884 ff.).

Christian Education (Philadelphia, 1916 ff.).

The Christian Movement in Japan (Tokyo, various publishers, 1903 ff.). An annual publication by Protestants.

The Chronicle. A Baptist Historical Quarterly (Scottdale, Pa., The American Baptist Historical Society, 1938 ff.).

Church History (Chicago, 1932 ff.). The official organ of the American Society of Church History.

Clark, Elmer T., *The Small Sects in America* (Nashville, Cokesbury Press, 1937, pp. 311). A useful survey.

Clark, Joseph B., *Leavening the Nation. The Story of American Home Missions* (New York, The Baker & Taylor Co., 1903, pp. vii, 362). An excellent survey.

Clark, S. D., *Church and Sect in Canada* (University of Toronto Press, 1948, pp. xiii, 458). A well-documented study of Canadian Protestantism, partly from a sociological angle and an Anglican standpoint.

Clarke, William Newton, *Sixty Years with the Bible* (New York, Charles Scribner's Sons, 1912, pp. 259). An autobiography.

Cleland, Robert Glass, *A History of Phelps Dodge 1834–1950* (New York, Alfred A. Knopf, 1952, pp. xiv, 307, xxli). Well written, based on careful research.

Cole, Charles C., *The Social Ideas of the Northern Evangelists 1826–1860* (New York, Columbia University Press, 1954, pp. 268). Begun as a doctoral dissertation.

Cole, Stewart G., *The History of Fundamentalism* (New York, Richard R. Smith, 1931, pp. xiv, 360). Carefully documented.

Coleman, William J., *The First Apostolic Delegation in Rio de Janeiro and Its Influence in Spanish America. A Study in Papal Policy, 1830–1840* (Washington, The Catholic University of America Press, 1950, pp. ix, 468). A doctoral dissertation.

Colvin, D. Leigh, *Prohibition in the United States. A History of the Prohibition Party and the Prohibition Movement* (New York, George H. Doran, 1926, pp. 678). Sympathetic.

Colwell, James, editor, *A Century in the Pacific: Scientific, Sociological, Historical, Missionary, General* (London, Charles H. Kelly, 1914, pp. xi, 781). Deals chiefly with the history of Methodism.

The Continuation Committee Conferences in Asia 1912–1913. A Brief Account of the Conferences Together with Their Findings and Lists of Members (New York, Chairman of the Continuation Committee, 1913, pp. 488).

Corwin, E. T., *History of the Reformed Church, Dutch* (in Vol. VIII of *American Church History*, pp. xi–xviii, 1–212. New York, The Christian Literature Co., 1895).

Cramer, C. H., *Royal Bob. The Life of Robert G. Ingersoll* (Indianapolis, The Bobbs-Merrill Co., 1952, pp. 314). Well written, based on careful research.

Crawford, Benjamin Franklin, *Religious Trends in a Century of Hymns* (Carnegie, Pa., Carnegie Church Press, 1938, pp. 204). Limited to Methodist hymns.

Crawford, William Rex, *A Century of Latin-American Thought* (Cambridge, Mass., Harvard University Press, 1945, pp. 320). An excellent, sympathetic survey.

Cross, Robert D., *The Emergence of Liberal Catholicism in America* (Cambridge, Mass., Harvard University Press, 1958, pp. ix, 328). Based on extensive research. Endeavours to be objective but is sympathetic with the liberals.

Cross, Whitney R., *The Burned-over District. The Social and Intellectual History of Enthusiastic Religion in Western New York, 1800–1850* (Ithaca, Cornell University Press, 1950, pp. xiii, 383). Readable; based on extensive research.

Curti, Merle Eugene, *The American Peace Crusade, 1815-1860* (Durham, N.C., Duke University Press, 1927, pp. viii, 250). Begun as a Harvard doctoral dissertation.

Curti, Merle, *Peace or War. The American Struggle 1636-1936* (New York, W. W. Norton & Co., 1936, pp. 374). By a competent historian.

Cyclopædia of Methodism: Containing Historical, Educational, and Statistical Information, Dating from the Beginning of the Work in the Several Provinces of the Dominion of Canada and Extending to the Annual Conferences of 1880 (Toronto, Methodist Book and Publishing House, 1881, pp. 850).

Dallet, Ch., *Histoire de l'Église de Corée* (Paris, Victor Palmé, 2 vols., 1874). By a member of the *Société des Missions Étrangères* of Paris. Based largely upon documentary reports by missionaries.

Dawson, C. A., *Group Settlement. Ethnic Communities in Western Canada* (Toronto, The Macmillan Co. of Canada, 1936, pp. xx, 395).

Dennis, James S., Beach, Harlan P., and Fahs, Charles H., editors, *World Atlas of Christian Missions* (New York, Student Volunteer Movement for Foreign Missions, 1911, pp. 133). Standard.

Decamps, Baron, *Histoire Générale Comparée des Missions* (Paris, Librairie Plon, 1932, pp. viii, 760). By several writers, principally on Roman Catholic missions.

Dickson, John, *History of the Presbyterian Church of New Zealand* (Dunedin, J. Wilkie & Co., 1899, pp. xviii, 532). An account town by town and district by district.

Dictionary of American Biography (New York, Charles Scribner's Sons, 21 vols., 1928-1944). Standard.

Dictionary of National Biography (London, Macmillan and Co., 63 vols., 1885-1900, 6 supplementary volumes through 1912). Standard.

Dombrowski, James, *The Early Days of Christian Socialism in America* (New York, Columbia University Press, 1936, pp. viii, 208). Based on a doctoral dissertation.

Dorchester, Daniel, *Christianity in the United States from thē First Settlement down to the Present Time* (New York, Phillips & Hunt, 1888, pp. 793). Contains much useful material.

Dorland, Arthur Garratt, *A History of the Society of Friends (Quakers) in Canada* (Toronto, The Macmillan Co. of Canada, 1927, pp. xiii, 343). Carefully done, well documented.

Dubbs, Joseph Henry, *History of the Reformed Church, German* (in Vol. VIII of *American Church History*, pp. 213-423. New York, The Christian Literature Co., 1895).

Du Plessis, J., *A History of Christian Missions in South Africa* (New York, Longmans, Green and Co., 1911, pp. xx, 494). A sympathetic account based on extensive research.

Du Plessis, J., *The Life of Andrew Murray of South Africa* (London, Marshall Brothers, preface 1919, pp. xvi, 553). Important not only as a biography but also for information on the history of the Dutch Reformed Church in South Africa.

Dwight, Henry Otis, *The Centennial History of the American Bible Society* (New York, The Macmillan Co., 2 vols., 1916). An official history.

The Education of American Ministers (New York, Institute of Social and Religious Research, 4 vols., 1934). By various authors. Based upon prolonged and extensive research. Mainly on the Protestant ministry.

Elder, John Rawson, *The History of the Presbyterian Church of New Zealand, 1840–1940* (Christchurch, Presbyterian Bookroom, preface 1940, pp. xv, 464). Sympathetically and carefully done.

Ellis, John Tracy, *American Catholicism* (University of Chicago Press, 1956, pp. xiii, 206). Sympathetic, popular, by an outstanding Roman Catholic authority.

Ellis, John Tracy, editor, *Documents of American Catholic History* (Milwaukee, The Bruce Publishing Co., 1956, pp. xxiv, 677). A comprehensive collection, with valuable prefaces to the documents.

Ellis, John Tracy, *The Life of James Cardinal Gibbons, Archbishop of Baltimore (1834–1921)* (Milwaukee, The Bruce Publishing Co., 2 vols., 1952). By a distinguished Roman Catholic scholar.

Encyclopedia of Southern Baptists (Nashville, Broadman Press, 2 vols., 1958). Officially compiled.

Everett, John Rutherford, *Religion in Economics. A Study of John Bates Clark, Richard T. Ely, Simon N. Patten* (New York, King's Crown Press, 1946, pp. xiii, 160). Based on a doctoral dissertation.

Faust, Albert Bernhardt, *The German Element in the United States, with Special Reference to Its Political, Moral, Social, and Religious Influence* (New York, The Steuben Society of America, 2 vols., 1927. Copyrighted 1909). A standard work.

Fergusson, E. Morris, *Historic Chapters in Christian Education in America* (New York, Fleming H. Revell Co., 1935, pp. 192). A popular survey.

Ferm, Vergilius, *The Crisis in American Lutheran Theology. A Study of the Issue between American Lutheranism and Old Lutheranism* (New York, The Century Co., 1927, pp. xiii, 409). Based upon extensive research in the sources.

Fides News Service (Rome, c. 1926 ff.). News releases issued in close coöperation with the Society for the Propagation of the Faith.

Findlay, G. G., and Holdsworth, W. W., *The History of the Wesleyan Methodist Missionary Society* (London, The Epworth Press, 5 vols., 1921–1924). An official history.

Finley, James B., *Autobiography of James B. Finley; or Pioneer Life in the West,* edited by W. P. Strickland. (Cincinnati, The Methodist Book Concern, 1850, pp. 455).

Fortescue, Adrian, *The Lesser Eastern Churches* (London, Catholic Truth Society, 1913, pp. xv, 468). Sympathetic, by a Roman Catholic, based on extensive research in the sources.

Fortescue, Adrian, *The Orthodox Eastern Church* (London, Catholic Truth Society, new issue, 1929, pp. xix, 451). By a fair-minded Roman Catholic specialist.

Fortescue, Adrian, *The Uniate Eastern Churches. The Byzantine Rite in Italy, Sicily, Syria, and Egypt,* edited by George D. Smith (London, Burns Oates & Washbourne, 1923, pp. xxiii, 244). Based on extended travel and research. Completed by the editor after the author's death.

504   The Nineteenth Century Outside Europe

Foster, Frank Hugh, *A Genetic History of the New England Theology* (University of Chicago Press, 1907, pp. xv, 568). A standard survey.

Foster, Frank Hugh, *The Modern Movement in American Theology. Sketches in the History of American Protestant Thought from the Civil War to the World War* (New York, Fleming H. Revell Co., 1939, pp. 219). A posthumously published continuation of the preceding volume.

Froom, LeRoy Edwin, *The Prophetic Faith of Our Fathers. The Historical Development of Prophetic Interpretation* (Washington, Review and Herald Publishing Co., 4 vols., 1950–1954). A work of great erudition by a Seventh-Day Adventist.

Gabriel, Ralph Henry, *The Course of American Democratic Thought. An Intellectual History since 1815* (New York, The Ronald Press Co., 1940, pp. xi, 452).

Gabriel, Ralph Henry, *Religion and Learning at Yale* (New Haven, Conn., Yale University Press, 1958, pp. x, 271).

Galdames, Luis, *A History of Chile,* translated and edited by Isaac Joslin Cox (Chapel Hill, University of North Carolina Press, 1941, pp. xii, 565). A standard text by a Chilean scholar.

Galpin, W. Freeman, *Pioneering for Peace. A Study of American Peace Efforts to 1846* (Syracuse, N.Y., The Bardeen Press, 1933, pp. ix, 237). Based on the sources.

Garraghan, Gilbert J., *The Jesuits of the Middle United States* (New York, The American Press, 3 vols., 1938). Heavily documented, by a Jesuit.

Giles, R. A., *The Constitutional History of the Australian Church* (London, Skeffington & Son, 1929, pp. 320). Carefully done by an Anglican clergyman. Contains significant documents.

Gill, Everett, *A. T. Robertson. A Biography* (New York, The Macmillan Co., 1943, pp. xvi, 250). By a friend.

Gillard, John T., *The Catholic Church and the American Negro* (Baltimore, St. Joseph's Society Press, 1929, pp. xv, 324). A sympathetic account.

Goodspeed, Thomas Wakefield, *Ernest DeWitt Burton. A Biographical Sketch* (University of Chicago Press, 1926, pp. vii, 93). Careful and admiring.

Goodykoontz, Colin Brummitt, *Home Missions on the American Frontier. With Particular Reference to the American Home Missionary Society* (Caldwell, Ida., The Caxton Printers, 1939, pp. 460). Based on extensive research.

Goslin, Tomas S., *Los Evangelicos en la América Latina. Siglo XIX Los Comienzos* (Buenos Aires, "La Aurora," 1957, pp. 127). An admirable survey.

Gregg, William, *History of the Presbyterian Church in the Dominion of Canada, from the Earliest Times to 1834; with a Chronological Table of Events to the Present Time, and Map* (Toronto, Presbyterian Printing and Publishing Co., 1885, pp. xv, 646).

Griffin, Joseph A., *The Contribution of Belgium to the Catholic Church in America (1523–1857)* (Washington, The Catholic University of America, 1932, pp. xvi, 235). A doctoral dissertation, based chiefly on printed materials.

Groves, C. P., *The Planting of Christianity in Africa* (London, Lutterworth Press, 4 vols., 1948–1958). Carefully done. Covers all Africa from the early Christian centuries, with primary emphasis on Protestant missions. Arranged by the main chronological divisions.

Grubb, Kenneth G., *The Northern Republics of South America. Ecuador, Colombia, and Venezuela* (London, World Dominion Press, 1931, pp. 151). A first-hand survey, chiefly of Protestant missions.

Grubb, Kenneth G., *Religion in Central America* (London, World Dominion Press, 1937, pp. 147). By an expert in missionary surveys.

Guilday, Peter, *The Life and Times of John England, First Bishop of Charleston (1786–1842)* (New York, The American Press, 2 vols., 1927). By an eminent Roman Catholic scholar.

Guilday, Peter, editor, *The National Pastorals of the American Hierarchy (1792–1919)* (Washington, National Catholic Welfare Council, 1923, pp. xiii, 358). A collection of documents.

Handlin, Oscar, *The Uprooted. The Epic Story of the Great Migration which made the American People* (Boston, Little, Brown and Co., 1952, pp. 310). Semi-popular.

Harvey, F. G., *Notes on Australian Church History* (Ms). Based on extensive research.

Heeney, Wm. Bertal, editor, *Leaders of the Canadian Church* (Toronto, The Musson Book Co., 1918, pp. 319). Sketches of bishops, by various authors.

Herring, Hubert, *A History of Latin America from the Beginnings to the Present* (New York, Alfred A. Knopf, 1956, pp. xx, 796, xxvi). A competent text-book.

Hofstadter, Richard, and Hardy, C. DeWitt, *The Development and Scope of Higher Education in the United States* (New York, Columbia University Press, 1952, pp. ix, 254). A thoughtful descriptive analysis.

Hogg, William Richey, *Ecumenical Foundations. A History of the International Missionary Council and Its Nineteenth-Century Background* (New York, Harper & Brothers, 1952, pp. xi, 466). The definitive history.

Hopkins, C. Howard, *History of the Y.M.C.A. in North America* (New York, Association Press, 1951, pp. xii, 818). The official centennial history.

Hopkins, Charles Howard, *The Rise of the Social Gospel in American Protestantism 1865–1915* (New Haven, Conn., Yale University Press, 1940, pp. xii, 352). A standard competent survey.

Huonder, Anton, *Der einheimische Klerus in den Heidenländern* (Freiburg im Breisgau, Herdersche Verlagshandlung, 1909, pp. x, 312). Based on wide reading.

Hynes, Michael J., *History of the Diocese of Cleveland. Origin and Growth 1847–1952* (Cleveland, Diocese of Cleveland, 1953, pp. xxiv, 520). An official history, based on extensive research.

The International Review of Missions (London, 1912 ff.). An official organ of the International Missionary Council, and long the standard Protestant journal on foreign missions.

Jacobs, Henry, *New Zealand. Containing the Dioceses of Auckland, Christchurch, Nelson, Waiapu, Wellington, and Melanesia* (London Society for Promoting Christian Knowledge, 1887, pp. xvi, 480). By the Dean of Christchurch, New Zealand.

Jacobs, Henry Eyster, *A History of the Evangelical Lutheran Church in the United States* (New York, The Christian Literature Co., 1893, pp. xvi, 539). A standard work, predominantly on the colonial period, but with some attention to the nineteenth century.

The Japan Christian Quarterly (Tokyo, The Federation of Christian Missions, and later The Christian Literature Society of Japan, 1926–1947).

Johnson, Charles A., *The Frontier Camp Meeting. Religious Harvest Time* (Dallas, Southern Methodist University Press, 1955, pp. ix, 325). Well written. Based on careful research.

Jones, Thomas Jesse, editor, *A Study of the Private and Higher Schools for Colored People in the United States* (Washington, Government Printing Office, 2 vols., 1917).

Journal of Negro History (Washington, 1916 ff.).

Keefe, Sister St. Thomas Aquinas, *The Congregation of the Grey Nuns (1737–1910)* (Washington, The Catholic University of America, 1942, pp. x, 373). A doctoral dissertation.

Kelley, Francis Clement, and Byam, Eber Cole, *Blood-Drenched Altars. Mexican Study and Comment* (Milwaukee, The Bruce Publishing Co., 2nd ed., revised, 1935, pp. xix, 521). From a Roman Catholic viewpoint.

Kennedy, John J., *Catholicism, Nationalism, and Democracy in Argentina* (Univercity of Notre Dame Press, 1958, pp. xii, 219). Scholarly.

Kiek, Edward Sidney, *An Apostle in Australia. The Life and Reminiscences of Joseph Coles Kirby, Christian Pioneer and Social Reformer* (London, Independent Press, 1927, pp. 316). Sympathetic.

King, H. E., *Australia* (Westminster, The Society for the Propagation of the Gospel in Foreign Parts, 1935, pp. 59). A competent survey of the Church of England in Australia.

Kittler, Glenn D., *The White Fathers* (New York, Harper & Brothers, 1957, pp. xv, 299).

Krout, John Allen, *The Origins of Prohibition* (New York, Alfred A. Knopf, 1925, pp. 339). Based on careful research.

Landon, Fred, *Western Ontario and the American Frontier* (Toronto, The Ryerson Press, 1941, pp. xvi, 305). Carefully done.

Latourette, Kenneth Scott, *A History of Christian Missions in China* (New York, The Macmillan Co., 1929, pp. xii, 930). Covers the entire range of Christian missions from the beginning to 1928, with extensive footnotes and bibliography.

Latourette, Kenneth Scott, *A History of the Expansion of Christianity* (New York, Harper & Brothers, 7 vols., 1937–1945).

Latourette, Kenneth Scott, *World Service. A History of the Foreign Work and World Service of the Young Men's Christian Association of the United States and Canada* (New York, Association Press, 1957, pp. xiv, 489). An official history.

Lemmons, Leonhard, *Geschichte der Franziskanermissionen* (Münster i.W., Aschendorffschen Verlagsbuchhandlung, 1929, pp. xx, 376). Carefully done, by a Franciscan.

Levy, George Edward, *The Baptists of the Maritime Provinces 1753–1946* (St. John, N.B., Barnes-Hopkins, 1946, pp. xii, 337). An official history, based on careful research.

Lindsey, Charles, *Rome in Canada. The Ultramontane Struggle for Supremacy over the Civil Authority* (Toronto, Lovell Brothers, 1877, pp. 398). Anti-Roman Catholic and especially against ultramontanism in Canada.

Loetscher, Lefferts Augustine, *The Broadening Church. A Study of Theological Issues in the Presbyterian Church since 1869* (Philadelphia, University of Pennsylvania Press, 1954, pp. 195). Competent, by a Presbyterian.

Lord, Robert H., Sexton, John E., and Harrington, Edward T., *History of the Archdiocese of Boston in the Various Stages of Its Development 1604 to 1943* (New York, Sheed & Ward, 3 vols., 1944). An official history.

Lovett, Richard, *The History of the London Missionary Society 1795–1895* (London, Henry Frowder, 2 vols., 1899). An official account.

Lowitt, Richard, *A Merchant Prince of the Nineteenth Century, William E. Dodge* (New York, Columbia University Press, 1954, pp. xii, 384). Based on careful research.

Lucas, Henry S., *Netherlanders in America. Dutch Immigration to the United States and Canada, 1789–1950* (Ann Arbor, University of Michigan Press, 1955, pp. xix, 744). A definitive work.

Lübeck, Konrad, *Die russischen Missionen* (Aachen, Xaverius-Verlagsbuchhandlung, 1922, pp. 68). Careful and objective, by a Roman Catholic.

The Lutheran Quarterly (Gettysburg, 1949 ff.).

MacGillivray, Donald, editor, *A Century of Protestant Missions in China 1807–1907* (Shanghai, The American Presbyterian Mission Press, 1907, pp. vii, 677, xl, 52). By many authors. A standard work.

Mackay, John A., *The Other Spanish Christ. A Study in the Spiritual History of Spain and South America* (London, Student Christian Movement Press, 1932, pp. xv, 288). By a scholarly former Protestant missionary in Spanish America.

McNeill, John Thomas, *The Presbyterian Church in Canada, 1875–1925* (Toronto, General Board, Presbyterian Church in Canada, 1925, pp. xi, 276). An early work of a distinguished church historian.

Maes, Camillus P., *The Life of Rev. Charles Nerinckx: with a Chapter on the Early Catholic Missions in Kentucky* (Cincinnati, Robert Clarke & Co., 1880, pp. xvii, 635). Valuable for extensive quotations from original sources.

Manross, William Wilson, *A History of the American Episcopal Church* (New York, Morehouse Publishing Co., 1935, pp. xvi, 404). Except for three chapters, based on original sources.

Marnas, Francisque, *La "Religion de Jesus" (Iaso Ja-kyo) Resuscitee au Japon dans la Seconde Moitie du XIX Siècle* (Paris, Delhomme et Briquet, 2 vols., c. 1897).

Maston, A. B., editor, *Jubilee Pictorial History of the Churches of Christ in Australasia* (Melbourne, Austral Publishing Co., 1903, pp. 424). By a member of the denomination.

Mathews, Basil, *John R. Mott, World Citizen* (New York, Harper & Brothers, 1934, pp. xiii, 469). Semi-autobiographical: written from material provided by Mott.

Mathews, Shailer, *New Faith for Old. An Autobiography* (New York, The Macmillan Co., 1936, pp. vi, 303). An attempt to tell an autobiography in the setting of the religious changes of a half-century.

Matthiessen, F. O., *American Renaissance. Art and Expression to the Age of Emerson and Whitman* (New York, Oxford University Press, 1941, pp. xxiv, 678).

Mayer, F. E., *The Religious Bodies of America* (St. Louis, Concordia Publishing House, 1954, pp. xiii, 587). A competent survey and book of reference from the standpoint of one connected with the Missouri Synod.

Maynard, Theodore, *The Story of American Catholicism* (New York, The Macmillan Co., 1941, pp. xviii, 694). A popular account by a Roman Catholic.

Mays, Benjamin Elijah, and Nicholson, Joseph William, *The Negro's Church* (New York, Institute of Social and Religious Research, 1933, pp. xiii, 321). Based on careful research.

Mead, Sidney Earl, *Nathaniel William Taylor, 1786-1858, a Connecticut Liberal* (University of Chicago Press, 1942, pp. xi, 259). A readable account by a competent specialist.

Mecham, J. Lloyd, *Church and State in Latin America. A History of Politico-Ecclesiastical Relations* (Chapel Hill, University of North Carolina Press, 1934, pp. viii, 550). A standard survey based on careful research.

Minutes of the Annual Conferences of the Methodist Episcopal Church for the Years 1773-1828 (Vol. I, T. Mason and G. Lane, 1840).

Morice, A. G., *History of the Catholic Church in Western Canada from Lake Superior to the Pacific (1659-1895)* (Toronto, The Musson Book Co., 2 vols., 1910). Sympathetic, based upon manuscript archives and printed sources.

Mott, John R., *Papers and Addresses* (New York, Association Press, 6 vols., 1946, 1947).

Moynihan, James H., *The Life of Archbishop John Ireland* (New York, Harper & Brothers, 1953, pp. xii, 441). Sympathetic, based largely on the correspondence of Ireland.

Murtagh, James G., *Australia: The Catholic Chapter* (New York, Sheed & Ward, 1946, pp. xviii, 261). Sympathetic, with emphasis on the social aspects.

Neill, Stephen, *Anglicanism* (Harmondsworth, Middlesex, Penguin Books, 1958, pp. 466). By an Anglican bishop.

Newman, A. H., *A History of the Baptist Churches in the United States* (Vol. II of *American Church History*. New York, The Christian Literature Co., 1894, pp. xv, 513).

Nichol, Francis R., *The Midnight Cry. A Defense of the Character and Conduct of William Miller and the Millerites, Who Mistakenly Believed that the Second Coming of Christ would take place in the year 1844* (Washington, Review and Herald Publishing Co., 1944, pp. 560). A sympathetic account based upon extensive, careful research.

Niebuhr, H. Richard, *The Kingdom of God in America* (Chicago, Willet, Clark & Co., 1937, pp. xvii, 215). A penetrating analysis.

Norlie, Olaf Morgan, *History of the Norwegian People in America* (Minneapolis, Augsburg Publishing House, 1925, pp. 602). Packed with information, but without footnote references to the sources.

O'Brien, Eric M., *The Dawn of Catholicism in Australia* (Sydney, Angus & Robertson, 2 vols., 1928). Sympathetic.

O'Brien, Joseph L., *John England, Bishop of Charleston. The Apostle to Democracy* (New York, The Edward O'Toole Co., 1934, pp. xiii, 222).

O'Donnell, John Hugh, *The Catholic Hierarchy of the United States, 1790–1922* (Washington, The Catholic University of America Press, *Studies in American Church History*, Vol. IV, 1922, pp. xiv, 223). Contains brief biographies of the bishops and extensive bibliographies.

O'Gorman, Thomas, *A History of the Roman Catholic Church in the United States* (New York, The Christian Literature Co., 1895, pp. xviii, 515). Three-fifths is on the period before 1815.

Padelford, Frank W., *The Commonwealths and the Kingdom. A Study of the Missionary Work of State Conventions* (Philadelphia, The Griffith and Rowland Press, 1913, pp. xiii, 209). An authoritative text-book of the home missions of the Northern Baptist state conventions.

Paik, L. George, *The History of Protestant Missions in Korea, 1832–1910* (Pyeng Yang, Union Christian College Press, 1929, pp. ix, 438, xiii). A doctoral dissertation.

Parker, Joseph I., editor, *Directory of World Missions* (New York, International Missionary Council, 1938, pp. xi, 255).

Pérez, Rafael, *La Compañía de Jesus en Colombia y Centro-América despues de su Restauración. Part I. Desde el llamamiento de los pp. de la Compañía de Jesus à la Nueva Granada en 1842, hasta su Expulsión y Dispersión en 1850* (Valladolid, Luis N. de Gaviria, 1896, pp. 453). By a Jesuit. Mostly on Colombia, with a little on Ecuador.

Pfeffer, Leo, *Church, State, and Freedom* (Boston, Beacon Press, 1953, pp. xvi, 675). A dependable study of the constitutional and legal picture in the United States of America.

Posey, Walter Brownlow, *The Development of Methodism in the Old Southwest 1783–1824* (Tuscaloosa, Ala., Weatherford Printing Co., 1933, pp. 151). Sympathetic, based on careful research.

Power, Edward J., *A History of Catholic Higher Education in the United States* (Milwaukee, The Bruce Publishing Co., 1958, pp. xiii, 383). Carefully and sympathetically done.

Price, Ernest, *Bananaland. Pages from the Chronicles of an English Minister to Jamaica* (London, The Carey Press, 1930, pp. x, 186). By a teacher in Kingston.

Purchas, H. T., *A History of the English Church in New Zealand* (Christchurch, Simpson & Williams, 1914, pp. xvii, 252). By an Anglican clergyman.

Rice, Edwin Wilbur, *The Sunday-School Movement and the American Sunday-School Union* (Philadelphia, The Union Press, 2nd ed., 1927, pp. 485). A standard work, sympathetic.

Richards, Thomas C., *Samuel J. Mills, Missionary Pathfinder, Pioneer and Promoter* (Boston, The Pilgrim Press, 1906, pp. 275). An admiring biography, based on good sources.

Rohne, J. Magnus, *Norwegian American Lutheranism up to 1872* (New York, The Macmillan Co., 1926, pp. xxiv, 271). Based on careful research.

Romanell, Patrick, *Making of the Mexican Mind. A Study in Recent Mexican*

Thought (Lincoln, Neb., University of Nebraska Press, 1952, pp. ix, 213). Vigorous, taking positive positions, and based on extensive research.

Rothan, Emmet H., *The German Catholic Immigrant in the United States (1830–1860)* (Washington, The Catholic University of America Press, 1946, pp. viii, 172). A doctoral dissertation.

Rothensteiner, John, *History of the Archdiocese of St. Louis in the Various Stages of Development from A.D. 1673 to A.D. 1928* (St. Louis, Blackwell Wielandy Co., 2 vols., 1928). An official history.

Rouse, Ruth, and Neill, Stephen Charles, editors, *A History of the Ecumenical Movement 1517–1948* (London, S.P.C.K., 1954, pp. xxiv, 822). The definitive official history, by various authors.

Ryan, Edwin, *The Church in the South American Republics* (Milwaukee, The Bruce Publishing Co., 1932, pp. viii, 119). By a Roman Catholic priest, scholarly, in a popular style.

Ryerson, Egerton, *The Story of My Life* (Toronto, William Briggs, 1883, pp. 613).

Sanderson, J. E., *The First Century of Methodism in Canada* (Toronto, William Briggs, 2 vols., 1908). Contains much first-hand material, largely arranged in the form of annals.

Schaff, David S., *The Life of Philip Schaff. In Part Autobiographical* (New York, Charles Scribner's Sons, 1897, pp. xv, 526). By a son.

Schlatter, Wilhelm, *Geschichte der Basler Mission 1815–1915* (Basel, Basler Missionsbuchhandlung, 3 vols., 1916). Based especially on unpublished sources.

Schmeckbier, Laurence F., *The Office of Indian Affairs. Its History, Activities and Organization* (Baltimore, The Johns Hopkins Press, 1927, pp. xiv, 591). Scholarly.

Schmidlin, Joseph, *Catholic Missionary History,* translated and edited by Matthias Braun (Techny, Ill., Mission Press, 1933, pp. xiv, 862). A standard survey. The English translation has added to it.

Schmidt, Martin, *Wort Gottes und Fremdlingschaft. Die Kirche vor dem Auswanderungsproblem des 19. Jahrhunderts* (Erlangen and Rothenburg o. Tauber, Martin Luther-Verlag, 1953, p. 179). Well done.

Schneider, Carl E., *The German Church on the American Frontier. A Study of the Rise of Religion among the Germans of the West* (St. Louis, Eden Publishing House, 1939, pp. xx, 579). A standard work, based on extensive research.

Schulze, Adolf, *200 Jahre Brüdermission II Band. Das zweite Missionsjahrhundert* (Herrnhut, Verlag der Missionsbuchhandlung, 1932, pp. xii, 715). Well documented.

Schwager, Friedrich, *Die katholische Heidenmission der Gegenwart in Zusammenhang mit ihrer Grossen Vergangenheit* (Steyl, Missiondruckerei, 1907, pp. 446). A standard work.

Shannon, James P., *Catholic Colonization on the Western Frontier* (New Haven, Conn., Yale University Press, 1957, pp. xiii, 302). Based upon extensive research. Deals primarily with Bishop John Ireland's efforts.

Shaughnessy, Gerald, *Has the Immigrant Kept the Faith? A Study of Immigration* and *Catholic Growth in the United States 1790–1920* (New York, The Macmillan Co., 1925, pp. 289). Based upon statistics.

Shedd, Clarence P., *Two Centuries of Student Christian Movements* (New York, Association Press, 1934, pp. xxii, 466). The definitive work, sympathetic.

Shortt, Adam, and Doughty, Arthur G., editors, *Canada and Its Provinces* (Toronto, Glasgow, Brock and Co., 23 vols., 1914–1917).

Silva Cotapos, Carlos, *Historia Eclesiástica de Chile* (Santiago, Imprenta de San José, 1925, pp. viii, 387). By a bishop.

Sissons, C. B., *Egerton Ryerson, His Life and Letters* (Toronto, Clarke, Irwin & Co., 2 vols., 1937, 1947). The standard biography.

Slosser, Gaius Jackson, editor, *They Seek a Country. The American Presbyterians. Some Aspects* (New York, The Macmillan Co., 1955, pp. xvi, 330). By various specialists.

Smith, H. Shelton, *Changing Conceptions of Original Sin. A Study in American Theology since 1750* (New York, Charles Scribner's Sons, 1955, pp. xi, 242). Carefully done by a specialist on the history of American theology.

Smith, Timothy L., *Revivalism and Social Reform in Mid-Nineteenth-Century America* (New York, Abingdon Press, 1957, pp. 253). Carefully and sympathetically done.

Stephenson, George M., *The Puritan Heritage* (New York, The Macmillan Co., 1952, pp. 282). Has chiefly to do with the revivals and the movements for moral reform which came from them.

Stephenson, George M., *The Religious Aspects of Swedish Immigration. A Study of Immigrant Churches* (Minneapolis, University of Minnesota Press, 1932, pp. viii, 542). Based upon sources and an extensive literature.

Stewart, Randall, *American Literature and Christian Doctrine* (Baton Rouge, Louisiana State University Press, 1958, pp. xiii, 155).

Stewart, Robert Laird, *Sheldon Jackson, Pathfinder and Prospector of the Missionary Vanguard in the Rocky Mountains and Alaska* (Chicago, Fleming H. Revell Co., 1908, pp. 488). Admiring, based on good sources.

Stock, Eugene, *The History of the Church Missionary Society: Its Environment, Its Men, and Its Work* (London, Church Missionary Society, 4 vols., 1899–1916). The standard history, by a secretary of the Society.

Stokes, Anson Phelps, *Church and State in the United States* (New York, Harper & Brothers, 3 vols., 1950). The standard work.

Streit, Carolus, *Atlas Hierarchious* (Paderborn, Typographia Bonifacius, 1913, pp. 35, 37, 128).

Strong, Esther Boorman, and Warnshuis, A. L., *Directory of Foreign Missions* (New York, International Missionary Council, 1933, pp. xii, 278).

Strong, Josiah, *The Challenge of the City* (New York, Eaton & Mains, 3rd ed., 1907, pp. xiv, 329). Issued for the Young People's Missionary Movement.

Strothmann, R., *Die Koptische Kirche in der Neuzeit* (Tübingen, J. C. B. Mohr [Paul Siebeck], 1932, pp. vi, 167). A careful comprehensive study, chiefly on the nineteenth and twentieth centuries.

Sweet, William Warren, *Religion in the Development of American Culture 1765–1840* (New York, Charles Scribner's Sons, 1952, pp. xiv, 338). By a distinguished specialist.

Sweet, William Warren, *The Story of Religion in America* (New York, Harper & Brothers, 1950, pp. ix, 492). A semi-popular survey by a specialist.

Swihart, Altman K., *Since Mrs. Eddy* (New York, Henry Holt and Co., 1931, pp. xii, 402). Largely on dissent within Christian Science.

Symons, John C., *Life of the Rev. Daniel James Draper . . . with Historical Notices of Wesleyan Methodism in Australia. Chapters also on the Aborigines and Education in Victoria* (Melbourne, Wesleyan Book Depot, 1870, pp. vii, 411). Sympathetic.

Taylor, William, *Story of My Life,* edited by John Clark Ridpath (New York, Hunt & Eaton, 1895, pp. 705).

Tewksbury, Donald G., *The Founding of American Colleges and Universities Before the Civil War, with Particular Reference to the Religious Influences Bearing upon the College Movement* (New York, Bureau of Publications, Teachers College, Columbia University, 1932, pp. x, 254). Based upon extensive research.

Theology Today (Princeton, N.J., 1944 ff.).

Thompson, H. P., *Into All Lands. The History of the Society for the Propagation of the Gospel in Foreign Parts 1701–1950* (London, S.P.C.K., 1951, pp. xv, 760). A standard official history.

Thompson, Robert Ellis, *A History of the Presbyterian Churches in the United States* (New York, The Christian Literature Co., 1895, pp. xxxi, 424). A standard work with strong New School sympathies.

Timpe, Georg, editor, *Katholisches Deutschtum in den Vereinigten Staaten von Amerika. Ein Querschnitt.* Vol. II of *Volksdeutsche Quellen und Darstellungen.* (Freiburg im Breisgau, Herder & Co., 1937, pp. xii, 248).

Tisserant, Eugene, *Eastern Christianity in India. A History of the Syro-Malabar Church from the Earliest Times to the Present Day.* Authorized adaptation from the French by E. R. Hambye (Calcutta, Orient Longmans, 1957, pp. xviii, 266). Largely on the Roman Catholic connexion.

Torbet, Robert G., *A History of the Baptists* (Philadelphia, The Judson Press, 1950, pp. 538). A careful, competent survey.

Torbet, Robert G., *Venture of Faith. The Story of the American Baptist Foreign Mission Society and the Woman's American Baptist Foreign Mission Society 1814–1954* (Philadelphia, The Judson Press, 1955, pp. xiv, 634). Based upon thorough use of the sources and the pertinent literature.

Tucker, William Jewett, *My Generation. An Autobiographical Interpretation* (Boston, Houghton Mifflin Co., 1919, pp. xii, 464). By a distinguished preacher, theologian, and educator.

Twentieth Century Encyclopedia of Religious Knowledge (Grand Rapids, Mich., Baker Book House, 2 vols., 1955).

Union of South Africa, Union Office of Census and Statistics, *Official Year Book of the Union and of Basutoland, Bechuanaland Protectorate, and Swaziland, No. 9,*

1926–1927 (Pretoria, The Government Printing and Stationery Office, 1928, pp. xix, 1157).

[U.S.] Bureau of the Census, *Religious Bodies, 1916* (Washington, Government Printing Office, 2 vols., 1919). From data supplied by the churches.

United States Department of Commerce, Bureau of the Census, *Religious Bodies: 1926* (Washington, Government Printing Office, 2 vols., 1929). From data provided by the churches.

Vernon, C. W., *The Old Church in the New Dominion. The Story of the Anglican Church in Canada* (London, Society for Promoting Christian Knowledge, 1929, pp. viii, 215). An excellent survey by an Anglican.

Waddilove, W. J. D., *The Stewart Missions. A Series of Letters and Journals Calculated to Exhibit to British Christians the Spiritual Destitution of the Emigrants Settled in the Remote Parts of Upper Canada* (London, J. Hatchard & Sons, 1838, pp. xvi, 252).

Wade, Mason, *The French Canadians* (Toronto, The Macmillan Co. of Canada, 1955, pp. xvi, 1106). A standard work.

Walker, Williston, *A History of the Congregational Churches in the United States* (New York, The Christian Literature Society, 1894, pp. xiii, 451). By an outstanding church historian, a Congregationalist.

Walsh, H. H., *The Christian Church in Canada* (Toronto, The Ryerson Press, 1956, pp. ix, 355). A competent, inclusive historical survey.

Wasson, Alfred W., *Church Growth in Korea* (New York, International Missionary Council, 1934, pp. xii, 175). By a Methodist missionary in Korea.

Watters, Mary, *A History of the Church in Venezuela 1810–1930* (Chapel Hill, University of North Carolina Press, 1933, pp. ix, 260). Based on careful research.

Weber, Herman C., *1933 Edition Yearbook of the American Churches* (New York, Round Table Press, 1933, pp. 400).

Weigle, Luther A., *American Idealism* (New Haven, Conn., Yale University Press, 1928, pp. 356). One of the *Pageant of America* series, built around pictures which so far as possible were contemporary.

Wentz, Abdel Ross, *A Basic History of Lutheranism in America* (Philadelphia, Muhlenberg Press, 1955, pp. viii, 430). By a distinguished specialist.

Wheeler, W. Reginald, and others, *Modern Missions in Chile and Brazil* (Philadelphia, The Westminster Press, 1926, pp. xviii, 434). A Presbyterian survey.

White, C. A., *The Challenge of the Years. A History of the Presbyterian Church of Australia in the State of New South Wales* (Sydney, Angus and Robertson, 1951, pp. xviii, 614). Based on careful research.

White, Charles L., *A Century of Faith . . . Centenary Volume Published for the American Baptist Home Mission Society* (Philadelphia, The Judson Press, 1932, pp. 320).

Williams, Daniel Day, *The Andover Liberals. A Study in American Theology* (New York, King's Crown Press, 1941, pp. viii, 203). Sympathetic, based on a doctoral dissertation.

Williams, Mary Wilhelmine, *The People and Politics of Latin America. A History* (Boston, Ginn & Co., 1938, pp. xi, 889). A competent survey.

Wilson, Robert, *Official Year Book of the Commonwealth of Australia,* No. 32, 1939 (Canberra, Commonwealth Government Printer, 1940, pp. xxxii, 992).

Wolf, Edmund Jacob, *The Lutherans in America. A Story of Struggle, Progress, Influence, and Marvelous Growth* (New York, J. A. Hill & Co., 1889, pp. 544). A popular, sympathetic account, primarily for Lutherans.

Woodson, C. G., *The Education of the Negro Prior to 1861. A History of the Education of the Colored People of the United States from the Beginning of Slavery to the Civil War* (New York, G. P. Putnam's Sons, 1915, pp. v, 454). Well documented.

Woodson, Carter G., *The History of the Negro Church* (Washington, The Associated Publishers, 2nd ed., 1921, pp. x, 330). Sympathetic to the Negro.

Worldmission (New York, 1951 ff.). A quarterly Roman Catholic review.

Ylvisaker, S. C., and Anderson, Chr., and Lillegard, etditors, *Grace for Grace. Brief History of the Norwegian Synod* (Mankato, Minn., Lutheran Synod Book Co., 1943, pp. vii, 211). An official history.

Zeitschrift für Missionswissenschaft (Münster i.W., 1911 ff.).

Zuretti, Juan Carlos, *Historia Eclesiastica Argentina* (Buenos Aires, "Huarpas," 1945, pp. 340). Sympathetic; based on extensive bibliographies. Has many short biographies.

Zwierlein, Frederick J., *The Life and Letters of Bishop McQuaid, Prefaced with the History of Catholic Rochester Before His Episcopate* (Rome, Desclee & Compagni, 3 vols., 1925–1927). By a well-trained scholar; sympathetic, based on extensive research.

Index

Abbott, Lyman, 164–165, 197, 232, 235
Acadians, 254
Activism, 13
Adams, John Quincy, 204
Advent Christian Church, 119
Africa, North, 384–399; south of the Sahara, 463–480; *see also various countries*
African Methodist Episcopal Church, 78, 79, 87, 281
Aglipay y Labayan, 428
Aguinaldo, 428
Ahrens, H., 293, 342
Alexander, Archibald, 167
Alexander, Charles McCallon, 34
Alexandria, Patriarchate of, 386
Alfaro, Eloy, 327
Allen, A. V. G., 174
Allen, Richard, 78
Alline, Henry, 260
American (and Foreign) Anti-Slavery Society, 97, 205
American Baptist Home (and Foreign) Mission Society, 23, 24, 42, 89, 90, 146
American Baptist Tract (Publication) Society, 25, 89
American Bible Society, 25, 203, 205, 210, 242, 301, 314, 321, 329, 340, 342, 348, 412
American Board of Commissioners for Foreign Missions, 74, 87, 97, 203, 205, 242, 301, 310, 397, 410, 418, 429, 454, 461, 462, 474
American Colonization Society, 205, 206–207
American Education Society, 97, 205
American Federation of Catholic Societies, 138
American Federation of Labour, 238
American and Foreign Christian Union, 43
American (Home) Missionary Society, 22–23, 42, 50, 97, 145, 203, 205, 206
American Peace Society, 97, 208, 209, 220
American Protective Association, 59
American Society for the Promotion of Temperance, 97
American Standard Version of the Bible, 190–191
American Sunday School Union, 25, 37–38
American Temperance Society (Union), 211
American Tract Society, 25, 97

American Unitarian Association, 154
"Americanism," 106, 107, 108–109
Amish, 45
Ancient Order of Hibernians, 106, 137
Andover case, 159
Andrew, James O., 88
Anglican Communion. *See* England, Church of
Anglo-Catholicism, 264, 470
Anne de Beaupré, Ste., 258
Anthony, Susan B., 217
Anti-Burghers, 265
Anti-Catholicism, 101
Anti-clericalism, 291, 318, 325
Antioch, Patriarchate of, 386
Anti-Saloon League, 214, 215
Anti-slavery movement, 203–207, 494
Apostolic Lutheran Church (Finnish), 56
Aquinas, Thomas, 492
Argentina, 291, 292, 293, 295, 298, 336–340
Armenian Church, 391–392
Armenian Uniates, 395
Arminianism, 36, 186
Arnold, Matthew, 5
Asbury, Francis, 20, 21
Asia, South-East, 416–424; Western, 384–399; *see also various countries*
Assyrian Church, 390–391
Atkinson, George H., 142
Atkinson, Henry A., 231
Atonement, Society of the, 69, 133
Augustana Synod, 51, 52
Augustinians, 403
Australia, 353–370; Protestantism in, 355–364; Roman Catholicism in, 364–367; education in, 367–368; missions within and outside, 368–369, 371
Azariah, Vedenayagam Samuel, 408, 411, 488

Bacon, Leonard, 235
Baillie, John, 488
Baker, Nelson H., 134
Bali, 425
Balmaceda, José Manuel, 333
Bangs, Nathan, 186–187
Baptist General Tract Society, 25
Baptist Triennial Convention, 86, 89

Baptist World Alliance, 486
Baptists, in the United States, 9, 11, 12, 17, 18, 19, 20, 22, 23, 24, 42, 78, 79, 88, 89–90, 177–185; in Canada, 260, 271–272; in Jamaica, 280; in Mexico, 310; in Latin America, 312, 313, 314, 330, 331, 340, 342, 348; in Australia, 355, 361–362; in New Zealand, 374–375, 376; in India, 409, 410; in Burma, 420; in the Philippines, 428; in Japan, 455
Barbados, 282
Barbosa, Ruy, 345
Barnard, Henry, 141
Barnabites, 419
Barreda, Gabino, 308
Barrios, Justo Rufino, 311, 312
Barton, Clara, 216
Basel Mission, 411
Bates, Katherine Lee, 202
Batlle y Ordóñez, José, 341, 342
Bechuanaland, 475–476
Beecham, John, 269
Beecher, Henry Ward, 27, 164, 197, 209, 235
Beecher, Lyman, 26, 27, 160, 161, 211
Beel, Annie C., 121–122
Bégin, Louis Nazaire, 258
Beguines, 61
Belgian Congo, 465, 477–478
Bellamy, Edward, 227
Bellamy, Joseph, 94
Bello, Andres, 332
Benedictines, 63, 133, 403
Berry, Martha McChesny, 218
Bible, American revision of, 190–191; in India, 412; in China, 439–440; in Japan, 456
Bible Christians, 269, 270, 361
Bible Class Union, New Zealand, 376
Bible societies, 25, 412; *see also* American Bible Society *and* British and Foreign Bible Society
Bilbao, Francisco, 332
Blackwell, Henry Brown, 218
Blakeslee, Erastus, 38
Blanchet, François Norbert, 75
Bliss, William Dwight, 228–229
Blue Button Army, 130
Boehm, Henry, 41
Bolívar, Simón, 290, 327, 328
Bolivia, 293, 295, 330–331
Booth, William and Ballington, 124
Borneo, 425, 427
Boudinot, Elias, 219
Bourget, Ignace, 257
Bowne, Borden Parker, 181, 186, 189–190, 198
Boxer uprising, 435, 439
Boy Scout movement, 126
Brace, Charles Loring, 219
Brahmo Samaj, 415
Brazil, 286, 287, 288, 291–292, 294, 298, 343–349
Breckinridge, Robert Jefferson, 142
Brent, Charles R., 489

Brethren, Church of the, 89
Briand, Jean Olivier, 251
Briggs, Charles Augustus, 169–170, 174, 197
Brigham, John C., 301
British and Foreign Bible Society, 25, 301, 329, 340, 342, 348, 396, 412
British Guiana, 282
British West Indies, 277, 279–282
Broadus, John Albert, 177–178
Brook Farm, 157
Brooke, James, 427, 430
Brooks, Charles, 141
Brooks, Phillips, 175, 218
Brothers of Christian Schools, 134, 339
Brotherhood of the Kingdom, 231
Broughton, William Grant, 356, 366
Brown, William Adams, 171
Browning, Robert, 5
Brownson, Orestes Augustus, 69
Buddhism, 457
Bunge, Carlos Octavio, 337
Burdette-Coutts, Baroness, 356
Burghers, 265
Burke, Edmund, 252
Burma, 419–420
Burns, Thomas, 373
Burritt, Elihu, 208
Burton, Ernest DeWitt, 185
Bush Brotherhoods, 357
Bushnell, Horace, 161–163, 197, 225
Butler, Johanna, 136
Butler, William, 410
Buttrick, Wallace, 222

Cahensly, Peter Paul, 103
Calvinism, 29, 167
Cambridge Mission to Delhi, 408
Campbell, Alexander, 11, 113, 261
Campbell, John, 267
Camp-meetings, 12, 17, 19–20
Canada, 247–76; and the United States, 248–250; Roman Catholic Church in, 250–259; Protestants in, 259–274
Capers, William, 78
Capuchins, 339, 346, 403, 406
Carey, Felix, 419
Carey, William, 402, 485
Caribbean area, 315–317
Carlyle, Thomas, 5
Carmelites, 135, 403, 405, 406
Carnegie, Andrew, 210, 221
Carranza, 308
Carrera, Rafael, 311
Carroll, John, 58, 61, 101
Cassinese, 133
Castors, 257
Castro, Cipriano, 320
Catholic Knights of America, 137
Catholic missionary societies, 65, 70, 80, 133, 134, 246

Catholic Total Abstinence Union, 213
Celebes, 426
Central America, 310–315
Ceylon, 416–419
Chaldean Uniates, 395, 404
Channing, William Ellery, 154–155
Chapman, John Wilbur, 34, 36
Chauncy, Charles, 153
Chautauqua movement, 144
Chile, 291, 293, 296, 298, 331–334
China, 431–445; Roman Catholic Church in, 433–436; Protestantism in, 436–443; Russian Orthodox Church in, 444
China Inland Mission, 438, 439
Chiniquy, Charles, 258
Chisholm, Caroline Jones, 366
Christian Brothers, 134, 339
Christian Catholic Church in Zion, 123
Christian Commonwealth Colony, 229
Christian Endeavour, Young People's Society of, 11, 13, 130–131, 273
Christian Instruction, Brothers of, 134
Christian Labour Union, 226, 228
Christian Literature Society for India and Africa, 412
Christian and Missionary Alliance, 334, 424, 429
Christian Reformed Church, 57
Christian Science, 11, 120–122, 203
Christians (denomination), 11, 17, 22
Chuntokyo, 449
Church of Jesus Christ of Latter Day Saints, 11, 18, 113, 114–116, 203
Church membership, U.S., 12, 16, 59, 78, 79, 80, 81, 88, 91, 104, 110, 113, 115, 117, 119, 120, 123
Church Missionary Society, 259, 371, 372, 374, 376, 396–397, 418, 477
Church Peace Union, 210, 221
Churches of Christ, 89, 113, 355, 363
Cicero, Father, 347
Circuit riders, 17, 21
Cities, U.S., growth of, 6, 7; reform in, 215
City missions, 129–130
Clark, Francis E., 130
Clark, John Bates, 228
Clark, Myron A,, 303
Clarke, Col. and Mrs. George R., 130
Clarke, James Freeman, 155
Clarke, William Newton, 181–182
Classes, Methodist, 17, 21
Clausen, C. L., 54
Clemens, Samuel L., 191
Clergy, training of, 27, 28, 93–96, 109–110, 157–163, 166, 169, 177, 178, 196, 197, 267, 282, 357, 359, 363, 373, 397, 413; *see also* Education
"Clergy reserves," 263, 265
Coffin, Henry Sloane, 171
Coillard, François, 474
Coke, Thomas, 280, 418

Colombia, 290, 292, 297, 298, 311, 314, 318, 321–324
Colonial and Continental Church Society, 259
Colonial Missionary Society (Congregational), 260, 362, 363
Coloured Methodist Episcopal Church, 79, 146
Colwell, Stephen, 225
Commission for Catholic Missions . . . , 80
Committee on Coöperation in Latin America, 489
Confucianism, 431
Congo, 465–466, 477–478
Congregational Home Missionary Society, 23
Congregationalists, in the United States, 12, 18, 22, 23, 24, 25, 86, 153–165; in Canada, 260, 272; in British Guiana, 282; in Latin America, 348; in Australia, 355, 362–363; in Japan, 455
Constantinople, Patriarchate of, 385–386
Continental Missions Conferences, 487
Conwell, Russell H., 233–234
Cook, Joseph, 226
Cooper, Thomas, 5
Coptic Church, 388–389
Copts, Uniate, 394–395
Cornell, Ezra, 150
Corrigan, Michael Augustine, 106, 148, 238, 239
Cortés, Juan Donoso, 325
Costa Rica, 311, 314
Cousin, Victor, 69
Cowley Fathers, 408
Cuba, 288, 291, 292, 316, 317
Cumberland Presbyterian Church, 11
Cunha, Euclydes da, 345
Curaçao, 279
Cyprus, 387
Cyril II, 387
Cyril IV, 388
Cyril V, 388–389

Dana, James Dwight, 164
Danish Evangelical Lutheran Church in America, 56
Darrow, Clarence, 184
Darwin, Charles, 5, 493
Daughters of Charity, 66
Davenport, Ira Erastus, 120
Davis, Andrew Jackson, 120
Dedham case, 154
Deism, 4
Demers, Modeste, 75, 254
Denominationalism, U.S., 10, 11, 14, 17–18, 85, 96, 112–123; *see also various denominations*
De Salle, John Baptist, 134
De Smet, Pierre-Jean, 75
Devereux, Nicholas, 133
Dewey, John, 5
Díaz, José de la Cruz Porfirio, 307–308, 309
Dietrichson, J. W., 54–55

Dillard, James Hardy, 147
Disciples of Christ, in the United States, 11, 12, 17, 22, 89, 113; in Canada, 261; in Mexico, 310; in Latin America, 340; in the Philippines, 428
Divine Scientists, 122
Divine Word, Society of the, 403
Dix, Dorothea Lynde, 215–216
Dodge, David Low, 207
Dodge, Grace H., 129
Dodge, William Earl, 99, 213, 220
Dodge, William Earl, Jr., 220
Domestic and Foreign Missionary Society, 24, 264
Dominican Republic, 289, 316
Dominicans, 61, 63, 66, 133, 134, 423, 424, 433
Dow, Neal, 212
Dowie, John Alexander, 123
Draper, John William, 191
Drew, Daniel, 223
Drexel, Katherine, 76
Drumgoole, John Christopher, 239–240
Drummond, Henry, 31, 193
Du Bose, William Porcher, 174
Duff, Alexander, 409–410, 487
Dukhobors, 273
Dunant, Henri, 486
Durant, Henry F., 144
Dutch Guiana, 277, 278, 282
Dutch Reformed Church, 57, 468, 469–470, 474
Dwight, Timothy, 26, 153, 159

East, Church of the, 390–391
East Indies, 424–427
Eastern (Orthodox) Churches, 76, 110, 385–392, 398, 444, 449, 453
Ecuador, 290, 325–327
Ecumenical Methodist Council, 486
Ecumenical Missionary Conference, 488
Ecumenical Movement, 486, 487, 488
Eddy, Asa Gilbert, 120
Eddy, Mary Baker, 120, 121
Eddy, Sherwood, 33, 411
Edinburgh Conference (1910), 14, 487, 488, 489; Continuation Committee of, 489
Education, in the United States, 94, 140–151, 182, 183–185, 222 (theological schools, 27, 28, 94–95, 109–110, 157–158, 159–163, 166, 169, 171, 177, 178, 183–185, 188, 196, 197); in Canada, 255–256, 262–263, 264, 270–271, 272; in Latin America, 287, 288, 299, 300, 333; in Australia, 357, 363, 367–368; in New Zealand, 375; in Western Asia, 395–396, 397; in India, 406, 411–412, 413; in China, 440–441; in Korea, 448; in Japan, 455; in South Africa, 473; *see also* Parochial schools
Edwards, Jonathan, 19, 26, 153, 159
Eielsen, Elling, 54
Eliot, George, 5

Elliott, Walter, 107
Ely, Richard Theodore, 227–228, 229
Emerson, Ralph Waldo, 5, 156
Emerson, William, 156
Emmons, Nathanael, 94, 141, 153
England, Church of, in Canada, 259, 261–264; in the West Indies, 279, 282; in Central America, 313; in Australia, 355–358; in New Zealand, 373–374, 376; in India, 407–409; in Burma, 420; in South Africa, 470, 473
England, John, 62, 109
Enlightenment, 9, 293, 300, 341, 344
Episcopalians, in the United States, 11, 43, 86, 174–175; in Canada, 261; in Mexico, 310; in Brazil, 348; in the Philippines, 429
Epworth League, 132, 273
Esbjörn, Lars Paul, 51, 52
Ethiopian (Abyssinian) Church, 389–390
Eucharistic congresses, 72
Evangelicalism, 4, 11, 19, 36, 49–56, 493–494
Evangelical Alliance, 98, 99, 485–486, 487
Evangelical Association, 11, 41, 89, 113, 264
Evangelical Synod, 17, 49, 50, 51
Evangelical Union of South America, 330, 348
Evangelists, 26–37

Fairchild, James H., 214
"Faith" missions, 302
Faith and Order, World Conference on, 489
Falkland Islands, 301, 302
Faribault plan, 67, 148
Farwell, Mrs. John V., Jr., 129
Fathers of the Precious Blood, 63
Fathers of St. John the Evangelist, 408
Federal Council of the Churches of Christ in America, 14, 99–100, 232, 275, 484
Fee, John G., 145
Fenwick, Edward Dominic, 61
Ferreira, Carlos Vaz, 341
Feuerbach, 5
Fidelis of the Cross, Father, 68
Fiji Islands, 461
Finney, Charles Grandison, 28–30, 36, 163, 204
Finnish Evangelical Lutheran Church of America, 56
Fisk, Wilbur, 187
Fiske, John, 191
Flores, Juan José, 325
Foreign missions. *See* Missionary enterprises and societies
Foreign Missions Conference of North America, 245, 487, 489
Foster, George Burman, 183–184
Fox, Margaret and Kate, 119
Francia, José Caspar Rodríguez de, 335
Franciscans, 63, 64, 133–134, 334, 347, 433
Franson, Frederick, 53
Freedmen's Aid Society, 146
French Guiana, 317
Friendly Islands, 460–461

Fundamentalism, 192–194, 198–199

Gallatzin, Demetrios Augustine, 65
Gallicanism, 250, 256, 257
Gambier Islands, 460
Gandhi, Mohandas Karamchand, 415, 443, 475
García Moreno, Gabriel, 325–326
Gardiner, Allen Francis, 301, 331, 340
Garfield, James A., 236
Garrison, William Lloyd, 204
Gates, Frederick T., 222
Gates, George A., 229
Gell, Frederick, 408
General Council of the Evangelical Lutheran Church in North America, 92
General Education Board, 147, 222
General Eldership of the Churches of God, 116–117
General Missionary Convention (Baptist), 242
George, Henry, 227, 239
German Evangelical Church of Brazil, 348
German Mission Conferences, Association of, 487
German Reformed Church, 49–51, 56, 172–173
Gibbons, James, 62, 103, 105, 106, 107, 149, 238, 239, 240
Giddings, Joshua R., 204
Gladden, Washington, 209, 225–226
Glasgow Colonial Society, 259–260
Goan schism, 404
God, Churches of, 116–117
Goethe, 5
Gómez, Juan Vicente, 320
Gonzáles, Joaquín V., 337
Good Shepherd, 135
Gordon, Adoniram Judson, 234
Gordon, George Angier, 165, 197
Gossner Mission, 411
Gough, John Bartholomew, 212
Grabau, J. A. A., 47
Grant, George Monro, 267
Gray, Robert, 470
Gray, W. H., 75
Great Awakening, 4, 12, 19
Greek Orthodox Church, 110
Greenland, 277, 278
Grenfell, Wilfred Thomason, 274
Grey Nuns, 250, 256
Grimké, Sarah Moore, Angelina Emily, and Thomas Smith, 208–209
Guadeloupe, 317
Guatemala, 311, 312
Guevara y Lira, Archbishop, 320
Guiana, 277, 278, 282, 317
Guinea, 467
Gützlaff, Karl Friedrich August, 437, 438
Guzmán Blanco, Antonio, 319–320

Hadley, Samuel H. and H. H., 130
Haiti, 288, 289, 292, 315–316

Hale, Edward Everett, 209, 224
"Hardshell" Baptists, 90
Hardy, Thomas, 5
Hare, William Hobart, 76
Harms, Ludwig, 474
Harper, William Rainey, 38, 144, 182–183, 193
Harris, George, 159
Harris, Samuel, 225
Harrison, Benjamin, 236
Hasselquist, Tuve Nilsson, 51, 52
Hawaii, 6, 459, 461–462
Hawthorne, Nathaniel, 157, 202
Heber, Reginald, 408
Hecker, Isaac Thomas, 69–70, 107
Hermannsburg Mission, 474
Herron, George D., 229
Hicks, Elias, 272
Hidalgo y Costilla, Miguel, 289
Hideyoshi, 446, 450
Hill, John C., 312
Hines, Joshua Vaughan, 118
Hodge, Archibald Alexander, 168, 197
Hodge, Charles, 166–168, 173, 197
Hodur, Francis, 104
Holiness movement, 117–118, 330
Holy Ghost Fathers, 403, 478
Holy Infancy and Youth of Jesus, Brothers of the, 134
Holy Sepulchre, Brotherhood of the, 387
Home Mission Board (Baptist), 42
Honduras, 282, 311, 313
Hopkins, Samuel, 153, 154, 203
Horner, Ralph, 273
Hovey, Alvah, 180
Howe, Julia Ward, 209, 216–217
Howe, Samuel Gridley, 216
Huerta, Francisco, 308
Hughes, John, 62, 67, 70, 102, 237
Hung Hsiu-ch'üan, 437
Hungarian Reformed Church in America, 57
Huntington, William Reed, 99
Hutterian Brethren, 45
Huxley, Thomas H., 5

Ibsen, Henrik, 5
Icelandic Evangelical Lutheran Synod in North America, 56
Immaculate Heart of Mary, Congregation of the, 477
Immigration to the Americas, 6, 7, 8, 10, 39–68, 81, 102, 259, 293
India, 400–415; Roman Catholic Church in, 402, 403–406; Protestantism in, 402, 407–413
Indians, United States, 7, 8, 72–77; in Canada, 255; in Latin America, 286, 287, 288, 347
Indo-China, French, 423–424
Industrial Revolution, 6, 7
Ingenieros, José, 337
Ingersoll, Robert G., 5, 176

Inglis, Charles, 261, 262
Inland Mission of the Cape Colony, 474
Inland Mission of China, 438, 439
Inland South American Missionary Union, 348
Inner Mission in Germany, 493
Institutional church, 233–234
Intercollegiate Peace Association, 210
International Congregational Council, 486
International Friendship, World Alliance for, 210
International Grenfell Association, 274
International Missionary Council, 14, 489
International Sunday School Committee (Association), 38
Ireland, John, 62, 65, 102, 103, 105, 106, 148, 149, 213, 238
Irish Catholic Benevolent Union, 137–138
Irish Catholic Colonization Association, 65
Islam, 388, 425
Iturbide, Augustin de, 290, 304, 310
Ives, Levi Silliman, 68
Iyeyasu, 450

Jackson, Sheldon, 23
Jacobite Church, 390, 401
Jacobs, Benjamin Franklin, 38
Jamaica, 279–281
James, Daniel and Daniel Willis, 220
James, Henry, 202
James, William, 191
Janson, Eric, 52
Japan, 450–457
Jarweh, Michael, 395
Java, 425
Jeanes, Anna T., 147
Jehovah's Witnesses, 11, 122–123
Jerusalem, Patriarchate of, 387; Anglo-Prussian bishopric in, 398
Jesuits, in the United States, 61, 133; in Canada, 250, 255; in Latin America, 288, 305, 306, 309, 311, 314, 319, 322, 326, 328, 334, 341, 342, 345, 346; in India, 403, 406; in China, 433; in Japan, 450
Jews in the United States, 40, 80–81
Johnson, Richard, 356
Jones, Jesse Henry, 227, 228
Juárez, Benito, 306, 307, 308
Judson, Adoniram, 419–420
Judson, Henry Pratt, 185

Kalley, Robert Reid, 348
Kasatkin, Ivan, 453
Keene, John Joseph, 106, 149, 238
Keller, Helen, 218
Kemper, Jackson, 24
King, Henry Churchill, 163
Kingdom, Brotherhood of the, 231
Kingdom Movement, 229–230
Kirby, Joseph Coles, 364

Kirchenverein des Westens, 50
Knights of Columbus, 137
Knights of Labour, 106, 229, 238
Know-Nothing movement, 58
Korea, 446–449
Korn, Alejandro, 337
Kozlowski, Anthony, 104
Krause, Karl Chr. Fr., 293
Krausism, 293, 308, 341
Krauth, Charles Porterfield and Charles Philip, 195
Kumiai, 455

Labour Temple, 233
Labour unions, 106, 229, 238, 258
Labrador, 247
Labuan, 427
Ladd, William, 208
Ladies' Christian Union, 128, 210
Laestadius, Lars Levi, 56
Laflèche, Louis-François Richer, 257
Lambeth Conferences, 99, 486
Lamennais, Jean Marie Robert de, 317
"Landmarkers," 90
Lang, John Dunmore, 358, 367
Lasterría, José Victorino, 332
Lathrop, Rose Hawthorne, 69, 136
Latin America, 284–352; colonial policies in, 286; independence of, 288–292; Roman Catholicism in, 294–300; Protestantism in, 300–303; see also various countries
Latter Day Saints, Church of Jesus Christ of (Mormons), 11, 18, 113, 114–116, 203
Laurier, Wilfred, 257
Lavigerie, Charles Martial Allemand, 393
Laws, Robert, 476
Laymen's Missionary Movement, 244
Lazarists, 133, 299, 339
League of Universal Brotherhood, 208
Lee, Jason, 74
Leigh, Samuel, 360, 371
Leo XIII, 103, 107, 149, 240, 257, 258, 394, 395, 404, 492
Leopold II, 465, 478
Leopoldine Society, 63
Lewis, Samuel, 141–142
Liberia, 206, 465
Libermann, Francis Maria Paul, 317, 478
Lievens, Constant, 405
Lincoln, Abraham, 212, 236
Livingstone, David, 382, 464, 465, 472, 476
Livingstone, John H., 94
Locke, John, 9
London Missionary Society, 409, 464, 472, 479
Looking Upward, Press Onward Society, 50
López, Basilio, Carlos Antonio, and Francisco Solano, 335
Love, Alfred Henry, 209
Lovejoy, Elijah Parish, 206
Ludwig-Missionsverein, 63

Lundy, Benjamin, 204
Luther League, 132
Lutheran Brethren of America, 55
Lutherans, in the United States, 11, 12–13, 17, 45–52, 53, 54–55, 56, 91–93, 98; in Canada, 272; in Brazil, 348; in Australia, 355, 363; in India, 411
Lyell, Charles, 5, 493
Lyon, Mary, 144

McAuley, Catherine, 135
McAuley, Jerry, 130
McConnell, Francis John, 233
McCosh, James, 168
Macdonell, Alexander, 252
Macdonnell, Daniel James, 267
McGiffert, Arthur Cushman, 170, 197
McGlynn, Edward, 106, 239
McGready, James, 19
Machray, Robert, 264
McKendree, William, 21
McKinley, William, 236
McLoughlin, John, 75
McMurdy, Robert, 209
McQuaid, Bernard John, 106, 110, 148, 149, 238, 239
Madagascar, 478–479
Madero, 308
Maine Temperance Union, 212
Malaya, 421–422
Manchus, 433, 434, 435
Mann, Horace, 141
Mar Thoma Christians, 409
Mariannhill, 475
Marist Brothers, 134, 371, 375
Maronites, 392–393, 395
Marsden, Samuel, 365, 360, 371
Marsden, Samuel Edward, 357
Marshman, Joshua, 402
Martinique, 317
Marx, Karl, 355, 493
Mary, devotion to, 492; Society of, 461
Mary Immaculate, Oblates of, 133, 254, 255, 256, 403
Maryknoll Fathers, 133, 134, 246
Mathew, Theobald, 212
Mathews, Shailer, 184, 185, 232
Maximilian, 306–307
Maximos III, 394
Mead, Charles M., 159
Mead, Silas, 362
Medical Missionary Association, Chinese, 440
Melanesian Mission, 376
Meletios, 386
Melkites, 394
Melville, Herman, 157, 202
Men and Religion Forward Movement, 232
Méndez, Archbishop, 319
Mennonites, 45, 89, 272
Mercersburg theology, 98, 172–173, 198

Methodist Council, 486
Methodist Episcopal Church, South, 78, 79, 88, 146
Methodists, in the United States, 11, 12, 17, 19, 20–22, 24, 41, 78, 86, 87, 88, 185–190; in Canada, 260, 268–271; in the West Indies, 280, 282; in British Guiana, 282; in Mexico, 310; in Latin America, 313, 315, 327, 329, 331, 334, 340, 342, 348; in Australia, 355, 360–361; in New Zealand, 374, 376; in India, 409, 410; in Burma, 420; in the Philippines, 428; in Korea, 447, 448; in Japan, 455; in the Pacific islands, 459, 460–461; in South Africa, 470, 473
Mexico, 287, 288, 289–290, 293, 295, 297, 299, 301, 303–310
Milan Society, 403
Miley, John, 189
Mill Hill fathers, 133, 403, 427, 477
Miller, William, 118–119
Mills, Samuel J., 25, 28, 206
Minnesota Irish Emigration Society, 65
Mission Friend movement, 53
Missionary conferences, 245, 413, 442–443, 456, 484, 487, 488, 489
Missionary enterprises and societies, 22–24, 33, 42, 64, 65, 70, 80, 127, 128, 133, 134, 242–246, 258, 264, 266–267, 270, 271–272, 330, 346, 348, 368–369, 371, 375–376, 396–398, 409, 411, 413, 426, 440, 464, 472, 474, 479, 489
Missions Étrangères. See Société des Missions Étrangères
Missouri Synod, 45, 46, 92, 272, 348, 494
Mitchell, Hinckley J., 190
Mitre, Bartolomé, 339
Modernism, 196, 492
Moffat, Robert, 464, 472
Mohammed Ali, 386, 388
Moluccas, 426
Monagas, José Tadeo and José Gregorio, 319
Mongols, 433
Montalvo, Juan, 326
Moody, Dwight Lyman, 30–33, 126, 244, 273, 411
Mora, José María Luis, 308
Moran, Patrick Francis, 367
Moravians, 278, 280, 282, 314, 437, 472
Morelos, José María, 289–290
Mormons, 11, 18, 113, 114–116, 203
Morris, William Case, 340
Morrison, Robert, 436–437
Morse, Rebecca F., 129
Morse, Richard Cary, 125
Morse, Samuel F. B., 58
Mott, John Raleigh, 33, 127, 216, 244–245, 376, 413, 443, 487, 488, 489
Mott, Lucretia Coffin, 216
Mountain, George Jehoshaphat, 262
Mountain, Jacob, 251, 261, 262

Mowat, John Bower, 267
Mtesa, 477
Muehlhauser, John, 49
Mühlenberg, Henry M., 48
Mukyokai, 456–457
Müller, George, 34
Mullins, Edgar Young, 178
Murray, Andrew, 468, 469, 474
Murray, John, 468
Muzi, Juan, 296, 333, 338

Napoleon III, 306, 307, 424
Nasmith, David, 129
Nast, William, 42
Nation, Carry Amelia Moore, 214
National Arbitration League, 209
National Baptist Convention, 90–91
National Missionary (Christian) Council of India, Burma, and Ceylon, 413
National Missionary Society of India, 411
National Temperance Society and Publication House, 213
"Nativism," 58
Nazarene, Church of the, 118, 330
Neesima, Joseph Hardy, 454–455
Negroes in the United States, 6, 8, 12, 77–78, 79, 80, 88, 91, 145–147, 203–207
Nerinckx, Charles, 61, 66
Nestorians, 390–391, 398, 433
Netherlands East Indies, 424–427
Netherlands Missionary Society, 426
Nettleton, Asahel, 27–28
Nevin, John Williamson, 172–173, 198
Nevius, John L., 448
New Caledonia, 461
"New divinity," 160, 161
New England Company, 259
New England theology, 153, 203
Newfoundland, 247; Society for Educating the Poor of, 259
New Granada. *See* Colombia
New Guinea, 459
New Thought, 122
New Zealand, 360, 371–377
Niagara Bible Conference (1895), 192–193
Nias, 426
Nicaragua, 311, 313
Nicolai (Ivan Kasatkin), 453
Nietzsche, 5
Nommensen, Ludwig Ingwer, 426
North, Frank Mason, 232
Northern Baptist Convention, 89, 185, 232
Northfield Schools, 33
Norton, Andrews, 155
Norwegian Lutherans in America, 54–55, 93
Notre Dame, School Sisters of, 63
Núñez, Rafael, 323
Nyasaland, 475–476

Oberlin, J. F., 163

Oblates of Mary Immaculate, 133, 254, 255, 256, 403
O'Brien, Matthew A., 134
O'Flynn, Jeremiah Francis, 365
O'Higgins, Bernardo, 296, 332
"Old Lutherans," 47
Oldham, Joseph H., 488, 489
Oldham, William F., 422
O'Quinn, James, 365
Orthodox Churches, in the United States, 11, 76, 110; in Western Asia and North Africa, 385–392; in China, 444; in Korea, 449; in Japan, 453
Orton, Joseph, 360
Owen, Robert, 45
Oxford Mission, 408

Pacific Islands, 458–462
Páez, José Antonio, 319
Paine, Thomas, 5
Pallegoix, 422
Pallotines, 64, 346
Panama, 311, 314–315
Papineau, Louis Joseph, 253
Paraguay, 287, 334–336
Park, Edwards Amasa, 158
Parker, Samuel, 74–75
Parker, Theodore, 155–156
Parochial schools, 59, 60, 65–68, 106, 140, 147, 148
Parvin, Theophilus, 301
Passionists, 339
Patagonian Missionary Society, 301
Patton, W. W., 146
Paul, Kanakarayan Tiruselvam, 411
Paulists, 70, 133
Peabody, Francis Greenwood, 232
Peace movement, 207–210, 217
Peck, John Mason, 23
Pedro I, 292, 344
Pedro II, 292, 343, 344, 345
Pella, 57
Pentecostal (holiness) movement, 11, 117–118, 330, 334, 349
Penzotti, Francisco G., 329
Peru, 287, 290, 291, 293, 301, 327–330
Peter, William Wesley, 440
Phelps, Anson Greene, 220
Philip, John, 472
Philippines, 6, 427–429
Phillips, Wendell, 204–205
Philpott, P. W., 273
Photios, 386, 387
Picpus Fathers, 460
Pictet, Benedict, 167
Pierce, John D., 141
Pietism, 4, 36, 493
Pious Society for Missions, 346
Pius IX, 297, 299, 320, 328, 344, 345, 394, 404

Plan of Union, Presbyterian-Congregationalist, 86–87, 161

Plessis, Joseph-Octave, 252

Plymouth Brethren, in the United States, 89; in Latin America, 312, 313, 321; in Australia, 355; in India, 409; in Indo-China, 424

Polding, John Bede, 365, 366

Polish National Catholic Church, 103–104

Pompallier, Jean Baptist François, 371, 375

Poor Sisters of St. Frances (Poor Clares), 61, 63

Positivism, 294, 299, 308–309, 317, 341, 345

Powderly, Terence V., 238

Powell, Joab, 18–19

Prada, Manuel González, 328

Prayer-meeting revival, 30

Presbyterians, in the United States, 9, 11, 12, 19, 22, 23, 24, 25, 43, 86, 87, 165–171 (New School and Old School, 87, 161, 166); in Canada, 259–260, 265–268; in British Guiana, 282; in Mexico, 310; in Latin America, 324, 340, 348; in Australia, 355, 358–360; in New Zealand, 374, 376; in Western Asia, 397; in India, 409, 410; in Siam, 423; in the Philippines, 428; in Korea, 447, 448; in Japan, 455; in South Africa, 470, 473

Preus, Adolph Carl and Herman Amberg, 55

Price, Thomas F., 246

Priestley, Joseph, 5

Prime, Samuel Irenaeus, 99

Primitive Methodists, 269, 270, 360, 361

Programme Catholique, 257

Prohibition, 212, 213, 214

Protestant Episcopal Church. *See Episcopalians*

Protestant Federation of France, 484

Protestantism, in the United States, 13; gains of, through immigration, 40, 41–57; converts to Catholicism from, 68–70; structural developments in, 86–93; clergy of, 93–96; coöperation within, 96–100, 243–245, 484–490; denominationalism of, *see* Denominationalism; nondenominational movements stemming from, 123–132; and education, 140–147; response of, to intellectual currents, 153–195; in Canada, 248, 249, 259–274; in the West Indies, 280–281; in Latin America, 300–303, 309–310, 312, 313, 314, 321, 324, 327, 329–330, 331, 333–334, 336, 340, 342, 347–349; in Australia, 355–364; in Western Asia and North Africa, 396–398; in India, 402, 407–413; in South-East Asia, 417, 418, 419–420, 421–423, 424, 426, 428–429; in China, 436–443; in Korea, 447–449; in Japan, 453–456; in the Pacific islands, 459, 460–461, 462

Provencher, Joseph Norbert, 254

Public School Society, 67

Puerto Rico, 6, 291, 292, 317

Purcell, Edward and John B., 237

Quakers, 202, 260–261, 272, 313, 315

Quebec Act, 251

Quimby, Phineas Parkhurst, 120

Radàma I, 478–479

Rainsford, William S., 233

Rankin, Melinda, 309–310

Rapp, Johann Georg, 45

Rappites, 45

Rauch, Frederick Augustus, 172

Rauschenbusch, Augustus, 42, 230

Rauschenbusch, Walter, 42, 181, 230–231, 237

Raymond, Miner, 188

Rechabites, Independent Order of, 212

Récollets, 250, 251

Redemptorists, 63, 70, 133, 254, 258, 339

Reform movements, 202–218

Reformed Churches, in the United States, 11, 17, 23, 49–51, 56, 57, 172–173; in South Africa, 468, 469–470, 474; Alliance of, 486

Regions Beyond Missionary Union, 330

Reid, Thomas, 158, 160

Religious Education Association, 39

Religious Tract Society, 25

Renan, 5

Rescue missions, 130

Rese, Frederick, 63, 64

Revell, Emma C., 31–32

Revivalism, 12, 19, 30, 36

Reynolds, Annie M. and James M., 129

Rhenish Missionary Society, 426, 472

Rhodes, Cecil John, 476

Rhodesia, 475–476

Ricci, Matteo, 433

Richard, Gabriel, 66

Richard, Timothy, 441

"Rites controversy," 434

Rivadavia, Bernadino, 337–338

Robertson, Archibald Thomas, 179

Robertson, Frederick W., 234

Robertson, James, 266

Rocafuerte, Vicente, 325

Rockefeller, John Davison, 147, 180, 182, 221–222

Rockefeller Foundation (and other philanthropies), 222–223

Rodó, José Enriqué, 341

Rogers, Edward H., 227

Roman Catholic Church, in the United States, 11, 12, 13, 27; gains of, through immigration, 40, 57–68; Protestant converts to, 68–70; worship and devotional practices of, 71–72; national structure of, 100–109; clergy of, 109–110 (see also Clergy); movements and organizations in, 132–138; and education, 147–149; response of, to intellectual currents, 195–196; effect of, on American life, 237–240; world mission of, 245–246; in Canada, 248, 249, 250–259; in the Caribbean area, 281, 282; in Latin America, 284, 285–286, 294–300, 304, 305–306, 311, 312, 313, 319–320,

321, 322, 323–324, 325–326, 328, 330–331, 333, 336, 337–340, 342, 343–347; in Australia, 364–367; in New Zealand, 375; in Western Asia and North Africa, 392–396; in India, 402, 403–406; in South-East Asia, 417–418, 419, 421, 422, 423, 426, 427–428, 429; in China, 433–436; in Korea, 446–447; in Japan, 452–453; in the Pacific islands, 460; in South Africa, 470–471; unity within, 484–485
Roosevelt, Theodore, 236
Rosas, Juan Manuel de, 338
Royce, Josiah, 191
Ruffner, William H., 142
Rush, Benjamin, 211
Russell, Charles Taze, 122–123
Russell, H. H., 214
Russell Sage Foundation, 218
Russia, expansion of, 6; influence of, in Western Asia and North Africa, 398
Russian Orthodox Church, 76, 110, 398, 444, 449, 453
Ruthenian Uniates, 253
Rutherford, Joseph Franklin, 123
Ryan, Abram J., 237
Ryerson, Egerton, 255, 270–271

Sacred Heart, Brothers of the, 134
Sacred Heart of Mary, Religious of the, 136
Sage, Margaret Olivia Slocum and Russell, 218
St. Catherine of Sinai, monastery of, 388
St. Charles Borromeo, Missionaries of, 64, 346
St. Cyril and St. Sergius, Brotherhood of, 398
St. Francis Xavier, Brothers of, 61, 134
St. Joseph's Society of the Sacred Heart, 133
St. Nazianz, Religious Society of, 64
St. Paul the Apostle, Missionary Society of, 70
St. Rafael Society, 103
St. Stephen, Community of, 408
Salesians, 339, 403
Salvador, El, 311, 312
Salvation Army, 124, 125, 330, 355, 409, 494
Salvatorians, 64, 403
Samoa, 6, 459
Sanford, Elias B., 99
Sankey, Ira D., 32, 33
San Martín, José de, 290, 291, 300
Santa Anna, Antonio López de, 305
Santa Cruz, Andrés, 330
Sarawak, 426–427
Sargeant, George, 280
Sargent, Henry, 69
Sarmiento, Domingo Faustino, 337, 339
Schaff, Philip, 98, 99, 172, 173, 190, 198
Schmucker, Samuel S., 47, 91, 92, 97, 98, 194
School Sisters of Notre Dame, 63
Schopenhauer, 5
Scofield, Cyrus Ingerson, 193, 312
Scotland, Church of, 260, 263, 265, 359, 410; National Bible Society of, 412
Seamen's Friend Society, 301

Sectionalism, U.S., 6, 85, 206
Selwyn, George Augustus, 371, 373–374
Seramphimites, 254
Servants of India Society, 415
Seton, Elizabeth Ann, 66, 69, 136
Seventh Day Adventists, in the United States, 118–119, 203; in Jamaica and British Guiana, 281, 282; in Latin America, 313, 314, 315, 327, 330, 331, 342, 348; in Australia, 355; in the Philippines, 429
Shaw, Barnabas, 473
Shaw, Bernard, 5
Sheldon, Charles Monroe, 228
Siam, 422–423
Sierra Leone, 467
Sihler, Wilhelm, 47
Silliman, Benjamin, 163
Simpson, Matthew, 209
Sisters of the Blessed Sacrament, 76
Sisters of Charity (Grey Nuns), 250
Sisters of Charity of Refuge, 135
Sisters of Charity of Nazareth, 66
Sisters of Charity of St. Joseph, 66, 136
Sisters of Mercy, 135
Sisters of Notre Dame de Namur, 61
Sisters of Our Lady of Compassion, 375
Sisters of the Presentation of the Blessed Virgin Mary, 135
Sisters of Providence, 256
Sisters of St. Joseph of Annecy, 403
Sisters of the Third Order of St. Dominic, 135, 136
Skogsbergh, E. August, 53
Slater, Edward Bede, 365
Slater, John Fox, 147
Slovak Evangelical Union; Slovak Lutheran Church, 56
Smiley, Albert Keith, 77, 209
Smith, George Adam, 31
Smith, Gerald Birney, 184
Smith, Gerrit, 219–220
Smith, Henry Preserved, 170, 197
Smith, Hyrum, 114
Smith, Joseph, 113–114
Smith, Joseph, Jr., 115
Smith, Rodney ("Gipsy"), 34
Smith, Samuel Francis, 201
Smyth, Egbert C., 159
Smyth, Newman, 159
Social Creed of Methodism, 231–232
Social gospel, 13, 223–234
Social Service, League (American Institute) for, 230
Social settlements, 234
Socialism, 228–229
Société d'Éducation (Quebec), 255
Société des Missionaires de Notre Dame d'Afrique, 393
Société des Missions Étrangères, 403, 419, 421, 422, 423, 433, 447, 452, 474, 479
Society Islands, 460

Society of Our Lady of Victory, 134
Society for Promoting Christian Knowledge, 259, 356, 408, 412, 470
Society for Promoting Collegiate and Theological Education in the West, 25
Society for the Propagation of the Faith, 61, 245, 259
Society for the Propagation of the Gospel in Foreign Parts, 262, 356, 408, 418, 421, 447–448, 470
Society for the Protection of Destitute Catholic Children, 68
Society of the Sacred Heart, 60
Society of St. Vincent de Paul, 375, 406
South Africa, 467–475
South America. *See various countries*
South American Missionary Society, 301, 331, 340
South India, Church of, 413
Southern Baptist Convention, 89–90, 100, 180; Home Mission Board of, 146
Spalding, Catherine, 66
Spalding, Henry H., 75
Spalding, John L., 149, 238
Spalding, Martin John, 149
Spencer, Herbert, 5, 493
Spiritualism, 119–120
Spurling, Richard G., Jr., 117
Stanley, Henry Morton, 464–465, 476
Stanton, Edwin M., 204, 205
Stanton, Elizabeth Cady, 217, 220
Stanton, Henry Brewster, 217
Stelzle, Charles, 233
Stephan, Martin, 45, 46
Stephen, Leslie, 5
Stetson, Augusta Emma Simmons, 121
Stewart, Charles James, 262
Stewart, Dugald, 158, 160
Stewart, James, 473, 476
Stewart, Lyman and Milton, 193
Stewart Mission Fund, 259
Stiles, Ezra, 154
Stirling, Waite Hocking, 301–302
Stone, Barton W., 11, 19, 20, 113
Stone, James Kent, 68
Stone, Lucy, 217–218
Storrs, Richard Salter, 165
Stowe, Calvin E., 142, 158
Stowe, Harriet Beecher, 158, 204
Strachan, John, 262–263
Strang, James Jesse, 114
Strauss, 5
Strong, Augustus Hopkins, 180–181
Strong, Charles, 364
Strong, Josiah, 99, 209, 230
Stuart, George H., 210
Stuart, Moses, 158
Studd, J. E. K., 33, 127
Student Volunteer Movement for Foreign Missions, 33, 127, 128, 244
Suárez, Agustín Enrique Alvarez, 337

Sucre, Antonio José de, 330
Sullivan, Anne Mansfield, 218
Sullivan, William Laurence, 196
Sulpicians, 109, 196, 250, 251, 256, 257
Sumatra, 426
Summers, Thomas Osmond, 188–189
Sumner, William Graham, 5, 232
Sun Yat-sen, 443
Sunday, William Ashley (Billy), 34–35, 36, 130
Sunday School Council of Evangelical Denominations, 38
Sunday Schools, 11, 13, 25, 37–39, 494
Suomi Synod, 56
Surinam, 278
Swedish Committee of Coöperation of Missionary Societies, 489
Swedish Evangelical Free Church, 53
Swedish Free Mission, Brazil, 348
Swedish Mission Covenant, 52–53
Swiss Churches, Conference of, 484
Syrian Church, 390, 401, 406, 408–409
Syrian Uniates, 395, 404

Taché, Alexander Antonin, 254
Taft, William Howard, 236
Tagore, Rabindranath, 415
Tahiti, 460
T'ai P'ing rebellion, 437–438
Talmadge, Thomas DeWitt, 170–171
Taney, Roger Brooke, 240
Tappan, Arthur and Lewis, 29, 205
Tappan, Benjamin, 205
Taschereau, Elzéar Alexandre, 256, 257
Tasmania, 354, 357, 359, 361, 362, 363, 365
Taylor, James Hudson, 438–439
Taylor, Nathaniel William, 26–27, 160, 161, 162
Taylor, William, 302–303, 327, 329, 334, 361, 410, 470
Taylor, William George, 361
Tejada, Ignacio de, 297, 298
Tejada, Sebastián Lerdo de, 307
Temperance movement, 210–215
Temple, William, 488
Tennent, William, 94
Tennyson, 5
Thailand, 422–423
Thayer, Joseph H., 159
Theology, Mercersburg, 98, 172–173, 198; New England, 153, 203; New Haven, 160, 161, 166; Methodists and, 185–190
Therry, John Joseph, 365
Thoburn, James Mills, 410, 422, 428
Thompson, Eliza J., 213
Thomson, James, 300–301, 309, 327, 329, 333, 340
Tientsin massacre, 435
Tierra del Fuego, 302
Tillett, Wilbur F., 189
Timan, John, 134

Timor, 425, 426
Tiradentes, 289
Tomlinson, A. J., 117
Tompkins, James J., 255–256
Tonga, 460–461
Tonghak, 449
Torrey, Reuben Archer, 34
Toussaint l'Ouverture, 289
Tranquebar Tamil Bible Society, 412
Transcendentalism, 156–157, 202, 224
Trappists, 133, 475
Trinidad, 277, 281
Truett, George Washington, 179
Trumbull, David, 334
Trumbull, Henry Clay, 39
Trusteeism, 101, 102, 104
Tucker, William J., 158
Tuckerman, Joseph, 224
Tupac Amaru, 289
Turretin, François, 167
Twain, Mark, 191
Tyler, Bennet, 161

Uchimura Kanzo, 456, 457
Uganda, 476–477
Ullathorne, William Bernard, 365, 366
Ulloa y Larrios, Bishop, 313
Ultramontanism, 256–257
Uniate Copts, 394–395
Uniates, 253, 393–395, 404–405, 406
Uniform Sunday School Lessons, 38
Unitarianism, 27, 153–157, 162, 175, 176, 202, 224
United Brethren in Christ, 11, 41, 89, 113
United Danish Evangelical Lutheran Church in America, 56
United Lutheran Church in America, 93
United Norwegian Lutheran Church, 55
United States, 4–246; distinctive characteristics of Christianity in, 8–15; Protestant gains from the older stock in, 16–37; Sunday Schools in, 37–39; immigration to, 39–68, 81, 102; Jews in, 40, 80–81; Roman Catholic gains in, from immigration and from Protestantism, 57–70; Roman Catholic worship in, 71–77; Negroes in, 77–80, 145–147, 203–207; ecclesiastical developments in, 84–111; movements emerging from Christianity in, 112–139; education in, 140–151; response of Christianity to intellectual currents in, 152–199; effect of Christianity on, 200–241; spread of Christianity from, 242–246; and Canada, 248–249; and the Philippines, 428
United States Christian Commission, 210
United States Sanitary Commission, 210
Unity School of Christianity, 14, 122
Universal Peace Society, 209
Universalism, 153
Universities' Mission to Central Africa, 476
Upper Canada Clergy Society, 259

Ursulines, 62, 135, 250
Uruguay, 292, 293, 298, 340–342
Utilitarianism, 308

Vanderkemp, John Theodore, 472
Varela y Morales, Felix, 316
Vaughan, Roger William, 366
Venezuela, 290, 295, 318–321
Veniaminoff, John, 76
Verbeck, Guido Herman Fridolin, 454
Verigin, Peter, 273
Verona y Pera, Enrique José, 317
Vincent, John H., 38, 144
Vincentians, 133
Virgin Islands, 278
Visitation Nuns, 135
Volunteers of America, 124

Wakefield, Edward Gibbon, 372, 373
Walsh, James A., 246
Walther, Carl Ferdinand Wilhelm, 45–46, 195
Walther League, 132
Wantage Sisters, 408
Ward, Henry Frederick, 232
Ward, Joseph, 142
Ward, William, 402
Warfield, Benjamin Breckinridge, 168
Warner, D. S., 117
Warnshuis, A. L., 489
Warren, William Fairfield, 188, 198
Washington, Booker T., 147
Washingtonian Temperance Movement, 212
Watch Tower Society, 122
Watson, John, 267
Watson, Richard, 186
Wattson, Lewis Thomas, 69, 133
Weidensall, Robert, 125
Weld, Theodore Dwight, 204
Wesley, John, 19, 20
Wesleyan Methodists, 360, 409, 420
West Indies, 277, 279–282
Westcott, Bishop, 357
Westminster Guild, 273–274
Whedon, Daniel Denison, 187–188, 198
White, Andrew Dickson, 191
White, Edward Douglas, 240
White Fathers, 393, 477, 478
Whitefield, George, 19, 20, 64
Whitman, Marcus, 75
Whitman, Walt, 192, 202
Whitsitt, William Heth; "Whitsitt controversy," 178
Whittier, John Greenleaf, 204
Wilder, Robert Parmelee, 244
Wiley, Calvin H., 142
Wilkes, Henry, 272
Willard, Frances E., 213, 214
Williams, S. Wells, 454
Willson, Robert William, 366
Wilson, Daniel, 408
Wilson, Woodrow, 236

Wimmer, Boniface, 63
Winebrenner, John, 116
Wishard, Luther D., 127
Woman's Christian Temperance Union, 213–214
Women leaders in reform, 214, 215–218
Women's rights movement, 208, 217–218
Worcester, Noah, 207
World Alliance for International Friendship, through the churches, 210
World Conference on Faith and Order, 489
World Council of Churches, 14, 487
World Missionary Conference, 14, 244, 487, 488, 489
World's Student Christian Federation, 14, 127, 128, 486, 487
World's Sunday School Association, 486
Wyneken, F. C. D., 47

Xavier, Francis, 433, 450
Xaverian Brothers, 61, 134

Youmans, Edward Livingston and William Jay, 191
Young, Brigham, 115
Young, George Paxton, 267
Young Men's Bible Camps, New Zealand, 376
Young Men's Christian Association, Young Women's Christian Association, in the United States, 11, 13, 14, 29, 33, 125–129, 210, 244; in Canada, 273; in Latin America, 303, 342, 348; in India, 411; in the Philippines, 429; in China, 442; many denominations in, 484; World's Alliance of, 486
Young People's Society of Christian Endeavour, 11, 13, 130–131, 273

Zelaya, José Santos, 313
Zenana Missionary Society; Zenana Bible and Medical Mission, 408
Zion City, 123
Zoarites, 45